Praise for 1–2 Chronicles

"What a gift to the church! Kaminski draws us into the sacred story of God's kingdom in the life of post-exilic Israel and helps the church see this same story continuing in our world today. With an engaging style, clear explanations, and rich theological insight, Kaminski has produced the go-to resource for pastors and Bible Study leaders who aim to savor 1–2 Chronicles and lead others to do the same."

— Andrew Abernethy, professor of Old Testament, Wheaton College

"Carol Kaminski's commentary on Chronicles is a wonderful gift to the church. Her reading of the book is historically aware, literarily sensitive, theologically informed, and pastorally astute. Chronicles has often been neglected in the church, but need be no more."

— David Firth, tutor in Old Testament, Trinity College, Bristol

"Composed to reassure God's followers in a time of instability and uncertainty, the books of Chronicles offer hope that God's purposes will be fulfilled, while at the same time reminding the people of the importance of praying with humility. Drawing on the best of recent research, Prof. Kaminski's commentary on Chronicles is an accessible and judicious explanation of the text that helpfully addresses its relevance for modern readers. Bible readers interested in Chronicles will undoubtedly find this to be an exceptionally valuable resource."

—T. Desmond Alexander, senior lecturer in biblical studies and director of postgraduate studies, Union Theological College

The Story of God Bible Commentary Series Endorsements

"Getting a story is about more than merely enjoying it. It means hearing it, understanding it, and above all, being impacted by it. This commentary series hopes that its readers not only hear and understand the story but are impacted by it to live in as Christian a way as possible. The editors and contributors set that table very well and open up the biblical story in ways that move us to act with sensitivity and understanding. That makes hearing the story as these authors tell it well worth the time. Well done."

Darrell L. Bock
Dallas Theological Seminary

"The Story of God Bible Commentary series invites readers to probe how the message of the text relates to our situations today. Engagingly readable, it not only explores the biblical text but offers a range of applications and interesting illustrations."

Craig S. Keener
Asbury Theological Seminary

"I love The Story of God Bible Commentary series. It makes the text sing and helps us hear the story afresh."

John Ortberg
Former Pastor of Menlo Park Presbyterian Church

"In this promising new series of commentaries, believing biblical scholars bring not only their expertise but their own commitment to Jesus and insights into today's culture to the Scriptures. The result is a commentary series that is anchored in the text but lives and breathes in the world of today's church with its variegated pattern of socioeconomic, ethnic, and national diversity. Pastors, Bible study leaders, and Christians of all types who are looking for a substantive and practical guide through the Scriptures will find these volumes helpful."

Frank Thielman
Beeson Divinity School

"I'm a storyteller. Through writing and speaking I talk and teach about understanding the Story of God throughout Scripture and about letting God reveal more of his story as I live it out. Thus I am thrilled to have a commentary series based on the story of God—a commentary that helps me to Listen to the Story, that Explains the Story, and then encourages me to probe how to Live the Story. A perfect tool for helping every follower of Jesus to walk in the story that God is writing for them."

Judy Douglass
Director of Women's Resources, Cru

"The Bible is the story of God and his dealings with humanity from creation to new creation. The Bible is made up more of stories than of any other literary genre. Even the psalms, proverbs, prophecies, letters, and the Apocalypse make complete sense only when set in the context of the grand narrative of the entire Bible. This commentary series breaks new ground by taking all these observations seriously. It asks commentators to listen to the text, to explain the text, and to live the text. Some of the material in these sections overlaps with introduction, detailed textual analysis and application, respectively, but only some. The most riveting and valuable parts of the commentaries are the stories that can appear in any of these sections, from any part of the globe and any part of church history, illustrating the text in any of these areas. Ideal for preaching and teaching."

Craig L. Blomberg
Denver Seminary

"Pastors and lay people will welcome this new series, which seeks to make the message of the Scriptures clear and to guide readers in appropriating biblical texts for life today."

Daniel I. Block
Wheaton College and Graduate School

"An extremely valuable and long overdue series that includes comment on the cultural context of the text, careful exegesis, and guidance on reading the whole Bible as a unity that testifies to Christ as our Savior and Lord."

Graeme Goldsworthy
author of *According to Plan*

1–2 CHRONICLES

The Story of God
Bible Commentary

1-2 CHRONICLES

Carol M. Kaminski

Tremper Longman III & Scot McKnight
General Editors

ZONDERVAN
ACADEMIC

ZONDERVAN ACADEMIC

1–2 Chronicles
Copyright © 2023 by Carol Kaminski

Requests for information should be addressed to:
Zondervan, *3900 Sparks Dr. SE, Grand Rapids, Michigan 49546*

Zondervan titles may be purchased in bulk for educational, business, fundraising, or sales promotional use. For information, please email SpecialMarkets@Zondervan.com.

Library of Congress Cataloging-in-Publication Data

Names: Kaminski, Carol M., author. | Longman, Tremper, III editor. | McKnight, Scot, editor.
Title: 1-2 Chronicles / Carol M. Kaminski, Tremper Longman III, Scot McKnight.
Other titles: Story of God Bible commentary
Description: Grand Rapids: Zondervan, 2023. | Series: The story of God Bible commentary. Old
    Testament series | Includes bibliographical references and index.
Identifiers: LCCN 2023013043 | ISBN 9780310490999 (hardcover) | ISBN 9780310491002 (ebook)
Subjects: LCSH: Bible. Chronicles--Commentaries. | BISAC: RELIGION / Biblical Commentary / Old
    Testament / Historical Books | RELIGION / Biblical Commentary / General
Classification: LCC BS1345.53 .K36 2023 | DDC 222/.607--dc23/eng/20230512
LC record available at https://lccn.loc.gov/2023013043

Cover design: Ron Huizinga
Cover photo: iStockphoto.com
Interior typesetting: Sara Colley

Printed in the United States of America

---

23 24 25 26 27 LBC 5 4 3 2 1

To my doctoral supervisor
and faithful servant of the Lord
Robert P. Gordon
Hebrews 13:7

Old Testament series

New Testament series

Contents

Acknowledgments

Throughout my teaching career I have been drawn to the stories of Israel's kings in Chronicles. Although my own academic research has focused on Genesis, when I was invited to contribute to the Story of God Bible Commentary, this seemed like the perfect opportunity to dive deeper into Chronicles and write a commentary on a book that has often been neglected in the church. My goal has been to bring to light Israel's stories in an accessible format, while also highlighting their relevance for the contemporary church. Like the returnees living in Jerusalem, we, too, are facing challenges that require us to return to the beloved stories of the faith so that we might gain a fresh vision of God's work in our midst.

This commentary would not be possible without the support and encouragement of others. I am grateful for Gordon-Conwell Theological Seminary's generous sabbatical program that enabled me to have extended times of research and writing. The support I have received from faculty colleagues and my dear friends, Tom and Donna Petter, David and Christine Palmer, Cathy McDowell, Jeff Arthurs, Quonekuia Day, and Mateus de Campos, has been a great blessing to me. Thanks for your prayers and encouragement along the way! I am indebted to the careful reading of the manuscript by the series editors, Tremper Longman and Mark Boda. Thank you for your helpful feedback and encouragement. Thanks also to Ruth Martin for preparing the Scripture Index. While any faults in this work are my own responsibility, the commentary has greatly benefited from Zondervan's editorial team, especially Lee Fields, for his meticulous and painstaking editorial work.

I had the opportunity to teach on Chronicles a few years ago at the West Coast Presbyterian Pastor's Conference at Mount Hermon, California. The input I received from this highly engaged group of pastors sharpened my focus on key areas of application and encouraged me to keep the church in view. My more recent women's Bible study on Chronicles at First Congregational Church Boxford was a blessing while I was doing final edits of the manuscript—thanks for praying for me! Lastly, I could not have completed this project without the support and encouragement from my husband and faithful friend, Matt. Many prayers were offered at our dinner table with our two boys, Robert and Ryan, "and let's pray for mom that she might finish Chronicles."

This commentary is dedicated to my doctoral supervisor, Robert P. Gordon, Emeritus Regius Professor of Hebrew, University of Cambridge. Over a decade ago, I had been invited to contribute to Professor Gordon's Festschrift in celebration of his upcoming retirement. I was serving as Dean of Faculty at Gordon-Conwell at the time, and this responsibility had regrettably prevented me from contributing to the volume in his honor. Now, in recognition of his outstanding scholarship, and more particularly, in gratitude for the years under his wise and kind tutelage, this book is dedicated to Robert P. Gordon.

CAROL M. KAMINSKI

The Story of God Bible Commentary Series

Why another commentary series?

In the first place, no single commentary can exhaust the meaning of a biblical book. The Bible is unfathomably rich and no single commentator can explore every aspect of its message.

In addition, good commentary not only explores what the text meant in the past but also its continuing significance. In other words, the Word of God may not change, but culture does. Think of what we have seen in the last twenty years: we now communicate predominantly through the internet and email; we read our news on iPads and computers. We carry smartphones in our pockets through which we can call our friends, check the weather forecast, make dinner reservations, and get an answer to virtually any question we might have.

Today we have more readable and accurate Bible versions in English than any generation in the past. Bible distribution in the present generation has been very successful; more people own more Bibles than previous generations. However, studies have shown that while people have better access to the Bible than ever before, people aren't reading the Bibles they own, and they struggle to understand what they do read.

The Story of God Bible Commentary hopes to help people, particularly clergy but also laypeople, read the Bible with understanding not only of its ancient meaning but also of its continuing significance for us today in the twenty-first century. After all, readers of the Bible change too. These cultural shifts, our own personal developments, and the progress in intellectual questions, as well as growth in biblical studies and theology and discoveries of new texts and new paradigms for understanding the contexts of the Bible—each of these elements work on an interpreter so that the person who reads the Bible today asks different questions from different angles.

Culture shifts, but the Word of God remains. That is why we as editors of The Story of God Bible Commentary, a commentary based on the New International Version 2011 (NIV 2011), are excited to participate in this new series of commentaries on the Bible. This series is designed to speak to this generation with the same Word of God. We are asking the authors to explain what the Bible says to the sorts of readers who pick up commentaries so they can understand not only what Scripture says but what it means for today. The Bible does not change, but relating it to our culture changes constantly and in differing ways in different contexts.

As editors of the Old Testament series, we recognize that Christians have a hard time knowing exactly how to relate to the Scriptures that were written before the coming of Christ. The world of the Old Testament is a strange one to those of us who live in the West in the twenty-first century. We read about strange customs, warfare in the name of God, sacrifices, laws of ritual purity, and more and wonder whether it is worth our while or even spiritually healthy to spend time reading this portion of Scripture that is chronologically, culturally, and—seemingly—theologically distant from us.

But it is precisely here that The Story of God Bible Commentary series on the Old Testament makes its most important contribution. The New Testament does not replace the Old Testament; the New Testament fulfills the Old Testament. We hear God's voice today in the Old Testament. In its pages he reveals himself to us and also his will for how we should live in a way that is pleasing to him.

Jesus himself often reminds us that the Old Testament maintains its importance to the lives of his disciples. Luke 24 describes Jesus's actions and teaching in the period between his resurrection and ascension. Strikingly, the focus of his teaching is on how his followers should read the Old Testament (here called "Moses and all the Prophets," "Scriptures," and "the law of Moses, the Prophets and Psalms"). To the two disciples on the road to Emmaus, he says:

> "How foolish you are, and how slow to believe all that the prophets have spoken! Did not the Messiah have to suffer these things and then enter his glory?" And beginning with Moses and all the Prophets, he explained to them what was said in all the Scriptures concerning himself. (Luke 24:25–27)

Then to a larger group of disciples he announces:

> "This is what I told you while I was still with you: Everything must be fulfilled that is written about me in the law of Moses, the Prophets and the Psalms." Then he opened their minds so they could understand the Scriptures. (Luke 24:44–45)

The Story of God Bible Commentary series takes Jesus's words on this matter seriously. Indeed, it is the first series that has as one of its deliberate goals the identification of the trajectories (historical, typological, and theological) that land in Christ in the New Testament. Every commentary in the series will, in the first place, exposit the text in the context of its original reception. We will interpret it as we believe the original author intended his contemporary audience to read it. But then we will also read the text in the light of the death and resurrection of Jesus. No other commentary series does this important work consistently in every volume.

To achieve our purpose of exposing the Old Testament in its original setting and also from a New Testament perspective, each passage is examined from three angles.

Listen to the Story. We begin by listening to the text in order to hear the voice of God. We first read the passage under study. We then go on to consider the background to the passage by looking at any earlier Scripture passage that informs our understanding of the text. At this point too we will cite and discuss possible ancient Near Eastern literary connections. After all, the Bible was not written in a cultural vacuum, and an understanding of its broader ancient Near Eastern context will often enrich our reading.

Explain the Story. The authors are asked to explain each passage in light of the Bible's grand story. It is here that we will exposit the text in its original Old Testament context. This is not an academic series, so the footnotes will be limited to the kinds of books and articles to which typical Bible readers and preachers will have access. Authors are given the freedom to explain the text as they read it, though you will not be surprised to find occasional listings of other options for reading the text. The emphasis will be on providing an accessible explanation of the passage, particularly on those aspects of the text that are difficult for a modern reader to understand, with an emphasis on theological interpretation.

Live the Story. Reading the Bible is not just about discovering what it meant back then; the intent of The Story of God Bible Commentary is to probe how this text might be lived out today as that story continues to march on in the life of the church.

Here, in the spirit of Christ's words in Luke 24, we will suggest ways in which the Old Testament text anticipates the gospel. After all, as Augustine famously put it, "the New Testament is in the Old Testament concealed, the Old Testament is in the New Testament revealed." We believe that this section will be particularly important for our readers who are clergy who want to present Christ even when they are preaching from the Old Testament.

The Old Testament also provides teaching concerning how we should live today. However, the authors of this series are sensitive to the tremendous impact that Christ's coming has on how Christians appropriate the Old Testament into their lives today.

It is the hope and prayer of the editors and all the contributors that our work will encourage clergy to preach from the Old Testament and laypeople to study this wonderful, yet often strange, portion of God's Word to us today.

TREMPER LONGMAN III, general editor Old Testament
GEORGE ATHAS, MARK BODA, AND MYRTO THEOCHAROUS, editors

Abbreviations

ANEP	*Ancient Near Eastern Pictures Relating to the Old Testament.* Edited by James B. Pritchard. 2nd ed. Princeton: Princeton University Press, 1969.
ANET	*Ancient Near Eastern Texts Relating to the Old Testament.* Edited by James B. Pritchard. 3rd ed. Princeton: Princeton University Press, 1969.
ASOR	*American Schools of Oriental Research*
AUSS	*Andrews University Seminary Studies*
BA	*Biblical Archaeologist*
BAR	*Biblical Archaeology Review*
BASOR	*Bulletin of the American Schools of Oriental Research*
BBR	*Bulletin for Biblical Research*
Bib	*Biblica*
BHS	Biblia Hebraica Stuttgartensia
BHQ	Biblia Hebraica Quinta
BTCB	Brazon Theological Commentary on the Bible
BSac	*Bibliotheca Sacra*
CBC	Cornerstone Biblical Commentary
CBQ	*Catholic Biblical Quarterly*
ESV	English Standard Version
JBL	*Journal of Biblical Literature*
JETS	*Journal of the Evangelical Theological Society*
JJS	*Journal of Jewish Studies*
JNES	*Journal of Near Eastern Studies*
JSOT	*Journal for the Study of the Old Testament*
JSOTSup	Journal for the Study of the Old Testament, Supplement Series
KJV	King James Version
LXX	Septuagint
MT	Masoretic Text
NAC	New American Commentary
NASB	New American Standard Bible
NCBC	New Century Bible Commentary
NICOT	New International Commentary on the Old Testament

NIV	New International Version
NRSV	New Revised Standard Version
NSBT	New Studies in Biblical Theology
NTS	*New Testament Studies*
OTE	*Old Testament Essays*
OTL	Old Testament Library
TynBul	*Tyndale Bulletin*
TOTC	Tyndale Old Testament Commentary
VT	*Vetus Testamentum*
WBC	Word Biblical Commentary

Introduction to 1–2 Chronicles

Chronicles tells the story of kingship and life in the kingdom, with joyful worship of God at its center. While the lives and exploits of Davidic kings will be rehearsed and principles for kingdom-living will be expounded, Chronicles is ultimately *God's story*. The Lord God is gloriously enthroned in the heavens, and he rules as king over all the nations. He is the creator and only God to whom all praise is due. Splendor and majesty belong to him alone, and this is surely *his* story of *his* mighty acts done in and through his people Israel. As we traverse the landscape of Chronicles, the goal of these stories is to lift our eyes beyond our individual lives and circumstances so that we might catch a vision of God's glorious and everlasting kingdom and discern how he is providentially at work and present in our world—even when the circumstances might look otherwise. Providing a counter-narrative to the powerful empires of the world, themes such as worship, prayer, seeking God's face, humility, repentance, trusting in God, obedience to his word, and listening to the Spirit permeate these stories, inviting us to inhabit the "real narrative" of the kingdom. Signs of *his* presence turn up in unexpected places, sometimes veiled but nevertheless present as we slow down to read deeply, with hearts intent on seeking God. The book of Chronicles is not for the faint-hearted, but it is for the thirsty. It will not leave the reader empty-handed, for it comes with the assurance from God himself that he will be found by those who seek him.

The contemporary church has much to learn from Chronicles. God's people had returned to Jerusalem after the exile, living at a time when the glory days of the monarchy were over. The kingdom established under David and Solomon had come to a catastrophic end. The temple had been destroyed and Judah's last king had been brought to Babylon, only after his sons had been hideously slaughtered and he himself had been brutally blinded. Having gone through the judgment of exile, the temple had been rebuilt and the returnees were living in Jerusalem as a small and insignificant province of Judah amid a vast and powerful Persian Empire. To be sure, their settlement in the land had begun, but it surely paled in comparison to the flourishing kingdom under David and Solomon when tribute from the nations streamed into Jerusalem. Now, the Judeans were forced to pay heavy taxes to Persia, and for some, such payments resulted in servitude and forfeiture of their land. Nations lived in close proximity to Judah, with the mixed population of Samaritans in the north, Edomites to the south, Ammonites to the east, and Phoenicians to the west. The returnees faced hostile opposition during their rebuilding efforts, and there was always the risk of religious compromise in a pluralistic environment. How were they to live in this new reality? What was their calling and how were they to see God at work?

Some of these questions may well resonate with us as we grapple with how to live as God's people in a post-Christendom world. In the church today, we do not face the destruction of the temple, nor have we lost the monarchy or experienced an exile to Babylon. But we are facing the erosion of a Christian worldview, causing us to wrestle with how we are to live in this new world. For some, the stories of the Christian faith are simply relics of the past, deemed irrelevant for our new world. Coupled with an increasing biblical illiteracy, we are in danger of losing the rich stories of the faith. Andrew Delbanco spoke presciently a few years ago in lectures he gave at Harvard: "we have gotten very good at deconstructing old stories . . . but when it comes to telling new ones, we are blocked."[1] Thus he concludes: "Here we arrive at the root of our postmodern melancholy. We live in an age of unprecedented wealth, but in the realm of narrative and symbol, we are deprived."[2] If the world has lost its story and needs new stories and symbols, then the task for the church in our age is surely to "tell the biblical narrative to the world in proclamation and to God in worship."[3] This is the true story that needs to be proclaimed and embodied in this age of transience, uncertainty, and lost identity. This is where the book of Chronicles provides a fresh vision for the church. By going back to Israel's stories of old, the Chronicler is reminding God's people—and the church today—of the irrevocable and unchanging plan of God. Israel's identity as a royal priesthood is to be found in the stories of the faith, *the sacred Scriptures*, which are being explained to a new generation in need of hope and vision. The Chronicler is reminding the returnees that God has not forgotten them, and he is accomplishing his creational plan, which is being realized on a *global* stage. Rather than fearing what lies ahead, they are to interpret their world in light of their sacred history and to understand that their circumstances are

---

1. Andrew Delbanco, *The Real American Dream: A Mediation on Hope* (Cambridge: Harvard University Press, 2019), 106.

2. Ibid., 107.

3. Robert W. Jenson, "How the World Lost Its Story," *First Things*, March 2010 (https://www.firstthings.com/article/2010/03/how-the-world-lost-its-story).

not outside God's sovereign plan. They are to be a witnessing and worshiping community among the nations.

With a compelling vision set before them, God's people are invited to inhabit the world of the kingdom that includes the sacred symbols of prayer, repentance, proclamation, and worship. This is a priestly kingdom with God's dynamic presence at its center. Regardless of how unpromising the circumstances might appear, this kingdom is filled with *joy* and *singing*—because a holy God is dwelling among his people. This is the vision—an eschaton of sorts—that is being set forth in Chronicles, and it stands as an invitation to the church today to see afresh what God is doing in our world and to inhabit the life of the kingdom, with worship at its center.

Since Chronicles is one of the more neglected books of the Old Testament, the goal of this commentary is to tell the story of Israel as it is being narrated in Chronicles. Although a good portion of the material relies upon Samuel and Kings (more about this shortly), our intention is not to be taken up with synoptic issues by comparing Chronicles with these other works (some excellent commentaries have already done this[4]) but is to keep the storyline the focus, as it is being told in Chronicles. Since the Chronicler interprets Israel's stories in light of the larger narrative of Scripture, additional Bible references have been included in the commentary. These cross references serve to highlight key concepts that are found elsewhere in the Old Testament and to remind the reader that Chronicles is deeply embedded in the larger narrative of Scripture.

Chronicles is saturated with theological commentary, sermonettes, prophetic speeches, and prayers. This means the author is not simply writing a history book (even though he is a historian), but he is also interpreting Israel's sacred history, carefully and meticulously explaining its significance for his own context. As noted by Selman, "the Chronicler's aim was to draw out spiritual and theological principles rather than produce an alternative history to Samuel and Kings."[5] The spiritual tone of the writing reverberates through his work, with calls to prayer, worship, trust in God, and even joy! The stories invite the reader into the habitable world of the kingdom, not as dispassionate or aloof bystanders, but as active participants who join Israel in celebratory

---

4. See Mark J. Boda, *1–2 Chronicles*, CBC (Carol Stream, IL: Tyndale House, 2010); Roddy L. Braun, *1 Chronicles*, WBC (Waco, TX: Word, 1986); Raymond B. Dillard, *2 Chronicles*, WBC (Waco, TX: Word, 1987); Sara Japhet, *I & II Chronicles* OTL (Louisville: Westminster John Knox, 1993); Ralph W. Klein, *1 Chronicles: A Commentary*, Hermeneia (Minneapolis: Fortress, 2006); Ralph W. Klein, *2 Chronicles: A Commentary*, Hermeneia (Minneapolis: Fortress, 2012); H. G. M. Williamson, *1 and 2 Chronicles*, NCBC (Grand Rapids: Eerdmans, 1982).

5. Martin J. Selman, *1 Chronicles: An Introduction and Commentary*, TOTC (Downers Grove, IL: InterVarsity Press, 1994), 29.

worship of the LORD God. As a commentator, my goal has been to reflect as much as possible the worshipful and homiletical tone of Chronicles with the intent of not only engaging the reader's mind, but also stirring the affections of the heart. This has led to the inclusion of hymns throughout the commentary, along with contemporary stories that speak to the heart and illustrate the relevance of these ancient stories for our world today. Before we embark on our journey through Chronicles, it is helpful to set the context for the book, which includes issues of authorship, historical context, literary structure, and theological themes. It is important to bear in mind that the Chronicler is retelling the stories of Israel's kings, but he is doing so hundreds of years after the events, writing from a different historical context (God's people are now living back in Jerusalem after the period of exile with no king on the throne). It is vital therefore that we understand the Chronicler's own circumstances, so that we might listen to these well-known stories that are being interpreted and applied in his own context. We rehearse these topics briefly since a good many of them will be included in the commentary.

Composition, Transmission, and Canonicity

Authorship and Date

Chronicles was written during the Persian period, after God's people had resettled in Jerusalem and rebuilt the temple. From early times, Jewish tradition identified Ezra as the author of Chronicles. Ezra's priestly heritage and skill as a scribe trained in the law of Moses makes him a good candidate, and the Levitical tone throughout Chronicles fits with his profile as a priest. According to this view, the books of Chronicles and Ezra-Nehemiah were originally a single work, noting that the last two verses of Chronicles are taken up in the opening verses of Ezra (2 Chr 36:22–23; cf. Ezra 1:1–3). A Greek text called 1 Esdras is seen to further support this view since it weaves together texts from Chronicles, Ezra, and selected chapters from Nehemiah, underscoring the close relationship between these books.[6]

The view that one author wrote Chronicles and Ezra-Nehemiah has been challenged by the more recent work of Sara Japhet. She has written extensively on Chronicles, seen especially in her highly technical and voluminous commentary on 1–2 Chronicles. In her seminal article on authorship, she argues persuasively that there are too many differences between Chronicles

---

6. For a helpful summary of authorship, along with a list of list of sources on the topic, see Eugene H. Merrill, *A Commentary on 1 & 2 Chronicles* (Grand Rapids: Kregel, 2015), 43–44; see also Selman, *1 Chronicles*, 65–75.

and Ezra-Nehemiah to identify them as the same author, including differences in language, literary style, biblical history, and theology.[7] Her work has been well-received in the scholarly community and finds further support by H. G. M. Williamson, resulting in a shift of scholarly opinion that now identifies the author of Chronicles as someone other than the author of Ezra-Nehemiah.[8] Since Chronicles is an anonymous work, it is commonplace to identify the author as "the Chronicler" or "the narrator," while recognizing that he was probably a Levite.

As we consider a possible date for Chronicles, it is important to bear in mind that the Chronicler has made extensive use of Samuel and Kings, with estimates that over fifty percent of his material relies on these two sources. This is relevant for the dating of Chronicles, since the concluding verses of 2 Kings can be dated to the middle of the sixth century BC when Jehoiachin was released from prison during the reign of Awel-Marduk (25:27–30). The final chapter of Chronicles notably concludes with a reference to the decree of Cyrus (2 Chr 36:22–23). The Persian king Cyrus II (559–530 BC) defeated Babylon in 539 BC and issued a decree in 538 BC that allowed the exiles to return to Jerusalem and rebuild the temple (cf. Ezra 6:3–5). A post-exilic date for Chronicles is confirmed by the list of exiles who returned to Jerusalem (1 Chr 9:2–34), and a reference to gold coins identified as "darics" (29:7) suggests a date after 515 BC since darics were minted during the reign of Darius I.[9] Lastly, the genealogy of Jehoiachin provides crucial information related to the date of composition (3:17–24). Not only are his seven sons mentioned, but Zerubbabel's children also extend the genealogy into the post-exilic period (vv. 19–20). Since his descendants extend several generations, this suggests a date of composition late in the fifth century BC.[10]

Canonicity and Title

The title given to this work in the Hebrew Bible is translated as "events of the days" (Heb. *dibre hayyamim*), which is a Hebrew phrase used elsewhere

---

7. Sara Japhet, "The Supposed Common Authorship of Chronicles and Ezra-Nehemiah Investigated Anew," *VT* 18 (1968): 332–72.

8. H. G. M. Williamson, "Did the Author of Chronicles also Write the Books of Ezra and Nehemiah?" *Bible Review* 3 (1987): 56–59.

9. See the discussion in Chapter 29 on 1 Chr 29:7, p. 278n6.

10. If the last member of the genealogy, Anani, is to be identified with Anani in the Elephantine papyri ("Ostan the brother of Anani"), dated to the reign of Darius II, this suggests the *terminus ad quem* is 407 BC (see the discussion in Chapter 3, Explain the Story on 1 Chr 3:24). It is possible that these last few names could have been added by a later editor to update the genealogy, thus not precluding the Chronicler from writing a few decades earlier.

to refer to royal archives and records (cf. 1 Kgs 14:19; 29; 15:7; 1 Chr 27:24; Neh 12:23, etc.). It is a fitting title for a work focused on Israel's kings, but it is important to bear in mind that the English title *Chronicles* did not come from a direct translation of the Hebrew title. The title for Chronicles in the Greek Septuagint is *Paraleipomenon* (meaning "omissions" or "things left out"), which refers to the fact that Chronicles includes material not found in Samuel and Kings. Some surmise that this title contributed to the view that Chronicles is simply supplemental to Samuel and Kings rather than being a historical record in its own right. In any case, the English title *Chronicles* did not come directly from the Greek translation, but rather, it made its way into our English Bible through a statement made by Jerome in the fourth century AD. In his prologue to his Latin translation of Samuel and Kings, Jerome suggested that the work known as *Paraleipomenon* might be more significantly called "the *chronikon* of the whole sacred history."[11] Williamson suggests that Jerome's employment of *chronikon* probably had Jewish tradition in view.[12] The influence of the Vulgate is seen in Luther's German title, *Die Chronika* and in the English title *Chronicles*. Despite having a circuitous history, the English title *Chronicles* is an appropriate heading for this work, and Jerome's comment that it chronicles the "whole of sacred history" represents the magnitude of the material.[13]

Even though Chronicles appears as two books in our English Bible, it is helpful to remember when reading Chronicles that it is one narrative, not two. Accordingly, the first verse of 2 Chronicles continues the storyline from 1 Chronicles. The placement of Chronicles in the canon falls into two traditions. In the standard scholarly edition of the Hebrew Bible, known as *Biblia Hebraica Stuttgartensia* (BHS), 1–2 Chronicles is located at the end of the third division of books, known as the Writings (*Ketuvim*). It appears after Ezra-Nehemiah, and thus it represents the conclusion to the Hebrew Bible. Some scholars see this order reflected in Jesus's reference to martyrs from "Abel to the blood of Zechariah" (Matt 23:35), since Abel is mentioned in Genesis (Gen 4:8–16) and Zechariah is mentioned in Chronicles (2 Chr 24:20–21), although this is disputed.[14] Notably, there is some manuscript evidence that Chronicles was located at the beginning of the Writings, represented in the

---

11. Cited by Williamson, *1 and 2 Chronicles*, 3.

12. Ibid., 3–4.

13. Gary N. Knoppers and Paul B. Harvey, Jr., "Omitted and Remaining Matters: On the Names Given to the Book of Chronicles in Antiquity," *JBL* 121 (2002): 227–43.

14. This is not as straightforward as it might appear, however. In Matthew's gospel, Zechariah is not identified as the son of Jehoiada (cf. 2 Chr 24:20) but as the son of Berekiah (cf. Zech 1:1); see Klein, *1 Chronicles*, 1n15.

more recent scholarly edition of the Hebrew Bible, known was *Biblia Hebraica Quinta* (BHQ).[15] According to the Greek Septuagint, 1–2 Chronicles is located after Samuel and Kings but before Ezra-Nehemiah. Even though its location within the canon may differ, the canonicity of 1–2 Chronicles has not been disputed in antiquity.

Literary Analysis

Genre

The Hebrew title given to Chronicles ("the events of the days") locates it within the corpus of historical records, especially among the royal archives (cf. 1 Kgs 14:19, 29; 15:7, 23, 31; 16:5, 14, etc.). The term *archive* perhaps best conveys the type of royal records that are being preserved, and the Chronicler's work as historian and archivist falls within this genre. The opening genealogies testify to the important task of record-keeping, which is summarized as follows: "All Israel was listed in the genealogies recorded in the book of the kings of Israel and Judah" (1 Chr 9:1). Accordingly, the verb "record, register" (Heb. *yahas*) occurs ten times in 1 Chr 4–9 (4:33; 5:1, 7, 17; 7:5, 7, 9, 40; 9: 1, 22) and elsewhere when records are in view (2 Chr 12:15; 31:16–19). As a historian, the Chronicler has made extensive use of sources throughout his work, many of which are no longer extant.[16] Especially important are the historical books of Samuel and Kings, which provide the content for about fifty percent of his work, but he also makes extensive use of the Torah (and other books), underscoring the abiding authority of Mosaic teaching for the post-exilic community. Given his reliance upon the Scriptures, it is appropriate to refer to him as a *biblical* historian, since his worldview and writings are deeply rooted in Israel's traditions. Allusions to Scripture throughout his work testify to his vast knowledge of Israel's sacred traditions.[17]

Yet the Chronicler not only appeals to the abiding authority of God's word, but he interprets it for his own generation, giving a homiletic and pastoral tone to his writing. Selman thus notes that for the Chronicler, "God's word is the

---

15. On its location as the *first* book of the Writings, see Klein, *1 Chronicles*, 2. For a more extensive discussion, see Edmond L. Gallagher, "The End of the Bible? The Position of Chronicles in the Canon," *TynBul* 65:2 (2014): 181–99.

16. For a list of sources and helpful analysis of them, see Boda, *1–2 Chronicles*, 13–16, and Merrill, *1 & 2 Chronicles*, 45, 54–55, 71–77.

17. It is remarkable to see how often the Chronicler refers to Moses and the law. This underscores the abiding authority of the Torah for the returnees; see Simon J. De Vries, "Moses and David as Cult Founders in Chronicles," *JBL* 107:4 (1988): 619–630. In his article De Vries highlights the authority of Moses, with respect to the law, and David, with respect to the cult.

ultimate standard upon which his dealings with his people are based in every generation. The principles underlying his word are unchanging though the ways in which they can be applied to new situations are surprisingly adaptable."[18] The Chronicler is a seasoned exegete who seeks to draw out principles from Israel's history that are important for his own generation. Writing with divine inspiration, he exhorts God's people to conform to God's will, living according to the values of the kingdom and devoting their lives to seeking him.

How to Preach from Chronicles

The stories of Chronicles are relevant for every generation, yet the complexity of the material (especially the extended genealogies) can cause even the seasoned pastor to be intimidated by Chronicles, not knowing *how* to preach from these books. Sermons on Chronicles could take a variety of forms. I have written a Bible study on Chronicles entitled *Cultivating Godliness*.[19] I have taken a thematic approach in the Bible study covering topics such as prayer, seeking God, humility, generosity, and joyful praise, just to mention a few. Throughout the commentary I make reference in the footnotes to sections where these topics are addressed. This should prove helpful for topical sermons or Bible studies on Chronicles. Contemporary illustrations and stories have been included in the Live the Story sections, which are intended to be used in sermons, as needed. Other thematic topics fertile for a preaching and teaching are prayer, worship, and leadership principles, just to name a few. Another approach might be to trace the stories of the kings chronologically, perhaps over the course of eight weeks. This preaching series could cover important southern kings such as David, Solomon, Asa, Jehoshaphat, Ahaz, Hezekiah, Manasseh, and Josiah. All the important themes in Chronicles will be found in the stories of these kings. Whatever approach taken, the book of Chronicles is not only rich theologically, but there are also many areas of application throughout the work that will prove beneficial for the church today.

Literary Structure

When reading 1–2 Chronicles (or preaching from this material), it is important to have a firm grasp of the larger structure of the work, originally presented as one continuous narrative but now in two books. The following four literary units can be identified in 1–2 Chronicles:

---

18. Selman, *1 Chronicles*, 43–44.
19. Carol M. Kaminski, *Cultivating Godliness: An Eight-Week Bible Study on 1–2 Chronicles* (n.p.: Casket Empty Media, 2023).

1. Genealogies, which end with a list of returnees (1 Chr 1–9).
2. The united kingdom under David, which includes the Davidic covenant (1 Chr 10–29).
3. The united kingdom under Solomon, with the building of the temple at its center (2 Chr 1–9).
4. The divided kingdom that results in the exile but ends with the hope of restoration (2 Chr 10–36).

Within the larger units, literary patterns and structures can be further identified,[20] although it is helpful to keep the big picture of the storyline in view.

Lastly, it is important to notice that the first literary unit ends with the return from exile (1 Chr 9), which effectively mirrors the storyline of the entire work, since the last two verses are an invitation to return to Jerusalem (2 Chr 36:22–23). This underscores the important theme of restoration that reverberates throughout Chronicles, shaping Solomon's prayer (2 Chr 6) and providing hope for God's people. This ending suggests, therefore, that we are always "figuratively starting again from Jerusalem on our way to the ends of the earth."[21]

Historical Setting of the Writing of Chronicles

The book of Chronicles tells the stories of Israel's southern kings, beginning with Saul (although only briefly since focus is on David) and continuing until the last king, Zedekiah. As noted above, Chronicles was written hundreds of years later, during the final period of the Old Testament. The Northern Kingdom of Israel had come to an end in 722 BC, with its inhabitants suffering great loss, exile, and the resettlement of foreigners in their land (2 Kgs 17). Yet the Chronicler is keen to show times when those from the northern tribes of Israel join the Southern Kingdom, keeping in view his vision for a united and restored people of God. After the demise of the North, the Southern Kingdom continues for a number of years, but the death of Josiah in 609 BC and the turbulent period that follows signals that the end of the kingdom is at hand.[22] God's people will be held accountable for their unfaithfulness, something demonstrated so vividly in their stiff-necked king Zedekiah, who refuses to

---

20. Some scholars argue for a chiastic structure to the book as a whole (and in smaller literary units), but these do not always fit as neatly as some suggest; see Merrill's judicious critique (*1 & 2 Chronicles*, 53–54). Literary patterns that are beneficial for interpretation will be noted in the commentary.

21. Richard Bauckham and Trevor Hart, *Hope Against Hope: Christian Eschatology at the Turn of the Millennium* (Grand Rapids: Eerdmans, 1999), 21. See also Chapter 65, Live the Story, pp. 569–71.

22. For the history of this period, see Chapter 65, Explain the Story, pp. 564–65.

humble himself. After graciously sending a series of prophets, God's judgment finally comes, resulting in the destruction of the temple and Jerusalem as well as the deportation of God's people to Babylon (2 Chr 36:1–21). But the Chronicler does not end on this somber note of exile, but rather, his entire work concludes with the hope of restoration and the call to return to Jerusalem (vv. 22–23). This topic permeates his writings and stands as an invitation to God's people, reminding them that God is *with them.*

Life in the Province of Judah and in the Diaspora under the Persians

The reign of Cyrus ushers in the return from exile in 538 BC (2 Chr 36:22–23; cf. Ezra 1–2), which is followed by the rebuilding of the temple under the leadership of Zerubbabel and Joshua, through the encouragement of Haggai and Zechariah (Ezra 5–6). A second wave of returnees travels to Jerusalem in 458 BC under the leadership of Ezra the priest (chs. 7–8), and covenant renewal follows (chs. 9–10). Nehemiah returns to Jerusalem in 445 BC, and under his leadership as governor, the walls are rebuilt with God's help, in spite of rising opposition (Neh 1–6). Restoration and covenant renewal characterize this period, as the community gathers to hear God's word read by Ezra and taught by the Levites (chs. 8–9). The historical books of Ezra and Nehemiah, along with the prophetical books of Haggai, Zechariah, and Malachi, provide insight into life back in Jerusalem as the returnees resettle in the land and adjust to their new circumstances.

In contrast to the glory days of the kingdom, the returnees belong to a small province within the vast Persian Empire. Instead of being ruled by Davidic kings in Jerusalem, they are subject to foreign Persian kings, such as Cyrus (559–530 BC), Cambyses (530–522 BC), Darius (522–486 BC), Xerxes (486–465 BC), and Artaxerxes I (465–424 BC). Excavations at Persian cities such as Pasargadae (the capital established by Cyrus), Susa (the administrative capital under Darius), and Persepolis (built by Darius) testify to the colossal administrative and palatial structures that were an important part of the flourishing Persian Empire.[23]

The Empire was comprised of provinces that were administered by local

23. An excellent resource on the Persian period is Edwin M. Yamauchi, *Persia and the Bible* (Grand Rapids: Baker Books, 1990). While more recent studies are available (see below), this volume provides a helpful and accessible introduction to this period. Yamauchi discusses each king at length, along with key Persian cites, providing historical and archaeological information that greatly enrich our understanding of this period. For a more recent and comprehensive history of the Persian period, see Pierre Briant, *From Cyrus to Alexander: A History of the Persian Empire.* Translated by Peter T. Daniels (Winona Lake, IN: Eisenbrauns, 2002).

governors (cf. Esth 1:1). The province of Judah was identified as *YHD* by the Persians, and thus it is commonly referred to as the province of Yehud.[24] Coins and seals found in the region with the official *Yehud* stamp testify to the resettlement of the returnees in Jerusalem and the surrounding towns.[25] It is estimated that the province extended north to south some twenty-five miles.[26] Lipschits estimates that the region surrounding Jerusalem (within approximately two miles of the city) saw an eighty-nine percent decline in the number of settlements in comparison to the flourishing kingdom at the end of the Iron Age (1200–1000 BC). He concludes that Jerusalem and its environs were almost completely empty during the period of the exile, although there is evidence that settlement continued in Judean villages and farms located in the northern region of Benjamin and south in Bethlehem.[27] This means that when the exiles returned to Jerusalem under Cyrus, they were facing the daunting task of not only rebuilding their own lives, but also their beloved city of Jerusalem, which had been desolate for a good many years. This would have required great faith and courage to start again with such a formidable task ahead of them.

Governors attested in the biblical accounts during the Persian period include Sheshbazzar (Ezra 1:8; 5:14), Zerubbabel (Hag 1:1, 14), and Nehemiah (Neh 5:14; 12:26).[28] The Persian king subjected the provinces to heavy taxation, resulting in vast amounts of gold and silver being drained from them, only to fill the royal treasuries. The vessels stamped with the *Yehud* seal were probably used for the collection of taxes.[29] With a heavy system of taxation imposed upon the provinces, this put pressure on those living in Jerusalem.[30] The Murashu texts discovered at Nippur attest to the kind of loans available in Mesopotamia by Murashu and Sons, which often came with high interest, up to an exorbitant forty percent.[31] Jewish names among the officials suggest that

---

24. Over four hundred seal impressions have been found, with concentrations at four major cities: Ramat-Rahel, Jerusalem, Mizpah, and Jericho; see Oded Lipschits, *The Fall and Rise of Jerusalem: Judah under Babylonian Rule* (University Park: Pennsylvania State University Press, 2005), 175–178.

25. Yamauchi, *Persia and the Bible*, 265–66. For a detailed analysis of settlement patterns during the Persian Period based on archaeology, see Lipschits, *The Fall and Rise of Jerusalem*, 206–71.

26. J. A. Thompson, *1, 2 Chronicles*, NAC (Nashville: Broadman & Holman, 1994), 31.

27. Lipschits, *The Fall and Rise of Jerusalem*, 217–218.

28. Yamauchi provides names of other governors not attested in the Bible (*Persia and the Bible*, 265). For a more detailed and technical analysis of the textual evidence, see H. G. M. Williamson, "The Governors of Judah under the Persians," *TynBul* 39 (1988): 59–82.

29. Lipschits, *The Fall and Rise of Jerusalem*, 175.

30. Yamauchi, *Persia and the Bible*, 274.

31. Ibid., 275–276. The Murashu texts found at Nippur (some 730 tablets) date from 454 to 404 BC (those translated). Yamauchi notes that approximately seventy of the 2,500 individuals named are Jewish. Nippur was one of the locations of the diaspora, with Jews being identified in 28

some of the diaspora had risen in power and wealth.[32] Yet the dire poverty facing others in Jerusalem causes Nehemiah to rebuke the wealthy among them for their usury that led to the servitude of their kinsmen (Neh 5:7, 11). Food shortages and economic deprivation further exacerbated the struggles of those living in the province of Yehud. Poverty could result in forfeiture of land, and with the highly inflated price of basic commodities, some found it a struggle to make ends meet (cf. Neh 5:1–13; Hag 1:9–11; 2:15–17). Despite the return from exile and rebuilding of the temple, life in the province was not without its difficulties.

The final point to keep in mind is that the province of Yehud was not only a small geographic region within the Persian Empire, but the returnees also faced political opposition and competing religious beliefs. Although temple-building efforts were supported by the Persian kings Cyrus (Ezra 1:1–4) and Darius (6:1–12), which was in accordance with their political strategy, the returnees had faced serious opposition to their rebuilding efforts (4:1–6:13). The temple was finally rebuilt and sacrifices were offered (6:14–22), but further opposition comes from Sanballat, governor of Samaria, Tobiah the Ammonite official, and Geshem the Arab (Neh 2:10, 19; 4:1; 6:1–2). Yamauchi provides a succinct summary of the situation: "The exiles returned to a tiny enclave surrounded by hostile neighbors: Samaritans to the north, Ammonites to the east, Arabs and Edomites to the south, and Phoenicians to the west."[33] An example of this opposition is seen during their early rebuilding efforts: "Then the peoples around them set out to discourage the people of Judah and make them afraid to go on building. They bribed officials to work against them and frustrate their plans during the entire reign of Cyrus king of Persia and down to the reign of Darius king of Persia" (Ezra 4:4–5; cf. Ezra 4:6–24; 5:3). While we are living thousands of years apart from this period, we have all experienced discouragement, and with unjust political practices that included bribery, it is easy to see why they were demoralized in their work.

Marriages with foreign women also take place during this period, including women from Ashdod, Ammon, and Moab (Neh 13:23; cf. Ezra 9:1–15).

---

of 200 settlements, showing their wide range of occupations, and perhaps suggesting why they did not return to Jerusalem (see ibid., 242–44).

32. Ibid., 244.

33. Ibid., 265. Knoppers has explored the relationship of Judah and Samaria, and concludes that during the Persian period, there is significant cultural and religious overlap between them; see Gary N. Knoppers, *Jews and Samaritans: The Origin and History of Their Early Relations* (Oxford: Oxford University Press, 2013), 102–34. His point is well-taken, but this should not undermine the level of conflict, as seen during the rebuilding efforts when the nations surrounding Judah are referred to as their enemies (Neh 4:11; 5:9; 6:1, 16) who sought to undermine their rebuilding activities (cf. Neh 2:19; 4:1–6, 15; 6:1–9, etc.); see also Briant, *From Cyrus to Alexander*, 586–587.

Marriage with a foreign spouse was not the primary issue,[34] but rather, such marriages had the potential to lead to syncretism and religious compromise. For example, ostraca found at Beersheba indicate that a third of the names were compounds that included the Edomite god Qos. Similarly, among the ostraca found at Arad, five had compound names with Yahweh, whereas four had compound names with Qos.[35] While the employment of theophoric names compounded with a foreign god does not automatically indicate worship of that deity, these names, at the very least, testify to the religious pluralism of the period.[36] The point to note is that the Judeans living in the small province of Judah were not only living amid the vast Persian Empire, but they were surrounded by nations with competing religious beliefs. The Jewish temple at Elephantine and the sacred site on Mount Gerizim indicate that worship of Yahweh (and other gods) took place beyond the borders of Jerusalem, adding further complexity to the religious climate of the period.[37] These were the realities facing the returnees living in Jerusalem. Yet amidst such uncertain and changing times, the Chronicler speaks a resounding message of hope—God's people are to look beyond their circumstances and remember God's irrevocable calling. They are to recognize that God *is* at work. While they might feel powerless and not know what to do, they are exhorted to *fix their eyes on God*.

Theological Themes

A Vision for a United People of God

The opening genealogies resound with a vision for a united people of God that hearkens back to Israel's original calling (1 Chr 2:1–2). Even though the division of the kingdom results in two concurrent kingdoms—often in opposition to each other—God's plan from the beginning was that there would be *one people of God*. Israel's calling to be a kingdom of priests and a holy

---

34. On this topic, see the Chapter 3, Explain the Story, pp. 51–55.

35. Yamauchi, *Persia and the Bible*, 265n103. Block notes that Qos appears as a theophoric element in names dated to the Persian period, especially in the ostraca from Arad and Beersheba. At Beersheba, at least one-third of names have the god Qos in them; see Daniel I. Block, *The Gods of the Nations: A Study in Ancient Near Eastern National Theology*, ETS Studies; 2nd ed. (Grand Rapids: Baker Academic, 200013), 42–43.

36. For a survey of names used in Samarian coins and inscriptions and in the fourth-century Samaria papyri, see Knoppers, *Jews and Samaritans*, 109–134; see also Yamauchi, *Persian and the Bible*, 247.

37. For example, there is evidence that Aramean gods were worshiped at Elephantine, in addition to the worship of Yahweh; see Briant, *From Cyrus to Alexander*, 586; Yamauchi, *Persia and the Bible*, 244–45.

nation has not changed, therefore, and this vision reverberates throughout Chronicles. While the introductory genealogies focus on the important tribes of Judah, Levi, and Benjamin, they also include the tribes of Simeon, Reuben, Issachar, Naphtali, Manasseh, Ephraim, and Asher. In spite of their turbulent and divided history, the Chronicler has not lost sight of the northern tribes, for they constitute "all Israel," a key term that speaks of unity and common ancestry.

The Chronicler's history of the united monarchy under David (1 Chr 11–29) and Solomon (2 Chr 1–9) serves the didactic purpose of presenting a unified and flourishing kingdom, with joyful worship of God at its center. The gathering of "all Israel" and the widespread support David receives from all the tribes testifies to the kind of unity in view (1 Chr 11–12). After giving much attention to preparing for Solomon's rule, David's reign concludes with a picture of a unified kingdom, as all his leaders and the people give generously toward the temple, with praises offered to their God (1 Chr 29). When Solomon builds the temple, all Israel rejoices when the ark arrives and God's glory fills the temple, and with one voice they sing praises to their God (2 Chr 5). During the divided monarchy, times when northerners join the Southern Kingdom are intentionally highlighted, especially during the reign of Hezekiah, when he invites northerners to the Passover (2 Chr 30). This chapter is a commentary on 2 Chronicles 7:14. The celebration presents a powerful vision of forgiveness and reconciliation, as a united people share the Passover meal together. Such unity of former enemies is not achieved through military victory or political alliances, but through repentance, humility, prayer, forgiveness, and healing. Ultimately, it is a gracious and forgiving God who stands behind this unified vision, giving his people one heart.

This picture of a restored and unified people of God is not insignificant for the returnees. The tribes of Judah, Benjamin, and Levi had returned to Jerusalem, but among the returnees were the northern tribes of Ephraim and Manasseh (1 Chr 9:3). Their new context afforded them the opportunity to practice their theology, not simply as an intellectual ideal but in their daily lives, as they allowed the Scriptures to shape and inform their community. Since there was no king on the throne, the reigns of David, Solomon, and Hezekiah present a future vision, an eschaton of sorts, for a unified people of God that will be fully realized when the son of David from the tribe of Judah rules over God's everlasting kingdom, a rule that will one day extend to the ends of the earth. This vision has much to offer the contemporary church, something that will be explored in this commentary.

A Vision for a Worshiping People of God

The temple in Jerusalem is central to the vision of the kingdom of the Lord presented in the book of Chronicles. Even before the temple had been built, the procession of the ark of the covenant—the place where a holy God is enthroned—marks a climactic moment in David's reign (1 Chr 13, 15). The Levites are set apart to sing and play music with harps, lyres, and cymbals, so that they might raise sounds of joyful worship to the Lord (15:16–26). Levitical musicians have an important role in leading Israel in praise and thanksgiving (25:1–31), and thus they are ever-present in the stories of Israel's kings, like a delightful melody of praise that bubbles forth from a joyful heart. Three musical families who trace their ancestry back to Aaron form the basis of Israel's worship team: Heman, the singer from the line of Kohath (6:33–38), Asaph, from the line of Gershon (6:39–43), and Ethan, from the line of Merari (6:44–47). Since a holy God dwells among his people, the Levites are set apart to give thanks and praise to God. Solomon goes to great lengths to build a glorious temple worthy of the Lord God (2 Chr 2–4), a temple embellished with Edenic imagery that signals to the imagination that it represents God's heavenly abode. When the ark of the covenant is brought into the temple, Levitical choirs sing praises to God with one voice, accompanied by an array of Levitical musicians (5:1–14; 7:1–3). With God's glorious presence in their midst, Solomon kneels before God on a large bronze platform with his hands spread out toward heaven. There he declares: "Lord, the God of Israel, there is no God like you in heaven or on earth—you who keep your covenant of love with your servants who continue wholeheartedly in your way" (6:14). Prayers offered to God, along with songs of thanksgiving and praise rooted in the Scriptures, reverberate throughout the stories of Israel's kings, reminding us that God has called Israel to be a worshiping people. Chronicles even envisions that the nations—and indeed, the whole creation—is to praise the Lord (1 Chr 16)!

The returnees living in Jerusalem had rebuilt the temple, yet even though there had been joy at its dedication, there is notably no procession of the ark into the temple, as there had been during the time of Solomon (2 Chr 5:1–10). Nor is there any reference to God's glory filling the temple, as there had been earlier (vv. 11–14). The absence of any reference to the ark of the covenant in the post-exilic books stands in stark contrast to the Chronicler's emphasis on the ark (1 Chr 13, 15; 2 Chr 5). It may well be that just like the Davidic kings provide an eschatological vision of a future reign of David's son, so too the Chronicler's focus on the ark gives the returnees an eschatological vision of God's glorious presence among his people, not unlike the prophets Haggai and Zechariah, who looked ahead to a *future* indwelling of God's glory. God has set apart his people to be a worshiping and witnessing people, and thus these stories invite the returnees to worship God and seek his face as they sing joyfully unto the LORD, while also giving them a vision for a future and glorious indwelling of God's presence, at which time the entire creation will praise his holy name.

A Vision for a Prayerful People of God

The elaborate and beautifully embellished temple in Jerusalem takes Solomon seven years to build, but what is central to the narrative is the presence of a holy God who has come to dwell among his people—he is restoring what was lost in Eden. This means, therefore, that the temple narrative does not conclude with God's glory filling it but with an extended *prayer*, underscoring that the temple is the place where God's people commune with their God. Solomon's prayer (2 Chr 6:12–42) and God's response to him (7:12–22) lie at the center of the narrative. Even though the highest heavens cannot contain the LORD, the mystery is that the temple is the place where heaven and earth meet. God's people are invited to humble themselves, pray and seek God's face, and remarkably, God promises to hear from heaven, forgive, and heal (2 Chr 7:14). Accordingly, the stories of Israel's kings have a didactic purpose, allowing the Chronicler to teach on the important topic of prayer. Stories of God's people desperately crying out to the LORD for help amidst insurmountable circumstances are especially instructive. Along with cries for help, prayers of repentance are critical (such as Manasseh's prayer), since forsaking God will lead to his wrath (a concept known as *divine retribution*). Time and time again, God proves himself faithful. He will be found by those who seek him, and he hears the prayers of penitent sinners. These are the beloved stories of Israel's kings that illustrate the centrality of prayer. They are intended to cultivate in the returnees the virtues of prayer, repentance, and reliance upon God in their own community.

A Vision for a Witnessing People of God

God has set apart Israel to be a worshiping and witnessing people. The opening genealogies testify that God has set apart Israel *from* the nations to be his people, but their sacred calling is to be lived out *among* the nations. Thus, the Chronicler provides a "world map" at the outset to underscore the global context of their calling (1 Chr 1:5–23). The LORD is the creator of humanity (including all the nations), not simply Israel, and the borders of his kingdom will one day extend to the ends of the earth. The psalms of praise sung by the Levites when the ark is brought into Jerusalem exhort God's people to make known his deeds among all the peoples (1 Chr 16:8, 24). They are to tell of his glory among the nations (v. 24). The psalm envisions that the nations will hear the resounding message that the LORD reigns (v. 31). David will later affirm that the LORD God is the creator of the whole earth, and thus everything belongs to him. He is "exalted as head over all" (29:11). With this cosmic vision in view, when Solomon builds the temple, the narrative is framed by declarations by foreigners (2 Chr 2:12; 9:8). The non-Israelite king of Tyre affirms that Israel's God is the creator when he gives words of praise: "Praise be to the LORD, the God of Israel, who made heaven and earth!" (2:12). Later, the queen of Sheba comes to Jerusalem with words of praise on her lips: "Praise be to the LORD your God" (9:8). Solomon's prayer had already anticipated that foreigners would hear of God's great name and pray to him. The vision is that "all the peoples of the earth" would know God's great name and fear him (6:33). Thus, even foreign dignitaries will come from afar and bring tribute into Jerusalem. There is the expectation, therefore, that the whole of creation will praise the LORD (1 Chr 16:30–33). Since the returnees were living in a small province amidst a vast Persian Empire with nations surrounding them, the opening genealogies and the stories that follow serve as reminders of their sacred calling. They are to make known the name of the LORD among the nations, for the LORD is great and "most worthy of praise" (v. 25).

Resources for Teaching and Preaching

There are many good commentaries that have been written on 1–2 Chronicles. Given that some of the discussions can be highly technical, especially when there are contested textual issues, I refer to the more technical commentaries in the footnotes. Although the volume by Sara Japhet is in this category, her commentary is thorough and comprehensive, so it has been cited below as an important resource. For the most part, the books selected as resources are more accessible and therefore highly beneficial for teaching and preaching. One of my favorite books on Chronicles is by Scott Hahn, *The Kingdom of God as Liturgical Empire*. It is essential reading for any pastor wanting to gain a deeper understanding of the theology of Chronicles. The commentary by Eugene Merrill is also rich in theology and includes appendixes on key topics that are helpful for preaching and teaching. For those wanting to do a Bible study on Chronicles, I have included my eight-week Bible study on Chronicles in the list below entitled, *Cultivating Godliness*. For those wanting to learn more about the Persian Period, the work by Edwin M. Yamauchi is an excellent resource.

Boda, Mark J. *1-2 Chronicles*. CBC. Carol Stream, IL: Tyndale House, 2010.

Hahn, Scott W. *The Kingdom of God as Liturgical Empire: A Theological Commentary on 1-2 Chronicles*. Grand Rapids: Baker Academic, 2012.

Japhet, Sara, *I & II Chronicles*. OTL. Louisville: Westminster John Knox Press, 1993.

Kaminski, Carol M. *Cultivating Godliness: An Eight-Week Bible Study on 1-2 Chronicles*. Casket Empty Media, 2023.

King, Phillip J. and Lawrence E. Stager. *Life in Biblical Israel*. Library of Ancient Israel Louisville: Westminster John Knox Press, 2001.

Merrill, Eugene H. *A Commentary on 1 & 2 Chronicles*. Grand Rapids: Kregel Publications, 2015.

McConville, J. G. *1 & 2 Chronicles*. Daily Study Bible Series. Philadelphia: Westminster, 1984.

Selman, M. J. *1 Chronicles: An Introduction and Commentary*. TOTC. Downers Grove, IL: InterVarsity Press, 1994.

Selman, M. J. *2 Chronicles: A Commentary.* TOTC. Downers Grove, IL, InterVarsity Press, 1994.

Williamson, H. G. M. *1 and 2 Chronicles.* NCB. Grand Rapids: Eerdmans, 1982.

Yamauchi, Edwin M. *Persia and the Bible.* Grand Rapids: Baker Books, 1990.

1 Chronicles 1:1–54

 LISTEN to the Story

¹Adam, Seth, Enosh, ²Kenan, Mahalalel, Jared, ³Enoch, Methuselah, Lamech, Noah.

⁴The sons of Noah:
  Shem, Ham and Japheth.

⁵The sons of Japheth:
  Gomer, Magog, Madai, Javan, Tubal, Meshek and Tiras.
⁶The sons of Gomer:
  Ashkenaz, Riphath and Togarmah.
⁷The sons of Javan:
  Elishah, Tarshish, the Kittites and the Rodanites.

⁸The sons of Ham:
  Cush, Egypt, Put and Canaan.
⁹The sons of Cush:
  Seba, Havilah, Sabta, Raamah and Sabteka.
The sons of Raamah:
  Sheba and Dedan.
¹⁰Cush was the father of
  Nimrod, who became a mighty warrior on earth.
¹¹Egypt was the father of
    the Ludites, Anamites, Lehabites, Naphtuhites, ¹²Pathrusites,
      Kasluhites (from whom the Philistines came) and Caphtorites.
¹³Canaan was the father of
    Sidon his firstborn, and of the Hittites, ¹⁴Jebusites, Amorites,
      Girgashites, ¹⁵Hivites, Arkites, Sinites, ¹⁶Arvadites, Zemarites
      and Hamathites.

¹⁷The sons of Shem:

Elam, Ashur, Arphaxad, Lud and Aram.

The sons of Aram:

Uz, Hul, Gether and Meshek.

¹⁸Arphaxad was the father of Shelah,

and Shelah the father of Eber.

¹⁹Two sons were born to Eber:

One was named Peleg, because in his time the earth was divided;

his brother was named Joktan.

²⁰Joktan was the father of

Almodad, Sheleph, Hazarmaveth, Jerah, ²¹Hadoram, Uzal,

Diklah, ²²Obal, Abimael, Sheba, ²³Ophir, Havilah and Jobab.

All these were sons of Joktan.

²⁴Shem, Arphaxad, Shelah,

²⁵Eber, Peleg, Reu,

²⁶Serug, Nahor, Terah

²⁷and Abram (that is, Abraham).

²⁸The sons of Abraham:

Isaac and Ishmael.

²⁹These were their descendants:

Nebaioth the firstborn of Ishmael, Kedar, Adbeel, Mibsam,

³⁰Mishma, Dumah, Massa, Hadad, Tema, ³¹Jetur, Naphish

and Kedemah. These were the sons of Ishmael.

³²The sons born to Keturah, Abraham's concubine:

Zimran, Jokshan, Medan, Midian, Ishbak and Shuah.

The sons of Jokshan:

Sheba and Dedan.

³³The sons of Midian:

Ephah, Epher, Hanok, Abida and Eldaah.

All these were descendants of Keturah.

³⁴Abraham was the father of Isaac.

The sons of Isaac:

Esau and Israel.

³⁵The sons of Esau:
  Eliphaz, Reuel, Jeush, Jalam and Korah.
³⁶The sons of Eliphaz:
  Teman, Omar, Zepho, Gatam and Kenaz;
  by Timna: Amalek.
³⁷The sons of Reuel:
  Nahath, Zerah, Shammah and Mizzah.

³⁸The sons of Seir:
  Lotan, Shobal, Zibeon, Anah, Dishon, Ezer and Dishan.
³⁹The sons of Lotan:
  Hori and Homam. Timna was Lotan's sister.
⁴⁰The sons of Shobal:
  Alvan, Manahath, Ebal, Shepho and Onam.
The sons of Zibeon:
  Aiah and Anah.
⁴¹The son of Anah:
  Dishon.
The sons of Dishon:
  Hemdan, Eshban, Ithran and Keran.
⁴²The sons of Ezer:
  Bilhan, Zaavan and Akan.
The sons of Dishan:
  Uz and Aran.

⁴³These were the kings who reigned in Edom before any Israelite king
  reigned:
  Bela son of Beor, whose city was named Dinhabah.
⁴⁴When Bela died, Jobab son of Zerah from Bozrah succeeded him as
  king.
⁴⁵When Jobab died, Husham from the land of the Temanites
  succeeded him as king.
⁴⁶When Husham died, Hadad son of Bedad, who defeated Midian in the
  country of Moab, succeeded him as king. His city was named Avith.
⁴⁷When Hadad died, Samlah from Masrekah succeeded him as king.
⁴⁸When Samlah died, Shaul from Rehoboth on the river succeeded
  him as king.

⁴⁹When Shaul died, Baal-Hanan son of Akbor succeeded him as
king.
⁵⁰When Baal-Hanan died, Hadad succeeded him as king. His city
was named Pau, and his wife's name was Mehetabel daughter of
Matred, the daughter of Me-Zahab. ⁵¹Hadad also died.

The chiefs of Edom were:
Timna, Alvah, Jetheth, ⁵²Oholibamah, Elah, Pinon, ⁵³Kenaz,
Teman, Mibzar, ⁵⁴Magdiel and Iram. These were the chiefs of
Edom.

Listening to the Text in the Story: Genesis 5:1–32; 10:1–32; 11:10–26

The Chronicler begins his account of Israel's history with a series of genealogies that begin with Adam and continue through Abraham, Isaac, and
Israel, extending to the twelve tribes of Israel and their settlement in the land.
These chapters span the entire history of God's people from creation until
the post-exilic period under the Persian Empire. As we traverse this landscape
through a plethora of names and intertwining relationships, it is helpful to
consider the larger purpose of these genealogies and how they contribute to
Chronicles as a whole.

First of all, it is important to bear in mind that, while the contemporary
reader is familiar with narratives, the genre of *genealogy* is less accessible. Old
Testament genealogies are often seen as archaic lists that have minimal relevance
or application for life today. Hebrew names can be difficult to pronounce, and
the endless and laborious repetition of descendants seems to have little value.
References to geographical locations like Gibeon, Kiriath Jearim, or Gilead do
not resonate with us, in contrast to the more familiar towns like Bethlehem
and Hebron. Yet the names and places *did* speak to ancient Israelites, who
connected towns with tribal territories and important people. Far from being
irrelevant, these families and locations were the fabric of their social structure,
governing their relationships and giving them a sense of identity and place.
We can be at a loss, however, since these ancient tribal affiliations and Israel's
families of origin are unfamiliar to us. So, while Perez might be remembered
as the ancestor of King David, other people like Ephrathah, son of Hur, or
Makir, son of Manasseh, are less well-known, but they *are* significant for
Israel's story. When reading these genealogies, we can feel like outsiders, as

those living in a foreign land trying to make sense of another culture and its web of relationships. This can lead to a cursory reading of the genealogies at best, as we quickly pass over them. The role of the commentary is to highlight and explain what is important and what might readily be known by ancient readers so that we can understand what is being communicated and gain confidence in preaching from this portion of Scripture.

As we listen to the texts in this chapter, it is important to recognize that the genealogies have been taken from the book of Genesis. More details will be provided in the commentary below, but it is helpful to identify three important genealogies that form the backbone of the chapter. The first genealogy traces the *linear* line of descent from Adam to Noah, as recorded in Genesis 5:1–32. This corresponds to the first ten names in 1 Chronicles 1:1–4. The next genealogy traces the lines of descent from Noah's three sons, Shem, Ham, and Japheth, as recorded in Genesis 10:1–32. Since these descendants represent nations, this *segmented* genealogy is often referred to as the Table of Nations (cf. 1 Chr 1:4–23).[1] The third genealogy traces the linear line of descent from Shem to Abram, as recorded in Genesis 11:10–26 (cf. 1 Chr 1:24–27). The significance of the two linear genealogies is that they trace the line of descent from Adam to Abraham, underscoring that God's purpose for his creation is being realized through Abraham or, more particularly, through Israel (1 Chr 2:1–2). The inclusion of the Table of Nations (1:5–23) and other non-elect genealogies (vv. 29–33, 35–44) indicates that God's calling of Israel is to be lived out on a global stage. God's people have been set apart to be a worshiping and witnessing people among the nations. We noted above that the Chronicler's writing is deeply embedded in the Scriptures, and this chapter is certainly a good example of the ongoing relevance of Israel's ancient texts for his own day.

EXPLAIN the Story

The Genealogy from Adam to Abraham (1:1–27)

Adam's linear genealogy is rehearsed in 1 Chronicles 1:1–4a. The genealogy is *linear* since only one son is named in each generation. It is highly selective,

---

1. Scholars distinguish between two types of genealogies: linear genealogies list only one son in each generation (Gen 5:1–32; 11:10–26), whereas segmented genealogies list more than one son in each generation (e.g., Gen 10:1–32). It is important to identify the type of genealogy, which is directly related to its function. For example, Adam's linear genealogy establishes a link between Adam and Noah, the tenth member, whereas the segmented genealogy in Gen 10:1–32 shows relationships between individuals and nations they represent. For further discussion, see Robert R. Wilson, "The Old Testament Genealogies in Recent Research," *JBL* 94 (1975), 169–89.

therefore, as each progenitor has other sons and daughters who are unnamed (Gen 5:4, 7, 10, etc.). Linear genealogies move quickly through time, providing a rapid succession of generations. Their purpose is not to show horizontal familial relationships, but to connect key figures in the genealogy, often by drawing attention to the first and tenth members. In the opening genealogy, Adam is the first member and Noah is its tenth. While the Chronicler has a highly abridged version of Adam's genealogy from Genesis (only giving their names), its purpose is to connect Adam to Noah, thereby showing that God's creational blessing first pronounced upon humanity is being taken up in his line (Gen 1:28; 5:1–2; 9:1, 7).

The second linear genealogy in 1 Chronicles 1:24–27, which has been taken directly from Genesis 11:10–26, extends the linear line another ten generations from Shem to Abraham. This identifies Abraham as the important tenth member (1 Chr 1:27). The result is that these two linear genealogies trace an unbroken genealogical line from Adam to Abraham. This communicates powerfully at the outset of Israel's history that the creation blessing given to humanity is being taken up by Abraham and his descendants. In the book of Genesis, language from the creation blessing, "be fruitful and increase in number" (Gen 1:28; 9:1), is reissued to Abraham, Isaac, and Jacob, but the imperatives shift to *promises* with God as subject (17:2, 6; 22:17; 26:4, 24; 28:3). The barrenness of Sarah serves as a tangible reminder that the creation blessing taken up by Abraham's descendants will be accomplished by God, in fulfillment of his promise (Gen 18, 21; cf. Rom 9:6–9; Gal 4:27–28). Genesis testifies, therefore, that the emergence of nations in Genesis 10:1–32 does not mark the fulfilment of the creation blessing, but rather, it is first being realized in the miraculous multiplication of Abraham's descendants according to divine promise (47:27; Exod 1:7).[2] The opening genealogies are the vehicle through which God's creation blessing is being realized. The line is first traced from Adam to Abraham, but it will lead to Israel (1 Chr 2:1–2) and even more narrowly to Judah (v. 3). The creation blessing will ultimately be fulfilled in the tribe of Judah, through David's line in particular, and, as we will see shortly, this is the most ethnically diverse tribe among all the tribes.

The Table of Nations located between these two linear genealogies traces the families of Noah's three sons, Shem, Ham, and Japheth (1:4b–23). It is identified as a *segmented* genealogy because more than one son is given in each

---

2. I have argued that the creation blessing is not fulfilled in the Table of Nations, but rather, it is first being fulfilled in Israel. The blessing then extends *to the nations* through Abraham's descendants; see Carol M. Kaminski, *From Noah to Israel: Realization of the Primaeval Blessing After the Flood* (JSOTSup, 413; London: T&T Clark, 2004).

generation. For example, seven sons of Japheth are listed in 1 Chronicles 1:5. The genealogies of Japheth (vv. 5–7), Ham (vv. 8–16), and Shem (vv. 17–23) correspond to their genealogies in Genesis 10:1–32. It is important to bear in mind that individuals named in the genealogy represent nations or people groups. Consider Ham's four sons (1 Chr 1:8): the name Cush refers to Africa; the second son is Egypt (Hebrew, "Mizraim"); the third son is Put (his identity is uncertain); and the last son, Canaan, refers to the Canaanites. While not every nation is represented, the highly stylized form with its emphasis on *seventy* conveys the idea of completeness.[3] It is functioning, therefore, as a genealogical "world map" intended to represent all the nations of the ancient world. Interest in the nations is seen in the inclusion of Israel's neighbors, including Philistines, Canaanites, Jebusites, Amorites, Girgashites, and Hivites (1:12–15; cf. Gen 15:18–21; Deut 7:1–2), along with the extended genealogy of Esau, whose descendants are known as the Edomites (1 Chr 1:35–54). We will encounter some of these people groups later in Chronicles, but at this point we simply note that the Chronicler is laying out a world map as the global context for Israel's calling. Since the returnees were living as a small province surrounded by nations, this presents a powerful vision for them as they grapple with how to live as God's people in their new context. The Table of Nations thus provides a theological lens and a "world map" through which the returnees are to interpret their own context and calling.

As we look more closely at the genealogy, it is important to notice that the order in which the descendants of Shem, Ham, and Japheth are presented has been reversed (Japheth, 1:5–7; Ham, vv. 8–16; and Shem, vv. 17–23). This reversal reflects the same literary feature found in Genesis 10:1–32, where Japheth's genealogy is given first (vv. 2–5), then Ham's (vv. 6–20), and finally Shem's (vv. 21–31). This is an ancient literary device intended to show that the lines of Japheth and Ham are secondary, whereas the line of Shem is the main line of promise. This means that the creation blessing, "be fruitful and increase in number" (1:28), is not being taken up by all three sons but by Shem's line in particular, which leads directly to Abraham (1 Chr 1:24–27). This indicates that the creation blessing will *first* be realized in Abraham's descendants (cf. Gen 17:2, 6; 28:3; 47:27; Exod 1:7), although it will eventually extend to all the nations.

By rehearsing these familiar genealogies from Genesis, the Chronicler has masterfully located Israel *among* the nations, as one people among many

---

3. The number seven is used in the ancient world to signify completeness or perfection. In accordance with ancient literary convention, the Table of Nations is highly stylized with a total number of seventy names being represented.

belonging to a world map (1 Chr 1:5–23), yet God's people are also *set apart* from the nations, since their particular linear genealogies speak of election and promise (vv. 1–4, 24–27). God's sovereign plan is that his covenant people are to be a worshiping and witnessing community, testifying to the nations that the LORD reigns. This gives a vision for the returnees: God's creational work is being accomplished in the particular people Israel, but the context is the world so that the name of the LORD might be known and proclaimed among the nations (1 Chr 16). The LORD is, after all, creator of *humanity*, not simply Israel, and the borders of his kingdom are global—they are intended to reach to the *ends of the earth* (Pss 2:8; 72:8–11)

Abraham's Two Sons: Isaac and Ishmael (1:28–34a)

The family tree narrows further to focus on Abraham's two sons, Isaac and Ishmael (1 Chr 1:28). Characteristic of the secondary line of descent, Ishmael's genealogy is given first (1:28–31; cf. Gen 25:12–16), followed by the sons of his concubine Keturah (1 Chr 1:32–33; cf. Gen 25:1–4). Isaac's sons are given next (1 Chr 1:34), which identifies him as the line of promise. This is consistent with Genesis, where Isaac is the heir of the Abrahamic promises and the covenant, rather than Ishmael (Gen 17:21; 25:5; 26:2–5, 23–24). We will see shortly, however, that the nations are not excluded from the line of promise, for they have been incorporated into the tribe of Judah (including an Ishmaelite, 1 Chr 2:17).[4] That the nations are included in David's family tree is an important signpost, pointing forward to the multi-ethnic kingdom of God that will be revealed in the advent of the Messiah.

Isaac's Two Sons: Esau and Israel (1:34b–54)

The genealogy continues with Isaac's two sons, Esau and Israel (1 Chr 1:34). In the genealogy, Isaac's younger son is not identified as *Jacob*, as one might expect from Genesis (cf. Gen 25:25–26), but *Israel*, the name given to him by God (cf. Gen 32:28; 35:9–12). The name Israel (which is a favorite of the Chronicler) serves as a reminder of God's promises of old, which included the reaffirmation of the creation blessing of multiplication (Gen 35:11; cf. 1:28; 9:1; 47:27), the promise of becoming a great nation and a "community of nations,"[5] (35:11; cf. 12:2), the promise of kings (35:11; cf. 17:6, 16; 49:10; Num 24:17), and the promise of land, originally given to Abraham (Gen 35:12; cf. 12:7; 13:14–17; 17:8, etc.). Therefore, the name Israel is deeply

---

4. See Live the Story in Chapter 2, pp. 46–48.
5. The Hebrew word *qahal*, translated as "community" can mean "sacred assembly." On the significance of this term, see Live the Story in Chapter 59, p. 512.

rooted in God's promises to the patriarch Israel. The Chronicler uses the name *Israel* to connect the returnees with their earlier history and to show that they are the continuation of this story.

Since Israel's sons are given *after* Esau's descendants (1 Chr 2:1–2), this identifies Israel as the line of promise. In the meantime, the descendants of Esau (as the secondary line of descent) are given first (1:35–37), along with the sons of Seir (vv. 38–42; cf. Gen 36:8, 20–30), followed by a list of Edomite kings and chiefs (1 Chr 1:43–54; cf. Gen 36:31–43). The Edomites, who were descendants of Esau, had been given Mount Seir (Gen 36:8–9; Deut 2:4–8), the region south-east of the Dead Sea. It is important to remember the earlier prophecies in Genesis about Jacob and Esau that identified them as two nations, with the older brother, Esau, serving his younger brother Jacob (Gen 25:23; 27:27–29, 39–40; cf. Num 24:17–19). While the two brothers finally reconcile after years of estrangement (Gen 27–28, 32–33), ongoing conflict between the nations they represent is seen in the animosity between the Edomites and Israelites.[6] It comes to a climax in the final days of the Southern Kingdom, and God will pronounce judgment against them for the treatment of Israel (Ps 137:7; Lam 4:21–22; Ezek 25:12–14). While it appears that the Edomites had abandoned their urban settlement, their presence in southern Palestine nevertheless continues into the Persian period, attested by Aramaic ostraca from Arad and Beer-sheba that include Edomite names.[7] The boundary for their pastoral life seems to have been just south of Hebron, indicating that they are one of Judah's close neighbors.[8]

The genealogy concludes with a list of Edomite kings who reigned in the land of Edom before any Israelite king ruled (1 Chr 1:43–54; cf. Gen 36:31–43).[9] In contrast to "dynastic succession" that will be central to Davidic kings (where each king is identified as the *son* of the previous king, cf. 1 Chr 3:10–14), in this genealogy, each king simply reigns in place of the previous king, not unlike what is seen in the Northern Kingdom (cf. 1 Kgs 16:22; 2 Kgs 1:17). For example, the genealogy records that when Bela died, Jobab, the son of Zerah (not "son of Bela"), becomes king in his place (1 Chr 1:44). The absence of dynastic succession may suggest that they are more like Israel's judges, or perhaps even chiefs (cf. Exod 15:15). This differentiates Edomite

---

6. See the discussion on 1 Chr 18:12–13, p. 191, and 2 Chr 25, pp. 465–68.

7. As noted above in the introduction, p. 13.

8. See Kenneth G. Hoglund, "Edomites," in *Peoples of the Old Testament World*, eds. Alfred J. Hoerth, Gerald L. Mattingly, and Edwin M. Yamauchi (Grand Rapids: Baker Books, 1994), 343–45.

9. It is important to note at the outset that many of the names in this genealogy are obscure and very little is known about these rulers and their towns. Some may have been leaders of administrative districts, although there is much uncertainty; see Klein, *1 Chronicles*, 77–81.

rulers from Judah's kings. Given that God's promises are realized in *linear* genealogies, it may suggest that the Edomites have a secondary role in comparison to Davidic kings (cf. Num 24:17–19). As with the earlier presentation of the nations (1 Chr 1:5–23), this final section contributes to the global map that sets the context for the story of Israel. The cumulative effect of the chapter is that it "implies the diversity *and* unity of the world and it suggests that Israel understood its role within the family of nations and as a witness to all humanity."[10]

LIVE the Story

Israel to Be a Worshiping and Witnessing Nation

God's people were living as a small province within an expansive Persian Empire, surrounded by nations that were sometimes hostile. Even though the Persian Empire was extending its kingdom, Israel was not to lose sight of the centrality of *God's kingdom*, which was rooted in his election of Israel that hearkens back to creation. The returnees who had resettled in Jerusalem and in the surrounding towns are being given a "big vision" of their role among the nations. The missional calling of God's people was first made known to Abraham (Gen 12:3), but it is important to recognize that this promise envisages that the nations will be blessed through Abraham's descendants, precisely, those identified in the Table of Nations. They are, indeed, "all peoples on earth" (12:3; cf. 10:5, 31), and these are the nations rehearsed by the Chronicler.

Israel's calling to be a blessing to the nations is articulated in 1 Chronicles 16, as their worship of God includes making his mighty deeds known *among the nations*. They are to testify among the nations that "The LORD reigns!" (v. 31). As noted above in the introduction (p. 17), when Solomon builds the temple, the entire narrative is framed by two public declarations by foreigners. The first one is on the lips of Hiram, the king of Tyre, who confesses: "Praise be to the LORD, the God of Israel, who made heaven and earth!" (2 Chr 2:12). This comes as a result of Solomon's bold testimony that his God was "greater than all other gods" (v. 5). The second proclamation that frames the temple-building narrative is on the lips of the queen of Sheba, when she begins her words with "Praise be to the LORD your God" (9:8). Even within Solomon's prayer, there is the expectation that foreigners will hear of God's great name

---

10. Ibid., *1 Chronicles*, 81.

and pray to God. The king implores God to answer "so that all the peoples of the earth may know your name and fear you" (6:33). This is the missional vision before the returnees, who are surrounded by nations, yet these are the very people who are to know the name of the LORD and fear him.

The church in the West is facing unchartered territory in a post-Christendom world. Todd Bolsinger writes on this new reality in his book, *Canoeing the Mountains*, where he advocates that our new context requires us to become communities transformed for mission. He recalls that when Lesslie Newbigin retired from forty years of missionary service in India, he returned to a Great Britain that was very different to what it was forty years earlier; he writes:

> What he found in his beloved homeland was a more difficult mission field than he had left behind. He wrote, "England is a pagan society and the development of a truly missionary encounter with this very tough form of paganism is the greatest intellectual and practical task facing the Church."[11]

Bolsinger notes that "in that one sentence Newbigin challenged the mental model of how the Christians in the West had seen their hometowns and resident cultures for what is now seventeen hundred years."[12] Our post-Christendom context means that the West has become the mission field, and so a renewed vision for mission is needed. This has been underscored by Phillip Jenkin's landmark book, *The Next Christendom: The Coming of Global Christianity*, where he rehearses the explosive growth of Christianity in the global south, along with the decline in what has traditionally been known as the West.[13] The decline in the West means that unreached people are now at *our* doorstep, and like the returnees, we are called to be a worshiping and witnessing people in our new context. This presents enormous challenges and unprecedented opportunities as the landscape of Christianity is undergoing a major transformation, all under the sovereign hand of God.

The returnees living back in Jerusalem were facing different and unfamiliar circumstances, and a vision *deeply rooted in Scripture* was needed for their new world. How were God's people to live in this new reality? How

---

11. Todd Bolsinger, *Canoeing the Mountains: Christian Leadership in Unchartered Territory* (Downers Grove, IL: IVP Books, 2018), 29, quoting Lesslie Newbigin, *Unfinished Agenda: An Updated Autobiography*, 2nd ed. (Edinburgh: St. Andrews Press, 1993), 236.

12. Ibid.

13. Phillip Jenkins, *The Next Christendom: The Coming of Global Christianity* (Oxford: Oxford University Press, 2002).

were they to see themselves in light of the powerful Persian Empire and the surrounding nations? The Chronicler reminds them of God's plan for his creation and their calling to make known his name among the nations. They were called to be a worshiping and witnessing kingdom, embodying a counter narrative to the kingdoms of the earth. The Scriptures were central for what it meant to live as God's kingdom-people. This is the call before the church today—the church in all parts of the globe: we are called to be a worshiping and witnessing community, testifying that Jesus reigns and that his kingdom is being established *globally*.

Jesus spoke about the kingdom after his resurrection when the disciples asked him when it was going to be restored. As they wrestled with their questions, Jesus responded by telling them they were to be *his* witnesses, not only in Jerusalem but "in all Judea and Samaria, and to the ends of the earth" (Acts 1:8). With this kingdom mandate in view, Philip proclaimed the good news about the kingdom of God to those in Samaria (8:9–12), and Paul spoke about the kingdom of God in Ephesus, so that the word of God was heard by Jews and Greeks (19:1–10; cf. 20:21). The book of Acts is a testimony to the early church witness in Jerusalem (chs. 1–7), Judea and Samaria (chs. 8–12), and finally, to the ends of the earth (chs. 13–28), culminating in Paul's teaching and preaching about the kingdom of God in Rome (28:23, 31). The kingdom envisioned here under the rule of Christ is a multi-ethnic kingdom, as people from all nations worship the King of Kings and Lord of Lords (Rev 4–5; 6:9–17; 15:1–8).

This was the call of God's people during the Persian period as their mission was being fulfilled amidst the nations. It is almost as though the Chronicler understood or saw from afar what Jesus would later teach his disciples—that the kingdom was like a mustard seed; even though smaller than other seeds and growing up amidst other plants, when fully grown it would become a great tree, and its branches would extend to the ends of the earth (Matt 13:31–32). This is the hope that is deeply embedded in these opening genealogies and throughout the book of Chronicles. Instead of focusing on their unpromising circumstances, which could lead to despondency and feelings of hopelessness (with no Davidic king on the horizon), God's people were not to forget what God had promised from long ago, for their calling was rooted in God's eternal plan. This is the kingdom that ought to capture our attention and give purpose to our lives, whether we are living as Christians in Africa, Asia, the Middle East, or even in a small New England town. While we may feel like a small minority amidst powerful and influential worldly kingdoms, God's heavenly kingdom *is* being established, and one day Jesus will return to judge all the nations and to rule over his creation. In the meantime, the church—the one people of God, with her rich mosaic of languages and cultures—is set apart to be a witnessing and worshiping community until Christ returns, as Jesus taught his disciples: "And this gospel of the kingdom will be preached in the whole world as a testimony to all nations, and then the end will come" (Matt 24:14).

LISTEN to the Story

¹These were the sons of Israel:
Reuben, Simeon, Levi, Judah, Issachar, Zebulun, ²Dan, Joseph,
Benjamin, Naphtali, Gad and Asher.

³The sons of Judah:
Er, Onan and Shelah. These three were born to him by a
Canaanite woman, the daughter of Shua. Er, Judah's firstborn,
was wicked in the LORD's sight; so the LORD put him to death.
⁴Judah's daughter-in-law Tamar bore Perez and Zerah to
Judah. He had five sons in all.

⁵The sons of Perez:
Hezron and Hamul.
⁶The sons of Zerah:
Zimri, Ethan, Heman, Kalkol and Darda—five in all.
⁷The son of Karmi:
Achar, who brought trouble on Israel by violating the ban on
taking devoted things.
⁸The son of Ethan:
Azariah.
⁹The sons born to Hezron were:
Jerahmeel, Ram and Caleb.

¹⁰Ram was the father of
Amminadab, and Amminadab the father of Nahshon, the leader
of the people of Judah. ¹¹Nahshon was the father of Salmon,
Salmon the father of Boaz, ¹²Boaz the father of Obed and
Obed the father of Jesse.

¹³Jesse was the father of

Eliab his firstborn; the second son was Abinadab, the third
Shimea, ¹⁴the fourth Nethanel, the fifth Raddai, ¹⁵the sixth
Ozem and the seventh David. ¹⁶Their sisters were Zeruiah and
Abigail. Zeruiah's three sons were Abishai, Joab and Asahel.
¹⁷Abigail was the mother of Amasa, whose father was Jether
the Ishmaelite.

¹⁸Caleb son of Hezron had children by his wife Azubah (and by
Jerioth). These were her sons: Jesher, Shobab and Ardon. ¹⁹When
Azubah died, Caleb married Ephrath, who bore him Hur. ²⁰Hur
was the father of Uri, and Uri the father of Bezalel.
²¹Later, Hezron, when he was sixty years old, married the daughter
of Makir the father of Gilead. He made love to her, and she
bore him Segub. ²²Segub was the father of Jair, who controlled
twenty-three towns in Gilead. ²³(But Geshur and Aram
captured Havvoth Jair, as well as Kenath with its surrounding
settlements—sixty towns.) All these were descendants of Makir
the father of Gilead.

²⁴After Hezron died in Caleb Ephrathah, Abijah the wife of Hezron
bore him Ashhur the father of Tekoa.

²⁵The sons of Jerahmeel the firstborn of Hezron:

Ram his firstborn, Bunah, Oren, Ozem and Ahijah. ²⁶Jerahmeel
had another wife, whose name was Atarah; she was the mother
of Onam.
²⁷The sons of Ram the firstborn of Jerahmeel:

Maaz, Jamin and Eker.
²⁸The sons of Onam:

Shammai and Jada.
The sons of Shammai:

Nadab and Abishur.
²⁹Abishur's wife was named Abihail, who bore him Ahban and
Molid.
³⁰The sons of Nadab:

Seled and Appaim. Seled died without children.

³¹The son of Appaim:

Ishi, who was the father of Sheshan.

Sheshan was the father of Ahlai.

³²The sons of Jada, Shammai's brother:

Jether and Jonathan. Jether died without children.

³³The sons of Jonathan:

Peleth and Zaza.

These were the descendants of Jerahmeel.

³⁴Sheshan had no sons—only daughters.

He had an Egyptian servant named Jarha. ³⁵Sheshan gave his daughter in marriage to his servant Jarha, and she bore him Attai.

³⁶Attai was the father of Nathan,

Nathan the father of Zabad,

³⁷Zabad the father of Ephlal,

Ephlal the father of Obed,

³⁸Obed the father of Jehu,

Jehu the father of Azariah,

³⁹Azariah the father of Helez,

Helez the father of Eleasah,

⁴⁰Eleasah the father of Sismai,

Sismai the father of Shallum,

⁴¹Shallum the father of Jekamiah,

and Jekamiah the father of Elishama.

⁴²The sons of Caleb the brother of Jerahmeel:

Mesha his firstborn, who was the father of Ziph, and his son Mareshah, who was the father of Hebron.

⁴³The sons of Hebron:

Korah, Tappuah, Rekem and Shema. ⁴⁴Shema was the father of Raham, and Raham the father of Jorkeam. Rekem was the father of Shammai. ⁴⁵The son of Shammai was Maon, and Maon was the father of Beth Zur.

⁴⁶Caleb's concubine Ephah was the mother of Haran, Moza and Gazez. Haran was the father of Gazez.

⁴⁷The sons of Jahdai:

Regem, Jotham, Geshan, Pelet, Ephah and Shaaph.

⁴⁸Caleb's concubine Maakah was the mother of Sheber and Tirhanah. ⁴⁹She also gave birth to Shaaph the father of Madmannah and to Sheva the father of Makbenah and Gibea. Caleb's daughter was Aksah. ⁵⁰These were the descendants of Caleb.

The sons of Hur the firstborn of Ephrathah:
    Shobal the father of Kiriath Jearim, ⁵¹Salma the father of
        Bethlehem, and Hareph the father of Beth Gader.
⁵²The descendants of Shobal the father of Kiriath Jearim were:
    Haroeh, half the Manahathites, ⁵³and the clans of Kiriath Jearim:
        the Ithrites, Puthites, Shumathites and Mishraites. From these
        descended the Zorathites and Eshtaolites.
⁵⁴The descendants of Salma:
    Bethlehem, the Netophathites, Atroth Beth Joab, half the
        Manahathites, the Zorites, ⁵⁵and the clans of scribes who lived
        at Jabez: the Tirathites, Shimeathites and Sucathites. These
        are the Kenites who came from Hammath, the father of the
        Rekabites.

Listening to the Text in the Story: Genesis 29:28–35; 30:1–24; 38:1–30;
    Micah 5:1–5

The story of God's people comes to a climax with the twelve sons of Israel (1 Chr 2:1–2). The genealogies that follow focus on their family trees and their settlement in the promised land. The northern tribes of Israel are represented in these genealogies (with the exception of Dan and Zebulun), but the focus is on the tribes of Judah (2:3–4:23), Levi (6:1–81), and Benjamin (7:6–12; 8:1–40). Emphasis on the royal line of Judah will narrow further to highlight David's line through Perez and his grandson Hezron (2:9–17; 3:1–24).

Several texts in Genesis provide important background information that helps us interpret Judah's genealogy in its present context. Jacob had two wives, Rachel and Leah, who each bore him sons (and a daughter named Dinah; Gen 30:21). Six sons were born to Leah: Reuben, Simeon, Levi, Judah, Issachar, and Zebulun (29:31–35; 30:17–20). Two sons were born to Rachel: Joseph and Benjamin (30:22–24; 35:16–18). Both wives had been barren before God had opened their wombs (29:31; 30:22), reminiscent of Sarah's barrenness (11:30; 18:11). Jacob fathered Dan and Naphtali through Rachel's maid, Bilhah (30:1–8), and he fathered Gad and Asher through Leah's maid, Zilphah (30:9–13), giving twelve sons in total (cf. 35:22–26; 46:8–27; Exod 1:1–5; 1 Chr 2:1–2).

Jacob's fourth-born son, Judah, is the focus of this chapter since interest lies with David and his descendants. Genesis 38 records that Judah had three sons, Er, Onan, and Shelah, who were born to him by his Canaanite wife, known as "the daughter of Shua" (38:12). Judah's firstborn son, Er, had married Tamar, but God took Er's life because he was evil in his sight (vv. 1–7; cf. Gen 46:12; Num 26:19). According to an ancient marriage custom, the brother-in-law of the childless widow was required to have sexual relations with his sister-in-law to raise up the family name by procuring a child (cf. Deut 25:5–10).[1] Yet Judah's second-born son, Onan, had disobeyed his father's request and had failed to meet his obligation as brother-in-law. He had wasted his seed, and his life had been taken by God (Gen 38:8–10). This left Shelah, the only remaining son of Judah. Yet Judah was hesitant to give Shelah to his daughter-in-law, for fear that he would die as well. After a considerable time of waiting, Tamar finally takes things into her own hands. She disguises herself as a prostitute, and Judah has sexual relations with her, resulting in her becoming pregnant (vv. 12–24). Judah's initial response was to have her killed, but after discovering that *he* was the father, he acknowledges his failure in providing for Tamar. Twins are born to Judah through Tamar: Perez and Zerah (vv. 27–30), and their genealogies will be taken up in this genealogy (1 Chr 2:4–6). As you read the genealogies, pay close attention to Perez's son, Hezron, and his three sons, Jerahmeel, Ram, and Chelubai (also known as Caleb). The line of Hezron through Ram is the most important, however, because David is from this line. As always, Davidic kingship is on the horizon.

EXPLAIN the Story

The Twelve Sons of Israel (2:1–2)

The linear genealogy tracing the line of descent from Adam to Abraham comes to a climax with the twelve sons of Israel: Reuben, Simeon, Levi, Judah, Issachar, Zebulun, Dan, Joseph, Benjamin, Naphtali, Gad, and Asher (1 Chr 2:1–2). As in Genesis, the reversal of primogeniture seen in the

---

1. See Kenneth A. Mathews, *Genesis 11:27–50:26*, NAC (Nashville: Broadman & Holman, 2005), 705–10.

preceding family history now comes to an end with Israel's twelve sons, who constitute the people Israel. Their genealogies can be traced back to Genesis (Gen 35:22–26; 46:8–25; cf. Exod 1:1–5), but the name *Israel* is used instead of Jacob (Gen 32:28; 35:10–12). All the tribes have a common ancestor, Israel, reminding God's people of his irrevocable plan for a united people of God. The unwavering commitment of the Chronicler to include the northern tribes has its origin in God's election of Israel, and his purpose still stands.

The Sons of Judah and His Line through Perez (2:3–8)

Judah's genealogy begins with his three sons, Er, Onan, and Shelah, who were born to him by his Canaanite wife, known as the daughter of Shua (translated as Bath-shua in some English translations, which simply means, "daughter of Shua"). In Genesis, marriage to someone outside of kin was looked upon negatively, especially a Canaanite, remembering that Noah had cursed Canaan (Gen 9:25–27). Prior to Judah's fathering children through a Canaanite woman, Judah's grandfather, Abraham, had instructed his servant to find a wife for his son Isaac. His servant had sworn by oath that he would not take a daughter from among the Canaanites, but instead, he would search for a wife from among Abraham's relatives (24:3–4, 37–38; cf. 27:46). Providently, God led Abraham's servant to Rebekah, who was a relative (24:15, 24–26, 47). Years later, Isaac similarly instructed his son Jacob not to take a wife from the daughters of Canaan (28:1–2, 6). By contrast, Jacob's brother Esau defiantly took an Ishmaelite wife, with full recognition that marriage to a foreigner displeased his father (28:8–9; cf. 36:2). That Judah's wife was *Canaanite* was not lost among early Jewish Targumic scholars, who tried to avoid this unsavory association by using a similar Hebrew word which meant *traders* instead of *Canaanite*.[2] Yet Judah's foreign marriage has not been glossed over by the Chronicler. To the contrary, it underscores that the line of Judah was not pure Israelite stock from the very beginning, a topic that is developed further in the Davidic genealogies, where non-Israelites are included in the tribe of Judah through marriage.[3]

As noted above, Jacob's firstborn son, Er, died, leaving his widow Tamar childless (1 Chr 2:3). Recalling Judah's illicit relationship with Tamar, the Chronicler notes that Judah's "daughter-in-law" (Heb. *kalla*) Tamar bore him Perez and Zerah (v. 4). According to Leviticus, a man who uncovered the

---

2. Victor P. Hamilton, *The Book of Genesis: Chapters 18–50*, NICOT (Grand Rapid: Eerdmans, 1995), 433n20.

3. See Live the Story below, pp. 46–48.

nakedness of his daughter-in-law (Heb. *kalla*) was to be put to death (Lev 18:15; 20:12). This is a sober reminder that Judah was not chosen as the royal line based on his own righteousness—quite the contrary!—and it highlights the grace of God shown to him.

The line continues with Tamar's two sons, Perez and Zerah, bringing Judah's sons to five in total (1 Chr 2:4). The two sons of Perez are given next, Hezron and Hamul (v. 5), followed by the sons of Zerah (vv. 6–8), which includes a brief reference to the sin of Achan, who belonged to the tribe of Judah (Josh 7:1–26). Many years earlier, a man named Achan had coveted gold and silver found among the spoil of Israel's enemy and had secretly taken it, even though it was strictly prohibited. As a result of his actions, the Israelites had suffered a tragic defeat with thousands being killed, thereby bringing "trouble" (Heb. *'akor*) on Israel. Recalling this history, the Chronicler refers to him as Achar (Heb. *'akar*). His presence in the genealogy serves as a reminder that Achan belonged to the tribe of Judah (cf. Josh 7:1, 16–18). Notably, his sin is identified as "violating [the ban]" (Heb. *ma'al*, 1 Chr 2:7), a key term in Chronicles that is usually translated "be unfaithful" in the NIV (5:25; 9:1; 10:13, etc.).[4] Here it underscores that Judah is not exempt from unfaithfulness (cf. 9:1; 2 Chr 36:14).

The Genealogy of King David through Perez's Son, Hezron (2:9–17)

The genealogy narrows further to focus on Perez's son Hezron and his three sons, Jerahmeel, Ram, and Caleb (also known as Chelubai). Their descendants are given in the following verses: Ram (1 Chr 2:10–17), Caleb (vv. 18–24, 42–55), and Jerahmeel (vv. 25–41). It is important to notice that Ram's genealogy is linear from Ram to Jesse (vv. 10–12), which is similar to the linear genealogy that concludes the book of Ruth (4:19–22). In Chronicles, the linear genealogy ends with Jesse, and David is introduced as the *seventh* son among his brothers, along with his sisters and their sons (2:13–17).[5] Several people in the genealogy are known from other texts. For example, Nahshon was a leader of Judah at the time of Moses (cf. Exod 6:23; Num 1:7; 2:3); Boaz was the husband of Ruth during the Judges period (Ruth 4:13); and Jesse was the father of David (v. 17; 1 Sam 16:1–13). The sons of David's sisters are also given, and a comment is made about Abigail's husband, Jether the Ishmaelite

---

4. For the meaning of the verb *ma'al*, see the discussion on 1 Chr 10:13 in Chapter 10, p. 119.

5. David is identified as the eighth-born son in 1 Sam 16:10, whereas in Chronicles he is the seventh, perhaps due to theological reasons identifying him as the important seventh member.

(1 Chr 2:17),[6] which highlights that a foreigner has been incorporated into the line of Judah.[7]

The Genealogy of Hezron's Son Caleb (2:18–24)

The genealogy of Hezron's son Caleb is given next (1 Chr 2:18–20, 24; cf. vv. 42–55). While the list of names can be daunting, it is helpful to keep in mind what is being emphasized in this genealogy. Caleb's sons through his two wives, Azubah and Jerioth, are noted (v. 18), yet his wife Azubah dies, and Caleb marries Ephrath. This is the line that is being highlighted, especially Caleb's fathering a son named Hur through Ephrath (vv. 19, 50–55; 4:1–4). Caleb's marriage to Ephrath is important because the name Ephrathah (an alternative spelling for Ephrath, 2:50; 4:4) is connected to King David. In the book of Ruth, Elimelek and his family are identified as "Ephrathites from Bethlehem, Judah" (Ruth 1:2). With this family background in view, David is identified as the "son of an Ephrathite named Jesse, who was from Bethlehem in Judah" (1 Sam 17:12). Ephrath is identified as Bethlehem in Genesis (cf. Gen 35:19; 48:7). The prophet Micah also refers to Bethlehem Ephrathah, which he identifies as a small clan in Judah, yet it will rise to prominence because of its association with messianic hope (Mic 5:2). By highlighting Caleb's wife *Ephrath*, the chapter anticipates Davidic kingship.

Similarly, a son named *Bethlehem* is included in Hur's descendants (1 Chr 2:51, 54; cf. 4:4), providing further connection to David. Boda summarizes the importance of the Hezron-Caleb line in this chapter, noting that "the Chronicler is highlighting a role played by the Hezron-Caleb line, that is, the founding not only of the towns throughout Judah that would become the power base of the royal line of Judah, but also of the key town (Bethlehem), which would nurture the royal line itself until David would arise."[8] He notes further that the Chronicler has emphasized Bethlehem by framing the chapter with references to this important town (2:51, 54; 4:4). We are reminded here that genealogies are not simply lists of names, but theology is embedded in them. By focusing on Caleb's marriage to Ephrath and their descendants, attention is on King David, whose anointing will take place in Bethlehem.

The second reason why Caleb's line is featured is because Hur's genealogy

---

6. The Hebrew of 2 Samuel 17:25 identifies Jether as an Israelite. Knoppers suggests that the Chronicler is dependent on a variant of 2 Sam 17:25 which agrees with 1 Chr 2:17. He notes further that Targum Chronicles (targums are the Aramaic, and sometimes interpretive, translations of the Hebrew OT) seeks to harmonize both texts; see Gary N. Knoppers, "Intermarriage, Social Complexity, and Ethnic Diversity in the Genealogy of Judah," *JBL* 120: 1 (2001), 19n21.

7. See below, Live the Story, pp. 46–48.

8. Boda, *1–2 Chronicles*, 47.

leads to a man named Bezalel (2:20), a well-known and skilled craftsman endowed with the Spirit. He had worked on the construction of the tabernacle (Exod 31:1–5; 35:30–35), and his altar will be used in the temple built by Solomon (2 Chr 1:5). His appearance in the genealogy connects the tribe of Judah to the temple, further highlighting the importance of Caleb's marriage to Ephrath.

The topic of inter-tribal relations is introduced with Hezron's marriage to the daughter of Makir (1 Chr 2:21). The book of Genesis records that Makir was a descendant of Joseph through his son Manasseh (Gen 50:23; Num 32:39–41). That a daughter of *Makir* marries into the tribe of Judah serves as an example of inter-tribal bonds contributing to the unity of the tribes, as does the reference to Gilead, which is located in the northern Transjordan (1 Chr 2:21–22). Later we will learn of occasions when the tribe of Manasseh joins with Judah (12:31, 37; 2 Chr 30:1, 10–11; 34:9) and when reforms are carried out in their territory (31:1; 34:6). Even Hezekiah's own son is named Manasseh, perhaps indicative of inter-tribal reconciliation. The tribe of Manasseh is also included among the returnees (1 Chr 9:3), something not mentioned in the parallel text in Nehemiah 11. This comment about Hezron's marriage to the daughter of Makir contributes to the vision for a united people of God. The genealogical fluidity of Makir will be highlighted later in the intermarriage of Manasseh with the tribe of Benjamin (see 1 Chr 7:14).

The Descendants of Hezron's Son Jerahmeel (2:25–41)

Next, focus is on the sons of Jerahmeel, the firstborn son of Hezron, whose descendants are given in two sections (1 Chr 2:25–32, 33–41). The clan of Jerahmeel had lived in the Negeb during the time of David. Identified as a seminomadic group, they are here fully incorporated into the line of Judah through Hezron. Within the genealogy, reference is made to an Egyptian servant named Jarha, who has been included in the line of Judah through marriage (vv. 34–35). His descendants are represented by a linear genealogy that is thirteen generations in length (vv. 35–41). This identifies it as one of the longest genealogies in the Old Testament, contributing to the important topic of the inclusion of the nations.[9]

Caleb's Descendants and the Towns They "Fathered" (2:42–55)

Additional descendants of Caleb are given, comprised of two lists (1 Chr 2:42–50a, 50b–55). The names in the genealogy refer to individuals and

---

9. Knoppers, "The Genealogy of Judah," 15–30; see below, Live the Story, pp. 46–48.

cities, and potentially both. The following names provide a sampling of names that are identified with cities: Ziph (2:42; cf. Josh 15:55), Mareshah (1 Chr 2:42; Josh 15:44), Hebron (1 Chr 2:43; cf. Josh 14:14–15; 15:13), Tappuah (1 Chr 2:43; cf. Josh 15:53), Maon (1 Chr 2:45; cf. Josh 15:55), and Beth Zur (1 Chr 2:45; cf. Josh 15:58).[10] A survey of these names indicates that they appear in Joshua 15, the chapter that outlines the territory of Judah. While not every name is known, it appears that both personal names and geographical locations are in view, and as Braun has noted, the territory for Caleb's descendants seems to be identified in the southern region of Judah's territory.[11]

The second list focuses on the sons of Hur, the firstborn of Ephrathah (1 Chr 2:50b). Hur's three sons are founders of important and well-known cities. Shobal is identified as the father of Kiriath Jearim, a border city belonging to Judah, formerly called Kiriath Baal (Josh 15:60; 18:14–15). This city is honored by being the place where the ark of the covenant is housed until it is transported to Jerusalem (1 Chr 13:5). The next son, Salma (alternative spelling, Salmon), is the founder of the well-known town of Bethlehem (2:51; cf. 1 Sam 16:1, 18; 17:12). His son is also called Bethlehem (1 Chr 2:54). Salma has already been identified as the father of Boaz, providing further connection to David (v. 11; cf. Ruth 4:21). It is clear from David's pedigree that he has strong ties to Bethlehem, the town associated with messianic expectations (Mic 5:2). The third son, Hareph, is the father of Beth Gader, a city otherwise unknown (1 Chr 2:51).

The genealogy concludes with the descendants of Shobal and their clans (vv. 52–53), which further links their towns to Judah (e.g., Zorah, Eshtaol; Josh 15:33). Finally, the descendants of Salma are given (1 Chr 2:54–55), connecting his family not only to Bethlehem, but also to other cities that suggest their migration north and south.[12] Braun notes that some of the names seem to have connection with Israel's neighbor, the Edomites, suggesting a potential relationship between Judah and the southern region.[13] Notably, the town of Netophah, located three miles southeast of Bethlehem, is among the post-exilic towns where Levites live, and some from this town were among the returnees (1 Chr 9:16; cf. Ezra 2:21–22; Neh 7:26; 12:28).

---

10. For a more extensive list, see Braun, *1 Chronicles*, 41–42.

11. Ibid., 42.

12. Klein, *1 Chronicles*, 107.

13. Braun, *1 Chronicles*, 42. For further information on the Edomites and their presence in Palestine after the exile, see the discussion in Chapter 1 on 1 Chr 1:34b–54, pp. 28–30.

LIVE the Story

The Grace of God Is on Center Stage

The introduction to the line of Judah—the most important line in the entire list of genealogies—has much to say about God's choice of Judah and his redemptive purposes. The opening verses highlight Judah's Canaanite wife and his illicit relationship with Tamar. The Chronicler has not avoided this family background, but in fact drawn attention to it. The significance of this has been noted by Hahn:

> To Judah are borne three sons by a foreign woman, a Canaanite, and David's direct line stems from Judah's illicit relationship with his daughter-in-law Tamar (Gen. 38; cf. Lev. 18:15; 20:12). The Chronicler is again pressing his theological points—that, against the ethnic exclusivist, even the royal line is not ethnically pure; in this case it contains Canaanite blood. He also seems to emphasize to his readers that God's ways are not our ways, that even out of human weakness and moral failure, God continues to work his purposes.[14]

In the story of David's family history, Judah not only marries a Canaanite woman, but he has an illicit sexual encounter with someone he thought was a prostitute, only to find out that she was his daughter-in-law. Things could not get much worse! This reminds us that the patriarchs were not chosen because of their righteousness—the story testifies to the contrary (cf. Gen 38:26). They are not chosen because they are good people, but because of God's sovereign and gracious plan.

This theme of God's grace reverberates throughout this line. Judah's firstborn son was "wicked in the Lord's sight" (1 Chr 2:3), which is the first reference to wickedness in Chronicles, yet it anticipates what will become all too evident in the stories of kings from the line of Judah. Kings such as Rehoboam (2 Chr 12:14), Jehoram (21:6), Ahaziah (22:3–4), Manasseh (33:2, 6), Amon (33:22), Jehoiakim (36:5), Jehoiachin (36:9), and Zedekiah (36:12) will be similarly described. We will even learn later that during the time of Manasseh, Judah will be charged with doing "more evil than the nations the Lord had destroyed before the Israelites" (33:9). God had dispossessed the

---

14. Scott W. Hahn, *The Kingdom of God as Liturgical Empire: A Theological Commentary on 1–2 Chronicles* (Grand Rapids: Baker Academic, 2012), 37.

nations because of their wickedness, but Judah is described as acting *more* wickedly than them. We also noted that Achar had acted unfaithfully (1 Chr 2:7), an important description that is used throughout Chronicles, but notably, it first appears with reference to the tribe of *Judah*. Saul will be charged with unfaithfulness (10:13), but so will southern kings, such as Rehoboam (2 Chr 12:2), Uzziah (26:16, 18), Ahaz (28:19, 22), and Manasseh (33:19), along with Judah (1 Chr 9:1). It is clear that the tribe of Judah is not exempt from wickedness and unfaithfulness, and the opening genealogies speak to this reality. Selman thus suggests that the presence of the verb "unfaithful" (Heb. *ma'al*; see discussion above, p. 40) in 2:7 and again in 9:1 indicates that "Israel is clearly riddled with 'unfaithfulness', from their entry into the promised land until their destruction by the Babylonians."[15] This is the place where sin *increases*, yet where sin increases, grace will abound all the more (Rom 5:20). This is, indeed, the genealogy of the Messiah (Matt 1:1–17). Even though Judah will be charged with unfaithfulness, the line of Judah has not come to an end. This is because of God's lavish grace.

The New Testament opens with a genealogy that traces the royal line of Judah, demonstrating that Jesus is Israel's promised Messiah (Matt 1:1). As Matthew rehearses the royal line, he does not gloss over unfavorable stories from the past, but instead, he recalls that Judah was the father of Perez and Zerah *by Tamar* (Matt 1:3); Salmon was the father of Boaz *by Rahab* (Matt 1:5); and David was the father of Solomon by *Bathsheba*, even identifying her as the *wife of Uriah* (Matt 1:6). When rehearsing our own family history, we may want to gloss over unsavory characters or family stories from our past that have the potential to tarnish our reputation, but in Chronicles and in Matthew's genealogy, these stories are remembered. Even ungodly kings such as Rehoboam, Ahaz, Manasseh, and Jehoiachin belong to this story. They serve as a testimony that the continuation of the line of Judah is due to God's grace and his faithfulness to his promises to David. Israel's most beloved and well-known king, David, knew the reality of God's grace in his own life, which was also evident in God's call of Israel (1 Chr 17:16–27). When confronted with the shameful reality of his own sin, he encountered God's mercy (2 Sam 12:1–25; 1 Chr 21:13; cf. Pss 32:1–5; 51:1–19). The genealogy of Judah reminds us from the outset that, in spite of human sin and failure, God's purposes still stand, and, remarkably, he uses sinners to accomplish his plans.

We can too easily assume that God chooses "good people" to accomplish his purposes. We rescript the stories of the key figures in the Old Testament

---

15. Selman, *1 Chronicles*, 96.

to make them our "heroes of the faith," yet often ascribe to them a level of perfection that is not found in the text. We can easily gloss over parts of their lives that put them in an unfavorable light, but this is not the testimony of Scripture. The apostle Paul identified himself as the greatest of sinners, yet he discovered the mercy of God. He was even called by God to be a witness to the Gentiles (Acts 9). Paul not only reminded the Corinthian church that those living immoral lives would not inherit the kingdom (his list includes the sexually immoral, idolaters, adulterers, men who have sex with men, thieves, the greedy, drunkards, slanderers, and swindlers; 1 Cor 6:9–10), but then he reminds them: "And that is what some of you were" (v. 11). They were to reflect on their calling and recognize that God has chosen the weak to shame the wise (1:26–29). Such lavish display of God's mercy in our lives does not lead to boasting, but to praise and worship, and to wholehearted service (Rom 12:1–2). Let us reflect upon God's call upon our lives, which is due to God's lavish grace and mercy. May we respond to the grace of God with hearts full of thanksgiving, remembering that God has not treated us as our sins deserve.

Judah's Place in God's Plan to Include All Nations

We noted above (pp. 28–30) that one of the purposes of the opening genealogies was to remind God's people that God's creational purposes were being fulfilled through Israel, and, more particularly, through Judah. God's people were to be a witnessing and worshiping community, testifying that the LORD reigns. God had promised Abraham that all the nations would be blessed in his descendants (Gen 12:3; cf. 18:18; 22:18; 26:4; 28:14), and such hope for the nations reverberates throughout the tribe of Judah. This is seen in six examples where non-Israelites have been included in Judah's genealogy: Judah's Canaanite wife, Shua (1 Chr 2:3; cf. Gen 38:2, 12); David's sister Abigail marries an Ishmaelite named Jether (1 Chr 2:17); Sheshan's daughter marries an Egyptian servant named Jarha (vv. 34–35); David's wife was Maakah, daughter of the king of Geshur (3:2); Mered married Bithiah, the daughter of Pharaoh (4:18); and Shelah's family is connected with Moab (vv. 21–22). Knoppers notes further that a number of non-Israelites who are only loosely associated with Israel have been incorporated into the Judahite genealogy, including Calebites, Jerahmeelites, and Kenizzites.[16] Building on the work of Knoppers, Hahn summarizes this feature, noting the following non-Israelites who have been included in the genealogy from groups such

---

16. For an insightful article on this topic, see Knoppers, "Genealogy of Judah," 15–30 (and on the textual issues related to the above texts, see especially pp. 19–25).

as "Canaanites, Ishmaelites, Arameans, Egyptians, Moabites, Calebites, Midianites, Jerahmeelites, Maacathites, Qenizzites, and Qenites, among others."[17] Non-Israelites also feature among David's military men, including Arabian Hagrites (1 Chr 11:38; cf. 27:31), Ammonites (11:39), Hittites (v. 41), and Moabites (v. 46). Two foreigners are also included among those who had charge of David's royal estate: Obil the Ishmaelite was in charge of the camels (27:30), and an Arabian Hagrite named Jaziz was in charge of the flocks (v. 31). That non-Israelites have been grafted into the line of Judah and are part of David's leadership underscores that God's plan to bless the nations through Abraham's descendants is being realized through the *line of Judah*. The inclusion of foreigners in David's genealogy makes this very point.

Sometimes there is the (false) assumption that the Old Testament is exclusively Jewish, whereas the New Testament is open to people from all nations. But this misinterprets the redemptive storyline of the entire Old Testament,[18] and it misses a key emphasis in the presentation of the tribe of Judah in Chronicles, which underscores that foreigners have been incorporated into the line of Judah. This is not to deny that there will be conflict with the nations,[19] as seen in Nehemiah's time (Neh 2:19–20; 4:1–8; 6:1–2, 16), but we need to keep both realities in view—God's people are to be a blessing to the nations, and they will be in conflict with those nations that oppose God (cf. 1 Chr 18–20). This chapter on David's genealogy focuses on the nations being incorporated into it.

The kingdom being established through David's line ultimately anticipates the Messiah, whose kingdom is comprised of both Jew and Gentile. The good news of the kingdom is to be preached to the ends of the earth as a witness for all nations (Matt 24:1–14). Jesus's disciples were to be his witnesses "in all Judea and Samaria, and to the ends of the earth" (Acts 1:8). The kingdom expanded as the disciples of Jesus were his witnesses in Jerusalem (Acts 1–7), Judea and Samaria (Acts 8–12), and finally, to the ends of the earth (Acts 13–28). This is how God's multi-ethnic kingdom is being established, as his salvation extends to the ends of the earth (Acts 13:47; cf. Matt 24:14). The book of Revelation gives us a glimpse of what is ahead for the people of God, as people from all tribes and nations worship the Lamb exalted on his throne (Rev 4–5; 6:9–17; 15:1–8). This is the kingdom to which we belong, and this is the kingdom that we are called to proclaim: the gospel of the kingdom of

---

17. Hahn, *The Kingdom of God*, 34.

18. One of the best books on this topic is Christopher J. H. Wright, *The Mission of God: Unlocking the Bible's Grand Narrative* (Downers Grove, IL: InterVarsity Press, 2006).

19. See the discussion on 1 Chr 18–20 in Chapters 18–20.

Christ which is for *all nations* (Matt 24:14; cf. Acts 8:9–12; 19:8–10; 20:21, 25; 28:23, 31). Just as God's people living in Jerusalem needed to have a fresh vision of their role among the nations, we, too, need a renewed vision of our role among the nations, with our eyes fixed on the multi-ethnic kingdom that Jesus is building. Instead of divisions in our churches among racial and ethnic lines, we are to represent God's eschatological community to the world, where people from all nations join together in worship of the one God. It is this vision that ought to shape our lives today, giving us hope and purpose, but also renewing our mission to proclaim the gospel to all nations until Jesus returns.

CHAPTER 3

1 Chronicles 3:1–24

 LISTEN to the Story

¹These were the sons of David born to him in Hebron:

The firstborn was Amnon the son of Ahinoam of Jezreel;

   the second, Daniel the son of Abigail of Carmel;

   ²the third, Absalom the son of Maakah daughter of Talmai king of Geshur;

   the fourth, Adonijah the son of Haggith;

   ³the fifth, Shephatiah the son of Abital;

   and the sixth, Ithream, by his wife Eglah.

   ⁴These six were born to David in Hebron, where he reigned seven years and six months.

David reigned in Jerusalem thirty-three years, ⁵and these were the children born to him there:

   Shammua, Shobab, Nathan and Solomon. These four were by Bathsheba daughter of Ammiel. ⁶There were also Ibhar, Elishua, Eliphelet, ⁷Nogah, Nepheg, Japhia, ⁸Elishama, Eliada and Eliphelet—nine in all. ⁹All these were the sons of David, besides his sons by his concubines. And Tamar was their sister.

¹⁰Solomon's son was Rehoboam,

   Abijah his son,

   Asa his son,

   Jehoshaphat his son,

   ¹¹Jehoram his son,

   Ahaziah his son,

   Joash his son,

   ¹²Amaziah his son,

   Azariah his son,

   Jotham his son,

   ¹³Ahaz his son,

Hezekiah his son,
Manasseh his son,
¹⁴Amon his son,
Josiah his son.
¹⁵The sons of Josiah:
Johanan the firstborn,
Jehoiakim the second son,
Zedekiah the third,
Shallum the fourth.
¹⁶The successors of Jehoiakim:
Jehoiachin his son,
and Zedekiah.

¹⁷The descendants of Jehoiachin the captive:
Shealtiel his son, ¹⁸Malkiram, Pedaiah, Shenazzar, Jekamiah,
Hoshama and Nedabiah.
¹⁹The sons of Pedaiah:
Zerubbabel and Shimei.
The sons of Zerubbabel:
Meshullam and Hananiah.
Shelomith was their sister.
²⁰There were also five others:
Hashubah, Ohel, Berekiah, Hasadiah and Jushab-Hesed.
²¹The descendants of Hananiah:
Pelatiah and Jeshaiah, and the sons of Rephaiah, of Arnan, of
Obadiah and of Shekaniah.
²²The descendants of Shekaniah:
Shemaiah and his sons:
Hattush, Igal, Bariah, Neariah and Shaphat—six in all.
²³The sons of Neariah:
Elioenai, Hizkiah and Azrikam—three in all.
²⁴The sons of Elioenai:
Hodaviah, Eliashib, Pelaiah, Akkub, Johanan, Delaiah and
Anani—seven in all.

Listening to the Text in the Story: 2 Samuel 7:8–17; Psalm 89:1–4, 36–37

Focus in this chapter is on the royal line of David. Although the Chronicler begins with David's sons born in Hebron (1 Chr 3:1–4) followed by his sons born in Jerusalem (vv. 5–9), attention shifts to Solomon (who is the tenth name in the list) and each son after him, with an unbroken line through to Josiah (vv. 10–14). Josiah's four sons are given, including Jehoiachin, "the captive" (vv. 15–17). The genealogy testifies that the exile of Jehoiachin does not bring an end to the Davidic line, but it remarkably continues with his sons born in Babylon (vv. 17–24). Since the line continues for several generations, this means that the royal line of David continues until the end of the Old Testament with the last member, Anani, dated to approximately 400 BC.

As we listen to the story of kingship set forth in this chapter, it is important to remember that God's promises to David concern one of his sons: "When your days are over and you go to be with your ancestors, I will raise up your offspring to succeed you, one of your own sons, and I will establish his kingdom" (1 Chr 17:11).[1] The recipient of God's promise is identified as "one of your own sons," something not mentioned in 2 Samuel 7. The genealogy in 1 Chronicles 3:10–14, with its relentless repetition of *his son* (e.g., "Abijah his son, Asa his son, Jehoshaphat his son;" v. 10) represents dynastic succession, thereby connecting each king to the Davidic promise. The linear genealogy thus testifies to God's promise to David, although it shifts with Josiah and his four sons (vv. 15–16). The shift to a segmented genealogy is indicative of the turbulent period that follows the death of Josiah, yet David's lamp has not been extinguished. Although kingship takes a more circuitous route with the exile of Jehoiachin (v. 17), the continuation of this genealogy testifies to the continuation of the royal line beyond the Babylonian exile (vv. 18–24), which resounds with hope that God's promises to David have not been forgotten.

EXPLAIN the Story

David's Sons Born to Him at Hebron and Jerusalem (3:1–9)

David's six sons born to him at Hebron are identified by their mothers: Amnon (by Ahinoam), Daniel (by Abigail), Absalom (by Maakah), Adonijah

---

1. See the discussion on 1 Chr 17 in Chapter 17.

(by Haggith), Shephatiah (by Abital), and Ithream (by Eglah; 1 Chr 3:1–4).[2] David's sons born to him in Jerusalem are given next (vv. 5–8; cf. 2 Sam 5:13–16), with four sons born to Bathsheba, identifying Solomon as the fourth (1 Chr 3:5; cf. 2 Sam 12:24–25).[3] When her sons are combined with the six born at Hebron, this positions Solomon as the important tenth name (1 Chr 3:5).[4] Moreover, when the other nine sons are given (vv. 6–8), this locates Solomon at the center of David's sons, with nine sons before him (vv. 1–5a) and another nine after him (vv. 6–8).[5] This elevates Solomon among his brothers, and it identifies him as the immediate heir of the Davidic promises (22:9–10; 28:4–7).

Solomon's mother was well-known as Bathsheba (2 Sam 11:3; 12:24; 1 Kgs 1:11, etc.), but she is called by an alternative Hebrew name, "Bath-shua," by the Chronicler (ESV, NASB, 1 Chr 3:5).[6] Since Judah's wife was named Bath-shua (lit. "daughter of Shua"), this alternative spelling establishes a subtle literary connection between Judah's wife and Solomon's mother, further legitimizing Solomon as royal heir (2:3–4; cf. Gen 38:12). The section is rounded off with a reference to David's sons by his concubines (1 Chr 3:6–9), along with their sister Tamar (v. 9). Reference to Tamar further reinforces the connection between David and Judah, whose daughter-in-law was named Tamar. She had become the mother of Judah's two sons Perez and Zerah (2:4; cf. Gen 38). Given that kingship is identified with Judah in the book of Genesis (Gen 49:8–10), echoes of kingship are implicit in this genealogy with the literary connections to the patriarch Judah. God's choice of Solomon will be stated clearly in the narrative leading up to Solomon's reign (1 Chr 22:9–10; 28:4–7; 29:1), but here the concept of election is being communicated through the genre of genealogy. It is not surprising to find, therefore, that the Chronicler takes up Solomon's linear genealogy next, as he traces David's line from Solomon to Zedekiah.

---

2. We noted above, pp. 41–42, that the line of Caleb is being highlighted (cf. 1 Chr 2:18–24). Reference to the town of Hebron provides further connection to Caleb since Hebron belonged to the Calebites (cf. Josh 14:13–15). For further connections with Caleb, see Jon D. Levenson and Baruch Halpern, "The Political Import of David's Marriages," *JBL* 99 (1980): 507–18.

3. That Solomon is *fourth* in this list underscores God's choice and election that is not according to primogeniture (cf. 2 Sam 12:24–25, where only Solomon is mentioned, not his three brothers).

4. The number ten is important in genealogies. For example, Noah is the tenth member in Adam's genealogy (1 Chr 1:1–4; cf. Gen 5:1–32), Abraham is the tenth member in Shem's genealogy (1 Chr 1:24–27; cf. Gen 11:10–26), and David is the tenth member in Perez's genealogy (Ruth 4:18–22).

5. Klein, *2 Chronicles*, 116.

6. The NIV simply has Bathsheba (perhaps not to confuse the reader), but the name Bath-shua is used by the Chronicler, which establishes an important literary link to the patriarch Judah.

The Royal Line from Solomon to Zedekiah (3:10–16)

Solomon is one among David's many sons (1 Chr 3:1–9), yet his linear gene-alogy indicates that he has been chosen to be David's successor. His father, David, acknowledges this fact when saying: "Of all my sons—and the LORD has given me many—he has chosen my son Solomon to sit on the throne of the kingdom of the LORD over Israel" (28:5). Focus is now on the singular line of descent, which is traced through Solomon's son, Rehoboam, and extends to Josiah, at which point the form shifts to a segmented genealogy (3:15). These are the kings whose stories are recounted in 2 Chronicles 10–35 (although the usurper Athaliah is not mentioned in the genealogy!).

The shift to segmentation is seen in Josiah's four sons: Johanan, Jehoiakim, Zedekiah, and Shallum (1 Chr 3:15). That there are *four* sons named in the genealogy is indicative of the precarious state of the kingdom after Josiah's death in 609 BC, which some scholars identify as the beginning of the seventy-year exile.[7] The absence of a singular line of descent indicates that the royal line is at risk as the stories of these puppet kings unfold. Except for Johanan, Josiah's three sons (and one grandson) will rule on the throne in Jerusalem. Their order of succession is outlined as follows, and their alternative names are noted:

Jehoahaz (= Shallum), son of Josiah (1 Chr 3:15; cf. 2 Chr 36:1–3)
Jehoiakim (= Eliakim), son of Josiah (1 Chr 3:15; cf. 2 Chr 36:4–8)
Jehoiachin (= Jeconiah/Coniah), son of Jehoiakim (1 Chr 3:16;
    cf. 2 Chr 36:8–10)
Zedekiah (= Mattaniah), son of Josiah[8] (1 Chr 3:15; cf. 2 Kgs 24:17;
    2 Chr 36:10–13)

Stories about these four kings are recorded in the last chapter of Chronicles. Despite the turbulent period leading up to the exile, the Davidic genealogy remarkably continues through Jehoiachin, son of Jehoiakim. The continuity of this royal line is traced next.

---

7. See Boda's discussion, *1–2 Chronicles*, 427; see also the discussion on 2 Chr 36:22–23, Chapter 65, pp. 568–69.

8. There is some question about the identity of the last king, Zedekiah, since there are two sons named Zedekiah in the genealogy (3:15, son of Josiah, and 3:16, son of Jehoiakim). In addition, the first Zedekiah is spelled with a longer form of the name (Heb. *tsidqiyyahu*) and the second is spelled with a short form (Heb. *tsidqiyyah*). It seems most likely that King Zedekiah was the son of Josiah (cf. Jer 37:1). This means that the last king on the throne was Jehoiachin's uncle (2 Kgs 24:17, spelled in Heb. *tsidqiyyahu*). For a more extensive discussion, see Japhet, *I & II Chronicles*, 97–99.

The Royal Line Continues During and After the Exile (3:17–24)

Jehoiachin is identified as the "captive" (Heb. *'asir*; 1 Chr 3:17), referring to his exile to Babylon in 597 BC. Nebuchadnezzar had brought Jehoiachin to Babylon, along with his mother, his wives, and leading citizens and artisans, including the prophet Ezekiel (2 Kgs 24:15–16; Ezek 1:1–2). The exile had been a watershed moment in Israel's history (1 Chr 9:1; 2 Chr 36:20; cf. Matt 1:11–12).

It is important to bear in mind that the last king on the throne was Zedekiah, Jehoiachin's uncle. Zedekiah's sons had been mercilessly killed by Nebuchadnezzar, at which time the rebellious Davidic king had been brutally blinded and brought to Babylon (2 Kgs 25:7–8; Jer 34:21). Since Jehoiachin represents the next generation *after* Zedekiah, the royal line of Judah extends furthest through him. This is why there is so much interest in Jehoiachin, even though he is among the ungodly kings who did evil in God's sight (2 Kgs 24:9; 2 Chr 36:9; cf. Jer 22:24–30). Clearly he has no godly character to merit his survival, yet remarkably, Jehoiachin lives another thirty-seven years in Babylon before being brought out of prison to eat at the king's table (2 Kgs 25:27–30; Jer 52:31–34). A Babylonian administrative document dated to the thirteenth year of Nebuchadnezzar records that oil and food were given to Jehoiachin and his five sons,[9] giving extra-biblical testimony to the royal line continuing amid this turbulent period. The significance of Jehoiachin was not lost on the Chronicler—he makes reference to his seven sons born in Babylon (1 Chr 3:17–18).

The names of Jehoiachin's seven sons are given (vv. 17–18), one of whom is Shenazzar (not to be identified with the well-known Sheshbazzar, cf. Ezra 1:8, 11; 5:14, 16, etc.).[10] The third son in the list, Pedaiah, will be particularly important, along with his brother Shealtiel. The genealogy extends further through Pedaiah's two sons, Zerubbabel and Shimei, and through Zerubbabel's sons and daughter (1 Chr 3:19–20). Zerubbabel was a well-known and important leader in the post-exilic community (Ezra 2:2; 3:2, 8; 5:2; Hag 1:1, 12; 2:1–9, etc.), serving as governor of the province of Yehud. Reference to the Davidic line being extended through his descendants underscores that the royal line continues beyond the exile. It is important to note that Zerubbabel's father is identified as Pedaiah in Chronicles, whereas elsewhere he is identified as Shealtiel (Ezra 3:2, 8; Neh 12:1; Hag 1:1; cf. Matt 1:12). One solution is

---

9. "The Court of Nebuchadnezzar," trans. A. Leo Oppenheim (*ANET*, 308); see also Isaac Kalimi, "Placing the Chronicler is His Own Historical Context: A Closer Examination," *JNES* 68:3 (2009), 186.

10. For further discussion, see Klein, *1 Chronicles*, 120.

that Shealtiel died before having children, and as such, his brother Pedaiah may have married Shealtiel's widow based on the levirate marriage, bearing Zerubbabel (Deut 25:5–10; cf. Gen 38). In this case, even though Pedaiah was Zerubbabel's biological father, the family name of Shealtiel was legitimately used to identify Zerubbabel, since the son born in a levirate marriage was to be called by the name of the childless dead brother (Deut 25:6).[11] While we cannot be certain, it is clear that Zerubbabel is the grandson of Jehoiachin, and as such, the royal line of David continues through him.

Zerubbabel's sons and daughter are given next (1 Chr 3:19–20), and their names serve as a testimony to God's faithfulness (see Live the Story below). The line continues as Zerubbabel's descendants are traced through several generations (vv. 19–24),[12] with the last member of the genealogy being identified as Anani (v. 24). Messianic hope may well have been connected with Anani, who is identified as the important seventh member. The Jewish Targum associates his name with messianic expectations (his name is a play on the expression "clouds of" in Dan 7:13), with the following comment given: "He is the king Messiah who will be revealed."[13] The name Anani also appears in the Elaphantine papyri, which records that Jewish mercenaries had sent a letter to the Persian governor of Yehud, as well as to the high priest Jehochanan, and to "Ostan the brother of Anani." If this figure is the same as Anani in 1 Chronicles 3:24 as scholars suggest, this dates him to 407 BC.[14]

LIVE the Story

The LORD Is Faithful!

The continuation of the royal line of David after the exile is a testimony to God's covenant loyalty to David and his faithfulness to his people. God had promised that he would restore his people and bring them back to Jerusalem. Despite the utter devastation around him, the prophet Jeremiah found hope in the character of the LORD, whose mercies are new every morning and whose faithfulness is great (Lam 3:21–24). God's faithfulness to his people is

---

11. Alternatively, Shealtiel could have been Zerubbabel's biological father, but his son was brought up by his brother Pedaiah, perhaps due to the death of Shealtiel and his wife. This would be analogous to Esther, who was cared for by her uncle Mordecai (Esth 2:7).

12. The exact number of generations from Jehoiachin to the end of the genealogy is debated, ranging anywhere from seven to fourteen.

13. As cited by Klein, *1 Chronicles*, 123n81.

14. "Petition for Authorization to Rebuild the Temple of Yaho," trans. H. L. Ginsberg (*ANET*, 492); cf. Kalimi, "Placing the Chronicler in His Own Historical Context," 186.

expressed in the names of Zerubbabel's descendants, something that is missed with a cursory reading of their names in English. Names can have significance in the ancient world, as they can today. Sometimes a name can recall a painful experience, such as Mara (Ruth 1:20–21) or Jabez (1 Chr 4:9–10), but they can also represent hope and promise. For example, when Lamech named his son Noah, it was with the hope that he would bring rest from the curse (Gen 5:29). In this chapter, the names of Zerubbabel's children resound with hope that testify to the character of the LORD ("Yahweh").[15] While the name Zerubbabel reflects his Babylonian context ("seed of Babylon"), the names of his sons and daughter (Shelomith) in 1 Chronicles 3:19–20 speak of the restoration:

> Meshullam (meaning "recompensed" or "restored"), Hananiah ("Yahweh is gracious"), Shelomith ("peace"), Hashubah ("consideration"), Ohel ("tent [of Yahweh]"), Berekiah ("Yahweh is blessed"), Hasadiah ("Yahweh has shown loyalty"), Jushab-Hesed ("let covenant loyalty be restored").[16]

The faithful character of the LORD ("Yahweh") is reflected in many of these names. God had revealed his name Yahweh to Moses many years earlier when the Israelites had made a golden calf and worshiped it. This is the content of the divine name that was revealed: "The LORD, the LORD, the compassionate and gracious God, slow to anger, abounding in love and faithfulness" (Exod 34:6). This is the character of God that permeates the entire Old Testament. Moses later exhorts the next generation of Israelites with these words: "Know therefore that the LORD your God is God; he is the faithful God, keeping his covenant of love to a thousand generations of those who love him and keep his commandments" (Deut 7:9). This is the character of the LORD that is on display when he restores his people. Zerubbabel's children are a powerful witness to the post-exilic community that the reason why they have returned was because *Yahweh has been gracious*. He has shown *covenant loyalty* to his people. Despite their struggles and their less-than-favorable circumstances, the returnees needed to remember that Yahweh is faithful, and he is accomplishing his redemptive purposes.

As we seek to live out the story, the question before us is whether we know

---

15. Some scholars believe that the sons and daughter in 1 Chr 3:19 refer to those born in Babylon, whereas those in 3:20 refer to those born after the return (see Klein, *1 Chronicles*, 120–21). Klein also notes that the name Shelomith appears on a bulla that dates to the late sixth century BC, which suggests she may have been a high-ranking functionary.

16. Boda, *1–2 Chronicles*, 56, citing Klein, *1 Chronicles*, 121.

the character of God. In the church today, God is often characterized as an angry and wrathful God, whereas Jesus is characterized by love and mercy. This can lead to a rejection of the Old Testament, but the Bible does not present two *different* images of God. On the contrary, Jesus explains and makes known the Father (John 1:18; cf. 8:21–30; 14:7–12). Those living inside the story of the Old Testament repeatedly testify that the Lord is gracious and compassionate, and that he is faithful (Exod 34:6–7; Num 14:18–19; Neh 9:16–37; Jonah 4:2; Mic 7:18).[17] We need to learn the stories of the Old Testament so that we might discover afresh the character of the Lord God. When explaining the meaning of God's character and attributes in Exodus 34:6–7, Boda notes that in human relationships we "do not first encounter a person's attributes, but rather their actions. We watch how they act and function in life and relationships and from this begin to discern certain patterns."[18] Similarly, we come to know God's character and his attributes by watching how he acts over time and in different circumstances. We cannot simply select a few Bible verses from the Old Testament, therefore, and assume that we know God's character. Study of the Scriptures is important, for God reveals his character and identity through his word. Paul thus exhorts the young Timothy to remain strong in the faith. He reminds him of God's faithfulness that was based on God's *character*; he said "if we are faithless, he remains faithful, for he cannot disown himself" (2 Tim 2:13). We are exhorted with the words from Hebrews, therefore: "Let us hold unswervingly to the hope we profess, for he who promised is faithful" (Heb 10:23). We can join with the hymn writer Thomas Chisholm and sing:

> Great is Thy faithfulness,
> O God my Father;
> There is no shadow of turning with Thee;
> Thou changest not,
> Thy compassions, they fail not;
> As Thou hast been Thou forever wilt be.

This is the testimony of those who returned from exile—*Yahweh is faithful!*

---

17. For a detailed and theologically rich analysis of Exod 34:6–7, see Mark J. Boda, *The Heartbeat of Old Testament Theology: Three Creedal Expressions, Acadia Studies in Bible and Theology* (Grand Rapids: Baker Academic, 2017), 29–44.

18. Ibid., 34.

LISTEN to the Story

¹The descendants of Judah:

Perez, Hezron, Karmi, Hur and Shobal.

²Reaiah son of Shobal was the father of Jahath, and Jahath the
father of Ahumai and Lahad. These were the clans of the
Zorathites.

³These were the sons of Etam:

Jezreel, Ishma and Idbash. Their sister was named Hazzelelponi.
⁴Penuel was the father of Gedor, and Ezer the father of
Hushah.

These were the descendants of Hur, the firstborn of Ephrathah and
father of Bethlehem.

⁵Ashhur the father of Tekoa had two wives, Helah and Naarah.

⁶Naarah bore him Ahuzzam, Hepher, Temeni and Haahashtari.
These were the descendants of Naarah.

⁷The sons of Helah:

Zereth, Zohar, Ethnan, ⁸and Koz, who was the father of Anub
and Hazzobebah and of the clans of Aharhel son of Harum.

⁹Jabez was more honorable than his brothers. His mother had named
him Jabez, saying, "I gave birth to him in pain." ¹⁰Jabez cried out to the
God of Israel, "Oh, that you would bless me and enlarge my territory! Let
your hand be with me, and keep me from harm so that I will be free from
pain." And God granted his request.

¹¹Kelub, Shuhah's brother, was the father of Mehir, who was the
father of Eshton. ¹²Eshton was the father of Beth Rapha, Paseah
and Tehinnah the father of Ir Nahash. These were the men of
Rekah.

¹³The sons of Kenaz:

Othniel and Seraiah.

The sons of Othniel:

Hathath and Meonothai. ¹⁴Meonothai was the father of Ophrah.
Seraiah was the father of Joab,

the father of Ge Harashim. It was called this because its people
were skilled workers.

¹⁵The sons of Caleb son of Jephunneh:

Iru, Elah and Naam.

The son of Elah:

Kenaz.

¹⁶The sons of Jehallelel:

Ziph, Ziphah, Tiria and Asarel.

¹⁷The sons of Ezrah:

Jether, Mered, Epher and Jalon. One of Mered's wives gave birth
to Miriam, Shammai and Ishbah the father of Eshtemoa.
¹⁸(His wife from the tribe of Judah gave birth to Jered the
father of Gedor, Heber the father of Soko, and Jekuthiel
the father of Zanoah.) These were the children of Pharaoh's
daughter Bithiah, whom Mered had married.

¹⁹The sons of Hodiah's wife, the sister of Naham:

the father of Keilah the Garmite, and Eshtemoa the Maakathite.

²⁰The sons of Shimon:

Amnon, Rinnah, Ben-Hanan and Tilon.

The descendants of Ishi:

Zoheth and Ben-Zoheth.

²¹The sons of Shelah son of Judah:

Er the father of Lekah, Laadah the father of Mareshah and the
clans of the linen workers at Beth Ashbea, ²²Jokim, the men
of Kozeba, and Joash and Saraph, who ruled in Moab and
Jashubi Lehem. (These records are from ancient times.)
²³They were the potters who lived at Netaim and Gederah;
they stayed there and worked for the king.

²⁴The descendants of Simeon:

Nemuel, Jamin, Jarib, Zerah and Shaul;
²⁵Shallum was Shaul's son, Mibsam his son and Mishma his son.

²⁶The descendants of Mishma:

Hammuel his son, Zakkur his son and Shimei his son.

²⁷Shimei had sixteen sons and six daughters, but his brothers did not have many children; so their entire clan did not become as numerous as the people of Judah. ²⁸They lived in Beersheba, Moladah, Hazar Shual, ²⁹Bilhah, Ezem, Tolad, ³⁰Bethuel, Hormah, Ziklag, ³¹Beth Markaboth, Hazar Susim, Beth Biri and Shaaraim. These were their towns until the reign of David. ³²Their surrounding villages were Etam, Ain, Rimmon, Token and Ashan— five towns—³³and all the villages around these towns as far as Baalath. These were their settlements. And they kept a genealogical record.

³⁴Meshobab, Jamlech, Joshah son of Amaziah, ³⁵Joel, Jehu son of Joshibiah, the son of Seraiah, the son of Asiel, ³⁶also Elioenai, Jaakobah, Jeshohaiah, Asaiah, Adiel, Jesimiel, Benaiah, ³⁷and Ziza son of Shiphi, the son of Allon, the son of Jedaiah, the son of Shimri, the son of Shemaiah.

³⁸The men listed above by name were leaders of their clans. Their families increased greatly, ³⁹and they went to the outskirts of Gedor to the east of the valley in search of pasture for their flocks. ⁴⁰They found rich, good pasture, and the land was spacious, peaceful and quiet. Some Hamites had lived there formerly.

⁴¹The men whose names were listed came in the days of Hezekiah king of Judah. They attacked the Hamites in their dwellings and also the Meunites who were there and completely destroyed them, as is evident to this day. Then they settled in their place, because there was pasture for their flocks. ⁴²And five hundred of these Simeonites, led by Pelatiah, Neariah, Rephaiah and Uzziel, the sons of Ishi, invaded the hill country of Seir. ⁴³They killed the remaining Amalekites who had escaped, and they have lived there to this day.

Listening to the Text in the Story: Joshua 15:1–63; 19:1–9; Judges 1:1–20

The descendants of Judah have already been introduced (1 Chr 2:3–3:24), but the tribe of Judah continues to be the focus in this chapter (4:1–23) with attention on Caleb's line through Hur. Within the genealogy, attention is given to the prayer of Jabez (recalling that Salma's descendants lived at Jabez; 2:54–55), along with linen workers and craftsmen who serve the king. Despite some repetition, this section reinforces the central role of Judah.

Families from the tribe of Simeon and their settlement in the land are included next (4:24–43). The placement of Simeon immediately after Judah is not due to birth order, but because of their inclusion within the territory of Judah (Josh 19:1–9; cf. Josh 15:26–32). Other tribes of Israel will be given in the next three chapters (1 Chr 5:1–26; 7:1–8:40), and notably, the important (and extensive!) genealogy of Levi is sandwiched in between (6:1–81). The genealogies conclude with the names of those who dwelt in Jerusalem after the exile (9:2–34), followed by the resumption of Saul's genealogy (vv. 35–44). This provides a bridge to the next chapter where the final days of Saul are rehearsed, which ushers in the transition to King David (10:1–14).

EXPLAIN the Story

The Descendants of Judah through Hur (4:1–16)

The genealogy begins with a list of Judah's descendants as key family members already mentioned are recalled, such as Hezron (1 Chr 4:1; cf. 2:5), Karmi (4:1; cf. 2:7), Hur (4:1; cf. 2:19), and Shobal (4:1; cf. 2:50). What follows, then, is a collection of fragmentary genealogies rather than a systematic presentation of lines of descent. Instead of attempting to trace or reconstruct particular genealogical lines, it is more fruitful to highlight key themes that present themselves in the chapter.

The descendants of Hur, who is himself identified as the first born of Ephrathah (1 Chr 4:4), recalls his earlier genealogy (4:4; cf. 2:50–51, 54). We have already noted that his line is important because of his connection with Ephrathah and Bethlehem (see the commentary on 1 Chr 2:18–24, pp. 41–42), since David is identified as the "son of an Ephrathite named Jesse, who was from Bethlehem in Judah" (1 Sam 17:12). Interest in Ephrathah and Bethlehem reinforces the connection with Judah.

Brief commentary is given about a man named Jabez (1 Chr 4:9–10). As is characteristic of the Chronicler, the figure of Jabez provides an opportunity to teach on the important topic of prayer. The name *Jabez* recalls that he had been born in "pain" (v. 9),[1] reminiscent of Eve's pain in childbearing

---

1. The three consonants (*'-ts-b*) of the root that serve as the basis for the Hebrew word for "pain" (and the verb in v. 10) appear also in the Hebrew name rendered in English as Jabez. Although the

(Gen 3:16). Yet the story recounts how Jabez had called out to God amid his painful circumstances. The verb "to call" (Heb. *q-r-*) is used of people such as David (1 Chr 21:26) and Asa (2 Chr 14:11) who call out to God in their distress, and even foreigners who call out to the LORD (6:33). The prayer of Jabez is also important because this is the first time in Chronicles where God is referred to as the "God of Israel" (1 Chr 4:10; cf. 15:12, 14; 16:4, 36; 2 Chr 6:4, 7, 10, etc.), underscoring God's unique covenant-relationship with his people Israel (Exod 5:1; 24:10; 32:27; 34:23, etc). Jabez prays to God: "Oh, that you would bless me and enlarge my territory! Let your hand be with me, and keep me from harm so that I will be free from pain" (1 Chr 4:10). Even though his name resounds with pain, God graciously grants him his request (see Live the Story below).

Another key figure in the genealogy is Othniel, Israel's first judge, whose descendants are given, along with a comment about their craftsmanship (4:13–14; cf. Judg 3:9–11). A well-known leader during the time of Moses is mentioned next, Caleb, along with his descendants (1 Chr 4:15–16; cf. Num 13:6; Josh 14:6–15). These two figures indicate that leaders had come from the tribe of Judah even before David had become king. Other lesser-known families are mentioned (1 Chr 4:17–20), but Mered's marriage to Bithia (a daughter of an Egyptian pharaoh) is noteworthy, since it highlights ethnic diversity within the tribe (v. 17–18).[2] The genealogy concludes with the descendants of Shelah, the son of Judah through his Canaanite wife, the daughter of Shua (vv. 21–23; cf. 2:3). The name of Shelah's deceased brother is preserved in the name of his firstborn son, Er (4:21; cf. Gen 38:3, 7; 1 Chr 2:3). While the descendants of Shelah are not prominently featured, they nevertheless have an important contribution through their craftsmanship, which includes working with linen and making pottery (4:21–23). David himself wore a robe of linen (15:27). Fine linen was used in the temple (2 Chr 2:14; 3:14) and it was worn by Levitical musicians (5:12), underscoring Judah's association with the temple.

The Descendants of Simeon (4:24–43)

The descendants of Simeon and their settlements are given next (1 Chr 4:24–43). Simeon was Jacob's second born son through Leah (Gen 29:33), whose sons became leaders within the tribe (46:10; Exod 6:15). It is important to

---

last two consonants are reversed (the consonants of the name are *y-'-b-ts*), a play on his name is clearly intended.

2. See Judah's Place in God's Plan to Include All Nations in Live the Story, Chapter 2, pp. 46–48.

recall some of the family history, as this accounts for the placement of Simeon within the genealogies. Jacob's firstborn son, Reuben, had been disqualified from honor as firstborn because of his illicit relationship with his father's concubine (Gen 35:22; 49:4; 1 Chr 5:1), While it is expected that preeminence will be given to Simeon as the next son in line, the vengeance he carried out against the men of Shechem leads to his father's judgment against him and the dispersal of the tribe (Gen 49:5–7; cf. ch. 34). Their tribal allotment is outlined in Joshua (Josh 19:1–9), although it is important to recognize that a number of their towns are included in Judah's territory, since their inheritance fell within the larger tribe of Judah (Josh 15:26–32; 19:9). Their small number in comparison to the many descendants of Judah testifies to this reality and their history (1 Chr 4:27; cf, Josh 19:9). Simeonite towns located in the southern region of Judah are reminiscent of their earlier territorial allotment (1 Chr 4:28–33; cf. Josh 19:1–9). While the cities mentioned in the genealogy reflect the period of the united monarchy ("until the reign of David"; 1 Chr 4:31), several of their towns, such as Beersheba, Moladah, Hazar Shual, Ziklag, Ain, and Rimmon (vv. 28, 30, 32), are also mentioned in Nehemiah 11:26–29,[3] indicating that they were inhabited by the returnees (thus giving contemporary relevance to the list).[4] Names of clan leaders are given next (1 Chr 4:34–38), along with their acquisition of good pastureland for their flocks (vv. 39–40). Further procurement of land is achieved through military victories, including over the Amalekites (vv. 41–43; cf. Exod 17:8–16), something Saul had failed to do (1 Sam 15:1–33). Despite these accomplishments, the tribe of Simeon is largely inconsequential and overshadowed by the important tribe of Judah.

LIVE the Story

The Prayer of Jabez

The book of Chronicles is perhaps best known for the prayer of Jabez embedded in the genealogy of Judah. While the focus of the chapter is on Judah's genealogy, it is characteristic of the Chronicler to include narrative material in genealogies that highlight important themes (cf. 1 Chr 5:18–22; 6:49). Since prayer is central to Chronicles, the prayer of Jabez provides an opportunity for the Chronicler to teach on this important topic. The prayer of Jabez has

---

3. The towns Ain and Rimmon are sometimes listed as two towns (Josh 19:7; 1 Chr 4:32), but in Neh 11:29 Ain and Rimmon are listed as one town, En Rimmon. On the identification of the site, see Klein, *1 Chronicles*, 150.

4. Boda, *1–2 Chronicles*, 59.

become known to us through Bruce Wilkinson's bestselling book, *The Prayer of Jabez: Breaking through to the Blessed Life* (Colorado Springs: Multnomah Books, 2000). When it was first published in 2000, it sold over two million copies in just over a year. Sales continued with *The Prayer of Jabez Devotional* (Colorado Springs: Multnomah Books, 2006), along with additional volumes of the Prayer of Jabez for kids (2001), teens (2001), and women (2002 by Darlene Marie Wilkinson). In 2008 the book had sold over ten million copies, becoming the recipient of the Diamond Book Award.[5] It is characteristic of the Chronicler to give brief theological "sermons" in his narratives, and this is precisely what he is doing here when commenting on Jabez.

Prayer is an important theme that permeates Chronicles. Jabez is an example of someone who prays to God, and his request is granted. Hahn thus notes that prayer is the "subtext of the genealogy," but even more, it is the message of the "entire book of Chronicles: God hears prayers. He is found by those who seek him."[6] The prayer of Jabez is intended to encourage the returnees to pray to God amid their difficult circumstances, reminding them (and us) that God answers prayer. The returnees had not only experienced the loss of the monarchy, but there had been a drought (Hag 1:5–11), some had faced poverty and forfeiture of their land (Neh 5:1–13), and they had faced opposition from foreign leaders that threatened their lives (4:1–11). Jabez serves as a reminder that God's people were to cry out to him amid their own painful circumstances.

Yet this prayer is not intended to be used as some kind of magical prayer or mantra that guarantees success. Wilkinson's own story of his failed ministry in Africa has drawn criticism from *Christianity Today* and the *Wall Street Journal*, precisely since it contradicts the main premise of his book that blessing is achieved by praying this prayer in particular.[7] Herein lies the danger. The prayer of Jabez is not intended to guarantee financial or ministry success, nor does it guarantee that life will be free from pain or suffering. Consider for a moment that the Chronicler's *own context* mitigates against this kind of prosperity gospel and triumphalism. Answered prayer is surely an important theme in Chronicles (2 Chr 14:11–12; 18:31; 20:1–22; 32:20–21; 33:12–13), and Ezra and Nehemiah serve as examples in the post-exilic community of those who pray amid challenging circumstances and witness answered prayer (Ezra

---

5. See the blog by Tim Challies, "The Best Sellers: The Prayer of Jabez," May 4, 2014 (www .challies.com).

6. Hahn, *The Kingdom of God*, 41.

7. Known as his "Dream for Africa" and his "African Dream Village" initiative; see the blog by Tim Challies, "The Best Sellers: The Prayer of Jabez," May 4, 2014.

8:21–23, 31–32; Neh 4:9–10; 6:16). Yet this is not a prosperity gospel, but rather, these stories are intended to encourage us to call out to God in prayer.

It is too easy in the Christian life to become self-sufficient and to think that *we* have the ability to solve all problems. Instead of *self*-sufficiency, God wants us to bring our needs and concerns to him. The psalms provide us with prayers of those who call out to God amid the trials of life, such as Psalm 18:6: "In my distress I called to the LORD; I cried to my God for help. From his temple he heard my voice; my cry came before him, into his ears." Many psalms testify to these heartfelt prayers of God's people who call out to God for help.

Prayer is the hallmark of the people of God throughout the ages. Jesus not only modeled prayer (Matt 14:23; Luke 5:16; 6:12; 9:28–29), but he taught his disciples *how* to pray (Matt 6:9–15; cf. Luke 11:1–13; 18:1–8). The early church continued in the tradition of prayer (Acts 1:14; 2:42; 14:23), and we, too, are exhorted to pray (1 Thess 5:17; Jas 5:13–15). But fervent and consistent prayer does not exempt us from trials and persecution, as many in the early church experienced, such as John the Baptist (Matt 14:1–12), Stephen (Acts 7:54–60), James (Acts 12:2), Paul (e.g., 2 Cor 11:23–27), John (Rev 1:9), and other believers (see Heb 11:32–40; 1 Pet 4:12–19; 5:9–10).[8] There are no guarantees that we will be free from harm or pain, but God does answer prayer according to his perfect will and purpose. The book of Chronicles resounds with this word of encouragement *to pray*.

---

8. For a thought-provoking book that recounts stories from the suffering church, see Nick Ripken and Greg Lewis, *The Insanity of God: A True Story of Resurrected Faith* (Nashville: B&H, 2013).

LISTEN to the Story

¹The sons of Reuben the firstborn of Israel (he was the firstborn, but when he defiled his father's marriage bed, his rights as firstborn were given to the sons of Joseph son of Israel; so he could not be listed in the genealogical record in accordance with his birthright, ²and though Judah was the strongest of his brothers and a ruler came from him, the rights of the firstborn belonged to Joseph)—³the sons of Reuben the firstborn of Israel:

Hanok, Pallu, Hezron and Karmi.

⁴The descendants of Joel:

Shemaiah his son, Gog his son,

Shimei his son, ⁵Micah his son,

Reaiah his son, Baal his son,

⁶and Beerah his son, whom Tiglath-Pileser king of Assyria took into exile. Beerah was a leader of the Reubenites.

⁷Their relatives by clans, listed according to their genealogical records:

Jeiel the chief, Zechariah, ⁸and Bela son of Azaz, the son of Shema, the son of Joel. They settled in the area from Aroer to Nebo and Baal Meon. ⁹To the east they occupied the land up to the edge of the desert that extends to the Euphrates River, because their livestock had increased in Gilead.

¹⁰During Saul's reign they waged war against the Hagrites, who were defeated at their hands; they occupied the dwellings of the Hagrites throughout the entire region east of Gilead.

¹¹The Gadites lived next to them in Bashan, as far as Salekah:

¹²Joel was the chief, Shapham the second, then Janai and Shaphat, in Bashan.

¹³Their relatives, by families, were:

Michael, Meshullam, Sheba, Jorai, Jakan, Zia and Eber—seven in all.
¹⁴These were the sons of Abihail son of Huri, the son of Jaroah, the son of Gilead, the son of Michael, the son of Jeshishai, the son of Jahdo, the son of Buz.
¹⁵Ahi son of Abdiel, the son of Guni, was head of their family.
¹⁶The Gadites lived in Gilead, in Bashan and its outlying villages, and on all the pasturelands of Sharon as far as they extended.
¹⁷All these were entered in the genealogical records during the reigns of Jotham king of Judah and Jeroboam king of Israel.

¹⁸The Reubenites, the Gadites and the half-tribe of Manasseh had 44,760 men ready for military service—able-bodied men who could handle shield and sword, who could use a bow, and who were trained for battle. ¹⁹They waged war against the Hagrites, Jetur, Naphish and Nodab. ²⁰They were helped in fighting them, and God delivered the Hagrites and all their allies into their hands, because they cried out to him during the battle. He answered their prayers, because they trusted in him. ²¹They seized the livestock of the Hagrites—fifty thousand camels, two hundred fifty thousand sheep and two thousand donkeys. They also took one hundred thousand people captive, ²²and many others fell slain, because the battle was God's. And they occupied the land until the exile.

²³The people of the half-tribe of Manasseh were numerous; they settled in the land from Bashan to Baal Hermon, that is, to Senir (Mount Hermon).
²⁴These were the heads of their families: Epher, Ishi, Eliel, Azriel, Jeremiah, Hodaviah and Jahdiel. They were brave warriors, famous men, and heads of their families. ²⁵But they were unfaithful to the God of their ancestors and prostituted themselves to the gods of the peoples of the land, whom God had destroyed before them. ²⁶So the God of Israel stirred up the spirit of Pul king of Assyria (that is, Tiglath-Pileser king of Assyria), who took the Reubenites, the Gadites and the half-tribe of Manasseh into exile. He took them to Halah, Habor, Hara and the river of Gozan, where they are to this day.

Listening to the Text in the Story: Genesis 48:8–20; 49:22–26; Deuteronomy 33:13–17

The tribes of Judah (1 Chr 2:2–4:23) and Simeon (4:24–43) have been rehearsed thus far, but since the focus of the genealogies is on all Israel, attention now shifts to the tribes living east of the Jordan, beginning with Reuben (5:1–10), moving northward with Gad (vv. 11–22), and further north with the half-tribe of Manasseh (vv. 23–26). Drawing from sources in the Pentateuch, these lists are highly selective and abridged, with some generational gaps. Genealogies and settlement patterns of the tribes west of the Jordan will be resumed in 1 Chronicles 7 after a lengthy presentation of Levi (ch. 6). It is important to rehearse briefly Reuben's family history and his relationship with his younger brother Joseph, since these two figures are central in this chapter (remembering that Joseph is represented in the genealogy through his son Manasseh).

Reuben was the firstborn son of Jacob through Leah (Gen 29:32; 35:23). As firstborn, a double portion was due to him (cf. Deut 21:15–17), yet Reuben's illicit sexual relationship with his father's concubine, Bilhah, resulted in him forfeiting his firstborn status (Gen 49:3–4; cf. 35:22). One scholar thus writes: "Reuben's primordial status was no guarantee of circumstantial preeminence with the larger Israel group. Instead, not only is Reuben characterized negatively in historical memory, it is precisely his lack of social standing that is perceived negatively."[1] This "lack of social standing" is attested in the Chronicler's ordering of the genealogies with Reuben's demotion from first place. In Jacob's deathbed blessing, Reuben's loss of preeminence is contrasted with the prophetic hope of kingship in the line Judah (49:8–10). Further, the extended blessing given to Joseph distinguishes him above his brothers (vv. 22–26; cf. Deut 33:13–17).

EXPLAIN the Story

The Descendants of Reuben (5:1–10)

The Chronicler explains at the outset that Reuben's genealogy could not be listed according to birthright (as firstborn) because he had defiled his father's bed (1 Chr 5:1). His birthright had been given to Joseph, although Judah prevailed over his brothers and a ruler came from him (v. 2; cf. Ps 78:67–72). Reuben's four sons are mentioned (1 Chr 5:3; cf. Exod 6:14; Num 26:5–6), followed by the descendants of Joel (possibly reflecting a generational gap) that extend several generations (1 Chr 5:4–5). A leader among the Reubenites named Beerah had been carried away into exile by Pul (an alternative name

---

1. Thomas D. Petter, *The Land between the Two Rivers: Early Israelite Identities in Central Transjordan* (Winona Lake, IN: Eisenbrauns, 2014), 100.

for Tiglath-Pileser). The backstory to this comment is that the Assyrian king Tiglath-Pileser III (745–727 BC) had attacked the Northern Kingdom during the reign of Pekah, capturing key towns and bringing their inhabitants to Assyria (2 Kgs 15:29). The Chronicler comments that the tribe of Reuben had been among the exiles, as suggested by the reference to Gilead (located in the Transjordan) coming under Assyrian control (cf. 2 Kgs 15:29).

Further comment is made about the Reubenite settlement east of the Jordan, which was due to their increased cattle (1 Chr 5:7–9). The Reubenites and Gadites were known as herdsmen who had much livestock (Num 32:1), and their settlement east of the Jordan hearkens back to their earlier history when they had requested this fertile region as their inheritance (vv. 1–42; Josh 1:12–18; 13:8–23). Settlement in the towns of Aroer, Nebo, and Baal Meon (1 Chr 5:7–8) are among the towns that had been allotted to them in the Transjordan (Num 32:3, 34, 38). An ancient stela dated to the ninth century BC records the victories of a Moabite king named Mesha. In the inscription, Mesha claims victory over Israel, which included the three cities of Aroer, Nebo, and Baal Meon.[2] There has been a long history of competing claims for the region between the Arnon and Jabbok rivers, as this text highlights. One scholar thus writes: "In the vicissitudes of frontier life, tribal groups may have appeared and disappeared on the historical scene, following the patterns of abatement and intensification that were indelibly etched in the *longue durée* history of the region (see Judges 3, 5, 10; 1 Chr 5:9)."[3] Some scholars suggest that the Reubenite settlement in these towns refers to an earlier period prior to the Moabite victory, although alternative solutions are proposed by other scholars.[4] The Chronicler rounds off the Reubenite genealogy with a comment about their victory over the Hagrites (an Arab people dwelling in the Transjordan; cf. Ps 83:6) during the time of Saul, which resulted in their settlement east of Gilead (1 Chr 5:10). With this rather brief genealogy (vv. 1–10), focus shifts to the northern tribe of Gad.

The Descendants of Gad (5:11–17)

The tribe of Gad lived north of Reuben, and like the Reubenites, they had requested to live east of the Jordan (Num 32:1–42; cf. Josh 13:24–28), which

---

2. See "The Moabite Stone" (also known as the Mesha Inscription), trans. W. F. Albright (*ANET*, 320–32).

3. Petter, *The Land between the Two Rivers*, 100.

4. Selman, for example, suggests that these verses refer to an earlier Reubenite expansion and that this territory was later captured by Mesha, king of Moab (Selman, *1 Chronicles*, 105–106). For more technical discussions, see Japhet (*I & II Chronicles* 135) and Klein (*1 Chronicles*, 162–63).

included the fertile land of Bashan (1 Chr 5:11; Josh 13:11), another contested region. The genealogy of Gad is noticeably brief (1 Chr 5:11–17) in comparison to the lengthy genealogies of Judah and Levi (2:3–4:23; 6:1–81), indicating where the Chronicler's sympathies lie. Four clan leaders are named, along with seven of their relatives (5:12–13), followed by names of those who lived in Gilead, in Bashan and its towns, and in the pastures of Sharon (vv. 14–16). These people had been enrolled in genealogies during the days of Jotham king of Judah and in the days of Jeroboam king of Israel (v. 17). This is another example of the many sources used by the Chronicler to compile his history, even if they are no longer extant.[5]

Military Exploits of Reuben, Gad, and the Half-Tribe of Manasseh (5:18–22)

Focus shifts to the valiant men from the tribes of Reuben, Gad, and the half-tribe of Manasseh, who had waged war against the Arabian Hagrites (cf. Ps 83:6). Jetur, the first of the three names, appears elsewhere as a descendant of Ishmael (1 Chr 5:19; cf. Gen 25:13–15; 1 Chr 1:31). The reason for their military victory is given: "They were helped in fighting them, and God delivered the Hagrites and all their allies into their hands, because they cried out to him during the battle. He answered their prayers, because they trusted in him" (5:20). As is characteristic of Chronicles, a key teaching moment is taken up in this genealogy that highlights godly qualities (see Live the Story below). After defeating their enemy, the tribes acquire prized livestock, including cattle, camels, sheep, and donkeys, along with a large number of men (vv. 21–22).

The Descendants of the Half-Tribe of Manasseh (5:23–26)

The Chronicler continues to trace the tribes northward with the half-tribe of Manasseh (the other half-tribe of Manasseh lived west of the Jordan; cf. 1 Chr 7:14–19). As with the tribe of Gad, attention is first on the individual tribe (5:23–24), which is followed by commentary on three tribes (vv. 25–26). The descendants of Manasseh are numerous, and as such, their territory extends to the northern region of Bashan as far as Mount Hermon (v. 23). Seven heads of families known for their military stature are mentioned (v. 24), although a stinging indictment follows: "But they were unfaithful to the God of their ancestors and prostituted themselves to the gods of the peoples of the land, whom God had destroyed before them" (v. 25). The verb "to act unfaithfully"

---

5. See the helpful list provided by Boda, for example (*1–2 Chronicles*, 14).

(Heb. *ma'al*) is a key term employed in Chronicles.[6] It is first used to describe Achan's violation of the ban that led to Israel's devastating defeat (2:7), and it will be used shortly to describe Judah's unfaithfulness that leads to their exile (9:1).

The tribes of Reuben, Gad, and the half-tribe of Manasseh are charged with unfaithfulness because of their idolatry, which will lead to their exile by Tiglath-Pileser III (5:25–26). The Northern Kingdom had been characterized by flagrant and persistent idolatry, not only in their worship of the two golden calves (1 Kgs 12:28–33), but also in their worship of Baal that was widespread under Ahab.[7] The Northern Kingdom comes to an end in 722 BC (cf. 2 Kgs 17), but the unraveling of the kingdom is seen earlier during the reign of Tiglath-Pileser III (745–727 BC), for God had "stirred up the spirit of Pul king of Assyria (that is, Tiglath-Pileser king of Assyria), who took the Reubenites, the Gadites and the half-tribe of Manasseh into exile" (1 Chr 5:26). God will later stir up the Persian king Cyrus to rebuild Jerusalem (2 Chr 36:22–23; cf. Ezra 1:1–4; Hag 1:14), but at this point he is stirring up an Assyrian king to bring judgment, which results in the exile of the Transjordanian tribes (2 Kgs 15:29; cf. 17:1–6). Their settlement in "Halah, Habor, Hara and the river of Gozan" (1 Chr 5:26) anticipates the exile of the Northern Kingdom to this region (cf. 2 Kgs 17:24–41). The Chronicler notes that the tribes were exiled into Assyrian territory "to this day" (1 Chr 5:26), underscoring the dire consequences of their religious compromise.

LIVE the Story

An Exhortation to Trust in God for Help

Amid this story of the territorial expansion of the Transjordanian tribes, along with a warning against adopting the religious practices of the nations, there is an exhortation to trust in God. In just one verse, the theology of Chronicles is given in a nutshell: "They were helped in fighting them, and God delivered the Hagrites and all their allies into their hands, because they cried out to him during the battle. He answered their prayers, because they trusted in him" (1 Chr 5:20). We noted in the introduction that the Chronicler recalls Israel's history in order to draw out spiritual and theological principles (pp. 7–8). Selman thus writes that in Chronicles, the Scriptures are unchanging "though the ways in which they can be applied to new situations are surprisingly

---

6. See the discussion in Chapter 10 on 1 Chr 10:13, pp. 118–19.
7. See the discussions in Chapter 47, pp. 413–14, and Chapter 50, pp. 437–38.

adaptable."[8] This is one of those "spiritual principles" that can be applied to our contemporary context.

First of all, the people *cry out* to God (Heb. z-ʿ-q). This is precisely what Jehoshaphat does amidst a battle when facing the onslaught of an enemy attack (2 Chr 18:31). On another occasion, when facing an insurmountable challenge, he remembers God's promise that if his people cry out to him in their distress, he will hear and deliver (20:9; cf. ch. 6). Hezekiah and Isaiah the prophet will similarly "cry out" to God in prayer when facing an Assyrian attack (32:20; cf. Neh 9:4, 28). This prayer is a heartfelt cry to God during a crisis or amidst difficult circumstances. Israel's early history was founded on the Exodus from Egypt, when God *heard* the heartfelt cry of his people (Exod 2:23–24; 3:9). This message resounds throughout the Scriptures: God wants his people to cry out to *him* for help, and he has demonstrated time and time again that he is not a dispassionate God who is removed from the cries of his people. The book of Hebrews reminds us that we have a great high priest who sympathizes with our weakness. We are encouraged to approach God's throne of grace with confidence, "so that we may receive mercy and find grace to help us in our time of need" (Heb 4:16).

Second, we learn that God answered their prayer *because they trusted in him* (1 Chr 5:20). They did not trust in their military might, even though they were equipped with weapons and were skilled in battle (v. 18). Instead, they trusted in the LORD, echoing Psalm 44:6: "I put no trust in my bow, my sword does not bring me victory." When Nehemiah faced opposition, the people gathered with their weapons, but they prayed to God and *trusted* that *he* would fight on their behalf (Neh 4:9–23). The psalms are full of examples of God's people who put their trust in the LORD (Pss 9:10; 22:4–5; 28:7, etc.). We, too, are called to put our trust in God alone, not in our own abilities, our achievements, our wealth, or in anything else.

Lastly, we read that the men were *helped* by God (Heb. ʿ-z-r). Contrary to the popular myth that "God helps those who help themselves,"[9] this story testifies that God helps those who put their *trust in him*. King David experienced this when he was going through a difficult period in his life, at which time he had received divine help (Heb. ʿ-z-r, 1 Chr 12:1, 17, 18, 19, 21, 22). Even names of those who came to help him contain the Hebrew root ʿazar (Ahiezer, Azarel, Joezer, and Ezer; vv. 3–6, 9)! The prophet Amasia made

---

8. Selman, *1 Chronicles*, 43–44.

9. For the history of this popular saying, see the discussion on 2 Chr 14 in Live the Story, Chapter 43, pp. 389–90.

known to David that his helper was God (v. 18)![10] Affirmation that God helps his people permeates the psalms, as they trust *him*. Such help from God leads to joy, as the psalmist affirms: "The LORD is my strength and my shield; my heart trusts in him, and he helps me. My heart leaps for joy, and with my song I praise him" (Ps 28:7).

While we do not face military opposition, nor does God promise us military victory (as he did to Israel under the Mosaic covenant, contingent on obedience), we are exhorted to call upon God in our circumstances of life; we are not to trust in our own achievements or abilities or in our wealth and success, but in God alone. The great hymn by Isaac Watts, which begins, "O God, our help in ages past, Our hope for years to come," testifies to this reality, causing us to lift our voice in praise to God for his help throughout the ages. This is the word of exhortation for us today from Chronicles.

---

10. See the discussion on 1 Chr 12 in Chapter 12.

LISTEN to the Story

¹The sons of Levi:
Gershon, Kohath and Merari.
²The sons of Kohath:
Amram, Izhar, Hebron and Uzziel.
³The children of Amram:
Aaron, Moses and Miriam.
The sons of Aaron:
Nadab, Abihu, Eleazar and Ithamar.
⁴Eleazar was the father of Phinehas,
Phinehas the father of Abishua,
⁵Abishua the father of Bukki,
Bukki the father of Uzzi,
⁶Uzzi the father of Zerahiah,
Zerahiah the father of Meraioth,
⁷Meraioth the father of Amariah,
Amariah the father of Ahitub,
⁸Ahitub the father of Zadok,
Zadok the father of Ahimaaz,
⁹Ahimaaz the father of Azariah,
Azariah the father of Johanan,
¹⁰Johanan the father of Azariah (it was he who served as priest in
    the temple Solomon built in Jerusalem),
¹¹Azariah the father of Amariah,
Amariah the father of Ahitub,
¹²Ahitub the father of Zadok,
Zadok the father of Shallum,
¹³Shallum the father of Hilkiah,
Hilkiah the father of Azariah,

¹⁴Azariah the father of Seraiah,
   and Seraiah the father of Jozadak.
¹⁵Jozadak was deported when the LORD sent Judah and Jerusalem
   into exile by the hand of Nebuchadnezzar.

¹⁶The sons of Levi:
   Gershon, Kohath and Merari.
¹⁷These are the names of the sons of Gershon:
   Libni and Shimei.
¹⁸The sons of Kohath:
   Amram, Izhar, Hebron and Uzziel.
¹⁹The sons of Merari:
   Mahli and Mushi.
These are the clans of the Levites listed according to their
   fathers:
²⁰Of Gershon:
   Libni his son, Jahath his son,
   Zimmah his son, ²¹Joah his son,
   Iddo his son, Zerah his son
   and Jeatherai his son.
²²The descendants of Kohath:
   Amminadab his son, Korah his son,
   Assir his son, ²³Elkanah his son,
   Ebiasaph his son, Assir his son,
   ²⁴Tahath his son, Uriel his son,
   Uzziah his son and Shaul his son.
²⁵The descendants of Elkanah:
   Amasai, Ahimoth,
   ²⁶Elkanah his son, Zophai his son,
   Nahath his son, ²⁷Eliab his son,
   Jeroham his son, Elkanah his son
   and Samuel his son.
²⁸The sons of Samuel:
   Joel the firstborn
   and Abijah the second son.
²⁹The descendants of Merari:
   Mahli, Libni his son,

Shimei his son, Uzzah his son,
³⁰Shimea his son, Haggiah his son
and Asaiah his son.

³¹These are the men David put in charge of the music in the house of the LORD after the ark came to rest there. ³²They ministered with music before the tabernacle, the tent of meeting, until Solomon built the temple of the LORD in Jerusalem. They performed their duties according to the regulations laid down for them.

³³Here are the men who served, together with their sons:

From the Kohathites:

Heman, the musician,
the son of Joel, the son of Samuel,
³⁴the son of Elkanah, the son of Jeroham,
the son of Eliel, the son of Toah,
³⁵the son of Zuph, the son of Elkanah,
the son of Mahath, the son of Amasai,
³⁶the son of Elkanah, the son of Joel,
the son of Azariah, the son of Zephaniah,
³⁷the son of Tahath, the son of Assir,
the son of Ebiasaph, the son of Korah,
³⁸the son of Izhar, the son of Kohath,
the son of Levi, the son of Israel;

³⁹and Heman's associate Asaph, who served at his right hand:

Asaph son of Berekiah, the son of Shimea,
⁴⁰the son of Michael, the son of Baaseiah,
the son of Malkijah, ⁴¹the son of Ethni,
the son of Zerah, the son of Adaiah,
⁴²the son of Ethan, the son of Zimmah,
the son of Shimei, ⁴³the son of Jahath,
the son of Gershon, the son of Levi;

⁴⁴and from their associates, the Merarites, at his left hand:

Ethan son of Kishi, the son of Abdi,
the son of Malluk, ⁴⁵the son of Hashabiah,
the son of Amaziah, the son of Hilkiah,
⁴⁶the son of Amzi, the son of Bani,
the son of Shemer, ⁴⁷the son of Mahli,

the son of Mushi, the son of Merari,
the son of Levi.

⁴⁸Their fellow Levites were assigned to all the other duties of the tabernacle, the house of God. ⁴⁹But Aaron and his descendants were the ones who presented offerings on the altar of burnt offering and on the altar of incense in connection with all that was done in the Most Holy Place, making atonement for Israel, in accordance with all that Moses the servant of God had commanded.

⁵⁰These were the descendants of Aaron:
Eleazar his son, Phinehas his son,
Abishua his son, ⁵¹Bukki his son,
Uzzi his son, Zerahiah his son,
⁵²Meraioth his son, Amariah his son,
Ahitub his son, ⁵³Zadok his son
and Ahimaaz his son.

⁵⁴These were the locations of their settlements allotted as their territory (they were assigned to the descendants of Aaron who were from the Kohathite clan, because the first lot was for them):
⁵⁵They were given Hebron in Judah with its surrounding pasturelands. ⁵⁶But the fields and villages around the city were given to Caleb son of Jephunneh.
⁵⁷So the descendants of Aaron were given Hebron (a city of refuge), and Libnah, Jattir, Eshtemoa, ⁵⁸Hilen, Debir, ⁵⁹Ashan, Juttah and Beth Shemesh, together with their pasturelands. ⁶⁰And from the tribe of Benjamin they were given Gibeon, Geba, Alemeth and Anathoth, together with their pasturelands.
The total number of towns distributed among the Kohathite clans came to thirteen.
⁶¹The rest of Kohath's descendants were allotted ten towns from the clans of half the tribe of Manasseh.
⁶²The descendants of Gershon, clan by clan, were allotted thirteen towns from the tribes of Issachar, Asher and Naphtali, and from the part of the tribe of Manasseh that is in Bashan.

⁶³The descendants of Merari, clan by clan, were allotted twelve towns from the tribes of Reuben, Gad and Zebulun.

⁶⁴So the Israelites gave the Levites these towns and their pasturelands. ⁶⁵From the tribes of Judah, Simeon and Benjamin they allotted the previously named towns.

⁶⁶Some of the Kohathite clans were given as their territory towns from the tribe of Ephraim.

⁶⁷In the hill country of Ephraim they were given Shechem (a city of refuge), and Gezer, ⁶⁸Jokmeam, Beth Horon, ⁶⁹Aijalon and Gath Rimmon, together with their pasturelands.

⁷⁰And from half the tribe of Manasseh the Israelites gave Aner and Bileam, together with their pasturelands, to the rest of the Kohathite clans.

⁷¹The Gershonites received the following:
From the clan of the half-tribe of Manasseh
    they received Golan in Bashan and also Ashtaroth, together with their pasturelands;
⁷²from the tribe of Issachar
    they received Kedesh, Daberath, ⁷³Ramoth and Anem, together with their pasturelands;
⁷⁴from the tribe of Asher
    they received Mashal, Abdon, ⁷⁵Hukok and Rehob, together with their pasturelands;
⁷⁶and from the tribe of Naphtali
    they received Kedesh in Galilee, Hammon and Kiriathaim, together with their pasturelands.

⁷⁷The Merarites (the rest of the Levites) received the following:
From the tribe of Zebulun
    they received Jokneam, Kartah, Rimmono and Tabor, together with their pasturelands;
⁷⁸from the tribe of Reuben across the Jordan east of Jericho
    they received Bezer in the wilderness, Jahzah, ⁷⁹Kedemoth and Mephaath, together with their pasturelands;
⁸⁰and from the tribe of Gad

they received Ramoth in Gilead, Mahanaim, [81]Heshbon and Jazer, together with their pasturelands.

Listening to the Text in the Story: Exodus 6; Joshua 21:1–45

The tribe of Levi is now on center stage. The sheer length of this genealogy (eighty-one verses!) underscores its importance for Chronicles, for with Levi "the Chronicler reaches the central point of his genealogical lists, doubtless reflecting his estimation of the significance of the priestly tribe for the community of his own day."[1] This chapter begins with the genealogy of the high priests (1 Chr 6:1–15), followed by the names of Levitical families (vv. 16–30), Levitical singers (vv. 31–48), and Aaron's descendants (vv. 49–53). It concludes with a list of Levitical cities that are dispersed among the tribes (vv. 54–81). The names of Aaron's descendants and their families are listed elsewhere in the Old Testament (e.g., Exod 6:16–25; Num 3:1–4, 17–20), and Levitical cities hearken back to the time of Joshua (Josh 21:4–40). While a contemporary reader might wonder why it was necessary to record so many names, it is important to remember that the priesthood was hereditary, and only Levites could serve in the temple. One of the functions of the genealogies was to provide credentials for priests and Levites. Accurate records were essential, since they verified who could legitimately minister in the temple (cf. Ezra 2:62), and thus they had an ongoing legal function in the life of the post-exilic community.

As we listen to the story, it is helpful to rehearse briefly the significance of the tribe of Levi and the priesthood. Levi was Jacob's third-born son through Leah (Gen 29:34). Levi and his brother Simeon were known in Genesis for their vengeance on behalf of their sister Dinah (ch. 34). Recalling this story, Jacob pronounces that Levi would be dispersed among Israel (49:5–7). Yet, concern for God's holiness characterized this tribe (Exod 32:26–29; cf. Num 25:7–13), and they were even willing to obey God's word without regard for their family (Deut 33:8–11).[2] Levi had three sons, Gershon, Kohath, and Merari (1 Chr 6:1; cf. Gen 46:11; Exod 6:16). These three families are the

---

1. Williamson, *1 and 2 Chronicles*, 68.

2. Tremper Longman notes that although Jacob had pronounced judgment on Simeon and Levi because of their violence against the men of Shechem, which would result in their being scattered among Israel (Gen 49:5–6), the histories of the tribes are vastly different. Simeon becomes absorbed into Judah (see discussion above in Chapter 4 on 1 Chr 4:24–43, p. 61, but the tribe of Levi is one of the most important of all the tribes. Longman argues that their actions in the golden calf story (Exod 32) led to God turning their curse into a blessing when they were set apart for service (cf. Exod 32:29);

basis of the organizational structure of the Levites (see 1 Chr 23), including where each family resided in relation to the tabernacle and their particular tasks and responsibilities in relation to the priesthood and the tabernacle (Num 3–4). The Levites were chosen by God to assist the priests and to provide all kinds of practical support for the tabernacle, including dismantling, moving, and reassembling it. The Levites were guardians of sacred space, ensuring that it was protected from lay encroachment. Yet the Levites had limitations imposed upon them, for the priesthood belonged exclusively to Aaron and his sons (Num 16).

Aaron's four sons, Nadab, Abihu, Eleazar, and Ithamar, were set apart for priestly service (Exod 28:1–2; cf. 1 Chr 6:49). They were adorned with colorful and elaborate priestly garments that radiated the holiness and beauty of those consecrated to serve in the presence of a holy God (Exod 28–29). Some have even suggested that the priest is intended to serve as "visual model of what ideal humanity is to look like, humankind in their original dignity and honor in relation to God and the world around them."[3] As priests, they had the privileged calling of officiating at the altar before a holy God and making atonement for Israel's transgressions so that they might have fellowship with God (cf. 1 Chr 6:49).

But since Nadab and Abihu had been killed (because they had entered the tabernacle with unauthorized fire; cf. Lev 10), the priestly line was taken up by Aaron's two sons Eleazar and Ithamar (Num 3:1–4, 10; 16:9–10, 39–40; 18:1–2, 7). Aaron's two sons and their descendants served as priests, but only one son in each generation served as high priest. Only the high priest was permitted to go beyond the veil into the most holy place, one day a year, and not without blood (Exod 30:10; Lev 16). The line of succession was through Eleazar, who is identified as the "chief" of the leaders of Levi (Num 3:32), as was his father Aaron (cf. Ezra 7:5). Eleazar thus assumes the role of high priest after his father dies (Deut 10:6; cf. Lev 16:32), which is symbolized by the transfer of priestly garments to his son, Eleazar (Num 20:23–29). The significance of Eleazar's line is underscored by the covenant God made with his son Phinehas, who was granted an enduring priesthood (25:10–13). Given that the office of high priest was hereditary, it is not surprising that priestly genealogies are important, and this is precisely why the Chronicler gives so much attention to them.

---

see Tremper Longman III, *Immanuel in Our Place: Seeing Christ in Israel's Worship* (Phillipsburg, NJ: P&R, 2001), 131–34.

3. John A. Davies, *A Royal Priesthood: Literary and Intertextual Perspectives on the Image of Israel in Exodus 19:6* (JSOTSup 395; London: T&T Clark, 2004), 156–57.

EXPLAIN the Story

The Linear Genealogy of the Priestly Line from Aaron to Jozadak (6:1–15)

The genealogy that follows traces the priestly line from Aaron to the time of the exile, noting that the last member, Jozadak, was the priest who went with Judah to Babylon (1 Chr 6:15). The genealogy is selective since not all the priests we encounter elsewhere in Chronicles appear in this genealogy, such as Jehoiada (2 Chr 22:11–24:17) and Azariah (26:20), and it is important to bear in mind that term "son" can also mean "descendant," thereby creating a genealogical gap.[4] As noted by Williamson: "In the Chronicler's symbolism, at the heart of the theocracy this perfectly arranged tribe is seen to revolve around the person of the high priest."[5] Other biblical books provide further information about priestly ancestry (e.g., Exod 6:16–25; Ezra 7:1–5), and all these contribute to our understanding of the priesthood.[6] When reading these genealogies and locating them within the larger story of the Old Testament, it is helpful to identify several key figures, such as Eleazar (1 Chr 6:4), Phinehas (v. 4), Zadok (v. 12), Seraiah (v. 14), and Jozadak (v. 14).

The genealogy begins with Levi and his three sons, Gershon, Kohath, and Merari (v. 1), but the Chronicler passes over Gershon and Merari to focus attention on the most important son, Kohath, and his four sons: Amram, Izhar, Hebron, and Uzziel (v. 2). Kohath is important because the priestly line will come from his line, thus the genealogy narrows further to focus on *Amram*, who is the father of Aaron, Moses, and Miriam (v. 3). At the outset, this family line is elevated, with particular interest on Aaron, the high priest.

The four sons of Aaron are introduced next, Nadab, Abihu, Eleazar and Ithamar, but attention is on Aaron's line through *Eleazar* (v. 4). Aaron's four sons had been anointed as priests (Exod 28:1), yet his eldest son Nadab and his brother Abihu had tragically died (Lev 10). Eleazar had been given a position of leadership (Num 3:32; 4:16), and he had become high priest after his father died (cf. 20:26–28). He had served as high priest when the Israelites were journeying to the promised land, and his leadership is noted throughout the

---

4. Williamson (*1 and 2 Chronicles*, 70–71) proposes that that there are twelve generations from Aaron to the building of the temple, and another twelve to the rebuilding of the temple through Jehozadak's son, Joshua.

5. Ibid., 69.

6. For a helpful (and not too technical) comparison of names appearing in these texts, see Merrill, *1 & 2 Chronicles*, 126–127, and the chart by Braun, *1 Chronicles*, 84.

period of Joshua (26:1–4, 63; 27:2; 31:12; cf. Josh 14:1; 19:51; 24:33). His son Phinehas is another important figure. He had zealously turned away God's wrath and made atonement for Israel (Num 25:1–13). As a result, God had honored him by promising that he and his descendants would have a perpetual priesthood (vv. 10–13; Ps 106:30).

The linear genealogy moves at a rapid pace from one generation to the next (1 Chr 6:4–9), pausing to focus attention on the priesthood during the time of Solomon (v. 10). The genealogy continues in relentless succession, glossing over several generations,[7] yet it pauses to focus on the last high priest, Jozadak, who had been brought into exile with Judah (v. 15). It's important to bear in mind that when Nebuchadnezzar destroyed Jerusalem, he had killed Zedekiah's seventy sons at Riblah, along with key leaders (Jer 52:8–11). Seraiah, the chief priest and father of Jozadak (1 Chr 6:14), had been brutally killed, along with temple personnel, court advisers, the scribe of the king's army, and sixty men of Judah (Jer 52:24–27). But Seraiah's son, Jozadak, had survived and been brought to Babylon with the other exiles (1 Chr 6:15). The priesthood will continue through him, therefore, and more particularly through his son Joshua, who has an important leadership role after the exile (Ezra 2:2; 3:2, 8; 5:2; Hag 1:1; Zech 3:1–10; 6:11–15). The priestly genealogy in this chapter extends to the turbulent period of the exile (1 Chr 6:15), although the story of the priesthood is resumed in chapter 9 since priests and Levites are among the returnees.

Descendants of Levi (6:16–30)

The genealogy that began in 1 Chronicles 6:1 with the three sons of Levi, Gershon (Gershom), Kohath, and Merari, is resumed in verse 16 with Gershon's two sons (v. 17), followed by Kohath's four sons (v. 18) and Merari's two sons (v. 19). The genealogy extends further with Gershon's descendants through his son Libni (vv. 20–21) and with Kohath's descendants through his son Amminadab (vv. 22–27). Ellkanah's son Samuel is among the list of names (vv. 27–28; cf. 1 Sam 8:2), suggesting that the prophet Samuel has Levitical ancestry.[8] The genealogy concludes with the descendants of Merari (1 Chr 6:29–30), with the last son in the list identified as Asaiah, who is among those who helped move the ark into Jerusalem (v. 30; cf. 1 Chr 15:6).

---

7. See Merrill, *1 & 2 Chronicles*, 126–27.

8. Samuel's father Elkanah lived in the hill country of Ephraim (cf. 1 Sam 1:1). Selman suggests that reference to Ephraim in Samuel may well be *geographical* rather than tribal (*Chronicles*, 111).

Levitical Singers Appointed to Lead God's People (6:31–48)

Focus shifts to the Levites whom David appointed to sing songs of worship (1 Chr 6:31–48). King David had instructed the Levites to appoint their relatives to sing and play music with harps, lyres, and cymbals, so that they might raise sounds of joy (cf. 15:16–26).[9] The tribe of Levi had a rich history of leading in worship from their early days with Moses and Miriam (Exod 15:1–21; cf. Deut 32:1–44). A variety of instruments are played when the Levites lead God's people in worship as the ark of the covenant is being brought into Jerusalem (1 Chr 16). Musicians will have an important role leading Israel in praise and thanksgiving (25:1–31).[10] Singing praises to God was central to Israel's life as a worshiping community (see Ps 68:4; cf. Pss 98:1; 105:2; 149:1), and since the Levites were given this sacred responsibility, their genealogies are important.

Three musical families appointed by David are given: Heman, the singer from the line of Kohath (1 Chr 6:33–38), Asaph, from the line of Gershon (vv. 39–43), and Ethan, from the line of Merari (vv. 44–47). Asaph stood on the right side of Heman (v. 39), Ethan stood on the left (v. 44), and Heman stood in the middle. These three worship leaders play a key role when the ark is brought to Jerusalem, and Asaph is a prominent worship leader during the reign of King David. Several psalms are attributed to him and to his sons (Pss 50, 73–83; cf. 2 Chr 29:30), and he is identified as lead musician (1 Chr 16:5; cf. 25:2, 9). Asaph's descendants will continue to have an ongoing role leading worship in the post-exilic community (cf. Ezra 2:41; Neh 7:44; 11:17; 12:46). Asaph and Heman are both identified as "seers," hinting at their prophetic role (Asaph, 2 Chr 29:30; Heman, 1 Chr 25:5). We will learn later that Heman and his family are important worship leaders under King David (25:4–6) and also under Solomon (2 Chr 5:12–14).

The Priestly Role and Aaron's Genealogy (6:49–53)

This section concludes with a brief statement about the role of Israel's priests that distinguishes them from the Levites: "But Aaron and his descendants were the ones who presented offerings on the altar of burnt offering and on the altar of incense in connection with all that was done in the Most Holy Place, making atonement for Israel, in accordance with all that Moses the servant of God had commanded" (1 Chr 6:49). Their important role will be seen throughout the stories of the kings. While the Levites had been chosen by God to assist the priests, the sacred task of ministering in the most holy place

---

9. On the topic of joy, see Live the Story in Chapter 34, pp. 319–21.
10. See the discussion in Chapter 25 on 1 Chr 25.

was assigned to Aaron and his sons. They were appointed to make atonement for the sins of Israel (Lev 1–7), with the most sacred responsibility performed on the Day of Atonement (ch. 16). Their priestly role was in accordance with all that Moses had commanded, underscoring the ongoing significance of the Torah in the life of Israel.

The sacred task assigned to Aaron and his sons is immediately followed by Aaron's linear genealogy through Eleazar and his son Phinehas (1 Chr 6:50–53; cf. vv. 4–8). The genealogy extends as far as Zadok and his son Ahimaaz, who serve during the time of David (2 Sam 15:36; 17:20; 18:22). This genealogy provides a transition to the next section, which describes the settlement of the Levites in their allotted cities, and it is not surprising to find that the towns given to the sons of Aaron are presented first.

Levitical Cities (6:54–81)

During the time of Moses, provision had been made for forty-eight Levitical cities that would be apportioned from all the tribes (Num 35:1–34). The Levites did not have their own territory, but instead, they had been dispersed among the tribes since the LORD was their inheritance (Deut 18:1–2; cf. Josh 13:14). The Levites were not only to live in these cities, but six of them functioned as places of refuge, where the manslayer who had killed someone unintentionally could flee and thus be protected from the blood avenger (Num 35:6–34). The specific cities and their pasture lands were first allocated during the time of Joshua, when Levitical leaders approached Eleazar and Joshua, requesting that towns be given to them according to God's command through Moses (Josh 21:1–3).[11] Using the ancient practice of lots, Joshua assigned forty-eight towns that were dispersed among the tribes to the families of Kohath, Gershon, and Merari. The Chronicler's presentation of the settlement of the priests and Levites in their cities has been drawn from the list in Joshua 21:1–39,[12] yet his arrangement gives priority to the settlement of Aaron's sons. While there is some debate about the exact settlement period in view,[13] the latter part of David's reign seems to be most likely.[14] This fits

---

11. For some of the historical issues regarding the allotment of Levitical cities (especially whether the cities were actually settled by the Levites during the time of Joshua or simply allotted); see Sara Japhet, "Conquest and Settlement in Chronicles," *JBL* 98 (1979): 205–218. Japhet argues that Levites were settled in these cities by the time of David.

12. A number of commentaries have detailed discussions about this chapter, including possible reconstructions of the text (such as Japhet and Klein). For a less technical but helpful comparison of towns, see Merrill, *1 & 2 Chronicles*, 127–29.

13. For a summary of the various views, see Klein, *1 Chronicles*, 186–189.

14. Following Braun, *1 Chronicles*, 98–99.

with the immediate context where the priestly genealogy ends with Ahimaaz (1 Chr 6:53).

Levitical towns had been assigned according to the three major families. While the section that follows is recorded in two parts (vv. 54–65 and vv. 66–81), there is symmetry since both sections represent the three major families of Kohath (vv. 54–61, 66–70), Gershon (vv. 62, 71–76), and Merari (vv. 63, 77–81). The Levitical towns may well have been functioning as provincial administrative centers where oversight of the king's estate could be carried out,[15] and we know that the Levites had an important judicial and teaching role (Deut 17:8–13; 2 Chr 17:7–9). The presentation of towns seems to be arranged according to geography.[16] Thirteen priestly towns are identified among the southern tribes of Judah, Benjamin, and Simeon, including the important city of Hebron where David will be anointed as king. The non-priestly Levites are allocated towns in the central region within the tribal territories of Ephraim and Manasseh (1 Chr 6:54–61, 65–70). The next family, Gershon, settled further north, in the territories of Issachar, Asher, and Naphtali, and in the region east of the Jordan in Bashan where the half-tribe of Manasseh lived (vv. 62, 71–76). The Levitical towns belonging to Merari are given last (vv. 63, 77–81). Their cities are located in the Transjordanian region, in the territories of Reuben and Gad, but also north-west in the territory of Zebulun. As with the genealogies as a whole, the distribution of Levitical cities among the twelve tribes (with the exception of Dan[17]) contributes to the theme of "all Israel," and it underscores the sacred nature of the kingdom.

 LIVE the Story

Jesus Is the Great High Priest

God had set apart Aaron and his sons for priestly service. They had the sacred task of officiating at the altar, but we do well to remember that perfection was not in the priesthood, for its priests had been taken from among humanity, and they, too, shared in sinful human nature. This is reflected in the consecration rites required before a priest could minister in the presence of a holy God. Priests had to wash themselves before putting on holy garments, and when they officiated at the altar, they had to offer sacrifices, *first* for their own sin, before offering sacrifices on Israel's behalf (Lev 4:3–12; 16:6, 11, 17; cf. Heb 5:1–4;

15. Ibid., 99.
16. As noted by Japhet, *1 & II Chronicles*, 160–61.
17. See the discussion in Chapter 7 on 1 Chr 7:12, pp. 92–93.

7:27–28). The well-known stories of the priesthood testify to the weaknesses of Israel's priests: Aaron had tragically acquiesced when the Israelites asked him to make a golden calf (Exod 32:1–6, 21–26, 35), and God would have destroyed him had it not been for Moses's intercession (Deut 9:20). Aaron's two sons, Nadab and Abihu, were judged by God for bringing unauthorized fire into the tabernacle (Lev 10). Eli's sons, Hophni and Phinehas, not only despised God's offerings, but they also had illicit relationships with the women who served at the doorway of the tent of meeting (1 Sam 2:12–17, 22–36). They, too, would be judged by God (1 Sam 4:1–22). While there are many priests who serve God faithfully (and we will encounter them in Chronicles), in the period prior to the exile the prophets denounce the priests for leading Israel astray (Jer 2:8, 26; Ezek 22:26). The corruption of the priesthood is seen after the exile, when Nehemiah rebukes the priests (Neh 13:4–9, 28–30) and when Malachi pronounces judgment against them (Mal 1:6–14; 2:1–9). This is not to say that every priest was corrupt, for we have a number of godly examples of priests who serve God faithfully, such as Joshua (Ezra 3:2; 5:2) and Ezra (7:6, 10), but the sober reality of the Old Testament is that Israel's priests were human beings, and they, too, were beset with weakness.

The writer to the Hebrews contrasts Jesus, the great high priest, with the priests under the old covenant. Jesus is the *perfect* and *faithful* high priest, who is described as "holy, blameless, pure, set apart from sinners, exalted above the heavens," and who now sits at the right hand of God's throne, making intercession on our behalf (Heb 7:26–27). Unlike the many priests in the Old Testament (as this genealogy testifies!) whose priesthood was for a limited term due to their mortality, Jesus *always* lives to make intercession on our behalf.

Jesus was not from the tribe of Levi (Heb 7:13–14), for his credentials were not based on physical ancestry but on the "power of an indestructible life" (v. 16). Instead of coming from the tribe of Levi, Jesus's priestly office is from the earlier order of Melchizedek, a priest without Levitical ancestry who was both priest and king (Gen 14:18–24; Ps 110:4; cf. Heb 3:1–19; 4:14–16; 5:1–10; 6:20; 7:1–28; 8:1–6). The superior priesthood of Melchizedek is seen in the fact that Abraham had given *him* a tithe (Gen 14:20). Moreover, since Levi was in the loins of Abraham, so to speak, the priestly tribe of Levi is thereby giving honor to Melchizedek (Heb 5:5–6; 7:1–10)! This testifies to the superior priesthood of Melchizedek, which is confirmed by the declaration in Psalm 110: "You are a priest forever, in the order of Melchizedek" (Ps 110:4; cf. Heb 5:6; 7:17, 21). Accordingly, Jesus's priestly ministry is modeled on the royal priesthood of Melchizedek, something that David represents in his priestly role (cf. 1 Chr 15:27–28).[18] Jesus is the anointed king who rules over the cosmos (Heb 1:1–14; 2:5–8), but also the merciful and faithful high priest who intercedes on our behalf (2:17; 5:1–10; 7:1–28; 8:1–6). This means that the priesthood in the Old Testament is the shadow of the good things to come—it anticipates Jesus's priestly ministry.

Israel's priests were to present "offerings on the altar of burnt offering and on the altar of incense in connection with all that was done in the Most Holy Place, making atonement for Israel" (1 Chr 6:49), but their sacred task points to something *greater* that is fulfilled in Jesus. The Old Testament sacrificial system was a temporary provision, for the reality was that the blood of goats and bulls could never take away sin (Heb 9:1–28; 10:11). Israel's priests under the old covenant had to daily offer sacrifices, which served as a reminder of sins (10:1–4). The Old Testament was a shadow of the good things to come, for it prepares us for the perfect and "once-for-all" sacrifice of Jesus, who offered up his own blood (chs. 9–10). He is the one who finally deals with the problem of human sin—something that the blood of goats and bulls can never do—for his atoning sacrifice *takes away* sin.[19] The genealogies of Levi highlight the importance and necessity of atonement in the Old Testament, and they remind us that Israel has been set apart as a kingdom of priests, but even more so, they look ahead to the great high priest, whose atoning sacrifice enables us to enter God's presence. Jesus is the new and living way that enables us to draw near to the throne of grace. This is surely good news for us today.

---

18. For a helpful summary of the priesthood of Melchizedek, see Eugene H. Merrill, "Royal Priesthood: An Old Testament Messianic Motif," *BSac* 150 (1993): 50–61 (esp. 51–57). For a summary of the tithe, see the discussion in Chapter 60 on 2 Chr 31.

19. For a helpful study designed for laypeople and pastors on sacrifices in the Old Testament and Jesus as the once-for-all sacrifice, see Longman, *Immanuel in Our Place*, 77–115.

LISTEN to the Story

¹The sons of Issachar:

Tola, Puah, Jashub and Shimron—four in all.

²The sons of Tola:

Uzzi, Rephaiah, Jeriel, Jahmai, Ibsam and Samuel—heads of their
families. During the reign of David, the descendants of Tola
listed as fighting men in their genealogy numbered 22,600.

³The son of Uzzi:

Izrahiah.

The sons of Izrahiah:

Michael, Obadiah, Joel and Ishiah. All five of them were chiefs.
⁴According to their family genealogy, they had 36,000 men
ready for battle, for they had many wives and children.

⁵The relatives who were fighting men belonging to all the clans of
Issachar, as listed in their genealogy, were 87,000 in all.

⁶Three sons of Benjamin:

Bela, Beker and Jediael.

⁷The sons of Bela:

Ezbon, Uzzi, Uzziel, Jerimoth and Iri, heads of families—five in
all. Their genealogical record listed 22,034 fighting men.

⁸The sons of Beker:

Zemirah, Joash, Eliezer, Elioenai, Omri, Jeremoth, Abijah,
Anathoth and Alemeth. All these were the sons of Beker.
⁹Their genealogical record listed the heads of families and
20,200 fighting men.

¹⁰The son of Jediael:

Bilhan.

The sons of Bilhan:

> Jeush, Benjamin, Ehud, Kenaanah, Zethan, Tarshish and
> Ahishahar. [11]All these sons of Jediael were heads of families.
> There were 17,200 fighting men ready to go out to war.

[12]The Shuppites and Huppites were the descendants of Ir, and the
Hushites the descendants of Aher.

[13]The sons of Naphtali:

> Jahziel, Guni, Jezer and Shillem—the descendants of Bilhah.

[14]The descendants of Manasseh:

> Asriel was his descendant through his Aramean concubine. She
> gave birth to Makir the father of Gilead. [15]Makir took a wife
> from among the Huppites and Shuppites. His sister's name
> was Maakah.
>
> Another descendant was named Zelophehad, who had only
> daughters.
>
> [16]Makir's wife Maakah gave birth to a son and named him Peresh.
> His brother was named Sheresh, and his sons were Ulam and
> Rakem.

[17]The son of Ulam:

> Bedan.

These were the sons of Gilead son of Makir, the son of Manasseh.

> [18]His sister Hammoleketh gave birth to Ishhod, Abiezer and
> Mahlah.

[19]The sons of Shemida were:

> Ahian, Shechem, Likhi and Aniam.

[20]The descendants of Ephraim:

> Shuthelah, Bered his son,
> Tahath his son, Eleadah his son,
> Tahath his son, [21]Zabad his son
> and Shuthelah his son.
>
> Ezer and Elead were killed by the native-born men of Gath,
> when they went down to seize their livestock. [22]Their father
> Ephraim mourned for them many days, and his relatives

came to comfort him. ²³Then he made love to his wife again, and she became pregnant and gave birth to a son. He named him Beriah, because there had been misfortune in his family. ²⁴His daughter was Sheerah, who built Lower and Upper Beth Horon as well as Uzzen Sheerah.

²⁵Rephah was his son, Resheph his son,
Telah his son, Tahan his son,
²⁶Ladan his son, Ammihud his son,
Elishama his son, ²⁷Nun his son
and Joshua his son.

²⁸Their lands and settlements included Bethel and its surrounding villages, Naaran to the east, Gezer and its villages to the west, and Shechem and its villages all the way to Ayyah and its villages. ²⁹Along the borders of Manasseh were Beth Shan, Taanach, Megiddo and Dor, together with their villages. The descendants of Joseph son of Israel lived in these towns.

³⁰The sons of Asher:
Imnah, Ishvah, Ishvi and Beriah. Their sister was Serah.
³¹The sons of Beriah:
Heber and Malkiel, who was the father of Birzaith.
³²Heber was the father of Japhlet, Shomer and Hotham and of their sister Shua.
³³The sons of Japhlet:
Pasak, Bimhal and Ashvath.
These were Japhlet's sons.
³⁴The sons of Shomer:
Ahi, Rohgah, Hubbah and Aram.
³⁵The sons of his brother Helem:
Zophah, Imna, Shelesh and Amal.
³⁶The sons of Zophah:
Suah, Harnepher, Shual, Beri, Imrah, ³⁷Bezer, Hod, Shamma, Shilshah, Ithran and Beera.
³⁸The sons of Jether:
Jephunneh, Pispah and Ara.
³⁹The sons of Ulla:
Arah, Hanniel and Rizia.

⁴⁰All these were descendants of Asher—heads of families, choice men, brave warriors and outstanding leaders. The number of men ready for battle, as listed in their genealogy, was 26,000.

Listening to the Text in the Story: Genesis 46:8–27; Numbers 26:1–51; Joshua 16—17

The extended genealogy of the tribe of Levi (1 Chr 6:1–81) is now followed by the genealogies of six tribes that settle west of the Jordan: the tribes of Issachar (7:1–5), Benjamin (vv. 6–12), Naphtali (v. 13), the half-tribe of Manasseh (vv. 14–19), the tribe of Ephraim (vv. 20–29), and the tribe of Asher (vv. 30–40). The tribes (with the exception of Benjamin) belong to the northern kingdom of Israel, yet, despite their apostasy, they have not been forgotten, underscoring the irrevocable calling of God's people Israel (2:1–2).

Three texts central to Israel's history lie behind this chapter (Gen 46:8–27; Num 26; Josh 16–17). Jacob's seventy descendants had journeyed to Egypt because of a famine. God had told Jacob not to be afraid to go to Egypt, for he would make him into a great nation there, and he would bring his people out of Egypt. Some of the names of Jacob's descendants are recalled in this chapter, the details of which are noted below (cf. Gen 46:8–27). The census of the twelve tribes of Israel after the generation had died in the wilderness is the second text that is recalled in this chapter (Num 26). Several names occurring in Genesis 46 and Numbers 26 appear in the Chronicler's presentation of the tribes of Issachar (1 Chr 7:1–5; cf. Gen 46:13; Num 26:23–24), Naphtali (1 Chr 7:13; cf. Gen 46:24; Num 26:48–49), and Asher (1 Chr 7:30–40; cf. Gen 46:17; cf. Num 26:44–46). The territory of Ephraim and Manasseh is given in Joshua 16–17, the two tribes representing Joseph. By recalling the names of Israel's forefathers, the post-exilic community is reminded of this early and formative period when they were a united people of God, thereby underscoring their common ancestry. In spite of their history of division, these tribes still belong to the people of Israel. Even though the tribes of Judah, Levi, and Benjamin constitute the southern kingdom of Judah, the inclusion of the northern tribes in the opening genealogies (with the exception of Dan and Zebulun) presents a powerful vision of "all Israel" that is central to the theology of Chronicles.

Military Men from the Tribe of Issachar (7:1–5)

Issachar was Jacob's fifth born son through Leah (Gen 30:17–18). The descendants of Issachar are traced through several generations (1 Chr 7:1–5), although the focus is not on their settlement in the land (cf. Josh 19:17–23) but on military men from the tribe who served during the time of David (1 Chr 7:2). Boda thus suggests that Issachar "represents a key military resource for David's kingdom, foreshadowing their participation in David's army in the Chronicler's narrative in 12:32, where they will be singled out as those who 'understood the signs of the times and knew the best course to take.'"[1] Their inclusion among the northern tribes anticipates their key military role during the time of David, and it further demonstrates the widespread support David receives from all the tribes.

Military Men from the Tribe of Benjamin (7:6–12)

Focus shifts to the tribe of Benjamin, beginning with the patriarch's three sons, Bela, Beker and Jediael (1 Chr 7:6; cf. 8:1–2), followed by leaders of family units: Bela (v. 7), Beker (vv. 8–9), and Jediael (vv. 10–11). As with Issachar in the previous section (vv. 1–5), the list is military in nature, suggesting those prepared for battle associated with the time of David (cf. v. 2). Their inclusion in the genealogy may well show their availability to "bolster David's kingdom, again foreshadowing their participation in David's army in the Chronicler's narrative."[2] That men from the tribe of Benjamin (Saul's own tribe) support David signals waning support for Saul, another indication that God was turning the kingdom over to David (cf. 12:2, 29). Included in the list of Benjaminites was a man named Hushim (cf. NASB, ESV, 7:12)[3] who is elsewhere identified as a son of Dan (Gen 46:23), suggesting a loss of his former tribal affiliation. It is important to remember that the Danites had abandoned their original tribal allotment when they settled further north (Judg 17–18). Accordingly, two Danite cities mentioned in the previous chapter have been incorporated into the territory of Ephraim (1 Chr 6:66, 69; cf. Judg 19:42). Boda makes the insightful observation that

---

1. Boda, *1–2 Chronicles*, 83.
2. Ibid.
3. The NIV has "Hushites" in 1 Chr 7:12 instead of "Hushim," although the NIV footnote gives "Hushim" as an alternative reading. It is preferable to read "Hushim" in 1 Chr 7:12, which would identify him as the son of Dan, according to Gen 46:23.

the tribe of Dan may have been "singled out by the Chronicler because of its blatant abandonment of its territorial allotment, as well as its creation of a rival cult, which led to the northern tribes being led astray (for both of these acts of Dan, see Judg 18; 1 Kgs 12:29–30; 2 Chr 11:14–15; 13:8–12)."[4] This is probably the reason why Dan's son, Hushim, is listed among the Benjaminites in 1 Chronicles 7:12. While it could be due to a scribal error or loss in transmission, when interpreted within the genealogies as a whole, it is more likely that it is due to the idolatrous history of Dan and their abandonment of their inheritance.

The Tribe of Naphtali (7:13)

The genealogy continues with the sons of Naphtali, Jacob's son through Rachel's servant, Bilhah (Gen 30:7–8). The tribe was located in the northern region, bordering Issachar and Zebulun (cf. Josh 19:32–39), yet only a brief genealogy is given here (cf. Gen 46:24). That the focus is not on Naphtali is further seen in the absence of any reference to the adjoining northern tribe, Zebulun (cf. Josh 19:10–16; Isa 9:1), which may have been due to its association with the idolatrous northern tribes (although the tribe of Naphtali did give support to David, and some from Zebulun humbled themselves during the time of Hezekiah; cf. 1 Chr 12:34; 2 Chr 30:11).

The Tribes of Manasseh (7:14–19)

The tribes of Manasseh and Ephraim are given next (1 Chr 7:14–29). Unlike the tribal lists of Issachar, Benjamin, and Asher, which are military in nature, the focus in the first section is on Manasseh's son Makir, who was a well-known figure in Israel's history (cf. Gen 50:23; Num 26:29; 32:39–40; Josh 17:1). Makir's son was Gilead (cf. Num 26:29–34), whose name is associated with the region of Gilead, east of the Jordan. The city bearing his name had a long history in connection with the tribe of Manasseh (cf. Num 32:39–40; 36:1; Josh 17:1–6).

Relevant to Manasseh's genealogy are the eighth century BC inscribed potsherds that have been uncovered by archaeologists at ancient Samaria. The Samaria Ostraca attest to luxury goods that were used in the royal court of the time, including wine and body oil. The significance of the ostraca for the tribe of Manasseh is highlighted in what follows:

---

4. Boda, *1–2 Chronicles*, 86. This whole section on 1 Chr 7 by Boda is insightful and theologically rich (see especially, pp. 82–87).

The topographical data they contain constitute the largest number of
Israelite place names found outside the Bible, and are invaluable for locating a number of cities surrounding Samaria, some of which appear in the
Bible. All of the clan names given in the second group of ostraca belong to
the tribe of Manasseh. That all but one of them appear in clan lists found
in the Bible (Num 26:29–34; Josh 17:2–3) demonstrates the longevity of
ancient tribal divisions and their administrative purposes.[5]

These ostraca provide important information about the distribution of goods,
clan systems, and key sites, reminding us that although the genealogies in this
chapter are far removed from our contemporary context, ancient Israel had
its own tribal organizational structure, and thus names and geography were
important aspects of social life.

Lastly, we note that several women are prominently featured in this genealogy, including the daughters of Zelophehad, which recalls an earlier story
about inheritance given to them (cf. Num 27:1–11; 36:1–12; Josh 17:3–6).
Wives chosen from Huppim and Shuppim connect the tribe of Manasseh with
Benjamin (1 Chr 7:15; cf. 7:12), just as the marriage of Makir's daughter to
Hezron establishes a relationship with Judah (2:21). The Chronicler is keen
to show these inter-tribal relationships, since it further establishes the unity
of the tribes (cf. 2:1–2; 12:23–40; 2 Chr 30:1, 10–11; 34:9). The tribes of
Ephraim and Manasseh are included among those who gave their support to
David (1 Chr 12:30–31), and they were among those who joined the Southern
Kingdom at crucial times of reform (2 Chr 15:9; 30:1, 10–11; 34:9). We
do well to remember that Ephraim and Manasseh are included among the
returnees (1 Chr 9:3); thus, reference to these inter-tribal relationships serves
to build unity in the post-exilic community.

The Tribe of Ephraim (7:20–29)

Focus shifts to Ephraim (1 Chr 7:20–29; cf. Num 26:35) and his three sons
Shuthelah, Ezer, and Elead (1 Chr 7:20–21). Shuthelah's line is represented
in his lineal genealogy (vv. 20–21), but his two brothers had been killed by
Philistines from Gath because they had tried to steal their livestock. Their
father, Ephraim, had mourned for them for many days, after which time his
wife conceived again and gave birth to a son named Beriah, whose name recalls

---

5. Scott B. Noegel, "The Samaria Ostraca," first published in *The Ancient Near East: Historical
Sources in Translation*, ed. Mark W. Chavalas (London: Blackwell, 2006), 397, now available online
(https://faculty.washington.edu/snoegel/PDFs/articles/Noegel%2048%20-%20ANEHST%202006c
.pdf).

the misfortune in the family (v. 23). Amidst this family crisis, hope emerges with the birth of a daughter named Sheerah. Remarkably, she builds three cities, one of which bears her name (v. 24). Further hope is seen in another descendant, Rephah, whose lineage leads to Joshua, one of Israel's most well-known leaders (vv. 25–27; cf. Josh 1:1). The genealogy concludes with a list of cities belonging to the tribe of Ephraim, which locates them west of the Jordan (1 Chr 7:28–29; cf. Josh 16:5–10). Finally, a comment is made that Ephraim and Manasseh were the sons of Joseph (1 Chr 7:29), recalling the list of Israel's sons (2:1–2) but also Israel's earlier history (Gen 48:13–20; 1 Chr 5:1–2).

The Tribe of Asher (7:30–40)

The chapter concludes with the descendants of Asher (cf. Gen 46:17; Num 26:44–46), the son born to Jacob through Leah's maid, Zilpah (Gen 30:12–13). As with the tribes of Issachar and Benjamin, the list is military in nature (cf. 1 Chr 7:40), anticipating that military men from Asher will give their support to David (12:36), and some from Asher will later join Judah in the Passover celebration (2 Chr 30:11).

Vision for a United and Reconciled People of God

The northern tribes presented in this chapter present a powerful vision for a united people of God. This is not to deny that sin has its impact on the northern tribes (as seen in the absence of the tribes of Dan[6] and Zebulun[7]), but there is nevertheless a vision for a unified people of God, since the northern tribes of Issachar (1 Chr 7:1–5), Naphtali (v. 13), Manasseh (vv. 14–19), Ephraim (vv. 20–29), and Asher (vv. 30–40) are included among the tribes, even though they had belonged to the apostate Northern Kingdom. Boda sums this up well:

> The Chronicler's inclusion of most of the Cisjordan northern tribes sent the message to his Judean audience that members of those northern tribes

---

6. The tribe of Dan had chosen territory further north instead of settling in the land allotted to them (Josh 19:40–48; Judg 18:1–31). Moreover, the city of Dan had become a key site for idolatry (1 Kgs 12:28–29; for the idolatry described without mentioning Dan see 2 Chr 13:8–9; cf. Judg 18:30–31). The Chronicler seems to have intentionally omitted Dan as an indictment against this tribe.

7. The tribe of Zebulun will be mentioned later (1 Chr 12:33; 2 Chr 30:10–11, 18), but their omission from the list may be intended to warn about the devastating results of disobedience that results in the loss of two tribes (see Boda, *1–2 Chronicles*, 87).

were to be considered as part of "Israel." This subtle call to unity was key in an era in which the territory of these tribes did not form a separate province in the Persian Empire.[8]

Judah's history with the Northern Kingdom had been fraught with conflict (2 Chr 10:16, 19; 13:2–9; 16:1–6; 28:5–15), and yet, King Hezekiah invites these same northern tribes to join him in the Passover celebration (ch. 30). Some from the tribes of Ephraim and Manasseh, Asher, Issachar, and Zebulun humble themselves and join Judah (vv. 11–12 18–19), and Hezekiah even prays on their behalf, asking that God might pardon those who had sought the LORD (vv. 18–19).[9] This is the painful work of forgiveness and reconciliation that is the outworking of 2 Chronicles 7:14.[10] This reminds us that the Chronicler is telling a story of "unmerited grace and the possibility of forgiveness. Again and again, sins are forgiven and out of sin and repentance, God brings even greater works."[11] This vision for a united people of God is not merely a matter of scholarly research or a theological ideal, but rather, it speaks to the necessary work of reconciliation of former enemies so that God's ideal might be embodied in the community.

Consider what took place many years earlier in Israel's history: the two estranged brothers, Jacob and Esau, had wept when they were finally reconciled after many years of conflict, at which time Jacob saw in his brother's acceptance of him the very face of God (Gen 33:1–17). Joseph had understood all too well the cost to him personally to be reconciled with his brothers, as he wept bitterly when they were finally united (Gen 45:14–15). Their reconciliation was a tangible demonstration of God's forgiveness and his sovereign hand (Gen 50:17–20). This is the painful journey of reconciliation between brothers. In Chronicles, this is played out on a national scale as estranged tribes are reconciled. God's people were not to forget that they were first and foremost brothers, belonging to the one people Israel. The prophets envision a time when Israel and Judah would form the one people of God (Jer 3:18; 50:4–5; Ezek 37:15–22), so that they would "never again be two nations or divided into two kingdoms" (v. 22). The breach of relationship between Judah and Israel was a great tragedy, but God is restoring and reuniting his people, and this is the vision being set forth in this chapter. Old divisions

---

8. Boda, *1–2 Chronicles*, 87.

9. See the discussion in Chapter 59 on 2 Chr 30, pp. 505–6.

10. On the connection between 2 Chr 7:14 and the story of Hezekiah, see the discussion in Chapter 36, p. 341.

11. Hahn, *The Kingdom of God*, 40.

and hostilities must be set aside in light of the greater purpose of God for a unified people.

In our churches today, we can easily divide over minor issues, such as the color of the carpet, the type of music that is played in worship services, or the size of the pulpit. Churches can even split over matters that are, in reality, inconsequential. The United States has become a divided nation, with different political views tearing at the fabric of society. We are a society of "us versus them," as Ben Sasse writes in his book entitled *Them: Why We Hate Each Other—and How to Heal.*[12] We are not only divided over politics, but we are also divided along ethnic and racial lines, which is a denial of the very gospel we claim to hold so dearly. Although the human story is filled with increasing conflict among peoples and nations, the solution for deeply felt animosity and hatred is found in Jesus's atoning death and the new life that he offers.

The reality of the gospel is that Jesus *has reconciled* believers into one body through the cross. Old hostilities *have been* broken down, and we *have been* created to be a new humanity in Christ (Eph 2:14–18). Where hostilities remain, it is a denial of the very gospel we seek to proclaim. We need to take seriously our unity that has been accomplished in Christ and to embody this unity in our relationships. Jesus taught his disciples that if they had something against a brother, they were to leave their offering and be reconciled with their brother first (Matt 5:22–24). They were to love their enemies and pray for those who persecuted them (vv. 44–48). Our churches need to be places that give testimony to the painful and hard work of reconciliation, as we seek to live out the reality of the gospel.

The reconciliation possible between estranged tribes and former enemies is seen in the powerful story of two families who reconcile after the Rwandan Genocide. A forty-year history of political conflict and injustice led to the eruption of violence in Rwanda in 1994, where it is estimated that one million Tutsis and moderate Hutus were massacred in one hundred days. Two men, Andrew and Callixte, had been childhood and family friends, but they would experience the conflict firsthand. In Andrew's neighboring village of Murambi, a staggering fifty thousand Tutsis were massacred in just eight hours. Andrew's wife, Madrine, lost her father, mother, and five siblings. It is unimaginable to consider the loss that she experienced, yet Andrew's childhood friend Callixte had been part of the mob that had killed his wife's family. This heart-wrenching tribal conflict put neighbor against neighbor, friend against friend.

After the genocide, local courts were established to try perpetrators of these

---

12. Ben Sasse, *Them: Why We Hate Each Other—and How to Heal* (New York: St Martin's, 2018).

crimes, and Andrew testified against his childhood friend Callixte, which led to his imprisonment for thirteen years. In 1994, World Vision started working in the area, providing food and caring for orphans. Counseling programs and reconciliation camps were established in an effort to bring healing to a people who had suffered so much trauma and pain. Andrew got involved with World Vision, and over time, he and his wife were learning about God's forgiveness.[13]

Remarkably, Andrew and Callixte now worship in the same church. Andrew preaches and Callixte reads Scripture alongside him. Their families even share meals together. This is a testimony to the amazing (and supernatural) reconciliation possible through Jesus. One pastor, Antoine, who serves in Rwanda comments: "You see in every country, people get wounded. People get hurt. They need to forgive." He comments further: "Your life becomes better when you repent, confess, and reconcile."[14] This is the powerful outworking of the gospel, and this is the vision that is being presented in Chronicles, as former tribal enemies are united as the one people of God.[15] This is the hard work of reconciliation, but it is possible through Christ, who has created us to be one new humanity, united *in him*.

---

13. The full story is told by Kari Costanza, "Rwanda: 20 Years Later," *World Vision*, 2014; see https://www.worldvision.org/disaster-relief-news-stories/rwanda-20-years-later.

14. Ibid.

15. See A Vision for Reconciliation in Live the Story, Chapter 59, pp. 510–11.

CHAPTER 8

1 Chronicles 8:1–40

 LISTEN to the Story

¹Benjamin was the father of Bela his firstborn,
Ashbel the second son, Aharah the third,
  ²Nohah the fourth and Rapha the fifth.
³The sons of Bela were:
    Addar, Gera, Abihud, ⁴Abishua, Naaman, Ahoah, ⁵Gera,
    Shephuphan and Huram.
⁶These were the descendants of Ehud, who were heads of families of
    those living in Geba and were deported to Manahath:
    ⁷Naaman, Ahijah, and Gera, who deported them and who was
    the father of Uzza and Ahihud.
⁸Sons were born to Shaharaim in Moab after he had divorced his
    wives Hushim and Baara. ⁹By his wife Hodesh he had Jobab,
    Zibia, Mesha, Malkam, ¹⁰Jeuz, Sakia and Mirmah. These were his
    sons, heads of families. ¹¹By Hushim he had Abitub and Elpaal.
¹²The sons of Elpaal:
    Eber, Misham, Shemed (who built Ono and Lod with its
    surrounding villages), ¹³and Beriah and Shema, who were
    heads of families of those living in Aijalon and who drove out
    the inhabitants of Gath.
¹⁴Ahio, Shashak, Jeremoth, ¹⁵Zebadiah, Arad, Eder, ¹⁶Michael, Ishpah
    and Joha were the sons of Beriah.
¹⁷Zebadiah, Meshullam, Hizki, Heber, ¹⁸Ishmerai, Izliah and Jobab
    were the sons of Elpaal.
¹⁹Jakim, Zikri, Zabdi, ²⁰Elienai, Zillethai, Eliel, ²¹Adaiah, Beraiah and
    Shimrath were the sons of Shimei.
²²Ishpan, Eber, Eliel, ²³Abdon, Zikri, Hanan, ²⁴Hananiah, Elam,
    Anthothijah, ²⁵Iphdeiah and Penuel were the sons of Shashak.

²⁶Shamsherai, Shehariah, Athaliah, ²⁷Jaareshiah, Elijah and Zikri were the sons of Jeroham.

²⁸All these were heads of families, chiefs as listed in their genealogy, and they lived in Jerusalem.

²⁹Jeiel the father of Gibeon lived in Gibeon.

His wife's name was Maakah, ³⁰and his firstborn son was Abdon, followed by Zur, Kish, Baal, Ner, Nadab, ³¹Gedor, Ahio, Zeker ³²and Mikloth, who was the father of Shimeah. They too lived near their relatives in Jerusalem.

³³Ner was the father of Kish, Kish the father of Saul, and Saul the father of Jonathan, Malki-Shua, Abinadab and Esh-Baal.

³⁴The son of Jonathan:

Merib-Baal, who was the father of Micah.

³⁵The sons of Micah:

Pithon, Melek, Tarea and Ahaz.

³⁶Ahaz was the father of Jehoaddah, Jehoaddah was the father of Alemeth, Azmaveth and Zimri, and Zimri was the father of Moza. ³⁷Moza was the father of Binea; Raphah was his son, Eleasah his son and Azel his son.

³⁸Azel had six sons, and these were their names:

Azrikam, Bokeru, Ishmael, Sheariah, Obadiah and Hanan. All these were the sons of Azel.

³⁹The sons of his brother Eshek:

Ulam his firstborn, Jeush the second son and Eliphelet the third.

⁴⁰The sons of Ulam were brave warriors who could handle the bow. They had many sons and grandsons—150 in all.

All these were the descendants of Benjamin.

Listening to the Text in the Story: Numbers 26:38–41; 1 Samuel 9:1–27

The tribe of Benjamin was introduced earlier, although its emphasis was military in nature (1 Chr 7:6–12). In this section, the Chronicler gives a more extensive list of Benjamin's descendants that focuses on Saul's family tree (8:1–40), drawing from earlier lists with some selectivity (e.g., Gen 46:21; Num 26:38–41). Benjamin was the beloved and youngest son of Jacob through Rachel (Gen 35:18; 42:4, 38). Even though a small tribe,

Israel's first king, Saul, would come from this tribe (1 Sam 9:1, 16, 21; 15:17). After the division, the tribe of Benjamin belonged to the Southern Kingdom (2 Chr 11:1, 3, 10, 12, 23, etc.). Selman thus notes that Judah and Benjamin usually appear together, and only rarely does Benjamin appear by itself in Chronicles or in Ezra-Nehemiah.[1] Its inclusion with the northern tribes reflects its role as a neutral "buffer" between Judah and the northern tribes of Ephraim and Manasseh.[2] The length of material devoted to the tribe of Benjamin (as the third most extensive after Judah and Levi) underscores its importance for the history of God's people, especially during this final period of the Old Testament. Settlement patterns in Israel during the exile indicate that even though Jerusalem was destroyed and her inhabitants were brought to Babylon, a remnant continued to live in villages and farms in the territory of Benjamin. During this period, the Benjaminite city of Mizpah became the administrative center, known for its storage facilities and large residential buildings.[3] So, while focus is clearly on Judah (1 Chr 2–4) and Levi (ch. 6), the tribe of Benjamin is next in importance. Emphasis on these three tribes is consistent with what we find in the post-exilic community that is comprised of people from Judah (Neh 11:4–6), Benjamin (vv. 7–9), and Levi (vv. 10–19). Although settlement in Benjamin slowly declined in the Persian Period as Jerusalem regained her central role,[4] the importance of Benjamin nevertheless remains. It is not surprising to find, therefore, that Benjamin's descendants are prominently featured after the exile (1 Chr 9:3, 7–9; cf. Ezra 1:5; 4:1; 10:9; Neh 11:7, etc.). Further, the geographical locations of Ono and Lod given in the genealogy (1 Chr 8:12) appear as individuals who are among the returnees (cf. Ezra 2:33; Neh 7:37), thus connecting this genealogy to the post-exilic community.

 EXPLAIN the Story

The Genealogies and Settlement of the Tribe of Benjamin (8:1–28)

The chapter begins with a list of Benjamin's sons, along with his descendants through his firstborn son, Bela, which extends for several generations (1 Chr 8:1–7). Geographical locations are noted throughout the genealogy, including Geba and Manahath (v. 6), Moab (v. 8), Ono and Lod (v. 12),

---

1. Selman, *1 Chronicles*, 118.
2. Boda, *1–2 Chronicles*, 87.
3. Lipschits, *The Rise and Fall of Jerusalem*, 237–39.
4. Ibid., 245–48.

Aijalon and Gath (v. 13), Jerusalem (v. 28, 32) and Gibeon (v. 29). Selman notes that the location of Benjamin at the end of the tribes "is paralleled by the account of the first tribe, Judah, which also emphasizes tribal geography (cf. 2:42–55; 4:1–23)."[5] Japhet argues further that the tribal allotment of land so central to the genealogies serves as an introduction to the reign of David; she writes: "The chapters set up the historical and geographical scene: the people of Israel in the land of Israel, as a continuous and uninterrupted reality from Jacob/Israel on. Thus, when the historical narrative starts with David's reign, the entity of people and the entity of land are established facts."[6] The two tribes of Judah and Benjamin function as bookends, emphasizing the geography of these two important tribes. Settlement patterns of the tribe of Benjamin are at the heart of this chapter, and the geographical expansion of the Benjaminite tribe is suggested by reference to the towns of Ono and Lod (8:12) and Aijalon (v. 13), which had originally been allotted to the tribe of Dan (Josh 19:42); here they fall within the territory of Benjamin.[7] Japhet notes that tribal expansion is also suggested by the southern (Manahath, v. 6), eastern (Moab, v. 8), and western (Lod, Ono, Gath, vv. 12–13) locations.[8]

After identifying five heads of families and their sons (Beriah, v. 16; Elpaal, v. 18; Shimei, v. 21; Shashak, v. 25, Jeroham, v. 27), the list of names concludes with a summary statement: "All these were heads of families, chiefs as listed in their genealogy, and they lived in Jerusalem" (v. 28). Although Jerusalem is located within the tribal territory of Benjamin (Josh 18:28), since it was a border town between Judah and Benjamin (15:8; 18:16), both tribes have connections to it (Judg 1:8, 21). The Jebusites continued to live in the city (formerly known as Jebus) until David conquered it and called it the City of David (1 Chr 11:4–8; cf. Josh 15:63; Judg 1:21). We will see shortly that the returnees—people from Judah, Benjamin, Ephraim and Manasseh—will live in Jerusalem, thus reference to the city anticipates what is to follow shortly (1 Chr 8:28; cf. 9:3; Neh 11:4, 7–8).

The Settlement of Benjaminites in Gibeon and Jerusalem (8:29–32)

This section focuses on those from Benjamin who lived in Gibeon and Jerusalem. The city of Gibeon was assigned to the tribe of Benjamin (Josh 18:25, 28; 21:17; 1 Chr 6:60; 9:35), and Saul's own family can be traced to

---

5. Selman, *1 Chronicles*, 118.
6. Japhet, "Conquest and Settlement in Chronicles," 218.
7. See the detailed discussion by Boda, *1–2 Chronicles*, 92–93.
8. Japhet, *I & II Chronicles*, 195.

this town (9:35–39).[9] Gibeon was an important religious site where the tabernacle was located (16:39; 21:29; 2 Chr 1:3). God also appears to Solomon at this location (1:3–4, 7), although Jerusalem becomes the central religious site after the temple has been built (1 Chr 22:1; 2 Chr 3:1). During the period of the exile, settlement in Gibeon continued, but like other towns in Benjamin, its population slowly declined with the rise of Jerusalem in the Persian Period.[10] Reference to the Benjaminites living in Gibeon (1 Chr 8:29) and Jerusalem (v. 32) thus serves to highlight two important religious sites that have ongoing significance in the life of the post-exilic community.

The Genealogy of Saul (8:33–40)

The chapter concludes with a brief reference to Saul's genealogy, which identifies Saul's grandfather as Ner and his father as Kish (1 Chr 8:33; cf. 9:35–39). Saul's four sons are named: Jonathan, Malki-Shua, Abinadab, and Esh-Baal, three of whom will feature shortly (10:2, 6). The genealogy of Saul's son Jonathan, the loyal friend of David, is here traced, possibly for the purpose of showing that his line continues for several generations through his son Merib-Baal (also known as Mephibosheth), recalling that David had shown kindness to him (8:34–38; cf. 2 Sam 9:1–13). The genealogy of the Benjaminites concludes with a reference to the sons of Ulam, who were military men well-equipped for war (1 Chr 8:40).

LIVE the Story

Commitment to Study the Scriptures

The extensive genealogy of the tribe of Benjamin brings these eight chapters of genealogies to a close. The following verse summarizes the task accomplished by the Chronicler: "All Israel was listed in the genealogies recorded in the book of the kings of Israel and Judah" (1 Chr 9:1). The next chapter shifts to focus on the returnees (vv. 2–34), followed by Saul's genealogy that functions as a bridge to Saul (vv. 35–44), who is the key figure in chapter 10. When considering how this chapter applies to our lives today, we could reflect upon God's faithfulness to his people, seen in the preservation of the tribe of Benjamin in spite of the judgment of 586 BC. We could also reflect upon the shift of the religious site from Gibeon to Jerusalem, reminding us that God

---

9. On the relationship between the towns of Geba, Gibeon, and Gibeah (Saul's hometown, 1 Sam 10:26; 15:34), see Boda, *1–2 Chronicles*, 89–90.

10. Lipschits, *The Rise and Fall of Jerusalem*, 243–44.

has a sovereign plan that he is establishing. Another way we can live the story is by considering for a moment the magnitude of the task accomplished by the Chronicler when compiling these extensive genealogies. Writing at a time when Judah's future was uncertain, he understood the times and the task God had set before him. The level of detail in the genealogies and the sheer length of the material underscores that the Chronicler has devoted himself to the study of the Scriptures.

In our Christian culture today, biblical illiteracy is all too pervasive, even in the church. We are too often looking for quick-fix Christianity, with two-minute devotions or pithy Bible verses that are seen to answer our problems, to the neglect of serious and extended study of the Scriptures. While the Bible remains an all-time bestseller, journalist and religion editor for the *New York Times* Kenneth Briggs found through his research that people are not reading it.[11] He notes that there are as many as eighty thousand versions of the Bible in more than five hundred languages, and yearly sales in the US are in the range of twenty-five million copies.[12] Yet he speaks alarmingly about a "Bibleless Christianity" that looms on the horizon. The book of Chronicles stands as a beacon of hope in our generation, a light unto our path, calling us to commit ourselves to studying and teaching the Scriptures. The word of God matters. Yet it requires earnest and consistent study. This is not to be taken lightly.

This is the challenge that the apostle Paul set before the young Timothy when he exhorted him with these words: "All Scripture is God-breathed and is useful for teaching, rebuking, correcting and training in righteousness, so that the servant of God may be thoroughly equipped for every good work" (2 Tim 3:16–17). The book of Chronicles is surely included among *all Scripture* that is useful for the church today. Yet Kenneth Briggs found in his research that the Old Testament Scriptures are being neglected in the church:

> As biblical literacy has decreased, churches have reduced the Bible's place in worship and congregational life. A growing tendency has been to minimize Scripture and go straight to Jesus, though the only near contemporary information about his person and mission comes from the New Testament.[13]

---

11. See the important research by journalist and commentator Kenneth A. Briggs in *The Invisible Best Seller: Searching for the Bible in America* (Grand Rapids: Eerdmans, 2016).

12. Ibid., 44.

13. Ibid., 9. More recently, in one of his sermons Andy Stanley has advocated "unhitching" the Old Testament from the church, which led to an onslaught of responses from Christian leaders; see Michael J. Kruger, "Why We Can't Unhitch from the Old Testament," *Gospel Coalition*, October 22, 2018, https://www.thegospelcoalition.org/reviews/irresistible-andy-stanley/.

This trend continues today and presents an urgent challenge to the church. Paul had studied the ancient Scriptures under the well-known and respected sage Gamaliel, a teacher of the law (Acts 5:34; 22:3). After his encounter with the risen Christ, he had spent countless hours teaching the Scriptures to others (13:14–15, 42–44, 48–49; 14:3; 17:1–4; 18:5; 19:8, 10; 20:20–21, etc.), including teaching at the well-known school of Tyrannus (19:9).

Keeping the centrality of God's word in view, Paul gave Timothy the following charge: "Preach the word; be prepared in season and out of season; correct, rebuke and encourage—with great patience and careful instruction" (2 Tim 4:2). Timothy was exhorted to be diligent in his work so that he might accurately handle the word of God (2:15). This is the challenge for every generation, and especially today with the potential for a "Bibleless Christianity" in the American church. Every generation needs preachers and teachers of the Scriptures who present themselves to God "as one approved, a worker who does not need to be ashamed and who correctly handles the word of truth" (v. 15). The Chronicler is one such preacher and teacher who has been diligent in his study of the Scriptures, and he serves as an example for us today.

A relentless commitment to study the Scriptures is seen in the life of William Tyndale, who spent his life translating the Bible into English for the common folk. Faced with the threat of imprisonment, he continued to labor for the cause God had set before him. Finally, after being charged with heresy, he would be imprisoned at Vilvorde Prison, yet his unwavering commitment to the word of God is seen in his letter to his prison warden. After asking for warmer and less worn out clothing for the bitter winter in prison and for a lamp, he writes: "But most of all I beg and beseech your clemency to be urgent with the commissary, that he will kindly permit me to have the Hebrew Bible, Hebrew grammar, and Hebrew dictionary, that I may pass the time in that study."[14] Rinehart comments, "Whether his requests were granted or not is unknown. But what is known is that Tyndale sat alone, in the dark, concerned to finish an English Old Testament and complete the work God had given him to do."[15]

As we reflect upon these opening genealogies and the importance of devoting ourselves to the study of the Scriptures, may our hearts be stirred to give priority to the word of God and to study it diligently. The word of God needs to be studied and applied in every generation; may this be true in our own generation.

---

14. For the complete letter (only an excerpt is noted above) and a helpful summary of Tyndale's life, see John Rinehart, *Gospel Patrons: People Whose Generosity Changed the World* (n.p.: Reclaimed, 2013), 53; see also www.gospelpatrons.org.

15. Ibid., 54.

LISTEN to the Story

¹All Israel was listed in the genealogies recorded in the book of the kings of Israel and Judah. They were taken captive to Babylon because of their unfaithfulness.

²Now the first to resettle on their own property in their own towns were some Israelites, priests, Levites and temple servants.

³Those from Judah, from Benjamin, and from Ephraim and Manasseh who lived in Jerusalem were:

⁴Uthai son of Ammihud, the son of Omri, the son of Imri, the son of Bani, a descendant of Perez son of Judah.

⁵Of the Shelanites:

Asaiah the firstborn and his sons.

⁶Of the Zerahites:

Jeuel.

The people from Judah numbered 690.

⁷Of the Benjamites:

Sallu son of Meshullam, the son of Hodaviah, the son of Hassenuah;

⁸Ibneiah son of Jeroham; Elah son of Uzzi, the son of Mikri; and Meshullam son of Shephatiah, the son of Reuel, the son of Ibnijah.

⁹The people from Benjamin, as listed in their genealogy, numbered 956. All these men were heads of their families.

¹⁰Of the priests:

Jedaiah; Jehoiarib; Jakin;

¹¹Azariah son of Hilkiah, the son of Meshullam, the son of Zadok, the son of Meraioth, the son of Ahitub, the official in charge of the house of God;

¹²Adaiah son of Jeroham, the son of Pashhur, the son of Malkijah; and Maasai son of Adiel, the son of Jahzerah, the son of Meshullam, the son of Meshillemith, the son of Immer.

¹³The priests, who were heads of families, numbered 1,760. They were able men, responsible for ministering in the house of God. ¹⁴Of the Levites:

Shemaiah son of Hasshub, the son of Azrikam, the son of Hashabiah, a Merarite; ¹⁵Bakbakkar, Heresh, Galal and Mattaniah son of Mika, the son of Zikri, the son of Asaph; ¹⁶Obadiah son of Shemaiah, the son of Galal, the son of Jeduthun; and Berekiah son of Asa, the son of Elkanah, who lived in the villages of the Netophathites.

¹⁷The gatekeepers:

Shallum, Akkub, Talmon, Ahiman and their fellow Levites, Shallum their chief ¹⁸being stationed at the King's Gate on the east, up to the present time. These were the gatekeepers belonging to the camp of the Levites. ¹⁹Shallum son of Kore, the son of Ebiasaph, the son of Korah, and his fellow gatekeepers from his family (the Korahites) were responsible for guarding the thresholds of the tent just as their ancestors had been responsible for guarding the entrance to the dwelling of the LORD. ²⁰In earlier times Phinehas son of Eleazar was the official in charge of the gatekeepers, and the LORD was with him. ²¹Zechariah son of Meshelemiah was the gatekeeper at the entrance to the tent of meeting.

²²Altogether, those chosen to be gatekeepers at the thresholds numbered 212. They were registered by genealogy in their villages. The gatekeepers had been assigned to their positions of trust by David and Samuel the seer. ²³They and their descendants were in charge of guarding the gates of the house of the LORD—the house called the tent of meeting. ²⁴The gatekeepers were on the four sides: east, west, north and south. ²⁵Their fellow Levites in their villages had to come from time to time and share their duties for seven-day periods. ²⁶But the four principal gatekeepers, who were Levites, were entrusted with the responsibility for the rooms and treasuries in the house of God. ²⁷They would spend the night stationed around the house of God, because they had to guard it; and they had charge of the key for opening it each morning.

²⁸Some of them were in charge of the articles used in the temple service; they counted them when they were brought in and when they were taken out. ²⁹Others were assigned to take care of the furnishings and all the other

articles of the sanctuary, as well as the special flour and wine, and the olive oil, incense and spices. ³⁰But some of the priests took care of mixing the spices. ³¹A Levite named Mattithiah, the firstborn son of Shallum the Korahite, was entrusted with the responsibility for baking the offering bread. ³²Some of the Kohathites, their fellow Levites, were in charge of preparing for every Sabbath the bread set out on the table.

³³Those who were musicians, heads of Levite families, stayed in the rooms of the temple and were exempt from other duties because they were responsible for the work day and night.

³⁴All these were heads of Levite families, chiefs as listed in their genealogy, and they lived in Jerusalem.

³⁵Jeiel the father of Gibeon lived in Gibeon.

His wife's name was Maakah, ³⁶and his firstborn son was Abdon, followed by Zur, Kish, Baal, Ner, Nadab, ³⁷Gedor, Ahio, Zechariah and Mikloth. ³⁸Mikloth was the father of Shimeam. They too lived near their relatives in Jerusalem.

³⁹Ner was the father of Kish, Kish the father of Saul, and Saul the father of Jonathan, Malki-Shua, Abinadab and Esh-Baal.

⁴⁰The son of Jonathan:

Merib-Baal, who was the father of Micah.

⁴¹The sons of Micah:

Pithon, Melek, Tahrea and Ahaz.

⁴²Ahaz was the father of Jadah, Jadah was the father of Alemeth, Azmaveth and Zimri, and Zimri was the father of Moza.

⁴³Moza was the father of Binea; Rephaiah was his son, Eleasah his son and Azel his son.

⁴⁴Azel had six sons, and these were their names:

Azrikam, Bokeru, Ishmael, Sheariah, Obadiah and Hanan. These were the sons of Azel.

Listening to the Text in the Story: Ezra 1:1–3; Isaiah 44:26–28; 45:1

The genealogies conclude with a list of those who returned from exile and settled in Jerusalem and its surrounding towns. This marks a key moment in the story of Israel since it signals that the restoration has begun. Judah had gone into exile for her unfaithfulness (1 Chr 9:1; cf. 2 Chr 36:14), and God had promised through the prophet Jeremiah that the exile would last for seventy years (Jer 25:11; cf. 2 Chr 36:21; Ezra 1:1; Dan 9:2). Many years earlier, God had promised his people Israel that if they confessed their unfaithfulness and humbled themselves before the LORD (Lev 26:40–42; cf. Dan 9:3–19), he would remember his covenant with Abraham, Isaac, and Jacob and remember the land. This is the restoration that is being highlighted in this chapter, when the exiles return to Jerusalem.

The importance of Jerusalem in the plan of God cannot be underestimated. Despite God's judgment against the city in 586 BC, his plan was always to bring his people back to Jerusalem. The prophet Isaiah had announced this message of hope to his people when prophesying about the Persian king Cyrus: "He is my shepherd and will accomplish all that I please; he will say of Jerusalem, 'Let it be rebuilt,' and of the temple, 'Let its foundations be laid'" (Isa 44:28). This prophecy stands behind the return that follows, and thus the proclamation of the Persian king Cyrus is an unmistakable sign that God's restoration has begun. Jerusalem will be inhabited! The book of Ezra thus begins with these words of prophetic fulfillment:

> In the first year of Cyrus king of Persia, in order to fulfill the word of the LORD spoken by Jeremiah, the LORD moved the heart of Cyrus king of Persia to make a proclamation throughout his realm and also to put it in writing: "This is what Cyrus king of Persia says: 'The LORD, the God of heaven, has given me all the kingdoms of the earth and he has appointed me to build a temple for him at Jerusalem in Judah. Any of his people among you may go up to Jerusalem in Judah and build the temple of the LORD, the God of Israel, the God who is in Jerusalem, and may their God be with them.'" (Ezra 1:1–3; see also 2 Chr 36:22–23)

This is the story that is taken up in this chapter as the names of those who return to Jerusalem and the surrounding towns are given. These are the people who have responded to the call of God to return, which undoubtedly required a step of faith and trust in God.

EXPLAIN the Story

Conclusion to the Genealogies (9:1)

The Chronicler's genealogies conclude with a summary statement, "All Israel was listed in the genealogies recorded in the book of the kings of Israel and

Judah" (1 Chr 9:1). One of the Chronicler's tasks in these opening chapters has been to provide accurate records (e.g., 4:33; 5:1, 7, 17, etc). Accurate record-keeping was essential since it documented tribal allotment of land, but priestly records were vital since failure to have one's priestly ancestry verified would mean exclusion from priestly service (Ezra 2:62; Neh 7:64). There are numerous references to records and royal archives throughout Chronicles, which point to the high level of scholarship that was required to write this history of Israel.[1]

The account begins with the statement that all Israel were "taken captive to Babylon because of their unfaithfulness" (1 Chr 9:1). The designation "all Israel" not only includes the northern tribes, but Judah as well (cf. ESV, 9:1). Reference to their "unfaithfulness" (Heb. *ma'al*) has already been anticipated (1 Chr 2:7; 5:25–26), but now we learn that the chosen and royal line of Judah is not exempt from this indictment. Reference to Israel's unfaithfulness at the beginning and end of the genealogies indicates that "Israel is clearly riddled with 'unfaithfulness', from their entry into the promised land until their destruction by the Babylonians."[2] But just as the entire work does not conclude with the exile but with a hopeful outcome (2 Chr 36:22–23), so, too, the Chronicler quickly shifts attention to focus on those who first dwelt in Jerusalem. God's judgment of exile is not the end of the story—God has a plan to restore his people! Even though all Israel had been unfaithful, God remains faithful to his promises.

Inhabitants of Jerusalem Include Those from Judah, Benjamin, Ephraim, and Manasseh (9:2–9)

Those who return to Jerusalem belong to a small province known as Yehud, which was simply one of several provinces within the Persian Empire (cf. Ezra 2:1; Neh 1:3; 7:6; 11:3; Esth 1:1; 3:8).[3] The Chronicler omits the term "province" (cf. Neh 11:3), perhaps suggesting an optimistic outlook. God's people are now resettling in their own property and in their towns (1 Chr 9:2), although the extent of their land diminished significantly after the exile.[4] The returnees are identified as Israelites, priests and Levites, and temple servants

---

1. On sources used, see the introduction, Genre, pp. 7–8.
2. Selman, *1 Chronicles*, 96.
3. See the introduction for the historical setting for this period, pp. 9–10.
4. See the introduction, Life in the Province of Judah and in the Diaspora under the Persians, pp. 10–13. Based on archaeological evidence of settlement patterns, Lipschits estimates the population of the province of Judah at around thirty thousand, which he notes fits with the numbers given in Neh 11, where only those who lived in Jerusalem are given (one-tenth of the population live in Jerusalem); see Lipschits, *The Rise and Fall of Jerusalem*, 270.

(v. 2). The community can be defined, therefore, as a "collaboration of laity (Israelites) and clergy (priests, Levites, Temple servants)," but even within the clergy, there is further collaboration among the priests, Levites, and temple servants.[5] These groups provide the structure for the list that follows: laity, comprised of four tribes (vv. 3–9), clergy, including priests (vv. 10–13), Levites (vv. 14–16), and temple servants, along with gate keepers (vv. 17–34).

Central to the return is the vision for a united people of God, seen in the comment that some from "Judah, from Benjamin, and from Ephraim and Manasseh" lived in Jerusalem (v. 3). The tribes of Ephraim and Manasseh have a representative function (cf. 2 Chr 30:1, 10; 31:1); thus in some sense "all Israel" is in view. The prophet Ezekiel had announced that God would unite Judah and Ephraim to become one nation (Ezek 37:15–22), and Zechariah similarly prophesied that Judah and Ephraim would be saved and brought back to Jerusalem (Zech 10:6–12). This contributes to an important theme in Chronicles that identifies Jerusalem as the dwelling place of all Israel, and as such, it represents in microcosm what God intends for the cosmos.

Three main clans of Judah are traced through Perez (1 Chr 9:4; cf. 2:3–5; Ruth 4:18–22), Shelah (1 Chr 9:5; cf. 4:21), and Zerah (9:6; cf. 2:4–6), bringing the number of family members to 690. These three clans trace their ancestry back to the time of Moses: "The descendants of Judah by their clans were: through Shelah, the Shelanite clan; through Perez, the Perezite clan; through Zerah, the Zerahite clan" (Num 26:20). Their names in this chapter present the returnees as a continuation of the original tribe. The descendants of Benjamin are given next, with the following four heads of families: Sallu, Ibneiah, Elah, and Meshullam, bringing the number of family members to 956 (1 Chr 9:7–9; cf. Neh 11:6, 8).

Priests and Levites Who Returned to Jerusalem (9:10–16)

The next group mentioned are priests (1 Chr 9:10–13) and Levites (vv. 14–16). Several priestly families are well-known in the post-exilic period, especially Jedaiah, Immer, and Pashhur (Ezra 2:36–39; Neh 7:39–40). Azariah traces his descent through Zadok (1 Chr 9:11), an important priestly line that has already been introduced (6:11–14). He is identified as the "official in charge of the house of God" (9:11), which suggests a high priestly role (cf. 2 Chr 31:10). As with the other lists, their number of 1,760 is higher than the number given in Nehemiah 11:12–14, although Selman notes that the priestly numbers are lower than the number recorded in Ezra

---

5. Boda, *1–2 Chronicles*, 99.

2:36–39, perhaps indicating a waning of interest in the office, as suggested by the prophet Malachi (cf. Mal 1:13).[6]

Seven Levites are named, with the pedigree of four individuals given: Shemaiah (descendant of Merari; 1 Chr 9:14), Mattaniah (descendant of Asaph; v. 15), Obadiah (descendant of Jeduthun; v. 16), and Berekiah (descendant of Elkanah; v. 16). In Nehemiah, Mattaniah, is identified as the "director who led in thanksgiving and prayer" (Neh 11:17), which is not surprising, given that he is a descendant of Asaph, the head musician during King David's time (1 Chr 16:5) and the author of several psalms (Pss 50, 73–83; cf. 2 Chr 29:30). His descendants continued to have an important role in worship in the post-exilic community (cf. Ezra 2:41; Neh 7:44; 11:17; 12:46). Similarly, Obadiah is from the well-known musical family of Jeduthun, whose name is associated with several psalms (Pss 39; 62; 77). His family also played an important leadership role (1 Chr 16:41–42; 2 Chr 5:12; 35:15).[7] Berekiah is probably another musician, who lived in the villages of the Netophathites (1 Chr 9:16), apparently a location where other musical families had resided when the wall of Jerusalem was dedicated during the time of Nehemiah (Neh 12:27–28).

Levitical Gatekeepers Who Returned to Jerusalem (9:17–34)

Attention now turns to the duties of the gatekeepers in the post-exilic community (1 Chr 9:17–27). Gatekeepers not only guarded the temple, but four Levites also had oversight of the chambers and the treasuries in the temple (v. 26; cf. 26:20–28).[8] Levitical guards worked throughout the night, protecting the temple and opening the house of God in the morning. Their job description entailed taking care of utensils, equipment, and food supplies used in the temple (9:28–29), which included mixing spices and preparing bread for the weekly showbread (vv. 31–32). Gatekeepers had an important role in the post-exilic community. Nehemiah appoints them to guard the gates of Jerusalem in order to ensure that the Sabbath was kept (Neh 13:19–22). Focus is on four major families who were assigned this important responsibility: Shallum, Akkub, Talmon, and Ahiman (1 Chr 9:17). Shallum is identified as their leader, whose pedigree can be traced to Korah (v. 19; cf. 26:1). He had oversight of the gatekeepers on the important eastern side, which marked the entrance to the tent (9:18–19; cf. 26:14, 17). The list of temple personnel is followed by reference to singers, who may well have also

---

6. Selman, *1 Chronicles*, 127.
7. See the discussion in Chapter 25 on 1 Chr 25, pp. 244–45.
8. See the discussion in Chapter 26 on 1 Chr 26, pp. 252–53.

served as gatekeepers (9:33). This section concludes with the statement that "All these were heads of Levite families, chiefs as listed in their genealogy, and they lived in Jerusalem" (v. 34).

The Genealogy of Saul (9:35–44)

The genealogy of Saul is given next (1 Chr 9:35–44; cf. 8:29–38), forming a bridge to the following chapter where Saul's death is described (10:1–14). Especially important are the names of Saul's four sons: Jonathan, Malki-Shua, Abinadab, and Esh-Baal (9:39), three of whom will be featured in the story that follows (10:2, 6). Their deaths will bring an end to Saul's dynasty (v. 6). That they die in battle ensures that David is free from any charge that he has taken the throne by force. Although Esh-Baal (also known as Ish-bosheth) serves as king over Israel for two years, he, too, is finally killed (2 Sam 4:1–12). With the genealogies now complete, the narrative section begins with the final days of Saul (1 Chr 10:1–14), which signals that God is turning the kingdom over to David.

LIVE the Story

Hope in the Promises of God

The Chronicler concludes his extended genealogies with a message of hope as he records the names of those who returned to Jerusalem after the exile. For the returnees, the glory days of the flourishing kingdom under David and Solomon must have felt like a bygone era. There was no king on the throne in Jerusalem, but instead, the returnees were living under Persian kings. Opposition had come from the surrounding nations in an attempt to thwart their rebuilding efforts. Their resettlement in the land paled in view of the extensive boundaries under Solomon, and some among the returnees were facing dire poverty.[9] Such adverse circumstances might have caused despondency among God's people. Yet the Chronicler's work is hopeful, joyful, and full of optimism! It is not optimism based on circumstances but on the sovereign plan of God that hearkens back to creation and to God's promises made to Israel. To be sure, there had been a period of exile, but the restoration has begun. God is on the move!

The Chronicler is reminding the returnees of God's irrevocable calling

---

9. See the introduction, Life in the Province of Judah and in the Diaspora under the Persians, pp. 10–13.

and their purpose to proclaim the name of the LORD among the nations. This serves as a message of hope against the despondency of the time. McConville sums this up well when considering their less-than-hopeful circumstances:

> To such defeatism the Chronicler answers that his small community is in reality the successor of Israel at its greatest, and that all God's commitments to their forefathers still stand, and are now focused on them. The function of ch. 9 is to show that God's plans, which are plans for the whole world (hence the scope of ch. 1), were centred upon Israel throughout its history (chs. 2–8) and are now being taken forward in the unlikely remnant that clustered around Persian Jerusalem.[10]

He raises the question whether such genealogies can have any relevance for the church today. He concludes: "Wherever the Church in the twentieth century feels itself to be of little account in the world, to have a precarious existence, despised and without real hope, its situation is in all essential respects like that of the Chronicler's Judah."[11] There is a sure and certain hope for God's people—not based on their circumstances but on the sure purposes and promises of God!

The Chronicler's "big vision" presented in these opening genealogies reminds God's people then, as it does for us today, that the sovereign LORD is in control over all the nations. His purposes still stand. He will be exalted among the nations. We are called to be faithful and trust in his sovereign and good plan that will not be thwarted. We are not to measure our circumstances simply by our own feeble and limited assessment, but we are to look beyond them and remember the character of God. He is faithful. He has a purpose that will surely come to pass. We are to be patient, waiting and watching to see signs of the kingdom and to be about the work of the kingdom. God rules as king over his everlasting kingdom. The genealogies, along with the return to Jerusalem, ultimately resound with a message of hope, and they call us to remember what God has done in the past and to hope in what he will do in the future.

---

10. J. Gordon McConville, *1 & 2 Chronicles*, Daily Study Bible Series (Philadelphia: Westminster, 1984), 12.
11. Ibid., 13.

1 Chronicles 10:1-14

 LISTEN to the Story

¹Now the Philistines fought against Israel; the Israelites fled before them, and many fell dead on Mount Gilboa. ²The Philistines were in hot pursuit of Saul and his sons, and they killed his sons Jonathan, Abinadab and Malki-Shua. ³The fighting grew fierce around Saul, and when the archers overtook him, they wounded him.

⁴Saul said to his armor-bearer, "Draw your sword and run me through, or these uncircumcised fellows will come and abuse me."

But his armor-bearer was terrified and would not do it; so Saul took his own sword and fell on it. ⁵When the armor-bearer saw that Saul was dead, he too fell on his sword and died. ⁶So Saul and his three sons died, and all his house died together.

⁷When all the Israelites in the valley saw that the army had fled and that Saul and his sons had died, they abandoned their towns and fled. And the Philistines came and occupied them.

⁸The next day, when the Philistines came to strip the dead, they found Saul and his sons fallen on Mount Gilboa. ⁹They stripped him and took his head and his armor, and sent messengers throughout the land of the Philistines to proclaim the news among their idols and their people. ¹⁰They put his armor in the temple of their gods and hung up his head in the temple of Dagon.

¹¹When all the inhabitants of Jabesh Gilead heard what the Philistines had done to Saul, ¹²all their valiant men went and took the bodies of Saul and his sons and brought them to Jabesh. Then they buried their bones under the great tree in Jabesh, and they fasted seven days.

¹³Saul died because he was unfaithful to the Lord; he did not keep the word of the Lord and even consulted a medium for guidance, ¹⁴and did

not inquire of the LORD. So the LORD put him to death and turned the kingdom over to David son of Jesse.

Listening to the Text in the Story: 1 Samuel 9–31

After an impressive nine chapters of genealogies that lead up to the return from exile (1 Chr 1–9), the storyline now backtracks to an earlier period that recalls Israel's first king. Saul has already been anticipated in the genealogies (8:33–38; 9:35–44), but the focus here is on his *death*, as it signifies that God is turning the kingdom over to David. Notice that only *one* chapter is devoted to Saul (a mere fourteen verses), whereas *nineteen* chapters are devoted to David (chs. 11–29). Although Saul's reign is inconsequential in the larger plan of God, it functions as a signpost, indicating that it is God's timing for David to rule over Israel. Thus, the Chronicler's primary concern when recalling the reign of Saul is to describe his defeat by the Philistines, along with the hideous dismembering of his body, which becomes a prized trophy of war.

In order to listen to the story of Saul's death within the context of Israel's story, it is important to recount briefly the events leading up to it. The Israelites had asked Samuel to give them a king like the nations, who would fight their battles (1 Sam 8:1–22). God had promised to defeat Israel's enemies, but his people rejected him by asking for a king to lead them in battle (10:18–19). In spite of Samuel's objection, God gives the people what they ask, and Saul is chosen to be Israel's first king (chs. 9–10). Yet Saul was from the tribe of Benjamin (chs. 9:1–2), whereas God's chosen king was to come from the tribe of Judah (Gen 49:8–12; Ruth 1:1–2; 4:18–22; 1 Sam 16; cf. Mic 5:1–2), as the Chronicler has reminded us through his extensive genealogies.

Saul's reign is described in detail in 1 Samuel 9–31, but three key events in Saul's life lead to God's judgment against him (13:1–23; 15:1–35; 28:1–25). The prophet Samuel announces God's word to Saul: "But now your kingdom will not endure; the LORD has sought out a man after his own heart and appointed him ruler of his people, because you have not kept the LORD's command" (13:14). On another occasion, Saul had refused to carry out God's instructions against the Amalekites, and Samuel tells the king: "You have rejected the word of the LORD, and the LORD has rejected you as king over Israel!" (15:26). It is not coincidental that David is anointed king after God had pronounced judgment against Saul (see ch. 16). While there will be many years of conflict between the house of Saul and the house of David, Saul's death signals that God is now turning the kingdom over to David.

EXPLAIN the Story

The Death of Saul (10:1–7)

Saul has already been introduced in the genealogies, but the Chronicler now picks up his reign with his final battle against the Philistines (1 Chr 10:1). The Philistines were one of Israel's key enemies during the period of the monarchy (e.g., 1 Sam 13–14; 17; 23; 28–29; 31). They occupied the coastal region and were especially known for the five city-states of Gaza, Ashkelon, Ashdod, Gath, and Ekron (cf. Josh 13:3; 1 Sam 6:4, 17). Cities within their territory had been allotted to Israel (Josh 13:3; 15:45-47; cf. Judg 1:18), yet the conquest of the land had been incomplete, resulting in the Philistines remaining a persistent and troubling enemy of Israel. Saul had fought them on several occasions, and notably, his death will take place while in battle against them, which is ironic since he had been chosen as king because of his military stature (1 Sam 9:1–2; cf. 8:20).

The story is picked up with the tragic defeat of Israel by the Philistines, with their bodies slain in the northern region of Mount Gilboa that overlooked the Jezreel Valley (1 Chr 10:1). This sets the scene for Saul's final days. With the smell of victory pulsating through them, the bloodthirsty Philistines doggedly pursue Saul and his three sons, Jonathan, Abinadab, and Malki-Shua. After the successful slaughter of the royal sons, the battle rages, resulting in Saul suffering a fatal wound, ironically by archers, since his tribe was known for its skill with bows (10:3; cf. 12:2). Fearing that the Philistines would humiliate and torture him (cf. Judg 16:21), Saul gives his armor bearer one final command: he is to unsheathe his sword and thrust it through him. But the gravity of the request made by his king prevents his armor bearer from committing such a dishonorable act. Saul is then left with the unsavory task of killing himself, which he does with his own sword when he falls on it, and his armor-bearer quickly follows. Now, both king and armor-bearer lie dead (1 Chr 10:4–5).

When the Israelites learn that their king and his sons are dead, they desperately abandon their homes and the Philistines take full possession of them. The significance of Saul's sons lying dead was not lost on the Chronicler. With singular focus he makes the terse but astute observation that "all his house died together" (v. 6). The Chronicler was undoubtedly well-aware that Saul's son Ish-Bosheth remained alive and would reign as king for a few short years until murdered (2 Sam 2:8–11; 4:1–12).[1] He has also recorded that Saul's descendants extend for many generations (cf. 1 Chr 8:33–40), but the theological significance of what has just taken place is that Saul's royal dynasty has now come to an end. This signals that God is turning the kingdom over to David.

The Body of Saul (10:8–12)

The next day the Philistines find the prized bodies of Israel's king and his sons. Like an animal playing with its captured and dead prey, the Philistines strip off Saul's clothes, cut off his head (cf. 1 Sam 17:54; 2 Kgs 10:7–8), and parade it and his armor throughout the land of the Philistines to carry the "good news" (NASB, ESV) to their idols and to the people (1 Chr 10:9). The defeat of Israel's first king is seen as a historic victory for the Philistines and their gods. In the biblical account, Dagon is identified as the Philistine god (Judg 16:23–24; 1 Sam 5:1–7). Dagon was well-known in ancient literature throughout Mesopotamia from the third millennium onwards. In the ancient world, gods were thought to have authority in the military sphere. In an earlier period prior to the reign of Saul, the Philistines had taken the ark of the covenant and had brought it to their god Dagon (1 Sam 4–5). The next morning Dagon had strangely toppled over, and the idol was curiously found bowing in submission before the ark (5:1–5). But here the situation has been tragically reversed. The Philistines put Saul's armor in the house of their gods as a trophy of war, and they hideously fasten his head to the house of Dagon in acknowledgment of the victory accomplished by their god (1 Chr 10:9–10). In a heroic act of courage, Israel's valiant men from Jabesh Gilead retrieve the headless body of Saul, along with the bodies of his sons, and bury their bones at Jabesh as they lament for their dead king (vv. 11–12).

God Turns the Kingdom over to David (10:13–14)

The Philistines attribute their victory to their god Dagon, but the Chronicler interjects with an alternative explanation that points to God's sovereign hand, reminding us that the LORD is the one who changes the times and epochs; he removes and establishes kings (cf. Dan 2:21). Lest there be any doubt, the Chronicler states clearly that these events have come about by God because

---

1. The Chronicler has already made reference to Saul's son Ish-Bosheth, who is also known as Esh-Baal (cf. 1 Chr 8:33; 9:39).

of Saul's ungodly behavior, and they serve as a warning to the post-exilic community: "Saul died because he was unfaithful to the LORD; he did not keep the word of the LORD and even consulted a medium for guidance, and did not inquire of the LORD. So the LORD put him to death and turned the kingdom over to David son of Jesse" (1 Chr 10:13–14).

Saul is charged with being "unfaithful" (Heb. *ma'al*), a key term used throughout Chronicles to describe those who act contrary to God's laws and stipulations (10:13; see also 2:7; 5:25; 9:1).[2] The Chronicler makes the comment that Saul had not kept God's word (10:13), which probably has in view two well-known stories about Saul. The first event took place when Saul gathered his army to fight against the Philistines (1 Sam 13). He had been outnumbered by the Philistine army, but instead of waiting for Samuel to arrive, he took it upon himself to offer the pre-battle sacrifice, resulting in God's judgment (vv. 13–14). Saul's focus on counting his army points to his underlying (false) belief that the battle would be won by the size of his army, but God's kings were to trust *in him* to fight on their behalf—a key theme that we will encounter throughout Chronicles.

The second event took place when God had commanded Saul to completely destroy the Amalekites because they had fought against the Israelites when they had left Egypt (1 Sam 15:1–3; cf. Exod 17:8–16; Deut 25:17–19). Instead of following God's command, Saul had foolishly spared the Amalekite king Agag, along with the best of the livestock (1 Sam 15:8–9). Samuel pronounced judgment against him for not obeying God's voice, and he was rejected as king (vv. 22–28; cf. 28:17–18). This was signified by the ominous departure of God's presence from Saul (16:14). The Chronicler probably has these two stories in view when describing him as acting unfaithfully (1 Chr 10:13).

The second reason given for Saul's death is that he had sought counsel from a spirit medium (1 Sam 28:7–25) instead of "inquiring" (Heb. *d-r-sh*) of God, one of the hallmarks of godly kings.[3] Spirit mediums were strictly prohibited under Mosaic law (Lev 19:31; 20:27; Deut 18:10–12). Accordingly, Saul is again told his kingdom will be torn away from him because he has not obeyed God (1 Sam 28:17–18). Saul will be defeated by the Philistines and his sons

---

2. The term "unfaithful" (Heb. *ma'al*, appearing in both the verb and noun forms) is used in the Old Testament to refer to sin in general (Lev 5:15; 6:2; 26:40), but also more specifically to actions such as adultery (Num 5:12, 27), worshiping of idols (Num 31:16; 1 Chr 5:25; 2 Chr 28:22–23), taking goods under the ban (Josh 7:1; 1 Chr 2:7), and breaching God's holiness (2 Chr 26:16, 18). It is used to describe kings such as Rehoboam (12:2), Ahaz (28:22), and Manasseh (33:19), and it describes the southern kingdom of Judah, who were brought into exile because of their unfaithfulness (1 Chr 9:1).

3. See the discussion in Chapter 30 on 2 Chr 1:5, pp. 291–93.

will die (v. 19). Upon hearing these words, an overwhelming fear had gripped Saul as he fell to the ground. But instead of prostrating himself before God in repentance, he had listened to his own men who had urged him to partake in a gluttonous feast (vv. 20–24). Saul's death now signals a decisive turning point in Israel's history—for David's enthronement as king is on the horizon.

LIVE the Story

God's Profile of a Leader

God's people had wanted a king "such as all the other nations have" (1 Sam 8:5) who would fight their battles, but God's king was not to rely upon military strength or the size of his army (Ps 33:16). He was to rely upon God and wait for *his* deliverance. Saul preferred to trust in his own military strength, adopting a secular model of leadership. From all external appearances and according to the secular profile of a king, Saul looked like a strong military leader who would lead Israel in victory, but his heart was not fully devoted to God.

By way of contrast, Israel's king was to be governed by different standards. He was not to multiply horses for himself, nor was he to multiply wives for himself (that is, political alliances), nor accrue gold or silver (Deut 17:16–17). Instead, Israel's king was to write for himself a copy of God's law; he was to meditate on it day and night, for the king was to fear God and follow his commandments (vv. 18–20). This was the type of leader God's people needed. Their first king failed to follow God's commandments, and ultimately, he feared the people more than God himself (1 Sam 15:19–24). The Chronicler's indictment against Saul is suggested in the single chapter devoted to him. Futher, Saul's gruesome death depicted in this chapter indicates that Israel's attempt to model their kingdom on the surrounding nations would end in utter failure. The returnees were surrounded by nations, yet their leaders were not to follow their practices. God's people back then—and now—are called to be separate from the nations. Yet it is all too easy to try to emulate leadership models and qualities found in the surrounding culture, especially when their models seem to lead to success. In doing so, we can easily forget that we are called to reflect the values of the heavenly kingdom.

Jesus taught his disciples that leaders in his kingdom were to be different than the surrounding culture. When his disciples were discussing among themselves who was the greatest, Jesus taught them: "The kings of the Gentiles lord it over them; and those who exercise authority over them call themselves

Benefactors. But you are not to be like that. Instead, the greatest among you should be like the youngest, and the one who rules like the one who serves" (Luke 22:25–26). God's leaders were first and foremost *servants*, a description God uses with reference to David when he directs Nathan to confront the king (Heb. *'ebed*, 1 Chr 17:4, 7, 17, 18, 19, 23, etc.). By way of contrast, the final hours of Saul's life tell us a great deal about how the king lived his life. Nowhere is it said that Saul humbled himself before God when facing military defeat, as we will encounter with Rehoboam (2 Chr 12:6–7). Nowhere is it recorded that he cried out to God for help amid the battle, as we will encounter with Jehoshaphat (18:31). And nowhere do we read that he entreated his God in his distress, as we will encounter with Manasseh (33:12–13). Instead, as is characteristic of a self-made man, Saul's final words are not a cry for help but a command to his armor-bearer, as he takes his life into his own hands in his final act of self-reliance. This is not the model of godly leadership, and it is certainly not the model on display in Jesus, the humble servant of the Lord who lays down his life for us. Jesus's model is the posture that we need to cultivate in our own lives.

The Chronicler's Vision for Leadership

Saul had all the trappings of a military leader—he was a mighty man of valor and a tall and impressive man (1 Sam 9:1–2). Saul had all the external qualifications one might want in a king, but his failure to walk with God and to follow his commandments would be his undoing. The Chronicler's depiction of Saul's final days illustrates what happens when a leader is unfaithful to God (1 Chr 10:13–14). In Chronicles, seeking God is the hallmark of godly leadership, but Saul fails to seek God and his life ends in disgrace. This is the legacy he leaves behind, portrayed so powerfully by the Chronicler.

Our culture is obsessed with celebrity personalities, those whose lives look like they are successful, yet their inner world can be morally bankrupt. Worldly values can too easily creep into the church. Christian leaders can be highly esteemed based on worldly categories of success, such as how many followers they have on Twitter or Instagram or how many thousands watch their videos or read their blogs, yet these are not the criteria for godly leadership. God cares about a leader's character and moral life. We are all too familiar with public stories of a Christian leader who has misappropriated finances for personal gain or used power and authority to gain sexual favors. Jesus warned Israel's religious leaders about the danger of the outward appearance of piety: "Woe to you, teachers of the law and Pharisees, you hypocrites! You clean the outside of the cup and dish, but inside they are full of greed and self-indulgence"

(Matt 23:25). He exhorted them to clean the inside of the cup first, so that the outside might be clean, further rebuking them: "You are like whitewashed tombs, which look beautiful on the outside but on the inside are full of the bones of the dead and everything unclean" (v. 27). This description characterizes Saul—he had the outward appearance of a leader, but he lacked integrity and a willingness to follow God's laws. The Chronicler's depiction of Saul's gruesome death underscores his failure as a king.

Rather than focus on the appearance of godliness, we need to cultivate a godly character. This is especially the case for church leaders. A recent poll shows that fifty-two percent of monthly churchgoers consider members of the clergy untrustworthy, and that doctors, teachers, members of the military, and scientists are viewed more positively.[4] Similar conclusions were drawn from a 2018 Gallup survey of the public's view of a variety of occupations' commitment to high ethical standards, which found that honesty and high ethical standards were not seen to be highly-demonstrated qualities among clergy.[5] The Bible is clear that God's leaders are called to a higher standard: they are to be above reproach, demonstrating godly qualities such as being "temperate, self-controlled, respectable" and "not given to drunkenness, not violent but gentle, not quarrelsome, not a lover of money" (1 Tim 3:2–3; cf. Titus 1:7–9), which includes having a good reputation with those outside the church (1 Tim 3:7). We are thus exhorted to pursue righteousness, godliness, faith, love, perseverance, and gentleness (6:11; 2 Tim 3:10), and to live sensibly, righteously, and godly in the present age (Titus 2:12). Integrity matters to a watching world, and it surely matters to God.

---

4. Yonat Shimron, "New poll shows growing view that clergy are irrelevant," 2019; see https://religionnews.com/2019/07/16/new-poll-shows-growing-view-that-clergy-are-irrelevant/.

5. Megan Brenan, "Nurses Again Outpace Other Professions For Honesty, Ethics," n.p. Online: https://news.gallup.com/poll/245597/nurses-again-outpace-professions-honesty-ethics.aspx?utm_source=alert&utm_medium=email&utm_content=morelink&utm_campaign=syndication.

LISTEN to the Story

¹All Israel came together to David at Hebron and said, "We are your own flesh and blood. ²In the past, even while Saul was king, you were the one who led Israel on their military campaigns. And the LORD your God said to you, 'You will shepherd my people Israel, and you will become their ruler.'"

³When all the elders of Israel had come to King David at Hebron, he made a covenant with them at Hebron before the LORD, and they anointed David king over Israel, as the LORD had promised through Samuel.

⁴David and all the Israelites marched to Jerusalem (that is, Jebus). The Jebusites who lived there ⁵said to David, "You will not get in here." Nevertheless, David captured the fortress of Zion—which is the City of David.

⁶David had said, "Whoever leads the attack on the Jebusites will become commander-in-chief." Joab son of Zeruiah went up first, and so he received the command.

⁷David then took up residence in the fortress, and so it was called the City of David. ⁸He built up the city around it, from the terraces to the surrounding wall, while Joab restored the rest of the city. ⁹And David became more and more powerful, because the LORD Almighty was with him.

¹⁰These were the chiefs of David's mighty warriors—they, together with all Israel, gave his kingship strong support to extend it over the whole land, as the LORD had promised—¹¹this is the list of David's mighty warriors:

Jashobeam, a Hakmonite, was chief of the officers; he raised his spear against three hundred men, whom he killed in one encounter.

¹²Next to him was Eleazar son of Dodai the Ahohite, one of the three mighty warriors. ¹³He was with David at Pas Dammim when the

Philistines gathered there for battle. At a place where there was a field full of barley, the troops fled from the Philistines. ¹⁴But they took their stand in the middle of the field. They defended it and struck the Philistines down, and the LORD brought about a great victory.

¹⁵Three of the thirty chiefs came down to David to the rock at the cave of Adullam, while a band of Philistines was encamped in the Valley of Rephaim. ¹⁶At that time David was in the stronghold, and the Philistine garrison was at Bethlehem. ¹⁷David longed for water and said, "Oh, that someone would get me a drink of water from the well near the gate of Bethlehem!" ¹⁸So the Three broke through the Philistine lines, drew water from the well near the gate of Bethlehem and carried it back to David. But he refused to drink it; instead, he poured it out to the LORD. ¹⁹"God forbid that I should do this!" he said. "Should I drink the blood of these men who went at the risk of their lives?" Because they risked their lives to bring it back, David would not drink it.

Such were the exploits of the three mighty warriors.

²⁰Abishai the brother of Joab was chief of the Three. He raised his spear against three hundred men, whom he killed, and so he became as famous as the Three. ²¹He was doubly honored above the Three and became their commander, even though he was not included among them.

²²Benaiah son of Jehoiada, a valiant fighter from Kabzeel, performed great exploits. He struck down Moab's two mightiest warriors. He also went down into a pit on a snowy day and killed a lion. ²³And he struck down an Egyptian who was five cubits tall. Although the Egyptian had a spear like a weaver's rod in his hand, Benaiah went against him with a club. He snatched the spear from the Egyptian's hand and killed him with his own spear. ²⁴Such were the exploits of Benaiah son of Jehoiada; he too was as famous as the three mighty warriors. ²⁵He was held in greater honor than any of the Thirty, but he was not included among the Three. And David put him in charge of his bodyguard.

²⁶The mighty warriors were:

Asahel the brother of Joab,

Elhanan son of Dodo from Bethlehem,

²⁷Shammoth the Harorite,

Helez the Pelonite,

²⁸Ira son of Ikkesh from Tekoa,

Abiezer from Anathoth,
29Sibbekai the Hushathite,
Ilai the Ahohite,
30Maharai the Netophathite,
Heled son of Baanah the Netophathite,
31Ithai son of Ribai from Gibeah in Benjamin,
Benaiah the Pirathonite,
32Hurai from the ravines of Gaash,
Abiel the Arbathite,
33Azmaveth the Baharumite,
Eliahba the Shaalbonite,
34the sons of Hashem the Gizonite,
Jonathan son of Shagee the Hararite,
35Ahiam son of Sakar the Hararite,
Eliphal son of Ur,
36Hepher the Mekerathite,
Ahijah the Pelonite,
37Hezro the Carmelite,
Naarai son of Ezbai,
38Joel the brother of Nathan,
Mibhar son of Hagri,
39Zelek the Ammonite,
Naharai the Berothite, the armor-bearer of Joab son of Zeruiah,
40Ira the Ithrite,
Gareb the Ithrite,
41Uriah the Hittite,
Zabad son of Ahlai,
42Adina son of Shiza the Reubenite, who was chief of the
    Reubenites, and the thirty with him,
43Hanan son of Maakah,
Joshaphat the Mithnite,
44Uzzia the Ashterathite,
Shama and Jeiel the sons of Hotham the Aroerite,
45Jediael son of Shimri,
his brother Joha the Tizite,
46Eliel the Mahavite,
Jeribai and Joshaviah the sons of Elnaam,

Ithmah the Moabite,
⁴⁷Eliel, Obed and Jaasiel the Mezobaite.

Listening to the Text in the Story: 1 Samuel 16; 2 Samuel 5:1–10; 23:8–39

The death of Saul and the end of his dynasty signals a decisive movement in the story of Israel. That the next nineteen chapters are devoted to King David underscores the centrality of his reign for the story of God's people (1 Chr 11–29). Even though the Chronicler was writing when there was no king on the throne, the stories of David provide hope and assurance for what God will do in the days ahead because God had made promises to David that stand as messianic expectations for the returnees living in Jerusalem. These stories are cherished because of the inviolability of God's promise to David—he will surely have a son ruling over God's everlasting kingdom.

The story of David's enthronement at Hebron is taken up in the next two chapters, as all Israel gathers to establish him as king (1 Chr 11:1; 12:23, 38). The unequivocal message that is communicated in 1 Chronicles 11–12 is that David's kingship has come about because of God's sovereign plan and with God's help. The Jebusites are defeated because God is with David (11:4); David becomes king according to the prior word of God (vv. 3, 10; 12:23); David's mighty men are victorious even when the numbers are against them because of God's help (12:14, 20, 23); David receives military support while he is fleeing from Saul as evidence of God's help (vv. 1, 17, 21, 22); and the Philistines are defeated because God is saving his people (11:14). That the sovereign hand of God is at work is demonstrated by the military support David receives from other tribes, including those from Saul's own tribe who give David their undivided support (12:2, 8, 19, 20, 29, 37, 38). David's army is thus likened to the army of God (v. 22). The people named in these chapters and their military victories resound with the unmistakable testimony that God is turning the kingdom over to David (10:14; 12:22).

As we listen to the story of David's enthronement at Hebron, it is important to recall that David first became king over Judah, reigning for seven years at Hebron (2 Sam 5:5; cf. 1 Chr 3:4; 29:26–27). During this initial period, Saul's son Ish-bosheth had reigned as king over Israel for two years (2 Sam 2:10). It was a tumultuous time of conflict between the house of David and the house of Saul (chs. 2–4). It is only after Ish-Bosheth is murdered (4:1–12), however, that David finally becomes king over all Israel (5:1–5). With singular focus, the Chronicler passes over the period when David's kingship was more tenuous and resumes the story with David's enthronement over all Israel.

When reading this account, it is important to notice that the Chronicler has not kept a strict chronology when drawing together these earlier stories about David. Initially taking his cues from the Samuel narrative, David's enthronement at Hebron (1 Chr 11:1–3; cf. 2 Sam 5:1–3) is immediately followed by his victory over the Jebusites at Jerusalem (1 Chr 11:4–9; cf. 2 Sam 5:6–10). The list of mighty men who give their support to David at Hebron probably recalls an earlier time in David's life (1 Chr 11:10–47; cf. 2 Sam 23:8–39). Although the list of mighty men in 2 Samuel is located toward the end of David reign, Bergen argues that it probably refers to an earlier period.[1] Emphasis in the following chapter on the help David receives continues by means of a "flashback," where the names of men who helped David at Ziklag are recalled (1 Chr 12:1–7; cf. 1 Sam 27). This means that thematic interests are given priority, reminding us that the Chronicler is rehearsing Israel's stories for a particular purpose that is relevant for his own context. This is the task of any good preacher. The theme of divine help is a common thread that marked David's time in the wilderness (1 Chr 12:8–18; cf. 1 Sam 22:1–5) and the period when he lived in Ziklag (1 Chr 12:19–22). The implication is that David would not have survived without God's sovereign support and protection, a topic that is surely relevant for the remnant living under Persian rule. By drawing upon earlier stories, the Chronicler is assembling a powerful testimony of the widespread support given to David under the sovereign hand of God, notably, *before* he had become king at Hebron. The final scene shifts back to Hebron with the list of men who had come to make David king (1 Chr 12:23–40). From a literary point of view, the chiastic structure begins with all Israel gathering at Hebron to anoint David as king (11:1–3), and it concludes with a great celebration at Hebron (12:38–40).

EXPLAIN the Story

David Is Anointed King at Hebron after the Death of Saul (11:1–3)

All Israel gathers to anoint David as king at Hebron, a city located within the territory of Judah (1 Chr 11:1; cf. 2 Sam 2:1–4; 5:3). Located nineteen miles south of Jerusalem, Hebron had religious significance from the time of

---

1. Robert D. Bergen, *1, 2 Samuel*, NAC (Nashville: Broadman & Holman, 1996), 441. 2 Sam 23:8–9 is located at the end of David's reign, but the last four chapters are usually identified as an epilogue or appendix that cover several periods earlier in David's life.

Abraham onward, especially as a family burial place for the patriarchs (Gen 23:1–20; 49:31; 50:13). After the Babylonian exile it was also inhabited by the returnees (it is identified by its former name Kiriath Arba in Neh 11:25; cf. Gen 35:27). Since all Israel gathers at Hebron, it underscores the widespread support David receives and the unity of the tribes under him (1 Chr 11:1, 10; 12:38; 13:5; 14:8). The name "Israel" identifies the people by their common ancestral father (2:1), and thus the description of "all Israel" evokes a united people, who were the focus of the genealogies (2:1–9:1). Now, at David's enthronement, the entire community gathers for this sacred moment in their history.

The people acknowledge that David has always been their leader (1 Chr 11:2), for even though Saul had been on the throne, David had nevertheless received support from the tribes. The people testify, therefore, that David had been their true leader from days gone by, which was in accordance with God's word that he would shepherd the people and be their prince (11:2; cf. 17:7; Ps. 78:70–72). David had been anointed by Samuel privately in his father's home (1 Sam 16:13), but now David is publicly anointed as king before all Israel (1 Chr 11:3; cf. 2 Sam 2:4; 5:3). The Spirit of God had come upon him when he was first anointed (1 Sam 16:1, 13; 2 Sam 23:1–2; cf. Zech 4:6), signifying that he had been set apart for this sacred task. Other leaders in the Old Testament are anointed, such as Moses and the elders (Num 11:17, 24–30), Joshua (27:18), specific judges (Judg 3:10; 6:34; 11:29), and especially prophets (Num 11:25), who play a key role in Chronicles (e.g., 1 Chr 12:18; 2 Chr 15:1; 20:14; 24:20). When the Spirit came upon David (1 Sam 16:13), the Spirit had ominously departed from Saul, another indication that the kingdom was being turned over to David (v. 14). The anointing of David by all Israel marks the culmination of his prior anointing, as he is publicly confirmed as Israel's legitimate and divinely appointed king.

David Defeats the Jebusites and Jerusalem Becomes the Capital (11:4–9)

After being anointed as king, David and the people journey toward Jerusalem (1 Chr 11:4). The city was formerly known as Jebus since it had been inhabited by the Jebusites (Judg 19:10–11; cf. 1 Chr 1:14). The Jebusites had been living in Canaan (Num 13:29; Josh 11:3), but their land had been promised to Abraham and his descendants (Gen 15:18–21; Exod 3:8). Accordingly, the Jebusites were one of seven nations the Israelites were to destroy as they took possession of the land (Deut 7:1–2; 20:17–18). Yet, the conquest of the land had been incomplete (Josh 15:63; Judg 1–2), and as such, David's conquest of Jebus is significant. The Chronicler introduces Joab at this point, who leads the attack against the Jebusites (1 Chr 11:6). As commander of David's army (2 Sam 8:16; 1 Chr 27:34), Joab has a strategic position in the kingdom, as we will see later (cf. 19:10–19; 20:1–8; 21:1–6). With Jebus now conquered, David takes up residence in the stronghold; the city is rebuilt and identified as the City of David (11:7–9). David becomes powerful because God is with him (v. 9).

David's Mighty Men Give Their Support to David at Hebron (11:10–47)

The Chronicler provides an extensive list of warriors who had given their support to David, which seems to refer to an earlier period in his life prior to his kingship (cf. 2 Sam 23:8–39).[2] Their inclusion at this point in the story is to show the widespread support given to David: "they, together with all Israel, gave his kingship strong support to extend it over the whole land, as the LORD had promised" (1 Chr 11:10).

The first section highlights David's highest-ranking military leaders, Jashobeam and Eleazar, and although not mentioned, Shammah is probably included among the three (cf. 2 Sam 23:11–12). Military exploits are here rehearsed, which demonstrate not only courage, but also loyalty shown to David (1 Chr 11:11–19). Stories of exceptional heroism are recalled, although they are not to be surpassed by David's three military officers who had distinguished themselves. Amid these stories of valor, we are reminded that military victory is due to God's intervention (v. 14), another indication of God's sovereign hand at work. The extraordinary military feats of two other warriors are noted, Abishai and Benaiah, resulting in their being given leadership positions (vv. 20–25).

The next section provides a more extensive list of David's military men (1 Chr 11:26–47; cf. 2 Sam 23:8–39).[3] Sometimes a man's father is identified, such as "Elhanan son of Dodo" (1 Chr 11:26), which can include his city of origin, such as "Elhanan son of Dodo from Bethlehem," and sometimes a person's ethnic background is given, such as "Zelek the Ammonite" (v. 39). This additional information can make the list seem somewhat convoluted and difficult to read since the names are not presented in a concise formula, but there is a purpose to these names. They demonstrate that David's military men came from a variety of cites in Israel, such as Bethlehem (v. 26), Gibeah

---

2. Bergen, *1, 2 Samuel*, 441.
3. For a discussion of textual issues regarding some of the names, see Klein, *1 Chronicles*, 292–95.

(v. 31), and Carmel (v. 37); from various tribal backgrounds, such as Benjamin (v. 31) and Reuben (v. 42); and from nations outside of Israel, such as Zelek the Ammonite (v. 39), Uriah the Hittite (v. 41), and Ithmah the Moabite (v. 46). Their purpose is to highlight the diverse group of people who have given their support to David. Their ethnic diversity contributes to a vision of the nations being part of the kingdom,[4] and notably, this is taking place amid unlikely circumstances—while David is hiding out in caves and fleeing for his life! This surely provides hope for the Chronicler's audience, who are living under Persian rule, and it provides hope for God's people today: God is establishing his kingdom amid *all* the circumstances of life, even when those circumstances seem less than promising.

Next, the high number and variety of military leaders supporting David *before* he had become king demonstrate that God had been at work establishing the kingdom while Saul was still on the throne. The loyalty shown to David during these difficult years will not be forgotten by the young leader. Notably, several of David's military men listed in 11:26–47 are appointed to leadership positions when the king sets up his organizational structure, at which time he appoints twelve military divisions (27:1–15). This means that David's loyal supporters will have important responsibilities when the kingdom is firmly established.

 LIVE the Story

God's Work in Unlikely Circumstances

The story of David's enthronement by all Israel at Hebron comes about after many difficult years. David had been anointed as a youth, but shortly thereafter he was forced to flee for his life, living as a fugitive for an extended period of time while Saul had relentlessly pursued him, seeking to kill him (1 Sam 18–27). David's enthronement at Hebron marks a climactic moment in his life, yet the call of God which began when he was a youth had required him to face ongoing trials, live without the safety and comfort of his home, and roam as a fugitive estranged from his family. During this difficult period in his life, David had the opportunity to kill Saul and put an end to his trials (chs. 24, 26), but he refused to stretch out his hand against God's anointed, thereby acknowledging the sovereign hand of God who was accomplishing his divine plan *his* way.

---

4. See Live the Story, Judah's Place in God's Plan to Include All Nations in Chapter 2, pp. 46–48.

The story of David, with his climatic enthronement at Hebron, is a reminder that God's calling upon our lives can include suffering and trials along with times of success. Yet the influential and pervasive prosperity gospel has set up false expectations of what it means to live the Christian life. Suffering is seen to be contrary to the plan of God, something that needs to be (and can be!) prayed away if sufficient faith can be garnered. An example is the *New York Times* bestselling author, Joel Osteen, whose book, *I Declare*, gives thirty-one promises for people to speak over their lives. One such promise reads: "I declare there is an anointing of ease on my life." This promise includes the declaration that "I will not continually struggle."[5] David had been anointed with oil (1 Sam 16), but his anointing was anything but an "anointing of ease." Quite the contrary! God's call upon David required him to suffer and struggle for many years without safety, family, and the comforts of home. This chapter recalling David's enthronement at Hebron is climatic, to be sure, but it comes after many difficult years, for David was required to wait for *God's* timing (cf. 1 Chr 10:14; 12:23). During these years, military men had given their support to him, and the king had learnt to rely on God's help through them. This reminds us that suffering and trials are not simply something to be prayed *away* (or "declared" away!), but we are to find comfort in God's presence and the help he provides amidst the struggles of life.

These stories of David are a testimony that God *is* present and at work accomplishing his sovereign plan, not only during times of success, but also amid seemingly hopeless circumstances. This provides encouragement for us today. When we face the hardships of life, whether sickness, financial insecurity, job loss, family strife, or even persecution, we need to have eyes to recognize his presence and to discern what he *is* doing. God has not forgotten his people, and he has not forgotten us. It is all too easy in our affluent and success-orientated society to gravitate towards times of success, assuming that it is *the* sign of God's blessing. God was with David not only when he became king, but throughout the years that led up to his enthronement at Hebron, reminding us that the difficult years were part of his sovereign plan (cf. 1 Chr 17:8).

Joel Osteen writes in another declaration that we need to live victoriously, declaring that we have royal blood flowing through our veins. Osteen writes: "By faith you need to walk like a king, talk like a king, think like a king, dress like a king, smile like a king."[6] The question is, what kind of king does Osteen

---

5. Joel Osteen, *I Declare: 31 Promises to Speak Over Your Life* (New York: Faith Words, 2012), 102.
6. Ibid., 118.

have in mind? Contrary to Osteen's view of kingship, the king we encounter in the gospels was a *suffering king* who laid down his life, and he calls us to take up our cross daily (Matt 10:38; 16:24; 24:9; Mark 8:34; Luke 9:23; 14:27). The apostle Paul understood that the call upon his life would entail suffering, and it was part of the path God had set before him (Acts 9:15–16; 20:23; 21:11; 2 Cor. 6:4–5; 11:23–27). Thus Paul would know not only the power of Jesus's resurrection but also the fellowship of his sufferings (Phil 3:10). This is the journey that is already anticipated in the life of David, and when his years draw to a close, he will acknowledge that he is simply a sojourner before God and that his days on earth were but a shadow in view of the larger plan of God (1 Chr 29:15). When we face the difficult seasons of life, this story of David's life reminds us that God *is* present and at work in our lives, even when our circumstances look less than promising.

CHAPTER 12

1 Chronicles 12:1–40

 LISTEN to the Story

¹These were the men who came to David at Ziklag, while he was banished from the presence of Saul son of Kish (they were among the warriors who helped him in battle; ²they were armed with bows and were able to shoot arrows or to sling stones right-handed or left-handed; they were relatives of Saul from the tribe of Benjamin):

³Ahiezer their chief and Joash the sons of Shemaah the Gibeathite; Jeziel and Pelet the sons of Azmaveth; Berakah, Jehu the Anathothite, ⁴and Ishmaiah the Gibeonite, a mighty warrior among the Thirty, who was a leader of the Thirty; Jeremiah, Jahaziel, Johanan, Jozabad the Gederathite, ⁵Eluzai, Jerimoth, Bealiah, Shemariah and Shephatiah the Haruphite; ⁶Elkanah, Ishiah, Azarel, Joezer and Jashobeam the Korahites; ⁷and Joelah and Zebadiah the sons of Jeroham from Gedor.

⁸Some Gadites defected to David at his stronghold in the wilderness. They were brave warriors, ready for battle and able to handle the shield and spear. Their faces were the faces of lions, and they were as swift as gazelles in the mountains.

⁹Ezer was the chief,
Obadiah the second in command, Eliab the third,
¹⁰Mishmannah the fourth, Jeremiah the fifth,
¹¹Attai the sixth, Eliel the seventh,
¹²Johanan the eighth, Elzabad the ninth,
¹³Jeremiah the tenth and Makbannai the eleventh.

¹⁴These Gadites were army commanders; the least was a match for a hundred, and the greatest for a thousand. ¹⁵It was they who crossed the

Jordan in the first month when it was overflowing all its banks, and they put to flight everyone living in the valleys, to the east and to the west.

¹⁶Other Benjamites and some men from Judah also came to David in his stronghold. ¹⁷David went out to meet them and said to them, "If you have come to me in peace to help me, I am ready for you to join me. But if you have come to betray me to my enemies when my hands are free from violence, may the God of our ancestors see it and judge you."

¹⁸Then the Spirit came on Amasai, chief of the Thirty, and he said:

"We are yours, David!
We are with you, son of Jesse!
Success, success to you,
   and success to those who help you,
      for your God will help you."

So David received them and made them leaders of his raiding bands.

¹⁹Some of the tribe of Manasseh defected to David when he went with the Philistines to fight against Saul. (He and his men did not help the Philistines because, after consultation, their rulers sent him away. They said, "It will cost us our heads if he deserts to his master Saul.") ²⁰When David went to Ziklag, these were the men of Manasseh who defected to him: Adnah, Jozabad, Jediael, Michael, Jozabad, Elihu and Zillethai, leaders of units of a thousand in Manasseh. ²¹They helped David against raiding bands, for all of them were brave warriors, and they were commanders in his army. ²²Day after day men came to help David, until he had a great army, like the army of God.

²³These are the numbers of the men armed for battle who came to David at Hebron to turn Saul's kingdom over to him, as the LORD had said:
   ²⁴from Judah, carrying shield and spear—6,800 armed for battle;
   ²⁵from Simeon, warriors ready for battle—7,100;
   ²⁶from Levi—4,600, ²⁷including Jehoiada, leader of the family of Aaron, with 3,700 men, ²⁸and Zadok, a brave young warrior, with 22 officers from his family;
   ²⁹from Benjamin, Saul's tribe—3,000, most of whom had remained loyal to Saul's house until then;
   ³⁰from Ephraim, brave warriors, famous in their own clans—20,800;

³¹from half the tribe of Manasseh, designated by name to come and make David king—18,000;

³²from Issachar, men who understood the times and knew what Israel should do—200 chiefs, with all their relatives under their command;

³³from Zebulun, experienced soldiers prepared for battle with every type of weapon, to help David with undivided loyalty—50,000;

³⁴from Naphtali—1,000 officers, together with 37,000 men carrying shields and spears;

³⁵from Dan, ready for battle—28,600;

³⁶from Asher, experienced soldiers prepared for battle—40,000;

³⁷and from east of the Jordan, from Reuben, Gad and the half-tribe of Manasseh, armed with every type of weapon—120,000.

³⁸All these were fighting men who volunteered to serve in the ranks. They came to Hebron fully determined to make David king over all Israel. All the rest of the Israelites were also of one mind to make David king. ³⁹The men spent three days there with David, eating and drinking, for their families had supplied provisions for them. ⁴⁰Also, their neighbors from as far away as Issachar, Zebulun and Naphtali came bringing food on donkeys, camels, mules and oxen. There were plentiful supplies of flour, fig cakes, raisin cakes, wine, olive oil, cattle and sheep, for there was joy in Israel.

Listening to the Text in the Story: 1 Samuel 27:1–12

The story that follows recalls the time in David's life when military men from Israel had come to him at Ziklag while he was fleeing from Saul (1 Sam 27:1–12). David had fled to the Philistines as a desperate measure out of fear for his life. The Philistine king Achish had given Ziklag to David as a place of refuge. The city had originally been given to the tribe of Simeon and was located in the southern towns of Judah (Josh 15:21, 31; 19:5). The Philistines had taken over Ziklag, and David now finds refuge there.[1] David and his six hundred men, together with their wives and children, had lived

---

1. Archaeologists have proposed various sites for biblical Ziklag including, more recently, Khirbet al Ra`I, but the exact location of biblical Ziklag remains a matter of dispute.

in the city for over a year. The Chronicler describes the military help David had received during this earlier period in his life (1 Chr 12:1–22), along with the support shown to him by all the tribes at his enthronement at Hebron (vv. 23–40). In both situations, the support David receives is surprising in view of his less-than-hopeful circumstances. While David had been hiding out in the Philistine territory and in caves, military men from Israel (even from Saul's own tribe of Benjamin) had joined him and had given him their full support. At David's enthronement, men from all the tribes, including the tribe of Benjamin, joined together with "one mind" to make David king (v. 38). Among the tribe of Issachar were those who "understood the times and knew what Israel should do" (v. 32). This was God's appointed time for the kingdom to be established, and the men of Issachar had discernment to understand the significance of these events. The remarkable support that David receives testifies to the fact that God was helping him (vv. 18, 22; cf. 11:9, 14), and as such, David's army is likened to the "army of God" (12:22). The chapter concludes with a great celebration at Hebron as a united people of God, who have gathered from afar, join together with one heart to make David king.

EXPLAIN the Story

David Receives Help from the Tribe of Benjamin (12:1–7)

The chapter begins by focusing on the names of the men who had helped David when he was in Ziklag (1 Chr 12:1; cf. 1 Sam 27:1-12). David's activities had been restricted because of Saul (1 Chr 12:1), not unlike someone whose activities are restricted due to imprisonment (cf. Jer 33:1; 36:5; 39:15), yet Chronicles resounds with the message that God was not restricted from doing *his* work—a message that would have instilled hope in the returnees who were living under Persian rule. The Chronicler recalls that during this difficult period in David's life, men from the tribe of Benjamin had joined him and given him their full support, with bows in-hand (1 Chr 12:2–7). That the Benjaminites were able to shoot arrows and sling stones with both hands speaks of their exceptional military capabilities (v. 2; cf. Judg 3:15; 20:16). The support David receives from the tribe of Benjamin is especially notable since Saul was from this tribe.

Names of men who give their support to David at Ziklag are listed, with their chief being Ahiezer ("my brother is my help"). His name anticipates an important theme of "help" that permeates the chapter.[2] The verb "to help" (Heb. *'-z-r*) appears seven times in the chapter (1 Chr 12:1, 17, 18 [2x], 19, 21, 22), and several names contain the root, such as Azarel and Joezer (v. 6) and Ezer (v. 9). David was experiencing *God's help* through the men coming to his aid. Such divine help causes the psalmist to praise God: "On my bed I remember you; I think of you through the watches of the night. Because you are my help, I sing in the shadow of your wings" (Ps 63:6–7).

The Mighty Men Who Help David (12:8–18)

The Chronicler rehearses the time when the Gadites had defected to David at his stronghold in the desert (1 Chr 12:8; cf. 1 Sam 22:1–5; 23:14). David had hidden from Saul near the cave of Adullam (22:1–5), but he had also taken refuge in the wilderness of En Gedi (23:29; 24:22). While David was living in these precarious hideouts, he had gathered a motley group of four hundred men from among those who were "in distress or in debt or discontented" (22:2). This group does not look very promising! At this time, military men from the tribe of Gad come to David in the wilderness. They are described as "brave warriors, ready for battle and able to handle the shield and spear. Their faces were the faces of lions, and they were as swift as gazelles in the mountains" (1 Chr 12:8; cf. Deut 33:20). Lion imagery speaks of their military prowess (Deut 33:20; cf. Gen 49:19), and their loyalty to David is seen in their traveling from the more remote Transjordan region, even when the water level of the Jordan was at its highest levels, requiring more effort (1 Chr 12:15).

Some of the men from Benjamin and Judah join him at the stronghold (vv. 16–18). As a fugitive in danger of being killed at any moment, David needs to know quickly if they have come to him in peace or if they have come to betray him (v. 17). He invokes God to look on the situation and decide. The answer that follows gives him the assurance he needs: God has indeed been watching over David, and the answer comes through a new and unexpected subject of the next verb—the Spirit! This is the first reference to God's Spirit in Chronicles (Heb. *ruach*, v. 18; cf. 28:12; 2 Chr 15:1; 20:14; 24:20, etc.). Here, the less common description of being "clothed" (NIV "came on") is used of the Spirit's activity (Heb. *l-b-sh*; see also Judg 6:34; 2 Chr 24:20). Amasai,

---

2. The idea of divine help is a dominant theme throughout Chronicles (e.g., 1 Chr 5:20; 15:26); see especially the commentary on Asa (2 Chr 14:11, Chapter 43, pp. 387–88), Jehoshaphat (2 Chr 18:31, Chapter 47, p. 416), and Hezekiah (2 Chr 32:8, Chapter 61, pp. 526–27).

clothed with the Spirit, gives words of encouragement to David.[3] He affirms that the men of Judah and Benjamin belong to him, and they are with him. He then says: "Peace, peace to you, and peace to your helpers! For your God helps you" (ESV, 1 Chr 12:18). These men have come in peace to support David, but even more importantly, Amasai lets David know that the help he is receiving has come from God! This is a moment of great encouragement and it serves as a tangible demonstration that God is with him.

David Receives Help from the Tribe of Manasseh (12:19–22)

As noted above, David had sought refuge at the Philistine city of Ziklag for over a year (1 Chr 12:19-22; cf. 1 Sam 27:1-7). First Samuel 29 picks up the story with David and his men assembling for battle as they attempt to join the Philistines against Saul. Yet the commanders of the Philistine army refuse to let David and his men join them in battle, for fear that they might turn against them (29:1-11). This is when David receives military support from the tribe of Manasseh, for they had defected in order to help David (1 Chr 12:19–22). At this time, however, the Amalekites had made a raid on the city of Ziklag, and David had initially suffered great loss (1 Sam 30:1–6), although with God's help, David is victorious, and he and his men are able to recover their women and children (30:7–20). The Chronicler alludes to this difficult period, noting that the men of Manasseh were among those who had helped David (1 Chr 12:20–21). The section concludes with a statement that David was being helped "until he had a great army, like the army of God" (v. 22). That David's army is compared to God's army underscores its size, as will be seen in what follows (vv. 24–41). Yet it is important to remember that Israel's military battles were never entirely secular, for God was fighting on their behalf.[4] Accordingly, the Chronicler's reference to God's army may well suggest the "human and divine participation in David's military adventures,"[5] which fits nicely with the theme of divine help.

David Receives Further Support at Hebron (12:23–40)

The section concludes with a list of military men from all the tribes who gathered at Hebron to turn Saul's kingdom over to David (1 Chr 12:23–40; cf. 10:14). With literary symmetry, this section now resumes the narrative

---

3. On the role of the Spirit to give encouragement, see the discussions on 2 Chr 15:1–7 (Chapter 44, pp. 393–94) and 20:14–17 (Chapter 49, p. 431).

4. See the discussion on the spiritual conflict between the kingdom of God and the nations in Chapters 14 and 19, Live the Story, pp. 153–54, 199–201.

5. Klein, *1 Chronicles*, 321.

from 1 Chronicles 11:1–3 with its focus on David's enthronement at Hebron, which is taking place according to the word of the LORD (12:23; cf. 11:3, 10). The list begins with the southern tribes of Judah, Simeon, Levi, and Benjamin (12:24–29), followed by the northern tribes of Ephraim, the half-tribe of Manasseh, Issachar, Zebulun, Naphtali, Dan, and Asher (vv. 30–36). Lastly, the more remote Transjordan tribes are listed: Reuben, Gad, and the half-tribe of Manasseh (v. 37). All the tribes are represented at this key moment in the story of Israel as they give their full support to David. The tribes number in the thousands, yet scholars have noted that the Hebrew word translated as "thousand" (Heb. *'eleph*) can mean a tribal sub-unit (rather than a literal headcount), which would result in a much smaller number.[6] Although we cannot be certain about the exact size of the tribal sub-units (and scholarly views vary), the point of the chapter is to underscore the widespread support given to David by all Israel. This is an affirmation of David's leadership and God's calling on him.

Amidst the list of the tribes, some additional comments are made: Jehoiada is identified as the "leader of the family of Aaron" (1 Chr 12:27–28), and Zadok is identified as a "brave young warrior" (v. 28).[7] Men from the tribe of Benjamin are highlighted since they had formerly given their allegiance to Saul (who was from their own tribe), but it is significant that they now give their support to David (v. 29; cf. vv. 2–6). The men of Issachar are highlighted as those who "understood the times and knew what Israel should do" (v. 32), suggesting that they are exemplary in their wisdom (cf. 2 Chr 2:12; Job 38:4). They were able to discern "the times," that is, they discerned what God was doing (cf. Esth 4:14), and with this in view, they give David their undivided support. Reference to the Spirit earlier in the chapter underscores that spiritual

---

6. See Braun, *1 Chronicles*, 169–70. High numbers in the OT are not easily resolved, although there is some level of scholarly consensus that in military census lists and military contexts, the Hebrew term *'eleph* probably refers to a military unit or a contingent of troops rather than a literal headcount (see George E. Mendenhall, "The Census Lists of Numbers 1 and 26," *JBL* 77:1 [1958]: 52–56. Common scholarly approaches include the following: a) the term *'eleph* is a social unit or sub-tribal unit (in the army), in which case the numbers would be much smaller; b) the term *'eleph* means "thousand," but the numbers are hyperbolic rather than literal headcounts; c) the term *'eleph* is repointed as *'alluf*, meaning "commander, colonel." In addition to these approaches, some high numbers may be due to scribal errors. For a helpful summary of various approaches, see Dillard, *2 Chronicles*, 106–107, 135 and Klein, *1 Chronicles*, 314–16. For the hyperbolic interpretation and ancient Near Eastern examples, see David M. Fouts, "A Defense of the Hyperbolic Interpretation of Large Numbers in the Old Testament," *JETS* 40:3 (1997): 377–87. For numbers in Chronicles, see J. Barton Payne, "The Validity of Numbers in Chronicles," *BSac* 136 (1979), pp. 109–128, 206–220. For a comprehensive analysis of high numbers along with pertinent textual issues, see John W. Wenham, "Large Numbers in the Old Testament," *TynBul* 18 (1967): 19–53.

7. Zadok will be later distinguished for his priestly role (1 Chr 15:11; 16:39; 24:3, 6, 31, etc.).

insight is needed to discern the movement of God. With such widespread support from all the tribes, this gives a vision for a unified kingdom, serving as an example to the returnees who are comprised of southern and northern tribes. The Chronicler is, as Boda suggests, "leveraging the past to stimulate hope for the future."[8]

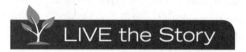

LIVE the Story

God's Kingdom and David's Mighty Men

In this story, the Chronicler is describing the widespread support David receives as God is establishing the kingdom. We are reminded in this story that, although David is God's anointed king, he is not doing this on his own, but rather, he needs the support of others so that the kingdom might be established. God is at work in the lives of these mighty men, who are successful in battle because of God's help. The central theme of help is not only seen in the repetition of the verb, but also in the names given, something that is missed in our English Bible. Imagine people coming to you while you were facing difficult circumstances, saying: "My name is Helper," "My name is Helpful," "My name is Helpmate," "My name is Helping," "My name is Helpfulness"—one gets the point! This is precisely what is being communicated in the Hebrew text. Most importantly, the prophet Amasai testifies that the help David receives is a demonstration of God's help (1 Chr 12:18). This echoes the message that permeates the psalms: "God is our refuge and strength, an ever-present help in trouble" (Ps 46:1). God is providing the help that David needs, and he is using others in the kingdom as his instruments. Later in David's reign, he exhorts his trusted and loyal leaders to help to his son Solomon (1 Chr 22:17). Just as David could not lead Israel without help from others, Solomon will need help from David's trusted leaders if he is to be successful. These stories underscore that God is establishing the kingdom under David, but they also offer us a glimpse into *how* he does this—through *people*—giving us hints about the future kingdom under the Messiah.

Jesus is the promised son of David who announces that the kingdom is at hand. Remarkably, he invites us to participate in his kingdom-work. As disciples of Jesus, we are to proclaim the gospel of the kingdom to all nations (Matt 24:14; cf. Acts 8:12; 19:8; 20:25; 28:23, 31), to live out the ethics of the kingdom (Matt 5–7; 1 Cor 6:9–10; Gal 4:21; Eph 5:5), to be "co-workers" in

---

8. Boda, *1–2 Chronicles*, 124.

the kingdom (Col 4:11), to use our talents for the sake of the kingdom (Matt 25:14–46), to suffer for the sake of the kingdom (2 Thess 1:5), to seek first the kingdom (Matt 6:33), to pray that God's kingdom might come on earth as it is in heaven (6:10), and to look forward to the time when "the kingdom of the world has become the kingdom of our Lord and of his Messiah, and he will reign for ever and ever" (Rev 11:15). This means that we are anything but passive bystanders. Jesus is establishing his kingdom on earth, but he is doing his kingdom-work through his followers who join him. In the movie *The Fellowship of the Ring*, the scene in Rivendell at the Council of Elrond comes to mind, where each person in the fellowship brings his weapon in support of Frodo, the ring-bearer. In the story of David, men from all the tribes bring their bows, slingstones, shields, and spears in service of the king. We, too, are called to participate in God's kingdom. Even though our circumstances might not aways look promising, God *is* building his kingdom, and this ought to be our priority, even as we pray that God's kingdom might come and be established on earth as it is in heaven.

LISTEN to the Story

¹David conferred with each of his officers, the commanders of thousands and commanders of hundreds. ²He then said to the whole assembly of Israel, "If it seems good to you and if it is the will of the LORD our God, let us send word far and wide to the rest of our people throughout the territories of Israel, and also to the priests and Levites who are with them in their towns and pasturelands, to come and join us. ³Let us bring the ark of our God back to us, for we did not inquire of it during the reign of Saul." ⁴The whole assembly agreed to do this, because it seemed right to all the people.

⁵So David assembled all Israel, from the Shihor River in Egypt to Lebo Hamath, to bring the ark of God from Kiriath Jearim. ⁶David and all Israel went to Baalah of Judah (Kiriath Jearim) to bring up from there the ark of God the LORD, who is enthroned between the cherubim—the ark that is called by the Name.

⁷They moved the ark of God from Abinadab's house on a new cart, with Uzzah and Ahio guiding it. ⁸David and all the Israelites were celebrating with all their might before God, with songs and with harps, lyres, timbrels, cymbals and trumpets.

⁹When they came to the threshing floor of Kidon, Uzzah reached out his hand to steady the ark, because the oxen stumbled. ¹⁰The LORD's anger burned against Uzzah, and he struck him down because he had put his hand on the ark. So he died there before God.

¹¹Then David was angry because the LORD's wrath had broken out against Uzzah, and to this day that place is called Perez Uzzah.

¹²David was afraid of God that day and asked, "How can I ever bring the ark of God to me?" ¹³He did not take the ark to be with him in the City of David. Instead, he took it to the house of Obed-Edom the Gittite.

¹⁴The ark of God remained with the family of Obed-Edom in his house for three months, and the LORD blessed his household and everything he had.

Listening to the Text in the Story: Exodus 25:10–22; 2 Samuel 6:2–11

Now that David is enthroned as king over all Israel, it is fitting that the ark of the covenant should be brought to Jerusalem (1 Chr 13–16).[1] David is not simply leading a secular or political kingdom, but it is first and foremost a *sacred* kingdom marked by the presence of a holy God in their midst (1 Chr 13:6; cf. 2 Chr 18:18). The central role of the ark is seen in the fact that the term "ark" (Heb. *'aron*) is mentioned forty-six times in Chronicles, twenty-nine of which are in 1 Chronicles 13–16.[2] At this sacred event, all Israel gathers at Kiriath Jearim, the current location of the ark, so that they might bring it to Jerusalem. A tragic event takes place, however, while the ark is being transported to the city. Uzzah, one of two men responsible to move it, stretches out his hand to take hold of it because it had become unstable. God's anger burns against him, and he is struck down and dies. As a result, David is afraid to move the ark, so he brings it to the house of Obed-Edom, where it remains for three months. At this time God blesses the house of Obed-Edom.

As we to listen to the story in its original context, it is important to consider the significance of the ark for the Israelite community and the laws governing its transportation. To the modern reader, God's anger against Uzzah seems like a capricious act by an angry God. Uzzah had simply wanted to prevent the cart from toppling over, yet he is killed instantly by God. How are we to understand this story? We begin by recalling that the ark of the covenant was *the* most holy and sacred object in Israel's worship. God had given Moses specific instructions about how to construct the tabernacle—because a *holy God* was to dwell among his people (Exod 25:8). This profound reality shaped every aspect of the covenant community. Detailed instructions were given to

---

1. The Chronicler does not follow a strict chronology in these chapters, but rather, placement of the stories is due to theological and thematic interests. In Chronicles, the final arrival of the ark into Jerusalem and the celebration that follows are presented as one uninterrupted narrative (1 Chr 15–16; cf. 2 Sam 5–6).

2. Christopher T. Begg, "The Ark in Chronicles," in *The Chronicler as Theologian: Essays in Honor of Ralph W. Klein*, eds. M. Patrick Graham, Steven L. McKenzie, and Gary N. Knoppers (JSOTSup 371; New York: T&T Clark, 2003), 133–45, esp. pp. 133–34.

Moses concerning the tabernacle, which included the ark of the covenant, the place where God would meet with his people (vv. 10–16, 22).

The ark was a box made of acacia wood, overlaid with pure gold. It was approximately forty-five inches long, twenty-seven inches wide, and twenty-seven inches high.[3] The lid of the ark, which was flanked by two golden cherubim reminiscent of the Garden of Eden, was called the "atonement cover" (NIV; "mercy seat" in NASB); it was the place where atonement was made (Lev 16:2). Prior to being moved, the ark was to be covered with a veil, along with durable leather and a cloth of pure blue (Num 4:6). It had four rings of gold on it, which enabled two poles to be attached. The Levites were to carry the ark by placing the poles on their shoulders (1 Chr 15:15; cf. Exod 25:14). Sacred objects in Egypt also had poles attached, which were used for transportation.[4] The holiness of the ark is underscored by the fact that it was located in the holy of holies (Exod 26:34), which was *the most* holy place in the tabernacle.[5]

The law stipulated that only the Levites could transport the ark (Deut 10:8; 18:5; cf. 1 Chr 15:12–15; 2 Chr 35:3). Given that David appoints Levites when moving the ark the second time, this suggests that Uzzah was not a Levite. As a lay person he was precluded from this task, and even Levites had to maintain a distance; the use of poles meant they did not carry it with their hands (Exod 25:12–15; Num 4:5–6; 1 Chr 15:13–15). These texts enable us to listen to the story in its original context and to interpret the events with this in view.

EXPLAIN the Story

David Consults with the People to Bring the Ark to Jerusalem (13:1–4)

The narrative begins with David seeking counsel from his leaders to discern whether or not to move the ark at this time, recalling that when Saul was king, the people had neglected to "seek" it (Heb. verb *d-r-sh*, 1 Chr 13:3; NIV "inquire"). Since the ark was the place of God's presence, not seeking it speaks

---

3. Measurements in the Old Testament are given in cubits (Exod 25:10); one cubit equals approximately eighteen inches.

4. See Aland Millard, "Tutankhamun, the Tabernacle and the Ark of the Covenant," *BSP* 7:2 (1994): 49–55.

5. On the various grades of holiness associated with the tabernacle, see Phillip P. Jenson, *Graded Holiness: A Key to the Priestly Conception of the World* (JSOTSup 206; Sheffield: JSOT Press, 2020), 89–114.

of their failure to seek God himself (Heb. *d-r-sh*, cf. 10:13–14).[6] By contrast, David's initiative sets the tone for his kingship, for he is a king who seeks God's presence and exhorts Israel to seek God's face continually (16:10–11). The ark of God, which is also called "the ark of the covenant law" (Exod 25:22; Num 4:5; 7:89), "the ark of the covenant of the LORD" (Num 10:33; 1 Chr 15:25, 26), or simply "the ark" (1 Chr 6:31; 13:9, etc.), was also the place where the Ten Commandments were kept (Exod 25:16); thus it held a sacred and central place in the covenant community.

David Gathers All Israel to Kiriath Jearim (13:5–6)

At this momentous occasion David assembles all Israel, including the priests and Levites, to Kiriath Jearim, located about eight miles north of Jerusalem. Kiriath Jearim (also known as Baalah and Kiriath-baal) was a border-town assigned to Judah (Josh 15:9, 60; 18:14–15). The families associated with Kiriath Jearim have already been introduced (1 Chr 2:50–53), but the location recalls the difficult period in Israel's history when the ark had been taken by the Philistines and later returned and brought to Kiriath Jearim, to the house of Abinadab (1 Sam 4–6). At David's initiative, the entire covenant community assembles at Kiriath Jearim to move the ark to Jerusalem, with people coming from the more remote regions of the Shihor River in Egypt and from Libo Hamath in the far north (cf. Josh 13:3).

God "Breaks Out" against Uzzah and He Dies (13:7–11)

The Israelites transport the ark by placing it on a new cart with Uzzah and Ahio guiding the oxen. Nowhere does the law mention that a *cart* was to be used to transport the ark! Even more telling, the Philistines had used a *new cart* when they had sent it away (1 Sam 6:7, 8, 11, etc.). The Israelites have curiously used the same mode of transport as the Philistines had used. It is perhaps not so surprising that things take a turn for the worse. While this is an occasion for celebrating (1 Chr 13:8),[7] the tone quickly shifts when Uzzah stretches out his hand to take hold of the ark in an effort to secure it (v. 9). God's anger burns against him and he is struck dead. In an instant, the singing turns to mourning. Lay people like Uzzah were not permitted to draw near to the ark, nor were they permitted to move it, as David later

---

6. On the meaning of the verb "to seek" (Heb. *d-r-sh*), see the discussion on pp. 291–93.

7. Even though the people are celebrating, the usual terms used in Chronicles for singing and joyful worship are not used here, but instead, the less common verb "to play, celebrate" (Heb. *s-h-q*; cf. 1 Chr 15:29) is used, perhaps hinting that something is awry.

recognized (cf. 15:12–15). Given that the ark was *the* most sacred object, it was presumptuous of Uzzah to think that he could reach his hand toward the ark unscathed.[8] Moreover, Uzzah does not take hold of the cart or even the oxen, but he stretches his hand to grasp the *ark itself*—the very place where God was enthroned! Uzzah's action represents an egregious failure to recognize that a holy God was in their midst (cf. 2 Chr 8:11). That God "breaks out" (Heb. *p-r-ts*) against Uzzah points to the unapproachable nature of his holiness (1 Chr 13:11; cf. 15:13). This becomes the event that is remembered when David names the place *Perez Uzzah* ("outbreak against Uzzah"), and the ark remains with the family of Obed-Edom for three months (13:13–14).

LIVE the Story

Jesus's Provision of the New, Living Way to Approach God

This story reminds us that God dwells in unapproachable holiness. The Old Testament uses the term "holy" to describe God's *otherness*—the LORD God is highly exalted and separated from his creation in his glorious splendor and in his moral purity. When God appeared at Mount Sinai in fire and smoke, the mountain shook violently and the people trembled at his presence. God had given Moses strict instructions about *how* he was to be approached and *who* could approach him. God had warned Moses that he would "break out" (Heb. *p-r-ts*) against his people[9] and they would die, should they attempt to draw near to him (Exod 19:1–25; cf. Heb 12:18–21). The people had to be consecrated in preparation for God's presence, which included washing their garments (Exod 19:10). Similarly, the Levites were consecrated before moving the ark (1 Chr 15:12–14), which most likely entailed an elaborate ritual including sacrifices, washing, and holy garments (cf. Exod 28–29; Lev 8:1–36). The entire sacrificial system, the purity laws, and the laws governing ethical conduct were based on the premise that God dwelt in unapproachable holiness. God told Moses that the people were to be holy, for "I am holy" (11:44; 19:2; cf. 20:7).[10] Aaron was painfully aware after the death of his two sons that those who draw near to God must treat him as holy (10:1–20;

---

8. The story of the ark being taken by the Philistines provides another example of its sacred nature (1 Sam 4–6). God smites the Philistines with tumors, and they return the ark for fear of their lives.

9. The term "break out" (Heb. *p-r-ts*) in Exod 19:22 and 19:24 is the same verb used to describe God "breaking out" against Uzzah (1 Chr 13:11; 15:13).

10. See Jay Sklar, *Leviticus: An Introduction and Commentary*, TOTC (Downers Grove, IL: Inter-Varsity Press, 2014), 37–49.

16:1–2). Hahn rightly notes that God's people are called "to intimacy with God—but on God's terms, not their own."[11]

As we reflect upon God's presence today, God's unapproachable and glorious holiness has not changed. The prophet Isaiah had received a vision of God's holiness when he saw him high and lifted up as he heard the seraphim calling out, "Holy, holy, holy is the LORD Almighty" (Isa 6:3). The vision that John receives is reminiscent of Isaiah's vision, when he beholds the living creatures who cry out: "'Holy, holy, holy is the Lord God Almighty, who was, and is, and is to come'" (Rev 4:8). God's unapproachable and incomprehensible holiness remains the same throughout the Scriptures. But what has changed is the means by which we approach a holy God and even the fact that we *can* approach him. Jesus's death enables us to draw near to God in a way that was not possible in the Old Testament. Under the new covenant, God has provided a *new* and *living* way for his people to draw near to him through the great high priest, Jesus, who is "holy, blameless, pure, set apart from sinners, exalted above the heavens" (Heb 7:26). Instead of God breaking out against *us* as he did with Uzzah, we can come into God's presence because Jesus has died in our place. We can draw near to God with confidence, precisely because Jesus has sprinkled our hearts and has cleansed us (10:19–22). Uzzah could not draw near to God, but Jesus's death has enabled *us* to draw near without the fear of death, yet we do so with reverence and awe, for our "God is a consuming fire" (12:29). The writer to the Hebrews exhorts us, therefore, to draw near to God with full confidence. This ought to invoke in us a deep and abiding sense of gratitude and thanks as we offer our lives consecrated in service to God (vv. 22–29).

Recapturing God's Holiness in the Church

It is vital for the church today to gain a fresh vision of God's holiness. David Wells has astutely observed that in our contemporary context we gravitate toward the love of God, yet we have tragically lost sight of God's holiness, which he defines as "everything that sets him [God] apart from the sinful creation" and "everything that elevates him above it in moral splendor."[12] We are drawn to love but repelled by holiness, Wells writes. As we selectively focus on God's love to the exclusion of his holiness, this means that we have failed to worship God based on his *self*-revelation. When God made known his name to

---

11. Hahn, *The Kingdom of God*, 56.
12. David F. Wells, *God in the Whirlwind: How the Holy-love of God Reorients Our World* (Wheaton: Crossway, 2014), 103; see especially Chapter 5, "The Splendor of Holiness," 101–127. For a concise summary of God's holiness, see Sklar, *Leviticus*, 39–41.

Moses, he revealed that his covenant-love and anger belonged *together* (Exod 34:6–7).[13] To be sure, God is *slow* to anger and his lovingkindness extends to thousands, but his judgment is nevertheless intrinsic to his character because it is rooted in his holiness.

We gain a vision of God's unapproachable holiness precisely through stories like Uzzah as they enable us to see the reality of God as *he* defines himself, rather than creating God in our image. Perhaps the loss of God's holiness in the church is the direct result of our neglect of the Old Testament in preaching and teaching.[14] Stories of God's unapproachable holiness are intended to draw us into a deeper understanding of God's character, resulting in praise and worship, but also fear and reverence for his holy name. This is exactly what happens in this story. When the ark is brought into Jerusalem, God's "*holy* name" is praised (1 Chr 16:10, emphasis added) and he is worshiped in the "splendor of *his holiness*" (v. 29, emphasis added). He is to be feared above all gods (v. 25). The praises of God's people join with the living creatures, who cry out, "Holy, Holy, Holy is the Lord God Almighty" (Rev 4:8). Stories like Uzzah's need to be preached in the church today so that we might gain a fresh vision of God's holiness.

---

13. Wells has argued that God's love and holiness should not be separated; he suggests that we refer to God's love as his *holy-love* (hence the subtitle of his book).

14. We noted earlier that Briggs in his research on the Bible in America laments that the Old Testament has been neglected (*The Invisible Bestseller*, 9).

LISTEN to the Story

¹Now Hiram king of Tyre sent messengers to David, along with cedar logs, stonemasons and carpenters to build a palace for him. ²And David knew that the LORD had established him as king over Israel and that his kingdom had been highly exalted for the sake of his people Israel.

³In Jerusalem David took more wives and became the father of more sons and daughters. ⁴These are the names of the children born to him there: Shammua, Shobab, Nathan, Solomon, ⁵Ibhar, Elishua, Elpelet, ⁶Nogah, Nepheg, Japhia, ⁷Elishama, Beeliada and Eliphelet.

⁸When the Philistines heard that David had been anointed king over all Israel, they went up in full force to search for him, but David heard about it and went out to meet them. ⁹Now the Philistines had come and raided the Valley of Rephaim; ¹⁰so David inquired of God: "Shall I go and attack the Philistines? Will you deliver them into my hands?"

The LORD answered him, "Go, I will deliver them into your hands."

¹¹So David and his men went up to Baal Perazim, and there he defeated them. He said, "As waters break out, God has broken out against my enemies by my hand." So that place was called Baal Perazim. ¹²The Philistines had abandoned their gods there, and David gave orders to burn them in the fire.

¹³Once more the Philistines raided the valley; ¹⁴so David inquired of God again, and God answered him, "Do not go directly after them, but circle around them and attack them in front of the poplar trees. ¹⁵As soon as you hear the sound of marching in the tops of the poplar trees, move out to battle, because that will mean God has gone out in front of you to strike the Philistine army." ¹⁶So David did as God commanded him, and they struck down the Philistine army, all the way from Gibeon to Gezer.

> [17] So David's fame spread throughout every land, and the LORD made all the nations fear him.

Listening to the Text in the Story: Psalms 2:1–12, 83:1–8

Now that David has become king over all Israel, he seeks to build a palace for himself. David recognizes that God has established him as king and has exalted his kingdom. The king of Tyre responds to David's kingship by providing wood and craftsmen for his royal palace, but not all the surrounding nations respond so favorably. David's kingship is met with hostility by the Philistines, who rise up against him after hearing that he had become king. As we read about David's battle with the Philistines, it is important to bear in mind that, even though several nations have been incorporated into the tribe of Judah,[1] the nations are also *in conflict* with the Davidic king and the kingdom.

Psalm 2 is an important and well-known psalm that provides an important theological lens as we read the story that follows. The psalmist asks the question: "Why do the nations conspire and the peoples plot in vain?" (v. 1). The following answer is given: "The kings of the earth rise up and the rulers band together against the LORD and against his anointed, saying, 'Let us break their chains and throw off their shackles'" (vv. 2–3). The Philistine attack of David and his kingdom (1 Chr 14:8–9) is a direct attack against the LORD, therefore. Similarly, Psalm 83 recounts that when Israel's enemies, such as Edom, Moab, Amon, Amelek, and Philistia, devise plans to wipe out the name of Israel, they are effectively rising up against *God himself.* The psalm underscores that Israel's enemies are in fact *God's* enemies (vv. 1–8). These two psalms provide an important theological lens as we read about David's battles against Israel's enemies (cf. 1 Chr 18–20).

 EXPLAIN the Story

David Builds a Palace (14:1–2)

The story begins with Hiram, king of Tyre, who provides cedar logs, stonemasons, and carpenters to build a palace for David (1 Chr 14:1). The Phoenician city of Tyre was a well-known coastal city famous for its maritime

---

1. See Chapter 2, Live the Story, Judah's Place in God's Plan to Include All Nations, pp. 46–48.

trade. The king of Tyre will later provide cedar and pine logs from Lebanon for Solomon when he builds the temple, along with skilled Phoenician artisans (1 Kgs 5:1–12; 7:13–46; 2 Chr 2:3–16).[2] The support David receives from the king of Tyre is tangible evidence that God's hand was upon him. David recognizes that "the LORD had established him as king over Israel and that his kingdom had been highly exalted for the sake of his people Israel" (1 Chr 14:2). We have already seen that God was sovereignly at work prior to David's enthronement (cf. chs. 11–12), but David now understands (lit. "knows") that God has established him as king, just as the men of Issachar "understood" (Heb. y-d-ʿ) the times and "knew" (Heb. y-d-ʿ) what Israel was to do (12:32). David recognizes what God is doing by exalting him as king. It was not for David's own glory but for the sake of God's people Israel. The establishment of the kingdom under David is a tangible demonstration of God's concern for his people!

David's Wives and Children (14:3–7)

The list of David's sons can be divided into two groups: those born while he was king of Judah for seven years (1 Chr 3:1–4) and those born during his longer reign in Jerusalem (vv. 5–9; 14:3–7; cf. 2 Sam 5:13–16). The first four sons named were born to David by Bathsheba, and the other nine sons were born to him by other wives. In the ancient world, royal marriages to foreign women were a strategic aspect of foreign policy.[3] Marriages to foreign women (especially princesses) will be central to Solomon's international policy, although they will lead to his ruin (1 Kgs 11:1–11). While no negative comment is made about David's wives, we do well to remember that Moses had warned that the king was not to take multiple wives (Deut 17:17).

The Philistines Rise Up against David (14:8–12)

When the Philistines hear that David has been anointed king over all Israel, they plan an attack against him (1 Chr 14:8). We have already encountered the Philistines in the story of Saul's death (ch. 10), at which time they had gruesomely dismembered his body and had paraded it as a trophy of war (vv. 8–12).[4] The Philistines, who lived adjacent to Israel on the Mediterranean coast, have been a constant and troubling enemy of Israel (cf. Judg 10:7–8;

---

2. For more background on the Phoenicians, see the discussion in Chapter 31 on 2 Chr 2.

3. See Jon D. Levenson and Baruch Halpern, "The Political Import of David's Marriages," *JBL* 99 (1980): 507–51, and Abraham Malamat, "Aspects of the Foreign Policies of David and Solomon," *JNES* 22:1 (1963): 1–17.

4. See the discussion in Chapter 10 on 1 Chr 10.

16:21–27; 1 Sam 4:2). Now, they assemble in the Valley of Rephaim, located near Jerusalem. As David is on route to meet them, we are told that he "inquired of God" (Heb. *sh-'-l*, 1 Chr 14:10), in contrast to Saul, who consulted a medium for guidance (10:13). It is characteristic of David, however, to seek counsel from God before a battle (1 Sam 23:2, 4; 30:7–8, etc.), for he understands that victory is in the hands of God (17:36–37). As divine warrior, the LORD fights on behalf of his people as they trust in him (2 Chr 13:15; 17:10; 20:15, 17, 29, etc.). In response to David's prayer, God tells the king to go up against the Philistines with the assurance of victory (1 Chr 14:10). David defeats the Philistines at a place named Baal Perazim ("Lord of the breaches"), which testifies that God had "broken out" against his enemies (Heb. *p-r-ts*, v. 11). God had "broken out" against Uzzah (Heb. *p-r-ts*, 13:11; 15:13), but now God breaks out against Israel's enemy, which underscores the sacred nature of Israel's holy wars.

The story concludes with a comment that the Philistines abandoned their gods, and David orders them to be burned with fire (14:12). The significance of this statement is not to be missed. After Saul had died in battle, the Philistines had stripped off his armor and dismembered his body. They had put Saul's armor in the temple of *their* gods and had put his head in the temple of Dagon (10:10), signifying that the Philistine gods had been victorious over Israel. Similarly, when the Philistines had defeated Israel during the days of Samuel, they had brought the ark of the covenant into the temple of Dagon (1 Sam 5:1–5). David's victory over the Philistines marks a decisive reversal of what had taken place under Saul. But David does not simply take their gods as trophies of war, nor does he offer them to his God. Rather, in accordance with God's law, he burns their gods with fire (1 Chr 14:12; cf. Deut 7:5, 25; 12:3). David's actions not only testify to his devotion to the LORD (1 Chr 16:7–36), but they serve as a testimony that the LORD alone is God (cf. 2 Chr 33:13, 15).

David's Second Victory over the Philistines (14:13–17)

The Philistines again raid the valley, and characteristically, David inquires of God (Heb. *sh-'-l*, 1 Chr 14:13–14; cf. 1 Sam 23:2, 4; 30:7–8; 1 Chr 14:10). Japhet notes that David is "depicted as receiving direct and constant guidance. He does not take one step without consulting God."[5] God answers his request, instructing him to circle around the Philistines and attack them in front of the poplar trees (v. 14). David and his men are to attack as soon as they hear the sound of marching, for it means that "God has gone out in front of you

---

5. Japhet, *I & II Chronicles*, 287.

to strike the Philistine army" (v. 15). Reminiscent of the Israelites' request that their king "go out before us and fight our battles" (1 Sam 8:20), now God is fighting on Israel's behalf, as he had promised (Deut 31:5–8 Josh 1:2–9). David follows God's command, and he and his men strike the Philistine army in an extensive battle "all the way from Gibeon to Gezer" (1 Chr 14:16). Gibeon was located six miles northwest of Jerusalem, falling within the tribal allotment of Benjamin and having connections with Saul (8:29; 9:35), but it was also the place where the tabernacle was located (21:29; 2 Chr 1:3). David's victory over the Philistines effectively stops their eastward advance, and as a result, his fame spreads to all the lands and God brings fear upon the nations (1 Chr 14:17).

LIVE the Story

Nations Opposing the Kingdom Will Be Judged

Battles in the Old Testament have been the source of much criticism, as God commands the Israelites to wipe out certain people groups.[6] David's battles in this chapter might be cited as yet another example, and there are more to come (cf. 1 Chr 18–20).[7] But these battles need to be interpreted from the perspective of Psalm 2, which underscores that nations arise against God's anointed, and thus they are an affront against God himself. Yet divine victory is assured, and kings of the nations are to take heed (Ps 2:10–12; cf. Ps 110:5–6). The book of Daniel is an example of the conflict between the kingdom of God and earthly kingdoms that oppose God and his people (Dan 7), and this spiritual conflict extends into the New Testament.

With this reality in view, Jesus taught that the growth of the kingdom was not without opposition (Matt 13:25, 28, 38–39). When he healed the sick and demon-possessed—signs of his kingdom—this often involved casting out of demons (12:28–29; Luke 11:21–22; 13:16). As divine warrior, Jesus comes to defeat the ultimate enemy, Satan himself (Col 2:13–15; Heb 2:14–15; 1 John 3:8). Conflict between the kingdom of God and the kingdom of darkness is thus exposed, a conflict which involves principalities and spiritual powers of wickedness that rise up against God and his kingdom (Eph 6:10–17). The

---

6. See Merrill, Excursus 6, "The Theological Ethics of Holy War," *1 & 2 Chronicles*, 256–61. Four approaches to this difficult topic are presented in the helpful Counterpoints volume, *Show Them No Mercy: Four Views on God and Canaanite Genocide*, ed. Stanley N. Gundry (Grand Rapids: Zondervan, 2003).

7. On this topic, see Chapter 19, Live the Story, p. 199–201.

spiritual nature of these battles is thus unveiled, and the ultimate adversary is identified as Satan himself and his demons (Matt 4:1–11; 12:25–26; Luke 10:18–19; Acts 26:18; cf. 1 Thess 2:18). In view of this spiritual battle, God's people are to be aware of the wiles of the enemy and not give Satan any foothold (Acts 5:3; 1 Cor 7:5; 2 Cor 2:11; 11:14).

This means that, even though all the nations are included in God's kingdom (cf. Dan 7:9–14; Rev 5:1–13), which is highlighted in the line of Judah,[8] the reality is that nations that *oppose* the kingdom of God will fall under divine judgment. The book of Revelation depicts an increasingly hostile world where opposition rises against God's people, seen especially in the Antichrist opponent,[9] yet hope is assured since these battles will ultimately result in the victory of the Lamb and the rule of the Messiah at his parousia (Rev 19–20; cf. 2 Thess 2:3–12).

In Western culture, God is often portrayed as loving and all-embracing, yet this is done to the exclusion of God's holiness and his wrath.[10] The Bible teaches that God is judge of the whole earth (Gen 18:25; Pss 7:6–8; 9:7–8; 82:8; 94:1–3; Dan 7:9–10), and as such, there will be a time of reckoning when all the nations will be held accountable at the return of Christ, whom God has appointed as judge over all (2 Thess 1:5–10; 2 Pet 2–3; cf. Dan 7:1–14).

With this final eschatological battle in view, Gard has argued that already in Chronicles Israel's battles have cosmic significance, noting: "What takes place on earth is, for the Chronicler, directly connected to and reflective of the cosmic and the spiritual."[11] Thus, the holy war tradition foreshadows the eschatological judgment, when Satan and his forces will be defeated and those nations who oppose God will finally be judged. David himself declared that the LORD was coming to judge the whole earth (1 Chr 16:33). One day every knee will bow before his throne. The reality of the return of Jesus in judgment has become unpopular, yet this story of David's victory over the Philistines anticipates, in some small measure, this future reality, and it serves as a sober reminder that God is the judge of the *all the earth*. One day every knee will bow in submission before his throne (Isa 45:20–25; cf. Phil 2:10–11).

---

8. See Live the Story, Chapter 2, Judah's Place in God's Plan to Include All Nations, pp. 46–48.

9. For a concise yet theologically rich summary of the Antichrist, see Bauckham and Hart, *Hope against Hope*, 110–16.

10. See Live the Story, Chapter 13, Live the Story, Recapturing God's Holiness in the Church, pp. 147–48.

11. Daniel L. Gard, "The Case for Eschatological Continuity," in *Show Them No Mercy: Four Views on God and the Canaanite Genocide*, ed. Stanley N. Gundry (Grand Rapids: Zondervan, 2003), 129.

LISTEN to the Story

¹After David had constructed buildings for himself in the City of David, he prepared a place for the ark of God and pitched a tent for it. ²Then David said, "No one but the Levites may carry the ark of God, because the LORD chose them to carry the ark of the LORD and to minister before him forever."

³David assembled all Israel in Jerusalem to bring up the ark of the LORD to the place he had prepared for it. ⁴He called together the descendants of Aaron and the Levites:

⁵From the descendants of Kohath,
Uriel the leader and 120 relatives;
⁶from the descendants of Merari,
Asaiah the leader and 220 relatives;
⁷from the descendants of Gershon,
Joel the leader and 130 relatives;
⁸from the descendants of Elizaphan,
Shemaiah the leader and 200 relatives;
⁹from the descendants of Hebron,
Eliel the leader and 80 relatives;
¹⁰from the descendants of Uzziel,
Amminadab the leader and 112 relatives.

¹¹Then David summoned Zadok and Abiathar the priests, and Uriel, Asaiah, Joel, Shemaiah, Eliel and Amminadab the Levites. ¹²He said to them, "You are the heads of the Levitical families; you and your fellow Levites are to consecrate yourselves and bring up the ark of the LORD, the God of Israel, to the place I have prepared for it. ¹³It was because you, the Levites, did not bring it up the first time that the LORD our God broke out in anger against us. We did not inquire of him about how to do it in the prescribed way." ¹⁴So the priests and Levites consecrated themselves in

order to bring up the ark of the LORD, the God of Israel. ¹⁵And the Levites carried the ark of God with the poles on their shoulders, as Moses had commanded in accordance with the word of the LORD.

¹⁶David told the leaders of the Levites to appoint their fellow Levites as musicians to make a joyful sound with musical instruments: lyres, harps and cymbals.

¹⁷So the Levites appointed Heman son of Joel; from his relatives, Asaph son of Berekiah; and from their relatives the Merarites, Ethan son of Kushaiah; ¹⁸and with them their relatives next in rank: Zechariah, Jaaziel, Shemiramoth, Jehiel, Unni, Eliab, Benaiah, Maaseiah, Mattithiah, Eliphelehu, Mikneiah, Obed-Edom and Jeiel, the gatekeepers.

¹⁹The musicians Heman, Asaph and Ethan were to sound the bronze cymbals; ²⁰Zechariah, Jaaziel, Shemiramoth, Jehiel, Unni, Eliab, Maaseiah and Benaiah were to play the lyres according to *alamoth*, ²¹and Mattithiah, Eliphelehu, Mikneiah, Obed-Edom, Jeiel and Azaziah were to play the harps, directing according to *sheminith*. ²²Kenaniah the head Levite was in charge of the singing; that was his responsibility because he was skillful at it.

²³Berekiah and Elkanah were to be doorkeepers for the ark. ²⁴Shebaniah, Joshaphat, Nethanel, Amasai, Zechariah, Benaiah and Eliezer the priests were to blow trumpets before the ark of God. Obed-Edom and Jehiah were also to be doorkeepers for the ark.

²⁵So David and the elders of Israel and the commanders of units of a thousand went to bring up the ark of the covenant of the LORD from the house of Obed-Edom, with rejoicing. ²⁶Because God had helped the Levites who were carrying the ark of the covenant of the LORD, seven bulls and seven rams were sacrificed. ²⁷Now David was clothed in a robe of fine linen, as were all the Levites who were carrying the ark, and as were the musicians, and Kenaniah, who was in charge of the singing of the choirs. David also wore a linen ephod. ²⁸So all Israel brought up the ark of the covenant of the LORD with shouts, with the sounding of rams' horns and trumpets, and of cymbals, and the playing of lyres and harps.

²⁹As the ark of the covenant of the LORD was entering the City of David, Michal daughter of Saul watched from a window. And when she saw King David dancing and celebrating, she despised him in her heart.

Listening to the Text in the Story: Psalm 132:1–18

The Chronicler resumes the story of the ark, which is now being transported into Jerusalem after being at the family of Obed-Edom for three months.[1] Psalm 132 describes the king's unswerving commitment to provide a resting place for God (Ps 132:2–5), which is seen in the story in 1 Chronicles 15. In this Song of Ascent, the psalmist depicts the worship of God in Zion as a joyous occasion when his people say: "Let us go to his dwelling place, let us worship at his footstool, saying, 'Arise, LORD, and come to your resting place, you and the ark of your might. May your priests be clothed with your righteousness; may your faithful people sing for joy'" (Ps 132:7–9).[2] This is the only place in the Psalter where the term "ark" is used (Heb. 'aron, Ps 132:8). The joy that comes as the ark finds its resting place in Jerusalem is seen in the story that follows, as David and the sacred assembly bring the ark into its resting place "with shouts, with the sounding of rams' horns and trumpets, and of cymbals, and the playing of lyres and harps" (1 Chr 15:28). Even the king is "dancing and celebrating" on this joyous occasion (v. 29). The arrival of the ark into Jerusalem marks a climactic moment in the life of the kingdom, for it signifies that God, who is enthroned above the cherubim, now resides in Jerusalem.

 EXPLAIN the Story

David Assembles All Israel at Jerusalem to Bring up the Ark (15:1–3)

David's building activity continues with focus on his palaces (1 Chr 15:1; cf. 11:4–9), but his preparation for the ark sets the context for what follows. David pitches a temporary tent, reminiscent of the tent of meeting in Israel's earlier period when God had moved from place to place with his people (15:1; see also 2 Chr 1:3–4; cf. 1 Chr 17:4–6). As David plans for the transportation of the ark, every precaution will be taken to ensure that the tragic event of Uzzah's death will not be repeated (see 1 Chr 13). Only the Levites are allowed to carry the ark, for they alone had been appointed to transport it (15:2; cf. Num 4:4–6, 15; Deut 10:8). All Israel gathers for this joyous event, and attention now turns to the Levitical leaders who are responsible to bring the ark from the house of Obed-Edom into Jerusalem.

---

1. For background information on the ark, see the discussion in Chapter 13 on 1 Chr 13.
2. Psalm 132:8–10 is recalled in Solomon's prayer when the temple is dedicated (cf. 2 Chr 6:41–42).

David Gathers Leaders among the Priests and the Levites (15:4–15)

David assembles the priests and Levites for this sacred task (1 Chr 15:4). This responsibility is assigned to six Levitical leaders from the three main families of Kohath (v. 5), Merari (v. 6), and Gershom (v. 7), with the important family of Kohath placed first. Three additional leaders from the Levites assemble: Elizaphan (v. 8; cf. Num 3:30), Hebron, and Uzziel (1 Chr 15:9–10; cf. Exod 6:18; 1 Chr 23:12, 19–20). The numbers given for the Levites from each family indicates that just over 850 Levites assemble, comprised of singers, musicians, and gatekeepers (15:16–24). This is a community-wide celebration!

In addition to the six Levitical leaders, David summons his two priests, Zadok and Abiathar (v. 11). Zadok comes from a long priestly line. He is named after Aaron's grandson through Eleazar (cf. 6:1–15). Abiathar is a descendant of Aaron, but his line is through Eleazar's brother, Ithamar (24:1–6). These two families represent the priesthood during this period. David instructs them to consecrate themselves and their relatives, as they have been appointed to bring up the ark. The law gave specific instructions about how priests and Levites were to be consecrated, for they were set apart to minister in the most holy place (Exod 28–29; Lev 8). Since the ark was a sacred object, priests and Levites were required to be ritually prepared to move it. David recalls the painful story of Uzzah, when God's holiness was demonstrated vividly in his death, at which time God had "broken out" against him (Heb. *p-r-ts*, 1 Chr 13:11; 15:13). Many years earlier, when God had appeared on Mount Sinai, anyone who touched the mountain would be put to death (Exod 19:12). The priests who came near were to consecrate themselves, lest God "break out" against them (Heb. *p-r-ts*, v. 22). The people were not to "force their way through" to come up to God, lest he "break out" against them (Heb. *p-r-ts*, v. 24). David now recalls that God had "broken out" against them (Heb. *p-r-ts*, 1 Chr 15:13; cf. 13:11), thus every precaution is to be taken before moving the sacred ark.

We noted earlier that only the Levites were permitted to transport the ark (Num 4:4–6; Deut 10:8; cf. 1 Chr 15:12–15; 2 Chr 35:3). The ark had hooks built into it so that poles could be used, and it was covered with solid blue cloth (Exod 25:12–15; Num 4:5–6; cf. 1 Kgs 8:6–8). David makes every effort to ensure that Moses's instructions are correctly followed, and thus the Levites carry the ark with poles on their shoulders "as Moses had commanded in accordance with the word of the LORD" (1 Chr 15:15).

David Appoints Singers, Musicians, and Gatekeepers (15:16–26)

David instructs the Levites to appoint their relatives to sing and play music with harps, lyres, and cymbals so that they might raise sounds of joy (1 Chr 15:16). Singing to the LORD is an important theme that runs through Chronicles. When the verb and the cognate noun are counted together (Heb. *sh-y-r*), there are over *thirty* occurrences in Chronicles![3] Not only are the psalms filled with the exhortation to: "Sing to God, sing in praise of his name, extol him who rides on the clouds; rejoice before him–his name is the LORD" (Ps 68:4; cf. Pss 98:1; 105:2; 149:1), but the Levites will exhort God's people to sing to the LORD (1 Chr 16:9, 23, 42). In fact, they exhort the *whole earth* to sing to the LORD!

An array of musical instruments was used in Israel's worship,[4] and attention will be given in Chronicles to the important role of Levitical musicians who lead Israel in praise and thanksgiving, with their duties assigned by lots (25:1–31). Several Levites are appointed, known for their skill in singing and playing music (15:17–22). Gatekeepers are chosen to have oversight over the ark (vv. 23–24; cf. 26:1–19), and priests are appointed to blow trumpets. The king and the people bring up the ark from the house of Obed-Edom with great "joy" (NIV "rejoicing;" 15:25), another important theme in Chronicles. God is even helping the Levites who are carrying the ark, and sacrifices are offered (v. 26).

The Arrival of the Ark into Jerusalem Is an Occasion for Celebration (15:27–29)

The Chronicler pauses for a moment to give background information about David's clothing, noting that he wore a "robe of fine linen" (1 Chr 15:27). Priests were adorned with priestly garments (Exod 28:4, 31, 34; 29:5; 39:22; Lev 8:7) and kings were also adorned with royal robes (1 Sam 24:5, 11), but fine linen was used to adorn the sacred temple (2 Chr 2:12–14; 3:14), and it was worn by Levitical singers who were set apart for God's service (5:12). Since David is wearing linen robes like the Levites, his clothing identifies him as one among them. Lest there be any doubt, the "linen ephod" David wears (1 Chr 15:27), which was worn exclusively by Israel's priests (Exod 28:1–43; cf. 25:7), identifies him as a priestly king. Since the ephod was made of gold with blue, purple and scarlet yarn and its precious jewels were engraved in

---

3. On the topic of joy, see Live the Story in Chapter 34 on 2 Chr 5, pp. 319–21.
4. See the discussion on 1 Chr 25 in Chapter 25, pp. 242–43.

its shoulder pieces, David must have stood out among the Levites, being beautifully adorned like one of Israel's priests! Psalm 110 describes the king as a priestly king, and the garments David wears thus identify him as a *priestly king* (cf. Ps 110:1–4; Zech 6:11–15).[5]

The procession into Jerusalem resounds with joyful music, "with shouts, with the sounding of rams' horns and trumpets, and of cymbals, and the playing of lyres and harps" (1 Chr 15:28). The jubilant procession as the ark is brought into Jerusalem is contrasted with David's wife, Michal, who despises him when she sees him leaping and celebrating (v. 29; cf. 2 Sam 6:16, 20). Even though Michal loved David, her relationship with him had been fraught with heartache (cf. 1 Sam 17:25; 18:18–30; 2 Sam 3:13–16). Michal views David's actions as shameful, but we learn from 2 Samuel that David responds by telling her why he has celebrated in this way: "It was before the LORD, who chose me rather than your father or anyone from his house when he appointed me ruler over the LORD's people Israel—I will celebrate before the LORD" (6:21). David is shameless in his devotion to the LORD who has chosen him to be ruler of his people. He has good reason to celebrate before his God!

LIVE the Story

Worship of God Is at the Center of the Sacred Assembly

The procession of the ark into Jerusalem marks a climactic moment in the reign of King David. After a failed first attempt that was deadly (1 Chr 13:1–14), this was an occasion for joyful singing and celebrating before the LORD. The ark signified that God was with his people. Solomon will later marvel when he asks the question: "But will God really dwell on earth with humans? The heavens, even the highest heavens, cannot contain you" (2 Chr 6:18). The ark residing in Jerusalem speaks of this profound reality—that God, the creator of the entire universe, the holy one enthroned on high, has indeed come to dwell among his people. The presence of God in Jerusalem means that the kingdom is not a political organization but a kingdom of priests, a *liturgical empire*, as Hahn describes it. He writes further:

> Israel is not primarily a national entity organized for military, political, or economic purposes; in Israel all those ordinary rationales for government

5. On this topic, see Merrill, "Royal Priesthood," 50–61 and William M. Schniedewind, "King and Priest in the Book of Chronicles and the Duality of Qumran Messianism," *JJS* 45 (1994): 71–78.

are to be ordered to the singular overriding reason of giving worship to God. This is what Israel exists for, and this is Israel's mission as God's firstborn status among the nations.[6]

This is why the procession of the ark into Jerusalem is so important and why the Chronicler gives so much attention to it, mentioning the ark *forty-six* times, even though it is entirely absent in the post-exilic books such as Ezra, Nehemiah, Haggai, Zechariah, and Malachi.[7] This is why *singing* praises to the LORD is mentioned so often in Chronicles (over thirty references when the verb and noun are combined)—God's presence among his people is an occasion for joy![8] This is also why the next chapter in Chronicles is all about *worship*, something absent in the Samuel account (cf. 2 Sam 6:12–17). In the next chapter, three psalms are brought together to form a symphony of praise to God. In fact, many of the themes that reverberate throughout Chronicles are found in 1 Chronicles 16, underscoring that *worship* shapes the entire community and it lies at the heart of what it means to be the people of God. This story reminds us yet again that God has set apart his people so that we might worship him.

Worship of God Continues in the Church

It is important to recognize that the Hebrew word translated as "assembly" (Heb. *qahal*, 1 Chr 13:2, 4; cf. the verb, v. 5; 15:3), which has its roots in Israel's early history (cf. Deut 4:10; 9:10), is prominently featured in Chronicles.[9] In this story, the sacred assembly gathers together to bring the ark into Jerusalem, which was a time for praising God in their midst (cf. 1 Chr 16). While it is not readily apparent, this story that depicts the sacred assembly giving praises to God anticipates what we find in the church when God's people join together in praises to God.

It is important to recognize that the Hebrew word used to describe the sacred "assembly" (Heb. *qahal*) is translated in the Septuagint (the Greek translation of the Old Testament) as *ekklesia* (1 Chr 13:2, 4). This is the same Greek word used to describe the church in the New Testament (e.g., Acts 5:11; 8:1, 3; 9:31, etc.). Fee notes that although the Greek term *ekklesia* (which means "assembly") was known in the Greek world for "any gathering

---

6. Hahn, *The Kingdom of God*, 57.
7. See the discussion in ibid., 54–55.
8. On the topic of joy, see Live the Story in Chapter 35, pp. 319–21.
9. Hahn notes that the term "assembly" (Heb. *qahal*) occurs thirty-seven times in Chronicles. For further discussion on this theologically rich topic, see Hahn, *The Kingdom of God*, 56.

of people for a common purpose,"[10] Paul's employment of the term was first and foremost based on its occurrence in the Old Testament. He notes that the Greek term *ekklesia* was a rendering for the Hebrew word *qahal*, which is "consistently used to refer to the *congregation* of Israel and had to do with the 'gathering together' of God's people."[11] The employment of *ekklesia* underscores the continuity between the sacred assembly in the Old Testament and the gathering of believers in the New Testament. The scene of joyful singing and worship that is described in 1 Chronicles 15 as the ark is brought into Jerusalem provides a rich image of what it means to be the people of God—with worship at the center.

This scene is repeated throughout the early church as believers gather together in homes, speaking to one another "with psalms, hymns, and songs from the Spirit" (Eph 5:19). They are to "sing and make music from your heart to the Lord" (v. 19; cf. 1 Cor 14:26). Paul exhorts believers at Colossae to "teach and admonish one another with all wisdom through psalms, hymns, and songs from the Spirit, singing to God with gratitude in your hearts" (Col 3:16).[12] Fee observes that Paul transferred the Psalter's hymnic pattern to Christian hymns so that "devotion previously given exclusively to Yahweh has for the early Christians transferred to Christ as 'Lord'—to the one who came to earth to both redeem and recreate us into the divine image."[13] He notes that "singing lay at the heart of Christian worship from the beginning, and as such, singing is full of assumed Christology."[14] This Christological focus of worship means that hymns in the Psalter that were sung "to" and "about" Yahweh are now sung "to" and "about" Christ. Thus, Christian worship is deeply rooted in Christology.[15] The scene of worship depicted in 1 Chronicles 15 anticipates what will become the reality for believers who gather together, singing hymns and making melodies in their heart.

Fee laments that our understanding of the English word "church" often misses this important connection with the Old Testament. In our contemporary

---

10. Gordon D. Fee, *Jesus the Lord according to Paul the Apostle: A Concise Introduction* (Grand Rapids: Baker Academic, 2018), 10.

11. Ibid.

12. Block has provided a helpful survey of the role of singing and music in the early church, which includes a discussion of two key Pauline texts (Eph 5:18–20; Col 3:15–17); see Daniel I. Block, *For the Glory of God: Recovering a Biblical Theology of Worship* (Grand Rapids: Baker Academic, 2014), 230–34

13. Fee, *Jesus the Lord*, 24.

14. Ibid., 22.

15. Ibid. Notably, when the disciples recognize Jesus as the Son of God, they worship *him* (Matt 14:33; cf. Matt 28:9, 17; Luke 24:52; Jn 9:38); the writer to the Hebrews says that when God brings his firstborn into the world, he says, "Let all God's angels *worship him*" (Heb 1:6).

context, the word "church" often "connotes a building—a meaning that did not exist in Paul's time—rather than a community of believers *gathered together for worship and fellowship*."[16] He observes that our concept of "going to church" is more like going to a sporting event or a function, but Paul's language is meant to encourage us "to 'assemble' as a church, so as to worship God and Christ as well as to be in fellowship with others."[17] The story of God's people celebrating his presence among them in 1 Chronicles 15 provides a vision for what it means to be *the church*, a people who gather together for worship. Deeply embedded in the Chronicler's retelling of Israel's history was the profound sense that God is *with his people*. This reality continues with believers in the New Testament, who celebrate the coming of Immanuel, "God with us." Jesus was not only present with his disciples, walking among them, but he told them: "For where two or three gather in my name, there am I with them" (Matt 18:20). The church is not a building, nor is it identified with any particular location (John 4:20–24), but as God's people gather for worship of the triune God—whether in homes, buildings, or even in prison—they are the *ekklesia*, the sacred assembly of old. We are God's people, his royal priesthood, and thus we are to declare "the praises of him who called you out of darkness into his wonderful light" (1 Pet 2:9). It is not coincidental that this climactic story of the ark's procession into Jerusalem ushers in an extended time of praise to the LORD (1 Chr 16), a subject to which we now turn.

---

16. Fee, *Jesus the Lord*, 10.
17. Ibid.

LISTEN to the Story

¹They brought the ark of God and set it inside the tent that David had pitched for it, and they presented burnt offerings and fellowship offerings before God. ²After David had finished sacrificing the burnt offerings and fellowship offerings, he blessed the people in the name of the LORD. ³Then he gave a loaf of bread, a cake of dates and a cake of raisins to each Israelite man and woman.

⁴He appointed some of the Levites to minister before the ark of the LORD, to extol, thank, and praise the LORD, the God of Israel: ⁵Asaph was the chief, and next to him in rank were Zechariah, then Jaaziel, Shemiramoth, Jehiel, Mattithiah, Eliab, Benaiah, Obed-Edom and Jeiel. They were to play the lyres and harps, Asaph was to sound the cymbals, ⁶and Benaiah and Jahaziel the priests were to blow the trumpets regularly before the ark of the covenant of God.

⁷That day David first appointed Asaph and his associates to give praise to the LORD in this manner:

> ⁸Give praise to the LORD, proclaim his name;
>   make known among the nations what he has done.
> ⁹Sing to him, sing praise to him;
>   tell of all his wonderful acts.
> ¹⁰Glory in his holy name;
>   let the hearts of those who seek the LORD rejoice.
> ¹¹Look to the LORD and his strength;
>   seek his face always.
>
> ¹²Remember the wonders he has done,
>   his miracles, and the judgments he pronounced,

¹³you his servants, the descendants of Israel,
  his chosen ones, the children of Jacob.
¹⁴He is the LORD our God;
  his judgments are in all the earth.

¹⁵He remembers his covenant forever,
  the promise he made, for a thousand generations,
¹⁶the covenant he made with Abraham,
  the oath he swore to Isaac.
¹⁷He confirmed it to Jacob as a decree,
  to Israel as an everlasting covenant:
¹⁸"To you I will give the land of Canaan
  as the portion you will inherit."

¹⁹When they were but few in number,
  few indeed, and strangers in it,
²⁰they wandered from nation to nation,
  from one kingdom to another.
²¹He allowed no one to oppress them;
  for their sake he rebuked kings:
²²"Do not touch my anointed ones;
  do my prophets no harm."

²³Sing to the LORD, all the earth;
  proclaim his salvation day after day.
²⁴Declare his glory among the nations,
  his marvelous deeds among all peoples.

²⁵For great is the LORD and most worthy of praise;
  he is to be feared above all gods.
²⁶For all the gods of the nations are idols,
  but the LORD made the heavens.
²⁷Splendor and majesty are before him;
  strength and joy are in his dwelling place.

²⁸Ascribe to the LORD, all you families of nations,
  ascribe to the LORD glory and strength.

²⁹Ascribe to the LORD the glory due his name;
> bring an offering and come before him.
Worship the LORD in the splendor of his holiness.
> ³⁰Tremble before him, all the earth!
> > The world is firmly established; it cannot be moved.

³¹Let the heavens rejoice, let the earth be glad;
> let them say among the nations, "The LORD reigns!"
³²Let the sea resound, and all that is in it;
> let the fields be jubilant, and everything in them!
³³Let the trees of the forest sing,
> let them sing for joy before the LORD,
> for he comes to judge the earth.

³⁴Give thanks to the LORD, for he is good;
> his love endures forever.
³⁵Cry out, "Save us, God our Savior;
> gather us and deliver us from the nations,
that we may give thanks to your holy name,
> and glory in your praise."
³⁶Praise be to the LORD, the God of Israel,
> from everlasting to everlasting.

Then all the people said "Amen" and "Praise the LORD."

³⁷David left Asaph and his associates before the ark of the covenant of the LORD to minister there regularly, according to each day's requirements. ³⁸He also left Obed-Edom and his sixty-eight associates to minister with them. Obed-Edom son of Jeduthun, and also Hosah, were gatekeepers.

³⁹David left Zadok the priest and his fellow priests before the tabernacle of the LORD at the high place in Gibeon ⁴⁰to present burnt offerings to the LORD on the altar of burnt offering regularly, morning and evening, in accordance with everything written in the Law of the LORD, which he had given Israel. ⁴¹With them were Heman and Jeduthun and the rest of those chosen and designated by name to give thanks to the LORD, "for his love endures forever." ⁴²Heman and Jeduthun were responsible for the sounding of the trumpets and cymbals and for the playing of the

other instruments for sacred song. The sons of Jeduthun were stationed at the gate.

⁴³Then all the people left, each for their own home, and David returned home to bless his family.

Listening to the Text in the Story: Psalms 96:1–13; 105:1–15; 106:1, 47–48

The arrival of the ark into Jerusalem is followed by a time of praise as those gathered remember God's mighty deeds and his faithfulness to his people. In this chapter, three psalms are brought together into one psalm, which is sung under the direction of Levitical singers and musicians, as all Israel joins together with one voice to give thanks and praise to the LORD. Each psalm is signaled by a word of exhortation: "Give praise to the LORD" (1 Chr 16:8), "Sing to the LORD, all the earth" (v. 23), and "Give thanks to the LORD" (v. 34), giving the following three literary units: Psalm 105:1–15 (= 1 Chr 16:8–22), Psalm 96:1–13 (= 1 Chr 16:23–33), and Psalm 106:1, 47–48 (= 1 Chr 16:34–36). The psalm is framed by references to "Asaph and his associates" (vv. 7, 37) and their ministry that takes place continually before the ark (vv. 6–7, 37), thus giving symmetry to the chapter.[1] David was probably responsible for the current arrangement, which was given to Asaph for use on this occasion and for future worship.[2] Praises sung to God consist of Israel's praise (vv. 9–11), international praise (vv. 23–30), and cosmic praise (vv. 31–33).[3] Since God now dwells in Jerusalem, it is entirely fitting that the sacred assembly joins together to sing praises and to give thanks to the LORD.

EXPLAIN the Story

The Ark Is Brought to Jerusalem and All Israel Celebrates (16:1–7)

The Levites bring the ark of the covenant into the tent in Jerusalem, although the tabernacle remains at Gibeon (1 Chr 21:29; 2 Chr 1:3–4). Burnt offerings and fellowship offerings are offered to God (1 Chr 16:1), which were central to Israel's worship (Exod 20:24; Num 10:10; Deut 27:6–7; cf. 1 Chr 16:40; 23:31). David's priestly role is highlighted as he offers sacrifices and blesses

---

1. Boda, *1–2 Chronicles*, 148.
2. Merrill, *1 & 2 Chronicles*, 203.
3. Ralph W. Klein, "Psalms in Chronicles," *Currents in Theology and Mission*, 32:4 (2005): 266.

the people (16:2; cf. 15:27). Burnt offerings were fully burnt on the altar,[4] but the fellowship offering (also known as the "peace offering" [e.g., NASB, ESV]) was shared among the people. The fat portion was offered to God, whereas the remaining portions were eaten by the laity (Lev 7:11–21) and the priest (vv. 32–35). God's people were in a covenant relationship with their God, and their shared meal was a tangible demonstration of their fellowship with God and with each other.[5] At this celebration, David generously provides food so that every person could share in the meal (1 Chr 16:3).

David appoints Levites as ministers before the ark; they are to lead the community in prayer, thanksgiving, and praise to God, with Asaph taking the lead (vv. 4–7). A number of psalms are attributed to Asaph and his sons (Pss 50, 73–83; cf. 2 Chr 29:30), and he is identified as the head musician (1 Chr 16:5; cf. 1 Chr 25:2, 9). Asaph's descendants will continue to have an ongoing role in leading worship in the post-exilic community (cf. Ezra 2:41; Neh 7:44; 11:17; 12:46). As will be seen later, three Levitical families—Asaph, Heman, and Jeduthun—are set apart for singing and playing musical instruments (1 Chr 25:1-8). Their genealogies have already been introduced, recalling that Heman was from the line of Kohath (6:33–38), Asaph was from the line of Gershon (vv. 39–43), and Ethan was from the line of Merari (vv. 44–47).

All Israel Joins Together in Thanksgiving to God (16:8–22)

The psalm begins with a call to worship as the Levites summon the sacred assembly to give thanks to the LORD and to call upon his name (1 Chr 16:8). A series of imperatives underscore the audible component of praise (such as, "give thanks," "proclaim," "make known," "sing," "sing praise," "tell," "glory," and "seek") as the community joins together in worship (vv. 8–9). Worship is at the very center of the Israelite community, for a holy God is enthroned in their midst. Their singing focuses on all that God has done, and they are to tell all of those deeds among the nations (v. 8). In the opening genealogies, the Chronicler located Israel among the nations as part of a "world map" (1:5–23), underscoring that they were called to be a worshiping and witnessing people in the midst of the nations. This is the vision being set forth in the opening verses of this psalm.

The hearts of those who seek the LORD are to "rejoice" (16:10), highlighting another important theme that runs through Chronicles. God's people

---

4. On the function of the burnt offering, see Sklar, *Leviticus*, 87–95 (especially, 94–95).
5. Ibid., 101–107.

rejoice in his goodness (v. 41; cf. 2 Chr 7:10) and in all that he has done for them (cf. 20:27; 29:36).[6] Those who rejoice have set their hearts to *seek* him (Heb. *b-q-sh*), and they are exhorted to "seek his face always" (1 Chr 16:11), which anticipates the well-known verse, "if my people, who are called by my name, will humble themselves and pray and *seek my face* (Heb. *b-q-sh*, 2 Chr 7:14, emphasis added).[7] The call to "remember" stands as an invitation to the returnees to reflect upon their past and to remember all that God has done for them (1 Chr 16:12). Throughout their history, God's people have been exhorted to remember God and his mighty works (cf. Deut 7:18; 8:2, 18; Pss 77:11; 78:35; 105:5).[8] Those gathered in Jerusalem are God's chosen people, and as such, they are the object of his love and election (Deut 4:37; 7:8; 10:15). He has not forgotten his chosen ones (cf. Isa 44:1–2; 45:4; 65:9), which surely includes the returnees living in Jerusalem. They are to remember that God has entered into a covenant with them, and thus they can declare that the LORD is their God (1 Chr 16:14). God had made a covenant with Abraham, Isaac, and Jacob, which he confirmed with Israel (vv. 15–18). The Chronicler has already recalled the genealogies of the patriarchs (cf. ch. 1), and thus the returnees are to see themselves in light of God's former promises, which included the promise of land (Gen 12:1–3; 15:7–21). Even though they were living under Persian rule after the exile, they were to *remember* their history and God's promises, which give them hope for their present circumstances. God had protected his people in the past, even when they were few in number and wandering from place to place (1 Chr 16:19–22). The returnees were to remember God's protective hand upon their ancestors, and he could surely be relied upon to preserve his people now.

The LORD Reigns as King over All the Earth (16:23–33)

The second part of the psalm is introduced with the exhortation: "Sing to the LORD, all the earth" (1 Chr 16:23), another key theme in Chronicles (cf. 15:16). Focus shifts to the declaration of God's glory among the nations. All the earth is summoned to sing praises to the LORD. His salvation is to be proclaimed from day to day. The reason they are to do so is because the LORD is great and "most worthy of praise" (16:25). Even though there were many

---

6. On the topic of joy, see Chapter 34, Live the Story, pp. 319–21.

7. See the discussion in Chapter 36 on 2 Chr 7:14, pp. 339–41.

8. On the important role of remembering in Israel's traditions (and in preaching), see Jeffrey D. Arthurs, *Preaching as Reminding: Stirring Memory in an Age of Forgetfulness* (Downers Grove, IL: IVP Academic, 2017).

gods in the ancient world, the LORD was to be feared *above* all gods, for the gods of the nations were mere idols (v. 26). The Old Testament reverberates with the teaching that the gods of the nations are simply idols, the work of man's hands (2 Chr 32:19; cf. Lev 19:4; Isa 2:8, 20; 31:7; Hab 2:18).

In contrast to man-made idols, the LORD alone is to be praised as creator (1 Chr 16:26; see also Gen 2:4; Isa 45:5–7, 18–19). Israel's worship is a powerful testimony to the nations that the LORD alone is God. The psalm exhorts God's people to reflect upon their God, who dwells in their midst: "Splendor and majesty are before him; strength and joy are in his dwelling place" (1 Ch 16:27). The description of God in the psalm, which is echoed throughout the Psalter, invites God's people to lift up their eyes and behold God's glorious dwelling place, where strength and joy are found (v. 27; cf. Pss 68:35; 104:1; 145:5).

The families of the nations are among those who are invited to worship the LORD (1 Chr 16:28–29), recalling God's promise to Abraham that all the families of the earth would be blessed through his seed (Gen 12:3). The nations are invited to ascribe to the LORD the glory due to his name and to bring an offering before him in worship (1 Chr 16:29). This theme is picked up in the temple-building narrative, which is framed by two declarations of praise offered by non-Israelites (2 Chr 2:11–12; 9:8). Foreign nations will even come bearing gifts into Jerusalem (9:9–10, 13–14, 24).[9] With this cosmic vision in view, *the whole earth* is exhorted to tremble before God in awe of his mighty presence (1 Chr 16:30; cf. Ps 114:7). The entire creation is to resound with praise among the nations, declaring, "The LORD reigns!" (1 Chr 16:31; Exod 15:18). Even the trees will sing for joy to the LORD (1 Chr 16:32–33)! No part of God's creation is outside of his domain. As Klein notes, "The Chronicler invites the whole tripartite cosmos—heaven, earth, sea—to join in to celebrate Yahweh's kingdom."[10] In this psalm, the entire cosmos is exhorted to praise the LORD and to acknowledge his reign over all (cf. Ps 148:1–14).

Prayer to God for Deliverance from the Nations (16:34–36)

The third section of the psalm is introduced with the exhortation: "Give thanks to the LORD" (1 Chr 16:34), recalling the opening of the psalm (v. 8). God is to be thanked for his goodness and his covenant loyalty (v. 34; cf. Ps 106:1). Regardless of what circumstances Israel might find themselves in,

---

9. See Live the Story in Chapter 38, pp. 359–60.
10. Klein, "Psalms in Chronicles," 268.

God's enduring covenant-love (Heb. *hesed*) remains forever. God's people call out to him, saying: "Save us, God our Savior; gather us and deliver us from the nations" (1 Chr 16:35; cf. Ps 106:47). Salvation belonged to God alone and, in this psalm, God is identified as Israel's Savior (1 Chr 16:35; Ps 65:5; 79:9; 85:4; cf. Isa 43:4, 11; 45:17). Many times throughout Israel's history, God has saved his people from their enemies (Exod 14:30; Num 10:9; Deut 20:4; 33:29; 1 Chr 18:6, 13; 2 Chr 20:9; 32:22). God's people pray, therefore, that he might deliver them from the nations, and this is surely something that resonated with those living in Jerusalem under Persian rule. Their salvation would result in thanks being offered to God's holy name (1 Chr 16:35). The psalm invites the returnees to give thanks to God even before the battle has been won (cf. 2 Chr 20:20–22), and it resounds with the hope that their praise will extend to the nations. The psalm concludes with Israel blessing the LORD and the people respond with a resounding "Amen" and "Praise the LORD" (1 Chr 16:36). God is to be praised in every generation, from everlasting to everlasting.

The Priests and Levites Are Assigned Duties (16:37–43)

David leaves Asaph and his fellow Levites to serve before the ark (1 Chr 16:37). The family of Obed-Edom had taken care of the ark for three months (cf. 13:14), and this extended family is given the responsibility to take care of it in Jerusalem, which includes the two gatekeepers, Obed-Edom and Hosah (16:38). Zadok the priest and his relatives are to remain at Gibeon where the tabernacle is located (v. 39; cf. 2 Chr 1:3). They are to offer burnt offerings on the altar morning and evening, according to God's law (1 Chr 16:40). Sacrifices will continue at Gibeon, but in the near future, they will be offered in the temple in Jerusalem (22:1; 2 Chr 7:1–7). Heman and Jeduthun, along with other singers and musicians, are chosen to give thanks to God (cf. 1 Chr 25:1–31). Their joyful worship is sung aloud, accompanied with trumpets and cymbals. After this time of celebration, the people return to their homes, and David returns to his house and blesses his family (16:43).

LIVE the Story

Worship of God Is Rooted in Scripture

The collection of psalms sung by God's people as they bring the ark into Jerusalem underscores the centrality of worship for the Israelite community. This extended psalm reminds us that worship of God is rooted in God's revelation of his character and saving actions on behalf of his people. In his book *Knowledge of the Holy*, A.W. Tozer underscores how important it is for God's people to have knowledge of who God is. He notes in the introduction that we do the "greatest service to the next generation of Christians by passing on to them undimmed and undiminished that noble concept of God which we received from our Hebrew and Christian fathers of generations past."[11] This is precisely what we see in this psalm of thanksgiving. In staccato-like fashion, it rehearses one reason after another from Israel's history for why God is worthy of all praise and glory. There is even the expectation that as the nations hear about the character of the LORD and all that he has done, they, too, will join Israel in praise of the LORD God.

In our contemporary context, there is an implicit word of caution embedded in this psalm. In a day of increasing biblical illiteracy, the stories of God's mighty acts in the Old Testament are not so familiar to us. While worship of God continues in the church, it can easily lead to praise songs that are not grounded in the Scriptures, but rather, focus can be on catchy lyrics or melodies that are more about entertainment than worship. Block has discussed contemporary worship in his book *For the Glory of God*, noting that too often choices governing worship songs are based on what people enjoy singing, rather than the content of the words that are sung. His section on contemporary worship is thought-provoking and challenging.[12] His critique is worth careful consideration by church leaders and lay folk alike, especially when one considers the centrality of the Scriptures in Israel's worship.[13]

As we reflect upon the psalm sung by the Levites, it is rich in theology. It is deeply rooted in the Scriptures. And it is sung by Levites who were trained in the Torah. The Levites knew their history. They could rehearse God's character and his mighty deeds because they had studied the Scriptures. While contemporary melodies and styles of worship can and should be employed in our worship, this psalm speaks powerfully to the need for worship rooted in Scripture. All our worship should be God-focused rather than self-focused. Block wisely cautions us to evaluate carefully the words we are singing to ensure that they are theologically rich and God-centered.

---

11. A. W. Tozer, *Knowledge of the Holy* (New York: Harper One, 1961), 4.

12. Block, *For the Glory of God*, 236. The section on contemporary worship is under the heading, "The Importance of Song in Worship Today," 236–245.

13. Ibid. Block also draws attention to the fact that the term "worship" is often equated with praise music, but the term is broader and includes proclamation; thus he argues that Christ-centered worship is *Word* driven (241). He notes further that Acts 2:42 suggest a broader concept of worship that includes instruction, fellowship, breaking of bread, and prayer—noting that nothing is said of *music* (241).

Worship Leaders Trained in Torah

David appoints Levites "to minister before the ark of the LORD, to extol, thank, and praise the LORD" (1 Chr 16:4; cf. 23:5–6). It is important to recognize that Levitical worship leaders were not only skilled musicians (cf. ch. 25), but they were also well-educated in the Torah (cf. Deut 31:9–13; 33:10). Later we learn that Jehoshaphat appoints Levites to teach the law to all Israel (2 Chr 17:7–9). Ezra is an example of a Levite who was skilled in the law of Moses. He had set his heart to study the law, to practice it, and to teach it in Israel (Ezra 7:6, 10; cf. 8:16; Neh 8:7–9, 12). The Levites also received the tithe, which enabled them to devote themselves to the study of the Scriptures.[14] Levites were worship leaders, musicians, and composers. Asaph and his sons wrote several psalms (Pss 50; 73–83; cf. 2 Chr 29:30). Even a cursory reading of these psalms underscores that they are theologically rich. What this means is that the Levitical families that led worship were not only skilled musicians, but they were also "seminary-trained" worship leaders, to use a modern-day analogy. Block laments that worship leaders today are often chosen for their musical ability with minimal emphasis on their theological background: "In our day the same distortions extend to the way we recruit staff. Ministers of music are hired for their musical skill, achievements, creativity, or enthusiasm on stage, without sufficient concern for their knowledge of Scripture, their orthodoxy, or their theology of worship."[15] The depth of theology seen in the psalms (and in this chapter) reminds us of this rich theological heritage and the need for theologically-trained worship leaders. It is surely a sacred task and high calling that ought to give us pause as we pay careful attention to what we sing, so that our words might be worthy of the God we seek to honor and praise.[16]

---

14. See Chapter 60, Live the Story, Supporting Our Modern-Day Levites, p. 520–21.

15. Block, *For the Glory of God*, 236.

16. On the central role of musicians and oral worship from the time of David onward, see the discussion in Chapter 25 on 1 Chr 25, pp. 244–45, and Chapter 34 on 2 Chr 5, Live the Story, pp. 319–21.

LISTEN to the Story

¹After David was settled in his palace, he said to Nathan the prophet, "Here I am, living in a house of cedar, while the ark of the covenant of the LORD is under a tent."

²Nathan replied to David, "Whatever you have in mind, do it, for God is with you."

³But that night the word of God came to Nathan, saying:

⁴"Go and tell my servant David, 'This is what the LORD says: You are not the one to build me a house to dwell in. ⁵I have not dwelt in a house from the day I brought Israel up out of Egypt to this day. I have moved from one tent site to another, from one dwelling place to another. ⁶Wherever I have moved with all the Israelites, did I ever say to any of their leaders whom I commanded to shepherd my people, "Why have you not built me a house of cedar?"'

⁷"Now then, tell my servant David, 'This is what the LORD Almighty says: I took you from the pasture, from tending the flock, and appointed you ruler over my people Israel. ⁸I have been with you wherever you have gone, and I have cut off all your enemies from before you. Now I will make your name like the names of the greatest men on earth. ⁹And I will provide a place for my people Israel and will plant them so that they can have a home of their own and no longer be disturbed. Wicked people will not oppress them anymore, as they did at the beginning ¹⁰and have done ever since the time I appointed leaders over my people Israel. I will also subdue all your enemies.

"'I declare to you that the LORD will build a house for you: ¹¹When your days are over and you go to be with your ancestors, I will raise up your offspring to succeed you, one of your own sons, and I will establish his kingdom. ¹²He is the one who will build a house for me, and I will establish his throne forever. ¹³I will be his father, and he will be my son. I will never take my love away from him, as I took it away from your predecessor. ¹⁴I will set him over my house and my kingdom forever; his throne will be established forever.'"

¹⁵Nathan reported to David all the words of this entire revelation.

¹⁶Then King David went in and sat before the Lord, and he said:

"Who am I, Lord God, and what is my family, that you have brought me this far? ¹⁷And as if this were not enough in your sight, my God, you have spoken about the future of the house of your servant. You, Lord God, have looked on me as though I were the most exalted of men.

¹⁸"What more can David say to you for honoring your servant? For you know your servant, ¹⁹Lord. For the sake of your servant and according to your will, you have done this great thing and made known all these great promises.

²⁰"There is no one like you, Lord, and there is no God but you, as we have heard with our own ears. ²¹And who is like your people Israel—the one nation on earth whose God went out to redeem a people for himself, and to make a name for yourself, and to perform great and awesome wonders by driving out nations from before your people, whom you redeemed from Egypt? ²²You made your people Israel your very own forever, and you, Lord, have become their God.

²³"And now, Lord, let the promise you have made concerning your servant and his house be established forever. Do as you promised, ²⁴so that it will be established and that your name will be great forever. Then people will say, 'The Lord Almighty, the God over Israel, is Israel's God!' And the house of your servant David will be established before you.

²⁵"You, my God, have revealed to your servant that you will build a house for him. So your servant has found courage to pray to you. ²⁶You, Lord, are God! You have promised these good things

to your servant. [27]Now you have been pleased to bless the house of your servant, that it may continue forever in your sight; for you, LORD, have blessed it, and it will be blessed forever."

Listening to the Text in the Story: Psalms 2; 89

After this wonderful time of praise to the LORD (1 Chr 16), the story of King David comes to a climax when God makes promises to him that will have far-reaching implications for the entire canon of Scripture. David is God's chosen king from the line of Judah in fulfillment of God's promises to Abraham (Gen 17:6, 16; 49:8–10; cf. Ruth 4:18–22). Special attention has already been given to the tribe of Judah in the opening genealogies (1 Chr 2:3–4:23), and most importantly, David was shown to be a direct descendant of Judah through Perez. This underscores the central role of David in the plan of God that began in Genesis, and his kingship may even hearken back to the creation story when God created human beings in his image to rule over his creation (Gen 1:26–28). But the promises God makes to David at this key moment in the story reveal an *even greater plan* that concerns David's *son* and his everlasting rule over the kingdom of God.

God promises David that one of his sons will rule over God's everlasting kingdom (1 Chr 17:11–14). God even promises that he will be a *father* to David's son, and David's son will be *God's son* (v. 13). In the ancient world, kings used familial terms when describing their relationship to the gods, thereby expressing the king's intimacy and dependency on the god as father.[1] Psalm 2 describes the installation of the Davidic king, at which time God makes this pronouncement: "You are my son; today I have become your father" (v. 7). The king ruling as God's son will have worldwide dominion, for his rule will extend to the ends of the earth and nations will bow down before him (vv. 8–12; cf. Ps 72:8–11).[2] This psalm not only provides the background for the promises God makes to David concerning his son (1 Chr 17:13), but it anticipates the reign of Solomon, when the borders of the kingdom expand and foreign dignitaries bring their gifts from afar.[3]

---

1. See Henri Frankfort, *Kingship and the Gods: A Study of Ancient Near Eastern Religion as the Integration of Society & Nature* (Chicago: University of Chicago Press, 1962), 295–312.

2. On the divine status of the king implied in this psalm and in other Davidic texts, see Markus Zehnder, "The Question of the 'Divine Status' of the Davidic Messiah," *BBR* 30:4 (2002): 485–514.

3. See Live the Story in Chapter 38, pp. 359–60.

Another psalm that is important to keep in mind is Psalm 89. After praising God for his covenant-loyalty, the psalmist recalls God's covenant with David: "You said, 'I have made a covenant with my chosen one, I have sworn to David my servant, "I will establish your line forever and make your throne firm through all generations"'" (vv. 3–4). As with Psalm 2, the psalmist notes that the Davidic king will say to God: "You are my Father, my God, the Rock my Savior" (v. 26). God promises to appoint the Davidic king as God's firstborn, "the most exalted of the kings of the earth" (v. 27), and he promises to maintain his covenant-love with him forever (v. 28), something that David recounts in this chapter (1 Chr 17:13). The Davidic covenant thus provides the contours for the story of the kings that is traced in Chronicles, but God's promises to David extend far beyond the period of kings, since they anticipate the reign of the Messiah (see Live the Story below).

 EXPLAIN the Story

Nathan Tells David That He Will Not Build the Temple (17:1–6)

With the ark now in Jerusalem, David has settled in his own palace (1 Chr 17:1). The "rest" mentioned in Samuel has been omitted (cf. 2 Sam 7:1), since it will not be fully realized until Solomon's reign (1 Chr 22:9) and only after David's military victories (v. 18; 23:25). The story initially focuses on David's conversation with the prophet Nathan as he reflects upon his recently built cedar palace, which far exceeds the temporary tent he has pitched for the ark. Nathan affirms David's intention to build a house for God, and he assures him that God is with him (17:2). But God's word comes to Nathan, revealing to him that David is not the one to build a house for God (v. 4).[4] Using a wordplay on a familiar Hebrew word that can have different meanings, Nathan tells David that he is not to build a "house" for God (Heb. *bayit*, meaning "temple," v. 4). Instead, as the prophet will make known shortly, God intends to build a "house" for David (Heb. *bayit*, meaning "dynasty," v. 10). Nathan reminds David that God had not dwelt in a permanent house from Israel's earliest days, nor had he requested any leaders to build him a temple; but instead he had moved from one dwelling place to another (vv. 5–6; cf. Num 9:15–23; 10:11–12). Reference to Israel's leaders recalls the period of the Judges and suggests that this "new royal phase is seen as the answer to the

---

4. David will later comment that the reason he was not to build the house was because he had shed much blood and had been a man of war (1 Chr 22:8; 28:3); see the discussion on 1 Chr 28:3 in Chapter 28, pp. 268–69.

oppression faced by Israel" during this period.[5] It had been an unstable period when judges had ruled, but hope for God's people is on the horizon now that David has become king.

God Makes Promises to David (17:7–10a)

Through the prophet Nathan, God reminds David that he had been taken from the pasture tending sheep to be leader of Israel, something firmly etched in David's own story (1 Sam 16:11–12; 2 Sam 6:21; 1 Chr 28:4) and in Israel's memory (11:1–2; Ps 78:70–71). The royal shepherd motif is at home in the ancient Near East, yet it is employed here to highlight David's humble beginnings; it serves as a reminder of the unexpected nature of the call of God. God's choice of David was not based on ancient laws of primogeniture (1 Sam 16; 1 Chr 2:15), nor was it based on outward appearances (1 Sam 16:7); David was chosen according to God's sovereign plan. Other ancient texts highlight a king's divine election while a youth, and such humble beginnings served as proof of the legitimacy of the king.[6] David will never forget his early years and God's call upon his life, for he is first and foremost God's servant.

God has been with David wherever he has gone (1 Chr 17:8), reminiscent of God's promise to the patriarchs (Gen 26:3; 28:15; 31:3–5) and his assurance given to other leaders, such as Moses (Exod 3:12), Joshua (Josh 1:5), and Gideon (Judg 6:12–13, 16). That God had been with David wherever he had gone underscores God's loyal and unswerving commitment to him, even during the difficult years when he had fled from Saul (cf. 1 Chr 12:18, 22). There is no place too far from God's abiding presence, as David himself acknowledges. Even if he were to ascend to heaven or dwell in the remotest part of the sea, God was still with him (Ps 139:1–12). God had been with David, cutting off all his enemies from before him (1 Chr 17:8; cf. 11:4–9), and his upcoming victories over his enemies serve as a testimony to God's abiding presence (chs. 18–20), as will be the case with other kings (2 Chr 13:8–12; 14:9–15; 20:1–30, etc.). God promises David that his name will become great (1 Chr 17:8; cf. Gen 12:2), yet even though the king is given this great honor, David's life is devoted to praising God's name (1 Chr 16:8–36; 29:10–16). He will never forget that God's name is to be exalted, not his own.

God promises to provide a place for his people and to plant them so that they would no longer be disturbed and oppressed (1 Chr 17:9). The language of "planting" (Heb. *n-t-ʿ*) not only recalls God's planting of his people in the

---

5. Boda, *1–2 Chronicles*, 155.

6. Gary N. Knoppers, *1 Chronicles 10–29: A New Translation with Introduction and Commentary*, Anchor Yale Bible (New Haven: Yale University Press), 668.

land of Israel (Ps 80:9, 14–16; Isa 5:7; Jer 2:21; 11:17), but also the promise of restoration, when God's people will once again be planted in the land after being uprooted in the exile (1:10; 24:6; 31:28; Ezek 36:36; Amos 9:15). The promise of peace and security is bound up with God's promise to "subdue" David's enemies (Heb. *k-n-ʿ*, 1 Chr 17:10), which recalls Israel's earlier period when their enemies had been subjugated (Deut 9:3; Judg 3:30; 4:23; 8:28, etc.), but it also anticipates David's forthcoming victories (1 Chr 18:1; 20:4). Although a different verb is used, the subjugation of Israel's enemies hearkens back to the creation mandate given to humanity (Heb. *k-b-sh*, Gen 1:28), which was partially realized (Num 32:22, 29; Josh 18:1), but it, too, anticipates David's victories (1 Chr 22:18). There is the expectation, indeed, that the rule of the Davidic king will extend to the ends of the earth (Ps 72:8–11; Zech 9:9–10), something hinted at during Solomon's reign (2 Chr 9:1, 22–24, 26).

God's Promises to David Concerning His "House" (17:10b–15)

The promises now shift to focus on David's dynasty (1 Chr 17:10). David had wanted to build a temple ("house") for God, but God promises that he will build a dynasty ("house") for David (v. 10). The temporal clause in 17:11 ("When your days are over and you go to be with your ancestors") indicates that the promises given in the next section concern a *future* son of David. God promises to raise up David's descendant, literally, his "seed" (Heb. *zeraʿ*), who will be one of his own sons (v. 11; cf. 3:10–17). Emphasis on David's "seed" (Heb. *zeraʿ*, 17:11; cf. Ps 89:4, 29, 36, etc.) is reminiscent of God's promise concerning Abraham's "seed" (Heb. *zeraʿ*, Gen 12:7; 13:15, 16; 15:5, 18, etc.), and it underscores why genealogies are important in both Genesis and Chronicles, since God's promises will be realized through a biological descendant (cf. Matt 1:1; Acts 13:23).

God promises that David's son will build the temple (1 Chr 17:12), a promise that will be realized with Solomon, the king chosen for this task (22:9–11; 28:5–6; 2 Chr 2:4, 12). The temple-building narrative is thus central to the reign of Solomon (chs. 2–7). God promises to establish the throne of David's son forever (1 Chr 17:12). Although Solomon will rule in place of his father, he is required to obey God's laws if he is to rule on God's everlasting throne (22:9–13; 28:5–7; 2 Chr 7:17–18), something that will be his undoing (cf. 1 Kg 11).

God promises David that he will be a father to David's son, and his son will be identified as God's son (1 Chr 17:13; 28:6). This is another theologically rich promise, hearkening back to Adam (Gen 1:26–28; cf. Gen 5:3), whose royal status as "son of God" is already suggested in the creation story when

God created humanity in his image (cf. Luke 3:38).[7] Since the Chronicler begins the story of kingship with Adam, this hints that the creation story is being taken up by the Davidic king, who is appointed as God's "son" to rule over God's everlasting kingdom (cf. Pss 2:6–7; 89:26).[8] Accordingly, human beings were originally given the royal task of "ruling" over the creation (Heb. r-d-h, Gen 1:28; Ps 8:6), but this is taken up with Israel's kings (1 Kgs 4:24; Ps 72:8), echoed in the priestly king of Melchizedek (cf. Heb. r-d-h, Ps 110:2, 4).[9]

God promises David that he will not take his "lovingkindness" (Heb. hesed; NIV "love") away from him as he had done to Saul (1 Chr 17:13). God's covenant-loyalty is the hallmark of his character (Exod 34:6–7; Num 14:18–19; 2 Chr 6:14; Neh 1:5; 9:17, 32, etc.).[10] Throughout Chronicles, God's people praise God for his goodness and covenant-love with the exhortation: "Give thanks to the LORD, for he is good; his love endures forever" (1 Chr 16:34; see also v. 41; 2 Chr 5:13; 7:3, 6; 20:21). Solomon will appeal to God's covenant-love (Heb. hesed) when he prays: "LORD God, do not reject your anointed one. Remember the great love promised to David your servant" (6:42, emphasis added). God's covenant with David is rehearsed in Psalm 89, and it is not surprising to find again that God's lovingkindness (Heb. hesed) is mentioned throughout the psalm (89:1, 2, 14, 24, 28, 33, 49). God's promise of his hesed to David is appealed to at the end of the psalm, with the hope that God would fulfill what he has promised (v. 49).

God makes the following promise concerning David's son: "I will set him over my house and my kingdom forever; his throne will be established forever" (1 Chr 17:14; cf. 2 Sam 7:13). In Chronicles, the Davidic kingdom is identified as God's kingdom, not David's (1 Chr 28:5; 29:23; 2 Chr 13:8). Williamson notes that this crucial shift to the kingdom of the LORD "introduces a further characteristic thought. God is the real king of Israel, and the

---

7. On Adam's royal status, see Catherine L. McDowell, *The Image of God in the Garden of Eden: The Creation of Humankind in Genesis 2:5–3:24 in Light of* mīs pî pīt pî *and* wpt-r *Rituals of Mesopotamia and Ancient Egypt* (Winona Lake, IN: Eisenbrauns, 2015), 136–42.

8. For a list of texts, see Merrill's Excursus 5: "David and Royal Sonship" (*1 & 2 Chronicles*, 254–56).

9. This promise concerning David's son finds its ultimate fulfillment in Jesus, who is God's Son ruling on his everlasting throne (Heb 1:1–14; 2:6–8), but Jesus is also the great high priest according to the order of Melchizedek, who was himself a priestly king (Heb 5:5–6; 7:17; cf. Ps 110:4). See Live the Story in Chapter 6, pp. 85–87.

10. The term *hesed*, translated by a variety of terms, such as "covenant loyalty, faithfulness, steadfastness love," occurs approximately 250 times in the Old Testament. God reveals that he is *abounding* in covenant-love (Exod 34:6; Num 14:18; cf. Deut 7:9, 12); his people are to praise him because his *hesed* endures forever (Ps 136). During Israel's darkest days, it is God's *hesed* that preserves his people, even when they have failed miserably (Exod 34:6-7; Num 14:18-19; Neh 9:17; Lam 3:22, 32). When circumstances look less hopeful, God's people can rely on his unfailing *hesed*.

kingdom is his. Consequently, the only legitimate kings are those whom he has confirmed and chosen."[11] God's people have sung praises to the Lord who *reigns* (1 Chr 16:31), but God is now revealing his sovereign plan that David's son is to rule over his kingdom. David recognizes this profound reality later, when he affirms that God has chosen his son Solomon "to sit on the throne of the kingdom of the Lord over Israel" (28:5; cf. 29:23). Remarkably, God is promising to place *his* kingdom into the hands of David's son (cf. 2 Chr 13:8)! God's throne and kingdom will last *forever*, a term occurring eight times in the chapter (1 Chr 17:12, 14, 22, 23, 24, 27; cf. Dan 2:44; 7:13–14). Words collapse before the enormity of what is being promised. No wonder David's response as he sits dumbfounded before the Lord is simply: "Who am I?"

David Responds to God's Promises in Praise and with Gratitude (17:16–27)

God's lavish and undeserved promises made to David cause the king to lift his voice in praise and worship. Upon hearing these promises, we read that David "went in and sat before the Lord" (1 Chr 17:16). This is an intimate moment as David sits before his God. There are no public prayers. Nathan is no longer with the king. Instead, we are drawn into David's intimate relationship with the Lord, as he reflects upon God's call on his life. David is fully known by his God and in his prayer we gain a glimpse into the heart of the king.

While the exact location is not given, since David sits "before the Lord," he appears to be sitting in God's presence, possibly before the ark (17:16; cf. 23:13, 31; 29:22; 2 Chr 1:6). As he sits before his God, he recognizes that he is unworthy of the honor God has bestowed upon him. Like others who have been called by God, David poses the question in utter amazement: "Who am I, Lord God, and what is my family, that you have brought me this far?" (1 Chr 17:16; cf. Exod 3:11; 1 Chr 29:14). David has been protected by God through many difficult years when he was fleeing from Saul, yet God had been his help (cf. ch. 12). David recognizes that God's promise concerning his house concerns the *future*. The full realization of the promise will not come to pass until another one thousand years with the arrival of the Messiah, the Son of David, who will rule over God's everlasting kingdom. This kind of honor might perhaps be shown to a man of high standing who was held in high esteem, yet David, an insignificant shepherd and the youngest among his brothers, is mindful that he is unworthy (17:18). He is simply God's servant (Heb. *'ebed*), a term used throughout this chapter that underscores David's

---

11. Williamson, *1 and 2 Chronicles*, 136.

humble posture before his God (vv. 17, 18, 19, 23, 24, 25, 26). God has made known all these great promises according to his will and for the sake of his servant. David sits in awe of his God.

As the king reflects on all that God has done, he bursts forth with praises, acknowledging: "There is no one like you, LORD, and there is no God but you, as we have heard with our own ears" (1 Chr 17:20). God's people had sung that the LORD was to be feared above all gods and that the gods of the nations were mere idols (16:25–26). These are the words that ruminate in the king's heart as he declares, "There is no one like you, LORD." This is the testimony of God's people throughout the ages, who witness God's mighty acts and his salvation (Deut 4:33–35, 39; Isa 45:5, 21; 64:3–4; Mic 7:18). The king meditates on all that God has done. He remembers the mighty Exodus redemption that was indelibly etched in Israel's history, when God performed signs and wonders in Egypt and made known the greatness of his name (1 Chr 17:21). David is amazed that God has called Israel to be his *own people*, and that "you, LORD, have become their God" (v. 22; cf. Exod 6:7; 20:2). The Chronicler has spent significant time tracing the descendants of Israel, underscoring that even in the post-exilic period, God's calling of his people Israel is irrevocable (1 Chr 2–8; 9:2–3). Even after the division, the northern tribes are not entirely lost, for God's plan includes all Israel (2 Chr 30:1–12, 18, 25; 34:9). David thus affirms that God has made his people Israel his own *forever* (1 Chr 17:22).

David now prays that God's words spoken might be established forever (v. 23), anticipating Solomon's prayer (2 Chr 1:9; 6:17). He asks God to act so that his name might be magnified as the people declare: "The LORD Almighty, the God over Israel, is Israel's God!" (1 Chr 17:24). David has found courage to pray, for he recognizes that God has revealed to him that his house will be built (v. 25). This kind of revelation comes from God alone (Deut 29:29), not unlike what prophets receive (1 Sam 3:7; 9:15; cf. Acts 2:30–31). David's prayer concludes with the resounding affirmation: "You, LORD, are God!" (1 Chr 17:26), and this reality gives him assurance that what God has promised will come to pass. God's blessing upon David and his house will continue forever (v. 27; cf. Num 23:19–20)!

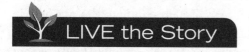 LIVE the Story

Jesus Is the Promised Son and Eternal King

God makes unconditional promises to David that his son will rule over God's everlasting kingdom and that his son will be *God's Son*. This is the story that is taken up in the Southern Kingdom with the succession of kings from David's line (cf. 1 Chr 3:1–16). Even though the promises are given unconditionally to David, the son who is to rule over God's everlasting kingdom is required to obey God's laws (1 Kgs 3:14; 6:11–12; 1 Chr 22:11–13; 28:7; 2 Chr 7:17; Ps 89:30–37). Solomon is the son of David who builds the temple (2 Chr 1:9; 6:10, 15), but he is not the recipient of God's everlasting throne and kingdom. On the contrary, his idolatry will ultimately result in the kingdom being torn away from his son, although for the sake of David it will not be torn away *fully* (1 Kgs 11:11–13, 31–36; 2 Chr 10:15). While there are a number of godly kings in the line of David, kings like Asa, Jehoshaphat, Hezekiah, and Josiah, the reality is that every king fails in some way.[12] Kingship finally comes to an end in 586 BC, yet the prophetic hope that God will one day raise up a righteous Davidic king remains a sure hope (Isa 9:6–7; Jer 23:5–6; 33:14–26; Mic 5:1–5, etc.).

The New Testament resounds with the good news that Jesus is the promised son of David, born in Bethlehem according to God's promises of old (Matt 1:1–17; 2:1–12; Luke 1:26–38; 2:1–20; cf. Rom 1:1–3). The angel thus reveals to Mary concerning her son: "He will be great and will be called the Son of the Most High. The Lord God will give him the throne of his father David, and he will reign over Jacob's descendants forever; his kingdom will never end" (Luke 1:32–33). Jesus begins his public ministry with the declaration that the kingdom of heaven has arrived (Matt 3:2), and at his baptism, a voice from heaven declares that he is God's beloved Son (Matt 3:16–17; Mark 1:10–11; cf. Ps 2:7). Many more texts could be cited that confirm Jesus's identity as the son of David and the eternal Son of God,[13] which would surely include his entrance into Jerusalem on a donkey, when he is hailed "Son of David" (Matt 21:1–11; Mark 11:1–11; cf. Zech 9:9–10) as the crowd shouts: "Blessed is the coming kingdom of our father David!" (Mark 11:10).

Yet the texts noted above would be incomplete without drawing attention to another promise given to David that Jesus marvelously (and unexpectedly) fulfills. God promises to "raise up" David's offspring and establish his everlasting kingdom (1 Chr 17:11; cf. 2 Chr 6:10). The Hebrew root "to stand, arise" (Heb. *q-w-m*) is used here in the causative stem: *God will cause* David's descendant to arise. While not readily apparent, the resurrection of Jesus lies at the center of this promise when read in light of the New Testament.

The book of Acts testifies that Jesus is the risen Lord. In Peter's sermon on

---

12. See Live the Story in Chapter 65, pp. 569–71.

13. For a concise yet theologically rich presentation of key Pauline texts, see Fee, *Jesus the Lord*, 93–116.

the day of Pentecost, he proclaims that even though Jesus had been nailed to a cross and put to death, God "raised him from the dead" (Acts 2:24). Peter uses the Greek verb "to raise up, resurrect" (Greek, *anistemi*), the same verb used in the Septuagint (the Greek translation of the Old Testament) in the promise that God would "raise up" David's son (Greek, *anistemi*, 1 Chr 17:11). This means that when interpreted in light of the New Testament, God's promise to "raise up" David's son anticipates the resurrection of Jesus.[14] Citing Psalm 16:8–11 (when David had proclaimed that God would not allow his holy one to undergo decay), Peter reminds his audience that David died and was buried, yet he was a prophet, for he knew that "God had promised him on oath that he would place one of his descendants on his throne" (Acts 2:30). Jesus is the promised son of David, born in Bethlehem to rule over his people (Matt 2:5–6), but his *resurrection* vindicates him as the righteous son of David whom God promised to raise up (cf. Rom 1:3–4)!

The apostle Paul in his sermon also refers back to David, proclaiming: "From this man's descendants God has brought to Israel the Savior Jesus, as he promised" (Act 13:23). As with Peter, Paul rehearses all that happened to Jesus, including his death on a cross and his burial (vv. 28–29), yet he proclaims that God raised him from the dead (v. 30). He further explains the significance of Jesus's resurrection in light of the Scriptures, saying:

> We tell you the good news: What God promised our ancestors he has fulfilled for us, their children, by *raising up* Jesus. As it is written in the second Psalm: "You are my son; today I have become your father." *God raised him* from the dead so that he will never be subject to decay. As God has said, "I will give you the holy and sure blessings promised to David." (italics mine, vv. 32–34)

As with Acts 2:24, the verb used to describe God's *raising* of Jesus from the dead in Acts 13:33–34 is the same verb used in the Greek translation of 1 Chronicles 17:11 (Greek, *anistemi*).[15] Jesus, who was born as a descendant of David, was declared the Son of God by his resurrection from the dead (Rom 1:3–4), and the promise to David lies at the center of the purposes of God. The sense of wonder over the resurrected Messiah and the salvation found in his name permeates the stories of the early church. The sermons preached

---

14. See N. T. Wright, *The Resurrection of the Son of God*, Christian Origins and the Question of God, Vol. 3 (Minneapolis: Fortress Press, 2003), 147–50.

15. The same verb appears in Jer 23:5, when the prophet announces that God would "raise up" a righteous branch of David (Greek, *anistemi*).

are deeply rooted in the Scriptures, and they testify that the resurrection of Jesus is the fulfillment of God's promise. N.T. Wright thus notes: "The resurrection was the sign to the early Christians that this living god had acted at last in accordance with his ancient promise, and had thereby shown himself to be God, the unique creator and sovereign of the world."[16] God has acted decisively in history by raising Jesus from the dead, and Jesus's disciples were changed by this reality.

We live in a culture that has lost hope in promises and the kind of "narratable world" that is found in the Bible. Robert Jenson has written an insightful and thought-provoking article entitled "How the World Lost Its Story," where he traces the shift from modernity to postmodernity, particularly as it relates to the loss of story and the incoherence that characterizes our current world. He summarizes at the outset the task of the church in this context:

> It is the church's constituent task to tell the biblical narrative to the world in proclamation and to God in worship, and to do so in a fashion appropriate to the content of that narrative, that is, as a promise claimed from God and proclaimed to the world. It is the church's mission to tell all who will listen, God included, that the God of Israel has raised his servant Jesus from the dead, and to unpack the soteriological and doxological import of that fact.[17]

This was the task of the early church as the gospel of Jesus was proclaimed, a gospel deeply rooted in the Scriptures and in God's promise of old. In contrast to the hopelessness that characterizes postmodernity, the biblical narrative resounds with hope and restoration, and it is the *true story* of the world. The resurrection of Jesus testifies that God is faithful to fulfill what he has promised—this has profound significance, as Wright notes: "The resurrection means that Jesus is the messianic 'son of god'; that Israel's eschatological hope has been fulfilled; that it is time for the nations of the world to be brought into submission to Israel's god."[18] The resurrection is central to the narrative plot of the entire Bible.[19] This also means that we have hope for our own resurrection. Our hope is not in this life only but in the life to come. Bauckham and Hart

---

16. Wright, *The Resurrection of the Son of God*, 726.

17. Robert Jenson, "How the World Lost Its Story," *First Things*, March 2010 (https://www.firstthings.com/article/2010/03/how-the-world-lost-its-story).

18. Wright, *The Resurrection of the Son of God*, 726.

19. The centrality of the resurrection for the entire biblical narrative is emphasized in the Bible series I have co-authored with David Palmer, which is structured around the acronym CASKET EMPTY, an acronym that testifies to Jesus's empty tomb as the center of the biblical story (for more information, see www.casketempty.com).

note that a vision of the Eschaton is missing from the church today, for they argue that biblical eschatology has been replaced by "every kind of progressivist utopianism."[20] Amidst competing worldviews, we are called to proclaim that God has raised Jesus from the dead and to embody the resurrected life found in the Son, thereby testifying to the "real narrative" of the kingdom and giving hope of an Eschaton to a world that has tragically lost the true story.

20. Bauckham and Hart, *Hope Against Hope*, 114–15.

LISTEN to the Story

¹In the course of time, David defeated the Philistines and subdued them, and he took Gath and its surrounding villages from the control of the Philistines.

²David also defeated the Moabites, and they became subject to him and brought him tribute.

³Moreover, David defeated Hadadezer king of Zobah, in the vicinity of Hamath, when he went to set up his monument at the Euphrates River. ⁴David captured a thousand of his chariots, seven thousand charioteers and twenty thousand foot soldiers. He hamstrung all but a hundred of the chariot horses.

⁵When the Arameans of Damascus came to help Hadadezer king of Zobah, David struck down twenty-two thousand of them. ⁶He put garrisons in the Aramean kingdom of Damascus, and the Arameans became subject to him and brought him tribute. The Lᴏʀᴅ gave David victory wherever he went.

⁷David took the gold shields carried by the officers of Hadadezer and brought them to Jerusalem. ⁸From Tebah and Kun, towns that belonged to Hadadezer, David took a great quantity of bronze, which Solomon used to make the bronze Sea, the pillars and various bronze articles.

⁹When Tou king of Hamath heard that David had defeated the entire army of Hadadezer king of Zobah, ¹⁰he sent his son Hadoram to King David to greet him and congratulate him on his victory in battle over Hadadezer, who had been at war with Tou. Hadoram brought all kinds of articles of gold, of silver and of bronze.

¹¹King David dedicated these articles to the Lᴏʀᴅ, as he had done with the silver and gold he had taken from all these nations: Edom and Moab, the Ammonites and the Philistines, and Amalek.

> [12]Abishai son of Zeruiah struck down eighteen thousand Edomites in the Valley of Salt. [13]He put garrisons in Edom, and all the Edomites became subject to David. The Lord gave David victory wherever he went.
>
> [14]David reigned over all Israel, doing what was just and right for all his people. [15]Joab son of Zeruiah was over the army; Jehoshaphat son of Ahilud was recorder; [16]Zadok son of Ahitub and Ahimelek son of Abiathar were priests; Shavsha was secretary; [17]Benaiah son of Jehoiada was over the Kerethites and Pelethites; and David's sons were chief officials at the king's side.

Listening to the Text in the Story: 1 Chronicles 16:35; 17:10

The story of King David continues with his military victories over surrounding nations (1 Chr 18–20), followed by a military census and the choice of Jerusalem as the site for the temple (ch. 21). Large sections from Samuel have been omitted (such as David's adultery with Bathsheba and the family strife that follows), but we noted in the introduction that the Chronicler is not simply writing another history, but he is explaining the theological significance of events and drawing out principles from Israel's history for his own audience.[1] What, then, is the purpose of these truncated stories that give singular attention to David's military victories?

First of all, they demonstrate that God is fulfilling his promise to David to "subdue" his enemies (Heb. *k-n-ʿ*, 1 Chr 17:10; cf. 18:1; 20:4). God is faithful to fulfill what he has promised. Second, these victories are not due to David's military expertise, but God's saving work (Heb. *y-sh-ʿ*, 18:6, 13). This recalls the psalm that God's people had sung: "Save us, God our Savior; gather us and deliver us from the nations" (16:35). Only God is able to save his people, and his saving work during the reign of David testifies to this reality. Third, these battles explain why David was precluded from building the temple—for he had waged many wars and had shed much blood (22:8; 28:3).[2] Fourth, David dedicates the spoil from his victories and the tribute he receives from the nations for sacred use, underscoring David's unswerving commitment to

---

1. See the introduction, Life in the Province of Judah and in the Diaspora under the Persians, pp 10–13.

2. See the discussion on 1 Chr 22:8 in Chapter 22, pp. 219–20, where I explain why David is precluded from building the temple.

prepare for the temple that will be built by Solomon. Lastly, David's military victories will establish peace in the kingdom, so that David's son can devote himself to the important task of temple-building.

EXPLAIN the Story

David's Victories over Surrounding Nations (18:1–6)

David's battles begin with the Philistines, who had earlier waged war against him (1 Chr 14:8–17). The gruesome tactics of the Philistines were noted when they had mercilessly dismembered Saul's body (10:1–12), and the same Philistines had even earlier gouged out Samson's eyes (Judg 16:21–25). Prior to the monarchy, the Philistines had fought against Israel and killed thousands (1 Sam 4:2), and they had taken the ark of the covenant (5:1–5). After Samuel had led Israel in repentance, the Philistines were finally subdued (7:13–14). We may recall further that when Davd was a young shepherd, he had confronted the Philistine champion named Goliath. David had recognized that Goliath would be defeated because this uncircumcised Philistine had taunted the armies of the living God (17:26). Now, David defeats the same Philistines and takes possession of the city of Gath (1 Chr 18:1).[3] Klein notes that the verb "defeat" (Heb, *n-k-h*, 18:1), which occurs eleven times in 1 Chronicles 18–20, "forms a steady drumbeat" in each of the following units.[4] Although David does not defeat the Philistines entirely, his victory signals their subjugation and effective containment.[5]

David's military victories continue with his defeat of the Moabites, who lived east of the Dead Sea. Israel's relationship with the Moabites had been marked by conflict from their early days (Num 22–24; Deut 23:3–6; Judg 3:12–30), although David had a family connection with Moab (Ruth 4:21–22), and his parents had sought safe-haven in the region (1 Sam 22:3–4). David's defeat of the Moabites leads to economic benefit, not only when he receives tribute, but these victories also signal that David has captured "the key to economic development in the Levant: the trade routes, which could be taxed as trade moved between Africa, Europe, and Asia."[6]

---

3. The town of Gath is probably to be identified as one of the cities belonging to the Philistine Pentapolis, although some scholars locate it further north in the vicinity of Gezer (see Klein, *1 Chronicles*, 391).

4. Ibid., 390.

5. See Malamat, "Aspects of Foreign Policies," 11–12.

6. Boda, *1–2 Chronicles*, 160–61.

David's victory over the Aramean king Hadadezer is recorded next, signifying his penetration into the northern region of Syria as far as Hamath, thereby securing important trade routes (1 Chr 18:3).[7] David's victory gives him control over the entire region as far as Zobah, a key Aramean state located north of Damascus. Later, Solomon will build store cities in Hamath to facilitate his extensive international trade (cf. 2 Chr 8:3–4). Since the Euphrates River marked the northern boundary of the promised land, David's territorial expansion is in fulfillment of God's promise (1 Chr 18:3; cf. Gen 15:18; Exod 23:31; Josh 1:4), and it anticipates Solomon's expanded boundaries (2 Chr 7:8; 8:3–4; 9:26). Chariots, horsemen, and foot soldiers are taken as spoil, but David hamstrings a number of horses (cf. Josh 11:6–9). Since Moses had prohibited the king from accruing many horses, David may well have had this in view (Deut 17:16). David's defeat of the Arameans of Damascus results in garrisons being placed in their region and tribute being given to him (1 Chr 18:5–6). Such victories were a testimony that God was saving David wherever he went (v. 6).

Spoils Are Dedicated to the LORD (18:7–11)

Among David's spoils were gold shields, which Hadadezer's officers bring to Jerusalem, and a large quantity of bronze from the towns of Tebah and Kun, which belonged to Hadadezer (1 Chr 18:7–8). Bronze was used to make the "Sea" in Solomon's temple (2 Chr 4:2), along with the elaborately engraved pillars that flanked the entrance to the temple (1 Kgs 7:14–22; 2 Chr 3:15–17). The spoils David receives will be used for the temple, thus they even anticipate the temple that Solomon will build.

When Tou, king of Hamath, hears that David has defeated Hadadezer, he dispatches his trusted emissary Hadoram (his son) to seek peace and to bless David on account of his victory (1 Chr 18:9–10). This suggests some kind of political alliance, which gives David control of the important northern region. Perhaps Hadoram's alternative name in Samuel (Joram, "Yahweh is exalted") is indicative of his allegiance to David and his God (2 Sam 8:10).[8] Hadoram brings articles of gold, silver, and bronze, which David dedicates to the LORD, along with the silver and gold he had taken from all the nations, including from Edom, Moab, the Ammonites and the Philistines, and Amalek (1 Chr 18:11; cf. 2 Chr 5:1). It was noted above that Psalm 83 includes Edom, Moab,

---

7. For a detailed account of David's victory over the Arameans and the political setting, see Malamat, "Aspects of the Foreign Policies," 1–17.

8. Klein notes further that there is eighth century BC evidence of two Yahwistic names in texts from the region, suggesting Israelite presence in the north (Klein, *1 Chronicles*, 395n46).

Ammon, Amalek, and Philistia among the list of nations that conspire against Israel (Ps 83:1–8). That *they* now bring tribute to David underscores that God has fought on David's behalf, bringing nations into submission, and their gold and silver are thus set apart for sacred use.

Victory over the Edomites (18:12–13)

Attention turns to Abishai, the son of Zuriah, who defeats thousands of Edomites in the Valley of Salt (1 Chr 18:12–13), which probably refers to the area south and east of the Dead Sea.[9] Zuriah was David's sister, who had three sons, Abishai, Joab, and Asahel (2:16). David's nephew Abishai was among the military men who had given him support and whose heroic deed was remembered: "He raised his spear against three hundred men, whom he killed, and so he became as famous as the Three" (11:20). His brother Joab was commander of the army (18:15; 19:8), but Abishai was also an important military leader. Although David subdues the Edomites at this time, they will later wage war against Judah (2 Chr 20:22; cf. 21:8–10; 25:5–13).[10] David is victorious because God "gave [him] victory wherever he went" (1 Chr 18:13), highlighting an important theme in the chapter.

David's Administrative Structure (18:14–17)

David's rule over all Israel is described as his "doing what was just and right for all his people" (1 Chr 18:14). God's throne was characterized by "righteousness and justice" (Pss 89:14; see also 97:2; 98:9; 99:4; 103:6), and as such, there was the expectation that the Davidic king would reflect God's righteous and ethical standards (Jer 22:2–4, 15; 23:5; 33:15). David will later appoint judges, who are to instruct God's people in his law (1 Chr 26:29–32). Their important role is encapsulated in Jehoshaphat's instructions to the judges he appoints: "Consider carefully what you do, because you are not judging for mere mortals but for the LORD, who is with you whenever you give a verdict. Now let the fear of the LORD be on you. Judge carefully, for with the LORD our God there is no injustice or partiality or bribery" (2 Chr 19:6–7; cf. Deut 16:18–20; 17:8–12).

The list of David's leaders begins with Joab, who was over his army, and Jehoshaphat, the recorder (1 Chr 18:15). Joab has a key role to play throughout David's reign (11:6–8; 19:10–19; 20:1–8; 21:1–6, etc.), although later in his life he will be loyal to Adonijah. He is finally killed under Solomon's rule,

---

9. Ibid., 396.

10. For more background on the Edomites, see the discussions in Chapter 1 on 1 Chr 1, pp. 27–30, and Chapter 54 on 2 Chr 25, pp. 466–69.

resulting in Benaiah becoming commander of the army (1 Kgs 2:28–35). Zadok, the son of Ahitub, and Abimelech, the son of Abiathar, were priests (1 Chr 18:16).[11] It is important to recall that Aaron had four sons, Nadab, Abihu, Eleazar, and Ithamar, but since Nadab and Abihu died (6:3; 24:2; cf. Lev 10), this meant Eleazar and Ithamar were the two remaining priestly lines from Aaron. Accordingly, Zadok was from the line of Eleazar, whereas Abimelech was from the line of Ithamar (cf. 1 Chr 24:1–3). They serve as priests while Shavsha serves as secretary; the priestly ministry will be divided among these two families of Eleazar and Ithamar, with a greater number assigned to Eleazar (vv. 1–31). David's leadership concludes by mentioning Benaiah, who was over the Kerethites and Pelethites,[12] and David's sons, who were chief officials (18:17; cf. 2 Sam 8:18).

 LIVE the Story

The Lord Saves His People

David has been victorious over his enemies because *God has saved him* (Heb. *y-sh-ʿ*, 1 Chr 18:6, 13). This salvation hearkens back to the mighty exodus from Egypt when God saved his people (Exod 14:30). God's people were to remember that "the LORD your God is the one who goes with you to fight for you against your enemies to give you victory" (Heb. *y-sh-ʿ*, Deut 20:4). Since God was fighting on Israel's behalf, their military battles were never entirely secular, thus they are referred to as *holy* war.[13] Under the leadership of Joshua, whose name speaks of God's salvation (Heb. *Yeshua*, "Yahweh is salvation"), the Israelites defeat their enemies by faith as God gives them the land. After Joshua had died, God raised up judges who would "save" his people from their enemies (Heb. *y-sh-ʿ*, Judg 2:16, 18; 3:9, 31, etc.). These texts illustrate the importance of God's salvation that is central to the Old Testament, and it is seen in this story of King David. Salvation belongs to God, and he alone is Israel's Savior (Ps 65:5; 79:9; 85:4; Isa 43:3, 11; 45:17). This is why the psalms sung by God's people when the ark was brought into Jerusalem conclude with the prayer: "Save us, God our Savior; gather us and deliver us from the nations" (Heb. *y-sh-ʿ*, 1 Chr 16:35; cf. Ps 106:47).

---

11. For a summary of the priestly line of Abiathar, especially how his genealogy is identified in different sources, see Merrill's helpful summary (*1 & 2 Chronicles*, 193).

12. See the discussion in Chapter 27 on 1 Chr 27:4, p. 260.

13. For a helpful summary of Holy War, see Merrill, *1 & 2 Chronicles*, 256–61.

Yet God's salvation in the Old Testament looks forward to an even greater salvation in the New Testament that is ultimately fulfilled in Jesus, whose name means "Yahweh saves."

In Matthew's gospel, after rehearsing Jesus's genealogy that traces his line back to Abraham and David (Matt 1:1–17), he recalls the angelic announcement when Joseph is told that Mary will give birth to a son (v. 21). The angel announces that her son is to be named *Jesus*, which is the Greek form of the Hebrew name Joshua ("Yahweh saves"). When the name Jesus is made known, the angel reveals that this child will be a deliverer, for he will "save his people from their sins" (v. 21). Already in the Old Testament there was the expectation that God's salvation and restoration would entail more than military or political liberation (see Isa 40–55). Isaiah looked forward to the time when God would accomplishing an "everlasting salvation" (Isa 45:17). It would be through the Suffering Servant who would atone for Israel's sin (Isa 52:13–53:12). Thus the prophet Ezekiel announced that God would save his people from their sin (Ezek 36:29). This salvation foreshadowed in the Old Testament is realized in Jesus, who is identified as *Savior*, something that had characterized Yahweh in the Old Testament. The angel thus announces at his birth: "Today in the town of David a Savior has been born to you; he is the Messiah, the Lord" (Luke 2:11). God's saving work is thus being accomplished through Jesus, Israel's Savior from the line of David (Acts 5:31; 13:23; cf. Eph 5:23; Phil 3:20, etc.).[14] Yet, when the crowds shout out, "Hosanna to the Son of David!" (Matt 21:9), they do not fully realize that the salvation Jesus accomplishes requires the Savior to die on a cross, for he will "save his people from their sins" (1:21).

Just as David was unable to save himself—he needed *God* to accomplish salvation on his behalf—so, too, we are unable to save ourselves. In the Old Testament, God's people were to learn through their countless military battles (especially during those times when they were outnumbered) that salvation was from *God alone*, as Jehoshaphat (2 Chr 20:9) and Hezekiah understand (32:22). The prophet Isaiah announces that God's people were to turn to the LORD and "be saved, all you ends of the earth; for I am God, and there is no other" (Isa 45:22; 46:7; Jer 2:28; 11:12). This is surely an important reminder for our lives today. We serve a wonderful Savior, but those who receive his

---

14. For a helpful summary of Jesus as Savior in Pauline texts, see Fee, *Jesus as Lord*, 106–108. He notes that Jesus's mission cannot be separated from his identity as God's eternal Son, and thus he is a fully divine Savior.

salvation must come on bended knee, turning away from false gods lurking in our heart and relinquishing any false hope that we can save ourselves. There is only one Savior, and his name is *Jesus*. The good news of the gospel that we proclaim is that "everyone who calls on the name of the Lord will be saved" (Acts 2:21; see also Rom 10:13). This is the saving work of Jesus that is anticipated in God's salvation of David some one thousand years earlier.

CHAPTER 19

1 Chronicles 19:1–19

 LISTEN to the Story

¹In the course of time, Nahash king of the Ammonites died, and his son succeeded him as king. ²David thought, "I will show kindness to Hanun son of Nahash, because his father showed kindness to me." So David sent a delegation to express his sympathy to Hanun concerning his father.

When David's envoys came to Hanun in the land of the Ammonites to express sympathy to him, ³the Ammonite commanders said to Hanun, "Do you think David is honoring your father by sending envoys to you to express sympathy? Haven't his envoys come to you only to explore and spy out the country and overthrow it?" ⁴So Hanun seized David's envoys, shaved them, cut off their garments at the buttocks, and sent them away.

⁵When someone came and told David about the men, he sent messengers to meet them, for they were greatly humiliated. The king said, "Stay at Jericho till your beards have grown, and then come back."

⁶When the Ammonites realized that they had become obnoxious to David, Hanun and the Ammonites sent a thousand talents of silver to hire chariots and charioteers from Aram Naharaim, Aram Maakah and Zobah. ⁷They hired thirty-two thousand chariots and charioteers, as well as the king of Maakah with his troops, who came and camped near Medeba, while the Ammonites were mustered from their towns and moved out for battle.

⁸On hearing this, David sent Joab out with the entire army of fighting men. ⁹The Ammonites came out and drew up in battle formation at the entrance to their city, while the kings who had come were by themselves in the open country.

¹⁰Joab saw that there were battle lines in front of him and behind him; so he selected some of the best troops in Israel and deployed them against the Arameans. ¹¹He put the rest of the men under the command of Abishai his brother, and they were deployed against the Ammonites. ¹²Joab said,

"If the Arameans are too strong for me, then you are to rescue me; but if the Ammonites are too strong for you, then I will rescue you. ¹³Be strong, and let us fight bravely for our people and the cities of our God. The LORD will do what is good in his sight."

¹⁴Then Joab and the troops with him advanced to fight the Arameans, and they fled before him. ¹⁵When the Ammonites realized that the Arameans were fleeing, they too fled before his brother Abishai and went inside the city. So Joab went back to Jerusalem.

¹⁶After the Arameans saw that they had been routed by Israel, they sent messengers and had Arameans brought from beyond the Euphrates River, with Shophak the commander of Hadadezer's army leading them.

¹⁷When David was told of this, he gathered all Israel and crossed the Jordan; he advanced against them and formed his battle lines opposite them. David formed his lines to meet the Arameans in battle, and they fought against him. ¹⁸But they fled before Israel, and David killed seven thousand of their charioteers and forty thousand of their foot soldiers. He also killed Shophak the commander of their army.

¹⁹When the vassals of Hadadezer saw that they had been routed by Israel, they made peace with David and became subject to him.

So the Arameans were not willing to help the Ammonites anymore.

Listening to the Text in the Story: Tiglath-pileser III Prism

David's victories over the Ammonites and Arameans are described in this chapter (1 Chr 19; cf. 2 Sam 10). The story about David's kindness shown to Jonathan's son Mephibosheth has been omitted (see ch. 9), giving singular focus to David's military victories. The material has been taken from 2 Samuel 10–12, with a large section omitted (11:2–12:25).[1] Given that David's war with the Arameans has already been recounted (1 Chr 18), it may seem strange that David fights yet another battle with the Arameans. It is important to recognize, however, that repeated military campaigns against the same enemy are not uncommon in this kind of contested region.

The Assyrian king Tiglath-pileser I (1114–1076 BC), for example, fought

---

1. In Samuel, the Ammonite war is the narrative context for David's adultery with Bathsheba; see John I. Lawlor, "Theology and Art in the Narrative of the Ammonite War (2 Samuel 10–12)," *Grace Theological Journal* 3 (1982): 193–205.

several battles with the Arameans.[2] Pitard notes that his military strategy included control over the trade routes, and this meant almost yearly attacks on the Arameans.[3] Tiglath-pileser's expedition into Syria is recorded on an octagonal prism, with a preserved fragment that boasts: "Twenty-eight times (I fought) the Ahlamu peoples and the Arameans, (once) I even crossed the Eurphrates twice in one year."[4] David's battle against the Arameans is not surprising, therefore, although in this case he is required to fight against them because they had come to the aid of the Ammonites.

EXPLAIN the Story

The Humiliating Actions of the Ammonites and Their Defeat Under Joab (19:1–15)

The account begins with the death of Nahash, king of the Ammonites, which results in his son, Hanun, ruling in his place (1 Chr 19:1). The Ammonites were descendants of Lot who lived east of the Jordan in the territory allotted to them (Gen 19:36–38; cf. Deut 2:19, 37). During the reign of Saul, Nahash had attacked Jabesh-Gilead. Facing immanent defeat, the men of Jabesh sought to enter into a covenant with Nahash, agreeing to become his servants (1 Sam 11:1). The king agrees to the covenant, but only with the horrific condition that he be allowed to gouge out their right eyes, thereby bringing disgrace on Israel (v. 2). In the story that follows (cf. vv. 1–11), Saul is able to defeat the Ammonites (and thus Nahash does not gouge out their right eyes), but the threat of the Ammonites reminds us about the kind of threats David faces and the weightiness of his role as king as he seeks to secure the safety of his people.

The Ammonites had suffered defeat under Saul, but Nahash had remained as king. After his death, his son Hanun rules in his place (1 Chr 19:1). David decides to show kindness to Hanun in return for the kindness that had been shown to him (v. 2).[5] David sends messengers to the Ammonite king to express his sympathy, but Hanun's commanders assume that David's real reason was

---

2. See Wayne T. Pitard, "Arameans," in Hoerth, Mattingly, and Yamauchi, *Peoples of the Old Testament World*, 207–30.

3. Ibid., 211.

4. Tiglath–Pileser I (1114–1076): "Expeditions to Syria, the Lebanon, and the Mediterranean Sea," trans. A. Leo Oppenheim (*ANET*, 275); see Pitard, "Arameans," in Hoerth, Mattingly, and Yamauchi, *Peoples of the Old Testament World*, 211. Pitard notes that Tiglath-pileser's son Ashur-bel-kala also fought against the Arameans.

5. It is difficult to know exactly what kindness David has in view, although the time when Shobi, the son of Nahash, provided food and supplies for David and his men is one example of kindness shown to him (2 Sam 17:27–29).

to spy out the land (v. 3). Hanun seizes the envoys and subjects them to humiliating treatment: he shaves their body hair, cuts off their garments at the buttocks, and sends them away in disgrace (v. 4; cf. 2 Sam 10:4). Exposing someone's nakedness was a shameful action (cf. Isa 47:3; Mic 1:11; Nah 3:5), and Hanun has degraded the men by shaving their hair from head to toe (cf. Isa 7:20).[6] When David hears that his men have faced such humiliation, he sends word to his men, instructing them to remain in Jericho until their hair grows back (1 Chr 19:5). This highly offensive action has made the Ammonites "obnoxious" to David (Heb. *b-'-sh*, v. 6). The verb "to stink, abhor" (Heb. *b-'-sh*) is used to describe the stench that comes from rotten food being eaten by maggots (Exod 16:20) and the stench from water containing dead fish (7:18). It can also refer to loathsome actions between people, such as when Absalom had sexual relations with his father's concubines on the rooftop of his house (2 Sam 16:21–22). What the Ammonites had done was highly grievous to David. But when the Ammonites learn that they had caused such a reaction (and they surely intended to incite David), Hanun prepares for battle, sending an exorbitant one thousand talents of silver (estimated at 67,300 pounds[7]) to hire horsemen and chariots from Aram Naharaim ("Aram of the two rivers"), a region north of the Euphrates, and from another two Aramean allies at Maakah and Zobah (1 Chr 19:6; cf. 18:3). Preparations for war are complete with the acquisition of chariots, along with military reinforcements that have assembled at Medeba, located in Moab about six miles south of Heshbon (cf. Num 21:30; Josh 13:9).[8]

When David hears of the coalition formed against him, he sends for his military commander, Joab, and his army as they prepare for battle (1 Chr 19:8–9). In recognition that the battle must be fought on two fronts (since the Ammonites were stationed in the city, whereas the Arameans were preparing for battle in the open fields with their assembled chariots), Joab gathers his choice soldiers to fight against the Arameans, but his brother Abishai, who was a proven military leader (cf. 11:20; 18:12–13), is to wage war against the Ammonites. They agree to support each other, depending on where the help is needed (19:12). Joab exhorts his brother to be strong so that they might fight bravely for their cities and people, with the encouragement that the LORD would do what was good in his sight (v. 13). Joab leads a successful battle against the Arameans, who flee before him. The Ammonites retreat upon hearing that the Arameans had fled, and Joab returns to Jerusalem (v. 15).

---

6. Boda, *1–2 Chronicles*, 166.
7. Klein, *1 Chronicles*, 403.
8. Not all scholars identify Medeba as this location (see Klein, *1 Chronicles*, 404).

David's Defeat of the Arameans (19:16–19)

The battle is not over, however, for the Arameans seek military reinforcements from other Arameans living beyond the Euphrates, whose army was under the command of Shopak (1 Chr 19:16). After news reaches David, he gathers all Israel and crosses the Jordan, leading Israel in a decisive victory (v. 17). Although some Arameans flee, David is able to kill thousands of charioteers and foot soldiers, along with their commander, Shophak (v. 18). Terms of peace are initiated by the Arameans in recognition that they had lost the battle. They become David's servants and refuse to give further support to the Ammonites (v. 19).

 LIVE the Story

The Kingdom of God Faces Hostility

The battles David wages against the surrounding nations and the humiliating treatment of his men underscore the level of hostility between God's people and the nations. To be sure, God has a plan to bless all the nations (Gen 12:3) and nations will become part of God's people, yet there is another reality that is evident in this story. As noted earlier, nations can also rise up against God's people, as Psalm 2 makes clear: "The kings of the earth rise up and the rulers band together against the LORD and against his anointed, saying, 'Let us break their chains and throw off their shackles'" (Ps 2:2–3).[9] God has installed his king in Zion and he will surely defeat all his foes, but the psalm unveils the spiritual conflict between God's anointed king and the kingdoms of the earth. Hanun's humiliating treatment of David's men and the alliance of Ammonites and Arameans formed against Israel serve as another reminder of this reality, something not entirely unfamiliar to the returnees who had faced opposition on all fronts.[10]

The conflict between God's people and those who are hostile to his kingdom is seen in the early church, as they faced intense opposition under the Roman Empire. John the Baptist was imprisoned and beheaded (Luke 3:19–20; 9:7–9), Stephen was stoned to death (Acts 7), James the brother of John was martyred (12:2), and the apostle Paul was severely beaten (2 Cor 6:1–10) and imprisoned in Rome (Acts 23:33–24:27; 28:16; cf. Phil 1:12–14).

In his Olivet Discourse, Jesus taught his disciples that there would be an

---

9. See the discussion in Chapter 14 on 1 Chr 14, p. 150.
10. On key biblical texts, see the introduction, Genre, pp. 7–8.

increased period of persecution and tribulation (Matt 24–25). The temple
and the holy city of Jerusalem would be destroyed, for nation would rise
against nation and kingdom against kingdom. Jesus warned: "Then you will
be handed over to be persecuted and put to death, and you will be hated by
all nations because of me" (24:9). Jesus had already warned his disciples that
they had a hard road ahead of them (10:23), but they were simply following
in the steps of their teacher (10:24–25, 38–39).

The Olivet Discourse also resounds with hope, looking ahead to the day
when the Son of Man "comes in his glory, and all the angels with him, he
will sit on his glorious throne.[11] All the nations will be gathered before him,
and he will separate the people, one from another, as a shepherd separates the
sheep from the goats" (25:31–32). At this time, the King will say to those
on his right, "Come, you who are blessed by my Father; take your inheritance, the kingdom prepared for you since the creation of the world" (v. 34).
This hearkens back to the battles in the Old Testament, which serve as a
precursor to the final judgment, as Merrill notes: "Holy War as sanctioned
and practiced in the days of ancient Israel was but an earthly and historical
expression of eschatological war that finally eliminates evil from God's perfect
new creation."[12] When interpreted within this larger cosmic battle, the church
is commissioned to proclaim the gospel to all nations and to recognize that
the gospel will be refused, rejected, and met with hostility. Amidst opposition,
God's people are to persevere and remain faithful, remembering that the Son
of David will reign victoriously. The parousia gives us hope and courage to
persevere in the present, for there is an end. As noted in the introduction, we
are exhorted in Chronicles to lift our eyes beyond our individual circumstances
so that we might catch a vision of God's glorious and everlasting kingdom and
to discern how he is providentially at work and present in our world—even
when the circumstances might look otherwise.[13] In the West, persecution can
take the form of slander, ridicule for beliefs, charges of discrimination, and
rejection by friends and family. In other parts of the world, following Christ
can result in conflict with one's own family, and for some, this can lead to

---

11. Bauckham and Hart note that in our contemporary context, eschatological hope and transcendence have been replaced by the myth of progress. They argue that the church in the West has
adapted its eschatology by embracing a kind of progressivist utopia, yet such "utopia" is not achieved
through history but through the *redemption* of history (*Hope Against Hope*, 26–43).

12. Merrill, *1 & 2 Chronicles*, 261; see also Gard, "The Case for Eschatological Continuity,"
in Gundry, *Show Them No Mercy*, 113–141, and Tremper Longman III, "The Case for Spiritual
Continuity," in Gundry, *Show Them No Mercy*, 161–95.

13. See the introduction, pp. 1–4.

estrangement, but also torture and death. Amid all the trials and tribulations, we are not to lose sight of the fact that we are citizens of a *heavenly* kingdom. We are called to persevere amidst persecution and to proclaim the gospel of the kingdom, being fully assured that the victory of the risen and reigning king has already been won—and he will one day return in all his glory: "Come Lord Jesus, Come."

LISTEN to the Story

¹In the spring, at the time when kings go off to war, Joab led out the armed forces. He laid waste the land of the Ammonites and went to Rabbah and besieged it, but David remained in Jerusalem. Joab attacked Rabbah and left it in ruins. ²David took the crown from the head of their king—its weight was found to be a talent of gold, and it was set with precious stones—and it was placed on David's head. He took a great quantity of plunder from the city ³and brought out the people who were there, consigning them to labor with saws and with iron picks and axes. David did this to all the Ammonite towns. Then David and his entire army returned to Jerusalem.

⁴In the course of time, war broke out with the Philistines, at Gezer. At that time Sibbekai the Hushathite killed Sippai, one of the descendants of the Rephaites, and the Philistines were subjugated.

⁵In another battle with the Philistines, Elhanan son of Jair killed Lahmi the brother of Goliath the Gittite, who had a spear with a shaft like a weaver's rod.

⁶In still another battle, which took place at Gath, there was a huge man with six fingers on each hand and six toes on each foot—twenty-four in all. He also was descended from Rapha. ⁷When he taunted Israel, Jonathan son of Shimea, David's brother, killed him.

⁸These were descendants of Rapha in Gath, and they fell at the hands of David and his men.

Listening to the Text in the Story: 2 Samuel 11–12

David's military battles against the surrounding nations continue with his war against the Ammonites. The Chronicler's singular focus on David's victories is underscored when considering the source of these stories in Samuel. The battle in 1 Chronicles 20:1 picks up the story in 2 Samuel 11:1, but the next two verses (1 Chr 20:2–3) resume the narrative in 2 Samuel 12:26 (the story of David and Bathsheba in 11:2–12:25 has been omitted). The next battle introduced in 1 Chronicles 20:4 picks up the story from 2 Samuel 21:18, which means that nine chapters in between have been omitted.[1] The Chronicler has, therefore, kept a singular vision on David's military victories that prepare the way for Solomon and the temple. The Chronicler's silence about David's adultery and the family strife that follows gives undivided attention to David's role to secure peace in the kingdom, and it may even point to a theology of grace that is characteristic of the Chronicler's work.

EXPLAIN the Story

David Defeats the Ammonites and Receives Spoils (20:1–3)

The story of David's battles continues with Joab leading Israel's army against the Ammonites as he lays waste their land and besieges the city of Rabbah, the capital of the Ammonites located along the strategic King's Highway (1 Chr 20:1). The Chronicler makes a passing comment, "but David remained in Jerusalem" (v. 1), which sets the context for David's adultery with Bathsheba and the murder of Uriah (2 Sam 11:1–12:25). Passing over these stories, the Chronicler picks up the narrative with Joab's defeat of the Ammonite capital of Rabbah (12:26), which was "left . . . in ruins" (Heb. *h-r-s*, 1 Chr 20:1). This language is used of God's defeat of Israel's enemies, including the Egyptians when God "threw down" those who arose against him (Exod 15:7; cf. Pss 28:5; 58:6; Isa 22:19; Mal 1:4). The account of David's involvement in the battle at Rabbah is omitted (see 2 Sam 12:27–29), but the story is resumed with the comment that David "took the crown from the head of their king" (1 Chr 20:2; cf. 2 Sam 12:30). Some scholars suggest that the crown belonged to the Ammonite god Milcom,[2] but it is more likely that it was a royal crown used by the Ammonite king. Sculptures depicting crowned heads have been discovered near Amman, although it is uncertain whether the god Milcom or an Ammonite king is being depicted.[3] Taking off someone's crown entailed stripping a person of his honor (Job 19:9; Ezek 21:26), and thus it was a symbolic action, signifying military

1. The Chronicler has omitted David's family strife, including Absalom's attempt to usurp the throne; see the detailed analysis of Braun (*1 Chronicles*, 201) and the summary of these chapters by Merrill (*1 & 2 Chronicles*, 272–73).

2. Klein, *2 Chronicles*, 406.

3. See Siegfried H. Horn, "The Crown of the King of the Ammonites," *AUSS* 11 (1973): 170–80.

defeat and submission (Jer 13:18; Lam 5:15–16). The crown belonging to the Ammonite king was made of gold and inlaid with precious stones (1 Chr 20:2). David's highly symbolic gesture at the conclusion of his wars signifies his victory over his enemies, along with the large amount of spoil he brings out of the city. We also learn that David "brought out the people who were there, consigning them to labor with saws and with iron picks and axes" (v. 3).[4] David follows this practice of subjecting defeated foes to servitude in other Ammonite cities (v. 3). Afterward, David and the people return to Jerusalem.

David's Defeat of the Philistines (20:4–8)

The Chronicler picks up the story with the temporal clause, "In the course of time" (1 Chr 20:4), which has been used to introduce earlier battles, thus providing literary unity to the chapters (cf. 18:1; 19:1). The war that breaks out in Gezer involves the Philistines (20:4) and it picks up the story from 2 Samuel 21:18–22.[5] David had struck down the Philistines from Gibeon to Gezer earlier (1 Chr 14:16), and Gezer is again in view, a city that bordered Philistine territory. A leader named Sibbekai is among David's mighty men of war (11:29), and he was one of his commanders (27:11). Sibbekai kills a man named Sippai, who is identified as a descendant of the Rephaites (20:4), a people well-known for their towering and formidable stature (Deut 2:10–11, 20; 3:11). They were notably among the inhabitants whose land is promised to Abraham's descendants (Gen 15:18–21; cf. Josh 16:10; Judg 1:29). The Chronicler differs from his source by noting that the Philistines were "subjugated" at this time (Heb. *k-n-'*, 1 Chr 20:4), which not only recalls God's promise to subdue Israel's enemies (Deut 9:3; Judg 3:30; 4:23; 8:28), but also his more recent promise to David: "I will also subdue all your enemies" (Heb. *k-n-'*, 1 Chr 17:10; see also 2 Chr 13:18; 28:19); thus this statement signals fulfillment of God's promise.

Another battle with the Philistines is recalled, when a man named Elhanan kills the brother of Goliath the Gittite (1 Chr 20:5).[6] The description of his

---

4. The NASB translation of 20:3 ("He brought out the people who were in it, and he cut *them* with saws and with sharp instruments and with axes") suggests that David mutilated the people, but the direct object of the verb ("them") is absent in the Hebrew text (as the italicized *them* in the NASB indicates); the NIV is the preferable reading, as cited above.

5. The story in Chronicles differs from 2 Sam 21:18–22 in a number of places (for example, the city Gezer is Gob in 2 Sam 21:9; Sippai is identified as Saph in 2 Sam 21:18; Saph is a descendant of Rapha in 2 Sam 21:18, instead of a descendent of the Rephaites in 1 Chr 20:4); Merrill suggests that the Chronicler may have been using a different source (*1 & 2 Chronicles*, 240–41); see also Braun, *1 Chronicles*, 209.

6. The text in 2 Sam 21:19 gives a different family of origin for Elhanan, and Goliath is killed instead of his brother. Notwithstanding some of the potential textual issues, since Goliath was killed

spear "with a shaft like a weaver's rod" (v. 5) is reminiscent of Goliath (1 Sam 17:7), but also other formidable foes (1 Chr 11:23). Another military man of great stature taunts Israel (20:6), evoking Goliath's earlier reproach (1 Sam 17:10, 25, 26), yet he, too, is killed by David's nephew, Jonathan (1 Chr 20:6–7). These defeated foes, who fell at the hands of David and his men, bring these two chapters on David's military victories to a conclusion, thus they establish a peaceful kingdom in preparation for Solomon.

LIVE the Story

The Kingdom Continues under God's Grace

Joab's war with the Ammonites sets the context for David's adultery with Bathsheba (1 Chr 20:1; cf. 2 Sam 11:1). The Chronicler's omission of David's sin and the family strife that follows enables him to give singular focus to David's military battles as he prepares the way for Solomon (cf. 1 Chr 22:8–10). But there may also be hints of God's grace in the Chronicler's presentation of David in this chapter.[7] In spite of David's serious moral failures, God continues to use him to establish his kingdom purposes. Selman thus notes that the Chronicler was not unaware of David's sins, but rather he "wishes to stress Samuel's concluding emphasis on the Uriah/Bathsheba tragedy on repentance, forgiveness, and restoration (2 Sa. 12:13, 24–25; cf. Ps. 51:13–19)."[8] With a similar emphasis, Hahn observes that the Chronicler from "beginning to end" tells a "story of unmerited grace and the possibility of forgiveness. Again and again, sins are forgiven and out of sin and repentance, God brings even greater works."[9] It is possible that the Chronicler's omission of David's sin contributes to this theme of grace and restoration. In spite of his sin, David is not disqualified from his leadership role in the kingdom. McConville comes to a similar conclusion about the Chronicler's presentation of David, suggesting that the "omission of huge misdemeanors reported in 2 Sam. 9–20, with all their debilitating consequences for the kingdom, is further dramatic evidence of God's willingness to use even the most inconstant of people in his service."[10] The same principle will later be seen during the reign of Manasseh.

---

earlier by David (1 Sam 17), it seems more likely that Goliath's brother is in view (see Merrill, *1 & 2 Chronicles*, 241).

7. On the topic of God's grace in the tribe of Judah, see Live the Story, The Grace of God Is on Center Stage, in Chapter 2, pp. 44–46.

8. Selman, *1 Chronicles*, 196.

9. Hahn, *The Kingdom of God*, 40.

10. McConville, *I & II Chronicles*, 64.

He is the worst southern king and the greatest of sinners (2 Chr 33:1–9), yet when he confesses his sin, God not only brings Manasseh back to Jerusalem, but remarkably, he restores him to his kingdom (v. 13). Thus, God uses the repentant sinner, and his restoration results in even greater works when the king establishes religious reforms in the kingdom (vv. 14–16).

An amazing truth of the Christian faith throughout the ages is that God uses sinners, those forgiven and restored, for his kingdom purposes (cf. 1 Cor 15:9–10). The reality of God's forgiveness means that David has been restored, and God continues to accomplish his purposes through him. God had made promises to David that he would subdue his enemies (Heb. *k-n-'*, 1 Chr 17:10), and in spite of David's sin, we read in this story that the Philistines were "subjugated" (Heb. *k-n-'*, 20:4; cf. 18:1). The subjugation of David's enemies is an important theme in these chapters. That David defeats the formidable Philistines even after his adultery with Bathsheba and the murder of Uriah (reading Chronicles in light of Samuel) underscores the reality of God's forgiveness and restoration. This ought to give us encouragement that, in spite of our sin, God uses us for his kingdom purposes and he is faithful to fulfill his promises. The apostle Paul understood this:

> Here is a trustworthy saying that deserves full acceptance: Christ Jesus came into the world to save sinners—of whom I am the worst. But for that very reason I was shown mercy so that in me, the worst of sinners, Christ Jesus might display his immense patience as an example for those who would believe in him and receive eternal life." (1 Tim 1:15–16)

LISTEN to the Story

¹Satan rose up against Israel and incited David to take a census of Israel. ²So David said to Joab and the commanders of the troops, "Go and count the Israelites from Beersheba to Dan. Then report back to me so that I may know how many there are."

³But Joab replied, "May the LORD multiply his troops a hundred times over. My lord the king, are they not all my lord's subjects? Why does my lord want to do this? Why should he bring guilt on Israel?"

⁴The king's word, however, overruled Joab; so Joab left and went throughout Israel and then came back to Jerusalem. ⁵Joab reported the number of the fighting men to David: In all Israel there were one million one hundred thousand men who could handle a sword, including four hundred and seventy thousand in Judah.

⁶But Joab did not include Levi and Benjamin in the numbering, because the king's command was repulsive to him. ⁷This command was also evil in the sight of God; so he punished Israel.

⁸Then David said to God, "I have sinned greatly by doing this. Now, I beg you, take away the guilt of your servant. I have done a very foolish thing."

⁹The LORD said to Gad, David's seer, ¹⁰"Go and tell David, 'This is what the LORD says: I am giving you three options. Choose one of them for me to carry out against you.'"

¹¹So Gad went to David and said to him, "This is what the LORD says: 'Take your choice: ¹²three years of famine, three months of being swept away before your enemies, with their swords overtaking you, or three days of the sword of the LORD—days of plague in the land, with the angel of the LORD ravaging every part of Israel.' Now then, decide how I should answer the one who sent me."

¹³David said to Gad, "I am in deep distress. Let me fall into the hands

of the LORD, for his mercy is very great; but do not let me fall into human hands."

[14]So the LORD sent a plague on Israel, and seventy thousand men of Israel fell dead. [15]And God sent an angel to destroy Jerusalem. But as the angel was doing so, the LORD saw it and relented concerning the disaster and said to the angel who was destroying the people, "Enough! Withdraw your hand." The angel of the LORD was then standing at the threshing floor of Araunah the Jebusite.

[16]David looked up and saw the angel of the LORD standing between heaven and earth, with a drawn sword in his hand extended over Jerusalem. Then David and the elders, clothed in sackcloth, fell facedown.

[17]David said to God, "Was it not I who ordered the fighting men to be counted? I, the shepherd, have sinned and done wrong. These are but sheep. What have they done? LORD my God, let your hand fall on me and my family, but do not let this plague remain on your people."

[18]Then the angel of the LORD ordered Gad to tell David to go up and build an altar to the LORD on the threshing floor of Araunah the Jebusite. [19]So David went up in obedience to the word that Gad had spoken in the name of the LORD.

[20]While Araunah was threshing wheat, he turned and saw the angel; his four sons who were with him hid themselves. [21]Then David approached, and when Araunah looked and saw him, he left the threshing floor and bowed down before David with his face to the ground.

[22]David said to him, "Let me have the site of your threshing floor so I can build an altar to the LORD, that the plague on the people may be stopped. Sell it to me at the full price."

[23]Araunah said to David, "Take it! Let my lord the king do whatever pleases him. Look, I will give the oxen for the burnt offerings, the threshing sledges for the wood, and the wheat for the grain offering. I will give all this."

[24]But King David replied to Araunah, "No, I insist on paying the full price. I will not take for the LORD what is yours, or sacrifice a burnt offering that costs me nothing."

[25]So David paid Araunah six hundred shekels of gold for the site. [26]David built an altar to the LORD there and sacrificed burnt offerings

and fellowship offerings. He called on the LORD, and the LORD answered him with fire from heaven on the altar of burnt offering.

²⁷Then the LORD spoke to the angel, and he put his sword back into its sheath. ²⁸At that time, when David saw that the LORD had answered him on the threshing floor of Araunah the Jebusite, he offered sacrifices there. ²⁹The tabernacle of the LORD, which Moses had made in the wilderness, and the altar of burnt offering were at that time on the high place at Gibeon. ³⁰But David could not go before it to inquire of God, because he was afraid of the sword of the angel of the LORD.

Listening to the Text in the Story: Genesis 23:1–20

The story of David's military battles escalates to focus on a new adversary who incites David to conduct a census. Although this will lead to a plague that kills thousands, this story nevertheless resounds with hope, since it is at *this* time that David purchases the threshing floor from Araunah, the place that will become the site for the temple (1 Chr 22:1; 2 Chr 3:1). When retelling this familiar story (see 2 Sam 24), the Chronicler uses language reminiscent of Abraham's purchase of the cave of Machpelah from Ephron the Hittite (Gen 23:1–20). Williamson notes that both stories involve a key figure purchasing property from a non-Israelite; both sites will be used for ongoing sacred purposes; both Abraham and David offer to "give" the full price for the site (Gen 23:9, 11; 1 Chr 21:22); and both individuals pay the "full price," an expression unique to these two stories (Gen 23:9, 11; 1 Chr 21:22, 24).[1] In the Abraham account, the negotiations, along with the full price paid, affirm that Abraham has legally acquired the property.[2] Given that God had promised the land of Canaan to Abraham, which included the land of the Hittites (Gen 15:20; cf. Exod 3:8, 17; 13:5; Deut 7:1; 20:17, etc), Abraham's purchase of land from a *Hittite* is not insignificant. Hamilton rightly notes that the crucial element in the chapter is not Sarah's death but "Abraham's acquisition of land from outsiders. As such, it is a harbinger of

---

1. Citing these parallels, Williamson notes: "David's purchase of the threshing floor from Ornan has been patterned by the Chronicler on Abraham's purchase of the cave of Machpelah from Ephron in Gen. 21" (see Williamson, *1 and 2 Chronicles*, 149–50).

2. Some have suggested that Abraham's negotiations reflect Hittite laws, noting also that the property was purchased from Ephron the Hittite (see Hamilton, *Genesis*, 123–36).

things to come."[3] That David purchases the threshing floor and surrounding field from Araunah the *Jebusite* underscores that he, too, has purchased property from outsiders (1 Chr 21:15, 18, 28; cf. 2 Chr 3:1), and it, too, is a harbinger of things to come.

EXPLAIN the Story

David Orders a Census Be Taken of Israel (21:1–7)

The account is introduced with Satan (simple transliteration of the Heb. *satan*) standing against Israel and inciting David to take a census (1 Chr 21:1). While the Hebrew noun *satan* can refer to a human "adversary" (1 Kgs 5:4, 11:14, etc.) or an angelic adversary (Num 22:22, 32), it can also refer to the accuser in God's heavenly court, known as Satan (Job 1:6, 7, 8, 9, 12; 2:1, 2, 3; Zech 3:1–2).[4] Williamson suggests that the Chronicler was influenced by Job (and Zech 3:1–2), noting that the verb "to incite" (Heb. *s-w-t*) is used of Satan in Job 2:3.[5] Since the noun *satan* occurs without the article in 1 Chronicles 21:1, this suggests the personal name Satan is in view (cf. NIV). While scholarly debate abounds,[6] a case can be made for interpreting the adversary as Satan himself.[7] Interpreting 1 Chronicles 21:1 in this way does not resolve all the issues, especially when comparing this text to 2 Samuel 24:1, where Yahweh incites David to number Israel,[8] but Robert Gordon observes that in these two accounts (and in Job) we are faced with the "complementarity of roles which is unresolvable simply because the biblical writers are grappling with the mystery of evil."[9] He notes further that Chronicles is one of several texts that indicate an increasing tendency to associate evil with Satan, something

---

3. Ibid., 136.

4. Most English Bibles translate the noun in Job and Zechariah as Satan, although not all scholars agree that Satan is in view since the proper noun is not used in these texts (*satan* occurs with the definite article, "the satan").

5. Williamson, *1 and 2 Chronicles*, 143.

6. For a summary of scholarly views, see Paul Evans, "Divine Intermediaries in 1 Chronicles 21: An Overlooked Aspect of the Chronicler's Theology," *Bib* 85 (2004): 545–65, and Ryan E. Stokes, "The Devil Made Me Do It . . . or Did He? The Nature, Identity, and Literary Origins of the Satan in 1 Chronicles 21:1," *JBL* 128 (2009): 91–106.

7. See the helpful and succinct discussion by Klein, *1 Chronicles*, 418–419.

8. In the Chronicler's source, Yahweh's anger burns against Israel and *he* incites David to number Israel (2 Sam 24:1), but in Chronicles it is *satan* who incites David. If *satan* is a member of God's heavenly council who is acting on his behalf (cf. Num 22:22, 32), as some scholars argue, then the two texts are not incompatible since Yahweh is still responsible for the action (see Braun, *1 Chronicles*, 216). But this interpretation raises the theological issue of whether God would incite evil.

9. Robert P. Gordon, *I & II Samuel: A Commentary*. Library of Biblical Interpretation (1986; repr., Grand Rapids: Zondervan, 1999), 317.

that is more fully developed in the New Testament (cf. 2 Cor 12:7; Jas 1:13).[10] Although Satan wreaks havoc in the kingdom, Williamson concludes that since 1 Chronicles 21 is ultimately about God's choice of the site for the temple, this story (like Job) shows that Satan is under God's sovereignty and is an instrument of the divine will.[11]

Since Satan entices David to number Israel, the question arises about the nature of David's sin that evokes God's wrath. While there are times when a census is taken without any negative repercussions (Exod 30:12; Num 1:2; 26:2), David's census implies that he is relying upon his military strength rather than trusting in the LORD. The king was not to put his trust in military strength, nor in a foreign power, but only in the LORD (Pss 20:7; 33:16–17; 147:10). If there was any doubt about David's actions, Joab's response of alarm serves to highlight the seriousness and offensive nature of the king's request. His opening exhortation, "May the LORD multiply his troops a hundred times over" (1 Chr 21:3), reminds David that God is able to provide all that he needs. David's actions are thus "an affront to Yahweh in that David seems to be more dependent on armies he can raise than on Yahweh's strong arm."[12] Joab's questions should have caused David to rethink his foolish and potentially perilous command that will cause guilt to come upon Israel (v. 3). The term "guilt, wrongdoing" (Heb. 'ashma), which occurs seven times in Chronicles, is used to describe guilt incurred through egregious sins (2 Chr 24:18; 28:10, 13 [3x]; 33:23). Joab foresees that David's action will bring guilt upon Israel (1 Chr 21:3; cf. vv. 7, 14, 17), but the command of the king prevails. Joab returns with the number of Israelites prepared for battle, which included thousands from Judah,[13] but Joab did not number Levi and Benjamin (vv. 5–6). The tribe of Levi was exempt from military service since they were set apart to serve in the tabernacle (Num 1:47–50). Benjamin may have been excluded from the census due to the location of the tabernacle at

---

10. Ibid.

11. Williamson, *1 and 2 Chronicles*, 144–45.

12. Merrill, *1 & 2 Chronicles*, 245.

13. The account in 2 Sam 24:9 has a significantly lower number for Israel at 800,000, with a comparable number of 500,000 for Judah, giving a total of 1,300,000. Different solutions are offered by scholars (see Williamson's estimates, for example, in *1 and 2 Chronicles*, 145) but even with creative solutions, the numbers remain high for David's military, who only represented a portion of the total population; see Yigal Shiloh, "The Population of Iron Age Palestine in Light of a Sample Analysis of Urban Plans, Areas, and Population Density," *BASOR* 239 (1980): 25–35 (especially, 32). On high numbers in the Old Testament and, more particularly, on the meaning of the Hebrew term *'eleph* as a military unit (rather than a literal headcount), see the discussion on 1 Chr 12:23–40 in Chapter 12, pp. 138–40.

Gibeon (cf. 1 Chr 21:29), which was in the territory of Benjamin.[14] While the king's command was abhorrent to Joab, even more so the matter was "evil in the sight of God," which results in his punishment of Israel (v. 7). Instead of David striking Israel's enemies (Heb. *n-k-h*, 1 Chr 18:1, 2, 3, 5, 9, translated in the NIV "defeat" or "strike down"), God now strikes *Israel*—and the king knows *he* is responsible.

David's Repentance and God's Judgment of a Plague Against Israel (21:8–17)

David immediately responds in repentance before God, confessing that he has sinned greatly, and yet he boldly asks that God might take away his guilt, acknowledging that he has been exceedingly foolish (1 Chr 21:8). God makes known through the prophet Gad that David is allowed to choose his punishment: three years of famine, three months to be swept away by enemies, or "three days of the sword of the LORD—days of plague in the land, with the angel of the LORD ravaging every part of Israel" (v. 12). Upon hearing these words, David chooses to fall into the hand of the LORD, for he knows that the mercies of God are great. As a result, God sends a plague upon Israel, and thousands are killed (v. 14).

The catastrophic scene shifts to focus on the angel sent to Jerusalem to destroy it, but at the last moment, God relents, saying to the angel "Enough! Withdraw your hand" (v. 15). The staying of God's hand is reminiscent of his mercy shown to Israel after they had worshiped the golden calf, when God relented from destroying them (Exod 32:12, 14; cf. Judg 2:18). David lifts up his eyes and sees the angel of the LORD, who had been standing near the threshing floor of Araunah. He now has eyes to see the gravity of the situation—the angel was standing between heaven and earth with his sword outstretched *toward Jerusalem* (1 Chr 21:16). The full weight of his sin now rests on David as he and the elders cover themselves with sackcloth and fall prostrate to the ground. The heavenly scene is not unlike the angel of the LORD who had stood against Balaam (Num 22:23, 31, 34) and the angel of the LORD who appeared to Joshua (Josh 5:13–15). With this heavenly scene casting a dark and ominous shadow over Jerusalem, David and the elders lie with their faces toward the ground. With a sense of urgency, David pleads with God, confessing that he has sinned and acted wickedly (1 Chr 21:17). He acknowledges that *he* was the one who had brought harm to the sheep,

---

14. Williamson, *1 and 2 Chronicles*, 145.

so he asks that God's judgment fall upon him and his family, but surely not
on the people.

David Is Instructed to Build an Altar to the LORD and God's Wrath Is Averted (21:18–30)

The angel of the LORD tells the prophet Gad that David is to build an altar
to the LORD on the threshing floor of Araunah the Jebusite (1 Chr 21:18).[15]
David obeys the word spoken by Gad, but in the meantime, the angel of the
LORD appears to Araunah while he is threshing wheat (v. 20), recalling the
divine visitation Gideon had many years earlier (Judg 6:11–24). With a sense
of God-fearing determination, David approaches Araunah, requesting that
he give him the "site" (Heb. *maqom*) of his threshing floor for the full price
so that he can build an altar to the LORD and thereby stop the plague from
killing even more people (1 Chr 21:22).

Many years earlier God had told Moses that he would choose "the place"
(Heb. *maqom*) for his name to dwell (Deut 12:5, 11, 18; 14:23, etc.). David
had seen the angel of the LORD standing by the threshing floor, which is "the
place" that David is buying from Araunah. Since the angel had appeared there,
it is now "the place" associated with God's presence, recalling the time when
Jacob had seen an angelic vision, leading to his acknowledgment: "Surely
the LORD is in this place, and I was not aware of it" (Gen 28:16). Jacob had
identified the "place" as the house of God (v. 17). The theophany that David
witnesses suggests that this, too, is a holy place, and it anticipates that it will
be "the place" for the house of God (1 Chr 22:1). The significance of this story
was not lost on Solomon. When he begins building the temple, he recalls the
location of Mount Moriah "where the LORD had appeared to his father David.
It was on the threshing floor of Araunah the Jebusite, the place provided by
David" (2 Chr 3:1).

As David seeks to secure the threshing floor, he asks Araunah to give it to
him for the "full price" so that the plague might be stopped. As noted above
(p. 209), the expression "full price" only occurs in this passage (1 Chr 21:22,
24) and in Genesis 23:9, when Abraham bought a burial site for Sarah from
Ephron. Araunah generously offers to give it to David and to provide oxen
for the burnt offerings, the threshing sledges for wood, and the wheat for the

---

15. The name Araunah appears in 2 Sam 24, but the alternative spelling, Ornan, is used in
Chronicles. The ESV and NASB have retained the name Ornan, whereas the NIV has used the
name Araunah that occurs in Samuel, probably for the sake of consistency. We have retained the
NIV translation throughout.

grain offering—he offers to give everything David needs (1 Chr 22:23)! But David insists on paying the full price, for he will not take these items from him, thereby giving to the LORD that which costs *him* nothing (v. 24).

While it is entirely appropriate for the nations to bring gifts of tribute (18:2, 6; 2 Chr 9:1), the context here is not tribute but David's sin, and as such, he cannot offer up a sacrifice to the LORD which does not belong to him—it must be *his* offering. Furthermore, a central theme in the sacrificial system was the idea of *sacrificial* giving—the sacrifice must cost the worshiper something. Burnt offerings were the most costly, since the entire animal was burnt on the altar. David gives Araunah six hundred shekels of gold,[16] recalling Abraham's payment to Ephron of four hundred shekels for the cave of Machpelah and the surrounding field (Gen 23:16; cf. Gen 25:9; 49:29–32; 50:13). After David purchases "the place," he builds an altar to the LORD (1 Chr 21:25). This is consistent with the patriarchs, who built altars and called upon the name of the LORD at key sites where God had appeared to them, such as Abram at Shechem (Gen 12:6–7), Isaac at Beersheba (26:23–25), and Jacob at Bethel (35:1–7). As with David, these sites have ongoing religious significance for Israel. David offers burnt offerings and peace offerings on the altar, and he calls upon the LORD (1 Chr 21:26). God answers him with fire from heaven, and he instructs his angel to withdraw his sword. When David sees that God has answered him on the threshing floor of Araunah, he offers sacrifices there. Williamson thus notes that the Chronicler "invites us in reading the narrative to trace in it the clear pointers to the divine will which, in spite of circumstances, led David specifically to the threshing floor of Araunah rather than to the expected high place at Gibeon, and then, through answering by fire, demonstrated the transfer to this altar of this focus of the nation's worship, formerly centered on the tabernacle."[17] Since the altar of burnt offering was located at Gibeon (v. 29; cf. 2 Chr 1:3), David's sacrifice (and God's acceptance of it) marks a shift to Jerusalem as the future site for atonement (cf. 1 Chr 22:1–2).

---

16. In 2 Sam 24:24 David pays fifty shekels (of silver), whereas in Chronicles he pays six hundred shekels (of gold). Since he purchases the "site" in Chronicles (21:25), this may suggest that in addition to the fifty shekels of silver for the threshing floor and oxen, David purchased the larger area from Araunah that would become the site for the temple, just as Abraham purchased both the cave and the field surrounding it (Williamson, *1 and 2 Chronicles*, 149–50).

17. Ibid., 151.

LIVE the Story

Not Offering to the LORD That Which Costs Us Nothing

When David had requested to buy the threshing floor, he had refused Araunah's generous offer. It would have been easy for David to obtain the threshing floor at no personal cost. But David recognized something about his offering that is instructive for us today. When the Israelites were to enter the land, they were required to give God the best of their flock and the best of their produce (e.g., Lev 1:3, 10; 2:1, 4, 5, 7). The sacrificial system emphasized that only unblemished animals could be offered to God. The prophet Malachi rebukes God's people for offering up blind, lame, and sick offerings to God (Mal 1:8), noting that even their governor would not accept these kinds of second-rate, low-quality offerings, how much more would God not accept them! Some had vowed a male in their flock, but then sacrificed a blemished animal to God (v. 14). The point is that God does not accept second-rate, token gifts—he is worthy of much more.

By way of illustration, when we "repackage" a gift, we are all aware that it is not the same as a gift carefully chosen and purchased. Giving someone a gift that someone had previously given to us might meet some kind of social requirement or expectation, but we all know that the gift does not come from the heart. Another example are gifts children give their parents. When children are young, parents often pay for the gifts that their children give to them or to their siblings, but when they are adults, there is the expectation that they will pay for the gifts *themselves*. The gift is not central, but the intention of the giver. David understood this. He knew that *he* needed to buy the threshing floor—Araunah could not give it to him. David refused to give to God that which cost him nothing.

While we do not offer sacrifices to God (since Jesus's costly sacrifice has paid the cost for our redemption), the principle of giving to God that which costs us something is worthy of further reflection. Jesus taught that it wasn't simply *how much* that was given but the level of *sacrifice*, as seen in the widow's mite (Mark 12:41–44). Mary is commended for the very costly perfume which she used to anoint Jesus's feet (John 12:1–11). The apostle Paul commends the churches of Macedonia for their generosity, even amid their poverty: "In the midst of a very severe trial, their overflowing joy and their extreme poverty welled up in rich generosity. For I testify that they gave as much as they were able, and even beyond their ability. Entirely on their own, they urgently pleaded with us for the privilege of sharing in this service to the Lord's people" (2 Cor 8:2–4). This was a testimony of their love for Christ as they first gave of themselves, and thus their financial support reflected their devotion. The apostle Paul also commends the Philippians for their generous giving to him, for they had provided for his needs and for his ministry (Phil 4:14–18), which was "a fragrant offering, an acceptable sacrifice, pleasing to God" (v. 18). Giving that is acceptable to God requires giving *sacrificially*, as a response of gratitude for all that we have received.

Rather than simply giving our financial resources, Paul takes this a step further when referring to our whole lives as *living sacrifices*, offered up to God in response to his mercy: "Therefore, I urge you, brothers and sisters, in view of God's mercy, to offer your bodies as a living sacrifice, holy and pleasing to God—this is your true and proper worship" (Rom 12:1). We are to offer our very lives to God in sacrificial service and in worship—to paraphrase the powerful declaration of David: "I will not give to the LORD that which costs me nothing." Our worship of God is captured in the last stanza of the well-known hymn by Isaac Watts:

> Were the whole realm of nature mine,
> that were a present far too small.
> Love so amazing, so divine,
> demands my soul, my life, my all.

David served the purpose of God in his generation (cf. Acts 13:36), and as his life is drawing to a close, he gives generously of his resources for the building of the temple (1 Chr 29). We, too, are called to serve the purposes of God in our generation with faithfulness, generosity, and with self-sacrificial living as we follow Jesus, our king, who gave himself up for us, paying the ultimate price with his own shed blood.

CHAPTER 22

1 Chronicles 22:1–19

¹Then David said, "The house of the LORD God is to be here, and also the altar of burnt offering for Israel."

²So David gave orders to assemble the foreigners residing in Israel, and from among them he appointed stonecutters to prepare dressed stone for building the house of God. ³He provided a large amount of iron to make nails for the doors of the gateways and for the fittings, and more bronze than could be weighed. ⁴He also provided more cedar logs than could be counted, for the Sidonians and Tyrians had brought large numbers of them to David.

⁵David said, "My son Solomon is young and inexperienced, and the house to be built for the LORD should be of great magnificence and fame and splendor in the sight of all the nations. Therefore I will make preparations for it." So David made extensive preparations before his death.

⁶Then he called for his son Solomon and charged him to build a house for the LORD, the God of Israel. ⁷David said to Solomon: "My son, I had it in my heart to build a house for the Name of the LORD my God. ⁸But this word of the LORD came to me: 'You have shed much blood and have fought many wars. You are not to build a house for my Name, because you have shed much blood on the earth in my sight. ⁹But you will have a son who will be a man of peace and rest, and I will give him rest from all his enemies on every side. His name will be Solomon, and I will grant Israel peace and quiet during his reign. ¹⁰He is the one who will build a house for my Name. He will be my son, and I will be his father. And I will establish the throne of his kingdom over Israel forever.'

¹¹"Now, my son, the LORD be with you, and may you have success and build the house of the LORD your God, as he said you would. ¹²May the LORD give you discretion and understanding when he puts you in

command over Israel, so that you may keep the law of the LORD your God. [13]Then you will have success if you are careful to observe the decrees and laws that the LORD gave Moses for Israel. Be strong and courageous. Do not be afraid or discouraged.

[14]"I have taken great pains to provide for the temple of the LORD a hundred thousand talents of gold, a million talents of silver, quantities of bronze and iron too great to be weighed, and wood and stone. And you may add to them. [15]You have many workers: stonecutters, masons and carpenters, as well as those skilled in every kind of work [16]in gold and silver, bronze and iron—craftsmen beyond number. Now begin the work, and the LORD be with you."

[17]Then David ordered all the leaders of Israel to help his son Solomon. [18]He said to them, "Is not the LORD your God with you? And has he not granted you rest on every side? For he has given the inhabitants of the land into my hands, and the land is subject to the LORD and to his people. [19]Now devote your heart and soul to seeking the LORD your God. Begin to build the sanctuary of the LORD God, so that you may bring the ark of the covenant of the LORD and the sacred articles belonging to God into the temple that will be built for the Name of the LORD."

Listening to the Text in the Story: The Story of Wen-Amon

With Israel's enemies subdued (1 Chr 18–20) and God's wrath averted (ch. 21), David now proceeds to make preparations for the temple, which will be built on the very site he has purchased from Araunah (22:1). The coastal cities of Sidon and Tyre are prominently featured in this chapter, since large cedars from Lebanon will be transported from these two well-known trading ports. The importance of securing prized wood from Lebanon is seen in the Egyptian story of Wen-Amon, an official from the Temple at Karnak, who was sent to Byblos on the Phoenician coast. His mission was to secure wood so that a ship could be constructed to transport the Egyptian god Amon across the Nile.[1] The hieratic text describing this expedition is dated to the eleventh century BC, which locates it in the period of the united monarchy. Such expeditions to Lebanon are known from other ancient texts. In the seventh century BC, the Assyrian king Esarhaddon had requested that wood,

---

1. "The Journey of Wen-Amon to Phoenicia," trans. John A. Wilson (*ANET*, 25–29).

including logs, long beams, and thin boards of cedar and pine, be brought from Lebanon to Nineveh for his palace.[2] The Phoenicians were accomplished maritime traders who were highly skilled at transporting large cedars on cargo ships from Lebanon, and they play a key role in this story and in the reign of Solomon (cf. 2 Chr 2:8–9).[3]

EXPLAIN the Story

David Acquires Building Materials for the Construction of the Temple (22:1–5)

With the threshing floor of Araunah still in view, David acknowledges that the "house of the LORD God is to be here, and also the altar of burnt offering for Israel" (1 Chr 22:1). The king begins to gather building materials, even though he will not build the temple himself. He assembles foreigners living in the land, who are conscripted to work on the temple (v. 2). Stonecutters will be needed to hew out stones; iron is gathered for nails and clamps; and cedar is brought to Jerusalem by the Sidonians and Tyrians. David's activities anticipate the extensive construction of the temple under his son Solomon (2 Chr 2–4). David recognizes that his son is young and inexperienced, and he is mindful that the temple built for God should be "of great magnificence and fame and splendor in the sight of all the nations" (1 Chr 22:5), so he devotes his energies and resources to make preparations for it. David affirms that the goal is that God's glory might extend to the *all the earth*, a topic that will be further illustrated when the temple is built (2 Chr 2:11–12; 9:8).

David's Charge to Solomon (22:6–16)

David calls his son Solomon and charges him to build a house for the LORD (1 Chr 22:6). He recalls that even though he had intended to build the temple, God had precluded him from this task because he had shed much blood and had fought many wars (v. 8; cf. 28:3). The chapters describing David's military battles testify to this reality (chs. 18–20), but they underscore that God has now given rest to Israel through David (cf. 22:18; 23:25). Murry suggests further that David's shedding of blood has had a polluting effect

---

2. Esarhaddon (680–669): "The Syro-Palestinian Campaign," Prism B, trans. A. Leo Oppenheim (*ANET*, 291); cf. Ashurnasirpal II (883–859): "Expedition to Carchemish and the Lebanon," trans. A. Leo Oppenheim (*ANET*, 275–76).

3. See the discussion in Chapter 31 on 2 Chr 2, pp. 295–99, for more information about the Phoenicians.

on the land (cf. Num 31:19–24), making him unfit to build the sacred site.[4] Murray thus concludes: "David's unusual degree of ritual defilement is in irresolvable tension with the demand for a unique degree of ritual purity in the temple-builder."[5] In contrast to David, who is a man of war, Solomon is a "man of peace and rest" (1 Chr 22:9), thus the time is at hand for the temple to be built, according to God's promise (2 Sam 7:11; cf. Josh 1:13; 21:44). Solomon's name, which means "peace, peaceful," signifies the peaceful kingdom that he inherits (1 Chr 23:25; cf. 2 Chr 20:30). David affirms that Solomon has been chosen to build God's house, and God will establish the throne of his kingdom forever (1 Chr 22:10).[6]

David pronounces a blessing upon Solomon that the LORD might be with him and that he might be successful in building the temple. God had been with David (1 Chr 17:8) as he had been with the patriarchs of old (Gen 26:3; 28:15). David understands that God's abiding presence has sustained him and given him success, and he now prays that God might be with his son. He asks further that God would give Solomon discretion and understanding so that he might keep the law of the LORD (1 Chr 22:12; cf. Neh 8:8, 13). David reminds Solomon that he will have success, but only if he follows God's laws (1 Chr 22:13). Reminiscent of Moses's charge to Israel and to Joshua (Deut 31:6–7, 23; Josh 1:6–9), David charges Solomon with the words: "Be strong and courageous. Do not be afraid or discouraged" (1 Chr 22:13; cf. 1 Chr 28:20; 2 Chr 32:7). These words foreshadow Haggai's exhortation to Zerubbabel, who is patterned after Solomon (Hag 2:4). Even though the task might seem overwhelming, God's presence will help and sustain Solomon. David reminds his son that he has "taken great pains to provide for the temple" (1 Chr 22:14). David had not simply given out of his surplus, but his giving costs him something (cf. 21:24). The extent of his generosity will be seen in the final chapter of his life (cf. 29:12–17), and other kings will be generous with their resources as well (2 Chr 7:5; 30:24; 35:7). David's commitment to God in these final years of his life underscores his thankfulness to the LORD and his priority to see God's kingdom established. He is preparing for a new work of God under the leadership of Solomon. After rehearsing the provisions of gold and silver that he has given, David concludes with a blessing upon his son, "and the LORD be with you" (1 Chr 22:16).

---

4. See Donald F. Murray, "Under Yhwh's Veto: David as Shedder of Blood in Chronicles," *Bib* 89 (2001): 457–67.

5. Ibid., 475.

6. See the discussion in Chapter 17 on 1 Chr 17 for an explanation of these promises, especially pp. 179–81.

David's Charge to the Leaders to Help Solomon and Seek the Lord (22:17–19)

David turns his attention to the leaders of Israel, instructing them to "help" (Heb. '-z-r) his son Solomon (1 Chr 22:17). David himself had received help from leaders during a critical period in his life (cf. ch. 12).[7] Now, he exhorts his trusted leaders to help his son Solomon, who is the chosen and legitimate heir to the throne (22:17; cf. 3:10–14; 17:11; 22:9–10). David reminds his leaders that God is with them, and he affirms that God has given the inhabitants of the land into his hand (v. 18; cf. 20:8). With echoes of the creation mandate (Gen 1:28) and Israel's entrance into the land under Joshua (Josh 18:1; cf. Num 32:22, 29), David affirms that the land has now been made "subject" (Heb. k-b-sh, 22:18). The subjugation of the land means, therefore, that it is the time for the temple to be built. David's final word of exhortation to his leaders is that they should set their heart and soul "to seek" the LORD their God (Heb. d-r-sh, v. 19; cf. 28:9; 2 Chr 1:5). They are to build the sanctuary of the LORD so that the ark of the covenant and the holy vessels can be brought into God's house, a temple built for the name of the LORD (cf. 2 Chr 2:4; 6:10).

 LIVE the Story

Wise Use of Time and Resources in Our Final Years

David devotes his time, energy, and resources for God's work during the final years of his life. He resolves to make preparations for the temple before he dies (1 Chr 22:5), and thus the next seven chapters describe all that David accomplishes prior to his death (29:28). These chapters testify that David's final years have a *purpose*—he is intent on using his resources for God's kingdom. David secures skilled workers to work on the temple. He provides building materials for the temple, requiring him to negotiate trade with the Phoenicians. He gives wise counsel to his son and warns him about the importance of following God's law. He provides large quantities of gold, silver, bronze, and iron, telling his son that he has "taken great pains to provide for the temple of the LORD" (22:14). Lastly, he exhorts his leaders to give their support to his son. Even though David will not live to see the finished temple and he will not receive the wide-spread recognition that his son will receive (cf. 2 Chr 8–9), he is living his final years with a *kingdom* purpose.

---

7. On the topic of divine help, see Live the Story in Chapter 5, pp. 71–73, and the discussion in Chapter 12 on 1 Chr 12, especially pp. 135–36.

When we consider our own contemporary context, our culture gives much weight to retirement years, which are depicted as a time of playing golf, living in a warm climate, traveling, and spending our hard-earned resources on ourselves. It is estimated that an average of ten thousand Baby Boomers in the United States are retiring every day, and that in the next twenty years an estimated seventy million Baby Boomers will no longer be working.[8] This presents an unprecedented challenge to the church, and it raises the question of how Christians approaching the age of retirement will use their time, energy, and resources.

A group of Christian leaders in Colorado has been rethinking what it means for Christians to retire. Their *Retirement Reformation Manifesto* begins with the bold claim: "Reforming retirement requires a reframing of our thinking, allowing us to shine a light into the purposeless retirement void and finding freedom from unending leisure, indulgence, and self-gratification." Their manifesto is intended to inspire retirees to view their final years of life as an opportunity "to find spiritual fulfillment and meaning using their life experiences and resources to serve and enrich others."[9]

David's final years are about establishing *God's kingdom*. David's devotion to the LORD challenges us to consider how we are using our time and resources, especially those of us who are approaching this final season of life. Do we simply adopt the cultural values of retirement, or do we consider how we might use our time and resources for the kingdom? The call of God does not end at sixty-five years old! In fact, Abraham was seventy-five when God called him to be a blessing to the nations (Gen 12:1–3). Sometimes biblical characters protest that they are too young to be called to a particular task, but in our culture, some may think they are too old. Moses served God until he died at age 120 (Deut 34:7), and Joshua served God until he died at age 110 (Josh 24:29). These servants of God continued to serve God throughout their lives, even when they were elderly. Their lives challenge us to consider our own expectations and pursuits. Are we focused on building God's kingdom or on accruing personal wealth for our own pursuit of pleasure? Like David, we need to recognize that we are sojourners on this earth and that everything

---

8. For these statistics and others, along with a thoughtful article, see Jeff Haanen, "Don't Waste Your Retirement," March 15, 2019 (https://www.thegospelcoalition.org/article/dont-waste-your -retirement/).

9. In the Christian Post article by John Stonestreet and Warren Cole Smith, "What should Christians do with their retirement?", the authors cite the Retirement Reformation Manifesto, and they recall Chuck Colson's commitment to use the latter years of his life in service of the kingdom, noting that while one's work may end, God's kingdom-work never ends (https://www.christianpost .com/voice/what-should-christians-do-with-retirement.html).

has come from God. We ought to weigh carefully how we use the final years of our lives so that we might live with a *kingdom* purpose. The apostle Paul reminded his listeners of this when he preached his sermon at Antioch. King David died after he had "served God's purpose in his own generation" (Acts 13:36). David lived with a kingdom-purpose. May this also be said of our lives, that we might serve God's purpose in our own generation.

LISTEN to the Story

¹When David was old and full of years, he made his son Solomon king over Israel.

²He also gathered together all the leaders of Israel, as well as the priests and Levites. ³The Levites thirty years old or more were counted, and the total number of men was thirty-eight thousand. ⁴David said, "Of these, twenty-four thousand are to be in charge of the work of the temple of the LORD and six thousand are to be officials and judges. ⁵Four thousand are to be gatekeepers and four thousand are to praise the LORD with the musical instruments I have provided for that purpose."

⁶David separated the Levites into divisions corresponding to the sons of Levi: Gershon, Kohath and Merari.

⁷Belonging to the Gershonites:
Ladan and Shimei.
⁸The sons of Ladan:
   Jehiel the first, Zetham and Joel—three in all.
⁹The sons of Shimei:
   Shelomoth, Haziel and Haran—three in all.
   These were the heads of the families of Ladan.
¹⁰And the sons of Shimei:
   Jahath, Ziza, Jeush and Beriah.
   These were the sons of Shimei—four in all.
   ¹¹Jahath was the first and Ziza the second, but Jeush and Beriah
      did not have many sons; so they were counted as one family
      with one assignment.

¹²The sons of Kohath:
Amram, Izhar, Hebron and Uzziel—four in all.

¹³The sons of Amram:

Aaron and Moses.

Aaron was set apart, he and his descendants forever, to consecrate the most holy things, to offer sacrifices before the LORD, to minister before him and to pronounce blessings in his name forever. ¹⁴The sons of Moses the man of God were counted as part of the tribe of Levi.

¹⁵The sons of Moses:

Gershom and Eliezer.

¹⁶The descendants of Gershom:

Shubael was the first.

¹⁷The descendants of Eliezer:

Rehabiah was the first.

Eliezer had no other sons, but the sons of Rehabiah were very numerous.

¹⁸The sons of Izhar:

Shelomith was the first.

¹⁹The sons of Hebron:

Jeriah the first, Amariah the second, Jahaziel the third and Jekameam the fourth.

²⁰The sons of Uzziel:

Micah the first and Ishiah the second.

²¹The sons of Merari:

Mahli and Mushi.

The sons of Mahli:

Eleazar and Kish.

²²Eleazar died without having sons: he had only daughters. Their cousins, the sons of Kish, married them.

²³The sons of Mushi:

Mahli, Eder and Jerimoth—three in all.

²⁴These were the descendants of Levi by their families—the heads of families as they were registered under their names and counted individually, that is, the workers twenty years old or more who served in the temple of the LORD. ²⁵For David had said, "Since the LORD, the God of Israel, has granted rest to his people and has come to dwell in Jerusalem forever, ²⁶the

Levites no longer need to carry the tabernacle or any of the articles used in its service." [27]According to the last instructions of David, the Levites were counted from those twenty years old or more.

[28]The duty of the Levites was to help Aaron's descendants in the service of the temple of the LORD: to be in charge of the courtyards, the side rooms, the purification of all sacred things and the performance of other duties at the house of God. [29]They were in charge of the bread set out on the table, the special flour for the grain offerings, the thin loaves made without yeast, the baking and the mixing, and all measurements of quantity and size. [30]They were also to stand every morning to thank and praise the LORD. They were to do the same in the evening [31]and whenever burnt offerings were presented to the LORD on the Sabbaths, at the New Moon feasts and at the appointed festivals. They were to serve before the LORD regularly in the proper number and in the way prescribed for them.

[32]And so the Levites carried out their responsibilities for the tent of meeting, for the Holy Place and, under their relatives the descendants of Aaron, for the service of the temple of the LORD.

Listening to the Text in the Story: Exodus 19:6; Numbers 3–4

With David's final years drawing near, he is concerned to appoint Levites to serve in the temple. The tribe of Levi has already been introduced, recalling that Levi's three sons were Gershon, Kohath, and Merari (1 Chr 6:1).[1] These three families form the basis of the Levitical administrative structure according to the three divisions of Gershon (23:7–11), Kohath (vv. 12–20), and Merari (vv. 21–23). The tribe of Levi had been set apart for service in the tabernacle. Their primary responsibility was to serve the priests and provide logistical support and labor for the tabernacle (Num 3–4). God tells Moses: "Bring the tribe of Levi and present them to Aaron the priest to assist him. They are to perform duties for him and for the whole community at the tent of meeting by doing the work of the tabernacle" (Num 3:6–7). The duties of the Levites are rehearsed in this chapter (1 Chr 23:26–32), yet, unlike their earlier tasks which included dismantling and moving the tabernacle and its sacred vessels, this aspect of their job description has now changed with the permanent temple on the horizon (v. 26). The central role of the

---

1. For background about the Tribe of Levi, see the discussion in Chapter 6 on 1 Chr 6.

priests and Levites in the administrative structure of the kingdom reminds us that God's people were a "kingdom of priests and a holy nation" (Exod 19:6). The kingdom was not only ruled by a king from the line of Judah, but it was also a *sacred* kingdom—the kingdom of the LORD—and thus the role of the Levites is not secondary or tangential but central to Israel's identity and purpose.

EXPLAIN the Story

Solomon Is Appointed King (23:1–2)

As David's years are drawing to a close, he appoints his son Solomon as co-regent while he remains king until his death (1 Chr 23:1). The more formal and public anointing will take place later (cf. 29:22b–25), but the backstory recounted in Kings indicates that Solomon's succession to the throne is under serious threat (cf. 1 Kgs 1). Thus, David's decision to make his son co-regent is both necessary and a matter of some urgency.[2] The Chronicler does not mention the turbulent period prior to Solomon's succession to the throne, yet it is helpful to rehearse it briefly here. Absalom (a son of David by Maacah) had attempted to usurp the throne from his father, but after a series of events he is finally killed (2 Sam 15:1–18:18). When David is elderly, Adonijah (another son of David, by Haggith) sets his eyes on the throne, but his plans are thwarted when Zadok the priest and Nathan the prophet intervene. With the support of Bathsheba, Solomon is confirmed as the legitimate heir to the throne (1 Kgs 1). During a period of co-regency, David sets the kingdom in order in preparation for Solomon's reign and the building of the temple. Solomon thus rules as "apprentice-king" while David remains king until his death.[3] This is the context for the chapters that follow, as David appoints key political and religious leaders to ensure the smooth transition of leadership. Over the course of five chapters, names of key leaders and their responsibilities will be given, which include Levites (1 Chr 23), priests (ch. 24), musicians (ch. 25), gatekeepers (ch. 26), and commanders and officers (ch. 27).

---

2. For a discussion on Solomon's co-regency, see Merrill, *1 & 2 Chronicles*, 272–73. Ball provides a helpful list of co-regencies that existed in Egypt; he suggests David's co-regency could have been based on an Egyptian model. While this is difficult to establish with certainty, his article underscores that co-regencies were known in the ancient world; see E. Ball, "Co-Regency of David and Solomon (1 Kings 1)," *VT* XXVII (1977): 268–79.

3. Merrill, *1 & 2 Chronicles*, 273.

The Levites Divided into Divisions According to the Three Families (23:3–6)

In accordance with Mosaic tradition (Num 4:3–39), David numbers the Levites thirty years and older (1 Chr 23:3). Since the age of Levitical service is elsewhere identified as twenty (1 Chr 23:24, 27; 2 Chr 31:17; Ezra 3:8), the age of thirty may suggest an older source or it may indicate that the age of service could change depending on the particular needs. The Levites are assigned four primary tasks: oversight of the temple, officers and judges, gatekeepers, and worship leaders (1 Chr 23:4–5).[4] The Levites are divided according to the three Levitical families of Gershon, Kohath, and Merari.

The Levitical Family of Gershon (23:7–11)

Names of leaders from the family of Gershon are given first, although it is important to note that the list is selective, and some of the names and relationships are not easily resolved (1 Chr 23:7–11).[5] For example, the firstborn son of Gershon in the genealogy is Ladan, yet elsewhere he is identified as Libni (Exod 6:17; Num 3:18; 1 Chr 6:17). This suggests generational gapping (a feature known in other genealogies), which would identify Ladan as a descendant of Libni (rather than a literal son). Ladan's family will be assigned the responsibility over the treasuries of the house of the LORD (26:22). Shemei may be a reference to the original son of Gershon (Num 3:21; 1 Chr 6:17), but since this is a popular name (occurring over forty times in the Old Testament), it is equally possibly that he is a later descendant. The genealogy seems to skip generations, focusing on the current Levites assigned to work on the temple,[6] yet the genealogy (even with its gaps) ensures that Levitical ancestry is preserved for the purpose of establishing the legitimacy of temple personnel.

The Levitical Family of Kohath (23:12–20)

The second Levitical family traced is Levi's son Kohath, who fathers four sons: Amram, Izhar, Hebron, and Uzziel (1 Chr 23:12; see also 6:2). Given that Amram was the father of Aaron and Moses (6:3), this genealogy is given the place of preeminence in 1 Chronicles 6, especially the priestly genealogy

---

4. For a comparison of the numbers of Levites in various periods, see Klein, *I Chronicles*, 451.

5. Given the complexity of the lists here, along with textual issues, I refer the reader to the more technical commentaries that address specific issues, such as Klein, *I Chronicles*, 443–59.

6. For example, Jehiel, Zetham, and Joel (23:8) were in charge of the temple treasuries (1 Chr 26:22; cf. 29:8). Joel may also be the chief mentioned earlier (1 Chr 15:7, 11), although since this is a common name, one cannot be certain.

through Aaron's son Eleazar, whose line leads to important priestly figures such as Zadok, Azariah, and Jehozadak, the priest who was brought into exile by the Babylonians (vv. 1–15).

The Chronicler notes that Aaron was "set apart, he and his descendants forever" (23:13). From Israel's early and formative period, God had "set apart" (Heb. *b-d-l*) Israel from the nations to be a holy people (Lev 20:24, 26; cf. 1 Kgs 8:53; Ezra 6:21; 9:1). There is further separation within Israel, for God had "set apart" the Levites from their fellow Israelites for his service (Num 8:14; 16:9). Among the Levites, God had further "set apart" Aaron and his sons to serve as priests (16:1–40). The priestly line continues through Eleazar's son Phinehas, who is promised an enduring priesthood (25:10–13). The task of Israel's priests was to "consecrate the most holy things, to offer sacrifices before the Lord, to minister before him and to pronounce blessings in his name forever" (1 Chr 23:13). Reference is made to Moses, the man of God, who is appropriately included here (v. 14) since he was a descendant of Levi; he thus shares with the Levites the sacred task of drawing near to God and mediating between God and Israel (Exod 3, 24, 32–34). Since Moses's two sons, Gershom and Eliezer, belong to the tribe of Levi, they are included in the genealogy, along with their descendants (1 Chr 23:15–20; cf. Exod 18:3–4). As with the previous genealogy, some of the Levites in the list are known for their leadership role during David's reign (cf. 1 Chr 26:20–25).

The Levitical Family of Merari (23:21–23)

The family of Levi's third son, Merari, is noted briefly. Merari had two sons, Mahli and Mushi (1 Chr 23:21; Exod 6:19; 1 Chr 6:29–30), but the line is first traced through Mahli, whose sons were Eleazar and Kish. Eleazar had daughters but he died before having sons, so the sons of Kish marry them. Descendants of Kish are later mentioned during the reign of Hezekiah (2 Chr 29:12). The sons of Mushi are noted in passing, bringing the short list to completion.

The Responsibilities of the Levites (23:24–32)

The Levites were registered by their families with heads of families recorded by name, those who were twenty years old and upward (1 Chr 23:24; cf. Num 1:2–3). The need to generate records of temple personnel was due to the rest achieved under David; thus construction of the temple is on the horizon (1 Chr 23:25; cf. 22:18). Instead of being taken up with disassembling and moving the tabernacle, the Levites were to fulfill their responsibilities by serving in the temple.[7] Their task is described here: they were in charge of the "courtyards, the side rooms, the purification of all sacred things and the performance of other duties at the house of God. They were in charge of the bread set out on the table, the special flour for the grain offerings, the thin loaves made without yeast, the baking and the mixing, and all measurements of quantity and size" (23:28–29). Worship of God is at the center of life in the kingdom, and the Levites are given the privilege of ministering before the LORD and leading Israel in thanksgiving and praises to the LORD (vv. 30–31; cf. 1 Chr 15–16).[8]

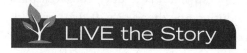

LIVE the Story

God's People Are Set Apart for His Service

In the Old Testament, God sets apart the tribe of Levi to minister before the LORD. God further sets apart Aaron and his sons for priestly service, and among them, the high priest is given unique access into God's presence beyond the veil, one day per year (see Lev 16). The prerequisite for service in the temple was Levitical ancestry, which is why the genealogy of Levi is so important in Chronicles. In the post-exilic community, families whose Levitical ancestry could not be found in the records were considered unclean and thus excluded from the priesthood (see Ezra 2:61–63). Ancestral heritage was no small matter!

The Levites had been set apart to draw near to God and to serve him, yet their vocation hearkens back to an earlier period, when Adam was given a priestly role in the Garden of Eden to "work it and take care of it" (Gen 2:15).[9] Wenham notes that the two verbs used in Genesis 2:15 (Heb. *sh-m-r* and *'-b-d*) appear together in passages that describe Levitical duties (Num 3:7–8; 8:26; 18:5–6). Wenham thus concludes: "If Eden is seen as an ideal sanctuary, then perhaps Adam should be described as an archetypal Levite."[10] That the Levites

---

7. For a detailed analysis of the Levitical tasks, including the Chronicler's employment of priestly language based in Israel's traditions and his innovations, see Gary N. Knoppers, "Hierodules, Priests, or Janitors? The Levites in Chronicles and the History of the Priesthood," *JBL* 118:1 (1999): 49–72.

8. On the topic of worship, see the discussions in Chapters 15 and 16 on 1 Chr 15–16, pp. 155–73, and Live the Story in Chapter 34, pp. 319–21.

9. For the connections between the Garden of Eden and the Jerusalem Temple, see the discussions in Chapters 32 and 33 on 2 Chr 3–4, pp. 305–8, 311–15.

10. Gordon J. Wenham, "Sanctuary Symbolism and the Garden of Eden," in *I Studied Inscriptions from before the Flood*, ed. Richard S. Hess and David T. Tsumara (Winona Lake, IN: Eisenbrauns, 1994), 401; see https://www.godawa.com/chronicles_of_the_nephilim/Articles_By_Others/Wenham-Sanctuary_Symbolism_Garden_of_Eden.pdf. See also Greg K. Beale, *The Temple and the Church's*

are described in language reminiscent of Adam suggests that in some sense their role of drawing near to God and offering praises to him is intended for *humanity*, that is, the Levitical identity and calling points to a greater reality.

John A. Davies has conducted an extensive study on Exodus 19:5 and concludes that God's setting apart of Israel means that his people are to enjoy the privileged status of royalty and priesthood, which includes having access to God's heavenly court.[11] The temple itself reflects God's heavenly throne,[12] thus Israel's priests and Levites are given access into the divine realm as they draw near before a holy God. But Exodus 19:5 indicates that God's intention was that *all Israel* would enjoy this special relationship as God's treasured possession.[13] Hahn makes the astute observation that during the reign of Hezekiah when the sacred assembly gathers for worship, they are invited to draw near to God and bring him their offerings (2 Chr 29:31). He notes that language describing their consecration and drawing near to God is used of Israel's priests,[14] thus suggesting that Hezekiah is addressing the people as if they were priests.[15] In the story that follows, the gathered assembly includes foreigners, reminding us that the sacred assembly was not limited to ethnic Israelites (30:25).

The prophet Isaiah looked forward to a time when Levitical ancestry would no longer be the prerequisite for priestly service. In a vision of a glorified Zion where nations stream to it, the prophet envisions God taking priests and Levites from *among the nations*. He looks forward to the time when *foreigners* will join themselves to the LORD (Isa 56:6; 66:20–21). When God rebuilds the ancient ruins, he will call his gathered people "priests of the LORD" and God's "minsters" (61:6). This anticipates the time when *all* of God's people—even those from among the nations—will be given this privileged vocation, enabling them to have access into God's presence.

With this rich history in view, the writer to the Hebrews explains that through Jesus's sacrificial death, believers are given free and unrestricted access into God's presence. In the Old Testament, the Levites served in the temple, being assigned all kinds of temple-related tasks, yet even *their* access to God's

---

Mission: A Biblical Theology of the Dwelling Place of God, NSBT (Downers Grove, IL: InterVarsity Press, 2004), 77–78.

11. John A. Davies, "A Royal Priesthood: Literary and Intertextual Perspectives on the Image of Israel in Exodus 19:6," *TynBul* 53:1 (2002): 157–59.

12. See the discussions in Chapters 32–33 on 2 Chr 3–4.

13. See the discussion by Christopher J. H. Wright, *Exodus*, SGBC (Grand Rapids, Zondervan Academic, 2021), 339–45.

14. See the discussion in Chapter 58 on 2 Chr 29, pp. 498–99.

15. For a theologically rich and detailed analysis, see Hahn, *Kingdom of God*, 174; cf. the discussion in Chapter 58 on 2 Chr 29, p. 498.

presence was limited. The priests officiated at the altar, but only the high priest could enter the holy of holies, one day per year (Lev 16; Heb 9:1–14). The astounding reality is that through Jesus, the great high priest (according to the order of Melchizedek), we can have confidence to enter God's heavenly sanctuary—*beyond the veil* (Heb 10:19–22).[16] The hiddenness and inaccessibility of God that characterized God's presence in the temple has now been opened up through Jesus—*the temple veil was torn in two*. We can approach God in worship because Jesus has established a new and living way. He has entered into heaven itself and accomplished the definitive purgation through his own shed blood.

Peter makes the remarkable statement that believers in Christ are "being built into a spiritual house to be a holy priesthood, offering spiritual sacrifices acceptable to God through Jesus Christ" (1 Pet 2:4–5). Isaiah had seen that foreigners would become priests and ministers of God, and now Peter reminds God's people, including Gentiles: "But you are a chosen people, a royal priesthood, a holy nation, God's special possession, that you may declare the praises of him who called you out of darkness into his wonderful light" (1 Pet 2:9; cf. Rev 1:6; 5:10). This is our privilege and high calling, seen from afar in the Old Testament through the Levites but fulfilled through Jesus, our great high priest, who serves as a priest forever. The Levites were to stand every morning and evening to thank and to praise the LORD (1 Chr 23:30), thus for the Chronicler, "life is for perpetual worship," and this is to be a "joyous, heartfelt affair."[17] We are exhorted to avail ourselves of all that has been accomplished in Christ and to draw near to God in worship—and in keeping with Chronicles, may this be a joyous, heartfelt affair.

---

16. For Jesus's high priestly role, see Live the Story, Chapter 6, pp. 85–87.
17. Hahn, *The Kingdom of God*, 127.

CHAPTER 24

1 Chronicles 24:1-31

 LISTEN to the Story

¹These were the divisions of the descendants of Aaron:

The sons of Aaron were Nadab, Abihu, Eleazar and Ithamar. ²But Nadab and Abihu died before their father did, and they had no sons; so Eleazar and Ithamar served as the priests. ³With the help of Zadok a descendant of Eleazar and Ahimelek a descendant of Ithamar, David separated them into divisions for their appointed order of ministering. ⁴A larger number of leaders were found among Eleazar's descendants than among Ithamar's, and they were divided accordingly: sixteen heads of families from Eleazar's descendants and eight heads of families from Ithamar's descendants. ⁵They divided them impartially by casting lots, for there were officials of the sanctuary and officials of God among the descendants of both Eleazar and Ithamar.

⁶The scribe Shemaiah son of Nethanel, a Levite, recorded their names in the presence of the king and of the officials: Zadok the priest, Ahimelek son of Abiathar and the heads of families of the priests and of the Levites— one family being taken from Eleazar and then one from Ithamar.

⁷The first lot fell to Jehoiarib,
the second to Jedaiah,
⁸the third to Harim,
the fourth to Seorim,
⁹the fifth to Malkijah,
the sixth to Mijamin,
¹⁰the seventh to Hakkoz,
the eighth to Abijah,
¹¹the ninth to Jeshua,
the tenth to Shekaniah,
¹²the eleventh to Eliashib,

the twelfth to Jakim,
[13]the thirteenth to Huppah,
the fourteenth to Jeshebeab,
[14]the fifteenth to Bilgah,
the sixteenth to Immer,
[15]the seventeenth to Hezir,
the eighteenth to Happizzez,
[16]the nineteenth to Pethahiah,
the twentieth to Jehezkel,
[17]the twenty-first to Jakin,
the twenty-second to Gamul,
[18]the twenty-third to Delaiah
and the twenty-fourth to Maaziah.

[19]This was their appointed order of ministering when they entered the temple of the LORD, according to the regulations prescribed for them by their ancestor Aaron, as the LORD, the God of Israel, had commanded him.

[20]As for the rest of the descendants of Levi:
from the sons of Amram: Shubael;
     from the sons of Shubael: Jehdeiah.
     [21]As for Rehabiah, from his sons:
     Ishiah was the first.
[22]From the Izharites: Shelomoth;
     from the sons of Shelomoth: Jahath.
[23]The sons of Hebron: Jeriah the first, Amariah the second, Jahaziel
     the third and Jekameam the fourth.
[24]The son of Uzziel: Micah;
     from the sons of Micah: Shamir.
     [25]The brother of Micah: Ishiah;
     from the sons of Ishiah: Zechariah.
[26]The sons of Merari: Mahli and Mushi.
     The son of Jaaziah: Beno.
[27]The sons of Merari:
     from Jaaziah: Beno, Shoham, Zakkur and Ibri.
[28]From Mahli: Eleazar, who had no sons.
[29]From Kish: the son of Kish:
     Jerahmeel.

³⁰And the sons of Mushi: Mahli, Eder and Jerimoth.

These were the Levites, according to their families. ³¹They also cast lots, just as their relatives the descendants of Aaron did, in the presence of King David and of Zadok, Ahimelek, and the heads of families of the priests and of the Levites. The families of the oldest brother were treated the same as those of the youngest.

Listening to the Text in the Story: Leviticus 10

As David continues to prepare for the rule of Solomon and the temple he will build, he organizes the priesthood into twenty-four divisions, according to the two priestly families of Eleazar and Ithamar.[1] During the time of Moses, Aaron and his four sons, Nadab, Abihu, Eleazar, and Ithamar, had been set apart to serve as priests (Exod 28:1–2). Yet Aaron's two sons Nadab and Abihu had died because they had offered unauthorized fire before God (Lev 10:1–2; cf. Lev 16:1). With the death of Aaron's two sons, the division of the priesthood is based on Aaron's two remaining sons, Eleazar and Ithamar (cf. Num 3:1–4, 10; 16:9–10, 39–40, etc.). Their families had the sacred calling of officiating at the altar and making atonement for Israel's sins. Yet only one son in each generation would serve as high priest, and this line of succession is through Eleazar (3:32), who assumes this responsibility after his father dies (Deut 10:6; cf. Lev 16:32; Num 20:23–29). Since the priestly office was hereditary, the Chronicler gives much attention to genealogies, and at the outset of this chapter, the Chronicler notes that Zadok (who serves as priest during the time of David) was a descendant of Eleazar (1 Chr 24:3). This chapter focuses on the two priestly lines of Eleazar and Ithamar, for their descendants will serve as Israel's priests.

 EXPLAIN the Story

The Priestly Lines of Eleazar and Ithamar (24:1–6)

The chapter is divided into two sections, beginning with the divisions of the priesthood (1 Chr 24:1–19), followed by names of additional Levites

---

1. The origin of the twenty-four divisions has been the subject of some debate (see Selman, *1 Chronicles*, 229–30).

(vv. 20–31). The names of Aaron and his four sons are noted at the outset, although the priesthood is taken up in the lines of Eleazar and Ithamar (v. 1; cf. 15:11), represented by Zadok (from the line of Eleazar) and by Ahimelek (from the line of Ithamar) at the time of David. We have already seen that Zadok and Ahimelek had a key leadership role when the ark was brought into Jerusalem (vv. 11–14; 16:39–40).

Zadok proved to be a trusted and loyal servant of David (2 Sam 15:24–29; 17:15–29; 1 Kgs 1:8, 32–40). He became high priest during the reign of Solomon after the previous high priest, Abiathar, had been disloyal to Solomon (2:27, 35; cf. 1 Sam 2:27–36). The more prominent role of Zadok's family is seen in their higher numbers: sixteen heads of families represent the division of Zadok, whereas eight heads of families represent the division of Ithamar (1 Chr 24:4). The division of labor among these two priestly families was determined by lots, and Shemaiah the scribe (who was a Levite) records their outcome in the presence of the king, the princes, Zadok and Ahimelek, and the heads of the priestly and Levitical households (v. 6).

The Division of the Priesthood According to Lots (24:7–19)

The use of lots is unfamiliar in our contemporary context, however, they were commonly used in the ancient world (Joel 3:3; Jonah 1:7; Nah 3:10; cf. Ps 22:18). Lots were employed when the land was apportioned among the tribes (Num 26:55, 56; 33:54; 34:13–14; see also Josh 14:2; 1 Chr 6:61, 63, 65, etc.).[2] In the Old Testament, lots were used to determine God's will, as there was the expectation that God was working through them (see Lev 16:8–10). One proverb summarizes this succinctly: "The lot is cast into the lap, but its every decision is from the LORD" (Prov 16:33; see also Acts 1:23–26). Accordingly, when Joshua used lots, he had done so "before the LORD" (Josh 18:6, 8, 10), and in this chapter, lots are cast in the presence of the king and Israel's religious leaders (1 Chr 24:5–6). Another benefit of lots was that they ensured the equitable distribution of responsibilities and rotation among priestly families, so that one family was not favored or given preferential treatment.

Twenty-four names are recorded that identify families from Eleazar and Ithamar who serve as priests, with sixteen coming from Eleazar and eight coming from Ithamar (1 Chr 24:7–18). These names provide a "roster," not unlike church rosters when people or families are assigned certain tasks over

---

2. Although the NIV does not always translate the term "lot" in these verses (probably so that the text is more readable for a contemporary reader less familiar with lots), these verses nevertheless testify to the use of lots in the allotment of cities.

the course of a year. Jehoiarib is first, underscoring the prominence of his family, and notably, the Maccabean family that will be important in later Jewish history is from this line (cf. 1 Mac 2:1).[3] The list concludes by emphasizing the purpose of the list: "This was their appointed order of ministering when they entered the temple of the LORD, according to the regulations prescribed for them by their ancestor Aaron, as the LORD, the God of Israel, had commanded him" (1 Chr 24:19). Focus is on the orderly and systematic appointment of priests to serve in the temple, according to the regulations prescribed by Aaron.

Levitical Families According to Lots (24:20–31)

The chapter concludes with a list of Levites who served as temple personnel (1 Chr 24:20–30). Since these Levitical families have already been introduced (23:16–23), Boda suggests that their inclusion in this chapter may be to draw attention to the non-priestly lines of Levi, possibly even to heal rifts between the Levites and the priests and between the two priestly lines of Aaron, thereby affirming that all are called by God to serve in the temple.[4] As with the priestly division, lots are again used, and they are cast publicly before David, Zadok, Ahimelek, and other leaders (24:31).

LIVE the Story

Equitable Distribution of Tasks

The priesthood is central to this chapter but, since we have discussed this topic elsewhere,[5] we will consider another important issue raised in this chapter, namely, the use of lots along with the equitable distribution of tasks. David used lots to determine the priestly and Levitical allocation of tasks, and they will feature in the next two chapters when musicians and gatekeepers are assigned responsibilities (1 Chr 25:8–9; 26:13–14). One of the functions of lots was to ensure the equitable distribution of tasks among the Levitical families without favoring one above another. The Chronicler draws attention to this on several occasions, noting that the two priestly families were divided "impartially" (ESV, "all alike," 24:5) and later noting that families of an older brother were treated the same as families of a younger brother (v. 31). Similarly, when Levitical musicians are assigned responsibilities, their tasks were distributed "young and old alike, teacher as well as student" (25:8).

---

3. As pointed out by Williamson, *1 and 2 Chronicles*, 164.
4. Boda, *1–2 Chronicles*, 193.
5. See Live the Story in Chapter 6, pp. 85–87.

As with the musicians, lots were cast for the gate-keepers "according to their families, young and old alike" (26:13). Use of lots ensured that there was no favoritism or preferential treatment among the priestly and Levitical families, and since lots were ultimately used to discern God's will, this meant that their tasks were appointed by God.

In our contemporary church context, it is not uncommon for certain musical families or musicians to gain prominence in a church, especially when it comes to who plays the piano or the organ. We are all too familiar with the story of one or two prominent musicians who assume that they have the "right" to be the primary musician or worship leader. Certain musical families can be favored, which inevitably excludes other musicians from using their gifts in service to God. The principle of equitable distribution of tasks in this story could readily be applied to the church by adopting some kind of rotation system, which ensures that one or two individuals are not favored above others.

Further, Japhet notes that in the post-exilic period, there were more priests and Levites than needed. Their organization according to divisions (see Neh 10) ensured that those who were competing for the right to serve and to enjoy the privileges of the clergy could have this opportunity, but not all the time.[6] Similarly, when there are more qualified musicians in a particular church than needed, some kind of rotation enables everyone to use their gifts.

A key concept underlying these chapters is that the Levites were called to *service* (Num 8:14–22; 16:9). It is not surprising to find, therefore, that the word "service" is used throughout these chapters (1 Chr 23:24, 26, 28, 32; 24:3, 19; 25:1, etc., variously translated "served" and "ministering/ministry" in the NIV), underscoring that individual preferences were secondary in view of a higher calling to serve God. We are called to be faithful with the gifts God has given us, but they are given by the Spirit for the common good (1 Cor 12:1–31) so that the body might be built up in love (Eph 4:1–16). This ought to be the goal of our service. Our gifts are not to be used to glorify ourselves or to be self-serving. The church is not the place for favoritism or partiality (Jas 2:1–9), but rather, we are called to use our gifts for the building up of the body.

As I was reflecting on this topic, I was reminded of a senior faculty member at the institution where I have served for the past twenty years. Over a decade ago, I had spoken to our digital education department about recording an online version of my Old Testament Survey course. I was told at the time that a senior Old Testament colleague had already spoken to them about teaching this online course. I was happy to defer to my senior colleague but, upon

---

6. Japhet, *I & II Chronicles*, 423–24.

returning to my office, I received a call from him. He told me he had heard that I was interested in developing this course and, to my surprise, he informed me that he had withdrawn his name since he wanted *me* to teach the course. As God's *servant*, he was willing to relinquish his rights. God has designed his church in such a way that we all need each other; thus, one person is not more valuable than the other (1 Cor 12:4–31). Divisions due to preferential treatment or competition over certain privileged tasks have no place in the body of Christ. Our own personal preferences ought to be secondary in view of our primary calling to serve the Lord. This theme of service continues in the following chapter as Levitical musicians are appointed to lead Israel in worship—and, again, the assignment of tasks is by lots.

LISTEN to the Story

¹David, together with the commanders of the army, set apart some of the sons of Asaph, Heman and Jeduthun for the ministry of prophesying, accompanied by harps, lyres and cymbals. Here is the list of the men who performed this service:

²From the sons of Asaph:
Zakkur, Joseph, Nethaniah and Asarelah. The sons of Asaph were under the supervision of Asaph, who prophesied under the king's supervision.
³As for Jeduthun, from his sons:
Gedaliah, Zeri, Jeshaiah, Shimei, Hashabiah and Mattithiah, six in all, under the supervision of their father Jeduthun, who prophesied, using the harp in thanking and praising the LORD.
⁴As for Heman, from his sons:
Bukkiah, Mattaniah, Uzziel, Shubael and Jerimoth; Hananiah, Hanani, Eliathah, Giddalti and Romamti-Ezer; Joshbekashah, Mallothi, Hothir and Mahazioth. ⁵(All these were sons of Heman the king's seer. They were given him through the promises of God to exalt him. God gave Heman fourteen sons and three daughters.)

⁶All these men were under the supervision of their father for the music of the temple of the LORD, with cymbals, lyres and harps, for the ministry at the house of God.

Asaph, Jeduthun and Heman were under the supervision of the king. ⁷Along with their relatives—all of them trained and skilled in music for the LORD—they numbered 288. ⁸Young and old alike, teacher as well as student, cast lots for their duties.

⁹The first lot, which was for Asaph, fell to Joseph,
    his sons and relatives   12
the second to Gedaliah,
    him and his relatives and sons   12
¹⁰the third to Zakkur,
    his sons and relatives   12
¹¹the fourth to Izri,
    his sons and relatives   12
¹²the fifth to Nethaniah,
    his sons and relatives   12
¹³the sixth to Bukkiah,
    his sons and relatives   12
¹⁴the seventh to Jesarelah,
    his sons and relatives   12
¹⁵the eighth to Jeshaiah,
    his sons and relatives   12
¹⁶the ninth to Mattaniah,
    his sons and relatives   12
¹⁷the tenth to Shimei,
    his sons and relatives   12
¹⁸the eleventh to Azarel,
    his sons and relatives   12
¹⁹the twelfth to Hashabiah,
    his sons and relatives   12
²⁰the thirteenth to Shubael,
    his sons and relatives   12
²¹the fourteenth to Mattithiah,
    his sons and relatives   12
²²the fifteenth to Jerimoth,
    his sons and relatives   12
²³the sixteenth to Hananiah,
    his sons and relatives   12
²⁴the seventeenth to Joshbekashah,
    his sons and relatives   12
²⁵the eighteenth to Hanani,
    his sons and relatives   12

²⁶the nineteenth to Mallothi,
     his sons and relatives   12
²⁷the twentieth to Eliathah,
     his sons and relatives   12
²⁸the twenty-first to Hothir,
     his sons and relatives   12
²⁹the twenty-second to Giddalti,
     his sons and relatives   12
³⁰the twenty-third to Mahazioth,
     his sons and relatives   12
³¹the twenty-fourth to Romamti-Ezer,
     his sons and relatives   12.

Listening to the Text in the Story: Psalm 150:1–6

David's preparation for the temple continues with the appointment of Levitical musicians who are to lead Israel in praise and worship. Since David himself was a gifted musician and songwriter (1 Sam 16:18; 2 Sam 22:1), it is not surprising to find that he gives so much attention to the appointment of musicians, a topic already introduced (1 Chr 6:31–32; 13:8; 15:16, 19). This is, indeed, one of David's legacies, marking an important development in the traditions of the cult.[1] Praising God is central to Israel's life before a holy God, and so attention is rightly given to this sacred task. The final psalm in the Psalter resounds with praise as a variety of musical instruments are played, with each one being used to give praise to the LORD:

Praise the LORD.

Praise God in his sanctuary;
    praise him in his mighty heavens.
Praise him for his acts of power;
    praise him for his surpassing greatness.
Praise him with the sounding of the trumpet,
    praise him with the harp and lyre,
praise him with timbrel and dancing,

---

1. See the article by De Vries, "Moses and David as Cult Founders," 619–630.

praise him with the strings and pipe,
praise him with the clash of cymbals,
        praise him with resounding cymbals.

Let everything that has breath praise the LORD.

Praise the LORD. (Ps 150:1–6)

This invitation to praise the LORD underscores the centrality of worship, and it is fitting that David places so much importance on the appointment of Levites for this sacred task.

Musical instruments were known in the ancient world, and several artifacts depicting musicians playing them provide some delightful examples. A terracotta cult stand dated to the late eleventh or early tenth century BC found at Ashdod depicts a musical ensemble, with musicians playing the flute, cymbals, lyre, and a tambourine.[2] Another terracotta figure on display in the Israel Museum, dated to the seventh century BC, depicts a musician playing a double flute.[3] Several ancient flutes have been found in Israel, one of which was made of bone about eleven centimeters (about four and a half inches) in length.[4] These kind of archaeological discoveries provide a rich sampling of instruments that help to locate this chapter in its ancient context.[5]

EXPLAIN the Story

David Sets Apart Three Levitical Families to Lead Israel in Worship (25:1–7)

David and the commanders of his army set apart musicians from the sons of Asaph, Heman, and Jeduthun to lead Israel in worship (1 Chr 25:1). While it might seem unusual that military commanders are involved in the selection process, Merrill notes that musicians often accompanied Israel in battles since they were *holy* wars and songs were sung to the LORD (cf. Exod 15:1–18, 20–21; Judg 5:1–31; see also 2 Chr 20:20–22).[6] The three Levitical families

---

2. The cult stand is in the Israel Museum collection; see www.imj.org.il/en/collections/369806
3. See the Israel Museum; https://www.imj.org.il/en/collections/370866
4. See the Israel Museum: https://www.imj.org.il/en/collections/369521
5. For a helpful summary of ancient musical instruments according to the three basic types of string, wind, and percussion, see Phillip J. King and Larry E. Stager, *Life in Biblical Israel*, Library of Ancient Israel (Louisville: Westminster John Knox Press, 2001), 290–300.
6. Merrill, *1 & 2 Chronicles*, 281.

of Asaph, Heman, and Jeduthun are mentioned elsewhere as having a key role in worship, and their various instruments include cymbals, trumpets, harps, and lyres. They and their families will have a prominent role when the temple is dedicated: "All the Levites who were musicians—Asaph, Heman, Jeduthun and their sons and relatives—stood on the east side of the altar, dressed in fine linen and playing cymbals, harps and lyres. They were accompanied by 120 priests sounding trumpets" (2 Chr 5:12). These are the three families that had been chosen and designated by name to give thanks to God in song and with instrument (1 Chr 16:4, 41–42). The Levites were to offer thanksgiving and praise to God every morning and every evening (23:30). Praising God was not relegated to one day per week on the Sabbath or during major festivals, but it was done *daily*.

Three Levitical families are set apart "for the ministry of prophesying" (25:1). The verb "to prophesy" (Heb. *n-b-ʾ*) occurs three times in the opening verses, marking the first occurrence of the verb in Chronicles (vv. 1–3; cf. 2 Chr 18:7, 9, 11, 17; 20:37). The language is used elsewhere to describe Israel's elders, who prophesied after the Spirit had come upon them (Num 11:25–27), and of prophets in general (e.g., 2 Chr 18:7, 17; 20:37). That Levites prophesy may suggest some kind of spontaneous utterance by the Holy Spirit (cf. Acts 2:4) accompanied by music (cf. 1 Sam 10:5–6), or it may indicate that the psalms have a prophetic quality, inspired by the Spirit. Notably, Asaph (a Levite) held the office of prophet (1 Chr 25:2), and Asaph, Heman, and Jeduthun are elsewhere identified as "seers" (Asaph, 2 Chr 29:30; Heman, 1 Chr 25:5; Jeduthun, 2 Chr 35:15).[7] It may well be that Levites are functioning as prophets in the royal court.[8] This language of "prophesy" underscores their important role within the sacred assembly, and it reminds us of the Spirit's role in worship. Accordingly, when the Spirit of the LORD comes upon a man named Jahaziel, he gives a prophetic word to Jehoshaphat, but he is notably identified as a Levite, belonging to the sons of Asaph (20:14–17). In another passage, the Spirit comes upon Zechariah, son of Jehoiada the priest; he gives a word of warning to Joash, using the common prophetic formula, "This is what God says." Although his word is rejected and he is killed (24:20–21), these passages suggest some kind of prophetic activity among the Levites.

The descendants of Asaph, Jeduthun, and Heman are given next (1 Chr 25:2–4), beginning with Asaph, who has a key leadership role. A number

---

7. Prophets such as Gad (2 Sam 24:11; 1 Chr 21:9; 2 Chr 29:25), Iddo (2 Chr 9:29; 12:15), and Jehu (2 Chr 19:2) are identified as "seers," which is another term used to describe Israel's prophets.

8. See the helpful summary by Boda (*1–2 Chronicles*, 185–86).

of psalms are attributed to him (Pss 50, 73–83; cf. 2 Chr 29:30), and he is identified as the head musician (1 Chr 16:5). It is important to bear in mind that his descendants continue to have a central role in worship in the post-exilic community (cf. Ezra 2:41; Neh 7:44; 11:17; 12:46). Jeduthun's descendants are given next (1 Chr 25:3). His name appears in relation to three psalms (Pss 39:1; 62:1; 77:1), and as with Asaph, his family is prominently featured in relation to worship (1 Chr 16:41, 42; 2 Chr 5:12; 35:15). Heman's descendants are given last (1 Chr 25:4–5). His large family is due to God's promise to exalt him, and he is the only one whose daughters are mentioned (v. 5). The presence of women among the Levitical musicians hearkens back to Miriam, who was from the tribe of Levi (Exod 15:1, 21). These three musical families are under the leadership of their fathers, whereas Asaph, Jeduthun, and Heman are under the direct leadership of King David. Their service in the house of the Lord includes singing accompanied by musical instruments, such as cymbals, harps, and lyres (1 Chr 25:6). The number of descendants from these three families totals 288 musicians. As with the divisions of priests and Levites, lots were cast for their specific duties, thereby ensuring that there was no favoritism or preferential treatment (v. 8).[9]

Lots Are Cast for the Duties of Levitical Musicians (25:8–31)

The first lot came out for Asaph, and the process continues until twenty-four lots are cast. Some of the names mentioned in this list have already been introduced, such as Joseph (1 Chr 25:2) and Gedaliah (v. 3), whereas other names are not mentioned elsewhere. The division of the musicians into twenty-four groups (vv. 8–31) is consistent with David's system of appointing twenty-four divisions of priests (24:7–18). David's military will be divided into twelve divisions, but the number 24,000 dominates,[10] providing further symmetry in David's administrative structure.

 LIVE the Story

The Church Continues in Praise and Thanksgiving

God's presence in the midst of his people was what distinguished them from the surrounding nations (cf. Exod 33:16), and as such, worship of the Lord in the temple was at the center of their life. Israel's praises were to resound

---

9. On the use and purpose of lots, see the discussion in Chapter 24 on 1 Chr 24:7–19, pp. 236–37.

10. See the discussion in Chapter 27 on 1 Chr 27:1–15, pp. 259–61.

with joy as the Levites made a loud sound in celebration to the LORD (1 Chr 15:16–22, 28). The Psalter testifies that the entire community is exhorted to sing to the LORD. Psalm 68:4 invites the community to "Sing to God, sing in praise of his name, extol him who rides on the clouds; rejoice before him—his name is the LORD" (see also Pss 98:1; 105:2; 149:1; Jer 20:13). In fact, the *whole earth* is exhorted to sing to the LORD (Pss 68:32; 96:1)![11]

This longstanding tradition of singing praises to God continued when the Israelites returned from exile, as singers from the family of Asaph and other singers, both male and female, were listed among the returnees (Ezra 2:41, 65; see also Neh 7:44; 12:24). Key moments in Israel's story were marked by worship, such as when the foundation of the temple was dedicated (Ezra 3:10–11), when the second temple was completed (Ezra 6:16), and when the walls of Jerusalem were dedicated (Neh 12:27–47). Worship was central to what it means to be God's people.

The early church continued in this tradition of singing hymns and offering praises to God, although their new context necessitated gathering for worship in homes (Acts 2:42, 46–47). In Paul's letter to believers at Ephesus, he exhorts them not to get drunk with wine, but instead, they were to speak to one another "with psalms, hymns, and songs from the Spirit. Sing and make music from your heart to the Lord" (Eph 5:19; cf. 1 Cor 14:26). Similarly, he exhorts believers at Colossae that the message of Christ was to dwell in them, as they "teach and admonish one another with all wisdom through psalms, hymns, and songs from the Spirit, singing to God with gratitude in your hearts" (Col 3:16).[12] Fee observes that Paul transferred the Psalter's hymnic pattern to Christian hymns so that "devotion previously given exclusively to Yahweh has for the early Christians transferred to Christ as 'Lord'—to the one who came to earth to both redeem and recreate us into the divine image."[13] He sums this up by stating that hymns in the Psalter that were sung "to" and "about" Yahweh are now sung "to" and "about" Christ, so that Christian worship is deeply rooted in Christology. Accordingly, hymnic material in the New Testament focuses on Jesus (Phil 2:5–11; Col 1:15–20; 1 Tim 2:5–6, etc.). The early church thus testifies that the Psalms witness to Christ (Luke 20:42; 24:44; Acts 13:33).

---

11. For an excellent overview of the place of music and singing in Israel, see Block, *For the Glory of God*, 222–30.

12. Block has provided a helpful survey of the place of song and music in the early church, which includes a discussion of two key Pauline texts (Eph 5:18–20; Col 3:15–17); see Block, *For the Glory of God*, 230–34; see also Allen P. Ross, *Recalling the Hope of Glory: Biblical Worship from the Garden of Eden to the New Creation* (Grand Rapids: Kregel, 2006), 262–68.

13. Fee, *Jesus the Lord*, 24.

One of the hallmarks of the people of God throughout the ages is that we are first and foremost a worshiping community. Block has noted that, while music is an important part of worship, there is more to worship than music, and not all Christian music is to be identified as biblical worship. Block notes that "proclamation" is central to worship, and Christ-centered worship is *Word* driven.[14] Bonhoeffer made the same point in his book *Life Together* when he noted that we do not simply hum a melody together, but our worship is the "sung *Word*." He continues: "All devotion, all attention should be concentrated on the Word in the hymn." This "sung Word" includes words of praise to God, words of thanksgiving, confession, and prayer, so that the "music is completely the servant of the Word."[15] I was reminded recently of a song I had learnt as a teenager at youth camps, which begins:

> Therefore the redeemed of the Lord shall return,
> And come with singing unto Zion,
> And everlasting joy shall be upon their head.

This song has been taken almost word-for-word from the book of Isaiah (cf. 35:10; 51:11). This is the "sung Word," and I can still remember this song forty years later. Songs and hymns that are theologically rich and faithful to the Scriptures have a didactic function, reinforcing central tenets of Christian theology.

In contemporary worship today, God's word has sometimes become the servant of music. Since the Levitical musicians were well-trained in Torah with several of them writing a number of psalms, we are reminded that the *content* of the songs we sing matters. This does not preclude using an array of musical instruments, even those that make a loud noise (see Ps 150), but careful attention needs to be given to ensure that the words we sing are biblically sound and Christ-centered. If Fee's statement is correct, that songs sung by the early church were creedal in nature, "full of theological grist" and giving evidence of what Christians actually believed about God and Christ,[16] then we need to pay careful attention to the content of our hymns and songs of praise to ensure that they are in accordance with sound biblical teaching—so that they are worthy of the God whom we serve.

---

14. Block, *For the Glory of God*, 240–41. On the topic of worship rooted in Scripture, see Live the Story, Worship of God Is Rooted in Scripture, in Chapter 16, pp. 171–72.

15. Dietrich Bonhoeffer, *Life Together*, trans. John W. Doberstein (New York: Harper Collins, 1954), 59.

16. Fee, *Jesus the Lord*, 23.

CHAPTER 26

1 Chronicles 26:1–32

 ## LISTEN to the Story

¹The divisions of the gatekeepers:

From the Korahites: Meshelemiah son of Kore, one of the sons of Asaph.
²Meshelemiah had sons:
    Zechariah the firstborn,
    Jediael the second,
    Zebadiah the third,
    Jathniel the fourth,
    ³Elam the fifth,
    Jehohanan the sixth
    and Eliehoenai the seventh.
⁴Obed-Edom also had sons:
    Shemaiah the firstborn,
    Jehozabad the second,
    Joah the third,
    Sakar the fourth,
    Nethanel the fifth,
    ⁵Ammiel the sixth,
    Issachar the seventh
    and Peullethai the eighth.
    (For God had blessed Obed-Edom.)

⁶Obed-Edom's son Shemaiah also had sons, who were leaders in their father's family because they were very capable men. ⁷The sons of Shemaiah: Othni, Rephael, Obed and Elzabad; his relatives Elihu and Semakiah were also able men. ⁸All these were descendants of Obed-Edom; they and their sons and their relatives were capable

men with the strength to do the work—descendants of Obed-Edom, 62 in all.

⁹Meshelemiah had sons and relatives, who were able men—18 in all.

¹⁰Hosah the Merarite had sons: Shimri the first (although he was not the firstborn, his father had appointed him the first), ¹¹Hilkiah the second, Tabaliah the third and Zechariah the fourth. The sons and relatives of Hosah were 13 in all.

¹²These divisions of the gatekeepers, through their leaders, had duties for ministering in the temple of the LORD, just as their relatives had. ¹³Lots were cast for each gate, according to their families, young and old alike.

¹⁴The lot for the East Gate fell to Shelemiah. Then lots were cast for his son Zechariah, a wise counselor, and the lot for the North Gate fell to him. ¹⁵The lot for the South Gate fell to Obed-Edom, and the lot for the storehouse fell to his sons. ¹⁶The lots for the West Gate and the Shalleketh Gate on the upper road fell to Shuppim and Hosah.

Guard was alongside of guard: ¹⁷There were six Levites a day on the east, four a day on the north, four a day on the south and two at a time at the storehouse. ¹⁸As for the court to the west, there were four at the road and two at the court itself.

¹⁹These were the divisions of the gatekeepers who were descendants of Korah and Merari.

²⁰Their fellow Levites were in charge of the treasuries of the house of God and the treasuries for the dedicated things.

²¹The descendants of Ladan, who were Gershonites through Ladan and who were heads of families belonging to Ladan the Gershonite, were Jehieli, ²²the sons of Jehieli, Zetham and his brother Joel. They were in charge of the treasuries of the temple of the LORD.

²³From the Amramites, the Izharites, the Hebronites and the Uzzielites:

²⁴Shubael, a descendant of Gershom son of Moses, was the official in charge of the treasuries. ²⁵His relatives through Eliezer: Rehabiah his son, Jeshaiah his son, Joram his son, Zikri his son and Shelomith his son. ²⁶Shelomith and his relatives were in charge of all the treasuries for the things dedicated by King David, by the heads of families who were the commanders of thousands and commanders of hundreds,

and by the other army commanders. ²⁷Some of the plunder taken in battle they dedicated for the repair of the temple of the LORD. ²⁸And everything dedicated by Samuel the seer and by Saul son of Kish, Abner son of Ner and Joab son of Zeruiah, and all the other dedicated things were in the care of Shelomith and his relatives.

²⁹From the Izharites: Kenaniah and his sons were assigned duties away from the temple, as officials and judges over Israel.

³⁰From the Hebronites: Hashabiah and his relatives—seventeen hundred able men—were responsible in Israel west of the Jordan for all the work of the LORD and for the king's service. ³¹As for the Hebronites, Jeriah was their chief according to the genealogical records of their families. In the fortieth year of David's reign a search was made in the records, and capable men among the Hebronites were found at Jazer in Gilead. ³²Jeriah had twenty-seven hundred relatives, who were able men and heads of families, and King David put them in charge of the Reubenites, the Gadites and the half-tribe of Manasseh for every matter pertaining to God and for the affairs of the king.

Listening to the Text in the Story: 1 Chronicles 9:17–34; Hittite Instructions for Temple Officials

With singers and musicians in place, David now appoints Levitical gatekeepers (1 Chr 26:1–19), treasurers (vv. 20–28), and officials and judges (vv. 29–32). While these tasks might initially appear somewhat mundane, the appointment of trusted leaders is essential for the effective management of the kingdom. An ancient inscription from the Hittites illustrates the importance of having trusted and loyal temple personnel.[1] The inscription states that temple servants were not allowed to partake of any food and drink dedicated to the cult, such as bread, beer and wine. Similarly, trustworthy caretakers of gold, silver, and precious items were essential; the text reads: "Whatever silver, gold, garments or bronze implements of the gods you hold, you are (merely) (their) caretakers. You have no right to the silver, gold, garments (and) bronze implements of the gods, and none whatsoever to the things that are in the gods' houses. They belong to the god alone."[2] Gatekeepers had a particularly important task of

---

1. "Instructions for Temple Officials," trans. Albrecht Goetze (*ANET*, 207–210).
2. Ibid. (*ANET*, 208).

protecting the temple that required long hours of service: "Furthermore, there shall be watchmen employed by night who shall patrol all night through. Outside the enclosure guards shall watch, inside the temples shall the temple officials patrol all night through and they shall not sleep. Night by night one of the high priests shall be in charge of the patrols."[3] Temple guardians were prohibited from spending the night in their own homes while on patrol—it was a capital offense! David's appointment of key temple personnel and managers of his royal estate is crucial, for they are "essential workers" who manage the affairs of the kingdom. Appointment of trusted leaders will ensure the smooth transition to Solomon when he becomes king.

David appoints gatekeepers who protect the temple and its treasuries, but they also protected the sacred precincts from lay encroachment. Levites appointed to this task served as security guards, protecting the temple from unlawful entry and guarding the temple treasuries. Their important role as guardians will be seen later when young Joash is anointed as king, at which time the Levites are instructed—with weapons in hand!—not to allow anyone into the temple except priests and Levites (2 Chr 23:6–11; cf. 2 Chr 26:16–23). Since Levitical gatekeepers were among the returnees, this chapter has ongoing relevance for the post-exilic community (1 Chr 9:17–34; cf. Neh 13:19–22).[4]

EXPLAIN the Story

David Appoints Levitical Gatekeepers from Kohath and Merari (26:1–19)

The list of names in this chapter can be somewhat confusing, and some of the relationships are not easy to identify. Rather than attempt to rehearse these relationships, it is more fruitful to focus on key families that are represented in the chapter and the tasks assigned to them. Japhet's succinct summary of this section is helpful. She notes that the line of *Kohath* is represented by two sub-branches, Meshelemiah and Obed-Edom, whereas the line of *Merari* is represented by Hosah.[5] Keeping these two lines in view is helpful, while noting that the largest and most important family is Obed-Edom. He is blessed by God with eight sons (1 Chr 26:4–8), and we may recall that this family had taken care of the ark of the covenant after the troubling incident with Uzzah

---

3. Ibid. (*ANET*, 209).
4. On the responsibilities of gatekeepers, see the discussion in Chapter 9 on 1 Chr 9:17–34, pp. 112–13.
5. Japhet, *I & II Chronicles*, 451.

(13:13–14). The men are described as "very capable" (26:6) and "able" (v. 9), although the NASB translation ("mighty men of valor" and "valiant men") is to be preferred, since it rightly draws attention to their military capabilities (cf. 2 Chr 23:1–15). The Levites were security guards appointed to prevent unlawful entry into the temple, to maintain order, and to protect temple revenue, something that would have required military strength.[6] These responsibilities might seem more like secular or governmental positions, but since their work entailed protecting the sacred temple and its treasuries, only those from the tribe of Levi could serve in this role. Even though they are not given the more prominent position of leading worship, they nevertheless serve alongside their fellow Levites, "ministering in the temple of the LORD" (1 Chr 26:12). Levites who serve as gatekeepers are as valuable as Levites who assist the priests and who lead worship—all are doing their work as service to the LORD. As with the other Levitical tasks, lots are cast for the assignment of responsibilities (v. 13).[7]

The lot for the important East gate falls to the family of Shelemiah (1 Chr 26:14), which was identified earlier as the gate of the king (9:18). During the Persian period, protecting the gate of the king was an important political post; Wright thus likens the guards to important government officials.[8] The lot for the north gate falls to Zechariah, and the south gate to Odeb-Edom and his sons, which included oversight of the storehouse (26:15). Wright notes that temples "functioned as the banks of antiquity, and to extend the metaphor, the temple storehouses were the bank vaults. Assignment of the doorways of such storehouses would have entailed considerable control over the finances of the kingdom."[9] This trusted responsibility is given to the family of Obed-Edom, whereas lots for the gates on the western side fall to Shuppim and Hosah (v. 16). A description of the guards indicates that there were six Levites stationed each day on the east, four on the north, another four on the south, and two at the storehouse (v. 17). These were the duties assigned to the gatekeepers from the Levitical families of Korah and Merari (v. 19).

The Levitical Families Appointed to Keep the Treasuries (26:20–28)

The temple had treasuries where tithes, dedicated offerings, spoil, and royal gifts were stored, possibly in its side rooms. Two Levitical families

---

6. Wright argues persuasively that the Levites are military figures; see John W. Wright, "Guarding the Gates: 1 Chronicles 26:1–19 and the Role of Gatekeepers in Chronicles," *JSOT* 48 (1990): 69–74.

7. For the use of lots in the Old Testament, see the discussion in Chapter 24 on 1 Chr 24:7–19, pp. 236–37.

8. Wright, "Guarding the Gates," 74–76.

9. Ibid., 76.

are appointed to take care of the temple treasuries and the items that had been dedicated to the LORD (1 Chr 26:20). Large quantities of gold, silver, valuable metals, and precious stones were kept in the temple (cf. 29:1–8; 2 Chr 5:1; 32:27–28). Protecting them required a high level of trust, but also military capabilities in the event that a foreign king attempted to plunder them (12:9; 25:23–24; 36:18). Sacred vessels and sacred objects were among the prized possessions of foreign kings (cf. Dan 1:2; 5:1–3). It was no small task, therefore, to be guardians of the temple treasuries. In the treasuries were the dedicated gifts that David had taken as spoil (1 Chr 26:26–27; see also 18:6–11; 20:2), along with precious items acquired by Samuel and Saul (v. 28).

David's Officials and Judges (26:29–32)

David also appoints Levitical officers and judges (1 Chr 26:29–32). Judges had been appointed during Israel's earlier and formative period (Exod 18:13–24; Deut 16:18–20; 17:1–13; 19:17–18; cf. Num 25:5).[10] They were to make judicial decisions according to God's laws, and Israel's priests and Levites were to instruct the people to follow God's law (2 Chr 17:9; 19:8–10; 31:4; see also Ezra 7:10). David's appointment of judges ensures that God's justice and righteousness were established under his rule, and Jehoshaphat will later appoint judges throughout the fortified cities of Judah (2 Chr 19:5–8).

In addition to those appointed to the temple precincts, David appoints Levitical leaders to oversee his affairs west of the Jordan (1 Chr 26:30) and east of the Jordan, which included oversight of the Reubenites, Gadites, and the half-tribe of Manasseh (vv. 31–32; cf. Num 32:1–42; Josh 22:1–9). Although not working in the temple, this is nevertheless a sacred task since the Levites are called to administer God's justice and represent the king in any civil disputes.[11] Since the Levites were known to be educated in God's law, these appointments underscore David's desire to see God's justice and righteousness established throughout his kingdom. In this case, rather than lots being used, these men were carefully chosen (1 Chr 26:31), underscoring their important role in the kingdom. When Jehoshaphat later appoints judges, he gives them the following instruction: "Consider carefully what you do, because you are not judging for mere mortals but for the LORD, who is with you whenever you give a verdict. Now let the fear of the LORD

---

10. For more information about the judicial process in ancient Israel, see Roland De Vaux, *Ancient Israel: Social Institutions*, Vol. 2 (New York: McGraw-Hill, 1965), 152–63.

11. See Boda, *1–2 Chronicles*, 201.

be on you. Judge carefully, for with the LORD our God there is no injustice or partiality or bribery" (2 Chr 19:6–7).[12]

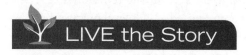

LIVE the Story

Service to the LORD

David has appointed Levitical gatekeepers, guardians of his treasuries, and officers and judges. Gatekeepers were the king's security guards, who were assigned the task of protecting the sacred temple and its treasuries. Gatekeepers had an important role among the returnees living in Jerusalem after the temple had been rebuilt (cf. 1 Chr 9:17–32). Japhet notes that their duties would have included "daily opening of gates, inventory and upkeep of the furniture and the holy utensils, and also guarding the supplies for the regular service, such as flour and oil for the bread offering, wine for the wine offering and frankincense and spices for the incense."[13] While some of these tasks might seem rather mundane, they held a position of trust (26:22, 26) and their service unto the LORD was essential. We are reminded in this chapter that the variety of duties performed by the Levites were needed for the temple to function effectively. They were the kingdom's "essential workers" who ensured that everything was done properly so that the entire community could worship the LORD.

As we consider the church today, all kinds of tasks are needed to enable the church to function effectively. Not only are there preachers and teachers, but also janitors, gardeners, property managers, ushers, greeters, sound technicians, treasurers, and those who prepare coffee and bake food for times of fellowship. Many of these tasks might seem mundane and less valuable than the role of preacher and worship leader, yet everyone joins together so that the entire body can function effectively and, most importantly, so that God can be worshiped as people gather together every Sunday. The Chronicler notes, indeed, that the gatekeepers were assigned duties for ministering in the temple "just as their relatives had" (1 Chr 26:12). Ultimately, every Levite served the LORD, whether small or great, young or old (24:5, 31; 25:8; 26:13), and thus all the work done was valuable.

When the apostle Paul describes the variety of spiritual gifts that are given to Christians, he makes clear that they are given for the common good (1 Cor 12:7). He not only teaches that every part is valuable to the body (vv. 12–17),

---

12. On the appointment of judges and the implications for today, see the discussion in Chapter 48 on 2 Chr 19:4–11, pp. 421–22.

13. Japhet, *I & II Chronicles*, 217.

but that God has placed each member in the body as he desires. He teaches further that "those parts of the body that seem to be weaker are indispensable" and thus they are to be honored in the body (vv. 22–23). David's appointment of Levites who served in a variety of tasks underscores that all kinds of jobs were needed for a flourishing kingdom with the temple at its center. Whatever ways God has called us to serve him, whether it is preaching and teaching or ensuring that the church property is properly maintained, all jobs are valuable, and we all serve one Lord. Selman thus writes: "As God's people pay proper attention to their status as a worshiping community, the distinction between sacred and the secular disappears. All have value in God's eyes."[14] This story reminds us of the variety of tasks needed in God's kingdom and that every task is valuable, since we all serve the one Lord.

---

14. Selman, *1 Chronicles*, 237.

CHAPTER 27

1 Chronicles 27:1-34

 LISTEN to the Story

¹This is the list of the Israelites—heads of families, commanders of thousands and commanders of hundreds, and their officers, who served the king in all that concerned the army divisions that were on duty month by month throughout the year. Each division consisted of 24,000 men.

²In charge of the first division, for the first month, was Jashobeam son of Zabdiel. There were 24,000 men in his division. ³He was a descendant of Perez and chief of all the army officers for the first month.

⁴In charge of the division for the second month was Dodai the Ahohite; Mikloth was the leader of his division. There were 24,000 men in his division.

⁵The third army commander, for the third month, was Benaiah son of Jehoiada the priest. He was chief and there were 24,000 men in his division. ⁶This was the Benaiah who was a mighty warrior among the Thirty and was over the Thirty. His son Ammizabad was in charge of his division.

⁷The fourth, for the fourth month, was Asahel the brother of Joab; his son Zebadiah was his successor. There were 24,000 men in his division.

⁸The fifth, for the fifth month, was the commander Shamhuth the Izrahite. There were 24,000 men in his division.

⁹The sixth, for the sixth month, was Ira the son of Ikkesh the Tekoite. There were 24,000 men in his division.

¹⁰The seventh, for the seventh month, was Helez the Pelonite, an Ephraimite. There were 24,000 men in his division.

¹¹The eighth, for the eighth month, was Sibbekai the Hushathite, a Zerahite. There were 24,000 men in his division.

¹²The ninth, for the ninth month, was Abiezer the Anathothite, a Benjamite. There were 24,000 men in his division.

¹³The tenth, for the tenth month, was Maharai the Netophathite, a Zerahite. There were 24,000 men in his division.

¹⁴The eleventh, for the eleventh month, was Benaiah the Pirathonite, an Ephraimite. There were 24,000 men in his division.

¹⁵The twelfth, for the twelfth month, was Heldai the Netophathite, from the family of Othniel. There were 24,000 men in his division.

¹⁶The leaders of the tribes of Israel:

over the Reubenites: Eliezer son of Zikri;

over the Simeonites: Shephatiah son of Maakah;

¹⁷over Levi: Hashabiah son of Kemuel;

over Aaron: Zadok;

¹⁸over Judah: Elihu, a brother of David;

over Issachar: Omri son of Michael;

¹⁹over Zebulun: Ishmaiah son of Obadiah;

over Naphtali: Jerimoth son of Azriel;

²⁰over the Ephraimites: Hoshea son of Azaziah;

over half the tribe of Manasseh: Joel son of Pedaiah;

²¹over the half-tribe of Manasseh in Gilead: Iddo son of Zechariah;

over Benjamin: Jaasiel son of Abner;

²²over Dan: Azarel son of Jeroham.

These were the leaders of the tribes of Israel.

²³David did not take the number of the men twenty years old or less, because the LORD had promised to make Israel as numerous as the stars in the sky. ²⁴Joab son of Zeruiah began to count the men but did not finish. God's wrath came on Israel on account of this numbering, and the number was not entered in the book of the annals of King David.

²⁵Azmaveth son of Adiel was in charge of the royal storehouses.

Jonathan son of Uzziah was in charge of the storehouses in the outlying districts, in the towns, the villages and the watchtowers.

²⁶Ezri son of Kelub was in charge of the workers who farmed the land.

²⁷Shimei the Ramathite was in charge of the vineyards.

Zabdi the Shiphmite was in charge of the produce of the vineyards for the wine vats.

²⁸Baal-Hanan the Gederite was in charge of the olive and sycamore-fig trees in the western foothills.

Joash was in charge of the supplies of olive oil.

²⁹Shitrai the Sharonite was in charge of the herds grazing in Sharon.

Shaphat son of Adlai was in charge of the herds in the valleys.

³⁰Obil the Ishmaelite was in charge of the camels.

Jehdeiah the Meronothite was in charge of the donkeys.

³¹Jaziz the Hagrite was in charge of the flocks.

All these were the officials in charge of King David's property.

³²Jonathan, David's uncle, was a counselor, a man of insight and a scribe. Jehiel son of Hakmoni took care of the king's sons.

³³Ahithophel was the king's counselor.

Hushai the Arkite was the king's confidant. ³⁴Ahithophel was succeeded by Jehoiada son of Benaiah and by Abiathar.

Joab was the commander of the royal army.

Listening to the Text in the Story: 1 Chronicles 11:10–47; Gezer Calendar

David's organization of the kingdom will be complete with his appointment of military commanders (1 Chr 27:1–15), tribal leaders (vv. 16–24), overseers of property and agricultural production (vv. 25–31), and wise counselors (vv. 32–34). Israel's leaders identified in this chapter present a picture of a unified and flourishing kingdom under David. Several of these leaders have already been introduced (see 11:10–47),[1] but it is important to recall what had been said about them: "These were the chiefs of David's mighty warriors—they, together with all Israel, gave his kingship strong support to extend it over the whole land, as the LORD had promised" (v. 10). It is important to keep in mind that these leaders are not merely secular or governmental officials, but rather, they have a key spiritual role in establishing the kingdom (22:17; 28:1–8), and these are the leaders who consecrate themselves and generously give of their

---

1. The two lists are not identical (there are differences in spelling and family associations), suggesting the list has been updated to reflect a later period (see Selman, *1 Chronicles*, 245). For a helpful comparison of names, see Braun, *1 Chronicles*, 259–60.

own resources toward the temple (29:6–10). As we will see shortly, a number of leaders have already given David their undivided loyalty. It is critical that trusted leaders are in place as David's own life is drawing to a close, thereby ensuring that the kingdom is in good hands for the next generation.

It was common in the ancient world for a king to have a large estate, which required oversight by trusted and capable managers. David's royal estate included vineyards and wine cellars, olive and sycamore trees, cattle, camels, donkeys, and flocks (27:27–31). Those of us who live in cities and in the suburbs are far removed from an agrarian lifestyle, but this was not the case in ancient societies. Life in ancient Israel was structured around the agricultural year, with its predictable seasons for planting and harvesting governed by climate and rainful. An ancient tablet found at Gezer underscores the importance of agricultural life in the tenth century BC; it reads:

> His two months are (olive) harvest,
> His two months are planting (grain),
> His two months are late planting;
> His month is hoeing up of flax,
> His month is harvest and *feasting*;
> His two months are vine-tending,
> His month is summer fruit.[2]

While the original purpose of the tablet is disputed, it reminds us of the importance of the agricultural calendar in ancient societies. King and Stager thus note: "Agriculture, the basis of the economy of ancient Israel, influenced practically every facet of daily life, especially the religious, economic, legal, and social spheres."[3] David's appointment of overseers and managers is not insignificant, therefore.

EXPLAIN the Story

David Organizes His Military into Twelve Divisions (27:1–15)

David's military is divided into twelve divisions, with one commander appointed over each division (1 Chr 27:1–15). While the military fought in Israel's battles, Japhet notes that their job description was probably wider

---

2. "The Gezer Calendar," trans. W. F. Albright (*ANET*, 320).

3. King and Stager, *Life in Biblical Israel*, 86. For an excellent summary of agriculture in ancient Israel, see Stager's chapter 3 ("The Means of Existence," 85–122).

in scope: "We may conjecture that in time of peace these reserves would be given the duty of guarding the kingdom's borders, doing police service and maintaining order in conquered territories, manning strongholds and castles, attending to the weapons and equipment—chariots, horses, etc."[4] Their service was to rotate among the twelve divisions, for the men were "on duty month by month," which refers to the changing of the guard (v. 1; cf. 2 Kgs 11:9; 2 Chr 23:8).[5] Each division numbers 24,000, but since the term *thousand* (Heb. *'eleph*) can refer to sub-units within the tribe (rather than a literal headcount), this would suggest eligible males selected for service "would be appreciably smaller than the clan pool from which they were drafted."[6] Israel's military had available to them both weapons and protective gear, which included shields, spears, helmets, coats of armor, bows, and slingstones (see 1 Chr 11:11, 20, 23; 2 Chr 26:14). Weapons in the ancient world included those used for hand-to hand combat (such as clubs, maces, axes, daggers, and swords), those thrown by the hand (such as spears, lances, and slingstones), and those used for long-range combat (such as bows and arrows).[7]

The names of David's military commanders begin with Jashobeam (1 Chr 27:2), a descendant of Perez from the tribe of Judah (vv. 2–3; cf. 2:5, 9–15). As first in rank, he was among those who had supported David and was known for his heroism (11:11). Jashobeam is given the first position, and his battalion will assume responsibilities for the first month (27:2–3). Dodai is second, and he had charge of the second month (v. 4). Benaiah, son of Jehoiada the priest, is appointed head of the third division (v. 5). It is important to recognize that Benaiah and his son Ammizabad were Levites, underscoring that military battles were never entirely secular. Military language was used earlier to describe Levitical gatekeepers (26:6, 9), so the presence of such a prominent priestly family in the military is not so surprising. Benaiah was among David's trusted thirty men and was known for killing two Moabite men, along with an Egyptian of considerable stature (11:22–25; cf. 2 Sam 23:20–23). Benaiah had been loyal to David when his son Adonijah had attempted to usurp the throne (1 Kgs 1:8–10), and he had been with Zadok and Nathan when Solomon was anointed as king, even offering a blessing (vv. 32–37). Benaiah, in fact, will be responsible for the deaths of Adonijah (2:25) and Joab (vv. 28–35), because of their disloyalty to Solomon (v. 35; see also 4:4).

---

4. Japhet, *I & II Chronicles*, 468.

5. Boda, *1–2 Chronicles*, 205.

6. King and Stager, *Life in Biblical Israel*, 241. On the different approaches to the Hebrew term *'eleph*, see the discussion in Chapter 43 on 2 Chr 14:8–9, p. 387.

7. For a description on ancient weapons of war, see King and Stager, *Life in Biblical Israel*, 224–31.

The fourth division is led by Asahel the brother of Joab, along with his son Zebadiah (1 Chr 27:7). Since Asahel had been killed earlier (before David had become king), this may explain why his son is named in the list (see 2 Sam 2:18–23). The fifth division was led by Shamhuth the Izrahite (1 Chr 27:8); the sixth was led by Ira, from the town of Tekoa and among David's thirty warriors (11:28). The seventh division was led by Helez, from Ephraim (27:10), the eighth by Sibbekai, known for his military capabilities (20:4; see also 2 Sam 21:18; 1 Chr 11:29), the ninth by Abiezer, from Benjamin (1 Chr 27:12), and the tenth by Maharai the Zerahite, connecting him to Judah (v. 13; cf. 2:4, 6). These four were among David's trusted thirty who had given him their undivided support (11:27–30). The final two divisions are led by Benaiah the Ephraimite (27:14; see also 2 Sam 23:30) and by Heldai, from the family of Othniel (1 Chr 27:15; cf. 4:13).

Tribal Leadership (27:16–22)

The next section deals with tribal leadership (1 Chr 27:16–22). The designation "leader" (Heb. *nagid*), translated as "chief officer" (ESV), is used to describe various leadership positions in the kingdom, including the king (1 Sam 10:1; 13:14; 25:30; 2 Sam 5:2), officials serving under the king (1 Chr 13:1; 2 Chr 11:11; 19:11; 28:7), and Levitical leaders (1 Chr 9:11, 20; 12:27; 26:24; 2 Chr 31:12). One leader from each tribe is identified (1 Chr 27:16–22), including the tribe of Levi. Hashabiah is identified as the chief officer of Levi, but Zadok is leader over Aaron (v. 17). Since the tribes of Gad and Asher are not included,[8] the number twelve is achieved with the inclusion of the two half-tribes of Manasseh (one half-tribe settled east of the Jordan). A brief comment is made that David did not number men twenty years of age and younger, recalling his earlier census when God's wrath had come upon Israel (27:23–24; see 1 Chr 21).[9] In this story, God's promise to multiply Israel as the stars of the heaven is noted, suggesting the flourishing of the kingdom is in accordance with God's promise to the patriarchs (27:24; cf. Gen 15:5; 22:17; 26:4).

Overseers of the King's Estate (27:25–31)

Azmaveth was assigned oversight of the king's storehouses, and Jonathan had oversight of the store cities in the country and villages (1 Chr 27:25). Grain

---

8. This is perhaps not surprising, since minimal attention had been given to them in the genealogies (Gad: 5:11–16; Asher: 7:30–40). Merrill suggests their absence from the list may reflect the historical and territorial situation of the Chronicler's time (*1 & 2 Chronicles*, 293).

9. See the discussion in Chapter 21 on 1 Chr 21, pp. 209–14.

was stored in granaries and silos, and there may have been storage rooms in tripartite pillared buildings in Israel.[10] Storage jars found by archaeologists, which are identified as *lmlk* jars ("belonging to the king") because of their handles stamped with this phrase, underscore the kind of storage vessels that were needed for the king's goods.[11] Solomon will build several store cities (2 Chr 8:4–6), as will Jehoshaphat (17:12–13; see also 32:28).

Ezri is appointed overseer of laborers in the fields (1 Chr 27:26), whereas oversight of the olive trees, vineyards, and the production of oil was divided between Shimei, Zabdi, Baal-Hanan, and Joash (vv. 27–28). Olive oil production was well-known in the Levant, and it was a major industry in Israel, even allowing for surplus oil to be exported. A major production site for oil was the Philistine city of Ekron, where over a hundred olive presses were found. One estimate is that Ekron produced a thousand tons of oil annually.[12] The responsibilities assigned to Shimei, Zabdi, and Baal-Hanan were not insignificant, therefore.

Shitrai and Shaphat had oversight of the cattle, one in the Sharon Plain and the other in the valleys (v. 29). Located on the Mediterranean coast, the Sharon Plain provided rich pastureland for cattle. Obil, the Ishmaelite, had charge of the camels (v. 30).[13] Camels were domesticated in the ancient world as beasts of burden; they were especially beneficial because of their ability to store water, making them ideal for long journeys (see 2 Chr 9:1). Another pack animal was the donkey, useful for local transportation, and Jehdeiah had charge of them (1 Chr 27:30). Lastly, Jaziz the Hagrite had oversight of the flocks (v. 31).[14] Sheep and goats provided meat, clothing, and milk, and thus they were an important domestic animal in ancient Israel. The list concludes with a comment that these men had oversight of the property owned by King David (v. 31).

Appointment of Counselors (27:32–34)

The list of David's leaders concludes with his counselors, which included his uncle Jonathan, who was known as a wise and skilled scribe (1 Chr 27:32).

---

10. King and Stager, *Life in Biblical Israel*, 91.

11. See Alfred J. Hoerth, *Archaeology & the Old Testament* (Grand Rapids: Baker Academic, 1998), 344 (fig. 17.3).

12. King and Stager, *Life in Biblical Israel*, 96.

13. That David has an Ishmaelite in a leadership position has already been anticipated in Judah's genealogy, where non-Israelites are included; see Live the Story, Judah's Place in God's Plan to Include All Nations, in Chapter 2, pp. 46–48.

14. On the Hagrites, see the discussion on 1 Chr 5:10 in Chapter 5, pp. 69–70. Their name derives from Hagar, thus they are connected to the Ishmaelites (Klein, *1 Chronicles*, 511).

Wisdom was prized in the ancient world, and the king needed wise counsel to run his estate. But wise counselors were especially needed to keep the king from turning aside from God's law. Rehoboam will forsake wise counsel from his elders, and it will have dire ramifications (2 Chr 10).[15] Jehiel took care of David's sons, which probably included instructing them. Ahithophel is identified as a counselor, along with Hushai, the king's confidant (1 Chr 27:33; cf. 2 Sam 15:32–17:29). The chapter concludes with an updated list of counselors, noting that Abiathar and Johoiada succeeded Ahithophel (1 Chr 27:33). Joab was the commander of David's army, but he is later disloyal to Solomon, which will result in his death (see 1 Kgs 2:34).

LIVE the Story

Succession Planning for the Next Generation of Leaders

This chapter concludes the leadership appointments David makes as he prepares the kingdom for the new king, Solomon (1 Chr 23–27). David ensures that the kingdom is in order with trusted and experienced leaders in place, who serve as temple personnel but also military commanders, security guards, and estate managers. These leaders are not to be viewed as secular appointments, but they are deeply committed to the LORD, as will be seen shortly when they consecrate themselves to God and give generously toward the temple. God's people will respond with joy "at the willing response of their leaders, for they had given freely and wholeheartedly to the LORD" (29:9). When we consider the role of David's leaders, it is evident that they are much more than secular military leaders and stewards of his estate. David finds it a source of great joy as he witnesses their generosity and devotion to God (v. 17). Unlike the preceding chapters, where lots were drawn to determine positions and responsibilities among the Levites (24:5, 7, 31; 25:8, 9; 26:13, 14), lots are not employed when David appoints his military, tribal, and estate-managers. The appointment of godly leaders is vital in every generation.

The New Testament teaches about the importance of selecting godly leaders and planning for the succession of leadership. In Paul's letters to Timothy and Titus, he makes known his intent to ensure that godly leaders are appointed for the next generation, as his own ministry is drawing to a close. Paul instructs Titus to appoint leaders in every city (Titus 1:5), and he outlines the kind of qualities he and Timothy should look for in a leader: "Now the overseer is to

---

15. On the important topic of wise counselors, see Live the Story in Chapter 39, pp. 365–66.

be above reproach, faithful to his wife, temperate, self-controlled, respectable, hospitable, able to teach, not given to drunkenness, not violent but gentle, not quarrelsome, not a lover of money" (1 Tim 3:2–3). These characteristics include being able to manage one's own household and having a good reputation with those outside the church. Paul writes to Timothy, hoping to come to him, but if delayed he wants Timothy to know how people ought to conduct themselves in God's household (vv. 14–15). It is clear that godly character is essential for church leaders (3:1–16; 5:17–25; Titus 1:5–9), along with an emphasis on teaching the word of God (2 Tim 4:1–5; Titus 1:9; cf. 1 Tim 4:13–16). Even though young, Timothy was an example of a godly leader, and Paul exhorts him to "set an example for the believers in speech, in conduct, in love, in faith and in purity" (v. 12).

The church in every age needs to ensure that godly leaders are appointed for the next generation. A major study done by Barna in 2017 found that in 1992, the average age of Protestant clergy in the US was forty-four years old. They note further that in 1992, one in three pastors was under forty years old, and one in four was over fifty-five. They compare this with the more recent situation: "Twenty-five years later, the average age is fifty-four. Only one in seven pastors is under forty, and half are over fifty-five. The percentage of church leaders sixty-five and older has nearly tripled, meaning there are now more pastors in the oldest age bracket than there are leaders younger than 40."[16] The study suggests possible reasons for an aging clergy, including increased life-expectancy, more "second career" clergy, and senior pastors unable to retire for economic reasons, but also "the lack of leadership development among Millennials and Gen-Xers and the lack of succession planning among Boomers."[17] The study reports that pastors are finding it a challenge to identify suitable candidates for the ministry. Another contributing factor may well be the level of student debt seminary students are required to take on as they prepare for ministry.[18] Succession planning not only involves selecting godly leaders, but also providing financially for seminary students so that they can enter the ministry without being burdened by enormous amounts of debt.[19] Providing the financial resources needed for the flourishing

---

16. Barna, "The Aging of Amercia's Pastors," March 1, 2017; see https://www.barna.com/research/aging-americas-pastors/.

17. Ibid.

18. On this topic (and the tithe), see Live the Story in Chapter 50, pp. 443–44.

19. See Live the Story in Chapter 29, where the generosity of a gospel patron named Lady Huntington is described. She gave generously to fund seminary students, including providing for their clothes, food, and ministry trips, using half of her annual income to cover their expenses. It is a remarkable story that serves as an example for us today.

of the kingdom is precisely what happens in the final chapter of David's life when he gathers the entire community and exhorts them to give generously to the work of the Lord (1 Chr 29). His succession plan entailed both the appointment of key leaders (chs. 23–27) *and* the giving of financial resources to enable Solomon to fulfill his calling to build the temple (chs. 28–29). That succession planning is important is seen in the number of chapters devoted to this task (chs. 23–29), and as one scholar suggests, this was David's chief legacy.[20] This serves as a challenge for us to consider our level of commitment to provide for the next generation of leaders for the church today.

20. John W. Wright, "The Legacy of David in Chronicles: The Narrative Function of 1 Chronicles 23–27," *JBL* 110:2 (1991): 229–42.

LISTEN to the Story

¹David summoned all the officials of Israel to assemble at Jerusalem: the officers over the tribes, the commanders of the divisions in the service of the king, the commanders of thousands and commanders of hundreds, and the officials in charge of all the property and livestock belonging to the king and his sons, together with the palace officials, the warriors and all the brave fighting men.

²King David rose to his feet and said: "Listen to me, my fellow Israelites, my people. I had it in my heart to build a house as a place of rest for the ark of the covenant of the LORD, for the footstool of our God, and I made plans to build it. ³But God said to me, 'You are not to build a house for my Name, because you are a warrior and have shed blood.'

⁴"Yet the LORD, the God of Israel, chose me from my whole family to be king over Israel forever. He chose Judah as leader, and from the tribe of Judah he chose my family, and from my father's sons he was pleased to make me king over all Israel. ⁵Of all my sons—and the LORD has given me many—he has chosen my son Solomon to sit on the throne of the kingdom of the LORD over Israel. ⁶He said to me: 'Solomon your son is the one who will build my house and my courts, for I have chosen him to be my son, and I will be his father. ⁷I will establish his kingdom forever if he is unswerving in carrying out my commands and laws, as is being done at this time.'

⁸"So now I charge you in the sight of all Israel and of the assembly of the LORD, and in the hearing of our God: Be careful to follow all the commands of the LORD your God, that you may possess this good land and pass it on as an inheritance to your descendants forever.

⁹"And you, my son Solomon, acknowledge the God of your father, and serve him with wholehearted devotion and with a willing mind, for the

LORD searches every heart and understands every desire and every thought. If you seek him, he will be found by you; but if you forsake him, he will reject you forever. ¹⁰Consider now, for the LORD has chosen you to build a house as the sanctuary. Be strong and do the work."

¹¹Then David gave his son Solomon the plans for the portico of the temple, its buildings, its storerooms, its upper parts, its inner rooms and the place of atonement. ¹²He gave him the plans of all that the Spirit had put in his mind for the courts of the temple of the LORD and all the surrounding rooms, for the treasuries of the temple of God and for the treasuries for the dedicated things. ¹³He gave him instructions for the divisions of the priests and Levites, and for all the work of serving in the temple of the LORD, as well as for all the articles to be used in its service. ¹⁴He designated the weight of gold for all the gold articles to be used in various kinds of service, and the weight of silver for all the silver articles to be used in various kinds of service: ¹⁵the weight of gold for the gold lampstands and their lamps, with the weight for each lampstand and its lamps; and the weight of silver for each silver lampstand and its lamps, according to the use of each lampstand; ¹⁶the weight of gold for each table for consecrated bread; the weight of silver for the silver tables; ¹⁷the weight of pure gold for the forks, sprinkling bowls and pitchers; the weight of gold for each gold dish; the weight of silver for each silver dish; ¹⁸and the weight of the refined gold for the altar of incense. He also gave him the plan for the chariot, that is, the cherubim of gold that spread their wings and overshadow the ark of the covenant of the LORD.

¹⁹"All this," David said, "I have in writing as a result of the LORD's hand on me, and he enabled me to understand all the details of the plan."

²⁰David also said to Solomon his son, "Be strong and courageous, and do the work. Do not be afraid or discouraged, for the LORD God, my God, is with you. He will not fail you or forsake you until all the work for the service of the temple of the LORD is finished. ²¹The divisions of the priests and Levites are ready for all the work on the temple of God, and every willing person skilled in any craft will help you in all the work. The officials and all the people will obey your every command."

Listening to the Text in the Story: Exodus 40:1–11; 2 Samuel 7:8–17; 1 Chronicles 17:1–15

As the life of David is drawing to a close, the king assembles his leaders and reminds them that God has chosen Solomon to build the temple. God's covenant with David is central to the story that follows (2 Sam 7:8–17). God had promised David: "When your days are over and you go to be with your ancestors, I will raise up your offspring to succeed you, one of your own sons, and I will establish his kingdom. He is the one who will build a house for me, and I will establish his throne forever" (1 Chr 17:11–12).[1] David has already rehearsed these promises to Solomon (22:7–16), but, like an elderly father who imparts final words of wisdom to his son, these promises are again percolating in David's heart. The covenant God made with David provides the background for all that follows, and it will resurface again after David has died and his son rules in his place (2 Chr 1:9).

 EXPLAIN the Story

David Affirms God's Choice of Solomon (28:1–7)

With the organizational structure of the kingdom in place (1 Chr 23–27), David assembles all his leaders in Jerusalem (28:1). Earlier David had "gathered" leaders, priests, and Levites (Heb. *'asap*, 23:2), but here the verb "to assemble" (Heb. *q-h-l*) is used, which refers to the gathering of God's people for a sacred assembly, often culminating in a cultic ceremony.[2] The king stands to his feet and addresses his assembled leaders. These are David's leaders who have been carefully appointed (chs. 23–27). David reminds those assembled that he had intended to build a permanent house for the ark, yet Nathan had made known to him that his son was to build the temple (17:1–15). David had made preparations for the temple, which included purchasing the threshing floor from Araunah (21:1–30), gathering large quantities of gold, silver, bronze, and iron (22:14) along with timber and stone (vv. 1–5, 14), and securing skilled workmen, stonecutters, masons, and carpenters (v. 15). Yet David had been precluded from building the temple because of the blood he had shed in his military battles that made him unfit to build a sacred temple (28:3; see also 22:8).[3]

With tenderness David remembers God's call upon his life, recalling that

---

1. See the discussion in Chapter 17 on 1 Chr 17:10b–15, pp. 179–81.
2. See Wright, "The Legacy of David," 230–31; see also Live the Story in Chapter 59, Live the Story, Vision for an "Assembly of Nations," pp. 512–13. There we note that the Hebrew noun, *qahal*, is translated in the Septuagint (the Greek translation of the Old Testament) as *ekklesia*.
3. See the discussion in the commentary on 1 Chr 22:8, pp. 218–19.

unforgettable day when Samuel had arrived at his house and had unexpectedly anointed him as king (1 Chr 28:4; see 1 Sam 16:1–13). That life-changing day would remain indelibly etched on David's heart and mind, as it was in Israel's memory (Ps 78:70–72). It had changed David's life forever—the young shepherd boy had been taken from tending sheep, and God had chosen him to shepherd Israel (1 Sam 16:1–13; cf. 1 Chr 11:2). Echoes of David's earlier prayer, "Who am I?" ruminate in David's heart, as he recalls with a sense of wonder that God had been pleased to make him king over all Israel (28:4). God had chosen the tribe of Judah as leader among the tribes, hearkening back to Jacob's death-bed blessing pronounced on his son Judah (Gen 49:8–10). Judah had prevailed over his brothers, and a leader would come forth from his line (1 Chr 5:1–2; see also 2:3–4:23). Standing behind David was the providential hand of God, who had been at work during unlikely circumstances (cf. 1 Sam 16; Ruth 4:18–22).

David acknowledges that God has chosen Solomon from among his many sons to sit on the throne (1 Chr 28:5; cf. 22:5–16); he recognizes that he is to rule over the "kingdom of the LORD" (28:5; 17:14; cf. 2 Chr 13:8; 20:6). Solomon has been chosen by God to build his house, but David further recalls that Solomon is to be God's *son* (1 Chr 28:6; cf. 17:13), underscoring his intimate relationship with God his father (Ps 2:7).[4] David rehearses these promises, but they come with a word of warning to his son: God will establish his everlasting kingdom, but only if he is "unswerving in carrying out my commands and laws, as is being done at this time" (28:7). God's throne was characterized by righteousness and justice, and thus there was the expectation that the Davidic king would represent God's law (cf. Pss 89:14; 97:2; 99:4; 103:6; Isa 9:6–7). As the prophet Isaiah announced concerning the king: he would reign on "David's throne and over his kingdom, establishing and upholding it with justice and righteousness from that time on and forever" (Isa 9:7). This underscores the critical role of obedience, something God will make known to Solomon in the days ahead (2 Chr 7:17–22).

David Exhorts the Leaders and Solomon (28:8–10)

David now addresses his leaders who have gathered in Jerusalem: "Be careful to follow all the commands of the LORD your God, that you may possess this good land and pass it on as an inheritance to your descendants forever" (1 Chr 28:8). Israel's leaders have a vital role in ensuring that God's commands are

---

4. See Chapter 17 on 1 Chr 17 for further discussion.

followed, for failure to do so would lead to the uprooting of God's people from their land (2 Chr 7:19–22; cf. 36:14–20).[5]

David now addresses Solomon directly: "And you, my son Solomon, acknowledge the God of your father, and serve him with wholehearted devotion and with a willing mind, for the LORD searches every heart and understands every desire and every thought. If you seek him, he will be found by you; but if you forsake him, he will reject you forever" (1 Chr 28:9). Solomon is exhorted to serve God with "wholehearted devotion," a godly virtue that is meant to characterize God's people (22:19; 29:19; 2 Chr 15:12).[6] The tragic testimony of Solomon's later years is that his heart "was not fully devoted to the LORD his God, as the heart of David his father had been" (1 Kgs 11:4). David acknowledges that God searches every heart and he understands its inner thoughts (1 Chr 28:9; cf. 29:17). David encourages Solomon that if he "seeks" God (Heb. *d-r-sh*), he will be found by him (28:9). Seeking God is a central theme in Chronicles.[7] Solomon seeks God at the beginning of his reign (Heb. *d-r-sh*, 2 Chr 1:5), which signals an affirmation of the young king. David's warning to his son about not forsaking the LORD will be given later to Solomon by God directly (7:19–22; cf. 1 Kgs 11:1–11, 33). David's exhortation concludes with a reminder that God has not only chosen Solomon to be king, but also to build the temple (1 Chr 28:10; cf. vv. 5, 6). As he had done earlier, David again exhorts Solomon: "Be strong and do the work" (v. 10; cf. 22:11–13; 28:20).

David Gives the Architectural "Plan" of the Temple to Solomon (28:11–19)

The narrative shifts to focus on the architectural "plan" (Heb. *tabnit*) that God gives David (1 Chr 28:11–18), which included plans for the "portico of the temple, its buildings, its storerooms, its upper parts, its inner rooms and the place of atonement" (v. 11), and also for all its furnishings (vv. 13–18). The plan David is shown recalls Israel's earlier history, when God had given plans to Moses for the tabernacle (Heb. *tabnit*, Exod 25:9, 40).[8] Stories of architectural plans and models given to kings by the gods are found in ancient Near Eastern

---

5. On the significant impact one leader can have on the spiritual state of the kingdom, see Live the Story, Chapter 53, pp. 460–62.

6. On the topic of wholehearted devotion, see Live the Story, Chapter 54, pp. 470–72.

7. For a summary of this verb, see the discussion in Chapter 30 in Live the Story, pp. 291–93.

8. For the connections between the tabernacle and the temple, see the discussion in Chapter 32 on 2 Chr 3, especially Listen to the Story.

literature.[9] It is important to recognize that since *God* gives David the plan for the temple and its furnishings (by his own hand), *he* is its chief architect. Later, when we discuss the temple and furnishings that Solomon builds, it will become evident that the earthly temple represents God's heavenly abode.[10] The significance of this is not to be missed. Only God knows what his *heavenly temple* is like, yet, through the blueprints he gives to David, God is effectively giving the king a glimpse into his *heavenly* throne. The last piece of furniture mentioned is the ark of the covenant, described here as a golden chariot that was covered by wings of the cherubim (1 Chr 28:18; see also 2 Chr 3:10–13; 5:7–8). The plan David receives takes him into the holy of holies, the place of God's footstool on earth.

Since the temple will be built as a physical structure, this means that access into the heavenly realm will be found in the temple. Thus the elaborate and glorious temple built by Solomon points beyond itself to God's heavenly throne. God is the chief architect, which means that the earthly building is intended to stir in his people a longing for his *heavenly* abode, just as Abraham was looking for the heavenly city, whose builder and architect was God (Heb 11:10). At this point in the story, the heavenly realm is unveiled to David, who received plans "in writing as a result of the LORD's hand on me, and he enabled me to understand all the details of the plan" (1 Ch 28:19). It is remarkable to witness the extent of God's involvement in the blueprints. This underscores the significance of the temple in God's redemptive plan—something we will explore later in the temple-building narrative (2 Chr 2–5). These are the plans that the Spirit puts into David's mind (1 Chr 28:12), the same Spirit who had given wisdom to those working on the tabernacle (Exod 28:3; 31:3, 35:31).

David's Final Charge to Solomon (28:20–21)

This section concludes with a final exhortation to Solomon: "Be strong and courageous, and do the work. Do not be afraid or discouraged, for the LORD God, my God, is with you. He will not fail you or forsake you until all the work for the service of the temple of the LORD is finished" (1 Chr 28:20; cf.

---

9. See examples in Victor Hurowitz, *I Have Built You an Exalted House: Temple Building in the Bible in the Light of Mesopotamian and North-West Semitic Writings* (JSOTSup 115; Sheffield, JSOT Press, 1992), 168–70. Scholars differ in their view regarding the meaning of *tabnit*, that is, whether it refers to a plan or an actual replica. Hurowitz argues that Moses was given a model, whereas a blueprint seems to be the primary meaning in 1 Chr 28 (except for the chariot, which he thinks is an actual replica, 28:18).

10. Beale, *The Temple and the Church's Mission*, 31–45. See the discussion in Chapter 32 on 2 Chr 3, for connections between the temple and God's heavenly throne.

1 Chr 22:13).[11] David assures Solomon of God's presence, which will enable him to complete the sacred task before him, a subject that is taken up shortly (2 Chr 2–5). Solomon has the support of the priests and Levites, along with the officials and people, who will do whatever he commands (1 Chr 28:21).

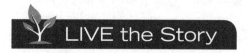

LIVE the Story

Gaining a Vision of God's Kingdom That Shapes Our Lives

God's superintending of the construction of the temple in this story reminds us that the temple is far more than merely an earthly building. When God reveals the blueprints to David, the king is given a window into God's *heavenly* temple, and this is the vision that impacts the use of his time, energy, and resources—David's focus is on God's kingdom. This might be described as an epiphany, as Wright notes: "God's direct manifestations in Chronicles are epiphanal—sporadic manifestations of the divine realm within the human realm."[12] These epiphanies are not open to all, but David is among those who is given insight into the divine realm as he beholds the plans for the temple.

Other people in the Old Testament are given glimpses into the divine realm. The prophet Isaiah was given a vision of God's heavenly and exalted throne when he heard the seraphim crying out: "Holy, holy, holy is the LORD Almighty; the whole earth is full of his glory" (Isa 6:3). The prophet Ezekiel receives a similar vision when the "heavens were opened" and he saw "visions of God" (Ezek 1:1). The glorious vision of God's heavenly and exalted throne caused him to fall on his face before the glory of the LORD (vv. 1–28). The prophet Daniel saw a vision of the heavenly throne room, where thousands upon thousands were attending the Ancient of Days. He was given a glimpse into the heavenly realm as he witnessed the glorious and everlasting kingdom given to the Son of Man (Dan 7:9–14). Like these prophets of old, David is given a glimpse into the heavenly realm.[13] The blueprints indicate that the earthly temple represents a much greater and glorious heavenly throne. But what impact does this heavenly vision have on the king? Does it have any *earthly* value?

---

11. See discussion in Chapter 22 on 1 Chr 22:13, pp. 219–20.

12. John W. Wright, "Beyond Transcendence and Immanence: The Characterization of the Presence and Activity of God in the Book of Chronicles," in *The Chronicler as Theologian: Essays in Honor of Ralph W. Klein*, ed. M. Patrick Graham, Steven L. McKenzie, and Gary N. Knoppers (London: T & T Clark International, 2003), 246.

13. On this topic, see Live the Story in Chapter 32, pp. 307–9.

Echoes of God's heavenly kingdom reverberate in his prayer that follows when he acknowledges: "Yours, LORD, is the greatness and the power and the glory and the majesty and the splendor, for everything in heaven and earth is yours. Yours, LORD, is the kingdom; you are exalted as head over all" (1 Chr 29:11). When people gain a glimpse of God's heavenly kingdom, their lives are transformed by it. As David's life is drawing to a close, it is not coincidental that he willingly and freely gives all of his wealth and riches to God for the construction of the temple. Similarly, when we gain a glimpse of God's *heavenly* kingdom, this shapes our lives. We are no longer focused on building our small kingdoms, but our priorities focus on *God's kingdom.*

As I reflect upon what it means to live with a kingdom focus, I'm reminded of a couple in Australia who were spiritual parents to me. Their lives were devoted to serving God on the mission field and in our local Baptist church. They had a beautiful and stately family home nestled in a wooded area next to a river, but what I remember most about them was that their house was always filled with youth from our church and guests who stayed with them. They had an open-door policy, always available for those who needed them. Their furniture was comfortable but showed signs of wear and tear. Their carpet was not the latest color, and it was well-worn from people in their home. Their kitchen bustled with people sharing cups of tea and hearty meals, but it did not have granite counter tops and the latest appliances. I can remember many conversations in that kitchen, even after leaving Australia to live in Massachusetts. Their focus was *on people* and their priority was God's kingdom. They were living as "strangers on the earth," so to speak, for they were looking for the city built by God. They didn't have to tell me this; I just knew it.

Our worldview needs to be shaped by a vision of God's kingdom, as we pray that his kingdom might come (Matt 6:10). The Scriptures, like David's blueprint he receives, give us a vision into God's heavenly kingdom. Our eyes need to be lifted up on high so that God's heavenly kingdom shapes how we live our lives on earth. Jesus teaches that we are to seek first his kingdom, and to pray that *his* kingdom might come. The apostle Paul recognized that David died after he had "served God's purpose in his own generation" (Acts 13:36). In these final years of David's life, we see his unswerving commitment to make preparations for the temple—he has a vision of something greater than himself. David's commitment to the LORD is seen in the story that follows, as he gives generously of all his earthly goods for the sake of God's heavenly kingdom. Like David, may our eyes gain a glimpse of God's heavenly kingdom, and may we be people who seek first *his* kingdom.

CHAPTER 29

1 Chronicles 29:1–30

 LISTEN to the Story

¹Then King David said to the whole assembly: "My son Solomon, the one whom God has chosen, is young and inexperienced. The task is great, because this palatial structure is not for man but for the LORD God. ²With all my resources I have provided for the temple of my God—gold for the gold work, silver for the silver, bronze for the bronze, iron for the iron and wood for the wood, as well as onyx for the settings, turquoise, stones of various colors, and all kinds of fine stone and marble—all of these in large quantities. ³Besides, in my devotion to the temple of my God I now give my personal treasures of gold and silver for the temple of my God, over and above everything I have provided for this holy temple: ⁴three thousand talents of gold (gold of Ophir) and seven thousand talents of refined silver, for the overlaying of the walls of the buildings, ⁵for the gold work and the silver work, and for all the work to be done by the craftsmen. Now, who is willing to consecrate themselves to the LORD today?"

⁶Then the leaders of families, the officers of the tribes of Israel, the commanders of thousands and commanders of hundreds, and the officials in charge of the king's work gave willingly. ⁷They gave toward the work on the temple of God five thousand talents and ten thousand darics of gold, ten thousand talents of silver, eighteen thousand talents of bronze and a hundred thousand talents of iron. ⁸Anyone who had precious stones gave them to the treasury of the temple of the LORD in the custody of Jehiel the Gershonite. ⁹The people rejoiced at the willing response of their leaders, for they had given freely and wholeheartedly to the LORD. David the king also rejoiced greatly.

¹⁰David praised the LORD in the presence of the whole assembly, saying,

"Praise be to you, LORD,
> the God of our father Israel,
> from everlasting to everlasting.

¹¹Yours, LORD, is the greatness and the power
> and the glory and the majesty and the splendor,
> for everything in heaven and earth is yours.

Yours, LORD, is the kingdom;
> you are exalted as head over all.

¹²Wealth and honor come from you;
> you are the ruler of all things.

In your hands are strength and power
> to exalt and give strength to all.

¹³Now, our God, we give you thanks,
> and praise your glorious name.

¹⁴"But who am I, and who are my people, that we should be able to give as generously as this? Everything comes from you, and we have given you only what comes from your hand. ¹⁵We are foreigners and strangers in your sight, as were all our ancestors. Our days on earth are like a shadow, without hope. ¹⁶LORD our God, all this abundance that we have provided for building you a temple for your Holy Name comes from your hand, and all of it belongs to you. ¹⁷I know, my God, that you test the heart and are pleased with integrity. All these things I have given willingly and with honest intent. And now I have seen with joy how willingly your people who are here have given to you. ¹⁸LORD, the God of our fathers Abraham, Isaac and Israel, keep these desires and thoughts in the hearts of your people forever, and keep their hearts loyal to you. ¹⁹And give my son Solomon the wholehearted devotion to keep your commands, statutes and decrees and to do everything to build the palatial structure for which I have provided."

²⁰Then David said to the whole assembly, "Praise the LORD your God." So they all praised the LORD, the God of their fathers; they bowed down, prostrating themselves before the LORD and the king.

²¹The next day they made sacrifices to the LORD and presented burnt offerings to him: a thousand bulls, a thousand rams and a thousand male

lambs, together with their drink offerings, and other sacrifices in abundance for all Israel. ²²They ate and drank with great joy in the presence of the LORD that day.

Then they acknowledged Solomon son of David as king a second time, anointing him before the LORD to be ruler and Zadok to be priest. ²³So Solomon sat on the throne of the LORD as king in place of his father David. He prospered and all Israel obeyed him. ²⁴All the officers and warriors, as well as all of King David's sons, pledged their submission to King Solomon.

²⁵The LORD highly exalted Solomon in the sight of all Israel and bestowed on him royal splendor such as no king over Israel ever had before.

²⁶David son of Jesse was king over all Israel. ²⁷He ruled over Israel forty years—seven in Hebron and thirty-three in Jerusalem. ²⁸He died at a good old age, having enjoyed long life, wealth and honor. His son Solomon succeeded him as king.

²⁹As for the events of King David's reign, from beginning to end, they are written in the records of Samuel the seer, the records of Nathan the prophet and the records of Gad the seer, ³⁰together with the details of his reign and power, and the circumstances that surrounded him and Israel and the kingdoms of all the other lands.

Listening to the Text in the Story: Exodus 25

In this final chapter of David's life, the king gathers all Israel together as they give generously to the LORD. Their generous contributions to be used for the temple are reminiscent of Israel's earlier days when their gifts had been used for the tabernacle (Exod 25). God had instructed Moses to gather contributions from the Israelites, for they were to make a sanctuary for God so that he might dwell among them (v. 8). We have noted that the "plan" (Heb. *tabnit*) God gives David for the temple (1 Chr 28:11–12, 18–19) recalls the "plan" (Heb. *tabnit*) God had given Moses for the tabernacle (Exod 25:9, 40). Under Moses's leadership, the Israelites were to contribute gold, silver, bronze, expensive blue, purple, and scarlet material, and other items needed for the construction of the tabernacle (Exod 25:1–8). The precious items David provides for the temple recall the materials used for the construction of the tabernacle (1 Chr 29:2; cf. Exod 25:3–7; 35:5–9, 22–28), including precious onyx stone (1 Chr 29:2;

cf. Exod 25:7; 28:9, 20, etc.).[1] Most importantly, the repetition of the term "give generously, offer willingly" (Heb. *n-d-b*) throughout this story (1 Chr 29:5, 6, 9 [2x], 14, 17 [2x]) recalls the Israelites' willing contributions given for the tabernacle (Heb. *n-d-b*, Exod 25:2; 35:5, 21, 22, 29), thus providing further connection between these two stories.[2] The cumulative effect is that the temple is not to be seen as something entirely new, but rather, it is a continuation of God's intention to dwell with his people that God had made known to Moses (25:8).

EXPLAIN the Story

David Gives His Treasures for the Temple (29:1–9)

David gathers the sacred assembly and testifies publicly that God has chosen Solomon to be king, although he recognizes that his son is still young and inexperienced (1 Chr 29:1; cf. 22:5). The work ahead is significant, given that the lavishly adorned temple was not to be built for man but for God. David has already provided resources for the house of God (22:14), including gold, silver, bronze, iron, and wood; these materials, along with "onyx for the settings, turquoise, stones of various colors, and all kinds of fine stone and marble—all of these in large quantities" had been given (29:2). In the ancient world, gold was used in temples since it was "rare, desirable, and very costly, and fittingly represents the dignity and power of those able to possess it, to a pre-eminent degree, God."[3] As will be seen shortly, gold is used in the temple and its furnishings, especially as one approaches the most holy place; as Jenson notes, the "costliness of an item is proportional to its closeness to God."[4]

David's delight in the temple leads him to give his "personal treasures" toward the house of his God (1 Chr 29:3). Earlier in Israel's history, God had identified his people as his "treasured possession" (Exod 19:5; Deut 7:6; 14:2; Ps 135:4), but David now gives *his* treasured possessions to God, over and above what he had already provided. The king gives large amounts of gold and silver, which are given for the temple and its furnishings (1 Chr 29:4–5;

---

1. Braun has a helpful summary of the precious metals used in relation to the tabernacle and priestly garments (*1 Chronicles*, 279–80).

2. For other connections between the tabernacle and the temple, see the discussion in Chapter 32 on 2 Chr 3.

3. Jenson, *Graded Holiness*, 103.

4. Ibid., 101; see especially Jenson's section on the material gradation of the tabernacle, 101–3.

cf. 2 Chr 2:7, 14).[5] Having provided his own personal treasures, David asks: "Now, who is willing to consecrate themselves to the LORD today?" (1 Chr 29:5). David, the chief leader in Israel has *first* offered up his own treasures, but now he calls for his *leaders* to follow. The repetition of the verb "to offer willingly" (Heb. *n-d-b*, 1 Chr 29:5, 6, 9 [2x], 14, 17 [2x]) in this section underscores the voluntary nature of the contributions, and it is reminiscent of the time under Moses when God's people had willingly contributed toward the tabernacle (Exod 25:2; 35:21, 29).

But David does not simply ask his leaders to contribute—he *first* asks them to willingly consecrate themselves to the LORD (1 Chr 29:5) or, more literally, he asks: "Who will willingly fill his hand today to the LORD?" Interestingly, the expression "to fill the hand" is used of priests who were set apart or "ordained" for the LORD's service (Exod 28:41; 29:9, 29, 33, 35; Lev 16:32, etc.). David asks his leaders to consecrate themselves *first* to the LORD. The gifts that follow are simply an act of worship by those who have first given themselves to God. What happens next is that all those in leadership, which included leaders of families, heads of tribes, military commanders, and officials, willingly give of their precious resources (1 Chr 29:6). This scene of freely giving is not unlike the rule of the priestly king, when people freely volunteer (cf. Ps 110:3). Large amounts of gold, silver, bronze, and iron are given, which underscore their generosity and devotion to God (1 Chr 29:7).[6] Those who had precious stones gave them to the treasury under the safe-keeping of Jehiel the Gershonite (v. 8; cf. 26:20–28).

The generosity of Israel's leaders does not go unnoticed by the people gathered in Jerusalem, who "rejoiced at the willing response of their leaders, for they had given freely and wholeheartedly to the LORD" (1 Chr 29:9). Leaders are called to serve God with wholehearted devotion (28:9; 2 Chr 19:9), and

---

5. See Merrill for estimated modern-day amounts given in 29:4 and 29:7 (Merrill, *1 & 2 Chronicles*, 302–303). Japhet suggests that the numbers three thousand and seven thousand are typological rather than literal (see Japhet, *I & II Chronicles*, 507). On quantities of gold in antiquity, see A. Millard, "King Solomon in his Ancient Context," in the volume edited by Lowell K. Handy, *The Age of Solomon: Scholarship at the Turn of the Millennium* (Leiden: Brill, 1997), 31–42. Millard notes that while the exact location of Ophir is still unknown, its historicity is confirmed by an eighth century BC receipt found at Tel Qasile that mentions gold from Ophir. For further discussion on gold, see the commentary in Chapter 38 on 2 Chr 9:13–24, pp. 357–58.

6. The term "daric" used in 29:7 refers to a coin named after Darius I and minted in the late sixth century BC (cf. Ezra 2:69; 8:27; Neh 7:70–72). Since the term was not in use until well after David, the Chronicler has used a modern term to describe the amount of gold coins given by David; see H.G.M. Williamson, "Eschatology in Chronicles," *TynBul* 28 (1977): 123–26. On some of the amounts in contemporary figures, see Merrill, *I & 2 Chronicles*, 302–3.

their generosity is a tangible demonstration of their commitment to God's kingdom. As David witnesses their generosity, this brings him great joy, and he rejoices along with all Israel (1 Chr 29:9).

David Praises God (29:10–22a)

On this joyous occasion, David's heart turns to praise the LORD, the God of Israel. His prayer begins: "Praise be to you, LORD, the God of our father Israel, from everlasting to everlasting" (1 Chr 29:10). David's voice rises in praise as he acknowledges that greatness, power, glory, majesty, and splendor belong to the LORD. He confesses that the kingdom belongs to God and that the LORD is exalted as head over all (v. 11). Even though David is king over the kingdom, he affirms publicly that the kingdom does not belong to him but to the LORD (cf. 17:14; 28:5; 2 Chr 9:8; 13:8). David understands that the earthly kingdom pointed to an even greater reality. God's throne was established in the heavens, and he rules over all (Pss 45:6; 103:19; 145:11, 13). God is exalted as head over everything (1 Chr 29:11).

David recognizes, therefore, that riches and honor come from God and that God is ruler over all (v. 12). This is precisely what Jehoshaphat will acknowledge in his prayer when he confesses: "LORD, the God of our ancestors, are you not the God who is in heaven? You rule over all the kingdoms of the nations" (2 Chr 20:6), as will Hezekiah (2 Kgs 19:15; Isa 37:16). The prophets envisage a time when the Messiah's rule will "extend from sea to sea and from the River to the ends of the earth" (Zech 9:10; cf. Ps 72:8), at which time God's heavenly rule will be extended to encompass the entire earth (cf. Mic 5:1–5).

David further acknowledges that strength and power belong to God and that God is the one who exalts and strengthens (1 Chr 29:12). David does not attribute his leadership position to his own qualities but to God, for he has not forgotten that God made him king, which he did for the sake of Israel. David gives thanks to God and praises his glorious name, as he joins with the sacred assembly to bless the LORD (v. 13). In view of God's greatness, David is overwhelmed with the privilege given to him and his people, who were able to give generously to God. David's heart-stirring question, "Who am I?" echoes his earlier response when he sat dumbfounded before his God, amazed that God had chosen *him* (17:16), even as Moses pondered the call of God upon his life (Exod 3:11). David acknowledges that everything has come from God's hand (1 Chr 29:14), which means that he and the people were simply giving to God what they had first received from him. This theology is rooted in God's gift of land to Israel. God's generosity to Israel was intended to foster reciprocity among his covenant people, leading Israel to give back to God with generosity and self-sacrifice.[7]

David confesses further: "We are foreigners and strangers in your sight, as were all our ancestors. Our days on earth are like a shadow, without hope" (1 Chr 29:15; cf. Ps 39:12). Like the patriarchs before him, who lived in tents as strangers on the earth (cf. Heb 11:9–10), David's statement has its theological roots in God's gift of land. The land was given to Israel but "enjoyment of the land and its benefits depends on a readiness to relinquish them."[8] Recognition that the land ultimately belonged to Yahweh and that his people were "foreigners and strangers" (1 Chr 29:15; cf. Lev 25:23) enables David and the people to hold their resources lightly. Those living back in Jerusalem after the exile had faced hardship, and they were grappling with the reality that their land belonged to others (see Neh 9:32–37). The words of David would have resonated with them, as they, too, were foreigners and strangers on the land. There was a future inheritance that was to shape their view of the earthly (cf. Heb 11:9–16). David is keenly aware that his days on earth were short, like a mere shadow (1 Chr 29:15; cf. Pss 102:11; 109:23; 144:4). These are words spoken by a king whose life is drawing to a close. He recognizes the transitory nature of his life in comparison to God's everlasting kingdom.

David returns to the theme of abundance that has been foremost in his mind, recognizing that everything has come from God's hand, and everything belongs to God (1 Chr 29:16). God tests the heart, and he is pleased with integrity (v. 17), a characteristic that reflects God's own rule (Pss 9:8; 96:10; 98:9; 99:4). David confesses that, with integrity of heart, he has willingly offered all these things to the LORD, and he has great joy as he witnesses others willingly giving to God (1 Chr 29:17). David prays that God might keep these thoughts and intentions in the heart of his people forever, and that God might direct their heart toward him (vv. 18–19). This comes from a shepherd who tenderly prays for his flock and who longs to see his people remain faithful to the LORD. He concludes his prayer by exhorting the assembly to bless the LORD, and the final scene is fittingly one of worship, as God's people bow down, "prostrating themselves before the LORD and the king" (v. 20). In light of the greatness, power, and majesty of God, worship is the only fitting response.

The next day, God's people offer a few thousand burnt offerings to God,

---

7. For the theology of reciprocity rooted in God's generous gift of land to Israel, see the insightful work of J. Gordon McConville, *Law and Theology in Deuteronomy* (JSOTSup 33; Sheffield: JSOT Press, 1984), 15–20, 82–86.

8. Ibid., 18.

along with drink offerings and other sacrifices in abundance (1 Chr 29:21). Among the five major sacrifices in the Old Testament, the burnt offering was entirely burnt on the altar (cf. Lev 1), and as such, it was the most costly sacrifice.[9] In light of the theme of generosity and wholehearted devotion that has permeated this story (1 Chr 29:1–9), it is fitting that several thousand burnt offerings are sacrificed to the LORD—given over *entirely* on the altar. If one of the purposes of the burnt offering was to "underscore the offerors' prayers, a type of exclamation point to what they were saying,"[10] then these burnt offerings serve as tangible expressions of their devotion to God. It is not surprising to read that their gathering concludes with resounding joy, as God's people "ate and drank with great joy in the presence of the LORD" (v. 22; cf. 1 Chr 12:39–40).[11]

Solomon Is Anointed King in Place of David (29:22b–25)

Attention now turns to the public anointing of Solomon (1 Chr 29:22b). David had appointed Solomon as co-regent earlier (23:1), but now the formal and public anointing ceremony takes place.[12] Zadok and Nathan have key roles in this sacred ceremony, although the Chronicler notes that Zadok was anointed along with Solomon (29:22), which emphasizes the dual leadership of king and priest.[13] The public and legal act of anointing serves to legitimize Solomon as the divinely appointed heir, which underscores that "his place on the throne has not been taken unlawfully or against the will of David."[14] The anointing ceremony identifies the king as the LORD's "anointed," an important title for the Davidic king (v. 22; cf. 2 Chr 6:42; Ps 2:2). The throne upon which Solomon sits is none other than the "throne of the LORD" (1 Chr 29:23; cf. 17:14; 28:5). Under God's blessing, Solomon prospers (29:23), echoing David's earlier exhortation that success would be achieved by God's presence (22:11, 13; cf. 2 Chr 7:17–18). Further, David's leaders

---

9. Sklar, *Leviticus*, 94.

10. Ibid.

11. On the topic of joy, see Live the Story in Chapter 34, 319–21.

12. In the Kings account, Solomon rides on his father's own mule as he is brought down to Gihon, the spring located on the eastern side of the City of David (1 Kgs 1:33). Zadok the priest, Nathan the prophet, and Benaiah have a central role in the anointing ceremony (vv. 32–40). Boda notes that having two anointings follows the pattern of Saul (1 Sam 10:1; 11:12–15) and David (1 Sam 16:13; 2 Sam 2:1–7; 5:1–5); see Boda, *1–2 Chronicles*, 221.

13. See Schniedewind, "King and Priest," 71–78. https://www.academia.edu/326665/King _and_Priest_In_the_Book_of_Chronicles_and_the_Duality_of_Qumran_Messianism

14. Åke Viberg, *Symbols of Law: A Contextual Analysis of Legal Symbolic Acts in the Old Testament*, Coniectanea Biblica Old Testament Series 34 (Stockholm: Almqvist & Wiksell International, 1992), 107.

and his sons "pledged their submission to King Solomon" (lit. "they put a hand under Solomon," 1 Chr 29:24). The symbolic act of putting one's hand under a person's thigh is used when swearing an oath of allegiance (cf. Gen 24:9; 47:29). Although the term "thigh" is not used, the symbolism carries the same legal function.[15] In view of the precarious nature of the throne (see 1 Kgs 1–2), their public support for Solomon affirms him as the legitimate heir. God exalts Solomon before all Israel, and he bestows on him royal splendor (1 Chr 29:25; cf. 2 Chr 1:1).

David's Death and Burial (29:26–30)

David has ruled as king over Israel for forty years, beginning with his seven-year reign at Hebron, followed by his thirty-three years in Jerusalem (2 Sam 5:1–5; 1 Kgs 2:11; 1 Chr 3:4; cf. 1 Chr 11:1–3). David dies "at a good old age, having enjoyed long life, wealth and honor" (29:28; cf. Gen 25:8; 35:29). The account of his reign concludes with references to written records that chronicle David's reign, such as the records of Samuel, Nathan, and Gad (1 Chr 23:29).[16]

 LIVE the Story

Storing up Treasures in Heaven

The final chapter in David's life resounds with heartfelt gratitude to God, which leads the king and the people to give generously toward the temple. These are not gifts given out of obligation. Nor are their gifts tithes, but rather, they are tangible expressions of their devotion to God. David had determined not to give to the Lord that which costs him nothing (1 Chr 21:24), and it is precisely this sacrificial giving that gets to the heart of the king. David's heart is filled with gratitude for all that God has done. His life is a testimony of one who has stored up treasures *in heaven*.

Jesus taught his disciples that they, too, were to store up treasures in heaven: "Do not store up for yourselves treasures on earth, where moths and vermin destroy, and where thieves break in and steal. But store up for yourselves treasures in heaven, where moths and vermin do not destroy, and where thieves do not break in and steal" (Matt 6:19–20). Use of their wealth was an outward and tangible demonstration of their willingness to do God's will.

When teaching through a parable about the rich man, Jesus spoke about a

---

15. Ibid., 45–51.
16. See the introduction (Genre, pp. 7–8) on sources used by the Chronicler.

man who had accrued an abundance of wealth, requiring him to build extra barns to store his worldly goods (Luke 12:16–20). He had wrongly assumed that he would have sufficient time to enjoy all of his precious goods, only to unexpectedly face death that very night. Unlike David, who understood that his days on earth were like a shadow (1 Chr 29:15), the foolish man had assumed that *he* was in control of his days. Unlike David, who recognized that *everything* belonged to God, the foolish man assumed that everything belonged *to him* ("my crops," "my barns," "my surplus grain"). Jesus concluded by teaching that we are not to be lavish on ourselves but stingy toward God (Luke 12:21).

Jesus taught further: "Sell your possessions and give to the poor. Provide purses for yourselves that will not wear out, a treasure in heaven that will never fail, where no thief comes near and no moth destroys. For where your treasure is, there your heart will be also" (Luke 12:33–34). Jesus taught that the kingdom of heaven was like treasure hidden in a field. Once found, a man sells all that he has to buy it (Matt 13:44). The kingdom of heaven was also like a merchant seeking fine pearls. After finding one precious pearl, he sells all that he has to buy it (Matt 13:45–46). Those who have tasted of the kingdom discover its incalculable worth—it is worth far more than earthly treasures, even one's most treasured possessions. Like a merchant who finds a precious pearl, these people make the kingdom their highest priority, and they willingly sacrifice their earthly goods because of its infinite worth.

The apostle Paul instructed the young Timothy to command those who were rich in this world not to put their hope in wealth but in God. They were to "do good, to be rich in good deeds, and to be generous and willing to share. In this way they will lay up treasure for themselves as a firm foundation for the coming age, so that they may take hold of the life that is truly life" (1 Tim 6:18–19). These verses summarize the final years of David's life. His generosity serves as an example for us as we consider how we are using our financial resources and whether our giving is marked by generosity, a tangible demonstration of our inward devotion to the LORD. The words of the abolitionist William Wilberforce could equally summarize David's life: "True Christians consider themselves not as satisfying some rigorous creditor, but as discharging a debt of gratitude." [17]

The book by John Rinehart, *Gospel Patrons: People Whose Generosity Changed the World*, is a moving and challenging book that traces the ministry

---

17. William Wilberforce, *A Practical View of Christianity* (1797; annotated repr., Peabody, MA: Hendrickson, 1996), 255.

of three gospel patrons who devoted themselves and their resources for the cause of the gospel.[18] The story of Lady Huntington, who supported the preaching efforts of George Whitefield, is told by Rinehart. It is remarkable to learn of her sacrificial giving and her unswerving commitment to God's word being preached. She not only supported the ministry of George Whitefield, but she had a burden to see the word of God preached and pulpits filled with well-trained preachers so that God's word could be made known. This led her to fund church buildings, to establish a seminary, and to fund seminary students who were training for the ministry, while deciding to use resources on herself only sparingly. Her support of seminary students, which included paying for their food, clothing, and ministry trips, would lead her to use half of her annual income for God's work. Rinehart writes: "What Lady Huntingdon and George Whitefield accomplished was truly incalculable. They reached into the unreached places of both England and America where there were no faithful churches and no gospel preachers."[19] The generosity of Lady Huntingdon and her devotion to the Lord challenges us to consider how we are using our time, energy, and resources for the expansion of God's kingdom.[20] Like David, may we recognize that our days on earth are like a shadow, quickly fading in comparison to God's everlasting kingdom, and like David, may our highest priority be serving God and using our resources for his kingdom.

---

18. For the story of William Tyndale, who was supported by Humphrey Monmouth, see Live the Story, Chapter 8, pp. 103–4. For the story of the third gospel patron, John Thorton, who supported the hymn writer, John Newton, see Live the Story, Chapter 37, pp. 350–52.

19. Rinehart, *Gospel Patrons*, 88.

20. Gospel Patrons has a website with helpful resources for the church, including how to implement in the local church the kind of giving highlighted in *Gospel Patrons;* see https://www.gospel patrons.org/.

LISTEN to the Story

¹Solomon son of David established himself firmly over his kingdom, for the LORD his God was with him and made him exceedingly great.

²Then Solomon spoke to all Israel—to the commanders of thousands and commanders of hundreds, to the judges and to all the leaders in Israel, the heads of families—³and Solomon and the whole assembly went to the high place at Gibeon, for God's tent of meeting was there, which Moses the LORD's servant had made in the wilderness. ⁴Now David had brought up the ark of God from Kiriath Jearim to the place he had prepared for it, because he had pitched a tent for it in Jerusalem. ⁵But the bronze altar that Bezalel son of Uri, the son of Hur, had made was in Gibeon in front of the tabernacle of the LORD; so Solomon and the assembly inquired of him there. ⁶Solomon went up to the bronze altar before the LORD in the tent of meeting and offered a thousand burnt offerings on it.

⁷That night God appeared to Solomon and said to him, "Ask for whatever you want me to give you."

⁸Solomon answered God, "You have shown great kindness to David my father and have made me king in his place. ⁹Now, LORD God, let your promise to my father David be confirmed, for you have made me king over a people who are as numerous as the dust of the earth. ¹⁰Give me wisdom and knowledge, that I may lead this people, for who is able to govern this great people of yours?"

¹¹God said to Solomon, "Since this is your heart's desire and you have not asked for wealth, possessions or honor, nor for the death of your enemies, and since you have not asked for a long life but for wisdom and knowledge to govern my people over whom I have made you king, ¹²therefore wisdom and knowledge will be given you. And I will also give

you wealth, possessions and honor, such as no king who was before you ever had and none after you will have."

¹³Then Solomon went to Jerusalem from the high place at Gibeon, from before the tent of meeting. And he reigned over Israel.

¹⁴Solomon accumulated chariots and horses; he had fourteen hundred chariots and twelve thousand horses, which he kept in the chariot cities and also with him in Jerusalem. ¹⁵The king made silver and gold as common in Jerusalem as stones, and cedar as plentiful as sycamore-fig trees in the foothills. ¹⁶Solomon's horses were imported from Egypt and from Kue—the royal merchants purchased them from Kue at the current price. ¹⁷They imported a chariot from Egypt for six hundred shekels of silver, and a horse for a hundred and fifty. They also exported them to all the kings of the Hittites and of the Arameans.

Listening to the Text in the Story: Exodus 25–40; 1 Kings 3:1–15; The Building of Ningirsu's Temple

The story of kingship continues with David's son Solomon, although his succession to the throne is not as smooth as it might appear (see 1 Kgs 1–2 for the backstory). The Chronicler picks up the story with Solomon securely on the throne under God's blessing. Trade relations with the king of Tyre are Solomon's top priority as he embarks on this massive building project. Phoenician artisans are secured to provide their expert craftsmanship for the beautification of the temple, and cedars are transported from Lebanon. Precious gold is brought on ships from the distant region of Ophir, and exotic animals are among the king's royal acquisitions. With international trade at its height, chariots and horses are acquired in great numbers, including prized Anatolian horses. As Solomon's kingdom expands and flourishes, foreign kings bring extravagant gifts into Jerusalem, and Solomon is greatly honored by a visit from the queen of Sheba. This is the prosperous kingdom under God's blessing that sets the context for Solomon's rule as the divinely appointed temple-builder.

The main focus of these chapters is on the construction of the temple and God's glorious presence filling it (2 Chr 2–5). Every effort will be made by Solomon to build a resplendent house worthy of his God. In the ancient world, high value was placed on the king's role as temple-builder, as Frankfort notes: "No greater service could be rendered to a god than the building of his house."[1] This was an honorable and sacred task, but it was often accompanied with fear and trepidation. The king needed confirmation through oracles that he was acting in accordance with the will of the gods before embarking on such a sacred task. Once divine confirmation had been given, every effort was made by the king to construct a magnificent temple worthy of his god.

The temple built by a Mesopotamian ruler named Gudea toward the end of the third millennium BC is an example of an ancient temple-building account. Written in cuneiform, the Gudea cylinders housed in the Louvre Museum describe the temple Gudea built for the god Ningirsu.[2] Two clay cylinders describe how Ningirsu appeared to Gudea in a dream, appointing him to build a temple and giving him plans, along with details about conscripting laborers, the materials to be used, and even specific decorations and furnishings.[3] The account mentions large stones that were quarried, cedars that were brought on ships, copper that was mined, and bricks that were molded. The extensive description concludes with the arrival of the god Ningirsu, as incense is burned and prayers are offered. Gudea even makes the whole city kneel down as they prostrate themselves to honor the god's arrival. With prayers and supplications being offered into the night, finally the god Ningirsu enters his house, signifying that the owner of the house has arrived. This is one of several temple-building texts known from antiquity.[4] Careful analysis of such texts help us to discern ancient formulaic features and to recognize the importance of temple-building in the ancient world.

Yet the Chronicler's presentation of Solomon's temple is first and foremost shaped by Israel's sacred traditions, with echoes of the creation story and the tabernacle narrative reverberating throughout these chapters.[5] The temple in Jerusalem is not to be seen as something entirely new, but rather it marks a climactic moment in the purposes of God that began in Eden. Botanical and arboreal imagery that decorate the temple walls and its furnishings, along with

---

1. Frankfort, *Kingship and the Gods*, 267. The important role of temple building in the ancient Near East has been highlighted in the superb volume edited by Mark J. Boda and Jamie Novotny, *From the Foundations to Crenellations: Essays on Temple Building in the Ancient Near East. Alter Orient und Altes Testament, Band 366* (Münster: Ugarit Verlag, 2010). For an analysis of the temple building account in Chronicles, see the article in this volume by Mark Boda, "Legitimizing the Temple: The Chronicler's Temple Building Account," 303–18.

2. We noted earlier that David was given the blueprint for the temple (1 Chr 28:11–19). A statue of Gudea seated and holding a plan of a temple is located at the Louvre Museum. I am grateful for Tremper Longman for pointing this out; see https://louvrebible.org.uk/oeuvre/102/louvre_departement_antiquites_orientales.

3. *The Building of Ningirsu's Temple* (Gudea, Cylinders A and B): http://etcsl.orinst.ox.ac.uk/cgi-bin/etcsl.cgi?text=t.2.1.7#.

4. Hurowitz, *I Have Built You an Exalted House*, 130–322.

5. For further discussion, see Boda, "Legitimizing the Temple," 313–16.

gold and precious jewels used to embellish it, are reminiscent of the Garden of Eden where God had walked with Adam and Eve, even as he walks among his people in the tabernacle and temple. The temple signifies the next stage of God's redemptive plan, as God now dwells among his people in the sacred building designed by him to be a microcosm of creation itself.

It is important to bear in mind that the temple built by Solomon is not the ultimate goal of the narrative, but rather, it is God's glorious presence among his people and the prayer that follows. What matters most is not the abundance of gold, the precious stones, the cedars from Lebanon, the horses from Egypt and Kue, the gifts from the nations, or even Solomon's extravagant ivory throne overlaid with gold. What matters most in these chapters is that the LORD God dwells with his people, as he is restoring what was lost in Eden. So while details about the temple will be given, the Chronicler lifts our attention beyond the building to reflect upon Solomon's extended prayer of dedication (2 Chr 6:12–42) and God's response to him (7:12–22), which lie at the center of a well-crafted chiastic structure.[6] Even though the highest heavens cannot contain the LORD, the mystery is that the temple will be the place where God's glory dwells. Unlike temples in the ancient world, there is no physical image installed in this temple, and the LORD surely does not need to be carried by any priest or brought to life by him. The true and living LORD, the creator and giver of life, is enthroned in heaven, yet he mysteriously descends to dwell among his people in the cloud, hovering above the Edenic cherubim and beyond the richly decorated and brightly colored veil.

The presence of God among his people is followed by Solomon's prayer, as the king kneels on a large bronze platform with uplifted hands toward heaven. This is a sacred moment when the king communes with his God. This is the place where heaven and earth meet. In contrast to the deaf and dumb idols of the ancient world, Solomon prays to the *living* God, who hears and sees (2 Chr 6:19, 20, 21, 23, 25, 27, 30, 33, 35, 39). The king exhorts God's people to pray to the LORD their God. We learn the remarkable truth from this story that God not only hears Solomon's prayer, but he also answers it, revealing that prayer is dialogue and the appropriate posture of one in communion with God is humility. God's people are thus invited to humble themselves, pray, and seek his face, and remarkably, God promises to hear from heaven, forgive, and heal (7:14). This promise reverberates throughout 2 Chronicles. In the ensuing

---

6. Scholars have observed the presence of a chiasm in these chapters. For a detailed analysis, see Dillard, *2 Chronicles*, 5–7. This literary structure is important, as it helps the reader identify parallel sections that are repeated for literary symmetry (e.g., 1:14–17 and 9:25, 28) and to discern the central role of prayer in the narrative.

commentary, we will consider the importance of self-humbling and prayer as set forth in 2 Chronicles 7:14, but for now, we note that the temple is first and foremost the place of God's presence. His glory is far more precious than gold and silver. It is far more precious than all the cedars of Lebanon, and it is surely far more precious than the fame that comes from foreign dignitaries. The God who dwells in unapproachable holiness, hidden beyond the veil in all his glory, invites his people to pray and seek his face. And he promises to be found by those who seek him. This is truly remarkable.

 EXPLAIN the Story

Solomon Worships the LORD at Gibeon (1:1–13)

God is with the young king Solomon (2 Chr 1:1; cf. 1 Chr 22:11, 16–18) even as he had been with his father David (17:8), and God exalts him greatly. Solomon assembles his leaders and all the people to Gibeon, a city approximately five miles north of Jerusalem, where the tent of meeting was located (2 Chr 1:1–3). During Israel's earlier history, the tabernacle had been located at Shiloh (Josh 18:1; 19:51; 1 Sam 1:3), but the Philistine attack had led to the departure of God's glory (1 Sam 4; cf. Jer 7:12). David had brought the ark of the covenant from Kiriath Jearim to Jerusalem and had placed it in a temporary tent (1 Chr 13, 15; 2 Chr 1:4). Asaph and his relatives had oversight of the ark, whereas Zadok the priest officiated at the tabernacle (1 Chr 16:37–40). The bronze altar had been made by Bezalel, the well-known craftsmen from the time of Moses (Exod 31:1–11; 36:1; cf. 1 Chr 2:20). Solomon and all the people inquire of the LORD, and Solomon offers a thousand burnt offerings on the altar (2 Chr 1:5–6).

In the evening God appears to Solomon in a dream, after he and the people had sought him (v. 7). That they seek the LORD is in accordance with what Moses had instructed many years earlier, for the Israelites were to seek God at the place he would choose for his name to dwell (Deut 12:5). David had exhorted his son to seek the LORD (1 Chr 22:19; 28:9), and God's answer to Solomon affirms that God is found by those who seek him (28:9; cf. Deut 4:29). God asks Solomon what he wants from him (2 Chr 1:7). Solomon acknowledges that God has shown covenant loyalty to his father David and that he now rules in his place. He asks God to confirm the promise he had made with his father, recognizing that he has become king over a great multitude (vv. 8–9).

Solomon asks God for wisdom and knowledge so that he might lead the people. Wisdom was an important quality for kings, enabling them to issue just decrees and to govern fairly (Prov 8:15–16; 29:12; cf. Isa 11:1–5). Solomon's desire for wisdom is thus received favorably, and God gives him wisdom and knowledge, something others will recognize in the days ahead (1 Kgs 4:29–34; 2 Chr 2:12; 9:5–6). But God also gives Solomon wealth, possessions, and honor—things for which he had not asked (1:11–12). Having received this word of assurance from God at Gibeon, Solomon returns to Jerusalem (v. 13).

Solomon's Extensive Wealth and Chariots (1:14–17)

Solomon musters an impressive number of chariots and horsemen and stations them at designated cities (2 Chr 1:14; see also 1 Kgs 9:19; 2 Chr 8:6). Chariots are attested in Canaan before the period of the monarchy, and David's military victories over nations included acquiring their chariots and horsemen (1 Chr 18:3–4). Now, with an expanding and flourishing kingdom (1 Kgs 4:20–25), extensive stables and caretakers are needed to provide shelter, food, and water. This responsibility is assigned to leaders appointed over Solomon's twelve administrative districts (vv. 26–28). Silver and gold are in abundance, and cedars are plentiful (2 Chr 1:15).[7]

Among Solomon's acquisitions are the well-bred horses he had imported from Egypt and Kue (v. 16). Kings in the ancient world were keen to acquire fine horses and chariots, not only for their use in warfare, but they were also sought after as symbols of status and glory.[8] Elaborately decorated chariots were given as royal gifts from one king to another, and they were among a king's prized treasures. Solomon's traders acquire horses from Egypt, but they are also able to purchase horses from Kue, a region in southeast Anatolia known for its stock of quality horses. They even secure an Egyptian chariot for the high price of six hundred shekels of silver, along with a horse for 150 shekels (v. 17). This expensive chariot was most likely a well-crafted royal chariot used by kings and dignitaries (Exod 15:4; 1 Sam 8:11; 2 Sam 15:1), similar to the Egyptian chariot Joseph had ridden in after he had been given a position of honor (Gen 41:42–43). In antiquity, royal chariots were elaborately decorated with gold and silver, and sometimes even with precious jewels. Since chariots were used in stately processions and ceremonies, they displayed the king's

---

7. On these use of gold in antiquity, and cedars, see the discussion in Chapter 31 and 32 on 2 Chr 2 and 3.

8. See the excellent article by Yutaka Ikeda, "Solomon's Trade in Horses and Chariots in Its International Setting," in *Studies in the Period of David and Solomon and Other Essays*, ed. Tomoo Ishida (Winona Lake, IN: Eisenbrauns, 1982), 215–38.

glory and status.[9] While the price for horses varied considerably depending on their age and quality, Solomon's payment of 150 shekels suggests that he had acquired a superior horse, probably well-trained for royal processions.[10] Solomon's traders exported horses to Hittite and Aramean kings in northern Syria (2 Chr 1:17). Trade of horses is known in the region, and Solomon was evidently a key player in international trade.

LIVE the Story

Seeking the LORD

The reign of Solomon begins on a high note as the entire community gathers at Gibeon. The Chronicler begins his account by noting that the king and the people "inquired" of the LORD (Heb. *d-r-sh*, 2 Chr 1:5). The high frequency of the verb "to inquire, seek" (Heb. *d-r-sh*) in Chronicles highlights its importance. By way of comparison, the verb appears three times in Samuel[11] and thirteen times in Kings,[12] but over forty times in Chronicles.[13] At key moments in Israel's story, the Chronicler pauses to highlight times when kings seek the LORD, such as Asa (2 Chr 14:4, 7; 15:2, 12) and Jehoshaphat (17:3–4; 19:3; 20:3), and when they fail to do so, such as Saul (1 Chr 10:13–14; 13:3). Emphasis on seeking the LORD throughout Chronicles raises the question of whether our lives are characterized by prayer. Seeking the LORD can mean inquiring of God as we seek him for wisdom or answers to situations. Sometimes it means devoting ourselves to God's work (22:19) and following his commands (2 Chr 14:4). Thus, it characterizes a God-focused life, as we seek to live according to his will and to rely upon him. Often difficult circumstances cause us to cry out to God in prayer (e.g., 1 Chr 4:10; 2 Chr 14:11; 15:4; 18:31; 20:3–4). Jehoshaphat had set his face to seek the LORD when facing an attack from his enemies (vv. 3–4). Rather than looking for help or finding solutions elsewhere, he had turned to God. The prophet Jeremiah looked forward to a time after the exile when God's people would seek the LORD with all their heart (Jer 29:13–14; cf. Deut 4:29), and this is an important virtue in Chronicles. The difficult years of exile in Babylon lead

---

9. See ibid., 223–25.

10. Ibid., 226–31.

11. Translated in the NIV by "inquire" (1 Sam 9:9; 28:7) and "find out" (1 Sam 11:3).

12. E.g., 1 Kgs 14:5 (NIV, "ask about"); 22:5 (NIV, "seek"), 7, 8 (NIV, "inquire").

13. E.g., 1 Chr 16:11; 22:19; 28:8, 9; 2 Chr 12:14; 14:4, 7; 15:2, 12, 13; 17:4; 18:4; 19:3; 20:3; 22:9; 26:5; 30:19; 31:21; 34:3. While translations of *d-r-sh* vary depending on the English version, the same Hebrew word is used throughout, which underscores its importance in Chronicles.

to a renewed emphasis on prayer, as seen in the lives of Ezra and Nehemiah (Ezra 8:21–23; 9:5–15; 10:1–2; Neh 1:4–11; 2:4; 4:9; 6:9; 9:1–37).

As I write this commentary, we are in the midst of a global pandemic caused by COVID-19. A study by the University of Copenhagen found that google searches for prayer in ninety-five countries increased exponentially during the global pandemic.[14] Researchers found that prayer was relatively flat before a country registered its first case of COVID-19, but as the virus became a global pandemic, internet searches on prayer skyrocketed, surging in March 2020 to the highest level in the past five years. The global pandemic has caused people to seek God for answers.

We are reminded in the story of Solomon that our lives ought to be characterized by seeking the LORD. This means that during difficult periods, God wants us to look to him for strength and help rather than put our trust in other things. But we are not simply to seek God during times of crisis, for the psalmist exhorts us to do this continually: "Look to the LORD and his strength; seek his face always" (1 Chr 16:11). We live in a time where our media-saturated culture fills us with ubiquitous images and messages that can easily drown out the voice of God, and we can become too distracted to pray.

By the first quarter of 2018, a study done by Nielson, a global data analytics company, estimated that American adults spend more than eleven hours daily "listening to, watching, reading, or generally interacting with" media.[15] Davis laments over our relentless obsession with online media when writing: "Never before in human history has it been possible for the human mind to be so over-stimulated, so distracted and so overloaded with a never-ending, Niagara Falls-like cascade of information, images, entertainment, texts, sounds, fantasies, pornography and commercial advertisements."[16] He suggests that the "One who has captured your imagination has captured your soul," followed by his probing question: "Where is your heart's true ontological home?"[17] The book of Chronicles stands as an invitation from the LORD to seek him, as he beckons us to give him our wholehearted devotion. What is remarkable in the story of Solomon is that God answers the king in a dream, and he gives him even more

---

14. The study led by Jeanet Sinding Bentzen is entitled, "In crisis, we pray: Religiosity and the COVID-19 pandemic," *Journal of Economic Behavior & Organization* 192 (December 2021): 541 -83. doi.org/10.1016/j.jebo.2021.10.014.

15. "Time Flies: U.S. Adults Now Spend Nearly Half A Day Interacting with Media," Nielson, July 31, 2018; https://www.nielsen.com/us/en/insights/news/2018/time-flies-us-adults-now-spend -nearly-half-a-day-interacting-with-media.html.

16. John Jefferson Davis, *Worship and the Reality of God: An Evangelical Theology of Real Presence* (Downers Grove, IL: InterVarsity Press, 2010), 15.

17. Ibid., 17.

than what he has asked (2 Chr 1:11–12; cf. Matt 7:7–11). This is the LORD God who invites us to dialogue with him, for he reveals himself through his *word*. When we consider that the highest of heavens cannot contain the LORD (2 Chr 2:6), it is remarkable that he graciously promises to be found by those who seek him (Deut 4:29; 2 Chr 7:14; 15:2). Yet in order for us to cultivate a habit of seeking God, we need to turn away from other competing voices and set aside things that draw our attention away from him. We need to turn off our mobile devices, unplug, and take time to read the Scriptures. The word of God is "alive and active" (Heb 4:12), and therein he is found. We need to take time to pray and seek his face. This is God's word of exhortation for us today.

LISTEN to the Story

¹Solomon gave orders to build a temple for the Name of the LORD and a royal palace for himself. ²He conscripted 70,000 men as carriers and 80,000 as stonecutters in the hills and 3,600 as foremen over them. ³Solomon sent this message to Hiram king of Tyre:

"Send me cedar logs as you did for my father David when you sent him cedar to build a palace to live in. ⁴Now I am about to build a temple for the Name of the LORD my God and to dedicate it to him for burning fragrant incense before him, for setting out the consecrated bread regularly, and for making burnt offerings every morning and evening and on the Sabbaths, at the New Moons and at the appointed festivals of the LORD our God. This is a lasting ordinance for Israel.

⁵"The temple I am going to build will be great, because our God is greater than all other gods. ⁶But who is able to build a temple for him, since the heavens, even the highest heavens, cannot contain him? Who then am I to build a temple for him, except as a place to burn sacrifices before him?

⁷"Send me, therefore, a man skilled to work in gold and silver, bronze and iron, and in purple, crimson and blue yarn, and experienced in the art of engraving, to work in Judah and Jerusalem with my skilled workers, whom my father David provided.

⁸"Send me also cedar, juniper and algum logs from Lebanon, for I know that your servants are skilled in cutting timber there. My servants will work with yours ⁹to provide me with plenty of lumber, because the temple I build must be large and magnificent. ¹⁰I will give your servants, the woodsmen who cut the timber,

twenty thousand cors of ground wheat, twenty thousand cors of barley, twenty thousand baths of wine and twenty thousand baths of olive oil."

[11]Hiram king of Tyre replied by letter to Solomon:

"Because the LORD loves his people, he has made you their king."

[12]And Hiram added:

"Praise be to the LORD, the God of Israel, who made heaven and earth! He has given King David a wise son, endowed with intelligence and discernment, who will build a temple for the LORD and a palace for himself.

[13]"I am sending you Huram-Abi, a man of great skill, [14]whose mother was from Dan and whose father was from Tyre. He is trained to work in gold and silver, bronze and iron, stone and wood, and with purple and blue and crimson yarn and fine linen. He is experienced in all kinds of engraving and can execute any design given to him. He will work with your skilled workers and with those of my lord, David your father.

[15]"Now let my lord send his servants the wheat and barley and the olive oil and wine he promised, [16]and we will cut all the logs from Lebanon that you need and will float them as rafts by sea down to Joppa. You can then take them up to Jerusalem."

[17]Solomon took a census of all the foreigners residing in Israel, after the census his father David had taken; and they were found to be 153,600. [18]He assigned 70,000 of them to be carriers and 80,000 to be stonecutters in the hills, with 3,600 foremen over them to keep the people working.

Listening to the Text in the Story: Ezekiel 26:1–28:19; The Story of Wen-Amon

The story of Solomon continues with preparations for the temple. Given the king's vast building project, an enormous amount of materials will be needed beyond what David had already given. Solomon enters into an alliance with the king of Tyre to procure wood and other building materials. We have already noted that the Phoenicians were seafaring traders who occupied the well-known ports of Byblos, Sidon, and Tyre.[1] The Egyptian emissary named Wen-Amon, who was an official of the Temple of Amon, describes his journey to Byblos to procure wood to be used for a ceremonial barge. After a somewhat arduous trip, Wen-Amon makes his request under the blessing of the god Amon, and goods from Egypt are supplied in exchange for wood. This lengthy account testifies to the lively and flourishing trade along the coast.[2] As experienced sea traders, Solomon understands that the Phoenicians were needed to transport large cedars from Lebanon on their impressive and well-built cargo ships (1 Chr 22:4; cf. Ezek 27:4–6). The importance of wood in antiquity is not to be underestimated, since it was highly sought after as the building material for temples, palaces, and boats. Solomon's alliance with the Sidonians through his marriage would have forged a strong and advantageous relationship with the Phoenicians (1 Kgs 11:1). The Phoenicians would receive luxury items, resulting in an abundance of wealth that was exchanged for their services.[3] It is not surprising to learn, therefore, that the cities of Tyre and Sidon become prosperous through their maritime trade, although they will become proud and fall under God's judgment (Isa 23:1–18; Jer 25:22; 47:4; Ezek 26:1–28:19; Amos 1:9–10; Zech 9:2–4).

 EXPLAIN the Story

Solomon Requests Wood and Craftsmen from Hiram, King of Tyre (2:1–10)

Solomon prepares to build the temple for the LORD, along with his royal palace (2 Chr 2:1). These two projects will take twenty years to complete (7:11; 8:1; cf. 1 Kgs 9:10–11). The temple is the most important structure, since its completion will signify the fulfillment of God's promise to David and the establishment of his eternal dynasty (1 Chr 17:12–14; 22:9–10; cf. 2 Chr 6:41–42). The temple Solomon is building is for the "name of the LORD my God" (2:4), which confirms that Jerusalem is the place where his *name* will dwell (Deut 12:18; 14:25; 15:20). Given the enormity of the building

1. See Chapter 22, Listen to the Story, pp. 217–18.

2. See ibid.; cf. "The Journey of Wen-Amon to Phoenicia," trans. John A. Wilson (*ANET*, 25–29).

3. Herbert Donner, "The Interdependence of Internal Affairs and Foreign Policy during the Davidic-Solomonic Period," in Ishida, *Studies in the Period of David and Solomon*, 205–14.

project, Solomon's laborers are in the thousands, as they quarry heavy stones and move them under appointed supervisors (2 Chr 2:2; cf. 1 Kgs 5:13–18; 2 Chr 2:17–18). Solomon approaches Hiram, the king of Tyre, for wood and skilled workers, recalling the favorable relationship Hiram had with his father David (1 Kgs 5:1; 1 Chr 14:1–2). By the end of the eleventh century BC, the island-city of Tyre, covering some forty acres, became the primary trading center, so it is not surprising that Solomon approaches Hiram to provide resources for his building project. The temple is the place where incense will be burned, showbread will be set out continually, and burnt offerings will be offered for daily worship and during Israel's religious festivals (2 Chr 2:4). With the temple in view, Solomon declares to Hiram that his God is greater than all gods (v. 5), echoing what is found in the psalms: "I know that the LORD is great, that our Lord is greater than all gods" (Ps 135:5; cf. Pss 95:3; 97:9). Solomon recognizes that he is unworthy to build a temple for the LORD who is highly exalted and above all gods.

Solomon requests that Hiram send him a skilled man to "work in gold and silver, bronze and iron, and in purple, crimson and blue yarn" (2 Chr 2:7). The Phoenicians were famous for their craftsmanship, as seen in Phoenician ceramics that are attested beyond their borders. Phoenician artisans worked with precious metals, making fine gold jewelry and metal dishes.[4] The temple would be adorned with precious gold, jewels and expensive material that would ensure it was a glorious house fitting for the LORD God. The Mediterranean coast was home to the *Murex* snail, which produced an expensive blue-violet dye.[5] A recent archaeological discovery at Timnah provides evidence of purple dyed fabric at the time of David and Solomon, based on radiocarbon dating.[6] The brightly colored fabric decorating the temple and adorning the priests was produced from this dye. It is estimated that several thousand mollusks were required for one priestly garment.[7] Solomon asks the king of Tyre to provide an artisan able to work with metal, and he requests cedar, juniper, and algum logs from Lebanon (vv. 8–9). The cedars of Lebanon, known for their towering height that

4. Glenn E. Markoe, "The Emergence of Phoenician Art," *BASOR* 279 (1990), 13–26.

5. Patricia M. Bikai, "Rich and Glorious Traders of the Levant," *Archaeology* 43:2 (1990): 22–30; R. R. Stieglitz, "Long-distance Seafaring in the Ancient Near East," *BA* 47 (1984): 134–42.

6. Jonathan Laden, "The Royal Purple of David and Solomon," *BAS*, 31 January 2021, https://www.biblicalarchaeology.org/daily/biblical-artifacts/artifacts-and-the-bible/the-royal-purple-of-david-and-solomon/.

7. Christine Palmer, "Israelite High Priestly Apparel: Embodying an Identity between Human and Divine," in *Fashioned Selves: Dress and Identity in Antiquity*. Megan Cifarelli, ed. (Oxford: Oxbow Books, 2019), 118–227 (120).

could reach 120 feet, were a sought-after and prized possession. In exchange, Solomon agrees to provide wheat, barley, wine, and oil (v. 10).

Solomon Secures Building Materials and Skilled Artisans to Work on the Temple (2:11–16)

The king of Tyre sends a letter to Solomon in response to his request. Hiram begins by affirming God's covenant-love for his people Israel (2 Chr 2:11), which is followed by his blessing: "Praise be to the LORD, the God of Israel, who made heaven and earth!" (v. 12). His words are reminiscent of the blessing pronounced by the foreign king Melchizedek many years earlier (Gen 14:19–20).[8] It is important to bear in mind that the Phoenicians had their own gods and goddesses that included a pantheon of gods, with chief deities venerated among them. Children were even sacrificed to their gods at the ancient Phoenician city-state of Carthage. Melqart ("king of the city") was the tutelary god of Tyre, and Hiram appears to have built temples for him and the goddess Astarte.[9] Given the plurality of gods worshiped by the Phoenicians, Hiram's praise of the LORD is not insignificant, and it gives us a glimpse into the purpose of the temple, which is to result in praise of the LORD among the nations. The Chronicler has, indeed, framed the temple-building narrative with two confessions uttered by non-Israelites, one here by Hiram, and the other by the queen of Sheba, who blesses the LORD God (2 Chr 9:8). It is not surprising that the temple narrative is framed by foreigners blessing the LORD since Israel's worship was intended to be proclaimed among the nations, and there was the expectation that the nations would join Israel in praising the LORD (1 Chr 16:8, 23–26, 31; cf. 2 Chr 6:32–33). Hiram acknowledges Solomon's wisdom, and this will be another reason why foreign dignitaries stream into Jerusalem, when all the kings of the earth seek audience with Solomon "to hear the wisdom God had put in his heart" (2 Chr 9:23). The confession by the king of Tyre hints at this international theme that reverberates throughout Chronicles.

The contributions of Hiram to the temple (along with Huram-Abi that follows) underscore that the temple is an "international project," built by Israel but with "Gentile helpers."[10] Thus, while Solomon initiates the project, non-Israelites "pitch in with material and skill."[11] The role of the nations to build the temple is envisioned by Isaiah in his description of a restored Zion (Isa

---

8. Williamson, *1 and 2 Chronicles*, 200.
9. Bikai, "Rich and Glorious Traders," 27.
10. Peter J. Leithart, *1 & 2 Chronicles*, BTCB (Grand Rapids, Brazos Press, 2019), 102.
11. Ibid.

60:1–14). Hiram agrees to send a skilled artisan named Huram-Abi, who was endowed with wisdom and understanding (2 Chr 2:13–14). These are qualities found among those Israelites who had worked on the tabernacle and on Israel's priestly garments (Exod 28:3; 31:6; 35:10; 36:1, 2, 4, 8). Huram-Abi was skilled in working with gold, silver, bronze, iron, stone, and wood, and he had experience working with expensive fabrics. Hiram agrees to bring logs from Lebanon and transport them to the coastal region of Joppa, and Solomon's servants are to bring supplies of wheat, barley, oil, and wine (2 Chr 2:15–16).

Laborers Are Appointed from among the Nations (2:17–18)

Preparations are now underway for the construction of the temple, and the Chronicler returns to the topic of conscripted labor, which forms a literary inclusio (2 Chr 2:2, 17–18). Samuel had warned the Israelites that their king would subject their sons to service (1 Sam 8:11–12), and this is precisely what Solomon does. Textual evidence from Alalakh and Ugarit attests to the practice of conscripted labor in Palestine.[12] David seems to have had his own labor force (2 Sam 20:24), but compulsory labor was extensive during the reign of Solomon due to these colossal building projects. Fellow Israelites were not to be subject to permanent service (Lev 25:35–46; cf. 2 Chr 8:9), although they could be conscripted for labor for limited periods as needed by the king (1 Kgs 5:13; 15:22). Emphasis on foreigners working on the temple (2 Chr 8:7–8; cf. 1 Chr 22:2) may even contribute to the idea that the temple is an international project (cf. Isa 60:10, 13). Later, when Rehoboam becomes king, the issue of heavy labor is a source of contention, especially among the northern tribes (2 Chr 10:1–19).[13]

LIVE the Story

God's Name Is to Be Exalted among the Nations

The lavishly adorned temple made of expensive building materials was to bring praise and glory to God's name (2 Chr 2:4). David had understood this when he made preparations, recognizing that the temple built for God "should be of great magnificence and fame and splendor in the sight of all the nations" (1 Chr 22:5). Glory is given to God's name through the elaborate temple that is built, but we find this same theme on the lips of Solomon when he publicly

---

12. I. Mendelson, "On Corvee Labor in Ancient Canaan and Israel," *BASOR* 167 (1962): 31–35.
13. See Jan A. Soggin, "Compulsory Labor under David and Solomon," in Ishida, *Studies in the Period of David and Solomon*, 259–66.

proclaims the greatness of his God. It is important to remember that Solomon lived in a polytheistic world surrounded by foreign gods. The Phoenicians worshiped gods and goddesses such as Melqart, Astarte, Baal-Shamem, Baal-Saphon, Eshumun, Baal-Sidon, Baalat Gubla, and Shadrapa.[14] Amid this religious pluralism, Solomon tells the Phoenician king that he is building a temple for the name of *his* God, the LORD. He boldly declares that "our God is greater than all gods" (2 Chr 2:5), which was surely an indictment against the Phoenician gods (cf. 1 Chr 16:25–26). His public confession results in the non-Israelite Hiram blessing the LORD and recognizing that the LORD was maker of heaven and earth (2 Chr 2:12; cf. Gen 14:19).

Solomon's public testimony to God's greatness provides an example for the returnees who were surrounded by nations, with Samaritans in the north, Ammonites to the east, Arabs and Edomites to the south, and Phoenicians to the west.[15] Notably, Phoenician deities continue to be worshiped in the Persian period, and Phoenician religious cults and temples spread as they colonized new regions. The post-exilic community lived amid a vast Persian Empire surrounded by nations, yet their calling to be a worshiping and witnessing community among them remained. This is why the first chapter of Chronicles locates Israel's genealogies alongside the Table of Nations, as it gives a visual "map" to show that Israel's calling was to be lived out *among* the nations (cf. 1 Chr 16:24). As descendants of Abraham, the returnees were called to be a blessing to the surrounding nations (Gen 12:3). In spite of their "day of small things" (Zech 4:10; cf. Hag 2:3, 23), God's calling had not changed and he was at work accomplishing his purposes.

This is the missional vision of the church today amid an increasingly pluralistic society. We are called to proclaim the gospel of the kingdom to *all nations* (Matt 24:14; cf. Acts 8:12; 19:8; 20:24–25; 28:23, 31). In our contemporary context, we can easily assume that proclamation of the gospel is to be done privately, for fear that we might offend someone or say something politically incorrect. Yet Solomon's declaration about the LORD's greatness is done publicly to a foreign king, and Israel's worship of their God at the temple served as a public witness to the surrounding nations that the LORD reigned. The gospel is to be lived out in our communities, but it also requires public declarations (while recognizing that in countries hostile to Christianity, this is not possible). Sometimes God calls his people to speak boldly to those in

---

14. William A. Ward, "Phoenicians," in Hoerth, Mattingly, and Yamauchi, *Peoples of the Old Testament World*, 202.

15. See the introduction, Life in the Province of Judah and in the Diaspora under the Persians, pp. 10–14.

authority and to take a stand for the sake of the gospel. The apostle Paul testifies before Roman governors, such as Felix and Festus (Acts 23:23–25:22), and before King Agrippa (25:23–26:32) and Caesar (26:32; 27:24). Peter and John proclaim the name of Jesus before rulers and elders (4:1–12), and when they are commanded not to speak in Jesus's name, they boldly refuse to stop speaking (vv. 18–20, 31). Jesus taught that we must be willing to confess him before others, even if this leads to hostility and suffering (Matt 10:32–36). In an increasingly pluralistic society, the uniqueness of Jesus is not always an acceptable message, yet we are reminded from Solomon's bold proclamation to Hiram—who had his own religious beliefs—that there is only one true God, and this message remains the same.

When the apostle Paul travelled to Athens, he was stirred by the city full of idols (Acts 17:16). He recognized that the men of Athens were very "religious," yet he made known to them that their worship was done in ignorance. He testifies boldly with these words: "The God who made the world and everything in it is the Lord of heaven and earth" (v. 24). He proceeds to tell them that life and breath are to be found *in him*, and that *he* made all the nations and appointed their times in history and their boundaries. He proclaims further: "God did this so that they would seek him and perhaps reach out for him and find him" (v. 27). Paul issues a call for repentance, and some of those listening "became followers of Paul and believed" (v. 34). This is the good news of the gospel. As Christians today, we are called to proclaim the gospel to all nations, making known that the name of Jesus is above all names, even as Solomon declares that the LORD was greater than all the gods of the nations.

CHAPTER 32

2 Chronicles 3:1–17

 LISTEN to the Story

¹Then Solomon began to build the temple of the LORD in Jerusalem on Mount Moriah, where the LORD had appeared to his father David. It was on the threshing floor of Araunah the Jebusite, the place provided by David. ²He began building on the second day of the second month in the fourth year of his reign.

³The foundation Solomon laid for building the temple of God was sixty cubits long and twenty cubits wide (using the cubit of the old standard). ⁴The portico at the front of the temple was twenty cubits long across the width of the building and twenty cubits high.

He overlaid the inside with pure gold. ⁵He paneled the main hall with juniper and covered it with fine gold and decorated it with palm tree and chain designs. ⁶He adorned the temple with precious stones. And the gold he used was gold of Parvaim. ⁷He overlaid the ceiling beams, doorframes, walls and doors of the temple with gold, and he carved cherubim on the walls.

⁸He built the Most Holy Place, its length corresponding to the width of the temple—twenty cubits long and twenty cubits wide. He overlaid the inside with six hundred talents of fine gold. ⁹The gold nails weighed fifty shekels. He also overlaid the upper parts with gold.

¹⁰For the Most Holy Place he made a pair of sculptured cherubim and overlaid them with gold. ¹¹The total wingspan of the cherubim was twenty cubits. One wing of the first cherub was five cubits long and touched the temple wall, while its other wing, also five cubits long, touched the wing of the other cherub. ¹²Similarly one wing of the second cherub was five cubits long and touched the other temple wall, and its other wing, also five cubits long, touched the wing of the first cherub. ¹³The wings of these cherubim extended twenty cubits. They stood on their feet, facing the main hall.

¹⁴He made the curtain of blue, purple and crimson yarn and fine linen, with cherubim worked into it.

[15]For the front of the temple he made two pillars, which together were thirty-five cubits long, each with a capital five cubits high. [16]He made interwoven chains and put them on top of the pillars. He also made a hundred pomegranates and attached them to the chains. [17]He erected the pillars in the front of the temple, one to the south and one to the north. The one to the south he named Jakin and the one to the north Boaz.

Listening to the Text in the Story: Genesis 22:1–19; Exodus 25–27; 30:1–31:11; 36–38; 40; 1 Kings 6:1–36; 1 Chronicles 21:1–30

With construction of the temple underway, its location is identified as Mount Moriah (2 Chr 3:1). Deeply embedded in Israel's traditions, stories of Abraham and David provide the background for Israel's most sacred site. The location of Moriah recalls the time when God tested Abraham, telling him to offer up his beloved son Isaac as a burnt offering (Gen 22:1–19).[1] This story took place on a mountain in the region of Moriah. The Chronicler further identifies Moriah as the place where God had appeared to David, recalling his purchase of the threshing floor from Araunah the Jebusite, which probably included the surrounding area (1 Chr 22:1). David had built an altar on this site, and he had sacrificed burnt offerings and fellowship offerings to the LORD. God had answered David with fire on the altar, and this site is now identified as the place where thousands of sacrifices will be offered. Both stories underscore that construction of the temple on Mount Moriah is indelibly etched in the plan and purposes of God.[2]

As we listen to the text in the story, it is important to hear echoes of the tabernacle in the description of the temple. God had given David the architectural plan of the temple (1 Chr 28:11–19), just as he had given a blueprint of the tabernacle to Moses (Exod 25:9, 40). The bronze altar built by Bezalel has its origin in the tabernacle narrative (31:1–11; 36:1; cf. 1 Chr 2:20), and his assistant from the tribe of Dan is mirrored in Huram-Abi's Danite pedigree (Exod 31:6; cf. 2 Chr 2:14). Language echoing the construction of

---

1. For connections between Gen 22 and 1 Chr 22, see the discussion in Chapter 21 on 1 Chr 21:18–30, pp. 213–14.

2. This point is contrary to Andy Stanley's popular teaching, who argues that the temple was Israel's attempt to be like the nations, but it was not God's plan—a view which misses a good many Scriptures that suggest otherwise (see especially 1 Chr 17:12; 22:19). Yet he writes, "The temple was a 'nice to have.' But it wasn't necessary. It wasn't his [God's] idea" (Andy Stanley, *Irresistible: Reclaiming the New that Jesus Unleashed for the World* [Grand Rapids: Zondervan, 2018], 41).

the tabernacle is seen in the repeated description that Solomon "made" or "built" (Heb. '-s-h) the building and its furnishings (2 Chr 3:8, 10, 14; 16; 4:1, 2, etc.; cf. Exod 38:2, 3, 4, 6, 8, 9, etc.) and in the completion of the building projects (39:32; 2 Chr 5:1).

Block has noted further that the tabernacle narrative is structured according to seven divine speeches ("and the LORD said/spoke to Moses"). Six speeches describe the creation of the tabernacle (Exod 25:1; 30:11, 17, 22, 34; 31:1), whereas the seventh divine speech concludes with the Sabbath (31:12). He suggests, therefore, that construction of the tabernacle corresponds to the six days of creation ("and God said"), followed by the Sabbath (Gen 2:2–3).[3] Emphasis on Solomon's "making" may even echo the creation story, where the verb "to make" (Heb. '-s-h) is used to describe God's creative activity (1:7, 16, 25, 31; 2:2–4), climaxing in his resting from all the work he had done (vv. 2–3; cf. Exod 40:33; 2 Chr 5:1; 7:11).

Echoes of creation may also be seen in the prominence of the number seven. Scholars note that it took *seven* years to build the temple (1 Kgs 6:38); it was dedicated on the *seventh* month (2 Chr 5:3; cf. 7:10); the celebration took place over *seven* days (7:9); and Solomon's prayer is structured around *seven* petitions.[4] The point to note here is the temple marks the fulfillment of God's plan to dwell with his people in the tabernacle, and there may even be hints that the temple has been modeled after creation itself.[5]

 EXPLAIN the Story

Solomon Builds the Foundation, Porch, and the Main Hall (3:1–7)

The location of the temple is identified as Mount Moriah, connecting the sacred site to the place where burnt offerings were offered by Abraham (Gen 22) and David (1 Chr 21). The site for the temple also becomes known as Mount Zion, God's holy hill and the place of his glorious enthronement (Pss 2:6; 48:1–3; 78:68–69; 132:6–18; cf. 1 Chr 11:5).[6] The Chronicler rounds off these introductory comments with a historical notice, stating that Solomon began to build the temple in the fourth year of his reign, which is dated to 966 BC (cf. 1 Kgs 6:1). Archaeologists have unearthed a number of temple

---

3. Block, *For the Glory of God*, 303.

4. Beale, *The Temple*, 61.

5. See Hahn, *The Kingdom of God*, 114–24; see the discussion in Chapter 33 on 2 Chron 4.

6. On the connection between Moriah and Zion, see Tremper Longman III, *Genesis*, SGBC (Grand Rapids: Zondervan, 2016), 302.

structures in the Levant indicating that several structures were used in antiquity. In his extensive survey, Davey surveys three basic architectural designs in the Levant that include three-room temples, broad-room temples, and long-room temples.[7] Solomon's temple was structured according to the well-known tripartite division that included a portico, a main hall (with storerooms along the outer walls), and an inner sanctuary, known as the most holy place.

Solomon's account begins with the foundation, which measures sixty cubits in length and twenty cubits in width (2 Chr 3:3). Since there were two different cubits in use, it is estimated that the temple would be either 90 by 30 feet, or 105 feet by 35 feet.[8] In the ancient world, the completion of a temple's foundation was often marked by a special ceremony, and texts were deposited in the foundation, invoking curses on later generations who might harm the structure. When the returnees had built the foundation of the second temple, it was accompanied by a special ceremony (Ezra 3:10–13; cf. Hag 2:15–19; Zech 4:6b–10a; 8:9–13).

The temple built by Solomon was lavishly embellished with pure gold that overlaid the interior walls, ceiling beams, door frames, and doors (2 Chr 3:4–7). While the description might sound rather extravagant, temples in Egypt were ornately decorated with luminous gold sheets that overlaid pillars, doorways, walls, and even floors. Textual evidence from Assyria attests to gold used to overlay walls that made them as bright as day.[9] Large quantities of gold and silver had already been contributed during David's reign (1 Chr 29:6–7; cf. 2 Chr 1:15). Solomon had acquired a vast amount of gold from the distant place known as Ophir (1 Kgs 9:28; 10:11), along with the gifts he had received (9:14; 10:14; 2 Chr 9:13–14).[10] Precious stones were used to decorate the temple, recalling the precious onyx, turquoise, and stones of various colors that had been given during David's reign (1 Chr 29:2; cf. Rev 21:18–20). Scholars have seen parallels between the Garden of Eden and Solomon's temple, not only with the precious materials used, but also in the winged cherubim engraved on the walls that unmistakably recall the cherubim in the Garden of Eden (Gen 3:24). This suggests that the temple is designed as a microcosm of creation.[11]

---

7. Christopher J. Davey, "Temples in the Levant and the Buildings of Solomon," *TynBul* (1979), 107–146.

8. On the length of the cubit, see Dillard, *2 Chronicles*, 28.

9. A. Millard, "King Solomon in his Ancient Context," 31–36.

10. For a detailed account on quantities, use, and sources of gold in antiquity, see ibid., 31–42. On Ophir, see the discussion in Chapter 29 on 1 Chr 29:4–5, pp. 277–78.

11. See Hahn, *The Kingdom of God*, 116–120.

Solomon Builds and Adorns the Most Holy Place (3:8–14)

Focus shifts to the construction and adornment of the most holy place, also called the holy of holies (2 Chr 3:8–14). Unlike the rectangular shape of the main temple structure, the inner sanctuary was a square, with its width and length measuring twenty cubits each. Precious gold was lavishly used to overlay the walls, and even the nails were coated with gold costing six hundred shekels, reminiscent of the price David paid for the altar (1 Chr 21:25). Palm trees, cherubim, and flowers were engraved on its doors (cf. 1 Kgs 6:32), adding to the beauty of the sacred building, but also evoking a luxuriant garden. Two sculptured cherubim adorned the most holy place, with their four wings spanning the entire room (2 Chr 3:10–13); they represented the heavenly creatures often associated with God's heavenly throne (Isa 37:16; cf. Ezek 1:4–21; 10:1–22). Standing side-by-side as guardians with their faces looking toward the entrance in the inner sanctuary (2 Chr 3:13), they evoke in the imagination the cherubim guarding the entrance to the Garden of Eden (Gen 3:24). Instead of preventing access, however, the high priest is permitted to enter the most holy place beyond the veil one day per year (Lev 16). The luminous inner sanctuary is completed with a description of a brightly colored veil that was made of costly blue, purple, and crimson yarn and linen, with cherubim woven onto it (2 Chr 3:14; cf. Exod 26:31–35). The cherubim embroidered into the veil provide further signals to the high priest that a holy God is enthroned in the inner sanctuary beyond the brightly colored veil.

Solomon Builds Two Decorative Pillars (3:15–17)

Two towering pillars with decorative capitals stood at the front of the main temple structure (2 Chr 3:15–17). They were elaborately decorated with pomegranates that encircled the capitals and were interwoven with gold chains at the top of the pillars. The description recalls the priestly garments that had pomegranates woven into the hem using purple-blue material (Exod 28:33, 34; 39:24, 25), along with braided gold chains woven into the breast piece (28:14, 22; 39:15). Solomon placed one of the pillars to the right, calling it Jakin ("he will establish"), and the other he placed to the left, calling it Boaz ("in strength," 2 Chr 3:17).[12] The towering pillars remind the worshiper of the strength and stability of the temple in contrast to the transitory period when the tabernacle had moved from place to place.

---

12. For scholarly views of these names and their significance, see Dillard, *2 Chronicles*, 30.

LIVE the Story

God's Presence with His People

God's plan to restore what was lost in Eden is being realized as he dwells among his people in the tabernacle and now in the temple. This is the place where his glory-cloud will reside above the golden cherubim beyond the brightly colored veil. Yet we do well to remember that only the high priest could enter the inner sanctuary. The ordinary Israelite was precluded from beholding God's glory. The writer to the Hebrews reflects upon the Jerusalem Temple, noting that "only the high priest entered the inner room, and that only once a year, and never without blood, which he offered for himself and for the sins the people had committed in ignorance" (Heb 9:7). In the Old Testament, God's glorious presence beyond the veil was mediated to the ordinary Israelite through the high priest. Palmer thus notes of the priestly garments: "The distinctive identity forged at his installation is lived out through his dressed body. Dress performatively fashions a bond between the worlds the high priest represents, making him an access point to the divine and his dressed body a meeting place of heaven and earth."[13] Adorned with sacral garments that identify him with the sacred tent, a walking tabernacle, God's people would gain a glimpse of God's glory through *him*.[14] He anticipates what will be fully revealed one day, when Jesus tabernacles among his people and we behold his glory (John 1:14). Under the old covenant, the high priest was the access point to the divine; as Palmer writes, "He is a man 'between worlds'—bridging them and embodying them as a microcosm of the divine-human relationship."[15]

With this priestly imagery in view, the writer to the Hebrews explains that Jesus, the great high priest, entered the "greater and more perfect tabernacle that is not made with human hands, that is to say, is not a part of this creation" (Heb 9:11). The earthly temple was a copy of God's heavenly sanctuary (v. 24; Rev 11:19; cf. 1 Chr 28:11–12), but the greater and more perfect sanctuary was heaven itself, where God was enthroned on high; thus the *whole earth* was filled with his glory (Num 14:21; Ps 72:19; Isa 6:3). Jesus does not enter the earthly holy of holies, as the priest would do once per year, but he "entered heaven itself, now to appear for us in God's presence" (Heb 9:24). Jesus enters

---

13. Palmer, "Israelite High Priestly Apparel," 117.

14. Palmer has argued that the Israelite high priestly garments indicate that the priest is an extension of the tent of meeting, "of one cloth and one purpose." She argues that God's presence is mediated through him to the ordinary Israelite (ibid., 124–26).

15. Ibid., 126.

before God's highly exalted and heavenly throne—something that the prophets had seen only dimly from afar (Isa 6:1; Ezek 1:26; 10:1; Dan 7:9). The astounding reality for our lives is that we can now enter the presence of God confidently through Jesus, for he has established a new and living way beyond the veil (Heb 10:19–20). This is the good news of the gospel. Fellowship with God has been restored through Jesus's atoning work, enabling us to draw near before God's heavenly throne. We join with all creation in praise and worship of our Lord and King (Rev 4:8–11; 5:13–14).

The glorious and lavishly embellished most holy place, where the Edenic cherubim flank the ark, gives us a glimpse into God's exalted throne. This rich imagery ought to shape our minds and inform our imaginations as we gaze upon the glory and holiness of our God. The book of Revelation helps us gain a preview of God's heavenly throne in all its glory. As the heavens are opened up to John, he sees a glimmering throne with someone sitting on it, whose appearance is likened to precious stones surrounded by a radiant rainbow. His throne is surrounded by twenty-four other thrones, with elders clothed in white and adorned with golden crowns (4:1–4). Before God's throne, John sees a sea of glass, with living creatures giving glory and honor to the one seated on the throne. In his heavenly vision, John sees the elders "fall down before him who sits on the throne and worship him who lives for ever and ever" (v. 10). As they lay their crowns before the throne, they proclaim that the Lord is worthy to receive glory and honor.

This is the heavenly throne that is foreshadowed in the temple built by Solomon, yet we now live after the coming of the Messiah, who has provided the way for us to enter into God's presence, beyond the veil, now before his heavenly throne. As we, too, fall down and worship the Lamb who was slain, we join with all creation, lifting our voice in praise, "To him who sits on the throne and to the Lamb be praise and honor and glory and power, for ever and ever!" (5:13). Our worship today is a foretaste of Christ's second coming, when we will one day join the myriads of living creatures and all the saints for all eternity, giving praise to the Lamb on the throne (4:1–11; 5:11–13; 15:2–8). The 1851 hymn written by Matthew Bridges, *Crown Him with Many Crowns*, invites us to worship the Lamb upon his throne in anticipation of his second coming:

> Crown him with many crowns,
> The Lamb upon his throne;
> Hark! how the heavenly anthem drowns
> All music but its own:

Awake, my soul, and sing
Of him who died for thee,
And hail him as thy matchless king
Through all eternity.

LISTEN to the Story

¹He made a bronze altar twenty cubits long, twenty cubits wide and ten cubits high. ²He made the Sea of cast metal, circular in shape, measuring ten cubits from rim to rim and five cubits high. It took a line of thirty cubits to measure around it. ³Below the rim, figures of bulls encircled it— ten to a cubit. The bulls were cast in two rows in one piece with the Sea.

⁴The Sea stood on twelve bulls, three facing north, three facing west, three facing south and three facing east. The Sea rested on top of them, and their hindquarters were toward the center. ⁵It was a handbreadth in thickness, and its rim was like the rim of a cup, like a lily blossom. It held three thousand baths.

⁶He then made ten basins for washing and placed five on the south side and five on the north. In them the things to be used for the burnt offerings were rinsed, but the Sea was to be used by the priests for washing.

⁷He made ten gold lampstands according to the specifications for them and placed them in the temple, five on the south side and five on the north.

⁸He made ten tables and placed them in the temple, five on the south side and five on the north. He also made a hundred gold sprinkling bowls.

⁹He made the courtyard of the priests, and the large court and the doors for the court, and overlaid the doors with bronze. ¹⁰He placed the Sea on the south side, at the southeast corner.

¹¹And Huram also made the pots and shovels and sprinkling bowls.

So Huram finished the work he had undertaken for King Solomon in the temple of God:

¹²the two pillars;

the two bowl-shaped capitals on top of the pillars;

the two sets of network decorating the two bowl-shaped capitals on
    top of the pillars;

¹³the four hundred pomegranates for the two sets of network (two rows of pomegranates for each network, decorating the bowl-shaped capitals on top of the pillars);
¹⁴the stands with their basins;
¹⁵the Sea and the twelve bulls under it;
¹⁶the pots, shovels, meat forks and all related articles.

All the objects that Huram-Abi made for King Solomon for the temple of the LORD were of polished bronze. ¹⁷The king had them cast in clay molds in the plain of the Jordan between Sukkoth and Zarethan. ¹⁸All these things that Solomon made amounted to so much that the weight of the bronze could not be calculated.

¹⁹Solomon also made all the furnishings that were in God's temple:

the golden altar;
the tables on which was the bread of the Presence;
²⁰the lampstands of pure gold with their lamps, to burn in front of the inner sanctuary as prescribed;
²¹the gold floral work and lamps and tongs (they were solid gold);
²²the pure gold wick trimmers, sprinkling bowls, dishes and censers; and the gold doors of the temple: the inner doors to the Most Holy Place and the doors of the main hall.

Listening to the Text in the Story: Genesis 2–3; Exodus 25–27; 31:1–11

The focus of this chapter shifts to the sacred furnishings and utensils made for use in the temple. While they clearly have a utilitarian function, imagery from the Garden of Eden is indelibly etched into their design. Botanical and arboreal images sculptured into the furnishings and engraved on the walls of the temple are intended to evoke the creation story and, more particularly, the Garden of Eden. God walks among his people in the tabernacle and temple (Lev 26:12; 2 Sam 7:6; 1 Chr 17:6), even as he had walked with Adam and Eve in the garden (Gen 3:8). The tabernacle, temple, and priestly garments are embellished with gold and precious stones (Exod 25:11–39; 28:6–27; 1 Chr 29:2; 2 Chr 3–4; Ezek 28:13; cf. Rev 21:19–20), reminiscent of the gold and precious stones found in Eden (Gen 2:12; cf. Ezek 28:13–14). The appointment of Levites as guardians of the tabernacle and temple (Num

3:7–8; 8:25–26; 18:5–6; 1 Chr 23:32) recalls Adam's priestly role as guardian of sacred space (Gen 2:15). Evoking a verdant garden, the walls of the temple are decorated with carvings of gourds and open flowers (1 Kgs 6:18), and its walls and doors are carved with cherubim, palm trees, and open flowers (vv. 29–35). Ornamental pomegranates are sculpted into the two bronze pillars (2 Chr 3:16; 4:12–13), and the large washing basin called the "Sea" stands on twelve bulls (1 Kgs 7:25), decorated with lions, bulls, cherubim, and palm trees (vv. 29, 36). The golden lampstand, with its flowering tree-like design, is reminiscent of the tree of life (2 Chr 4:7; cf. Exod 25:31–40). Cherubim engraved on walls and in the most holy place, along with the wings of the golden cherubim that flank the ark of the covenant, bring to mind the cherubim in the Garden of Eden (Gen 3:24; Ezek 28:14, 16).[1] Rich Edenic symbolism suggests that God designed the temple as a microcosm of creation itself.

EXPLAIN the Story

Solomon Makes the Furniture for the Temple (4:1–10)

The description of the furniture in the temple begins with an enormous bronze altar made by Solomon that measured twenty by twenty cubits, the same size as the most holy place.[2] An altar for burnt offerings had been located in the tabernacle (Exod 27:1–8; 40:6–7), but the altar built by Solomon was much larger due to the high volume of sacrifices that would be offered on it (cf. 2 Chr 7:4–5). A large circular washing basin called the "Sea" was made of cast metal. The basin stood on a stand made of twelve oxen, with their faces looking outward to the four corners of the earth (4:4–5). The number twelve may possibly represent the twelve tribes of Israel, as in Ezekiel's city gates (Ezek 48:30–34; cf. Rev 21:12, 14).[3] The unique description of the basin as "Sea" is perhaps intended to represent the waters of creation that flowed from Eden (Gen 2:10–11), which are depicted as flowing from the temple itself (Ezek 47:1–12; Joel 3:18; cf. Rev 21:6; 22:1–2).[4] The expansive basin was used exclusively by the priests for ritual washings (cf. Exod 30:17–21), but

---

1. For an insightful discussion on this topic, see Beale, *The Temple*, 66–80. He cites ancient Near Eastern texts that describe temples with garden-like features. See also, Wenham, "Sanctuary Symbolism and the Garden of Eden," 400–401.

2. On the length of the cubit, see discussion in Chapter 32 on 2 Chr 3:3, pp. 304–5.

3. Dillard, *2 Chronicles*, 35.

4. Hahn, *The Kingdom of God*, 117–18.

Solomon built ten additional basins, placing five on each side of the temple (2 Chr 4:6; cf. 1 Kgs 7:27–40).

Solomon made ten golden lampstands (2 Chr 4:7, 20; cf. Exod 25:31–40; 37:17–24), which may be intended to represent the light of God's presence.[5] Priests were responsible to maintain light in the tabernacle, and the lamps filled with oil were to burn continually (Lev 24:1–4; Num 8:2–4; cf. 2 Chr 13:11). Solomon also made ten tables, with five located on each side of the sanctuary, and one hundred gold sprinkling bowls (4:8). While only one table was used for the Bread of the Presence in the tabernacle (Exod 25:23–30; Lev 24:5–9), ten tables may have been used for this purpose, although elsewhere a single table is mentioned (2 Chr 13:11; 29:18; Ezek 41:22). Having made the sacred furniture and vessels, the courtyard used by the priests is constructed, along with the large court that was for the laity (2 Chr 4:9 cf. 1 Kgs 6:36; 7:12).

The Utensils and Furnishings Made by Huram-Abi and Solomon (4:11–22)

Furnishings and utensils made by Huram are described next that include two pillars with ornately decorated capitals, stands with their basins, the Sea and the twelve bulls under it, and the pots, shovels, meat forks, and other articles (2 Chr 4:12–16).[6] Huram-Abi had been employed for his craftsmanship (2:13–14), and the description of his artistic work in polished bronze gives literary symmetry to the narrative, but it also shows that the work Huram-Abi had been commissioned to do had been completed (4:16–17). The section concludes with a summary of the sacred furnishing made by Solomon that required large amounts of bronze (vv. 19–22).

 LIVE the Story

The Presence of God in the New Jerusalem

The temple built by Solomon represented God's heavenly sanctuary (cf. Ps 78:69). It was created to be an "earthly replica of YHWH's true heavenly residence," designed with Edenic and cosmic features.[7] Its furnishings, decorations, and structure suggest that it was designed by God to be a microcosm

---

5. Braun, *2 Chronicles*, 36.

6. See the discussion in Chapter 31 on 2 Chr 2 for the artistic contributions of the Phoenicians, pp. 297–98.

7. Block, *For the Glory of God*, 310.

of the cosmos.[8] Hahn states succinctly that the temple was an "architectural recapitulation of the cosmic temple of creation."[9] Although the temple built by Solomon was lavishly adorned with pure gold and decorated with botanical and arboreal images, it was simply a replica or copy of God's heavenly sanctuary. It ultimately pointed to something greater, something *beyond itself.*

The book of Revelation gives us insight into what lies *beyond* the earthly temple structure, as God's purpose for the temple is unveiled. This is especially seen in the last two chapters of Revelation, where the new heavens and earth are depicted as a temple-city (Rev 21–22). The heavenly city coming down from heaven is accompanied by a loud voice from the throne with these words: "Look! God's dwelling place is now among the people, and he will dwell with them" (21:3). This recalls God's plan to dwell with his people that is initially being realized in the tabernacle and the temple (Exod 25:8; Lev 26:11–12; Ezek 37:27). John sees the holy city shining with the glory of God, "its brilliance was like that of a very precious jewel, like jasper, clear as crystal" (Rev 21:11). The city was made of pure gold and decorated with every kind of precious stone (vv. 18–19), reminiscent of the elaborate and costly furnishings of the temple made of gold and precious stones. The new heavens and earth are described as a temple-city, in accordance with Ezekiel's temple vision many years earlier that spanned the entire city.[10] Now John sees the temple-city spanning even further. God's goal from the beginning was that his glorious presence would fill the entire earth (Num 14:21; Ps 72:19; Isa 6:3; Hab 2:14). John sees that the gloriously adorned New Jerusalem is in the shape of a square (Rev 21:16; cf. 2 Chr 3:8–14). This poetically depicts the inner sanctuary, indicating that the holy space has expanded to cover the entire cosmos, as Beale writes: "This is why the three sections of Israel's old temple (holy of holies, the holy place and then the outer courtyard) are no longer found in the Revelation 21 temple—because God's special presence, formerly limited to the holy of holies, has now burst forth to encompass the whole earth."[11] John's depiction of the golden temple-city embellished with precious stones in the shape of a square points to the greater reality beyond the earthly temple built by Solomon. God's intention to dwell with his people, which is being realized in some small measure in the temple, foreshadows the new heavens and new earth, where God's dwelling will be among his people *forever.* No longer will there be any temple "because the Lord God Almighty

---

8. For an extensive description, see Beale, *The Temple,* 29–80.
9. Hahn, *The Kingdom of God,* 119; see also Block, *For the Glory of God,* 297–314.
10. See Beale, *The Temple,* 367.
11. Ibid., 370.

and the Lamb are its temple" (Rev 21:22), and the throne of God and of the Lamb are now in the city (22:3; cf. Ezek 48:35). God's people—those clothed with robes washed in the blood of the Lamb—will enjoy fellowship with their God forever. As we read about Solomon's temple, may we keep our eyes fixed on the glorious hope that lies before us—the heavenly reality that lies beyond the earthly structure. May we wait in expectation until we hear the voice from God's throne saying: "Look! God's dwelling place is now among the people" (Rev 21:3). A few stanzas from the song by Matt Gilman, *New Jerusalem*, capture the longing of the heart of God's people:

> I'm looking for a city not made by human hands
> I'm longing for the garden where God once walked with man
> For eternity is written on my heart
> I'm longing for the day when we will never be apart
> When every tear will be wiped away, there'll be no sorry, hurt, or pain
> There'll be no more night
> All things will be made new, it will be a brand new way
> And in righteousness He'll reign and the Lamb will be the light
>
> Behold the tabernacle of God will be with men
> And He will be our God, and we will be His people
> And the bride she will marry the Lamb
> But until that day I'm longing for the New Jerusalem[12]

We join with God's people throughout the ages, saying, "Amen. Come, Lord Jesus."

---

12. Matt Gillman, *New Jerusalem* (https://www.youtube.com/watch?v=5-4R7rVaV2w).

LISTEN to the Story

¹When all the work Solomon had done for the temple of the LORD was finished, he brought in the things his father David had dedicated—the silver and gold and all the furnishings—and he placed them in the treasuries of God's temple.

²Then Solomon summoned to Jerusalem the elders of Israel, all the heads of the tribes and the chiefs of the Israelite families, to bring up the ark of the LORD's covenant from Zion, the City of David. ³And all the Israelites came together to the king at the time of the festival in the seventh month.

⁴When all the elders of Israel had arrived, the Levites took up the ark, ⁵and they brought up the ark and the tent of meeting and all the sacred furnishings in it. The Levitical priests carried them up; ⁶and King Solomon and the entire assembly of Israel that had gathered about him were before the ark, sacrificing so many sheep and cattle that they could not be recorded or counted.

⁷The priests then brought the ark of the LORD's covenant to its place in the inner sanctuary of the temple, the Most Holy Place, and put it beneath the wings of the cherubim. ⁸The cherubim spread their wings over the place of the ark and covered the ark and its carrying poles. ⁹These poles were so long that their ends, extending from the ark, could be seen from in front of the inner sanctuary, but not from outside the Holy Place; and they are still there today. ¹⁰There was nothing in the ark except the two tablets that Moses had placed in it at Horeb, where the LORD made a covenant with the Israelites after they came out of Egypt.

¹¹The priests then withdrew from the Holy Place. All the priests who were there had consecrated themselves, regardless of their divisions. ¹²All the Levites who were musicians—Asaph, Heman, Jeduthun and their sons

and relatives—stood on the east side of the altar, dressed in fine linen and playing cymbals, harps and lyres. They were accompanied by 120 priests sounding trumpets. [13]The trumpeters and musicians joined in unison to give praise and thanks to the LORD. Accompanied by trumpets, cymbals and other instruments, the singers raised their voices in praise to the LORD and sang:

> "He is good;
> his love endures forever."

Then the temple of the LORD was filled with the cloud, [14]and the priests could not perform their service because of the cloud, for the glory of the LORD filled the temple of God.

Listening to the Text in the Story: 1 Kings 8:1–11; 1 Chronicles 13, 16; Psalms 99:1–5; 132:7–8

Solomon now makes preparations to bring the ark of the covenant from the City of David into the newly built temple. As Israel's most holy object, every care is needed to follow the correct procedures outlined in the law (1 Chr 13; 15).[1] The ark had been kept at Kiriath-Jearim prior to David's transporting it to Jerusalem and placing it in a temporary tent (16:37–38; 2 Chr 1:4). The time has now arrived for the ark to be brought to its permanent place in the temple within the holy of holies. The significance of the ark is that it is identified as God's footstool, the place of his enthronement (1 Chr 28:2). God reigns from his heavenly throne above the cherubim (Ps 99:1; Isa 6:3), but the ark is the place where "his feet extended while sitting on his heavenly throne," as Beale poetically describes it.[2] God's presence above the ark points to his enthronement among his people, who are thus invited to exalt the LORD their God and "worship at his footstool" (Ps 99:5; cf. 132:7). As God arrives at his resting place above the ark, his people are to sing for joy (vv. 8–9). We will see shortly that the presence of God among his people is cause for great rejoicing and celebration.

---

1. See the discussion in Chapters 13 and 15 on 1 Chr 13 and 15.
2. Beale, *The Temple*, 370.

The Ark of the Covenant Is Brought into the Most Holy Place (5:1–10)

The temple took seven years to complete (1 Kgs 6:38), and Solomon's royal palace took another thirteen years (7:1), resulting in a twenty-year building project (2 Chr 8:1). The Chronicler only mentions the royal palace in passing (2:1; 7:11; 8:1; 9:11), allowing him to focus on the climatic event when the ark of the covenant is brought into the most holy place. As Solomon makes preparations, he places the silver, gold, and utensils that David had dedicated to God into the temple treasuries (5:1; cf. 1 Chr 29:1–5). He then gathers the elders of Israel, tribal leaders, and the ancestral heads on the seventh month during the Feast of Tabernacles (2 Chr 5:3; cf. Lev 23:33–43). The Levites are to transport the ark, the tent of meeting, and the holy vessels into the temple (cf. 1 Chr 15:11–15). Solomon and all the congregation sacrifice a multitude of sheep and oxen, just as David had done previously (v. 26; 16:1). The priests carry the ark into the inner sanctuary on poles, where it is placed under the wings of the golden cherubim (2 Chr 5:7–9). The Ten Commandments engraved on two stone tablets are placed in the ark, serving as a witness to the enduring covenant God had made with his people (v. 10; cf. Deut 10:2–5).

A Levitical Choir Leads Israel in Worship as God's Glory Fills the Temple (5:11–14)

As Israel celebrates the arrival of the ark into the temple, Levitical musicians stand on the east side of the altar "dressed in fine linen and playing cymbals, harps, and lyres" (2 Chr 5:12). The three Levitical families of Asaph, Heman, and Jeduthun had been set apart for singing and playing musical instruments (1 Chr 25:1–7). They and their sons join together with 120 priests who sound their trumpets as all join in unison to give thanks and praise to God (2 Chr 5:13). Accompanied by a variety of musical instruments, the singers lift their voices in praise to the LORD, singing the well-known refrain: "He is good; his love endures forever" (v. 13). As songs of praise are rising toward heaven, the temple fills with a thick cloud, preventing the priests from performing their service (vv. 13–14; cf. Exod 40:34–35; Rev 15:8). The cloud represents the heavenly realm (Ps 97:2). It is often associated with heavenly visions (Ezek 1:4, 28; cf. Dan 7:13) and theophanies (Exod 19:9, 16; 24:15–16). The descent of a visible cloud in the temple signifies that the invisible and exalted heavenly realm has in some sense come to earth.³ God's glory fills the temple, reminis-cent of God's glory descending on Mount Sinai (Exod 24:16–17; 33:18–23; 34:5–7) and in the tabernacle (40:34–35). It is surely an occasion for great rejoicing as the sacred assembly celebrates God's presence in their midst.

LIVE the Story

Worship the Lord Joyfully!

The presence of God's glory in the temple was an occasion for joyous celebra-tion, filled with singing and praise and accompanied by musical instruments, including cymbals, harps, lyres, and trumpets. This story recalls God's glory filling the tabernacle (Exod 40:34–35), yet Hahn notes that there is something new in the temple narrative—joyful praise and worship! It is not that there was an absence of singing in earlier times (cf. 15:1–18; Deut 32–33; Judg 5), but it is David who formally organizes the musicians, and thus they have a central role from the time of the monarchy onward (cf. 1 Chr 25). Hahn observes that for the "first time in Israel's history, psalms of thanksgiving were sung in the sanctuary, with horns, cymbals, harps and lyres (1 Chr 16:4, 7–36; 23:2–6; 25:1–31)."⁴ When David had brought the ark into Jerusalem (ch. 15), this was followed by an extended time of worship, as three psalms had been sung in praise to the Lord (ch. 16). Their worship had been accompanied by the sound of trumpets, cymbals, and other instruments used for playing sacred songs (v. 42). They had sung on the joyous occasion: "Let the hearts of those who seek the Lord rejoice" (v. 10). At that time, David had appointed Levites as musicians "to make a joyful sound with musical instruments: lyres, harps and cymbals" (15:16). In fact, the theme of joy permeates the Chronicler's writings. Hahn thus notes: "Chronicles, in a way unmatched elsewhere in the Bible, depicts the worship of God as a joyous, heartfelt affair. This was by design."⁵ He notes further that Israel's joy is the fulfillment of God's promise to Moses many years earlier (Deut 12:7, 12, 18). When referring to the place where God's name would dwell, Moses says: "And there rejoice before the Lord your God . . ."

---

3. See ibid., 36–37.

4. Hahn, *Kingdom of God*, 127. Block cautions that the absence of references to worship in the tabernacle does not mean it did not exist until David (Block, *For the Glory of God*, 222–31). While accepting his point, it is nevertheless clear that worship becomes formalized during the time of David, and thus it stands apart from the earlier periods. On the role of silence in the priestly concept of God, see Israel Kohl, "Between Voice and Silence: The Relationship between Prayer and Temple Cult," *JBL* (1996): 17–30.

5. Hahn, *Kingdom of God*, 127. See Hahn for a list of passages where joyful worship is mentioned.

(v. 12). At the climax of the temple-building account, the Levites now lead God's people in praise and worship with cymbals, harps, lyres, trumpets, and other instruments (2 Chr 5:12–13). Solomon exhorts them after his extended prayer, "may your faithful people rejoice in your goodness" (6:41).

The Chronicler's emphasis on joy throughout his work stands as an invitation to the post-exilic community and to us. We noted in the introduction (pp. 10–14) that life for the returnees had not been easy. They lived as a small province amidst a vast Persian Empire, occupying only a small portion of the land in comparison to the glory days of David and Solomon. Some had faced dire poverty, requiring them to sell their land and become indentured servants. They had faced opposition from the surrounding nations. Their situation could easily have led to despair, especially when they remembered their former days. Yet the Chronicler exhorts God's people to lift their eyes beyond their immediate circumstances and to recognize what God *was doing* in their midst.[6] God was ruling on his exalted and glorious throne, and this has not changed. Regardless of their circumstances, the returnees were to sing joyfully before their God. The prophet Habakkuk understood this—that in spite of the difficulties that lie ahead, he would find joy in God: "yet I will rejoice in the LORD, I will be joyful in God my Savior" (Hab 3:18). This is surely a good word for us today, for joy is not found in our circumstances but in God's presence. As the Levites sang, "strength and joy are in *his* dwelling place" (1 Chr 16:27, emphasis added). Joy is not something that we muster from within ourselves, but it is found in God's presence and in the reality that *he* reigns.

The apostle Paul understood that joy was not based on circumstances when writing his letter to believers at Philippi. Even though in prison, Paul found occasion for rejoicing when Christ was proclaimed (Phil 1:18). Paul's joy was not based in his circumstances, for he writes "But even if I am being poured out like a drink offering on the sacrifice and service coming from your faith, I am glad and rejoice with all of you" (2:17). Paul is joyful not because of his enjoyable surroundings, but because of the certainty and hope of the gospel. He exhorts the Philippians to rejoice with him (v. 18) with his well-known words: "Rejoice in the Lord always. I will say it again: Rejoice!"

---

6. In his thought-provoking article, Wright notes that the Chronicler (as narrator) "has the ability to discern and identify the divine presence and activity in the world, when it would otherwise be inaccessible to the reader." This key point is vital for the returnees (and for our contemporary context), as the Chronicler has insight into what God *is* doing in the world (even if the circumstances suggest otherwise), inviting God's people to recognize his dynamic presence, especially as it is manifest in the spoken word. See Wright, "Beyond Transcendence,"259.

(4:4; cf. 1 Thess 5:16). The poem written by Henry van Dyke in 1907 and set to Beethoven's melody "Ode to Joy" expresses this joy with the well-known first stanza:

> Joyful, joyful, we adore Thee
> God of glory, Lord of love;
> Hearts unfold like flowers before Thee,
> Praising Thee, their sun above,
> Melt the clouds of sin and darkness;
> Drive the dark of doubt away;
> Giver of immortal gladness,
> Fill us with the light of day!

May our lives be characterized by joyful praise and worship, so that Jesus's joy may be in us (John 15:11). May our voices arise in thanksgiving and praise as we take heed to receive Paul's exhortation: "Rejoice in the Lord always. I will say it again, Rejoice!"

CHAPTER 35

2 Chronicles 6:1–42

 LISTEN to the Story

¹Then Solomon said, "The LORD has said that he would dwell in a dark cloud; ²I have built a magnificent temple for you, a place for you to dwell forever."

³While the whole assembly of Israel was standing there, the king turned around and blessed them. ⁴Then he said:

"Praise be to the LORD, the God of Israel, who with his hands has fulfilled what he promised with his mouth to my father David. For he said, ⁵'Since the day I brought my people out of Egypt, I have not chosen a city in any tribe of Israel to have a temple built so that my Name might be there, nor have I chosen anyone to be ruler over my people Israel. ⁶But now I have chosen Jerusalem for my Name to be there, and I have chosen David to rule my people Israel.'

⁷"My father David had it in his heart to build a temple for the Name of the LORD, the God of Israel. ⁸But the LORD said to my father David, 'You did well to have it in your heart to build a temple for my Name. ⁹Nevertheless, you are not the one to build the temple, but your son, your own flesh and blood—he is the one who will build the temple for my Name.'

¹⁰"The LORD has kept the promise he made. I have succeeded David my father and now I sit on the throne of Israel, just as the LORD promised, and I have built the temple for the Name of the LORD, the God of Israel. ¹¹There I have placed the ark, in which is the covenant of the LORD that he made with the people of Israel."

¹²Then Solomon stood before the altar of the LORD in front of the whole assembly of Israel and spread out his hands. ¹³Now he had made a bronze platform, five cubits long, five cubits wide and three cubits high,

and had placed it in the center of the outer court. He stood on the platform and then knelt down before the whole assembly of Israel and spread out his hands toward heaven. ¹⁴He said:

"LORD, the God of Israel, there is no God like you in heaven or on earth—you who keep your covenant of love with your servants who continue wholeheartedly in your way. ¹⁵You have kept your promise to your servant David my father; with your mouth you have promised and with your hand you have fulfilled it—as it is today.

¹⁶"Now, LORD, the God of Israel, keep for your servant David my father the promises you made to him when you said, 'You shall never fail to have a successor to sit before me on the throne of Israel, if only your descendants are careful in all they do to walk before me according to my law, as you have done.' ¹⁷And now, LORD, the God of Israel, let your word that you promised your servant David come true.

¹⁸"But will God really dwell on earth with humans? The heavens, even the highest heavens, cannot contain you. How much less this temple I have built! ¹⁹Yet, LORD my God, give attention to your servant's prayer and his plea for mercy. Hear the cry and the prayer that your servant is praying in your presence. ²⁰May your eyes be open toward this temple day and night, this place of which you said you would put your Name there. May you hear the prayer your servant prays toward this place. ²¹Hear the supplications of your servant and of your people Israel when they pray toward this place. Hear from heaven, your dwelling place; and when you hear, forgive.

²²"When anyone wrongs their neighbor and is required to take an oath and they come and swear the oath before your altar in this temple, ²³then hear from heaven and act. Judge between your servants, condemning the guilty and bringing down on their heads what they have done, and vindicating the innocent by treating them in accordance with their innocence.

²⁴"When your people Israel have been defeated by an enemy because they have sinned against you and when they turn back and give praise to your name, praying and making supplication before you in this temple, ²⁵then hear from heaven and forgive the sin of

your people Israel and bring them back to the land you gave to them and their ancestors.

[26]"When the heavens are shut up and there is no rain because your people have sinned against you, and when they pray toward this place and give praise to your name and turn from their sin because you have afflicted them, [27]then hear from heaven and forgive the sin of your servants, your people Israel. Teach them the right way to live, and send rain on the land you gave your people for an inheritance.

[28]"When famine or plague comes to the land, or blight or mildew, locusts or grasshoppers, or when enemies besiege them in any of their cities, whatever disaster or disease may come, [29]and when a prayer or plea is made by anyone among your people Israel—being aware of their afflictions and pains, and spreading out their hands toward this temple—[30]then hear from heaven, your dwelling place. Forgive, and deal with everyone according to all they do, since you know their hearts (for you alone know the human heart), [31]so that they will fear you and walk in obedience to you all the time they live in the land you gave our ancestors.

[32]"As for the foreigner who does not belong to your people Israel but has come from a distant land because of your great name and your mighty hand and your outstretched arm—when they come and pray toward this temple, [33]then hear from heaven, your dwelling place. Do whatever the foreigner asks of you, so that all the peoples of the earth may know your name and fear you, as do your own people Israel, and may know that this house I have built bears your Name.

[34]"When your people go to war against their enemies, wherever you send them, and when they pray to you toward this city you have chosen and the temple I have built for your Name, [35]then hear from heaven their prayer and their plea, and uphold their cause.

[36]"When they sin against you—for there is no one who does not sin—and you become angry with them and give them over to the enemy, who takes them captive to a land far away or near; [37]and if they have a change of heart in the land where they are held captive, and repent and plead with you in the land of their captivity and say, 'We have sinned, we have done wrong and acted wickedly';

³⁸and if they turn back to you with all their heart and soul in the land of their captivity where they were taken, and pray toward the land you gave their ancestors, toward the city you have chosen and toward the temple I have built for your Name; ³⁹then from heaven, your dwelling place, hear their prayer and their pleas, and uphold their cause. And forgive your people, who have sinned against you.

⁴⁰"Now, my God, may your eyes be open and your ears attentive to the prayers offered in this place.

⁴¹"Now arise, Lord God, and come to your resting place,
    you and the ark of your might.
May your priests, Lord God, be clothed with salvation,
    may your faithful people rejoice in your goodness.
⁴²Lord God, do not reject your anointed one.
    Remember the great love promised to David your servant."

Listening to the Text in the Story: Leviticus 26:39–40; Deuteronomy 4:29–31; 12:1–28; 30:1–3; 1 Chronicles 17:12–14

The completion of the temple and God's glory filling it is followed by Solomon's prayer of dedication. Themes rehearsed in his prayer are deeply embedded in Israel's story. God told Moses many years earlier that when his people had been scattered afar (due to their sin), they were to seek him in prayer and he would be found by them (Deut 4:29). He exhorted them with these words: "When you are in distress and all these things have happened to you, then in later days you will return to the Lord your God and obey him" (v. 30). The call to return to God reverberates throughout this chapter as Solomon emphasizes the importance of prayer and repentance. This takes us to central theological themes in Chronicles. Solomon's prayer is crucial for the returnees. Dillard rightly notes that the Chronicler will "seek again and again to demonstrate the realization in Israel's history of the principles announced in Solomon's prayer and in God's response."[1] This chapter underscores the central role of prayer and repentance, and as such, Solomon's prayer functions as a paradigmatic prayer applicable to God's people throughout the ages.

---

1. Dillard, *2 Chronicles*, 7.

EXPLAIN the Story

Solomon Acknowledges That God Has Fulfilled His Promises to David (6:1–11)

Solomon recalls that God had said he would "dwell in a dark cloud" (2 Chr 6:1; cf. Deut 4:11; 5:22). Since clouds belong to the heavenly realm, they are a fitting vehicle to express the invisible and heavenly presence of God.[2] Solomon's description of the temple as a "magnificent" (NIV) or "lofty" (NASB) house (2 Chr 6:2) depicts an elevated place, likened to God's heavenly throne that is exalted above the earthly realm (cf. Isa 63:15). Beale thus concludes that the "temple is associated with the physically created firmament and the invisible heavenly dwelling of God to which the firmament pointed."[3] With this lofty dwelling in view, Solomon proceeds to bless all the people assembled before him as he praises God for his faithfulness in fulfilling his word to David (2 Chr 6:4; cf. 1 Chr 17:12–14). Solomon affirms that God has chosen Jerusalem as the place where his name would dwell (2 Chr 6:6; cf. Deut 12:5–28), and David is his chosen king (2 Chr 6:6; cf. 1 Sam 16). Even though David had intended to build the temple, God had told him that his son would build it (2 Chr 6:7–8; see also 1 Chr 17:4–15; 22:6–10). Solomon recognizes that he has succeeded his father and he now sits on the throne of Israel (2 Chr 6:10; see also 1 Chr 29:23) in fulfillment of God's promise to David (17:12, 14; 22:10; 28:5; 29:23).

Solomon's Prayer of Dedication (6:12–42)

Solomon stands before the altar in the presence of all the people (2 Chr 6:12). The king had built a raised platform of bronze in the court of the temple, and at this sacred moment he kneels on it with his hands spread out toward heaven (v. 13; cf. Exod 9:29, 33; Ezra 9:5; Ps 143:6; Isa 1:15). Solomon begins his prayer by affirming that there is no God like the LORD, in heaven or on earth (2 Chr 6:14). The LORD's uniqueness is affirmed throughout the Old Testament (Exod 15:11; Deut 4:39; Isa 44:6; 45:5–7, 21; 46:9), and this declaration stands in opposition to the ancient polytheistic world. Solomon praises God for his steadfast love, which is the hallmark of his character (Deut 7:9; Neh 1:5; 9:32), seen especially in his faithfulness to David (2 Chr 6:15; cf. Ps 89:30–37, 49).

---

2. Beale, *The Temple*, 36–37.
3. Ibid., 37.

Solomon asks God to keep his word given to David, when he had promised: "You shall never fail to have a successor to sit before me on the throne of Israel, if only your descendants are careful in all they do to walk before me according to my law, as you have done" (2 Chr 6:16). This underscores the certainty of God's promise, yet it highlights its conditional nature, for the recipient of the promise was required to keep God's laws (1 Kgs 2:3–4; 8:25; Ps 132:10–12). Even though Solomon has risen in the place of his father, he will only rule over God's everlasting kingdom if he obeys God's laws.[4] It would be unfathomable to have anyone other than a righteous Davidic king ruling on God's everlasting throne. Solomon thus prays, "And now, LORD, the God of Israel, let your word that you promised your servant David come true" (2 Chr 6:17).

Solomon marvels at God's choice of Jerusalem as his dwelling place when he poses the question: "But will God really dwell on earth with humans?" (v. 18). He recognizes that even the highest of heavens cannot contain God, how much less this house he has built! The prophet Isaiah, who had seen a glimpse of God's highly exalted and glorious throne, affirms that God's throne was in heaven (Isa 6:1–7), and earth was merely his footstool (66:1). The prophet Micaiah had received a similar vision: "I saw the LORD sitting on his throne with all the multitudes of heaven standing on his right and on his left" (2 Chr 18:18). The reality was that the temple could not contain the LORD God, who dwelt high above in heaven (6:21; 30:27). Accordingly, throughout his prayer Solomon asks God to hear *from heaven* (6:25, 27, 30, 33, 35, 39; cf. 7:14; 30:27). In view of God's exalted heavenly abode, Solomon rightly asks what kind of house could be built for God on earth. God's heavenly throne was far more glorious than the extravagant and lavish temple that Solomon had built. The temple was merely a copy of God's heavenly sanctuary (cf. Exod 25:9; 1 Chr 28:19; Heb 8:5) where God was enthroned (Pss 11:4; 47:7–8; 93:1–2; 103:19; Isa 66:1; Acts 7:49). The ark of the covenant was identified as God's footstool, where "his feet extended while sitting on his heavenly throne."[5] So while God's glory fills the earthly temple, Boda rightly notes that the temple "must be viewed as an entrance way into the heavenly throne room of God, rather than the entire throne itself."[6]

Solomon prays that God might listen to the prayers of his servant being offered, and that his eyes might be open toward this house, the place where

---

4. See the extended discussion on the Davidic covenant in the discussion in Chapter 17 on 1 Chr 17, pp. 176–82.

5. Beale, *The Temple*, 370.

6. Boda, *1–2 Chronicles*, 259.

his name would dwell (2 Chr 6:19–20). He asks that God might "hear . . . and . . . forgive" (v. 21), concepts repeated in a variety of expressions throughout his prayer (vv. 19, 20, 21, 23, 25, 27, etc.). God's ability to hear the prayers of his people serves as yet another reminder that God is unlike the idols, which have ears but cannot hear (Ps 115:1–8; Dan 5:23; cf. 1 Kgs 18:24–29). God promises Solomon that he will hear the prayers of his people when they humble themselves, seek his face, and turn from their wicked ways (2 Chr 7:14). Not surprisingly, the Chronicler draws attention to answered prayer, for it lies at the center of God's relationship with his people (30:20, 27; 33:13; 34:27).

Solomon asks God to "forgive" his people when they sin (Heb. *s-l-kh*, 6:21, 25, 27, 30, 39). God had revealed to Moses many years earlier that forgiveness was graciously available through the sacrificial system (Lev 4:20, 26, 31; 5:10, 13, 16). The sacred task of the priest was to "make atonement for the community" so that their sins would be forgiven (4:20; cf. 1 Chr 6:49). Yet at key moments in Israel's story, when God's people defiantly rebel against him (known as "high-handed" sins), he forgives Israel's sin based on his gracious character, even when no animal is sacrificed. In such instances, atonement was accomplished by a mediator (such as Moses) who prayed on Israel's behalf, thereby effecting atonement without a sacrifice.[7] Moses thus understood that he could always appeal to God's character, as he did in the golden calf story when he prayed: "if I have found favor in your eyes, then let the Lord go with us. Although this is a stiff-necked people, forgive our wickedness and our sin, and take us as your inheritance" (Exod 34:9). God revealed his name to Moses at this time: "The LORD, the LORD, the compassionate and gracious God, slow to anger, abounding in love and faithfulness, maintaining love to thousands, and forgiving wickedness, rebellion and sin" (vv. 6–7; cf. Num 14:18–19). Skar thus concludes that "atonement for sin is possible because of the Lord's proclivity to extend mercy; he does not treat his people as their sins deserve. It is not simply that atonement is rooted in grace (lesson one); it is that his very nature is to extend that grace because of his mercy."[8] Since

---

7. See Jay Sklar's insightful discussion of sin and atonement in the Pentateuch. He outlines three types of sins (unintentional, intentional but not necessarily high-handed, and high-handed sins), noting that there are seven examples in the Pentateuch where atonement is achieved for high-handed sins without a sacrifice being offered. In such cases, the mediation of a key figure (such as Moses, Aaron, and Phinehas) results in the restoration of Israel's relationship with God. To be sure, such atonement does not preclude God's discipline, but his people are not totally rejected. This is due to God's gracious character, but as Sklar notes, confession and repentance were necessary in the process of restoration. See Jay Sklar, "Sin and Atonement: Lessons from the Pentateuch," *BBR* 22:4 (2012): 467–91.

8. Ibid., 488.

the temple was the place where the LORD's *name* would dwell (Deut 12:5–28; 2 Chr 2:4), Solomon boldly prays to the LORD that he might forgive Israel's sins, as he has done in the past.

Solomon proceeds to rehearse a series of adverse circumstances in his prayer. The first situation concerns a man who sins against his neighbor and is required to take an oath (2 Chr 6:22–23). Oaths were sometimes part of legal procedures to resolve disputes (Exod 22:11), and they were used to determine a person's guilt or innocence (Num 5:11–31).[9] A person charged with a crime was required to appear before a judge, either to be condemned or acquitted (e.g., Exod 22:8–9; Deut 17:8–13; 25:1). Solomon asks God to act as judge and acquit the innocent.

The next circumstance entails being defeated before an enemy because of sin (2 Chr 6:24), which was one of the curses of the covenant (Lev 26:17; Deut 28:25, 48). The Southern Kingdom will be defeated by the Babylonians because of their unfaithfulness (1 Chr 9:1; 2 Chr 36:15–20), yet in his prayer Solomon exhorts God's people to "turn back and give praise to [his] name, praying and making supplication before [him] in this temple" (6:24). Even if the temple has been destroyed, prayers of repentance could be offered in Babylon, as Daniel understood when he implored God to hear and forgive (Dan 9:3–19). The requirement to "turn back, return" to God (Heb. *sh-w-b*, 2 Chr 6:24, 26, 37) is deeply rooted in God's promise of restoration given many years earlier (Deut 4:29–30; 30:1–3, 8, 10). The importance of repentance is thus underscored in Solomon's prayer (2 Chr 6:37–38; 7:14; cf. 15:4; 30:9), and the prophets repeatedly call God's people to return to the LORD (24:19; cf. Jer 35:15; 36:2–3, 7). Such repentance was accompanied by the giving of praise (Heb. *y-d-h*, 2 Chr 6:24), a hallmark of the people of God (1 Chr 16:4, 7–8, 34–35, 41; 23:30; 25:3, etc.).

God's people were to pray and make supplication before God in the temple (2 Chr 6:24). The verb "to pray" (Heb. *p-l-l*) occurs eight times in the chapter (vv. 19, 20, 21, 24, 26, 32, 34, 38), and the topic of prayer is also rehearsed elsewhere (7:1, 14; 30:18; 32:20, 24; 33:13). The critical role of prayer is exemplified in the story of Manasseh, who prays to God while in Babylon. God restores him because he has humbled himself and prayed to God (33:12–13, 19). The importance of prayer and confession is further seen in the post-exilic community (Ezra 10:1; Neh 1:4, 6; 2:4, etc.). The second verb for "to make supplication" (Heb. *h-n-n*) is best translated "to plead for mercy," as it evokes a heartfelt and desperate plea for mercy before a gracious God (Deut 3:23; Pss

---

9. For a helpful summary, see Boda, *1–2 Chronicles*, 261–63.

9:13; 30:8; 142:1). Since it is the LORD's character to be gracious (Exod 33:19; cf. Num 6:25), God's people are exhorted to appeal to his mercy.

Solomon implores God to "hear from heaven and forgive the sin of your people Israel and bring them back to the land you gave to them and their ancestors" (2 Chr 6:25). God had warned his people that if they disobeyed his laws, he would remove them from the land and send them into exile (Lev. 26:33–34, 38–39; Deut 28:32, 36, 41, 64), but he had also promised that if they returned to him, he would restore them (Lev 26:40–45; Deut 30:3–5). When rain is withheld due to Israel's sin (2 Chr 6:26; cf. Lev 26:19; Deut 11:17; 28:23–24), they are to pray, give praise to God's name, and turn from their sin. Solomon then asks God to provide rain, which would signify his blessing (2 Chr 6:27; cf. Lev 26:4; Deut 11:14; 28:12; Mal 3:10). Other adverse circumstances are rehearsed, such as famine, plague, blight, mildew, locusts, grasshoppers, enemy attack, or any other disaster or disease (2 Chr 6:28; cf. Lev 26:14–39; Deut 28:15–68). Whatever calamity comes upon God's people, the response should always be prayer and supplication before God (2 Chr 6:29). The goal is that God's people might learn to fear the LORD and walk in his ways (v. 31).

Solomon then turns his attention to the *foreigner*, "who does not belong to your people Israel but has come from a distant land because of your great name and your mighty hand and your outstretched arm" (2 Chr 6:32). Even the foreigner is invited to pray to God! Solomon audaciously asks God to "do whatever the foreigner asks of you" (v. 33). Answered prayer distinguishes God from the idols of the nations, for the LORD is the only true and living God who hears and answers prayers. Through answered prayer, the LORD reveals that he is God (cf. 33:13). Hope is expressed that all the peoples of the earth would know God's name and fear him (6:33; Ps 33:8). The psalmist thus envisions that answered prayer will lead to worship: "All the nations you have made will come and worship before you, Lord; they will bring glory to your name" (Ps 86:9). The international theme in Chronicles is again seen, underscoring that the temple is a house of prayer *for all nations* (cf. Isa 56:7).[10]

Next, Solomon rehearses what happens when his people go out in battle against their enemies and are sent into exile because of their sin (2 Chr 6:34–36). This is highly relevant for the returnees, whose recent history was shaped by their defeat and deportation to Babylon (1 Chr 9:1; 2 Chr 36:20). Amid such disaster, a cluster of verbs resound with the heartfelt repentance

---

10. On the international theme in Chronicles, see the introduction, The Vision for a Witnessing People of God, pp. 16–17, and Chapter 2, Live the Story, Judah's Place in God's Plan to Include All Nations, pp. 46–48.

required of God's people ("change of heart," "repent," "plead," "turn back," "pray," 6:37–38). In this case, prayers of repentance are accompanied by verbal confession: "We have sinned, we have done wrong and acted wickedly" (v. 37; cf. Ps 106:6; Dan 9:5, 15). In Chronicles there are several other confessions of sin (2 Chr 12:6–7; 29:5–9; 30:7–11; 33:12–13), but after the calamitous experience of exile, Solomon's prayer is more fully integrated into the life of the community, as extended prayers of confession are central to the restoration.

Solomon concludes his prayer by beseeching God to have his eyes open and his ears attentive to the prayers offered in the temple (6:40; cf. Dan 9:18–19). Psalm 132:8–10 is cited at the conclusion of Solomon's prayer, which draws attention to the ark's resting place in the temple and the joy that follows as God's faithful ones rejoice in his goodness (2 Chr 6:41). His prayer concludes with a plea that God might not reject his anointed one but remember his lovingkindness to David (v. 42 cf. 1 Chr 17:13; Ps 89:33). The Davidic king was not only anointed with oil (e.g., 1 Sam 16:3, 13; 1 Chr 29:22), but he is known simply as God's "anointed" (1 Sam 2:10; 12:3; 16:6; 24:6, 10, etc.). Solomon's prayer thus concludes where it began, with focus on God's covenant-loyalty shown to David (2 Chr 6:14–15).

LIVE the Story

Repentance and Forgiveness

The central role of repentance in Solomon's prayer is worth further reflection. God had made known to Moses many years earlier that repentance was vital for the restoration of God's people (Deut 4:29–31). Boda rightly remarks that "one cannot overestimate the impact of this second section of the prayer on the liturgical practices of the exilic and postexilic communities. This prayer provided guidance for the community living in the wake of the greatest disaster they could ever have imagined: the fall of the state and the exile of the people."[11] It is not surprising to find, therefore, that prayers of confession characterize the post-exilic period (Ezra 9:5–15; 10:1–2; Neh 1:7; 9:33–34; cf. Dan 9:3–19). It is important to bear in mind that, under the old covenant, sacrifices were God's provision for forgiveness for sins (Lev 5:15–19; Num 15:22–31), although intentional sins commonly required the death penalty (e.g., Lev 20). Yet we have noted that there are occasions in the Old Testament when Israel's sins that are worthy of death are forgiven without a sacrifice, through the prayers

---

11. Boda, *1–2 Chronicles*, 265–66

offered by a mediator.[12] Kings like David and Manasseh will experience God's forgiveness after acknowledging their own sins, yet no sacrifice is offered (2 Sam 12:1–15; 2 Chr 33:10–13; cf. Ps 32:1–5). In his prayer, Solomon now asks that God might forgive Israel's sins when *prayers of confession* are offered with genuine repentance. Herein lies the solution to Israel's sin and, indeed, the solution to the human plight of sin. Ultimately, it is to be found in the mercy of God and his willingness to forgive sin. Solomon knows that God has forgiven Israel's sins in the past, and it is his character to be gracious (see Exod 34:7; Ps 130:1–4; cf. Neh 9:17). The prayer of Solomon extends beyond the immediate temple, therefore, providing the theological vision for Israel's restoration (see Dan 9:4–19), something that is central for the ongoing life of the returnees (Ezra 9:5–15; 10:1, 10–11; Neh 1:4–11; 9:5–37).

The importance of repentance for Israel's story is seen in the last prophet, Malachi, who calls God's people to repent (Mal 3:1–15; 4:5–6). His prophetic words find their fulfillment in the ministry of John the Baptist, who announces: "Repent, for the kingdom of heaven has come near" (Matt 3:2). He is the prophet in the wilderness, preparing the way for the LORD's return (vv. 1–12; Mark 1:1–8; Luke 3:2–18). In response to his proclamation, people confess their sins and are baptized (Matt 3:6). The importance of repentance reverberates throughout the New Testament. When Jesus begins his public ministry, he announces: "Repent, for the kingdom of heaven has come near" (4:17; cf. Mark 1:15). Repentance is, therefore, a necessary condition of entrance into God's kingdom. Jesus identifies his own ministry as a call of sinners to repentance (Luke 5:32; 13:3, 5). His parables teach that there is great joy in heaven when one sinner repents (15:7, 10, 32). Jesus not only calls sinners to repentance, but he has divine authority to forgive sins (5:20–26). His atoning sacrifice is the means by which God's forgiveness is freely and graciously offered, enabling the new covenant promise of forgiveness to be realized (Matt 26:28). Even though thousands upon thousands of sacrifices will be offered in the temple Solomon builds, the reality is that they can never take away sin (Heb 10:1–18). But God himself provides the perfect atoning sacrifice when he offers up his beloved son for the sin of the world (Mark 10:45; John 3:16–17; Rom 3:21–26; cf. Isa 53:10). This is the forgiveness anticipated in Solomon's prayer.

Jesus taught his disciples that this message of "repentance for the forgiveness of sins" was to be preached in his name "to all nations, beginning at Jerusalem" (Luke 24:47). Solomon's temple was not simply a place of prayer

---

12. See Sklar, "Sin and Atonement," 485–90.

for Israel, but it was intended as a place of prayer for all nations (Isa 56:6–7; Mark 11:17). After the outpouring of the Holy Spirit, the disciples proclaimed the good news of the kingdom, calling people to repent. They announced that everyone who called upon the name of the Lord would be saved and receive forgiveness in the name of Jesus (Acts 2:38; 3:19; 4:12; 5:31). What Solomon saw only dimly has now become the reality in Christ.

In her book *Unbroken*,[13] Laura Hillenbrand tells the remarkable story of Louis Zamperini, who was drafted to fight in World War II. During his time of military service, his plane crashed and he and two others were left stranded on a raft for countless days, until they were finally found by the Japanese and sent to a prisoner of war camp for a grueling two years. After being released at the end of the war, Zamperini sought relief in alcohol while he and his wife lived in California. He continued to be tormented by horrific nightmares in the dark hours of the night, as he imagined himself strangling the prison guard known as "the Bird." The light of day provided no relief for his troubled soul, as rage filled his waking moments. After his wife had committed her life to Jesus, she invited her husband to join her at the Billy Graham rallies that were being held in California. Reluctantly, in 1949 Zamperini finally attended one of these rallies, at which time he heard the gospel message for the first time. Remembering a former vow he had made to God while adrift at sea, he knelt down before God in acknowledgment that he was a sinner in need of forgiveness. Forever etched in his heart and soul, he recalls what happened:

> When people come to the end of their rope and there's nowhere else to turn, they turn to God . . . I got on my knees and made my confession of faith. I couldn't believe what was happening to me there. I knew I was through getting drunk. I knew I had forgiven all my guards, including the Bird. It was just unbelievable. That was a genuine miracle.[14]

After giving his life to Christ, Zamperini testifies that the nightmares stopped from that day onward. He was even able to extend forgiveness to "the Bird." For his remaining years until his death in 2014, he worked with at-risk boys through the non-profit organization he established. That day in 1949, Louis Zamperini, the penitent sinner, received God's forgiveness that is found in

13. Laura Hillenbrand, *Unbroken: A World War II Story of Survival, Resilience, and Redemption* (New York: Random House, 2014).

14. "Be Hardy," by Louis Zamperini, January 2012 (https://www.coachayers.com/blog/2015/1/27/be-hardy-by-louie-zamperini#). See also an interview with him in Icons of the Faith Series (https://www.youtube.com/watch?v=S8Jq3_3DdxM).

Christ alone. This is what Solomon saw *from afar* when he knelt at the altar—that God hears the prayers of a repentant sinner and that he forgives sin. He alone can bring restoration and new life. This is the life-changing forgiveness found in Christ. A contemporary praise song by Elevation Worship, *O Come to the Altar*, expresses these profound truths well.[15] This is the reality that Solomon saw from afar as he knelt at the altar. Forgiveness lavishly offered by God was bought with the precious blood of Christ. This is what Louis Zamperini discovered as he knelt before the Lord, and this is the invitation offered to all who repent and seek God's face. Oh, what a Savior. Isn't he wonderful?

---

15. Wade Joye, Christopher Brown, Mack Brock, and Steven Furtick, "O Come to the Altar" by Elevation Worship, © Be Essential Songs. You may access a video performance of this song at https://www.youtube.com/watch?v=rYQ5yXCc_CA.

CHAPTER 36

2 Chronicles 7:1–22

 ## LISTEN to the Story

¹When Solomon finished praying, fire came down from heaven and consumed the burnt offering and the sacrifices, and the glory of the LORD filled the temple. ²The priests could not enter the temple of the LORD because the glory of the LORD filled it. ³When all the Israelites saw the fire coming down and the glory of the LORD above the temple, they knelt on the pavement with their faces to the ground, and they worshiped and gave thanks to the LORD, saying,

"He is good;
his love endures forever."

⁴Then the king and all the people offered sacrifices before the LORD. ⁵And King Solomon offered a sacrifice of twenty-two thousand head of cattle and a hundred and twenty thousand sheep and goats. So the king and all the people dedicated the temple of God. ⁶The priests took their positions, as did the Levites with the LORD's musical instruments, which King David had made for praising the LORD and which were used when he gave thanks, saying, "His love endures forever." Opposite the Levites, the priests blew their trumpets, and all the Israelites were standing.

⁷Solomon consecrated the middle part of the courtyard in front of the temple of the LORD, and there he offered burnt offerings and the fat of the fellowship offerings, because the bronze altar he had made could not hold the burnt offerings, the grain offerings and the fat portions.

⁸So Solomon observed the festival at that time for seven days, and all Israel with him—a vast assembly, people from Lebo Hamath to the Wadi of Egypt. ⁹On the eighth day they held an assembly, for they had celebrated the dedication of the altar for seven days and the festival for seven days more. ¹⁰On the twenty-third day of the seventh month he sent the people

to their homes, joyful and glad in heart for the good things the LORD had done for David and Solomon and for his people Israel.

[11]When Solomon had finished the temple of the LORD and the royal palace, and had succeeded in carrying out all he had in mind to do in the temple of the LORD and in his own palace, [12]the LORD appeared to him at night and said:

"I have heard your prayer and have chosen this place for myself as a temple for sacrifices.

[13]"When I shut up the heavens so that there is no rain, or command locusts to devour the land or send a plague among my people, [14]if my people, who are called by my name, will humble themselves and pray and seek my face and turn from their wicked ways, then I will hear from heaven, and I will forgive their sin and will heal their land. [15]Now my eyes will be open and my ears attentive to the prayers offered in this place. [16]I have chosen and consecrated this temple so that my Name may be there forever. My eyes and my heart will always be there.

[17]"As for you, if you walk before me faithfully as David your father did, and do all I command, and observe my decrees and laws, [18]I will establish your royal throne, as I covenanted with David your father when I said, 'You shall never fail to have a successor to rule over Israel.'

[19]"But if you turn away and forsake the decrees and commands I have given you and go off to serve other gods and worship them, [20]then I will uproot Israel from my land, which I have given them, and will reject this temple I have consecrated for my Name. I will make it a byword and an object of ridicule among all peoples. [21]This temple will become a heap of rubble. All who pass by will be appalled and say, 'Why has the LORD done such a thing to this land and to this temple?' [22]People will answer, 'Because they have forsaken the LORD, the God of their ancestors, who brought them out of Egypt, and have embraced other gods, worshiping and serving them—that is why he brought all this disaster on them.'"

Listening to the Text in the Story: Exodus 25:22; 40:34–38

As Solomon finishes praying, God's glory fills the temple and consumes the offering. Thousands of sacrifices are offered, and the festival draws to a close. The celebration is over and God's people return to their homes, but the temple narrative has not yet concluded, for God appears to Solomon at night, letting him know that he has *heard* his prayer (2 Chr 7:12). This reminds us that the temple is not simply a building, but it is the place where God *meets* with his people. Prayer is dialogue, since God's people not only pray to him, but he hears and responds. The Scriptures testify to the profound reality that the LORD is a God who speaks. When God had instructed Moses to build the tabernacle, God told him that he would speak to him there (Exod 25:22). God's people had remarkably heard God's voice speaking from the midst of the fire, and out of the heavens they had heard his voice (Deut 4:33, 36). In the story that follows, God now speaks to Solomon (2 Chr 7:12–22).

Wright notes that in Chronicles, God is mostly "physically" absent, for he dwells *in heaven*, as the prophet Micaiah explains: "I saw the LORD sitting on his throne with all the multitudes of heaven standing on his right and on his left" (2 Chr 18:18). Yet Wright makes the astute observation that in Chronicles, God is present *on earth* in his *speech*, which is precisely what we see in the story recounted in this chapter. When God appears to Solomon (1:7), his "appearance" is not visible but *audible*. Wright thus observes that as in 2 Chronicles 1:7, again in 7:12 God appears to Solomon, yet his appearance is in the *spoken word* (vv. 12–22). Wright concludes that God appears "only in dialogue with Solomon."[1] This is a fascinating study on the divine presence manifested in God's word, and the story of Solomon takes us to the heart of prayer as dialogue. God had instructed Moses to build a tabernacle so that he might dwell among his people (Exod 25:8), but the tabernacle was also the place where God would speak with Moses (v. 22). In the story that follows, God's glory fills the temple (2 Chr 7:1–3), but this also marks the occasion when God appears to Solomon through the divine word (vv. 12–22). God's word spoken to Solomon has ongoing significance for God's people throughout the ages.

EXPLAIN the Story

Sacrifices Are Offered and the Temple Is Dedicated (7:1–10)

When Solomon finishes praying, fire comes down from heaven and consumes the burnt offering and sacrifices, and God's glory fills the temple

---

1. Wright, "Beyond Transcendence," 246.

(2 Chr 7:1). This "dramatically underlines God's willingness to answer Solomon's request," as Williamson notes.[2] The priests are unable to enter the glory-filled temple (v. 2), as was the case earlier (5:14), but now God's glory is accompanied by fire as the offerings are consumed. The people respond by bowing down in worship with their faces toward the ground (7:3). Their posture of humility is fitting for the exalted LORD, whose fiery presence invokes not only joy, but reverence (Lev 9:23–24). The people respond in praise and thanksgiving with the refrain: "He is good; his love endures forever" (2 Chr 7:3). Their words of praise join with God's people throughout the ages who praise God for his goodness and covenant-loyalty (1 Chr 16:34; Pss 106:1; 107:1; 118:1; 136:1, etc.). Thousands of sacrifices are offered on the altar at this joyous dedication (2 Chr 7:5).[3] Priests and Levites stand at their appointed posts (v. 6; cf. 5:12–13), and Levitical musicians play their instruments made by David (cf. 1 Chr 23:5; 25:1–6). Solomon consecrates the middle of the court in front of the main temple precinct. Sacrifices are usually offered on the bronze altar (Exod 27:1–8; 29:10–14; Lev 1:1–8), but their large number required adjustment (2 Chr 7:7). The celebration covers an extended period, as the covenant community gathers in Jerusalem for a seven-day pilgrimage festival (vv. 8–9; cf. Lev 23:33–43). God's people travel into Jerusalem from the northern region of Hamath and as far south as the brook of Egypt, reflecting the outer boundaries of the land (2 Chr 7:8; cf. Gen 15:18; Num 34:5, 8; Josh 15:4, etc.). When the celebration concludes, people return to their homes "joyful and glad in heart for the good things the LORD had done for David and Solomon and for his people Israel" (2 Chr 7:10).[4]

God Answers Solomon's Prayer and Gives a Word of Hope (7:11–16)

The LORD appears to Solomon in the evening, as he had done previously, giving him the assurance that his prayer has been heard and that the temple has been chosen as a house of sacrifice (2 Chr 7:12). God thus "appears" to Solomon in the spoken word. This is how his presence *in heaven* (cf. 6:21, 25, 30, etc.) is manifest *on earth*. Solomon had asked whether God could indeed dwell with mankind on earth (v. 18), but his glorious presence in the temple

---

2. Williamson, "Eschatology in Chronicles," 146.

3. The text states that there were 22,000 oxen and 120,000 sheep sacrificed. Wenham has noted that these numbers would require twenty sacrifices a minute for ten hours a day, over the course of twelve days, thus he suggests the language is hyperbolic rather than literal (see Wenham, "Large Numbers," 49; see also Dillard, *2 Chronicles*, 57).

4. On the topic of joy, see Live the Story in Chapter 34, pp. 319–21.

(7:1–3) now comes to Solomon in the form of the divine word. One day, God's Word will become flesh and dwell with humanity on earth.

God makes known to Solomon three types of adverse circumstances that could come upon God's people, which include absence of rain, locusts, or a plague (v. 13). These are simply a sampling of the kind of adverse circumstances that could come upon God's people due to their sin, hearkening back to the Mosaic covenant (Lev 26:1–39; Deut 28:15–68).

Four responses of God's people are given next, along with a promise from God: "if my people, who are called by my name, will humble themselves and pray and seek my face and turn from their wicked ways, then I will hear from heaven, and I will forgive their sin and will heal their land. Now my eyes will be open and my ears attentive to the prayers offered in this place" (2 Chr 7:14–15). Williamson notes that terms found in these verses are used in the subsequent narrative and serve as "marks at one point or another to introduce one of the miraculous interventions that are such a characteristic feature of the Chronicler's work."[5] These verses are unique to Chronicles and take us to the heart of the Chronicler's theology.[6]

Humbling oneself is the first characteristic (Heb. *k-n-'*). Its importance for the restoration was already anticipated by Moses (Lev 26:41), and thus the Chronicler highlights key people who humble themselves, drawing attention to the aversion of God's wrath and the restoration that follows (Heb. *k-n-'*, 2 Chr 12:6–7, 12; 30:11; 32:26 [NIV, "repented"]; 33:12, 19; 34:27). Humbling oneself is not simply being a humble person, but rather, it entails submitting to God and his word. Accordingly, the opposite is not being proud, but *stiff-necked*. Judah's last king, Zedekiah, will refuse to humble himself when he hears God's word through Jeremiah, but instead, he stiffens his neck and hardens his heart (36:12–13). Refusing to submit to God and his word will lead to divine judgment (28:19; 33:23; 36:12), underscoring that the required posture of God's people is yielding to the LORD.

Prayer is the second response (Heb. *p-l-l*, 2 Chr 7:14). Solomon has already emphasized the important role of prayer (6:19, 20, 21, 24, 26, 32, 34, 38), but now it receives God's *own* commendation—God's people are exhorted to pray amidst their adverse circumstances. Taking this word to heart, the Chronicler highlights the role of prayer in the life of God's people (30:18; 32:20, 24). Manasseh is exemplary on the matter of prayer. Even though his sins are the most egregious of all the kings, yet, in his distress in Babylon, he

---

5. Williamson, "Eschatology in Chronicles," 150.
6. Several commentators have provided helpful summaries of the terms used here; see especially Dillard, *2 Chronicles*, 77–78, and Klein, *2 Chronicles*, 111.

humbles himself and prays to God (33:12–13, 19). God hears his prayer, and the repentant king is restored to his kingdom.

The next response God is looking for in his people is "seeking" his face (Heb. *b-q-sh*, 7:14). Many years earlier, Moses had taught God's people that if they sought the LORD, he would be found by them (Deut 4:29; cf. 2 Chr 15:2, 4, 15), and under David, they were exhorted to seek the LORD continually (1 Chr 16:10–11). The verb "to seek" (Heb. *b-q-sh*) describes the action of searching for a person in order to find someone (Gen 37:15–16; Josh 2:22; Judg 4:22; 1 Sam 10:21). That God's people are to seek God's *presence* is suggested by the object of their seeking, namely, God's *face*. This echoes the longing of the psalmist: "My heart says of you, 'Seek his face!' Your face, LORD, I will seek" (Ps 27:8), and it recalls the priestly blessing, "the LORD make his *face* shine on you and be gracious to you; the LORD turn *his face* toward you and give you peace" (Num 6:25–26, emphasis added). The Chronicler thus rehearses times when the king and people seek the LORD (2 Chr 11:16; 20:4; cf. Ezra 8:23), which serve as an exhortation to the returnees (and to us) to seek God and his favor. Alongside prayer and seeking God, the requirement of repentance ("turn from their wicked ways") is highlighted (Heb. *sh-w-b*, 2 Chr 7:14). Solomon has already emphasized this in his prayer (6:24, 26, 37), and the Chronicler highlights its importance elsewhere (15:4; 30:6, 9); but most importantly, failure to repent will have devastating consequences (36:13).[7]

God promises Solomon that he will hear from heaven, forgive their sin, and heal their land (2 Chr 7:14). The king has repeatedly asked God to hear the prayers of his people when they repent (6:20, 21, 23, 25, 27, etc.), and God now reassures Solomon that he *has* heard his prayer (7:12). It is important to bear in mind that the sacrificial system was God's provision for forgiveness (Lev 4–5; 19:22; Num 15:25, 28), for there was no forgiveness without the shedding of blood (Heb 9:22; cf. Lev 17:11). We have seen, however, that there are times in the Old Testament when God forgives Israel's ("high-handed") sin, even when sacrifices are not offered.[8] In such cases, confession and repentance were essential, as seen in David's prayer: "'I will confess my transgressions to the LORD.' And you forgave the guilt of my sin" (Ps 32:5; cf. 51:1–4). Now, God promises forgiveness to sinners who *repent*. God's gracious offer of forgiveness was always based on his character and his willingness to forgive sins (cf. Exod 34:9; Num 14:19–20). It is again God's character that stands behind his promise to forgive, and it will ultimately be revealed when God provides

---

7. On the importance of repentance, see Live the Story in Chapter 35, pp. 331–34.

8. See the discussion in Chapter 35 on 2 Chr 6:21, pp. 327–30, and Sklar's article, "Sin and Atonement," 467–91.

the "once-for-all" sacrifice required so that his forgiveness can be freely offered to those who repent.

God promises that he will "heal" their land (Heb. *r-p-*', 2 Chr 7:14). The promise of healing can refer to physical healing from a disease (Lev 13:18, 37; 14:3; 2 Chr 22:6, etc.), but sometimes sickness comes as a result of sin, in which case, physical restoration comes after the removal of God's wrath (Exod 15:26; Num 12:1–15; 1 Sam 6:3). Accordingly, the psalmist prays: "Have mercy on me, LORD; heal me, for I have sinned against you" (Ps 41:4; cf. Pss 103:3; 147:3; Isa 53:5). This kind of spiritual restoration ("healing") is seen in the story of Hezekiah, when he prays for northerners who humble themselves and turn from their evil ways (2 Chr 30:6–11, 20).[9] That God promises to heal *the land* suggests Israel's restoration is in view, rather than a physical healing from a disease.

Lastly, God promises that his eyes will be open and his ears will be attentive to the prayers offered in the temple, for he has chosen this as the place where his name will dwell (7:15–16). The prophet Daniel probably had this promise in mind when he prayed in Babylon, and notably, he did this in his room upstairs "where the windows opened toward Jerusalem" (Dan 6:10). Solomon's prayer gives the returnees further assurance that God hears the prayers of his people (cf. Ezra 9:5–15; Neh 1:4–11; 9:1–37).

God Warns Solomon and the People (7:17–22)

The focus now shifts to Solomon in particular, with the following divine promise: "'As for you, if you walk before me faithfully as David your father did, and do all I command, and observe my decrees and laws, I will establish your royal throne, as I covenanted with David your father when I said, 'You shall never fail to have a successor to rule over Israel'" (2 Chr 7:17–18). God had promised David that he would establish the throne of his son forever (v. 18; 1 Chr 17:12, 14), but the son who rules on God's throne is required to obey God's laws (28:5–7, 9; cf. Ps 89:30–37).[10] As Merrill writes, the Davidic covenant is "inextricably linked to the Mosaic because to disobey the latter is to jeopardize the former."[11] Solomon had been warned several times about the importance of following God's commands, not only by his father (1 Chr 22:11–13; 28:9), but also by God himself (1 Kgs 6:12–13 cf. 3:14; 9:2–9; 11:9). The Davidic king, who ruled over the kingdom of the LORD, was to rule

---

9. See the discussion in Chapter 59 on 2 Chr 30:18–21, pp. 505–7, for the practical outworking of 2 Chr 7:14.

10. See the discussion in Chapter 17 on 1 Chr 17.

11. Merrill, *1 & 2 Chronicles*, 360.

with justice and righteousness (2 Sam 8:15; 23:1–3; Ps 72:1–2; Jer 23:2–4). God's warning to Solomon is not an arbitrary requirement but is deeply rooted in Israel's traditions. It would be inconceivable, indeed, to have anyone other than a righteous Davidic king on the throne over God's kingdom—for he represents *God's rule* on earth.

God also warns Solomon what will happen if he forsakes God's laws and worships other gods: "I will uproot Israel from my land, which I have given them, and will reject this temple I have consecrated for my Name. I will make it a byword and an object of ridicule among all peoples" (2 Chr 7:20). Israel will be uprooted and brought into exile, and the temple will become a place of ruin and an object of ridicule. This verse foreshadows what will happen to Judah (1 Chr 9:1; 2 Chr 36:11–20), although at this point in the story, focus is on the flourishing kingdom under Solomon.

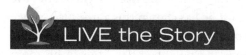

LIVE the Story

Cultivating a Posture of Humility before God

Self-humbling is the appropriate posture of those called by God's name. This can include admitting being in the wrong (2 Chr 12:6–7), repentance (30:11), humbly asking God for help (33:12–13), humbling one's pride (32:26), and submitting to the word of God (34:27). While circumstances may vary, what is common is an active, self-humbling posture before God in submission to his will. Williamson thus notes that the Chronicler is encouraging his readers to "return to God in self-humbling and prayer" so that God will "again intervene in their own generation as he had so manifestly done in the past in similar circumstances."[12]

This verse encourages us to return to God in "self-humbling and prayer," but it also raises a question about our own posture before God. We live in an age where individual rights have become a cardinal virtue, and oftentimes this is accompanied by arrogance and pride. David Brooks observes in his book *The Road to Character* that we have "seen a broad shift from a culture of humility to the culture of what you might call the Big Me, from a culture that encouraged people to think humbly of themselves to a culture that encouraged people to see themselves as the center of the universe."[13] The church is not exempt from this focus on the self and on individual rights, which can easily lead to pride

---

12. Williamson, "Eschatology in Chronicles," 153.
13. David Brooks, *The Road to Character* (New York: Random House, 2015), 6.

and arrogance. This kind of character trait manifests itself when we elevate our individual preferences to the detriment of the body. For example, many of us have probably been in churches where a major conflict occurs over issues like the color of the carpet, the size and location of the pulpit, whether there are hymns or contemporary songs, and the list could continue. It is important to recognize that these conflicts are not over doctrinal or moral issues, but they concern personal preferences, often embedded in our traditions; yet this is precisely where the cultural value of individual rights can creep into the church, causing division and conflict (cf. Jas 4:1–6). By way of contrast, the posture of self-humbling requires us to relinquish our individual rights and personal preferences for the sake of the body. This also means submission to pastoral leadership, as leaders are given the responsibility to shepherd the flock.

Jesus exemplified what it means to walk in humility and in submission to the will of God. He taught his disciples that they were first and foremost humble servants, for he came to serve, not to be served (Matt 20:28; Mark 10:45; John 13:1–17; cf. Phil 2:1–11). Those who exalted themselves would be humbled, but those who humbled themselves would be exalted (Matt 23:12). Jesus models for us what it means to humble ourselves and submit to the will of the Father (Phil 2:7–8); we are not to focus on our own interests but look to the interest of others. Rather than asserting our individual rights, even under the guise of religiosity, we are to clothe ourselves with humility and humble ourselves under the mighty hand of God (1 Pet 5:5–6; Jas 4:1–10). The posture of self-humbling is a lost virtue in our culture today, but as people called by God's name, we are called to cultivate a humble posture before him and in our church communities, reflecting the humility of our Lord.

God's Promise of Forgiveness and Healing Are Fulfilled in Jesus

God promises that if his people humble themselves, pray, and turn from our evil ways, he will forgive and heal.[14] This promise is encapsulated in Psalm 103, when the psalmist praises God, "who forgives all your sins and heals all your diseases" (v. 3). The generous offer of God to forgive and heal stands at the center of Chronicles; as Williamson notes, "there is an appeal here to the Chronicler's own readers to respond in like manner, for much of what follows is then designed to illustrate that no circumstances are too formidable to prevent God's immediate, direct and, if necessary, miraculous move to fulfil his promise."[15] This is especially seen in the forgiveness and healing under

---

14. On repentance, see Live the Story in Chapter 35, pp. 331–34.
15. Williamson, *1 and 2 Chronicles*, 225.

Hezekiah (see 2 Chr 30), but God's promise sets the stage for the forgiveness and healing that comes through Jesus, as seen in the description of his ministry:

> Jesus went throughout Galilee, teaching in their synagogues, proclaiming the good news of the kingdom, and healing every disease and sickness among the people. News about him spread all over Syria, and people brought to him all who were ill with various diseases, those suffering severe pain, the demon-possessed, those having seizures, and the paralyzed; and he healed them. (Matt 4:23–24)

Jesus's ministry was characterized by healing of the sick (8:1–17; 9:1–8, 18–38), with another summary statement that Jesus "went through all the towns and villages, teaching in their synagogues, proclaiming the good news of the kingdom and healing every disease and sickness" (9:35). Such healings were a demonstration that Jesus has authority to forgive sins (something only God could do), thus they were signs of spiritual restoration (cf. vv. 1–8). Jesus's healings signify that the kingdom of God has arrived, and they identify him as the promised Messiah (8:16–17; 11:1–5; cf. Isa 35:3–6; 53:4).

Jesus's healing ministry indicates that God's promise of forgiveness and healing is ultimately fulfilled through him. To apply the words of Williamson, the coming of the Messiah is God's "miraculous move to fulfil his promise."[16] Jesus's atoning sacrifice is the means by which God's forgiveness and restoration are available to all. Forgiveness of sins is offered freely to those who repent and believe in Jesus (John 3:16; Acts 5:31; 20:21; 1 Cor 15:3–4; 1 John 1:9–10; 2:2). This is the good news of the gospel that is anticipated in God's promise to Solomon in 2 Chronicles 7:14. God's people are characterized as those who have been forgiven by God and who freely extend forgiveness to others (Matt 18:21–35; Luke 17:3–4; cf. Eph 4:32; Col 3:13). The church, comprised of sinners forgiven and restored, serves as an ongoing testimony that no circumstances are too difficult for our God.

The story of six-time Grammy award winner and lead vocalist for the Imperials, Russ Taff, is a powerful testimony of the forgiveness and healing found in Jesus. In a recent documentary, *Russ Taff: I Still Believe*, the singer and songwriter tells of his early years of abuse and childhood trauma that left him feeling worthless and deeply wounded.[17] Even though highly successful, he sought relief for his depression and aching soul through alcohol. After many

---

16. Ibid.

17. Documentary: *Russ Taff: I Still Believe*, released October, 2018; see https://www.youtube.com/watch?v=yJHiOeIDspg.

years of rehab and with the support of his wife and family, Russ recounts the time when he experienced God's inner healing and forgiveness—in a hospital room, while he was visiting an elderly pastor dying of cancer. Russ had been invited to minister to the pastor, but to his surprise, the pastor asked to pray for *him*. On his knees in the hospital room, Russ began to weep as he heard prayers and words of affirmation from this elderly pastor. His fatherly hands, tenderly touching his head, were like ointment on his wounded soul. That day, Russ experienced God's forgiveness, healing, and restoration. In his own words Russ testifies: "I am living proof that Jesus is still about his Father's business, one broken person at a time."[18] Russ was the leading vocalist for the Imperials. The song *Forgiven* that he had sung earlier in his life became his personal testimony. He experienced what Solomon saw from afar, that God "forgives and forgets." Russ discovered how good it could be to stand in God's presence totally free—for he'd been *forgiven*.

---

18. Ibid.

LISTEN to the Story

¹At the end of twenty years, during which Solomon built the temple of the LORD and his own palace, ²Solomon rebuilt the villages that Hiram had given him, and settled Israelites in them. ³Solomon then went to Hamath Zobah and captured it. ⁴He also built up Tadmor in the desert and all the store cities he had built in Hamath. ⁵He rebuilt Upper Beth Horon and Lower Beth Horon as fortified cities, with walls and with gates and bars, ⁶as well as Baalath and all his store cities, and all the cities for his chariots and for his horses—whatever he desired to build in Jerusalem, in Lebanon and throughout all the territory he ruled.

⁷There were still people left from the Hittites, Amorites, Perizzites, Hivites and Jebusites (these people were not Israelites). ⁸Solomon conscripted the descendants of all these people remaining in the land—whom the Israelites had not destroyed—to serve as slave labor, as it is to this day. ⁹But Solomon did not make slaves of the Israelites for his work; they were his fighting men, commanders of his captains, and commanders of his chariots and charioteers. ¹⁰They were also King Solomon's chief officials—two hundred and fifty officials supervising the men.

¹¹Solomon brought Pharaoh's daughter up from the City of David to the palace he had built for her, for he said, "My wife must not live in the palace of David king of Israel, because the places the ark of the LORD has entered are holy."

¹²On the altar of the LORD that he had built in front of the portico, Solomon sacrificed burnt offerings to the LORD, ¹³according to the daily requirement for offerings commanded by Moses for the Sabbaths, the New Moons and the three annual festivals—the Festival of Unleavened Bread, the Festival of Weeks and the Festival of Tabernacles. ¹⁴In keeping with the ordinance of his father David, he appointed the divisions of the priests for their duties, and the Levites to lead the praise and to assist the priests

according to each day's requirement. He also appointed the gatekeepers by divisions for the various gates, because this was what David the man of God had ordered. ¹⁵They did not deviate from the king's commands to the priests or to the Levites in any matter, including that of the treasuries.

¹⁶All Solomon's work was carried out, from the day the foundation of the temple of the LORD was laid until its completion. So the temple of the LORD was finished.

¹⁷Then Solomon went to Ezion Geber and Elath on the coast of Edom. ¹⁸And Hiram sent him ships commanded by his own men, sailors who knew the sea. These, with Solomon's men, sailed to Ophir and brought back four hundred and fifty talents of gold, which they delivered to King Solomon.

Listening to the Text in the Story: 1 Kings 9:10–28; Psalm 72:7–11

Now that the temple in Jerusalem has been built and dedicated, Solomon expands his kingdom by building defensive and storage cities in the north as far as Hamath, thereby establishing an extensive infrastructure required for his flourishing trade in horses. Central to Solomon's foreign policy were his international marriages that forged important alliances. His marriage to the daughter of Pharaoh would have been one of his prized accomplishments. As the kingdom expands under Solomon, it is important to recognize that it signals that the Davidic kingdom is extending to the ends of the earth. Psalm 72 describes the Davidic king's rule as follows:

> In his days may the righteous flourish and prosperity abound till the moon is no more. May he rule from sea to sea and from the River to the ends of the earth. May the desert tribes bow before him and his enemies lick the dust. May the kings of Tarshish and of distant shores bring tribute to him. May the kings of Sheba and Seba present him gifts. May all kings bow down to him and all nations serve him. . . . Long may he live! May gold from Sheba be given him. May people ever pray for him and bless him all day long. (Ps 72:7–11, 15)

The geographical expansion of Solomon's kingdom (2 Chr 8:3–6; 9:26), his acquisition of gold and exotic animals from distant lands (8:17–18; 9:21), and the treasures and expensive commodities he receives from foreign dignitaries

(9:1, 9, 13–14, 24) contribute to an idealized kingdom that reverberates with messianic expectations.

EXPLAIN the Story

Solomon's Territory Extended through Building Projects (8:1–11)

Solomon spent twenty years building the magnificent temple in Jerusalem along with his own royal palace (2 Chr 8:1; cf. 1 Kgs 6:38; 7:1). It is estimated that Jerusalem covered about thirty-two acres during this period.[1] Solomon had given cities to Hiram in exchange for the wood he had supplied for the temple (see 9:11–14), and he had received the city of Gezer from Pharaoh as a dowry for his daughter (vv. 16–17). The Chronicler omits these details and picks up the story with Solomon building cities he had received from Hiram, perhaps further contributing to the topic of gifts and tribute received from foreign kings (2 Chr 8:2; cf. 9:24).[2] Solomon expands the kingdom north by capturing Hamath (8:3; cf. 1 Chr 18:9–10); his store cities were strategically located to facilitate trade, along with Tadmor in the desert. Solomon's extensive trade in prized Anatolian horses would have required a substantial infrastructure and access to trade routes.[3] Control in the north testifies to the expansion of the borders of Israel (cf. 2 Kgs 14:28; 17:24; 1 Chr 18:3), indicating it had reached its ideal northern border under Solomon, as seen when people assemble from northern Hamath all the way to the southern brook of Egypt (2 Chr 7:8). Securing the kingdom was further achieved through fortifying the strategic cities of Upper and Lower Beth Horon (8:5; cf. Josh 10:10–11; 1 Sam 13:18), along with Balath.[4] Solomon built storage cities for his chariots and horses, "whatever he desired to build in Jerusalem, in Lebanon and throughout all the territory he ruled" (2 Chr 8:6). Excavations at Megiddo point to the presence of horse stables, and although dated to the ninth century BC, they highlight the kind of infrastructure required for Solomon's many horses and chariots.[5]

Solomon secures his labor force from among the Hittites, Amorites, Perizzites, Hivites, and Jebusites who had remained in the kingdom (2 Chr

---

1. Hoerth, *Archaeology & the Old Testament*, 284.
2. Williamson, *1 and 2 Chronicles*, 228.
3. See Ikeda, "Solomon's Trade in Horses and Chariots," 234–38.
4. See Dillard for a helpful discussion of these cities, *2 Chronicles*, 65.
5. See Hoerth, *Archaeology & the Old Testament*, 286–288. See also King and Stager, *Life in Biblical Israel*, 186–89.

8:7; cf. 2:17–18). Israel's history attests to the continuation of foreigners living among them, who became forced laborers (cf. Josh 16:10; 17:13; Judg 1:28, 30, etc.). Israelites were exempt from such labor (Lev 25:39, 42, 44), unless needed for limited periods (1 Kgs 5:13; 15:22). They did serve as his fighting men, and commanders and captains were chosen from among them (2 Chr 8:9–10).

The palace Solomon builds for Pharaoh's daughter is mentioned briefly (v. 11). When Solomon entered into a political alliance with the king of Egypt by marrying his daughter (1 Kgs 3:1), the city of Gezer had been given as a dowry (9:16). Solomon's marriage to the daughter of Pharaoh attests to his far-reaching power and influence,[6] yet reliance upon political alliances usually meant that the king was not trusting in the LORD (cf. 2 Chr 16:7; 18:1; 19:2, etc.). When read with the Kings account in view, we know that Solomon's foreign wives will ultimately be his undoing (1 Kgs 11:1–13). The statement that his Egyptian wife lived in a palace *outside* the City of David because she could not be in proximity to the ark seems to have disapproving overtones (2 Chr 8:11).

Regular Worship Established at the Jerusalem Temple (8:12–16)

Solomon sacrifices burnt offerings to the LORD on the altar he had built (2 Chr 8:12), and such offerings were central to Israel's religious festivals (vv. 12–13). Continuing what David had already established, priests, Levites, and gatekeepers are appointed to perform their sacred duties.[7] Now that regular worship has been established in the newly built temple, Solomon's work as temple-builder is complete (v. 16).

Solomon's International Trade (8:17–18)

Solomon travels further south to Ezion Geber and Elath, located near the Gulf of Aqabah (2 Chr 8:17). Solomon's alliance with Hiram includes a joint maritime venture as they seek precious gold from Ophir (v. 18). The location of Ophir is a matter of some debate,[8] with East Africa or Western Arabia as the two most likely options.[9] Known for its gold, precious stones, and algum wood, Ophir was well worth an extended voyage. Shipbuilding in the ancient

---

6. On such political alliances, see Malamat, "Aspects of the Foreign Policies," 8–17.

7. For an extensive description of temple personnel, see the discussions in Chapters 23–26 on 1 Chr 23–26.

8. See Dillard for the various views, *2 Chronicles*, 66. See also the discussion in Chapter 29 on 1 Chr 29:4–5, pp. 277–78.

9. Kenneth A. Kitchen, "Sheba and Arabia," in Handy, *The Age of Solomon*, 143–45.

Near East has a long history, seen especially in artistic representations of boats in Egypt and Mesopotamia.[10] A sailing ship bearing a Hebrew inscription dated to the eighth to seventh century BC found on a miniscule seal may well represent an Israelite ship (cf. 20:36–37).[11] Since the Phoenicians were the maritime experts, Solomon wisely secures Hiram and his men for the expedition. The success of the expedition is seen in the 450 talents of gold brought to Solomon (8:18).

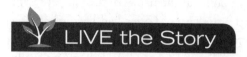 LIVE the Story

Using One's Resources to Glorify God—Not the Self

Solomon's flourishing kingdom has been highlighted in this chapter, with his building activities, his many horses and chariots, and his trade alliances resulting in an abundance of gold being brought into Jerusalem. Solomon's kingdom is clearly prosperous, yet we need to bear in mind that Moses had warned Israel many years earlier that the king was not to acquire "great numbers of horses for himself" (Deut 17:16).[12] Nor was he to take "many wives" or "accumulate large amounts of silver and gold" (v. 17). McConville rightly observes that Israelite kings were constrained in three areas that forbade trade with Egypt, acquiring a large harem, and accruing wealth. He notes that each of these "relates to established prerogatives of kings in the military, economic and political spheres, in all of which the king was supreme."[13] McConville notes further: "By conventional standards, therefore, these were the marks of success. And by them no Israelite king was more successful than Solomon."[14] As we have seen, these are precisely what characterizes Solomon's reign: he acquires many horses for himself (2 Chr 1:14, 16–17; 9:25), he has many wives (8:11; see also 1 Kgs 11:1), and he has gold and silver in abundance

---

10. On the maritime trade of the Phoenicians, see Chapters 30 and 31 on 2 Chr 1–2.

11. Robert R. Stieglitz, "Long Distance Seafaring in the Ancient Near East," 134–42, esp. 139.

12. On the negative view of horses in the prophets and psalms, see King and Stager, *Life in Biblical Israel*, 115. They note also that Israel's kings rode on donkeys or mules when performing royal functions (cf. 1 Kgs 1:33; Zech 9:9; Matt 21:5) and cite a text from Mari that suggests this was a practice known outside Israel. Mari is an ancient city located in northern Syria that has a rich history dating back to the third millennium BC. Thousands of administrative and economic texts unearthed at the site provide important information about economic, political, and religious life from the region.

13. J. Gordon McConville, *Deuteronomy*, Apollos Old Testament Commentary (Downers Grove, IL: InterVarsity Press, 2002), 294.

14. Ibid.

(2 Chr 8:17–18; 9:13–14, 20, 21). By way of contrast, David gives generously of all his treasures during the final years of his life (1 Chr 29). The final chapters in Solomon's life draw attention to his accumulation of wealth and the fame that comes as a result (seen in the next chapter as well), yet there is no reference to Solomon seeking the Lord, as he did early in his reign (2 Chr 1:5). Solomon is a highly successful king according to the ancient profile of a king, yet there is no affirmation about his *character*, as one finds with other kings. Compare what is said about Hezekiah's reign:

> This is what Hezekiah did throughout Judah, doing what was good and right and faithful before the Lord his God. In everything that he undertook in the service of God's temple and in obedience to the law and the. commands, he sought his God and worked wholeheartedly. And so he prospered. (31:20–21)

In fact, these kind of positive assessments of kings are made throughout Chronicles (14:2; 17:3–4; 24:2; 25:2; 26:4–5; 29:2; 34:2), but they are conspicuously absent in this chapter. We are reminded that success and prosperity can quickly lead to ruin when not accompanied by devotion to the Lord. Solomon's life serves as a warning for us today. While God may grant some of us wealth, which may even lead to an increase in status and power, we need to cultivate a posture of humility and recognize that everything belongs to God.

The book by John Rinehart, *Gospel Patrons*, was noted earlier. Rinehart traces the lives of three highly successful people who were known for their generosity. The third patron in Rinehart's book is John Thorton, a successful and wealthy businessman who became the gospel patron of the famous hymn writer John Newton. In a letter, he writes to Newton about his own devotional reading:

> I have been indulging this morning in a mediation and prayer and was glad to remain quiet till noon and devote a few hours to the remembrance of Proverbs 10:22, "The blessing of the Lord makes rich, and He adds no sorrow with it," which I can put my amen to. You will, I dare say, help us with your prayers. May the Lord keep every one of us looking with a single eye to Him, that we may not disgrace the holy profession.[15]

---

15. Cited by Rinehart, *Gospel Patrons*, 107.

Newton responds: "How worthless will money be found by those who over-value it now, in the hour of death and in the day of judgment. The hour is coming when everything else will be trifling and vain, but not so the knowl-edge and service of Jesus."[16]

The sense one gains from the story of Solomon is that his focus is on accruing wealth and prestige. By way of contrast, his father David never forgot his humble beginnings and God's call upon his life. At the end of his life, he was grateful for all that God had done, and he willingly offered his precious gifts unto the LORD (1 Chr 29). The life of Solomon serves both as a warning against self-reliance and an encouragement for us to cultivate thankfulness and generosity so that we might focus on God's glory, not our own. In the final analysis, money and fame will be found worthless, but as Thorton reminds us, "not so the knowledge and service of Jesus."

16. Ibid. For more information, see https://www.gospelpatrons.org/.

LISTEN to the Story

¹When the queen of Sheba heard of Solomon's fame, she came to Jerusalem to test him with hard questions. Arriving with a very great caravan—with camels carrying spices, large quantities of gold, and precious stones—she came to Solomon and talked with him about all she had on her mind. ²Solomon answered all her questions; nothing was too hard for him to explain to her. ³When the queen of Sheba saw the wisdom of Solomon, as well as the palace he had built, ⁴the food on his table, the seating of his officials, the attending servants in their robes, the cupbearers in their robes and the burnt offerings he made at the temple of the LORD, she was overwhelmed.

⁵She said to the king, "The report I heard in my own country about your achievements and your wisdom is true. ⁶But I did not believe what they said until I came and saw with my own eyes. Indeed, not even half the greatness of your wisdom was told me; you have far exceeded the report I heard. ⁷How happy your people must be! How happy your officials, who continually stand before you and hear your wisdom! ⁸Praise be to the LORD your God, who has delighted in you and placed you on his throne as king to rule for the LORD your God. Because of the love of your God for Israel and his desire to uphold them forever, he has made you king over them, to maintain justice and righteousness."

⁹Then she gave the king 120 talents of gold, large quantities of spices, and precious stones. There had never been such spices as those the queen of Sheba gave to King Solomon.

¹⁰(The servants of Hiram and the servants of Solomon brought gold from Ophir; they also brought algumwood and precious stones. ¹¹The king used the algumwood to make steps for the temple of the LORD and for the royal palace, and to make harps and lyres for the musicians. Nothing like them had ever been seen in Judah.)

¹²King Solomon gave the queen of Sheba all she desired and asked for; he gave her more than she had brought to him. Then she left and returned with her retinue to her own country.

¹³The weight of the gold that Solomon received yearly was 666 talents, ¹⁴not including the revenues brought in by merchants and traders. Also all the kings of Arabia and the governors of the territories brought gold and silver to Solomon.

¹⁵King Solomon made two hundred large shields of hammered gold; six hundred shekels of hammered gold went into each shield. ¹⁶He also made three hundred small shields of hammered gold, with three hundred shekels of gold in each shield. The king put them in the Palace of the Forest of Lebanon.

¹⁷Then the king made a great throne covered with ivory and overlaid with pure gold. ¹⁸The throne had six steps, and a footstool of gold was attached to it. On both sides of the seat were armrests, with a lion standing beside each of them. ¹⁹Twelve lions stood on the six steps, one at either end of each step. Nothing like it had ever been made for any other kingdom. ²⁰All King Solomon's goblets were gold, and all the household articles in the Palace of the Forest of Lebanon were pure gold. Nothing was made of silver, because silver was considered of little value in Solomon's day. ²¹The king had a fleet of trading ships manned by Hiram's servants. Once every three years it returned, carrying gold, silver and ivory, and apes and baboons.

²²King Solomon was greater in riches and wisdom than all the other kings of the earth. ²³All the kings of the earth sought audience with Solomon to hear the wisdom God had put in his heart. ²⁴Year after year, everyone who came brought a gift—articles of silver and gold, and robes, weapons and spices, and horses and mules.

²⁵Solomon had four thousand stalls for horses and chariots, and twelve thousand horses, which he kept in the chariot cities and also with him in Jerusalem. ²⁶He ruled over all the kings from the Euphrates River to the land of the Philistines, as far as the border of Egypt. ²⁷The king made silver as common in Jerusalem as stones, and cedar as plentiful as sycamore-fig trees in the foothills. ²⁸Solomon's horses were imported from Egypt and from all other countries.

²⁹As for the other events of Solomon's reign, from beginning to end, are they not written in the records of Nathan the prophet, in the prophecy of Ahijah the Shilonite and in the visions of Iddo the seer concerning Jeroboam son of Nebat? ³⁰Solomon reigned in Jerusalem over all Israel forty years. ³¹Then he rested with his ancestors and was buried in the city of David his father. And Rehoboam his son succeeded him as king.

Listening to the Text in the Story: 1 Kings 10:1–13; 11:41–43; Psalm 72; Isaiah 60:1–6

As Solomon's reign is drawing to a close, focus turns to the wealth of nations that streams into Jerusalem as Solomon's fame extends beyond Israel's borders. Since some of the less favorable stories are omitted (cf. 1 Kgs 11:1–40), some scholars conclude that the Chronicler has an idealistic view of Solomon. Yet the Chronicler's presentation of Solomon in this chapter is not simply to gloss over his sins, but rather, focus is on God's name extending to the nations, which provides vision and hope for the returnees living amidst a vast Persian Empire. Psalm 72 envisions that the Davidic king's rule will extend to the ends of the earth. Kings from Sheba and Seba come bearing gifts, and nations bow down before the king (Ps 72:8–11, 15). As nations are drawn to the glory of Zion, God's praises reach to the ends of the earth (Pss 48:10; 100:1; Isa 62:7). The prophet Isaiah similarly envisages that the wealth of nations will stream into Zion as foreign kings come from afar to see God's glory (60:3–5; cf. 61:6; 66:18–19). The prophet mentions gold and incense coming from Sheba: "And all from Sheba will come, bearing gold and incense and proclaiming the praise of the LORD" (60:6). This is the vision that reverberates throughout this chapter, underscoring that God is accomplishing his kingdom purposes in spite of human failure.

EXPLAIN the Story

The Visit by the Queen of Sheba (9:1–12)

The story begins with the queen of Sheba hearing about the fame of Solomon (2 Chr 9:1). She makes a lengthy journey to Jerusalem, traversing some 1,500 miles through the desert with her extensive caravan. The queen does not come empty-handed, however, for camels carry spices, and large quantities of gold and precious stones are among her gifts.[1] Camels were ideal for long-distance travel since they were able to carry aromatics and other exotic products across dry and hot deserts. Royal caravans are known in antiquity, such as the Hittite prince's visit to Egypt in the thirteenth century BC and the journey of the Babylonian king Nabonidus, who travelled to Western Arabia.[2] Sheba is identified as ancient Saba of Yemen, located in the southwestern Arabian Peninsula, known for its trade in incense and other aromatics and exotic products.[3] The rapid rise of the camel for long-distance travel in Western Arabia would have fostered trade and commerce in the region.[4] The queen travels to Jerusalem with her caravan to hear Solomon's wisdom firsthand. She may also have been concerned about Solomon's exploits in Ophir that were encroaching on her own trade in the region.[5] After hearing Solomon's wisdom and seeing his lavish spread of food, his richly clothed servants and cupbearers, and the burnt offerings he made in the temple (v. 4), she stands amazed before the king. All that she sees confirms the report that she had heard, and indeed, it exceeds it (vv. 5–6). Solomon's fame has surely extended to the nations!

Reminiscent of Hiram's affirmation of the LORD (2 Chr 2:11–12), the queen of Sheba gives words of praise in recognition of Solomon's kingship: "Praise be to the LORD your God, who has delighted in you and placed you on his throne as king to rule for the LORD your God. Because of the love of your God for Israel and his desire to uphold them forever, he has made you king over them, to maintain justice and righteousness" (9:8). Her affirmation contributes to the international theme in Chronicles, and it signifies that worship of the LORD is extending afar to the nations. The Chronicler identifies Solomon's throne as the LORD's throne (v. 8; cf. 1 Kgs 10:9, "the throne of Israel"), which is consistent with his theology elsewhere (1 Chr 17:14; 28:5; 29:23; 2 Chr 13:8). Dillard comments on the significance of this for the post-exilic community, noting that "Israel may be under foreign domination (Persia), but the kingdom remains secure; God always was and remains the real king of Israel, even when no descendant of David sits on the throne,

---

1. For a rich history of Sheba and Arabia, especially as it relates to the period of the monarchy, see Kitchen, "Sheba and Arabia," in Handy, *The Age of Solomon*, 126–53. Kitchen also discusses the identity of the Queen of Sheba and the location of Ophir. See also the discussion in Chapter 29 on 1 Chr 29:4–5, pp. 277–78.

2. Kitchen, "Sheba and Arabia," 142.

3. Ibid., 128.

4. Ibid., 135–36.

5. Ibid., 138–39.

and he promises that the kingdom will endure forever (9:8)."[6] The queen of Sheba gives 120 talents of gold, an abundance of spices, and precious stones to Solomon (9:9). Her gifts further contribute to the gold, algum trees, and precious stones that Hiram and his servants had brought to Solomon (v. 10; cf. 8:18); they were used to make the steps for the temple and palace, along with lyres and harps (9:11). Having travelled from afar, the queen of Sheba prepares to return home. Her generosity is met with reciprocity, for Solomon gives her everything that she desires, resulting in her leaving Jerusalem with more than she had brought with her (v. 12).

Solomon's Accumulation of Wealth and His Extravagant Throne (9:13–24)

Solomon accumulates an abundance of gold, with a yearly amount of 666 talents (2 Chr 9:13). His wealth increases further as revenue comes from traders and merchants, along with gold and silver brought by kings of Arabia and governors (v. 14). While the amount of gold might seem exorbitant when calculating these amounts in today's currency,[7] Kitchen notes that Tiglath-pileser II received 150 talents of gold from Metten II of Tyre, and the annual revenue the Persian Empire received from the Indus Basin was 360 talents of gold.[8] Set in its ancient context, such large quantities of gold are not inconceivable. In antiquity, high quantities of gold were stored in palaces and used to embellish temples for the gods.[9] Millard notes, for example, that Amenophis III boasts of giving the equivalent of 2.24 tons of refined gold to the temple of Montu in Karnak, and Tuthmosis II donated the equivalent of 13.6 tons to the temple of Amun in Karnak.[10] Millard gives other examples that demonstrate that the amount of gold Solomon receives is not without parallel in the ancient world. Solomon uses the contributions he receives to make six hundred large shields and three hundred smaller shields, all of hammered gold, which were put in the Palace of the Forest of Lebanon (v. 16; cf. 1 Kgs 7:1–12). These shields were most likely displayed in his palace, analogous to the golden shields that were on display in the shrine of Sargon II.[11]

Solomon's costly throne was embellished with an ivory veneer and overlaid

---

6. Dillard, *2 Chronicles*, 72.

7. Boda estimates Solomon's 666 talents to be valued at a staggering $879,120,000 in current rates (when writing in 2015), and Solomon's large shields would have cost $60,000 each (Boda, *1–2 Chronicles*, 371).

8. Kitchen, "Sheba and Arabia," in Handy, *The Age of Solomon*, 147.

9. See Millard, "King Solomon in his Ancient Context," 30–42.

10. Ibid., 40.

11. Ibid., 37.

with pure gold (2 Chr 9:17). In the ancient world, elaborate thrones and couches made of wood were not only covered with ivory veneer, but some were also embellished with precious stones and golden foil.[12] Solomon's throne had six steps and a footstool of gold. It was flanked by two lions on each side that supported the arms of the throne, and twelve carved lions stood on each side of the steps (vv. 18–19). The opulence of the period is further seen in Solomon's drinking vessels made of gold (v. 20). Golden vessels are mentioned in letters from Mari, and golden bowls and dishes are among the gifts listed in the El-Armana letters.[13] Kings in antiquity would have owned precious golden vessels, and Solomon is surely among them. Solomon received many luxury items from distant lands through his maritime venture with Hiram, enabling him to acquire gold, silver, ivory, and exotic animals (v. 21; cf. 8:18). The Chronicler summarizes this period, noting that Solomon "was greater in riches and wisdom than all the other kings of the earth" (9:22). Foreign kings sought audience with Solomon so that they might hear the wisdom God had put in his heart. Those who came to Solomon brought gifts of silver, gold, robes, weapons, spices, horses, and mules. As a result of Solomon's fame, the wealth of the nations is streaming into Jerusalem!

Solomon's Accumulation of Horses from the Nations and His Rule Extended Afar (9:25–28)

The Chronicler returns to the topic of Solomon's horse stalls, chariots, and horsemen, which were stationed in chariot cites in addition to those stationed in Jerusalem (2 Chr 9:25).[14] Reference to Solomon's horses at this point in the narrative forms a delightful literary inclusio (cf. 1:14, 16–17). Solomon's extensive kingdom is highlighted in the statement that he ruled "over all the kings from the Euphrates River to the land of the Philistines, as far as the border of Egypt" (9:26), further contributing to messianic expectations that a Davidic king's rule would extend to the ends of the earth (Ps 72:8; Zech 9:10).

The Final Years of Solomon (9:29–31)

The reign of Solomon draws to a close with references to the records of Nathan the prophet, the prophecy of Ahijah, and the visions of Iddo the seer (cf. 1 Chr 29:29; 2 Chr 12:15). Conspicuously absent from these closing remarks is any reference to Solomon's foreign marriages, his idolatrous practices, God's

---

12. Ibid., 37–38.
13. Ibid., 36–37.
14. The Chronicler appears to have combined two verses from Kings (1 Kgs 4:26 [MT 5:6]; 10:26). On this verse and some of the textual issues, see Japhet, *I & II Chronicles*, 642–43.

judgment, and the Edomite attack (1 Kgs 11:1–25). These stories were undoubtedly etched in Israel's history, and the Chronicler's terse reference to the prophecy of Ahijah is sufficient to recall these events (11:29–39). But focus is on the flourishing kingdom, reminding us that "despite Solomon's weaknesses, God was still working out his own purposes through him."[15] Selman's comments serve as a fitting conclusion to the reign of Solomon. The king dies and is buried (2 Chr 9:30–31), but one day, an even greater Solomon will arrive, and he will rule over God's everlasting kingdom.

LIVE the Story

A King Greater than Solomon Has Arrived

This chapter rehearses the many precious gifts Solomon had received from the queen of Sheba and from foreign dignitaries. As noted above, the prophets envisioned the time when tribute from the nations would stream into Zion (Isa 60:3–6; 61:6; 66:18–19). Gifts coming from Sheba are central to the expectation that nations would bow before the Davidic king (Ps 72:8–11, 15). These expensive gifts signal that God's praise is reaching the ends of the earth (Pss 48:10; 100:1; Isa 62:7). What is described in this chapter foreshadows what will take place when the ideal Davidic king rules on his throne. Gifts of gold, spices, and precious stones brought by the queen of Sheba point forward, therefore, to an even greater king who is worthy of greater glory and honor.

Some one thousand years later, Magi from the east are drawn to Jerusalem by a spectacular phenomenon in the sky that signals the birth of the Messiah. They make the arduous journey from afar so that they might worship the king. Upon arriving at the place where the child was, Matthew records that they "bowed down and worshiped him" (Matt 2:11), reminiscent of the angels who worship God when his firstborn comes into the world (Heb 1:6 cf. Luke 2:9–14). Yet the Magi from the east do no come empty-handed for, like the queen of Sheba, they bring gifts fitting for a king, as Matthew records: "Then they opened their treasures and presented him with gifts of gold, frankincense and myrrh" (2:11). Instead of bowing down before an earthly king, whose kingdom will not last, they bring precious gifts to the King of Kings, the true heir of the Davidic promises, whose everlasting kingdom will extend to the ends of the earth. Instead of seeing a glorious and lavishly decorated golden throne, they behold a child with his mother Mary. As the Magi bring gifts and

---

15. Selman, *1 Chronicles*, 251.

worship the king, they thereby signify that worship of the LORD is extending to the ends of the earth, and his kingdom is being exalted (Ps 72:8–11; cf. Mic 5:4; Zech 9:10).

Jesus's own ministry will begin with the royal announcement that the kingdom of God has arrived. Jesus is the king who is exalted above all kings and whose throne is everlasting. At his birth the angel announces: "He will be great and will be called the Son of the Most High. The Lord God will give him the throne of his father David, and he will reign over Jacob's descendants forever; his kingdom will never end" (Luke 1:32–33). As people from all nations worship the king, praises to God reach even to the ends of the earth (Pss 48:10; 100:1; Isa 62:7). Solomon's reign marks a time of flourishing of the kingdom, and he is even honored by a visit from the queen of Sheba, who comes from the ends of the earth to hear his wisdom (Matt 12:42). But Jesus exclaims that "now something greater than Solomon is here" (v. 42). His glory is far *greater* than the glory of Solomon's kingdom. He alone is worthy to receive glory and honor and thanks (Rev 4:9). With the saints of old, we bow down before the King who sits on the throne, casting our crowns before him, declaring that he alone is worthy (vv. 9–11). The hymn by Robert Grant, *O Worship the King*, which is a paraphrase of Psalm 104, lifts our hearts in praise to our King:

> O worship the King all glorious above,
> and gratefully sing his power and his love:
> our shield and defender, the Ancient of Days,
> pavilioned in splendor and girded with praise.
>
> O measureless Might, unchangeable Love,
> whom angels delight to worship above!
> Your ransomed creation, with glory ablaze,
> in true adoration shall sing to your praise![16]

Jesus is the King of Kings who fulfills God's promises of old. Regardless of our circumstances, the messianic hope embedded in the description of Solomon's reign reminds us that God's King, all glorious above, is enthroned on high, and his rule will one day extend to the ends of the earth.

---

16. Public domain; see https://www.jubilate.co.uk/songs/o_worship_the_king_all_glorious_above.

LISTEN to the Story

¹Rehoboam went to Shechem, for all Israel had gone there to make him king. ²When Jeroboam son of Nebat heard this (he was in Egypt, where he had fled from King Solomon), he returned from Egypt. ³So they sent for Jeroboam, and he and all Israel went to Rehoboam and said to him: ⁴"Your father put a heavy yoke on us, but now lighten the harsh labor and the heavy yoke he put on us, and we will serve you."

⁵Rehoboam answered, "Come back to me in three days." So the people went away.

⁶Then King Rehoboam consulted the elders who had served his father Solomon during his lifetime. "How would you advise me to answer these people?" he asked.

⁷They replied, "If you will be kind to these people and please them and give them a favorable answer, they will always be your servants."

⁸But Rehoboam rejected the advice the elders gave him and consulted the young men who had grown up with him and were serving him. ⁹He asked them, "What is your advice? How should we answer these people who say to me, 'Lighten the yoke your father put on us'?"

¹⁰The young men who had grown up with him replied, "The people have said to you, 'Your father put a heavy yoke on us, but make our yoke lighter.' Now tell them, 'My little finger is thicker than my father's waist. ¹¹My father laid on you a heavy yoke; I will make it even heavier. My father scourged you with whips; I will scourge you with scorpions.'"

¹²Three days later Jeroboam and all the people returned to Rehoboam, as the king had said, "Come back to me in three days." ¹³The king answered them harshly. Rejecting the advice of the elders, ¹⁴he followed the advice of the young men and said, "My father made your yoke heavy; I will make it even heavier. My father scourged you with whips; I will scourge you with scorpions." ¹⁵So the king did not listen to the people, for this turn of events

was from God, to fulfill the word the LORD had spoken to Jeroboam son of Nebat through Ahijah the Shilonite.

[16]When all Israel saw that the king refused to listen to them, they answered the king:

> "What share do we have in David,
>   what part in Jesse's son?
> To your tents, Israel!
>   Look after your own house, David!"

So all the Israelites went home. [17]But as for the Israelites who were living in the towns of Judah, Rehoboam still ruled over them.

[18]King Rehoboam sent out Adoniram, who was in charge of forced labor, but the Israelites stoned him to death. King Rehoboam, however, managed to get into his chariot and escape to Jerusalem. [19]So Israel has been in rebellion against the house of David to this day.

Listening to the Text in the Story: 1 Kings 11–12; 14:21–24

After the death of Solomon, his son Rehoboam becomes king, but this period is marked by the rebellion of the northern tribes that ushers in the divided kingdom. God had warned Solomon that his kingdom would be established forever, but only if he followed his commandments (2 Chr 7:17–22). Central to God's law was the prohibition against idolatry (Exod 20:3–5), yet Solomon flagrantly disobeys this command (1 Kgs 11:1–8). God had warned Solomon that his kingdom would be torn away from him, yet in spite of his egregious sins, the kingdom would not be entirely wiped out because of God's promises to David (vv. 9–13). The Chronicler does not mention Solomon's idolatry, but it was firmly etched in the history of God's people (Neh 13:26; cf. 2 Chr 9:29; 10:15). The prophet Ahijah had announced that the kingdom would be torn away from Solomon and that a military leader named Jeroboam would be given ten tribes (1 Kgs 11:29–39; cf. 2 Chr 10:15). With these prophetic words casting a foreboding shadow, Solomon had sought to kill Jeroboam, but he had escaped and found refuge in Egypt. Jeroboam had remained there until Solomon's death (1 Kgs 11:40; 2 Chr 10:2), but with Rehoboam now on the throne, the story is picked up with Jeroboam's arrival at Shechem.

EXPLAIN the Story

All Israel Gathers to Make Rehoboam King (10:1–2)

All Israel gathers at Shechem to make Rehoboam king (2 Chr 10:1). Shechem was located in northern Israel in the hill country of Ephraim (Josh 20:7; 1 Chr 6:67; 7:28). Shechem had an important and longstanding history, beginning with the patriarchs (Gen 12:6–7; 33:18–20). Joshua had also renewed the covenant at this location (Josh 8:30–35; 24:1–24). Given its religious significance, it is not surprising that all Israel gathers there, but David had been anointed king at *Hebron*, located in the territory of Judah (1 Chr 11:1–4). That all Israel now gathers in the northern territory of *Ephraim* is not promising for Rehoboam, especially since this was Jeroboam's own tribal territory (1 Kgs 11:26). With the prophecy of Ahijah lingering in the background and waiting to unfold, Jeroboam's arrival at Shechem has ominous overtones for Rehoboam.

Jeroboam and the People Request That Their Load Be Lightened (10:3–5)

Without further notice, Jeroboam assumes a leadership role as he and the people address the issue of hard labor. The extensive building activities of Solomon had placed a heavy burden on the people (cf. 1 Kgs 5:13–14; 2 Chr 2:17–18). Extensive work had been done over a period of seven years to construct the lavish temple in Jerusalem (1 Kg 6; 2 Chr 3–5), and another thirteen years had been spent constructing the royal palace. While artisans and skilled workmen had been employed, compulsory labor was necessary to complete such an extensive building project. Even though the burden fell on foreigners (8:7–9), the northern tribes of Israel were not exempt from involuntary labor (1 Kgs 5:13). While it was not permanent servitude, it had led to political unrest and tension in the kingdom. With these building projects completed and a new king on the throne, the people seek relief by asking that their workload be lightened (2 Chr 10:3–4). Their description of their work as a "heavy yoke" evokes the picture of oxen bearing a yoke around their neck (cf. Num 19:2; Deut 21:3), recalling Israel's many years of servitude in Egypt (Lev 26:13; Jer 2:20). As the people bring their request to Rehoboam, they give the king an ultimatum—they will serve the king, but only if their heavy yoke is lifted. Upon hearing their terms, Rehoboam agrees to consider the matter over a period of three days.

The Elders Give Rehoboam Counsel to Ensure a Smooth Transition (10:6–7)

Rehoboam seeks counsel from his elders who had served his father Solomon. Elders had been appointed at the time of Moses to share the leadership responsibilities (Exod 24:1; Num 11:16–30; cf. Josh 24:1), and they continue to have a leadership role in Israel (1 Sam 8:4; 2 Sam 3:17; 1 Chr 11:3). The elders counsel Rehoboam to treat the people well and give them a favorable answer (2 Chr 10:6–7). They wisely discern that a more lenient response by the king will secure the loyalty of the northern tribes and thereby ensure the stability of the kingdom.

Rehoboam Listens to the Advice of the Young Men (10:8–15)

Rehoboam foolishly rejects their counsel and seeks advice from young men who had grown up with him (2 Chr 10:8-9). With hubris they respond by telling the young king he should increase the workload. They even put words into the king's mouth, telling him that he should assert his right as king and make their yoke even heavier (vv. 10b–11)! The young men fail to discern that Rehoboam needed to secure the loyalty of the northern tribes and that subjecting them to labor would incite only rebellion. With the passing of three days, Jeroboam and all Israel return to Rehoboam, but the king foolishly listens to their advice instead of his elders (vv. 12–14). Rehoboam's rejection of wise counsel and his failure to discern what kind of leadership was needed result in the division of the kingdom (v. 15). The reader is to discern in these circumstances the divine orchestration of events, for the Chronicler notes that "this turn of events was from God, to fulfill the word the LORD had spoken to Jeroboam son of Nebat through Ahijah the Shilonite" (v. 15; cf. 1 Kgs 12:15).

The Division of the Kingdom Is in Fulfillment of God's Word through Ahijah (10:16–19)

When the people hear that their request has been rejected, they declare that they will have nothing to do with the house of David (2 Chr 10:16). They return to their tents with the curt statement that David was to look after his own house. The unrest among Israel has now become an outright rebellion. Recognizing the urgency of the situation, Rehoboam sends for Adoniram who was in charge of the forced laborers (v. 18; cf. 1 Kgs 4:6; 5:14), perhaps not the wisest choice, since compulsory labor had been the source of their discontent. The unrest that had been percolating under the surface violently erupts as the people stone Adoniram to death. Rehoboam hastily flees to Jerusalem in his chariot (2 Chr 10:18), and a final statement is made that "Israel has been in rebellion against the house of David to this day" (v. 19).

LIVE the Story

Failure to Listen to Wise Counsel

At the beginning of his reign, Rehoboam faced an uprising among his ranks. His response to the challenging circumstances had far-reaching ramifications for his kingdom. Rehoboam's initial instinct was to seek advice from his elders, which is consistent with the book of Proverbs that emphasizes the importance of seeking wisdom: "The way of fools seems right to them, but the wise listen to advice" (Prov 12:15). Another proverb similarly says, "Listen to advice and accept discipline, and at the end you will be counted among the wise" (19:20; cf. 20:18). Instead of listening to wise counsel, Rehoboam solicits ungodly advice from his younger friends. Their response reeks of hubris, as they tell the king that he can do whatever he pleases. Rehoboam failed to recognize that although king, he did not have unbridled authority.[1] He was required to humble himself and not elevate himself above his fellow Israelites. Rehoboam's friends overestimate his authority and assume that leadership was about position and power. They failed to understand that the hallmark of godly leadership was humility and the ability to listen to wise counsel. Godly wisdom was required so that they might know what to do (cf. 1 Chr 12:32). Throughout Chronicles the character of a king is seen in how he responds to counsel, whether he receives advice from people (13:1; 2 Chr 20:21; 30:2, 23; 32:3) or from prophets (25:16; cf. 1 Kgs 1:12). This is especially the case with prophets since they speak God's word to the king, and failure to give heed will lead to God's judgment. Rehoboam was a self-made man who does whatever he pleases. His failure to listen to wise counsel will lay the seed for his later rebellion when he forsakes the law of God (2 Chr 12:1).

This story serves as a reminder that we are required to humbly submit to others in the Christian community, whether a pastor, elder, teacher, or Christian friend. We need each other because we are all prone to pride and deception. It is not uncommon when hearing about a Christian leader whose sinful behavior has been exposed that warnings had been given by staff and by multiple church members, sometimes repeatedly, yet to no avail. This reminds us of the importance of humility, which includes a willingness to receive words

---

1. See the discussion in Chapter 55 on 2 Chr 26:16–23, pp. 477–78.

of warning and rebuke from others in the Christian community. We are all servants of Christ. Humility and submission to Christ ought to characterize our relationships with each other, which includes listening to advice and receiving rebuke from fellow believers (Matt 18:15–17; Luke 17:3; 1 Tim 5:20; Jas 5:19–20). We are called to "teach and admonish one another with all wisdom" (Col 3:16) so that the message of Christ might dwell among us. James teaches that the wisdom that comes from heaven is "first of all pure; then peace-loving, considerate, submissive, full of mercy and good fruit, impartial and sincere" (Jas 3:17). This is the wisdom Rehoboam needed but failed to seek. This kind of wisdom requires a posture of humility so that we might receive a word of correction, through others and through God's word (2 Tim 4:2). The story of Rehoboam underscores the consequences of failing to listen to wise counsel, but as we will see shortly, this was not an isolated incident, exposing further the posture of his heart.

CHAPTER 40

2 Chronicles 11:1–23

 LISTEN to the Story

¹When Rehoboam arrived in Jerusalem, he mustered Judah and Benjamin—a hundred and eighty thousand able young men—to go to war against Israel and to regain the kingdom for Rehoboam.

²But this word of the LORD came to Shemaiah the man of God: ³"Say to Rehoboam son of Solomon king of Judah and to all Israel in Judah and Benjamin, ⁴"This is what the LORD says: Do not go up to fight against your fellow Israelites. Go home, every one of you, for this is my doing.'" So they obeyed the words of the LORD and turned back from marching against Jeroboam.

⁵Rehoboam lived in Jerusalem and built up towns for defense in Judah: ⁶Bethlehem, Etam, Tekoa, ⁷Beth Zur, Soko, Adullam, ⁸Gath, Mareshah, Ziph, ⁹Adoraim, Lachish, Azekah, ¹⁰Zorah, Aijalon and Hebron. These were fortified cities in Judah and Benjamin. ¹¹He strengthened their defenses and put commanders in them, with supplies of food, olive oil and wine. ¹²He put shields and spears in all the cities, and made them very strong. So Judah and Benjamin were his.

¹³The priests and Levites from all their districts throughout Israel sided with him. ¹⁴The Levites even abandoned their pasturelands and property and came to Judah and Jerusalem, because Jeroboam and his sons had rejected them as priests of the LORD ¹⁵when he appointed his own priests for the high places and for the goat and calf idols he had made. ¹⁶Those from every tribe of Israel who set their hearts on seeking the LORD, the God of Israel, followed the Levites to Jerusalem to offer sacrifices to the LORD, the God of their ancestors. ¹⁷They strengthened the kingdom of Judah and supported Rehoboam son of Solomon three years, following the ways of David and Solomon during this time.

¹⁸Rehoboam married Mahalath, who was the daughter of David's son Jerimoth and of Abihail, the daughter of Jesse's son Eliab. ¹⁹She bore him sons: Jeush, Shemariah and Zaham. ²⁰Then he married Maakah daughter of Absalom, who bore him Abijah, Attai, Ziza and Shelomith. ²¹Rehoboam loved Maakah daughter of Absalom more than any of his other wives and concubines. In all, he had eighteen wives and sixty concubines, twenty-eight sons and sixty daughters.

²²Rehoboam appointed Abijah son of Maakah as crown prince among his brothers, in order to make him king. ²³He acted wisely, dispersing some of his sons throughout the districts of Judah and Benjamin, and to all the fortified cities. He gave them abundant provisions and took many wives for them.

Listening to the Text in the Story: 1 Kings 12:20–33; 14:21–31

Rehoboam now rules as king over a reduced Southern Kingdom, with ten tribes in the north. The tribes of Judah and Benjamin had rallied around David when Saul was king, requiring those from Benjamin to be disloyal to Saul, even though he was from their own tribe (1 Chr 12:16–18, 29). From the time of Rehoboam onward, the tribe of Benjamin joins the tribe of Judah to form the Southern Kingdom (2 Chr 11:12, 23; 14:8; 15:2, etc.), along with the tribe of Levi (11:13–14). Some from the northern tribes also join the Southern Kingdom (vv. 16–17), and their presence contributes to the theme of "all Israel" (cf. 15:9; 30:1, 10–11; 34:9). The returnees living in Jerusalem after the exile are from the tribes of Judah and Benjamin (1 Chr 9:3), along with Ephraim, Manasseh, and the Levites. The story of the Southern Kingdom is now taken up with Rehoboam, yet it is not off to a good start, for the king attempts to regain control of the northern tribes through military intervention. The unity of all Israel is an important theme that runs through Chronicles, yet reconciliation will not take place through military means but through prayer, repentance, and forgiveness (see 2 Chr 30).

 EXPLAIN the Story

Rehoboam Prepares for Battle against Israel, Obeys a Prophetic Rebuke (11:1–4)

Rehoboam had initially fled to Jerusalem after his officer who had over-seen his labor force was stoned to death (2 Chr 10:18). Upon arriving in

Jerusalem, he assembles thousands of military men from Judah and Benjamin to wage war against Israel so that his kingdom might be restored.[1] But the word of the LORD comes to Rehoboam through a prophet named Shemaiah, who gives the following warning: "This is what the LORD says: 'Do not go up to fight against your fellow Israelites. Go home, every one of you, for this is my doing'" (11:4). Given that the tribes of Israel all belonged to one family (1 Chr 2:1–2), Rehoboam is warned not to fight against his fellow Israelites, and he is to understand that these events are from God. Upon hearing these words, the king and the people give heed to the prophet and return to Jerusalem (2 Chr 11:4).

Rehoboam Fortifies His Kingdom (11:5–12)

Rehoboam focuses on building up and fortifying the kingdom. Fifteen cities are identified within the territory of Judah and Benjamin (2 Chr 11:6–10). Scholars have examined the geographical distribution of the cities to discern the rationale for the order of the list.[2] Japhet notes that cities are "situated at strategic points along major routes leading to the heart of the Judean hills, and the greatest attention is given to the western approaches, as the most common routes to Judah, from which danger was most imminent."[3] It is important to bear in mind that Shishak's attack against Jerusalem is described in the next chapter. This suggests that Rehoboam's fortifications were in anticipation of an Egyptian attack (cf. 12:4), although Japhet notes that he fortifies cities both before and after the attack.[4] Rehoboam stations officers at his fortified cities, and he ensures that they have ample supplies of food, oil, and wine, along with shields and spears (11:11–12).

Jeroboam Establishes His Rival Kingdom in the North (11:13–17)

Priests and Levites had been dispersed among the tribes of Israel in designated Levitical cities (1 Chr 6:54–81), but with idolatrous worship now established under Jeroboam, they return to Judah and Jerusalem, and Jeroboam appoints non-Levites as priests to officiate at the cult centers in Dan and Bethel

---

1. The text states he assembles 180,000 men, but we note elsewhere that the Hebrew word translated as "thousand" (Heb. *'eleph*) can refer to a smaller subdivision within a tribe, in which case the text would read that Rehoboam assembly 180 military units. See the discussion in Chapter 12 on 1 Chr 12:23–40, pp. 138–40.

2. See Klein, *2 Chronicles*, 169.

3. Japhet, *I & II Chronicles*, 665. Later, when the Cushites come against Asa, they arrive at Mareshah (14:10), thus suggesting its strategic location (11:8).

4. For a discussion of scholarly views, see ibid., 665–68. She argues that the description of the fortified cities in 2 Chr 11:5–12 is a summary of Rehoboam's building activities.

(cf. 1 Kgs 12:25–33). He makes two golden calves that are placed at Dan and Bethel, and he blasphemously identifies them as Israel's gods, saying: "Here are your gods, Israel, who brought you up out of Egypt" (v. 28; cf. Exod 32:4, 8). Included in their idolatrous worship was a goat idol (2 Chr 11:15), something strictly prohibited under the law (Lev 17:7). Amidst such flagrant idolatry, some from among the northern tribes set their hearts to seek the LORD, and they follow the Levites to Jerusalem, where they sacrifice to the LORD (2 Chr 11:16). They give their undivided support to Rehoboam, and the kingdom is strengthened (v. 17).

Rehoboam's Family (11:18–23)

The names of Rehoboam's wives and children that underscore family connections with members of David's royal household are given next (2 Chr 11:18–21). This is consistent with ancient Near Eastern practice among royalty to secure the royal blood line.[5] Rehoboam had eighteen wives and sixty concubines, fathering twenty-eight sons and sixty daughters (v. 21). Although it might seem like he is prospering under God's blessing, Moses had warned that the king was not to take multiple wives (Deut 17:17). Rehoboam's wife Maakah, identified as the daughter of Absalom, is especially loved by the king; he appoints her son, Abijah, as crown prince, for he intends him to be king (2 Chr 12:22; cf. 13:1–14:1). Rehoboam wisely disperses his sons throughout the territory of Judah and Benjamin to live in his fortified cities. He gives them provisions of food and takes many wives for them (v. 23).

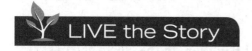

LIVE the Story

A United People of God

The division of the kingdom was a devastating and tragic event in light of the fact that all twelve tribes trace their ancestry back to the patriarch Jacob, who is known as Israel (1 Chr 2:1–2). Yet we are all too familiar with conflict between siblings from humanity's earliest period, as seen in the stories of Cain and Abel (Gen 4:1–16), Jacob and Esau (Gen 27–28), and Joseph and his brothers (Gen 37–50). This kind of familial estrangement that comes as a result of sin is now playing itself out on a national scale, as the twelve tribes of Israel divide into two kingdoms. Rehoboam had attempted to bring back the rebellious northern tribes by military force (2 Chr 11:1), yet this would have resulted in

---

5. Merrill, *1 & 2 Chronicles*, 389.

bloodshed, and Rehoboam is warned not to fight against his fellow Israelites (vv. 2–4; cf. 28:9–11). Reconciliation among the tribes would not take place by military force, but by humility, repentance, prayer, and forgiveness.[6] At the heart of the Chronicler's theology is the unwavering conviction that the twelve tribes were one people (1 Chr 1–9). God's vision for a restored and united people of God is an important message of the prophets (Jer 3:18; 50:4, 5; Ezek 36:10; 37:15–23; cf. Ps 133:1–3), and it is an important topic in Chronicles (cf. 1 Chr 9:3; 12:1–40; 2 Chr 30:1, 11, 18, etc.). This is why so many chapters are devoted to David and Solomon in Chronicles—they provide a vision for a unified people of God who are ruled by one king (cf. Ezek 34:23, 24; 37:22). The prophet's rebuke of Rehoboam contributes further to this vision, since God was opposed to brother fighting against brother.

The vision of a united people of God ultimately comes to fruition through the reconciling work of Jesus. Instead of the estrangement and hostility of Jew and Gentile, Jesus is creating "in himself one new humanity out of the two, thus making peace, and in one body to reconcile both of them to God through the cross, by which he put to death their hostility" (Eph 2:15–16). Paul writes to the church at Ephesus that they are "no longer foreigners and strangers, but fellow citizens with God's people and also members of his household" (v. 19). Jesus indeed prayed that his people might be one (John 17:11, 21–22). The condition of the human heart leads to conflict and estrangement among brothers and sisters, tribal groups, and nations, yet God's plan of redemption includes our restoration not only with God, but also with each other. While our contemporary culture elevates diversity as the supreme virtue, a biblical theology of diversity must be grounded in our unity in Christ. People from different races and ethnic groups are united together as they worship the one God (Rev 7:9–17). This theme reverberates throughout the Scriptures, and it ought to be reflected in our own lives and in our communities.

---

6. See the discussion in Chapter 59 on 2 Chr 30.

LISTEN to the Story

¹After Rehoboam's position as king was established and he had become strong, he and all Israel with him abandoned the law of the LORD. ²Because they had been unfaithful to the LORD, Shishak king of Egypt attacked Jerusalem in the fifth year of King Rehoboam. ³With twelve hundred chariots and sixty thousand horsemen and the innumerable troops of Libyans, Sukkites and Cushites that came with him from Egypt, ⁴he captured the fortified cities of Judah and came as far as Jerusalem.

⁵Then the prophet Shemaiah came to Rehoboam and to the leaders of Judah who had assembled in Jerusalem for fear of Shishak, and he said to them, "This is what the LORD says, 'You have abandoned me; therefore, I now abandon you to Shishak.'"

⁶The leaders of Israel and the king humbled themselves and said, "The LORD is just."

⁷When the LORD saw that they humbled themselves, this word of the LORD came to Shemaiah: "Since they have humbled themselves, I will not destroy them but will soon give them deliverance. My wrath will not be poured out on Jerusalem through Shishak. ⁸They will, however, become subject to him, so that they may learn the difference between serving me and serving the kings of other lands."

⁹When Shishak king of Egypt attacked Jerusalem, he carried off the treasures of the temple of the LORD and the treasures of the royal palace. He took everything, including the gold shields Solomon had made. ¹⁰So King Rehoboam made bronze shields to replace them and assigned these to the commanders of the guard on duty at the entrance to the royal palace. ¹¹Whenever the king went to the LORD's temple, the guards went with him, bearing the shields, and afterward they returned them to the guardroom.

¹²Because Rehoboam humbled himself, the LORD's anger turned from

him, and he was not totally destroyed. Indeed, there was some good in Judah.

¹³King Rehoboam established himself firmly in Jerusalem and continued as king. He was forty-one years old when he became king, and he reigned seventeen years in Jerusalem, the city the LORD had chosen out of all the tribes of Israel in which to put his Name. His mother's name was Naamah; she was an Ammonite. ¹⁴He did evil because he had not set his heart on seeking the LORD.

¹⁵As for the events of Rehoboam's reign, from beginning to end, are they not written in the records of Shemaiah the prophet and of Iddo the seer that deal with genealogies? There was continual warfare between Rehoboam and Jeroboam. ¹⁶Rehoboam rested with his ancestors and was buried in the City of David. And Abijah his son succeeded him as king.

Listening to the Text in the Story: 1 Kings 14:21–31; Karnak Stela of Shoshenq I

The story of the Southern Kingdom takes a turn for the worse when Rehoboam and all Israel forsake God's law. God sends Shishak, king of Egypt, against Judah, but the king and people humble themselves and the full wrath of God is averted. The Egyptian king Shoshenq I (known as Shishak in the Bible) was a military commander under Psusenes II, but when Psusenes died without an heir, Shoshenq I assumed the throne (945–924 BC). The Karnak Stela of Shoshenq I recounts his campaign in Palestine, with 175 cities mentioned, mostly in northern Palestine.[1] A fragmentary stele of Shoshenq I found at Megiddo may suggest that the king had entered into a treaty with Israel or that, perhaps, he was in control of the city.[2] Although the evidence is limited, it does testify to Shoshenq's presence in Palestine during this period.

The account in Kings provides important background information about the spiritual state of Judah at this time. Rehoboam's reign was characterized by rampant idolatry, and Judah was not exempt. Judah did evil in the sight of the LORD, provoking him to anger (1 Kgs 14:22). This is how the kingdom is described:

---

1. For a description and pictures of his campaign, see https://daahl.ucsd.edu/DAAHL/Shishak.php.
2. For a more extensive summary of Shoshenq's (also spelled Sheshonq, Shishak, etc.) campaign, and scholarship on the topic, see Klein, *2 Chronicles*, 182–183.

They also set up for themselves high places, sacred stones and Asherah poles on every high hill and under every spreading tree. There were even male shrine prostitutes in the land; the people engaged in all the detestable practices of the nations the Lord had driven out before the Israelites. (vv. 23–24)

With such flagrant apostasy, it is not surprising that God's wrath is unleashed when Shishak invades Judah.

EXPLAIN the Story

Forsaking God Leads to an Attack by Egypt (12:1–4)

When Rehoboam's kingdom becomes strong, he and all Israel abandon the law of the Lord (2 Chr 12:1). Strength can be seen positively, but there is the inherent danger that it can lead to pride. The king was supposed to meditate on the law of God and follow it (Deut 17:18–19), precisely what David had instructed Solomon to do (1 Chr 22:12; cf. 2 Chr 6:16). With this high priority placed on the word of God, priests and Levites were to instruct God's people in the ways of the Lord (17:9; 19:8–10; 31:4; cf. Ezra 7:10). Every aspect of Israel's conduct was to be governed by the law of the Lord (e.g., 2 Chr 23:18; 25:4; 36:16). Obedience would lead to covenantal blessings (Lev 26:1–13; Deut 28:1–14), but disobedience would lead to curses (Lev 26:14–39; Deut 28:15–68). Tragically, God's people abandon the law, and an enemy attack follows (2 Chr 12:2; cf. Deut 28:48–50). Shishak is identified as the Egyptian king, Shoshenq I of Libyan origin, who founded the Twenty-Second Dynasty.[3] His army consisted of various people, including Lubim, Sukkim, and Ethiopians (2 Chr 12:3). This ethnically diverse army is suggested in the Karnak Stela of Shoshenq I, which describes conflict between Egypt and Asiatics.[4] Shishak is able to capture some of the fortified cities of Judah and he arrives at Jerusalem, but God sends a prophet to Rehoboam to intervene (vv. 4–5).

The Prophet Shemaiah Gives the Theological Reasons for the Egyptian Invasion (12:5–8)

Rehoboam and the princes assemble in Jerusalem, at which time the prophet Shemaiah explains that God has abandoned them to Shishak because they

---

3. For a discussion of Egyptian epigraphic evidence, see Kenneth A. Kitchen, *On the Reliability of the Old Testament* (Grand Rapids: Eerdmans, 2003), 32–34; see also "The Campaign of Sheshonk I," trans. John A. Wilson (*ANET*, 263–64).

4. Kitchen, *On the Reliability*, 34.

have abandoned God (2 Chr 12:5; cf. 15:2). The verb "to abandon, forsake" (Heb. '-z-b) is a covenantal term commonly used by the Chronicler to describe a breach of the covenant-relationship (12:1; 15:2; 21:10; 24:20; 28:6; 29:6; cf. Deut 28:20; 29:25). God warns his people that if they forsake him, he will forsake them (2 Chr 15:2; 24:20, 24).

The response of Rehoboam and the leaders is critical at this point. The first thing they do is "humble themselves" (Heb. k-n-', 12:6–7). This act of self-humbling, which is central to Chronicles,[5] averts God's wrath (cf. 7:14; 30:11; 32:26; 33:12, 19; 34:27). Rehoboam and the leaders declare: "The LORD is just" (Heb. tsaddiq, 12:6). Using legal law-court language (Deut 16:19; 25:1), their declaration that the LORD was in the right is a confession of their guilt (cf. Neh 9:33–34; Dan 9:7, 14, 16). When God sees that they have humbled themselves, the prophet Shemaiah announces that God will not destroy them and his wrath will not be unleashed against Jerusalem (2 Chr 12:7–8, 12).

Shishak Succeeds in Plundering Jerusalem but the City Is Preserved (12:9–16)

Although Jerusalem is not destroyed at this time, Rehoboam is not entirely free from the consequences of his sin. Shishak succeeds in taking treasures from the house of God and from the palace, which are taken as trophies of war (cf. 2 Chr 36:7; Dan 1:2; 5:1–4). As the reign of Rehoboam is drawing to a close, the Chronicler returns to the theme of Rehoboam's humbling himself, underscoring its impact on averting God's wrath and the preservation of Jerusalem (2 Chr 12:12). This serves as a reminder that, in spite of their unfaithfulness that led to the Egyptian attack, there were some brighter moments when Rehoboam humbled himself in response to the prophetic word, representing "some good in Judah" (v. 12; cf. 19:3).

The story of Rehoboam concludes with formulaic statements made about his age when he became king and the length of his reign (2 Chr 12:13; cf. 1 Kgs 14:21). Focus shifts to Jerusalem, which is identified as the "the city the LORD had chosen out of all the tribes of Israel in which to put his Name" (2 Chr 12:13; cf. Deut 12:11, 14; 2 Chr 2:4; 6:6, 20, etc.). Reference is made to Rehoboam's mother, Naamah the Ammonite (2 Chr 12:13), hearkening back to Solomon's foreign wives (1 Kgs 11:1–8). Rehoboam's reign is summarized as follows: "He did evil because he had not set his heart on seeking the LORD" (2 Chr 12:14). Seeking the LORD (Heb. d-r-sh) is the hallmark of godly

---

5. See the discussion in Chapter 36 on 2 Chr 7:14, pp. 338–41.

leadership,[6] yet Rehoboam's failure to seek God had dire consequences for the kingdom. His ongoing war with Jeroboam indicates that his kingdom is not at peace (cf. 13:2), hinting at the spiritual state of the kingdom under his rule (12:15). Rehoboam's reign draws to a close with his death and burial, and the story of kingship continues with his son Abijah, who reigns in his place (v. 16).

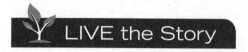 LIVE the Story

True Strength: Humility and Dependence upon the LORD

As noted above, the first thing Rehoboam does after the division in the kingdom is to wage war against the north (2 Chr 11:1). After a prophet intervenes, Rehoboam focuses on fortifying the kingdom and strengthening his defensive cities (vv. 11–12). But what is conspicuously missing in these stories is any reference to the king seeking the LORD, which sets him in contrast to kings like Asa (14:4), Jehoshaphat (17:4, 6), and Josiah (34:3). No such statement is made of Rehoboam, and in fact, we learn later that "he did evil because he had not set his heart on seeking the LORD" (12:14). His efforts were focused on becoming strong and building up the kingdom—something we can easily admire in leaders today—yet such strength without reliance upon God became his downfall.

It was after Rehoboam's "position as king was established and he had become strong" (2 Chr 12:1) that he and all Israel abandoned the law of God. Rehoboam was a capable and energetic leader, yet he was a self-made man whose accomplishments and strength became his undoing (v. 1). King Uzziah is another example of a king whose strength leads to pride, causing him to overstep his royal authority and fall under divine judgment (26:16–21). In the case of Rehoboam, emphasis throughout the narrative is placed on the strength of his kingdom (11:11, 12, 17; 12:13), but now his strength leads to his abandoning the law of God (12:1). The very cities that Rehoboam had fortified are ironically conquered by Shishak (v. 4).

Strength in leadership is a positive quality (e.g., 1 Chr 22:13; 28:10, 20; 2 Chr 15:7), but it usually comes as a result of God's help and presence (1 Chr 11:9–10; 22:11–19; 28:10, 20; 2 Chr 19:11; 26:7–8; 32:7–8). David thus exhorts Solomon to "Be strong and courageous," for God was with him (1 Chr 28:20). Similarly, Hezekiah exhorts God's people: "Be strong and courageous"

---

6. The Hebrew verb *d-r-sh* occurs over forty times in Chronicles; see the discussion in Chapter 30 on 2 Chr 1:5, pp. 291–93.

in face of the Assyrian attack, because God was with them (2 Chr 32:7–8). These passages teach that strength comes from the LORD, as the prophet Hannini taught: "For the eyes of the LORD range throughout the earth to strengthen those whose hearts are fully committed to him" (16:9; cf. 27:6). Strength achieved through self-effort can easily lead to pride and self-reliance and, in the case of Rehoboam, even turning away from God. While Rehoboam humbles himself when rebuked by a prophet and God's judgment is averted (12:6–8, 12), this could have been avoided had Rehoboam sought the LORD earlier in his reign.

In our contemporary culture, we can too easily value the strong and power-ful, and this secular value can easily influence the church. Instead of turning to God in prayer, we can rely upon ourselves and even pride ourselves in our ability to get a job done. Yet God often puts his people in situations where they are required to rely upon him. He does this so that we might not trust in ourselves but in God. The apostle Paul understood this when he said that he could do all things "through [Christ] who gives me strength," remembering that he was writing from a Roman jail (Phil 4:13). He understood that when he was weak, he was in fact strong, for he had learned to rely upon the Lord. This is the call of Christians today, to devote ourselves to the kingdom work, but to do so in dependence upon the Lord and to rely upon the strength of his might (Eph 6:10).

LISTEN to the Story

¹In the eighteenth year of the reign of Jeroboam, Abijah became king of Judah, ²and he reigned in Jerusalem three years. His mother's name was Maakah, a daughter of Uriel of Gibeah.

There was war between Abijah and Jeroboam. ³Abijah went into battle with an army of four hundred thousand able fighting men, and Jeroboam drew up a battle line against him with eight hundred thousand able troops.

⁴Abijah stood on Mount Zemaraim, in the hill country of Ephraim, and said, "Jeroboam and all Israel, listen to me! ⁵Don't you know that the LORD, the God of Israel, has given the kingship of Israel to David and his descendants forever by a covenant of salt? ⁶Yet Jeroboam son of Nebat, an official of Solomon son of David, rebelled against his master. ⁷Some worthless scoundrels gathered around him and opposed Rehoboam son of Solomon when he was young and indecisive and not strong enough to resist them.

⁸"And now you plan to resist the kingdom of the LORD, which is in the hands of David's descendants. You are indeed a vast army and have with you the golden calves that Jeroboam made to be your gods. ⁹But didn't you drive out the priests of the LORD, the sons of Aaron, and the Levites, and make priests of your own as the peoples of other lands do? Whoever comes to consecrate himself with a young bull and seven rams may become a priest of what are not gods.

¹⁰"As for us, the LORD is our God, and we have not forsaken him. The priests who serve the LORD are sons of Aaron, and the Levites assist them. ¹¹Every morning and evening they present burnt offerings and fragrant incense to the LORD. They set out the bread on the ceremonially clean table and light the lamps on the gold lampstand every evening. We are observing the requirements of the LORD our God. But you have forsaken

him. ¹²God is with us; he is our leader. His priests with their trumpets will sound the battle cry against you. People of Israel, do not fight against the LORD, the God of your ancestors, for you will not succeed."

¹³Now Jeroboam had sent troops around to the rear, so that while he was in front of Judah the ambush was behind them. ¹⁴Judah turned and saw that they were being attacked at both front and rear. Then they cried out to the LORD. The priests blew their trumpets ¹⁵and the men of Judah raised the battle cry. At the sound of their battle cry, God routed Jeroboam and all Israel before Abijah and Judah. ¹⁶The Israelites fled before Judah, and God delivered them into their hands. ¹⁷Abijah and his troops inflicted heavy losses on them, so that there were five hundred thousand casualties among Israel's able men. ¹⁸The Israelites were subdued on that occasion, and the people of Judah were victorious because they relied on the LORD, the God of their ancestors.

¹⁹Abijah pursued Jeroboam and took from him the towns of Bethel, Jeshanah and Ephron, with their surrounding villages. ²⁰Jeroboam did not regain power during the time of Abijah. And the LORD struck him down and he died.

²¹But Abijah grew in strength. He married fourteen wives and had twenty-two sons and sixteen daughters.

²²The other events of Abijah's reign, what he did and what he said, are written in the annotations of the prophet Iddo.

Listening to the Text in the Story: 1 Kings 15:1–7

Abijah had been appointed crown prince while his father Rehoboam had still been alive (2 Chr 11:22), but with the death of his father, he now assumes the throne. While not mentioned in Chronicles, it is important to keep in mind what is said about Abijah in Kings: "He committed all the sins his father had done before him; his heart was not fully devoted to the LORD his God, as the heart of David his forefather had been" (1 Kgs 15:3). Rehoboam had built high places for the worship of foreign gods, and he had set up male cult prostitutes (14:22–24). Abijah follows in the ways of his father, yet in spite of his sins, this chapter underscores that David's son rules over the kingdom of the LORD (2 Chr 13:8). While not stated directly, underlying this story is God's promise to David (1 Chr 17:11–14; 29:23). In spite of unfaithful kings, the kingdom does not come to an end (cf. 1 Kgs 15:4). At this time, civil war breaks out between Abijah and the northern king Jeroboam (cf. 2 Chr 12:15). While mentioned only briefly in Kings (1 Kgs 15:6), the Chronicler provides more information about this battle, which includes a negative assessment of idolatry in the north along with an affirmation of Davidic kingship and the kingdom of the LORD.

EXPLAIN the Story

Civil War between Abijah and Jeroboam (13:1–12)

Abijah reigns for three short years, but attention quickly turns to his war with Jeroboam (2 Chr 13:1–2). The scene is set with Abijah and his men being greatly outnumbered, since their army was half the size of Jeroboam's army (v. 3).[1] These insurmountable circumstances provide an opportunity for God's people to trust in him (cf. 15:8–11; 16:8; 20:1–25). Abijah and his army assemble in the hill country of Ephraim, which Klein locates in Benjaminite territory.[2] The king reminds Jeroboam that God has given kingship to David and his descendants by a covenant of salt (13:5; cf. 1 Chr 17:11–14), which emphasizes its perpetuity (cf. Num 18:19).[3] Waging war against the Davidic king was tantamount to resisting the kingdom of the LORD, which was in the hands of David's descendants (2 Chr 13:8). The Davidic king ruled over the kingdom of the LORD (1 Chr 17:14; cf. 28:5; 29:11, 23; 2 Chr 9:8). This meant that Jeroboam's war against Abijah was an affront against God himself. Abijah mocks Jeroboam and the people for taking their golden calves with them to battle (13:8). These so-called gods were simply man-made idols, not gods at all (v. 9; cf. Isa 37:19; 45:20; 57:6; Jer 2:11, 27–28; 3:9; Ezek 20:32; Hab 2:19, etc.). Reminiscent of Hosea's prophetic indictment (Hos 8:6), Abijah's declaration that the idols were "no-gods" marks a climactic moment in his speech.[4] The Northern Kingdom had even driven out priests and Levites who had dwelt among them (2 Chr 13:9; cf. 11:14), and this meant that *anyone* from the northern tribes could serve as priest—the office of priest was

---

1. On the high numbers (13:3) and the meaning of the Hebrew term *'eleph* as a military unit (rather referring to a literal headcount of 1,000), see the discussion in Chapter 12 on 1 Chr 12:23–40, pp. 138–40.

2. Klein, *2 Chronicles*, 200. He notes that the location of Mt Zemaraim (2 Chr 13:4) is uncertain.

3. Cole notes regarding the covenant of salt in Num 18:19 that "the concepts of preservation and permanence are conveyed by the function of salt in ancient Near Eastern society," citing its usage in the sacrificial system not only as an enhancer of flavor, but also as a preserver; see Dennis R. Cole, *Numbers*, NAC (Nashville: Broadman & Holman, 2000), 290.

4. Dillard, *2 Chronicles*, 105.

now *for sale!*[5] The futility of these self-appointed priests was that they were serving idols, not gods.

But Abijah affirms that the LORD was with Judah: "As for us, the LORD is our God, and we have not forsaken him. The priests who serve the LORD are sons of Aaron, and the Levites assist them" (2 Chr 13:10). This verse contrasts the idolatry in the north with worship of the LORD in the temple. While the south is not without idolatry (cf. 12:1), a contrast is being established between worship of "no-gods" in the north with non-Israelite priests and with worship of God in the temple with Aaron's sons serving as priests. Every morning and evening the Levites offered burnt offerings and burned incense. Showbread was set on the table and golden lampstands were lit every evening. Their daily worship was according to the requirements of the LORD, but the north had forsaken God (13:11; cf. 2:4). Abijah warns the Northern Kingdom not to fight against them, for they would be waging war against God, who was with them as their head; thus Jeroboam would not succeed (13:12).

The Southern Kingdom Is Victorious as God Helps Judah (13:13–19)

Judah faces attacks from the front and the rear, yet amidst the battle they cry out to the LORD, and the priests blow their trumpets (2 Chr 13:13–14). Israel's priests were to blow trumpets when they were attacked by an enemy so that the LORD might remember his people and save them (Num 10:1–10). Many times throughout Israel's history, God's people had cried out to their God (Exod 14:10; Num 20:15–16; Deut 26:6–9), especially during the period of the judges (Judg 4:3; 10:12; cf. Neh 9:27). God's people now desperately cry out to him, and as the trumpets are blasting, God "routed Jeroboam and all Israel before Abijah and Judah" (2 Chr 13:15). The verb "to strike, smite" (Heb. *n-g-p*), translated as "routed" in the NIV, is used of God's judgment of plagues when he struck the Egyptians (Exod 8:2; 12:13, 23, 27; cf. Exod 32:35; 2 Chr 21:14; 21:18), and it is also used of God's judgment against Israel's enemies (e.g., 1 Chr 19:16; 2 Chr 14:12; 20:22). When the northerners flee, Abijah and his army slaughter thousands, and the Northern Kingdom is subdued.[6] The people of Judah are victorious because they rely on the LORD (13:18; cf. 14:11; 16:8). Jeroboam is weakened at this time, and Abijah takes several northern cities (13:19). Jeroboam's death is anticipated because of God's judgment against him (v. 20), which will include his entire household (1 Kgs

---

5. Ibid., 109.

6. On the meaning of the term "thousand" (Heb. *'eleph*), see the discussion in Chapter 12 on 1 Chr 12:23–40, pp. 138–40.

14:7–11, 14–16; 15:29–30). On the other hand, Abijah grows in strength, and his household increases with many sons and daughters (2 Chr 13:21).

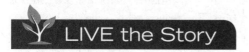
LIVE the Story

Trusting in God and Crying Out to Him

Military battles in ancient Israel provided opportunities for the king and the people to rely upon the LORD. Instead of trusting in foreign gods or even in their own military strength, they were to trust in the LORD for deliverance. It was during these insurmountable circumstances that the Israelites were to learn that help comes from the LORD. This is the testimony of God's people throughout the ages. The psalmist thus affirms: "God is our refuge and strength, an ever-present help in trouble. Therefore we will not fear, though the earth give way and the mountains fall into the heart of the sea" (Ps 46:1–2). The psalmist continues with these words of hope: "God is within her, she will not fall; God will help her at break of day" (v. 5). In another psalm, we are invited to join with Israel:

> Yes, my soul, find rest in God;
>> my hope comes from him.
> Truly he is my rock and my salvation;
>> he is my fortress, I will not be shaken.
> My salvation and my honor depend on God;
>> he is my mighty rock, my refuge.
> Trust in him at all times, you people;
>> pour out your hearts to him,
>> for God is our refuge. (62:5–8)

David discovered that God was indeed his help when he was fleeing from Saul (see 1 Chr 11–12). The psalms testify to this reality, that God can be trusted and that help comes from him alone (Pss 9:9; 18:30; 27:5; 37:5; 86:7; 118:5–6, 8; 125:1).

We do not face the same military battles today, nor are we promised military victory in earthly battles under the new covenant, as God had promised Israel. But throughout the ages, God wants his people to put their trust in him alone. Difficult and painful circumstances in our lives can draw us closer to God. James taught that when facing trials, we are to "consider it pure joy," for the testing of our faith produces perseverance (Jas 1:2–3). Believers in the early church were tested as they experienced trials, but they united together in prayer. While Peter was in prison, we read that "the church was earnestly praying to God for him" (Acts 12:5). After he had been miraculously released from jail, he arrives at Mary's house "where many people had gathered and were praying" (v. 12). This is a wonderful reminder that during difficult seasons of our life, we are to unite together in prayer to seek help from God.

Paul writes to the Corinthians about the afflictions he and Timothy had experienced in Asia, to the point that that they had despaired of life itself (2 Cor 1:8–9). But Paul understands God's sovereign hand at work, as he was teaching them to rely upon him. Perhaps we might ask ourselves what lessons God is teaching us through our adverse circumstances and how might we see them as an opportunity to rely upon God. Paul's words are instructive for us today, as he helps us to understand how God is at work amidst our circumstances: "But this happened that we might not rely on ourselves but on God, who raises the dead. He has delivered us from such a deadly peril, and he will deliver us again. On him we have set our hope that he will continue to deliver us, as you help us by your prayers" (2 Cor 1:9b–11a). This brings together several important themes: reliance upon God during difficult and seemingly hopeless situations, setting our hope on God alone, and receiving help from the saints through their prayers. Some of these themes have been rehearsed in the story of Abijah. The people had cried out to God amidst their distress, and God delivered them because they had trusted in him. These principles will be taught again in the story of Asa that follows.

LISTEN to the Story

¹And Abijah rested with his ancestors and was buried in the City of David. Asa his son succeeded him as king, and in his days the country was at peace for ten years.

²Asa did what was good and right in the eyes of the LORD his God. ³He removed the foreign altars and the high places, smashed the sacred stones and cut down the Asherah poles. ⁴He commanded Judah to seek the LORD, the God of their ancestors, and to obey his laws and commands. ⁵He removed the high places and incense altars in every town in Judah, and the kingdom was at peace under him. ⁶He built up the fortified cities of Judah, since the land was at peace. No one was at war with him during those years, for the LORD gave him rest.

⁷"Let us build up these towns," he said to Judah, "and put walls around them, with towers, gates and bars. The land is still ours, because we have sought the LORD our God; we sought him and he has given us rest on every side." So they built and prospered.

⁸Asa had an army of three hundred thousand men from Judah, equipped with large shields and with spears, and two hundred and eighty thousand from Benjamin, armed with small shields and with bows. All these were brave fighting men.

⁹Zerah the Cushite marched out against them with an army of thousands upon thousands and three hundred chariots, and came as far as Mareshah. ¹⁰Asa went out to meet him, and they took up battle positions in the Valley of Zephathah near Mareshah.

¹¹Then Asa called to the LORD his God and said, "LORD, there is no one like you to help the powerless against the mighty. Help us, LORD our God, for we rely on you, and in your name we have come against

this vast army. LORD, you are our God; do not let mere mortals prevail against you."

¹²The LORD struck down the Cushites before Asa and Judah. The Cushites fled, ¹³and Asa and his army pursued them as far as Gerar. Such a great number of Cushites fell that they could not recover; they were crushed before the LORD and his forces. The men of Judah carried off a large amount of plunder. ¹⁴They destroyed all the villages around Gerar, for the terror of the LORD had fallen on them. They looted all these villages, since there was much plunder there. ¹⁵They also attacked the camps of the herders and carried off droves of sheep and goats and camels. Then they returned to Jerusalem.

Listening to the Text in the Story: 2 Chronicles 6:34–35; Psalm 33:16–17

The reign of Asa marks a high point in the Southern Kingdom. At the outset of his reign, he establishes major religious reforms, thereby reversing the idolatrous practices of previous kings (1 Kgs 14:22–24; 15:1–3). The importance of Asa for the Chronicler is seen in the amount of attention devoted to him. Only a short section is given to him in Kings (15:9–24), but his reign is taken up in three chapters in Chronicles (2 Chr 14–16). As we listen to the text in the story, it is helpful to recall Solomon's prayer a few years earlier (6:12–42). The king had rehearsed in his prayer how God's people were to respond when facing an enemy attack: "When your people go to war against their enemies, wherever you send them, and when they pray to you toward this city you have chosen and the temple I have built for your Name, then hear from heaven their prayer and their plea, and uphold their cause" (vv. 34–35). Asa is an example of a king who prays amid the battle, and as we will see shortly, God answers the king. Psalm 33:16 encapsulates the theology that underlies the story of Asa, stating clearly that no king "is saved by the size of his army; no warrior escapes by his great strength. A horse is a vain hope for deliverance; despite all its strength it cannot save" (vv. 16–17). Instead of relying upon military strength, God's people were to trust in him for deliverance and hope in *him* (vv. 18–22). This is precisely what Asa does, thereby providing the Chronicler with rich material to teach on what it means to be faithful to God amid difficult circumstance. Much can be gleaned from Asa's life for the returnees living in Jerusalem and for our lives today.

EXPLAIN the Story

Asa Establishes Religious Reforms and He Fortifies His Kingdom (14:1–7)

The reign of Asa is introduced after the death of his father, Abijah, with the comment that during his days the country was at peace for ten years (2 Chr 14:1). This introduces one of several chronological notices by the Chronicler (15:10, 19; 16:1, 12-13), which underscores that the stories of Asa have been intentionally located in a chronological framework.[1] At the outset Asa is described as a king who did what was "good and right in the sight of the LORD his God" (14:2). This positive description characterizes other kings, such as Jehoshaphat (20:32), Joash (24:2), Amaziah (25:2), Uzziah (26:4–5), Hezekiah (29:2), and Josiah (34:2). Asa devotes his attention to the eradication of idolatrous worship, which includes the removal of foreign altars, high places, sacred pillars, and Asherim (14:3). These four objects associated with idolatrous worship were strictly prohibited in Israel (Exod 34:13; Deut 7:5; 12:3; cf. 2 Kgs 17:9–10). Moses had warned the Israelites upon entering the land that sacred pillars and Asherah poles used in pagan worship were to be destroyed. While worship of Asherah was widespread during Ahab's reign (1 Kgs 16:33; 18:19), the Southern Kingdom was not exempt from such pagan practices (2 Kgs 21:2–3, 7; 2 Chr 24:18; cf. 31:1). Religious reforms thus required the eradication of all objects pertaining to false worship (14:3; cf. 15:16; 17:6; 19:3; 31:1; 34:3–4, 7).

Asa replaces idolatrous worship with Yahweh worship—he commands Judah to seek the LORD and to follow his laws (14:4). The verb "to seek" (Heb. *d-r-sh*) occurs six times in these chapters (14:4, 7; 15:2, 12, 13; 16:12), underscoring its importance in this period.[2] This is precisely the kind of godly leadership that Judah needs, and it will be seen again during the reign of Jehoshaphat (20:3–4). It is not coincidental that the Chronicler devotes so much attention to these two kings, for they serve as examples for the returnees (chs. 14–20). Asa's kingship is under God's blessing, signified by the rest given at this time (14:5–6; cf. Josh 21:44; 23:1; 2 Sam 7:11), allowing Asa the opportunity to build and fortify cities (2 Chr 14:7).

---

1. The dates for Asa are not easily resolved, especially when comparing them with the chronological notices in Kings (1 Kgs 15:9-10, 33; 16:8). Various attempts have been made by scholars to reconcile the dates; for a summary of approaches, see Japhet, *1–2 Chronicles*, 703-704. For a more technical discussion, see Raymond B. Dillard, "The Reign of Asa (2 Chr 14–16): An Example of the Chronicler's Theological Method," *JETS* 23, 1980: 207–18.

2. See the discussion in Chapter 30, Live the Story, pp. 291–93.

The Cushite Army Advances toward Jerusalem (14:8–10)

Attention turns to Asa's army comprised of thousands of brave fighting men from Judah and Benjamin (2 Chr 14:8), although their weapons of mere shields, spears, and bows are no match for the many chariots used by the enemy! A man named Zerah, identified as a Cushite, comes against Asa with an enormous army and many chariots (v. 9). The Cushites were a sub-Saharan African people located south of Egypt in the region of Sudan. In the mid-eighth-century BC they conquered Egypt and established the Twenty-fifth Cushite Dynasty, which lasted for about one hundred years.[3] The Cushites will later come to the aid of Hezekiah (2 Kgs 19:9), but in this period they are waging war against Jerusalem. Zerah may have been an army general sent by the Egyptian pharaoh Osorkon I.[4] Asa's army numbered thousands, whereas Zerah's army numbered thousands upon thousands (2 Chr 14:9). The Hebrew word translated as "thousand" (Heb. *'eleph*) can refer to a smaller military unit, in which case the numbers would be much lower, depending on the size of the platoon.[5]

As with other holy wars in the Old Testament, it is not uncommon for the Israelites to be outnumbered by their enemy (cf. 2 Chr 20:2; 32:7). The prophet Hanani makes this point shortly when he recalls this battle: "Were not the Cushites and Libyans a mighty army with great numbers of chariots and horsemen? Yet when you relied on the LORD, he delivered them into your hand" (16:8). This great army coming from Egypt advances as far as Mareshah (14:9), a city included among those fortified by Rehoboam for their strategic location (11:8).[6] Asa and his army advance toward the battle, but what occurs on the battlefield takes us to the heart of the story.

Asa Calls upon God for Help and the Cushites Are Defeated (14:11–15)

As Asa and his army prepare for battle, the king calls out to God with heartfelt desperation: "LORD, there is no one like you to help the powerless against the

---

3. While often translated as Ethiopia (based on the Greek *Aethiopa*, cf. NASB, 2 Chr 14:9), the Cushites are not to be identified with the country of Ethiopia but with the African region south of ancient Egypt, known as Nubia. For a helpful summary of the Cushites, see Kevin Burrell, "Representing Cush in the Hebrew Bible," *BAR*, Winter, 2020 (https://www.baslibrary.org/biblical-archaeology-review/46/5/24), and Kevin Burrell, "The Cushites: Race and Representation in the Hebrew Bible, *ASOR* 8:1 (2020) (https://www.asor.org/anetoday/2020/12/cushites-hebrew-bible).

4. See the discussion by Dillard, *2 Chronicles*, 119–120.

5. On high numbers in the Old Testament, see the discussion in Chapter 12 on 1 Chr 12:23–40, pp. 138–40.

6. See Boda, *1–2 Chronicles*, 293.

mighty. Help us, LORD our God, for we rely on you, and in your name we have come against this vast army. LORD, you are our God; do not let mere mortals prevail against you" (2 Chr 14:11). Asa begins by affirming that help comes from God alone. He confesses that he and the people are weak and powerless in comparison to the mighty Cushite army. This is reminiscent of the men from Reuben, Gad, and Manasseh when they had cried out to God amid their battle against the Hagrites, and God had helped them (1 Chr 5:20). The psalms resound with the hope that God helps those who cry out to him (Pss 18:1-6; 22:19; 28:2, 6-9, etc.).[7] Now, Asa and the people cry out to the LORD and rely upon him. The verb "to rely upon, lean on" (Heb. *sh-ʿ-n*) is used several times in these chapters (2 Chr 14:11; 16:7, 8; cf. 13:18). Isaiah had warned about relying on chariots, for God's people were to rely upon him for deliverance (Isa 31:1; cf. 2 Chr 13:18). Facing an imminent attack, Asa does not rely on his military strength or on his army, but on the LORD. His cry for help anticipates Hezekiah's prayer when he acknowledges that "with us is the LORD our God to help us and to fight our battles" (32:8). In response to their cry for help, God strikes down the Cushites, who flee and are unable to recover (14:12–13). Asa plunders their cities and carries away much livestock, for the terror of God had fallen upon them (vv. 14–15), reminiscent of David's victories over his enemies in the days of old.

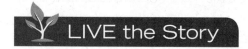

LIVE the Story

Prayer and Reliance upon God

Asa's victory over the Cushites is one of many battles in the Old Testament where the Israelites are greatly outnumbered by an enemy. The stories underscore that a king is not saved "by the size of his army; no warrior escapes by his great strength" (Ps 33:16). God is teaching his people through these military battles that they are to rely upon him. The turning point in this story is not military strength or expertise, but prayer and reliance upon God. An important spiritual lesson can be gleaned from this story, for the Chronicler has intentionally highlighted similar stories to teach the spiritual principle that he wants the returnees to cultivate in their own lives: God wants his people to call upon *him* for help.[8] While we do not face the same type of

---

7. On the topic of divine help, see the discussion in Chapter 12 on 1 Chr 12.

8. For stories with a similar theme, see 1 Chr 4:10; 5:20; 2 Chr 13:14–15; 18:31; 20:5–20; 32:20–22.

battles today, the principle of turning to God in prayer and relying upon him remains the same.

The question for our lives is whether we are relying on other things or people in place of God. The prophet Isaiah gave Israel the following warning: "Woe to those who go down to Egypt for help, who rely on horses, who trust in the multitude of their chariots and in the great strength of their horsemen, but do not look to the Holy One of Israel, or seek help from the LORD" (Isa 31:1). While we are not tempted to look to Egypt for help or rely on horses and chariots, there are other things that we can easily rely upon instead of turning to God. They can include our jobs, our own accomplishments, our retirement accounts, faculty tenure, and the list could continue. In the church and in Christian institutions, we can easily become reliant on marketing, networking, social media, and even on wealthy patrons—the list could continue. While God uses these things for his kingdom work, we are not to *rely* upon them or put our *trust* in them. Israelite kings had their own military, but they were not to rely upon their military but on the LORD. As Japhet notes, the king was expected "not only to possess military strength but to forego its use and to rely only on God for protection."[9] This is why God often has them outnumbered—so that they might learn to trust in him alone. We can too easily rely on our own strength and become self-sufficient, yet Proverbs teaches that those who trust in themselves are fools (Prov 28:26).

A 2017 Barna study found that fifty-two percent of practicing Christians "strongly agree" that the saying "God helps those who help themselves" is in the Bible.[10] The popularity of this saying is not the issue, but that Christians think it is *in the Bible*. Haynes traces the history of this familiar saying, noting that although Benjamin Franklin popularized it, it was written in the 1600s by an English politician named Algernon Sydney, with its roots tracing back to Greek mythology.[11] While the popular saying might seem harmless, it gets to the heart of the human problem. When we rely upon ourselves, our heart quickly turns away from the LORD. The prophet Jeremiah warns: "Cursed is the one who trusts in man, who draws strength from mere flesh and whose heart turns away from the LORD" (Jer 17:5). In Chronicles we discover that when a king becomes strong, this can easily lead to turning away from God

---

9. Japhet, *I & II Chronicles*, 792.

10. Barna, "Competing Worldviews Influence Today's Christians," May, 9, 2017 (https://www.barna.com/research/competing-worldviews-influence-todays-christians/).

11. See Clarence L. Haynes Jr. "Why 'God Helps Those Who Help Themselves' Is Presumed to Be Biblical," July 7, 2020 (https://www.christianity.com/wiki/christian-life/why-god-helps-those-who-help-themselves-is-presumed-to-be-biblical.html).

(see 2 Chr 12:1). Yet God often uses military battles—especially when God's people are outnumbered—to remind them that they *need* God's help. They had to *learn* the spiritual lesson that they were unable to fight their battles without God's help. The principle we are to learn from these stories is that when we are strong, we can easily rely upon ourselves, but when we are weak, God uses these circumstances to teach us to rely upon him. May we join with the apostle Paul, who had learnt this lesson: "That is why, for Christ's sake, I delight in weaknesses, in insults, in hardships, in persecutions, in difficulties. For when I am weak, then I am strong" (2 Cor 12:10). We call out to God with the prayer of Asa: "Help us, LORD our God, for we rely on you" (2 Chr 14:11). God is indeed our help, as reflected in the well-known hymn by Isaac Watts, *Our God, Our Help in Ages Past*:

> O God, our help in ages past,
> Our hope for years to come,
> Our shelter from the stormy blast,
> And our eternal home.
>
> Under the shadow of your throne,
> Your saints have dwelt secure;
> Sufficient is your arm alone
> And our defense is sure.

LISTEN to the Story

¹The Spirit of God came on Azariah son of Oded. ²He went out to meet Asa and said to him, "Listen to me, Asa and all Judah and Benjamin. The LORD is with you when you are with him. If you seek him, he will be found by you, but if you forsake him, he will forsake you. ³For a long time Israel was without the true God, without a priest to teach and without the law. ⁴But in their distress they turned to the LORD, the God of Israel, and sought him, and he was found by them. ⁵In those days it was not safe to travel about, for all the inhabitants of the lands were in great turmoil. ⁶One nation was being crushed by another and one city by another, because God was troubling them with every kind of distress. ⁷But as for you, be strong and do not give up, for your work will be rewarded."

⁸When Asa heard these words and the prophecy of Azariah son of Oded the prophet, he took courage. He removed the detestable idols from the whole land of Judah and Benjamin and from the towns he had captured in the hills of Ephraim. He repaired the altar of the LORD that was in front of the portico of the LORD's temple.

⁹Then he assembled all Judah and Benjamin and the people from Ephraim, Manasseh and Simeon who had settled among them, for large numbers had come over to him from Israel when they saw that the LORD his God was with him.

¹⁰They assembled at Jerusalem in the third month of the fifteenth year of Asa's reign. ¹¹At that time they sacrificed to the LORD seven hundred head of cattle and seven thousand sheep and goats from the plunder they had brought back. ¹²They entered into a covenant to seek the LORD, the God of their ancestors, with all their heart and soul. ¹³All who would not seek the LORD, the God of Israel, were to be put to death, whether small or great, man or woman. ¹⁴They took an oath to the LORD with loud acclamation, with shouting and with trumpets and horns. ¹⁵All Judah

rejoiced about the oath because they had sworn it wholeheartedly. They sought God eagerly, and he was found by them. So the LORD gave them rest on every side.

¹⁶King Asa also deposed his grandmother Maakah from her position as queen mother, because she had made a repulsive image for the worship of Asherah. Asa cut it down, broke it up and burned it in the Kidron Valley. ¹⁷Although he did not remove the high places from Israel, Asa's heart was fully committed to the LORD all his life. ¹⁸He brought into the temple of God the silver and gold and the articles that he and his father had dedicated.

¹⁹There was no more war until the thirty-fifth year of Asa's reign.

Listening to the Text in the Story: Judges 2:11–13

Asa and the people return to Jerusalem after defeating the powerful Cushite army with God's help. Yet their military victory was not to lead to complacency, but rather they were to give heed to the exhortation to seek God given by a prophet named Azariah, whose very name ("Yahweh helps") speaks to this central topic. The prophet recalls a period in Israel's history (most likely referring to the time of the judges) that serves to remind them of how quickly their ancestors had turned away from God each time after they had experienced his deliverance. They had done evil in God's sight when they had served the Baals; they had forsaken God, "who had brought them out of Egypt. They followed and worshiped various gods of the peoples around them. They aroused God's anger because they forsook him and served Baal and the Ashtoreths" (Judg 2:11–13). But when they cried out to God, he raised up deliverers who saved them (v. 18; 3:9; 4:3; 10:10, etc.). This well-known period in Israel's history is recalled among the returnees as they remember the times when their ancestors had rebelled against God and turned aside from his law (Neh 9:26). God had delivered them into the hands of their enemy, but when they had cried out to him amid their distress, he had heard from heaven and delivered them (v. 27). Yet the cycle had continued after they had rest from their enemies: "But as soon as they were at rest, they again did what was evil in your sight. Then you abandoned them to the hand of their enemies so that they ruled over them. And when they cried out to you again, you heard from heaven, and in your compassion you delivered them time after time" (v. 28). God had admonished his people by his Spirit through his prophets (v. 30), precisely what God is doing here through his prophet Azariah. God's people have experienced rest in the land (2 Chr 14:7; cf. 15:15), so Azariah's warning is timely.

EXPLAIN the Story

The Prophet Azariah Warns Asa (15:1–7)

The story begins with the Spirit of God coming on Azariah, son of Oded (2 Chr 15:1). The Spirit speaks through the prophet saying: "Listen to me, Asa and all Judah and Benjamin. The LORD is with you when you are with him. If you seek him, he will be found by you, but if you forsake him, he will forsake you" (v. 2). God had defeated the Cushites when his people had sought him and relied upon him, yet there is the danger that after the crisis is over, they might be tempted to forsake God, which would likely include the worship of idols (see 1 Sam 8:8; 2 Chr 7:22; 24:18, etc.), something that was widespread during the period of the judges (Judg 2:12–13; 10:6–7). The prophet announces that if they do this, God will forsake his people, and disaster will come upon them (2 Chr 7:22; 28:6; 29:6–10; 34:25). Azariah recalls the time when Israel was "without the true God, without a priest to teach and without the law" (15:3). This is probably referring to the period of the judges, which was characterized by idolatrous worship, thus they were "without the true God" (cf. Judg 2:11–19; 3:7; 10:6), "without a priest," since Micah had appointed his own son as priest (17:1–5; cf. 18:14), and they were "without the law," since everyone did what was right in their own eyes (17:6). Others argue that this refers to the Northern Kingdom (cf. Hos 3:4), since they worshiped the two golden calves ("without the true God"), they had non-Levites serve as priests ("without a priest to teach"), and they had failed to follow God's law ("without the law").[1] While the period of the judges seems to be in view, Azariah's point is to underline the "three essentials of the faith," which entail worship of the true God, priests to teach, and the law of God.[2] This crystalizes the core faith of Israel, and it underlines the importance of teaching the word of God in the covenant community. In what follows, the Chronicler describes the kind of havoc that comes as a result of idolatrous worship and the absence of God's word being taught: "In those days it was not safe to travel about, for all the inhabitants of the lands were in great turmoil.

---

1. On these two views, see Klein, *2 Chronicles*, 226–27.
2. Braun, *2 Chronicles*, 121.

One nation was being crushed by another and one city by another, because God was troubling them with every kind of distress" (2 Chr 15:5–6). This certainly characterized the period of the judges, and it is intended to motivate the Southern Kingdom in the reforms that follow (vv. 8–13). Thus, in contrast to these other examples, they were to "be strong and not give up, for [their] work will be rewarded" (v. 7). Calling God's people back to the LORD and his word is never in vain; it always has its rewards.

Religious Reforms and Covenant Renewal (15:8–19)

When Asa hears the prophetic words, he takes courage! He removes the detestable idols from the land of Judah and Benjamin, and even from the cities he had captured in the hill country of Ephraim (2 Chr 15:8). Asa not only removes the detestable idols from the land, but he also repairs the altar of the LORD in preparation for the sacrifices that will be offered (v. 8). He gathers Judah and Benjamin to Jerusalem, along with people from the northern tribes of Ephraim, Manasseh, and Simeon who had settled among them, for we are told that "large numbers had come over to him from Israel when they saw the LORD his God was with him" (v. 9; cf. v. 2). The Chronicler is keen to remind the returnees of times when northerners join the Southern Kingdom (11:16; 30:11–12, 18–19) as this would surely have encouraged them to be a unified people of God, living as the united tribes of Judah and Benjamin, along with Ephraim and Manasseh (1 Chr 9:3).[3] God's presence among his people draws the northerners to become part of the covenant community, anticipating what Zechariah sees when foreigners say, "Let us go with you, because we have heard that God is with you" (Zech 8:23).

The sacred assembly gathers to sacrifice thousands of cattle, sheep, and goats from the plunder (2 Chr 15:11). They enter into a covenant "to seek the LORD, the God of their ancestors, with all their heart and soul" (v. 12). The verb "to seek" (Heb. *d-r-sh*) marks the godly reign of Asa (14:4, 7; 15:2, 12, 13),[4] and doing it wholeheartedly is another important godly characteristic in Chronicles (1 Chr 22:19; 28:9; 29:19). Asa takes the bold step to put to death anyone who refuses to seek God (2 Chr 15:13). While this might seem rather extreme, the king is aware of the consequences of not following God, which will have even greater ramifications (cf. v. 3). In light of this, the king wants to ensure that this does not happen on his watch. Further, one person's unfaithfulness could have deadly consequences for an entire community

---

3. See the introduction, Historical Setting of the Writing of Chronicles, pp. 9–10, and Live the Story in Chapter 7.

4. See the discussion in Chapter 30 on 2 Chr 1:5, pp. 289–90.

(cf. Josh 7:1–26; 1 Chr 2:7).[5] Thus, wholehearted devotion to God was vital to ensure peace in the land. God's people join together in covenant renewal, which is accompanied by rejoicing over the oath they had sworn "because they had sworn it wholeheartedly. They sought God eagerly, and he was found by them" (2 Chr 15:15). Renewal of the covenant was accompanied by rest on every side (v. 15).

Asa takes the bold step to remove his grandmother, Maakah, from her position as queen mother (v. 16; see also 1 Kgs 15:2, 10). The queen mother had significant influence in the political sphere, as seen in Bathsheba's influence in the matter of royal succession (1 Kgs 1:11–31). Notably, her throne was located to the right of Solomon's (2:19)! The queen mother also had influence in the religious sphere, as seen in Jezebel's role in promoting worship of Asherah and Baal (16:31–33; 18:19). Asa's religious reforms necessitated the dismissal of his grandmother from her office, for she had set up an abhorrent image for Asherah (2 Chr 15:16; cf. 14:3). He destroys the image she had made and burns it in the Kidron Valley (15:16). Although the high places used for idolatrous worship are not completely destroyed (v. 17; cf. 17:6; 20:33; 28:4), Asa's heart is "fully committed to the Lord all his life" (15:17). As the chapter draws to a close, we are told that Asa brings into the temple the silver and gold that he and his father had dedicated, testifying to his devotion to God (v. 18). The land was at peace until the thirty-fifth year of Asa's reign (v. 19).[6]

LIVE the Story

The Importance of Teaching the Word of God

The prophet Azariah outlines succinctly "three essentials of the faith," which entail worship of the true God, priests to teach, and the law of God.[7] The prophet Malachi describes the role of a priest, whose lips "ought to preserve knowledge, because he is the messenger of the Lord Almighty and people seek instruction from his mouth" (Mal 2:7). Yet without a priest to teach the Scriptures, God's people are prone to wander away from God. Israel's history demonstrates how quickly they could worship false gods and adopt the practices and worldview of the surrounding nations. Their former history during

---

5. See the commentary on 2 Chr 21, Live the Story, pp. 204–5.
6. See the discussion in Chapter 45 on 2 Chr 16:1, p. 400, regarding this chronological notice.
7. Braun, *2 Chronicles*, 121.

the period of the judges serves as a powerful example of what happens when these "essentials" are lacking.[8] Klein's summary is instructive at this point:

> What was lacking was a priest who could teach with authority and apply the will of Yahweh to new situations. Not having the law does not mean for the Chronicler that Israel had a time in the land when it did not know of the revelation of Sinai but this law was not correctly taught or applied in the constantly changing challenges of life. While these were conditions in the distant past, they were also dangers in any period, including that of the Chronicler himself.[9]

The important role of the Levites to teach God's people is highlighted in a number of periods in Israel's history (e.g., 2 Chr 17:9; 31:4; 35:3; Ezra 8:16; Neh 8:7–9), which underlines the need to have teachers in every generation.[10]

Ezra is an example of a Levite skilled in the law of Moses during the postexilic period who was known as a teacher of the law (Ezra 7:10; cf. Neh 8:13). He had devoted himself to seek the law of God, to do it, and to teach its decrees and statutes in Israel. His public teaching ministry is especially seen when he stood on a podium and publicly read from the law over an extended period (Neh 8). This account highlights the role of the Levites who "instructed the people in the law" (v. 7) and made it clear, "giving the meaning so that the people understood what was being read" (v. 8). Careful searching of the Scriptures was vital for those teaching the word of God (vv. 13–14). Preaching of the word results in renewal of their relationship with the LORD during this time.

Teaching of the word of God is central to the life and well-being of the church in every generation. The book *The Invisible Best Seller* by Kenneth Briggs is just one of several studies that demonstrate that even though Bible sales are at an all-time high, there is a disconcerting decline in actual Bible *reading*.[11] Thus we are facing a crisis of biblical illiteracy, as noted by the Barna Group in a number of studies.[12] Biblical illiteracy does not simply mean the

---

8. See also Longman, *Immanuel in Our Place*, 140–43, who notes the dire consequences when Israel's priests turn away from God (cf. Judg 17–21) so that God's law is no longer taught.

9. Klein, *2 Chronicles*, 226.

10. The critical role of the priest is also seen in the reign of King Joash. Jehoiada was serving as priest at this time, but after his death we learn that the people "abandoned the temple of the LORD, the God of their ancestors, and worshiped Asherah poles and idols. Because of their guilt, God's anger came on Judah and Jerusalem" (2 Chr 24:18). See the discussion in Chapter 53 on 2 Chr 24, 457–59.

11. Briggs, *The Invisible Best Seller*.

12. See the 2016 Barna study, for example, "The Bible in America: 6-Year Trends," June 15, 2016 (https://www.barna.com/research/the-bible-in-america-6-year-trends/), and the 2019 Barna study,

loss of the biblical stories, but when the church fails to gain her categories of God from the Bible, the vacuum created leads to the adoption of cultural categories to define God that are idolatrous in nature.

The warning given by the prophet Azariah of the importance of teaching God's word requires us to reflect upon the role of the Scriptures in our lives and in the local church. Through his extensive research, this is what Briggs discovered: "The leading reason why people say they don't read the Scriptures is that they can't understand it. Language, style, and references to a lost world have made it unapproachable, they testify, despite hundreds of new translations."[13] He notes that while preachers base their sermons on the Bible, "they can no longer count on congregants to understand the larger settings from which the words came. The *sola Scriptura* is turning into a kind of 'nola Scriptura.'"[14] We discussed earlier in the commentary about the importance of studying the Scriptures,[15] and we might add that if the Scriptures are to be taught in the church, this will require an investment in seminary students so that they are not burdened with heavy debt. Seminary students are our contemporary "Levites," so to speak, who are training to teach God's word. This is all the more urgent in light of an aging protestant clergy in America and with fewer Millennials entering the ministry.[16] It will require generosity of God's people to provide for their needs.[17] We might recall that Humphrey Monmouth was the patron of William Tyndale. He not only supported him financially, but he gave Tyndale room and board in his home.[18] Financial support needs to be given to seminary students who are preparing for the ministry, but creative ideas, like giving room and board, are other ways to provide for them. The goal is that God's word would be preached and taught in the church, recalling Paul's timeless charge to Timothy: "Preach the word; be prepared in season and out of season; correct, rebuke and encourage—with great patience and careful instruction" (2 Tim 4:2). This is the sacred task of preachers and teachers, and it is the responsibility of the church in every generation to ensure that God's word is taught.

"State of the Bible 2019: Trends in Engagement," April 18, 2019 (https://www.barna.com/research/state-of-the-bible-2019/).

13. Briggs, *The Invisible Bestseller*, 57.

14. Ibid., 58.

15. See Live the Story in Chapter 8, pp. 103–5.

16. On the topic of generosity, student debt, and the importance of training the next generation of church leaders, see Live the Story in Chapter 27, p. pp. 263–65, and in Chapter 60, Generosity, pp. 519–20, and Supporting Our Modern-Day Levites, pp. 520–21.

17. See the discussion on the tithe in 1 Chr 29, Live the Story (Chapter 29, pp. 282–84), where Lady Huntington's generosity is noted, when she provided for food, clothing, and lodging of those training for ministry.

18. Rinehart, *Gospel Patrons*, 43.

LISTEN to the Story

¹In the thirty-sixth year of Asa's reign Baasha king of Israel went up against Judah and fortified Ramah to prevent anyone from leaving or entering the territory of Asa king of Judah.

²Asa then took the silver and gold out of the treasuries of the LORD's temple and of his own palace and sent it to Ben-Hadad king of Aram, who was ruling in Damascus. ³"Let there be a treaty between me and you," he said, "as there was between my father and your father. See, I am sending you silver and gold. Now break your treaty with Baasha king of Israel so he will withdraw from me."

⁴Ben-Hadad agreed with King Asa and sent the commanders of his forces against the towns of Israel. They conquered Ijon, Dan, Abel Maim and all the store cities of Naphtali. ⁵When Baasha heard this, he stopped building Ramah and abandoned his work. ⁶Then King Asa brought all the men of Judah, and they carried away from Ramah the stones and timber Baasha had been using. With them he built up Geba and Mizpah.

⁷At that time Hanani the seer came to Asa king of Judah and said to him: "Because you relied on the king of Aram and not on the LORD your God, the army of the king of Aram has escaped from your hand. ⁸Were not the Cushites and Libyans a mighty army with great numbers of chariots and horsemen? Yet when you relied on the LORD, he delivered them into your hand. ⁹For the eyes of the LORD range throughout the earth to strengthen those whose hearts are fully committed to him. You have done a foolish thing, and from now on you will be at war."

¹⁰Asa was angry with the seer because of this; he was so enraged that he put him in prison. At the same time Asa brutally oppressed some of the people.

¹¹The events of Asa's reign, from beginning to end, are written in the book of the kings of Judah and Israel. ¹²In the thirty-ninth year of

his reign Asa was afflicted with a disease in his feet. Though his disease was severe, even in his illness he did not seek help from the LORD, but only from the physicians. [13]Then in the forty-first year of his reign Asa died and rested with his ancestors. [14]They buried him in the tomb that he had cut out for himself in the City of David. They laid him on a bier covered with spices and various blended perfumes, and they made a huge fire in his honor.

Listening to the Text in the Story: Treaty of Kadesh

The reign of Asa continues in this chapter, yet the king faces a serious threat when the northern king Baasha advances southward, taking control of the city of Ramah, which was located in the territory of Benjamin. With Baasha's encroachment into his kingdom, along with his fear of being hemmed in, Asa's strategy is to secure military support from Ben-Hadad (an Aramean king ruling in Damascus) through a political alliance. A famous international peace treaty between Rameses II and Hattusilis underscores the kind of military aid a king could expect to receive from a treaty partner if he was attacked by an enemy. The Hittite version of the treaty is among the prized artifacts in the Istanbul Archaeological Museums. The treaty established peace after many years of wars between Egypt and the Hittite Empire, but what is noteworthy for our purposes is the commitment of each party to provide military reinforcements if the other king faced an enemy attack. An excerpt from the treaty reads as follows:

> If an enemy from abroad comes against the Hatti land, and Hattusilis, the great king, the king of the Hatti land, sends to me saying: "Come to me to help against him," Rea-mashesha mai Amana, the great king, the king of the land of Egypt, shall send his foot soldiers (and) his charioteers and they shall slay [his enemy] take revenge upon him for the sake of the Hatti land.[1]

Similarly, if an enemy invaded Egypt, Hattusilis was required to send military aid in the form of soldiers and chariots. Loyalty to the treaty required nothing less than each party coming to the aid of the other. This is precisely what Asa has in mind when he initiates an alliance with Ben-Hadad. The gold and silver

---

1. "Treaty between Hattusilis and Ramses II," trans. Albrecht Goetze (*ANET*, 202).

he pays is but a small price for such military reinforcements! While this may have been a shrewd and effective political strategy, the prophet Hanani will rebuke Asa for relying on the king of Aram instead of the LORD.

EXPLAIN the Story

Asa Enters into a Treaty with Ben-Hadad, Resulting in Baasha's Retreat (16:1–6)

King Baasha comes against Judah in the thirty-sixth year of Asa (2 Chr 16:1).[2] He fortifies the city of Ramah, a strategic city located approximately five miles north of Jerusalem. His advance southward into Benjaminite territory signaled a hostile move and was not to be taken lightly. But instead of turning to the LORD for help, as Jehoshaphat will do a few years later (20:1–4), Asa takes silver and gold from the temple treasuries and his own palace and sends them to Ben-Hadad,[3] the king of Aram (16:2; cf. 2 Kgs 12:18; 2 Chr 12:9). In doing so, Asa attempts to "buy protection" from the foreign king.[4]

When Asa sends silver and gold to the king, he makes his intentions clear: "'Let there be a treaty between me and you,' he said, 'as there was between my father and your father'" (2 Chr 16:3). His gifts are intended to induce Ben-Hadad to break his treaty with Baasha so that he would withdraw his support from him (v. 3). Treaties between kings required such loyalty, and Asa expects Ben-Hadad to demonstrate his allegiance by breaking his former treaty with Baasha. Ben-Hadad agrees and sends his armies against several northern towns of Israel, along with the store cities belonging to Naphtali (v. 4). The Aramean assault has a successful outcome: Baasha stops building at Ramah and abandons his work (v. 5). Asa then sends his own men to haul away the building materials from Ramah, which he uses to build two nearby cities of Geba and Mizpah (v. 6). Asa's political maneuver was successful, yet God's word through a prophet indicates that God was not pleased with how the king conducted himself.

---

2. The chronological notice is difficult to resolve in light of dates given elsewhere (cf. 1 Kgs 15:33; 16:6, 8). Various solutions have been proposed by scholars, although no consensus has emerged. For a helpful outline of the six chronological notices in Chronicles (2 Chr 14:1; 15:10, 19; 16:1, 12, 13), along with a summary of three different solutions proposed by scholars, see Dillard, *2 Chronicles*, 123–25. That the number thirty-six is the result of a scribal error is not to be ruled out, in which case, it originally read in the "sixteenth" year (see Boda, *1–2 Chronicles*, 311n2).

3. For a detailed analysis, see Klein, *1 Chronicles*, 237–38.

4. The name Ben-Hadad is attested in ancient inscriptions (his name simply means "son of the god Hadad"). For a discussion of possible identifications of the king, see ibid.

The Prophet Hanani Rebukes Asa (16:7–14)

God raises up prophets to bring words of rebuke to kings who stray from a godly path (2 Chr 12:5–8; 19:2; 20:37), reminding us that God does not leave the kings to their own devices. On this occasion, God raises up the prophet Hanani to rebuke Asa with these words: "Because you relied on the king of Aram and not on the LORD your God, the army of the king of Aram has escaped from your hand" (16:7). While Asa's alliance had resulted in Baasha's retreat, Asa learns that he could have had an even greater victory had he trusted in the LORD, for he could have "triumphed over two enemies, Israel and Aram."[5] Recalling Asa's earlier battle with the Cushites, the prophet reminds the king that God had delivered them into his hand (even though he had been greatly outnumbered) because he had relied on the LORD (v. 8; see 14:9–15). At that time, victory had not been achieved through Asa's military strength, nor had it been through a shrewd political move; rather, it was because he had relied on the LORD (14:11). The prophet explains further that the eyes of the LORD range "throughout the earth to strengthen those whose hearts are fully committed to him" (16:9; cf. Zech 4:10). Likened to a person earnestly looking for someone or something (Num 11:8; 2 Sam 24:2, 8; Jer 5:1), God is searching to find his faithful servants so that he might strengthen them. The causative verb in this verse indicates that people are not mustering their *own* strength, but rather, strength comes *from God*.[6]

Yet Asa has not relied upon the LORD, and as a result of his folly, he will have wars (2 Chr 16:9). Ironically, this is exactly what he had tried to avoid. When he hears these words, Asa is filled with rage. He puts the prophet in prison and treats some of his own people harshly (v. 10). The hardness of Asa's heart is tragically seen in his final days. Even when facing a disease in his feet (v. 12), which could have been due to the LORD's discipline (see 21:15, 18–19), the king does not seek help from the LORD, but from physicians (16:12). Asa dies two years later, and he is buried in his own tomb in the city of David (vv. 13–14).

 LIVE the Story

Listening to the Spirit

The story of Asa's reforms highlights the important role of God's Spirit. In the previous chapter, the prophet Azariah had brought God's word to the king

---

5. Ibid., 240.
6. On the topic of strength, see Live the Story in Chapter 41, pp. 376–77.

(2 Chr 15:1–7). The prophetic word had given Asa courage, and his religious reforms followed (vv. 8–14). But in the story we have just read, Asa's response to the prophet Hanani is rage (16:10), followed by the harsh treatment of the prophet and his people (v. 10). What we see in these stories are two different responses to the work of the Spirit, resulting in two very different outcomes. The Spirit of God is active throughout the Old Testament, coming upon key leaders who are empowered for a particular task (Num 11:17, 25; 27:18; 1 Sam 16:13), but especially coming upon prophets who proclaim God's word (2 Chr 11:2–4; 12:5–8; 16:7–9; 18:3–22; 20:14–17). When met with humility and obedience, words uttered by the Spirit lead to repentance and reformation, as seen in Asa's earlier life; when resisted, they lead to ungodliness and hardness of heart.

The Old Testament looked forward to a time when God would pour out his Spirit *on all flesh* (Isa 44:3; 61:1; Joel 2:28). He would place his Spirit *within* his people, causing them to walk in his ways and follow his laws (Ezek 36:26–27). The outpouring of God's Spirit at Pentecost indicates that Joel's prophecy has been fulfilled (Acts 2:1–13; cf. Joel 2:28–32), and we are now the beneficiaries. The outpouring of the Spirit, beginning at Pentecost and continuing in the early church (Acts 10:34–48; 11:15–18), marks the dawn of the new age. The Spirit of God was active in the Old Testament, but the same Spirit is present and active in our lives today, manifesting God's presence in our midst. The Holy Spirit gives us new life (John 6:63; Rom 7:6; 8:2, 11; 2 Cor 3:6), which we receive by faith (Gal 3:3, 14).

But notice also that the work of the Spirit brings about godliness in our lives, for the church has become the eschatological community, "whose members live in the present as those stamped with eternity."[7] Gordon Fee explains the implications of this: "Ethical life, therefore, does not consist in rules to live by. Rather empowered by the Spirit, we now live the life of the future in the present age, the life that characterizes God himself."[8] God's empowering Spirit within believers convicts of sin (John 16:8–11; Acts 7:51; 1 Cor 6:11), reveals God's truth (John 15:26; 16:13–15), and brings forth fruit pertaining to a godly character (Gal 5:22–23). Just as Israel's kings and the people were to give heed and pay careful attention to the Spirit's activity, we, too, are to be attentive to the work of the Spirit in our own lives and in the church. We are not to grieve or quench the Spirit (Eph 4:30; 1 Thess 5:19; cf. Acts 7:51) but,

---

7. Gordon D. Fee, *God's Empowering Presence: The Holy Spirit in the Letters of Paul* (Peabody, MA: Hendrickson, 1994), 804.

8. Ibid.

instead, be led by the Spirit (Rom 8:12–16; Gal 5:18) so that the fruit of the Spirit might be manifest in our lives.

Asa's reign had begun well, but it ended in tragedy. In this story we recognize the central role of the Spirit, yet, by way of contrast, we are now living as the eschatological community—the end of the ages has come *upon us* (cf. 1 Cor 10:11). This means, therefore, that our communal life through the Spirit stands in contrast to Asa, who forsook God and failed to listen to the Spirit. Fee thus notes that we have "entered the new aeon, where the Spirit is sufficient and stands over against the flesh in every way."[9] This serves as a great encouragement—unlike the Israelites in the Old Testament, we now experience life in the new age, empowered by God's own presence through his indwelling Spirit.

The Danger of Success without Humility

This story of Asa not only reminds us of the importance of listening to the Spirit, but it serves as a warning about the danger of success. We have seen that Asa's alliance with Ben-Hadad was a shrewd political move, and it was very successful: Ben-Hadad conquered several northern cities, Baasha stopped fortifying Ramah and retreated, and Asa took control of the city (2 Chr 16:4–6). It was clearly a major political victory, but the prophet Hanani tells Asa that he has acted *foolishly* (v. 9), reminiscent of the folly of Saul (1 Sam 13:13), but also David (1 Chr 21:8). What was Asa's folly? He had achieved success by relying on a foreign king instead of the LORD. This might seem like a minor offense, but the Scriptures resound with the message that God's people are to rely upon him alone—not on foreign nations or on military strength, but on the LORD. Asa's so-called success led to pride and a hard heart. When rebuked by the prophet, the king does not humble himself in repentance, but instead, he becomes even more ardent in his self-reliance, using his royal position to oppress one of God's servants and his own people. Ultimately, his so-called success came at great personal expense, resulting in ungodly character traits rising to the surface.

Many of us have seen people caught up in success and achievement and the impact this has on their character. Instead of godly virtues like kindness, gentleness, and self-control being cultivated, they become arrogant and self-serving, even treating those under them harshly, as Asa does with his own people. This story serves as a warning of the dangers of "success," when it is achieved through self-effort rather than reliance upon God. How things are accomplished matters to God. The end does not justify the means. God gives his kings success, but it is on *his* terms.

---

9. Ibid., 816.

LISTEN to the Story

¹Jehoshaphat his son succeeded him as king and strengthened himself against Israel. ²He stationed troops in all the fortified cities of Judah and put garrisons in Judah and in the towns of Ephraim that his father Asa had captured.

³The LORD was with Jehoshaphat because he followed the ways of his father David before him. He did not consult the Baals ⁴but sought the God of his father and followed his commands rather than the practices of Israel. ⁵The LORD established the kingdom under his control; and all Judah brought gifts to Jehoshaphat, so that he had great wealth and honor. ⁶His heart was devoted to the ways of the LORD; furthermore, he removed the high places and the Asherah poles from Judah.

⁷In the third year of his reign he sent his officials Ben-Hail, Obadiah, Zechariah, Nethanel and Micaiah to teach in the towns of Judah. ⁸With them were certain Levites—Shemaiah, Nethaniah, Zebadiah, Asahel, Shemiramoth, Jehonathan, Adonijah, Tobijah and Tob-Adonijah—and the priests Elishama and Jehoram. ⁹They taught throughout Judah, taking with them the Book of the Law of the LORD; they went around to all the towns of Judah and taught the people.

¹⁰The fear of the LORD fell on all the kingdoms of the lands surrounding Judah, so that they did not go to war against Jehoshaphat. ¹¹Some Philistines brought Jehoshaphat gifts and silver as tribute, and the Arabs brought him flocks: seven thousand seven hundred rams and seven thousand seven hundred goats.

¹²Jehoshaphat became more and more powerful; he built forts and store cities in Judah ¹³and had large supplies in the towns of Judah. He also kept experienced fighting men in Jerusalem. ¹⁴Their enrollment by families was as follows:

From Judah, commanders of units of 1,000:
> Adnah the commander, with 300,000 fighting men;
> ¹⁵next, Jehohanan the commander, with 280,000;
> ¹⁶next, Amasiah son of Zikri, who volunteered himself for the service of the LORD, with 200,000.
> ¹⁷From Benjamin:
> Eliada, a valiant soldier, with 200,000 men armed with bows and shields;
> ¹⁸next, Jehozabad, with 180,000 men armed for battle.

¹⁹These were the men who served the king, besides those he stationed in the fortified cities throughout Judah.

Listening to the Text in the Story: Deuteronomy 31:9–13

The story of the Southern Kingdom continues with the reign of Asa's son, Jehoshaphat (2 Chr 17–20). Klein notes that the account of his reign, which covers 102 verses, is longer than any other king of the divided monarchy, demonstrating his importance in Chronicles.[1] Many of the themes that reverberate throughout Chronicles can be found in these chapters, such as seeking the face of God, trusting in God amidst insurmountable obstacles, worshiping the LORD instead of idols, giving priority to God's word, and giving heed to a prophet. Yet Jehoshaphat's mistakes are not glossed over, reminding us that God uses ordinary people with their failures to accomplish his kingdom purposes, provided there is humility and repentance. In the final analysis, Jehoshaphat emerges as an outstanding and unforgettable king who calls God's people to prayer, fasting, and an unswerving trust in God. The cumulative effect of these stories provides an example of what it means to be *faithful*—something the Chronicler is keen to see cultivated in his audience, regardless of their circumstances.

The priority Jehoshaphat gives to teaching God's word has a longstanding tradition in the history of Israel, for priests and Levites had been assigned this sacred task (Lev 10:11; Deut 17:9–11; 31:9–13; 33:8–10; cf. Jer 18:18; Hag 2:11). At the end of every seven years, Israel's priests were to assemble the

---

1. Klein, *2 Chronicles*, 246.

entire community, including foreigners living among them, and read the law
before them so that they might learn to fear the Lord (Deut 31:10–13). This
is not unlike the post-exilic period, when Ezra was given these instructions:
"And you, Ezra, in accordance with the wisdom of your God, which you
possess, appoint magistrates and judges to administer justice to all the people
of Trans-Euphrates—all who know the laws of your God. And you are to
teach any who do not know them" (Ezra 7:25). The importance of teaching
the law among the returnees is not only seen in the ministry of Ezra (v. 6; cf.
Neh 8:1–18), but Yamauchi notes that this fits well with Persian policy, citing
the time when Darius had commissioned the codification of Egyptian laws in
demotic and Aramaic.[2] The Chronicler highlights the central role of the law
during the reign of Jehoshaphat (2 Chr 17:7–9; 19:4–11), which connects this
story to his own context while also being deeply rooted in Israel's traditions
(Deut 17:9–12; 31:9–13).

EXPLAIN the Story

God Establishes His Kingdom through King Jehoshaphat (17:1–6)

Jehoshaphat becomes king in place of his father, Asa, and strengthens himself over Israel (2 Chr 17:1). His first task is to fortify his kingdom, which
includes stationing military troops in the fortified cities of Judah (vv. 1–2).
Yet Jehoshaphat is not exemplary for his military strength, but rather, the
Chronicler notes at the outset of his reign: "The Lord was with Jehoshaphat
because he followed the ways of his father David before him. He did not
consult the Baals but sought the God of his father and followed his commands
rather than the practices of Israel" (vv. 3–4). His worship of the Lord is in
stark contrast to the proliferation of Baal worship during the reign of Ahab
(1 Kgs 16:29–32; cf. 2 Kgs 10:18–28), recalling that the prophet Elijah had
contended with 450 prophets of Baal at Mt Carmel (1 Kgs 18:1–46)! But
thankfully Jehoshaphat is *unlike* Ahab. The Lord establishes his kingdom,
which is none other than the kingdom of the Lord (1 Chr 17:14; 28:5;
29:23; 2 Chr 9:8; 13:8). In recognition of his kingship, Judah brings gifts to
Jehoshaphat, giving him great wealth and honor (17:5). Jehoshaphat's devotion to the Lord is seen in his removal of the high places and Asherim from
Judah (v. 6).[3]

---

2. Yamauchi, *Persia and the Bible*, 256–57.
3. For a description of high places and Asherim, see the discussion in Chapter 43 on 2 Chr
14:2–5, p. 386.

Jehoshaphat Ensures That God's Law Is Taught throughout Judah (17:7–9)

In the third year of Jehoshaphat's reign, he sends his officials to teach in the towns of Judah, along with Levites and two priests named Elishama and Jehoram (2 Chr 17:7–8). The term "official" (Heb. *sar*) often refers to some kind of military leader or official (12:10; 16:4; 17:14, 15, etc.), which may indicate that lay people are among the teachers, although the term is also used for Levitical and priestly leaders (1 Chr 12:28; 15:5–10). Priests and Levites had been given the sacred task of teaching the law (Deut 17:9–13; 33:8–11; cf. 2 Chr 35:3; Neh 8:7–8), and Ezra is a well-known example among the returnees (Ezra 7:10; Neh 8:1–8). Hezekiah will later collect tithes so that the Levites can devote themselves to God's law (2 Chr 31:4). Under Jehoshaphat's leadership, priests and Levites travel to the various cities of Judah, taking the "Book of the Law" with them so that they can instruct God's people (17:9).[4]

Jehoshaphat Gains Military Strength and His Kingdom Is Firmly Established (17:10–19)

The fear of the LORD falls upon the surrounding nations, leading to a time of peace (2 Chr 17:10). Fear upon the nations usually comes after military victories (1 Chr 14:17; 2 Chr 14:14; 20:29), but on this occasion, Jehoshaphat's piety results in tribute being given from Judah and the nations. Even the Philistines, one of Israel's enemies, bring tribute to Jehoshaphat, and the Arabians bring thousands of animals from their flock (17:11; cf. 9:14). Tribute from the nations streaming into Jerusalem is reminiscent of the flourishing kingdom under David and Solomon (1 Chr 18:2, 10–11; 2 Chr 9:1–14, 24), and it signals the ideal Davidic king, whose rule extends to the ends of the earth (Ps 72:8–11).[5] The flourishing kingdom under Jehoshaphat is not due to his military strength, nor is it due to his leadership abilities. Rather, he has sought the LORD God, and God has been with the king, establishing the kingdom.

Jehoshaphat becomes more and more powerful, building fortresses and store cities (2 Chr 17:12) as Rehoboam and Asa had done (11:5–12; 14:6–7). The chapter concludes with a description of his standing army, with

---

4. This text is problematic for scholars who hold to a late date for the Pentateuch (some argue this is a reference to a royal law code), but Klein has demonstrated convincingly that the "Book of the Law" refers to the Torah (also known as the Pentateuch); thus he suggests that the Chronicler had a "precritical view of the date of the Pentateuch" (see *2 Chronicles*, 251, especially the array of biblical references in his footnotes).

5. See Live the Story on 2 Chr 9 in Chapter 38, pp. 359–60.

a concentration of soldiers stationed in Jerusalem (17:13). Names of five military commanders are given who have oversight of an extensive conscripted army (vv. 14–19).[6] That soldiers have been stationed in Jerusalem means Jehoshaphat is well-prepared for an enemy attack, something that will be important in the days ahead (see 20:1).

LIVE the Story

The Priority of Teaching God's Word in the Church

Jehoshaphat ensures that God's word is taught throughout the kingdom. The ancient Scriptures were central to the well-being of the covenant community. Moses had not only taught the law to Israel (Deut 4:1, 5, 10, 14; 6:1), but he had exhorted God's people to learn it and obey it (5:1). The king himself was to study and meditate on God's law (17:18–20), and the success of Israel's leaders was contingent on their obedience (Josh 1:7–8; 1 Chr 22:12–13; 28:7). Azariah had warned Jehoshaphat's father about what happens when his people were "without a priest to teach and without the law" (2 Chr 15:3).[7] With this warning lingering in the background, Jehoshaphat takes the initiative to ensure that God's word is taught as priests and Levites (and possibly lay leaders) travel to the cities of Judah. These itinerant teachers bring the book of the law with them (17:9; cf. Josh 1:8), underscoring the abiding authority of the Scriptures. God's word was central to the life of the returnees, highlighting yet again that God's word needs to be taught in every generation (Ezra 7:6, 10, 25–26; Neh 8:1–18).

As believers today, the New Testament testifies to the ongoing priority of God's word in the life of the church, which includes the Old Testament Scriptures. While this might seem like an obvious point, since Paul taught, "All Scripture is God-breathed and is useful for teaching, rebuking, correcting and training in righteousness" (2 Tim 3:16), this cannot be assumed today. The well-known pastor and author Andy Stanley advocates "unhitching" the Old Testament from the church. He argues that the Old Testament is what gets the contemporary church into so much trouble, especially when we blend the old with the new. Instead, he advocates that Jesus is beginning an entirely

---

6. On the meaning of the Hebrew term *'eleph* (translated as "thousand") and its meaning as a smaller military unit (rather than a literal headcount), see the discussion in Chapter 12 on 1 Chr 12:23–40, pp. 138–40.

7. See Live the Story on 2 Chr 15 in Chapter 44, pp. 395–97.

new movement.[8] His book, entitled *Irresistible*, is filled with false assumptions about the Old Testament, including the following (as a sampling): God never intended his people to be ruled by a king; the temple was not God's idea; the old covenant was exclusively Jewish; and the Old Testament is not to be used as a guide for moral lessons or application.[9] That Stanley's book is ranked twenty-two on Amazon's Best Seller Rank for Christian Church Growth underscores the dire need of the church for solid biblical teaching.

Paul repeatedly warns about false teaching (1 Tim 1:3–7; 4:1–2; 6:3–5; 2 Tim 4:3–4; Titus 1:9–11, 13–14; cf. 2 Pet 2:1; 1 John 4:1–6), and he exhorts others to devote themselves to the teaching of God's word (1 Tim 5:17; 2 Tim 1:13–14; 2:2; 4:2–5; Titus 1:11; 2:1), recognizing that the Holy Spirit has gifted some to be teachers (1 Cor 12:28–29; Eph 4:11; cf. Rom 12:7; Heb 5:12; Jas 3:1). This task of the church to teach the word of God is especially important today, since we face an increasing biblical illiteracy, what Kenneth Briggs refers to as a "Bibleless Christianity."[10]

Jehoshaphat ensured that God's word was taught by appointing itinerant teachers who taught the Scriptures throughout the cities of Judah. In the contemporary church, priority needs to be given to the faithful teaching of the Scriptures in the pulpit, in small-group Bible studies, and in theological institutions that educate future pastors and church leaders. Ed Setzer has considered various approaches to teaching God's word in the local church. After surveying a number of statistics that highlight the problem, he raises the question: "So how do we get people to pull the Bible off their bookshelves and put it into their lives?"[11] Based on his research, he suggests nine factors that may lead to a higher engagement of the Bible, one of which is studying it in small groups, as he notes: "Small groups are key to combating and changing the epidemic of biblical illiteracy. Our research shows that as Christians increase their participation in small groups, their Bible engagement scores go up."[12] Just as Jehoshaphat developed a strategy to ensure that God's word was taught in the kingdom, pastors and church leaders need to think strategically

---

8. For a helpful critique, see Michael J. Kruger, "Why We Can't Unhitch from the Old Testament," Gospel Coalition, October 22, 2018, https://www.thegospelcoalition.org/reviews/irresistible-andy-stanley/.

9. Andy Stanley, *Irresistible*.

10. Briggs laments: "After centuries of highlighting the printed Word, the specter of Bibleless Christianity, or something close to it, looms on the horizon. . . . The *sola Scriptura* is turning into a kind of 'nola Scriptura'" (*The Invisible Bestseller*, 58); see also Live the Story in Chapter 8, pp. 103–5.

11. Ed Setzer, "The Epidemic of Biblical Illiteracy in our Churches," *Christianity Today*, July 2015, https://www.christianitytoday.com/pastors/2017/bible-engagement/epidemic-of-bible-illiteracy-in-our-churches.html.

12. Ibid.

about how God's word is taught in their own church context. The focus is always on the abiding word of God—this has not changed—yet *how* we teach God's word is based on the changing contexts for ministry.

One pastor I know has developed a new strategy in his church after reading Moses's instruction that the law was to be read every seven years (Deut 31:9–13). He and his leadership team have made the commitment to preach and teach through the entire Bible every seven years.[13] When I visited the church to teach on the Old Testament, the hunger for God's word was palpable among those attending the conference. Other pastors I know have been teaching weekly Bible studies on Zoom, making use of this platform during the pandemic when in-person teaching was not possible. Whatever the strategy used, the important principle is that God's word needs to be taught in every generation. The increase in biblical illiteracy certainly presents a challenge, but it is also an opportunity that requires an intentional commitment to teach the Scriptures. The apostle Paul gave special instructions to Timothy, who was to devote himself to the preaching and teaching of God's word (1 Tim 4:11–16; 2 Tim 2:15; 3:14–17; 4:2). We do well to recall these timeless words of affirmation given by Paul: "All Scripture is God-breathed and is useful for teaching, rebuking, correcting and training in righteousness" (2 Tim 3:16; cf. Rom 15:4). This is our calling today. It is all the more urgent in light of an increasing biblical illiteracy. We need pastors who are committed to study the Scriptures and to ensure that their congregants are taught the word of God.

---

13. Lead Pastor, Travis Simone, Williamsburg Community Chapel, Williamsburg, VA, USA.

CHAPTER 47

2 Chronicles 18:1–34

 LISTEN to the Story

¹Now Jehoshaphat had great wealth and honor, and he allied himself with Ahab by marriage. ²Some years later he went down to see Ahab in Samaria. Ahab slaughtered many sheep and cattle for him and the people with him and urged him to attack Ramoth Gilead. ³Ahab king of Israel asked Jehoshaphat king of Judah, "Will you go with me against Ramoth Gilead?"

Jehoshaphat replied, "I am as you are, and my people as your people; we will join you in the war." ⁴But Jehoshaphat also said to the king of Israel, "First seek the counsel of the LORD."

⁵So the king of Israel brought together the prophets—four hundred men—and asked them, "Shall we go to war against Ramoth Gilead, or shall I not?"

"Go," they answered, "for God will give it into the king's hand."

⁶But Jehoshaphat asked, "Is there no longer a prophet of the LORD here whom we can inquire of?"

⁷The king of Israel answered Jehoshaphat, "There is still one prophet through whom we can inquire of the LORD, but I hate him because he never prophesies anything good about me, but always bad. He is Micaiah son of Imlah."

"The king should not say such a thing," Jehoshaphat replied.

⁸So the king of Israel called one of his officials and said, "Bring Micaiah son of Imlah at once."

⁹Dressed in their royal robes, the king of Israel and Jehoshaphat king of Judah were sitting on their thrones at the threshing floor by the entrance of the gate of Samaria, with all the prophets prophesying before them. ¹⁰Now Zedekiah son of Kenaanah had made iron horns, and he declared, "This is what the LORD says: 'With these you will gore the Arameans until they are destroyed.'"

¹¹All the other prophets were prophesying the same thing. "Attack Ramoth Gilead and be victorious," they said, "for the LORD will give it into the king's hand."

¹²The messenger who had gone to summon Micaiah said to him, "Look, the other prophets without exception are predicting success for the king. Let your word agree with theirs, and speak favorably."

¹³But Micaiah said, "As surely as the LORD lives, I can tell him only what my God says."

¹⁴When he arrived, the king asked him, "Micaiah, shall we go to war against Ramoth Gilead, or shall I not?"

"Attack and be victorious," he answered, "for they will be given into your hand."

¹⁵The king said to him, "How many times must I make you swear to tell me nothing but the truth in the name of the LORD?"

¹⁶Then Micaiah answered, "I saw all Israel scattered on the hills like sheep without a shepherd, and the LORD said, 'These people have no master. Let each one go home in peace.'"

¹⁷The king of Israel said to Jehoshaphat, "Didn't I tell you that he never prophesies anything good about me, but only bad?"

¹⁸Micaiah continued, "Therefore hear the word of the LORD: I saw the LORD sitting on his throne with all the multitudes of heaven standing on his right and on his left. ¹⁹And the LORD said, 'Who will entice Ahab king of Israel into attacking Ramoth Gilead and going to his death there?'

"One suggested this, and another that. ²⁰Finally, a spirit came forward, stood before the LORD and said, 'I will entice him.'

"'By what means?' the LORD asked.

²¹"'I will go and be a deceiving spirit in the mouths of all his prophets,' he said.

"'You will succeed in enticing him,' said the LORD. 'Go and do it.'

²²"So now the LORD has put a deceiving spirit in the mouths of these prophets of yours. The LORD has decreed disaster for you."

²³Then Zedekiah son of Kenaanah went up and slapped Micaiah in the face. "Which way did the spirit from the LORD go when he went from me to speak to you?" he asked.

²⁴Micaiah replied, "You will find out on the day you go to hide in an inner room."

²⁵The king of Israel then ordered, "Take Micaiah and send him back

to Amon the ruler of the city and to Joash the king's son, ²⁶and say, 'This is what the king says: Put this fellow in prison and give him nothing but bread and water until I return safely.'"

²⁷Micaiah declared, "If you ever return safely, the LORD has not spoken through me." Then he added, "Mark my words, all you people!"

²⁸So the king of Israel and Jehoshaphat king of Judah went up to Ramoth Gilead. ²⁹The king of Israel said to Jehoshaphat, "I will enter the battle in disguise, but you wear your royal robes." So the king of Israel disguised himself and went into battle.

³⁰Now the king of Aram had ordered his chariot commanders, "Do not fight with anyone, small or great, except the king of Israel." ³¹When the chariot commanders saw Jehoshaphat, they thought, "This is the king of Israel." So they turned to attack him, but Jehoshaphat cried out, and the LORD helped him. God drew them away from him, ³²for when the chariot commanders saw that he was not the king of Israel, they stopped pursuing him.

³³But someone drew his bow at random and hit the king of Israel between the breastplate and the scale armor. The king told the chariot driver, "Wheel around and get me out of the fighting. I've been wounded." ³⁴All day long the battle raged, and the king of Israel propped himself up in his chariot facing the Arameans until evening. Then at sunset he died.

Listening to the Text in the Story: 1 Kings 16:30–33; 21:25–26

The story of Jehoshaphat takes a turn for the worse when he foolishly enters an alliance with the idolatrous northern king Ahab. An important text in Kings sets the context for the story that follows, and it underscores what a disastrous move it was for Jehoshaphat to forge a relationship with the northern king. Several chapters are devoted to Ahab's reign (1 Kgs 16:29–22:40), but the introductory comments about the king reveal at the outset his ungodly character:

Ahab son of Omri did more evil in the eyes of the LORD than any of those before him. He not only considered it trivial to commit the sins of Jeroboam son of Nebat, but he also married Jezebel daughter of Ethbaal king of the Sidonians, and began to serve Baal and worship him. He set up an altar for Baal in the temple of Baal that he built in Samaria. Ahab also made an Asherah pole and did more to arouse the anger of the LORD, the God of Israel, than did all the kings of Israel before him. (1 Kgs 16:30–33)

It is even said of Ahab that there was "never anyone like Ahab, who sold himself to do evil in the eyes of the LORD, urged on by Jezebel his wife. He behaved in the vilest manner by going after idols, like the Amorites the LORD drove out before Israel" (21:25–26). This is the king whom Jehoshaphat visits in Samaria, and tragically, Jehoshaphat is enticed by him to go into battle, something that will have dire consequences, almost costing him his life.

EXPLAIN the Story

Jehoshaphat Foolishly Enters into an Alliance with Ahab (18:1–8)

Great wealth and honor are attributed to Jehoshaphat, yet he foolishly allies himself with Ahab by marriage (2 Chr 18:1).[1] International marriages had been central to Solomon's foreign policy (8:11), yet alliances with foreign kings demonstrated a failure to trust in the LORD. Jehoshaphat visits Ahab in the capital city of Samaria—the very city that housed a temple for Baal (18:2; cf. 1 Kgs 16:29–33)! Jehoshaphat had not sought the Baals (2 Chr 17:3), yet one wonders *why* he would enter into an alliance with the wicked king Ahab (cf. 19:2). Hoerth notes, indeed, that Ahab was one of the most powerful northern kings, seen in the strategic role he played in the Battle of Karkar.[2] Ahab was the son of Omri, the northern king whose dynasty extends beyond Ahab for another two generations. Thus, the land of Israel becomes known in ancient texts as the "land of Omri," and his dynasty is identified as the "house of Omri." We will see shortly that this dynasty continues to exert its ungodly influence on the Southern Kingdom, culminating in the rise to power of the murderous usurper Athaliah, who was Ahab's daughter.[3] Given that Ahab was a powerful northern king, Jehoshaphat may well have felt it was advantageous to be on friendly terms with him. Whatever the reason, we will see shortly that an alternative (godly) path is always available for the king who seeks help from the LORD (ch. 20).

---

1. Jehoshaphat is allied with Ahab through the marriage of his son Jehoram to Ahab's daughter, Athaliah (cf. 2 Chr 21:6; 22:2).

2. Hoerth, *Archaeology & the Old Testament*, 312–13.

3. On the influence of Ahab's house on the south, see the discussion in Chapter 50 on 2 Chr 21, pp. 438–39.

When Jehoshaphat and those with him arrive in Samaria, a city located about thirty-five miles north of Jerusalem, Ahab puts on an impressive show by sacrificing many sheep and oxen. Ahab's intent is to entice his honored guest to go against Ramoth Gilead, located about fifty to sixty miles from Samaria (18:2). Ramoth Gilead may have fallen to Ben-hadad in an earlier campaign (1 Kgs 22:3), but no rationale is given here, making Jehoshaphat "look gullible and on shaky moral grounds."[4] The dialogue that follows shows that Jehoshaphat is committed to be Ahab's ally in battle, although he wisely instructs the king to "seek the counsel" of the LORD (*d-r-sh*, 2 Chr 18:4; see also vv. 6, 7). The verb "to seek" is frequently used in Chronicles to describe the pious king (cf. 19:3; 20:3),[5] and Jehoshaphat does the right thing to inquire of LORD, since holy wars required divine authorization before proceeding. Ahab assembles four hundred prophets and inquires of them if they should fight against Ramoth Gilead. They unanimously assure the kings that they will be victorious, but Jehoshaphat discerns that another prophet is needed. Ahab summons the prophet Micaiah, although the king gives an unfavorable assessment of him "because he never prophesies anything good about me, but always bad" (18:7)! Micaiah is nevertheless summoned at the request of Jehoshaphat (v. 8).

The Prophet Micaiah Prophesies That Ahab Will Be Defeated (18:9–27)

In the meantime, attention turns to Ahab and Jehoshaphat, who are robed with royal vestments, sitting on thrones by the gate of Samaria while the four hundred (false) prophets are before them (2 Chr 18:9). A prophet named Zedekiah takes horns to symbolically depict the defeat of the Arameans, giving further assurance of victory! As Micaiah is summoned, he is cautioned by a messenger to give a favorable verdict (v. 12). Micaiah refuses, swearing solemnly, "As surely as the LORD lives"; he tells the messenger that he will only speak what *God* tells him (v. 13). He initially tells the kings what they want to hear, but when urged to speak the truth, he tells them of the vision that he had seen of all Israel being scattered like sheep without a shepherd. Given that a shepherd was a well-known royal image in the ancient world, this was a portentous and unmistakable sign of military defeat (v. 16; cf. Nah 3:18). Micaiah's attention turns to a vision he had of the LORD's exalted throne, which underscores his sovereign rule over human affairs (2 Chr 18:18),

---

4. Klein, *2 Chronicles*, 261.

5. The verb "to seek" (Heb. *d-r-sh*) occurs over forty times in Chronicles; see the discussion in Chapter 30 on 2 Chr 1:5, pp. 291–93.

reminiscent of Isaiah's vision of God's heavenly throne (Isa 6:1–13). Prophets are sometimes given a glimpse into the heavenly realm (vv. 1–7; Ezek 1:4–28; Dan 7:9–14; Zech 3:1–5; cf. Jer 23:18–22), and on this occasion, Micaiah is to understand that God is bringing about the downfall of the idolatrous Ahab.

In the heavenly scene the LORD asks, "Who will entice Ahab king of Israel into attacking Ramoth Gilead and going to his death there?" (2 Chr 18:19). In the midst of a heavenly dialogue, one spirit responds: "I will entice him" (v. 20). The spirit will become a deceiving spirit in the mouth of his prophets, and the LORD affirms his plan with the command: "Go and do it" (v. 21). As Micaiah makes known the disaster that will come upon Ahab (who is being judged by God), the false prophet Zedekiah strikes Micaiah on the cheek. Instead of giving heed to the prophet, Ahab puts him in prison, with the instructions that he is to be given nothing except bread and water until Ahab returns safely. Micaiah retorts that if Ahab returns safely, God has not spoken by him (v. 27; cf. Deut 18:15–22)! As the death of Ahab unfolds shortly, we are to understand that God is at work behind the scenes, using his heavenly emissaries to execute judgment against Ahab, whose reign has been character-ized by blatant idolatry (1 Kgs 16:30–33; 21:25–26). False prophets in the Old Testament are condemned by God for leading people astray (Deut 18:19-22; Jer 23:9-26), but in this story, the LORD is actively bringing about Ahab's demise through them. The prophet Elijah had earlier announced judgment against him (1 Kgs 21:17–21), and now the LORD reveals through Micaiah his plan to judge Ahab, for the "LORD has decreed disaster for you" (2 Chr 18:22).

Ahab Is Killed, but Jehoshaphat Cries Out to God (18:28–34)

Contrary to the advice of Micaiah, Ahab and Jehoshaphat foolishly go up against Ramoth Gilead. Ahab plans to disguise himself, but he then instructs (the gullible!) Jehoshaphat to wear his royal garments (2 Chr 18:28–29). Not realizing the implications of what lies ahead, Jehoshaphat soon discovers the folly of his actions. The Arameans assume that *he* is the king of Israel. In a desperate plea, Jehoshaphat cries out to the LORD (v. 31), which takes us to the heart of the Chronicler's theology—God helps those who cry out to him for help. In response to Jehoshaphat's desperate cry, the LORD helps the king and draws away the enemy. But Ahab is severely wounded, and while the battle is raging, he props himself in his chariot until he finally dies that evening (v. 34). The account in Kings records that his blood-drenched chariot was cleaned by the pool of Samaria, with the dogs licking up his blood in accordance with God's word of judgment (1 Kgs 22:34–38; cf. 1 Kgs 21:18–19). On the other hand, Jehoshaphat narrowly escapes and arrives safely in Jerusalem.

LIVE the Story

Warnings Against False Prophets and Teachers

When Jehoshaphat had met with Ahab in Samaria, he had wisely told the king that they needed to inquire of the LORD, yet he was ambushed by false prophets (many of them!) who assure the kings that God will give them victory. This is perhaps just what they wanted to hear—God's blessing on *their* plans. Moses had warned the Israelites to be careful of false prophets (Deut 18:9–22). False prophets in this story claim to speak directly for God, using the authoritative formulate: "This is what the LORD says" (2 Chr 18:10). The Old Testament has numerous examples of those who claim to speak God's word (cf. Jer 28:1–17; Ezek 34:1–10), yet they end up tragically leading God's people astray. This reminds us that simply *claiming* to have heard from God or giving a word in "God's name" (even with a sign!) does not mean it is actually from God.

It is not uncommon to hear in Christian circles or on social media, "Thus says the LORD," by self-proclaimed prophets. Ruth Graham, a writer for the *New York Times*, comments on the alarming rise of Christian prophets. She observes that these kinds of "prophets" are the "stars within what is now one of the fastest-growing corners of Christianity: a loose but fervent movement led by hundreds of people who believe they can channel supernatural powers—and have special spiritual insights into world events."[6] These self-appointed prophets are filling a void, as Brad Christerson, faculty member at Biola University, comments: "It's a symptom of our time. People don't trust institutions, and people think that all mainstream institutions are corrupt: universities, science, government, and the media. They're searching for real sources of truth."[7] Yet, as the article rehearses, the so-called "prophecies" of these self-appointed prophets do not pass the test for a prophet—it must come true, as Micaiah stated unambiguously.

When we consider the New Testament, prophets are attested in the early church (Acts 11:28; 13:1; 15:32; 21:10; 1 Cor 12:28–29; 14:29; Eph 2:20; 4:11). This is not surprising, since the prophet Joel had announced that the pouring forth of God's Spirit would result in sons and daughters prophesying

---

6. Ruth Graham, "Christian Prophets are On the Rise. What Happens When They're Wrong," February 11, 2021, https://www.nytimes.com/2021/02/11/us/christian-prophets-predictions.html. See also the article in *Christianity Today* by Craig Keener, "When Political Prophecies Don't Come to Pass," November 11, 2020, https://www.christianitytoday.com/ct/2020/november-web-only/political-prophecy-false-bible-scholar-trump-election.html.

7. Cited by Ruth Graham in her *New York Times* article, "Christian Prophets are On the Rise."

(Joel 2:28). Yet, Jesus also warned about the dangers of false prophets, those who claim to speak in *his* name, casting out demons and healing, yet Jesus says he never knew them (Matt 7:15–23). This is the kind of false prophet Paul encountered, who was full of lies and deceit (Acts 13:6–12).

The New Testament writers are careful to warn fellow believers both about false prophets and teachers and the importance of testing words that are claimed to have come directly from God. John warns about false prophets, urging believers to test the spirits "to see whether they are from God, because many false prophets have gone out into the world" (1 John 4:1). Paul similarly teaches the Corinthians that they should "weigh carefully what is said" by prophets (1 Cor 14:29). Peter also warns about false teachers who secretly introduce destructive heresies, comparing them to false prophets in the Old Testament (2 Pet 2:1). They, too, will fall under God's judgment. False prophets are also identified in the book of Revelation as those who deceptively lead God's people away from worship of the Lord (Rev 13:11–18; 16:13; 19:20), especially seen in the malevolent intent of the Antichrist, who seeks to usurp God's sovereign rule.

As Christians today, the words and character of those who claim to be prophets need to come under careful scrutiny. Jesus taught that prophets are to be identified by their good fruit (Matt 7:16–20). God has also given us discernment through his Spirit. In contrast to the Old Testament, where the Spirit only came upon a select people, God now pours out his Spirit on all flesh (Isa 44:3; Joel 2:28; Acts 2:17). This elevates the role of every believer within the church community (Rom 5:5; 8:9; 1 Cor 2:12; 3:16; Gal 3:2; 4:6), and notably, it was through the Holy Spirit that Paul discerned that the Jewish false prophet was speaking lies (Acts 13:9–10). This ought to encourage us to listen to what God might be saying through the Holy Spirit, but also to evaluate people by their fruit and by their words, since both should be consistent with Scripture. While prophecy is not to be despised, believers are urged to "test them all" and "hold on to what is good" (1 Thess 5:21; cf. 1 John 4:1–6; cf. 2 John 7–9).

In his article "7 Traits of False Teachers," Colin Smith argues that we should expect to find false teachers and prophets in the church since Satan, the counterfeiter, is alive and well. Smith outlines seven ways to test a false teacher that include: considering a person's source, message, position, character, appeal, and fruit, citing biblical references to support this kind of testing.[8] In the Old

---

8. Colin Smith, "7 Traits of False Teachers," March 18, 2012, https://www.thegospelcoalition.org/article/7-traits-of-false-teachers/.

Testament, the ultimate test for a prophet was that their words come to pass (Deut 18:20–22; 2 Chr 18:27). This story serves as a warning and a reminder that we, too, need to scrutinize carefully words spoken by those who claim to have heard directly from God. This means, therefore, that simply *claiming* to be a prophet doesn't make one a prophet. Further, the test of prophecy is not how many thousands or millions of followers someone has on Twitter or Instagram, just as the many "prophets" uttering their words before Ahaz and Jehoshaphat were no indication that they were real prophets. In fact, there was only one true prophet who spoke God's word, and his prophetic word came to pass. This the most important test, and based on what is heard on social media, not too many seem to pass this test.

LISTEN to the Story

¹When Jehoshaphat king of Judah returned safely to his palace in Jerusalem, ²Jehu the seer, the son of Hanani, went out to meet him and said to the king, "Should you help the wicked and love those who hate the LORD? Because of this, the wrath of the LORD is on you. ³There is, however, some good in you, for you have rid the land of the Asherah poles and have set your heart on seeking God."

⁴Jehoshaphat lived in Jerusalem, and he went out again among the people from Beersheba to the hill country of Ephraim and turned them back to the LORD, the God of their ancestors. ⁵He appointed judges in the land, in each of the fortified cities of Judah. ⁶He told them, "Consider carefully what you do, because you are not judging for mere mortals but for the LORD, who is with you whenever you give a verdict. ⁷Now let the fear of the LORD be on you. Judge carefully, for with the LORD our God there is no injustice or partiality or bribery."

⁸In Jerusalem also, Jehoshaphat appointed some of the Levites, priests and heads of Israelite families to administer the law of the LORD and to settle disputes. And they lived in Jerusalem. ⁹He gave them these orders: "You must serve faithfully and wholeheartedly in the fear of the LORD. ¹⁰In every case that comes before you from your people who live in the cities—whether bloodshed or other concerns of the law, commands, decrees or regulations—you are to warn them not to sin against the LORD; otherwise his wrath will come on you and your people. Do this, and you will not sin.

¹¹"Amariah the chief priest will be over you in any matter concerning the LORD, and Zebadiah son of Ishmael, the leader of the tribe of Judah, will be over you in any matter concerning the king, and the Levites will

serve as officials before you. Act with courage, and may the Lord be with those who do well."

Listening to the Text in the Story: Deuteronomy 16:18–19

The story of Jehoshaphat continues with his safe return to Jerusalem. After being rebuked by the prophet Jehu for his alliance with Ahab, Jehoshaphat is instrumental in bringing Judah back to the Lord, seen especially in his appointment of judges to ensure that God's law is followed. The appointment of judges to administer justice can be traced back to the time of Moses, when those well-respected in the community were appointed to share in the judicial task (Exod 18:17–26; Deut 1:13–18; cf. Judg 4:4). Moses had instructed Israel: "Appoint judges and officials for each of your tribes in every town the Lord your God is giving you, and they shall judge the people fairly. Do not pervert justice or show partiality. Do not accept a bribe, for a bribe blinds the eyes of the wise and twists the words of the innocent" (Deut 16:18–19; cf. 17:8–12). In keeping with this longstanding tradition, judicial reforms are established under Jehoshaphat, whose very name ("Yahweh judges") speaks to this important topic.

EXPLAIN the Story

Jehoshaphat Is Rebuked for His Alliance with Ahab (19:1–3)

After arriving safely back in Jerusalem (see 2 Chr 18 for the back story), the prophet Jehu meets Jehoshaphat and says to him: "Should you help the wicked and love those who hate the Lord?" (19:2). Given the blatant idolatry that characterized Ahab's reign (1 Kgs 16:30–34), Jehoshaphat should not have entered into an alliance with him. Instead of falling under divine judgment, he responds rightly by removing the Asherah poles and by setting his heart to seek the Lord (2 Chr 19:3). His judiciary appointments that follow underscore his commitment to seek God.

Jehoshaphat Appoints Judges (19:4–11)

Jehoshaphat lives in Jerusalem, but his personal commitment to bring people back to the Lord is seen in his travels throughout the kingdom as he travels from Beersheba to the hill country of Ephraim (2 Chr 19:4). Encountering the king in these cities would have undoubtedly been a great honor, but most importantly, it had the result of turning people back to the LORD (v. 4). The king appoints judges to ensure that God's law is taught and upheld (vv. 5–7), thereby ensuring that God's standards of righteousness and justice were followed in the kingdom (cf. Jer 22:2–4; 23:5–8). Judges had a sacred task, as Japhet notes: "the presence of the Lord makes every legal judgment a religious act, to be observed with proper awe of the divine presence."[1] Scripture teaches that the LORD hates injustice, partiality, and bribery (cf. Deut 16:19; Mic 3:1–4, 9–11), thus the decisions of the judges were to reflect God's righteousness, who was judge of all the earth (cf. Pss 7:11; 9:7–8; 50:6; 82:1–8). Priests and Levites serve as the judiciary body in Jerusalem, offering legal advice for the courts within the towns of Judah (2 Chr 19:8).[2] In their sacred task, Jehoshaphat charges them: "You must serve faithfully and wholeheartedly in the fear of the LORD" (v. 9). When a matter came before the priests and Levites in Jerusalem, they were to apply God's laws in the administration of justice and to warn God's people not to sin against the LORD, lest his wrath come upon them (v. 10). The wrath of God was to be taken seriously, as Hezekiah will later understand (29:6–9; 32:25–26). Jehoshaphat appoints Amariah, the chief priest, over the priests and Levites and Zebadiah, the ruler of the house of Judah, over everything that relates to the king (19:11). As was seen during the reign of King David, the appointment of leaders by the king was critical to the flourishing of the kingdom.[3] Jehoshaphat gives his leaders an exhortation: "Act with courage, and may the LORD be with those who do well" (v. 11).

LIVE the Story

Resolving Disputes within the Christian Community

Judicial reforms established under Jehoshaphat testify to the reality of disputes within the covenant community and the need for leaders who are able to resolve them based on God's righteous standards. Within the church today, this underlying principle of resolving conflict within the Christian community remains the same, since believers are called to reflect God's holiness and righteousness. Disputes among believers are to be resolved following biblical principles, rather than adopting secular practices. Jesus taught his disciples that if a person sins, a

---

1. Japhet, *I & II Chronicles*, 775.
2. Klein, *2 Chronicles*, 276.
3. See Live the Story in Chapter 27, p. 263–65.

fellow believer was to address the issue with a brother or sister privately; if the person refuses to listen, one or two believers are invited into the conversation, so that it might be resolved. The church is required to take disciplinary action if the matter cannot be resolved in a smaller, more private context (Matt 18:15–17).

We live in a highly litigious society, and America has more lawsuits per 100,000 than any other country, with studies showing lawsuits are four times higher than Canada, 3.8 times higher than Australia, and 3.3 higher than Japan. There are also more lawyers per capita in the US (except Israel) and more judges per capita (except France) than any other country in the world.[4] It is all too easy for this litigious culture to influence how Christians resolve disputes with each other. When conflict arises within the church body, Paul instructs believers not to seek resolution through secular legal courts, but instead, he urges the church at Corinth: "If any of you has a dispute with another, do you dare to take it before the ungodly for judgment instead of before the Lord's people?" (1 Cor 6:1). While Romans 13:1–7 affirms the right of government to adjudicate in matters pertaining to criminal cases, Paul addresses civil litigation in 1 Corinthians 6:1–8. Civil cases in Roman Corinth covered matters such as "legal possession, breach of contract, damages, fraud and injury."[5] The judiciary process in Corinth entailed the appointment of one or two honorary magistrates who served for the year. Cases were brought before the magistrate, and sometimes juries were used, selected from Roman citizens with social status. Bribery was common practice, having the potential to influence the outcome of a trial.[6] Winter notes further that the judicial process exacerbated personal grievances, since the prosecutor's rhetorical strategy entailed attacking his opponent with hostile speeches and defamation of character (what the Romans called *reprehensio vitae* or *vituperatio*, "a personal attack on the character of one's opponents"). Divisions among believers already existed in the church at Corinth (1:10–17; 3:1–7), and Winter suggests that litigation in Roman courts may have been used to express publicly the animosity already present in the community.[7] Paul's point is that minor offenses should be resolved by arbitrators from within the church community

---

4. For these statistics, see the article by Alex Berezow, "Blame and Claim: Can We Fix America's Uniquely Litigious Society?," *American Council on Science and Health*, December 28, 2019 (https://www.acsh.org/news/2019/12/27/blame-and-claim-can-we-fix-americas-uniquely-litigious-culture-14477).

5. Bruce W. Winter, "Civil Litigation in Secular Corinth and the Church: The Forensic Background to 1 Corinthians 6:1–8," *NTS* 37:4 (1991), 561.

6. Ibid., 561–64.

7. Ibid., 567–68. One could argue that social media has this function today, where disputes within the Christian community are taking place in the public domain with divisive rhetoric instead of being done privately, in love, and face-to-face within the church community. The use of social media to vent anger is problematic at several levels, not the least of which is the impact this has on the witness of the gospel.

who were well-able to act in a legal capacity. Winter thus concludes that the Corinthian church

> failed dismally to judge the insider when they should have done so, 5.13. On the other hand, they had allowed the unrighteous outsides to judge the insiders, 6.1, when they should have resorted to the use of a fellow Christian from their number, who, by reason of his legal training, would have had the requisite qualifications to act as private arbitrator.[8]

Gordon Fee notes further that what lies behind Paul's teaching is an understanding that the church is an eschatological community, and this means grievances should not be resolved in secular courts. Fee notes that their eschatological existence "trivializes such grievances—and puts believers in the awkward position of asking a ruling by the very people they themselves will eventually judge."[9] Requiring secular courts to adjudicate disputes among believers also impacts the witness of the gospel. While our contemporary judicial system is not identical to the first century legal context, one may well wonder whether our highly litigious secular culture has had undue influence on the church. Winter notes, indeed, that the initiation of legal proceedings at Corinth was "a sign of defeat in relationships long before the verdict was pronounced in court."[10] Paul thus contends that it is far better to be wronged than seek solutions to disputes in secular courts of the day.

We have seen that in the Old Testament leaders were appointed from among the covenant community to settle disputes. Minor disputes were to be settled locally, yet priests and Levites were appointed to give counsel on weightier matters. God has appointed leaders within the church to address sin and disputes, yet there are also Christian organizations that are able to provide Christian arbitration so that conflict can be resolved biblically and within the Christian community. One such organization is Peacemaker Ministries.[11] The goal of this organization is to help Christians respond to disputes biblically, but also to provide legal Christian arbitration services so that Christians can resolve disputes within the Christian community. While the secular culture flaunts its individual rights, the Christian community is called to embody humility and self-sacrifice under the Lordship of Christ.

---

8. Ibid., 572.
9. Fee, *God's Empowering Presence*, 804.
10. Winter, "Civil Litigation," 571.
11. For more information about this organization, see www.peacemakerministries.org.

LISTEN to the Story

¹After this, the Moabites and Ammonites with some of the Meunites came to wage war against Jehoshaphat.

²Some people came and told Jehoshaphat, "A vast army is coming against you from Edom, from the other side of the Dead Sea. It is already in Hazezon Tamar" (that is, En Gedi). ³Alarmed, Jehoshaphat resolved to inquire of the Lord, and he proclaimed a fast for all Judah. ⁴The people of Judah came together to seek help from the Lord; indeed, they came from every town in Judah to seek him.

⁵Then Jehoshaphat stood up in the assembly of Judah and Jerusalem at the temple of the Lord in the front of the new courtyard ⁶and said:

"Lord, the God of our ancestors, are you not the God who is in heaven? You rule over all the kingdoms of the nations. Power and might are in your hand, and no one can withstand you. ⁷Our God, did you not drive out the inhabitants of this land before your people Israel and give it forever to the descendants of Abraham your friend? ⁸They have lived in it and have built in it a sanctuary for your Name, saying, ⁹'If calamity comes upon us, whether the sword of judgment, or plague or famine, we will stand in your presence before this temple that bears your Name and will cry out to you in our distress, and you will hear us and save us.'

¹⁰"But now here are men from Ammon, Moab and Mount Seir, whose territory you would not allow Israel to invade when they came from Egypt; so they turned away from them and did not destroy them. ¹¹See how they are repaying us by coming to drive us out of the possession you gave us as an inheritance. ¹²Our God, will you not judge them? For we have no power to face this vast

army that is attacking us. We do not know what to do, but our eyes are on you."

[13]All the men of Judah, with their wives and children and little ones, stood there before the LORD.

[14]Then the Spirit of the LORD came on Jahaziel son of Zechariah, the son of Benaiah, the son of Jeiel, the son of Mattaniah, a Levite and descendant of Asaph, as he stood in the assembly.

[15]He said: "Listen, King Jehoshaphat and all who live in Judah and Jerusalem! This is what the LORD says to you: 'Do not be afraid or discouraged because of this vast army. For the battle is not yours, but God's. [16]Tomorrow march down against them. They will be climbing up by the Pass of Ziz, and you will find them at the end of the gorge in the Desert of Jeruel. [17]You will not have to fight this battle. Take up your positions; stand firm and see the deliverance the LORD will give you, Judah and Jerusalem. Do not be afraid; do not be discouraged. Go out to face them tomorrow, and the LORD will be with you.'"

[18]Jehoshaphat bowed down with his face to the ground, and all the people of Judah and Jerusalem fell down in worship before the LORD. [19]Then some Levites from the Kohathites and Korahites stood up and praised the LORD, the God of Israel, with a very loud voice.

[20]Early in the morning they left for the Desert of Tekoa. As they set out, Jehoshaphat stood and said, "Listen to me, Judah and people of Jerusalem! Have faith in the LORD your God and you will be upheld; have faith in his prophets and you will be successful." [21]After consulting the people, Jehoshaphat appointed men to sing to the LORD and to praise him for the splendor of his holiness as they went out at the head of the army, saying:

"Give thanks to the LORD,
for his love endures forever."

[22]As they began to sing and praise, the LORD set ambushes against the men of Ammon and Moab and Mount Seir who were invading Judah, and they were defeated. [23]The Ammonites and Moabites rose up against the men from Mount Seir to destroy and annihilate them. After they finished slaughtering the men from Seir, they helped to destroy one another.

[24]When the men of Judah came to the place that overlooks the desert

and looked toward the vast army, they saw only dead bodies lying on the ground; no one had escaped. ²⁵So Jehoshaphat and his men went to carry off their plunder, and they found among them a great amount of equipment and clothing and also articles of value—more than they could take away. There was so much plunder that it took three days to collect it. ²⁶On the fourth day they assembled in the Valley of Berakah, where they praised the LORD. This is why it is called the Valley of Berakah to this day.

²⁷Then, led by Jehoshaphat, all the men of Judah and Jerusalem returned joyfully to Jerusalem, for the LORD had given them cause to rejoice over their enemies. ²⁸They entered Jerusalem and went to the temple of the LORD with harps and lyres and trumpets.

²⁹The fear of God came on all the surrounding kingdoms when they heard how the LORD had fought against the enemies of Israel. ³⁰And the kingdom of Jehoshaphat was at peace, for his God had given him rest on every side.

³¹So Jehoshaphat reigned over Judah. He was thirty-five years old when he became king of Judah, and he reigned in Jerusalem twenty-five years. His mother's name was Azubah daughter of Shilhi. ³²He followed the ways of his father Asa and did not stray from them; he did what was right in the eyes of the LORD. ³³The high places, however, were not removed, and the people still had not set their hearts on the God of their ancestors.

³⁴The other events of Jehoshaphat's reign, from beginning to end, are written in the annals of Jehu son of Hanani, which are recorded in the book of the kings of Israel.

³⁵Later, Jehoshaphat king of Judah made an alliance with Ahaziah king of Israel, whose ways were wicked. ³⁶He agreed with him to construct a fleet of trading ships. After these were built at Ezion Geber, ³⁷Eliezer son of Dodavahu of Mareshah prophesied against Jehoshaphat, saying, "Because you have made an alliance with Ahaziah, the LORD will destroy what you have made." The ships were wrecked and were not able to set sail to trade.

Listening to the Text in the Story: Psalm 44

The reign of Jehoshaphat comes to a climax when a coalition of foreign nations wages war against him. The response of the king enables the Chronicler to teach on godly virtues that includes self-humbling, prayer, reliance upon

God, and faith. When Jehoshaphat is faced with an enemy, he calls God's people to prayer and fasting. At the center of this story lies Jehoshaphat's corporate prayer of lament (2 Chr 20:5–12), followed by an oracle of salvation uttered by Jahaziel (vv. 13–19). As we listen to the text in this story, it is helpful to remember that individual and corporate prayers of lament found in the Psalter have common features that enable scholars to categorize them as a "lament" (cf. Pss 3–7; 22; 44; 51; 80). Examining these elements briefly will help us read Jehoshaphat's prayer with this genre in view.

Psalm 44 is a good example of a communal lament. The psalmist recalls God's past saving activity:

> We have heard it with our ears, O God;
>   our ancestors have told us
> what you did in their days,
>   in days long ago.
> With your hand you drove out the nations
>   and planted our ancestors;
> you crushed the peoples
>   and made our ancestors flourish.
> It was not by their sword that they won the land,
>   nor did their arm bring them victory;
> it was your right hand, your arm,
>   and the light of your face, for you loved them. (vv. 1–3)

As with the psalmist, Jehoshaphat begins his prayer by affirming God's might and power and by recalling God's past activity when he drove out the inhabitants of the land (2 Chr 20:6–7). The psalmist calls out to God, affirming that victory will come through him (Ps 44:4–5). The psalmist declares his trust in the LORD when he says: "I put no trust in my bow, my sword does not bring me victory" (v. 6), even as Jehoshaphat acknowledges his dependence upon the LORD in view of his own weakness (2 Chr 20:12). The psalmist concludes with a plea to God for help: "Rise up and help us; rescue us because of your unfailing love" (Ps 44:26). His prayer reflects Jehoshaphat's cry to God for help, when the king prays: "Our God, will you not judge them? For we have no power to face this vast army that is attacking us. We do not know what to do, but our eyes are on you" (2 Chr 20:12).

The king's prayer of lament is followed by an oracle of salvation pronounced by Jahaziel that begins with a characteristic exhortation, "Do not be afraid or discouraged because of this vast army. For the battle is not yours, but God's"

(2 Chr 20:15). This serves as a word of encouragement, not only for the people of Judah during Jehoshaphat's time, but also for the post-exilic community living as a small remnant with powerful nations surrounding them. They, too, are not to be afraid or discouraged, and they, too, are to call upon the LORD.

EXPLAIN the Story

Nations Wage War against Jehoshaphat (20:1–4)

The story begins with the Moabites, Ammonites, and Meunites waging war against Jehoshaphat (2 Chr 20:1).[1] David had defeated the Moabites a few decades earlier, and he had received tribute from them and from the Ammonites (1 Chr 18:2, 11). The Meunites are rarely mentioned in the Old Testament (cf. 4:41; 2 Chr 26:7), thus their identity is uncertain. They may have been located in the southern Negeb, which would be compatible with Mount Seir mentioned later (20:10, 22–23). Jehoshaphat hears the news that a "vast army is coming against you from Edom, from the other side of the Dead Sea" (v. 2). King Asa had faced a multitude coming against him, yet amidst his distress, he had cried out to God for help and was delivered (14:9–12). Jehoshaphat now faces a military threat that is beyond his own military capabilities. The urgency of the situation is underscored by the fact that the army has advanced to En Gedi, located approximately thirty-five miles from Jerusalem, west of the Dead Sea (20:2). En Gedi belonged to the tribe of Judah, thus they are encroaching into Israelite territory (Josh 15:62; cf. 1 Sam 23:29).

The king is rightly alarmed when he hears the news, but instead of calling up his standing army stationed in Jerusalem (cf. 2 Chr 17:13), Jehoshaphat sets his face to seek the LORD (20:3). The verb "to seek, inquire" (Heb. *d-r-sh*) can mean to investigate a situation (Deut 13:14; 17:4; 19:18; Judg 6:29), but also to seek an answer (Deut 17:9). Earlier, Jehoshaphat had inquired of prophets to see whether he and Ahab should go to battle (2 Chr 18:4, 6–7), but he had not listened to Micaiah, and he was almost killed as a result. Having learned the hard lesson, this time Jehoshaphat inquires of God, and, as we will see shortly, he gives heed to the prophetic word. Jehoshaphat's earnest desire to seek God is seen in the fast he proclaims. In the Old Testament, fasting was associated with mourning (e.g., 2 Sam

---

1. The Hebrew text identifies the third group as Ammonites, a people already mentioned in the list. Following the Septuagint, it is preferable to identity the third group as Meunites (NIV, ESV, NASB), a people mentioned elsewhere (2 Chr 26:7). On the textual issues and possible identity of the Meunites, see Williamson, *1 and 2 Chronicles*, 293–94.

1:12; 1 Chr 10:12), but sometimes it accompanied prayers, underscoring a person's earnest desire to seek an answer from God (2 Sam 12:16, 21–23; Ezra 8:21, 23; Neh 1:4). Jehoshaphat's posture is one of humility as he calls the entire community to pray and fast.

Jehoshaphat Beseeches God for Help (20:5–12)

Jehoshaphat stands before the people in the house of the LORD. He publicly confesses that the LORD is ruler over all the kingdoms of the nations and power and might belong to him (2 Chr 20:5–6). This recalls David's prayer when he had acknowledged: "Yours, LORD, is the greatness and the power and the glory and the majesty and the splendor, for everything in heaven and earth is yours. Yours, LORD, is the kingdom; you are exalted as head over all" (1 Chr 29:11). David had uttered these words during a time of celebration, but now, as Jehoshaphat faces the enemy's onslaught, he turns his attention to God, reminding God's people *who* is in their midst. This is an important principle when facing fearful situations—remembering that God is in control. The king remembers what God has done for his forefathers, for he had driven out the nations before them and given them the land (2 Chr 20:7–8). With echoes of Solomon's prayer reverberating in his own prayer, he recalls that if evil should come upon God's people, they were to stand before God in his house and cry out to him in their distress (v. 9; cf. 6:28–30). Instead of being overtaken with fear, he rehearses the sacred Scriptures, putting on the full armor of God, as it were, so that he might stand firm against the enemy. With the shield of faith, he confesses that God will deliver his people.

The king rehearses their dire circumstances, noting that these foreign nations are now coming against them, seeking to drive them out of their possession (20:10–11). Japhet perceptively observes that this is not "a common campaign for a limited military victory or territorial gains," but rather, it is "total war, a threat to the very existence of Israel."[2] Their assault against Jerusalem is a "direct affront to God's plan for the world."[3] We noted earlier that David's battles with foreign nations had a spiritual component, recalling that Psalm 2 describes the kings of the earth rising up against the LORD and against his anointed (Ps 2:1–3).[4] The nations were advised to take warning, however, because of God's wrath (vv. 10–12). It is not surprising to find, therefore, that Jehoshaphat calls upon God to bring judgment against those

---

2. Japhet, *I & II Chronicles*, 791.
3. Ibid.
4. On the spiritual nature of Israel's battles, see Live the Story in Chapter 14, pp. 153–54, Chapter 19, pp. 199–201, and Chapter 61, pp. 531–32.

who are attacking him (2 Chr 20:10–11). He acknowledges that he and the people are powerless in comparison to the vast army coming against him. He concludes his prayer with utter dependence upon God: "We do not know what to do, but our eyes are on you" (v. 12). As a leader, Jehoshaphat acknowledges his own weakness and inability to know what to do, but he is doing exactly what he *should* be doing—he is turning to the LORD for help. God is the one who will fight his battle.

The Spirit of the LORD Brings Encouragement through Jahaziel (20:13–19)

With the entire assembly standing before the LORD, the Spirit of God comes upon a man named Jahaziel, who is a Levite from the line of Asaph (2 Chr 20:14). The Spirit of God is active throughout the period of the kings, bringing both rebuke and encouragement (1 Chr 12:18; 2 Chr 15:1; 20:14; 24:20). In this story, the immediate response through the Spirit affirms that God *has* heard Jehoshaphat's prayer, and he is now helping Jehoshaphat know what to do—he is to wait for God's deliverance. This is how he fights his battle.

Jahaziel now brings a much-needed word of exhortation to the people: They are not to be afraid of the great multitude before them, for the battle is not theirs, but God's (20:14–15)! They are to go out the next day by the Pass of Ziz (which was probably located on the western shore of the Dead Sea in the region of Tekoa). Remarkably, they are not to fight themselves, but instead, they are to *wait* for the salvation of God (v. 17).[5] David had learnt through his military battles that salvation came from God alone, for he alone was Israel's Savior (1 Chr 16:35; cf. Ps 65:5; 79:9; 85:4; Isa 43:3, 11; 45:17). Many times, God had saved his people from their enemies, and he could be relied upon (cf. Exod 14:30; Num 10:9; Deut 20:4; 33:29; 1 Chr 18:6, 13; 2 Chr 20:9; 32:22). Upon hearing the oracle of salvation, Jehoshaphat "bowed down with his face to the ground, and all the people of Judah and Jerusalem fell down in worship before the LORD" (20:18). With faces lying on the ground, the scene is one of utter dependence before God. They are unable to save themselves, and this is precisely what God was teaching his people—he alone is Israel's Savior. We have become familiar with the songs sung by the Levites, and they now rise to the occasion, praising the God of Israel with a very loud voice (v. 19).

---

5. On the topic of salvation, see the discussion in Chapter 16 on 1 Chr 16:34–36, pp. 170–71, and especially Chapter 18, Live the Story, pp. 192–94.

God Gives Victory and People Give Praise (20:20–28)

Jehoshaphat and the people arise early in the morning and travel to the Desert of Tekoa, located a few miles south of Jerusalem (2 Chr 20:20). Jehoshaphat exhorts the people to have faith in the LORD their God. Jehoshaphat had learned what it meant to get ahead of God (cf. ch. 18), but now he rises to this "faith challenge" by trusting in God and exhorting others to have faith in God. He had previously not given heed to God's prophet (cf. ch. 19), but now he exhorts Judah to put their faith in God and his prophets so that they will be successful (20:20). The verb "to have faith, believe" (Heb. '-m-n) was first used of Abraham, who believed in the LORD (Gen 15:6). Faith has always been central to people of God (Hab 2:4; cf. Rom 1:17). In fact, kingdoms are conquered "by faith" (Heb 11:32–34), and it is through faith that the weak are made strong (v. 34). Now, the king exhorts God's people to have faith in the LORD in spite of their insurmountable circumstances. He assures them that that they will have *success*—something that Ahab's prophets had falsely promised (2 Chr 18:11, 14). Success is achieved by trusting in the LORD and giving heed to his Spirit.

Jehoshaphat appoints singers and musicians to lead God's people in praise and thanks, singing: "Give thanks to the LORD, for his love endures forever" (2 Chr 20:21; cf. 1 Chr 16:34). The people are singing their praises to God amidst this crisis, for they are holding onto God's steadfast love. In faith, they praise God even before the battle has been won. At the moment when they *begin* to praise and thank God,[6] the LORD sets ambushes against the men of Ammon, Moab, and Mount Seir, and they are struck down (2 Chr 20:22). Instead of the coalition joining forces, they turn against each other in self-destruction, resulting in a great slaughter (v. 23). As the men of Judah find corpses of the slain spread out in the desert, they take equipment and anything of value, finding so much plunder that it takes them three days to collect it (v. 25). On the fourth day, Jehoshaphat and the people return to Jerusalem with great joy, for God had made them rejoice over their enemies (vv. 26–28)![7]

God Gives Judah Rest from Their Enemies (20:29–34)

Reminiscent of God's salvation in their earlier days, the dread of the LORD falls upon all the surrounding kingdoms as the people hear that God has given the Israelites victory (2 Chr 20:29; cf. Exod 15:16; Deut 2:25; 11:25). The

---

6. The verb "to begin" (Heb. *h-l-l*) is used in other places to describe the beginning of an activity (see 1 Chr 27:24; 2 Chr 3:1, 2; 29:17).

7. On the topic of joy in Chronicles, see Live the Story in Chapter 34, pp. 319–21.

kingdom is at peace, recalling God's earlier promise to David (2 Sam 7:11; 1 Chr 22:9; 23:25). As Jehoshaphat's reign is drawing to a close, the Chronicler notes that he walked in the ways of his father Asa, doing that which is right in the sight of the LORD (2 Chr 20:32). The high places, however, were not entirely removed, as this will take place later during the reign of Josiah.

Jehoshaphat's Foolish Alliance with Ahaziah (20:35–37)

The story of Jehoshaphat concludes on a somber note, however, with the comment that he allied himself with the (ungodly) king of Israel, Ahaziah, in an effort to build a fleet of ships at the southern port of Ezion Geber (2 Chr 20:35–36). The prophet Jehu had previously rebuked Jehoshaphat for his alliance with Ahab (19:2), and it not surprising, therefore, that this alliance is met with a word of judgment by the prophet Eliezar. As a result, Jehoshaphat's ships are ruined and unable to sail. The Chronicler's candid assessment of Jehoshaphat at the end of his reign reminds us that every king fails in some way.[8]

 LIVE the Story

Walking by Faith, Not by Military Might

When Jehoshaphat hears of the enemy advance, it is important to notice what the king does *not do*. He does not call up his military, who were stationed in Jerusalem and in the cities of Judah (2 Chr 17:13, 14–18). Compare the story of Amaziah, who assembles a large army when preparing for battle (25:5–13). This is not what Jehoshaphat does. Instead, he seeks God in prayer (20:3). This is truly remarkable. Japhet makes the insightful comment that, although military power is attributed to the southern kings, the "the pious king is expected not only to possess military strength but to forego its use and to rely only on God."[9] Thus she notes that this is one of the paradoxes in the Chronicler's thought.[10] Even though Jehoshaphat's army is stationed in Jerusalem, his priority is to pray. Turning to God in prayer is one of the hallmarks of the people of God, and this story provides an example for the returnees living in Jerusalem so that they, too, might seek the LORD. While we are not promised military victory in earthly battles under the new covenant,[11] we are assured

---

8. See Live the Story in Chapter 65, p. 569.

9. Japhet, *I & II Chronicles*, 792.

10. Ibid.

11. On the topic of spiritual warfare and Jesus's victory, see Live the Story in Chapter 14, pp. 153–54.

of God's presence, and we are called to walk by faith, even as Jehoshaphat and the people who believe in the LORD did (v. 20). This story challenges us to consider what we do amid times of crisis or when facing unsurmountable circumstances. Do we turn to our own devices and rely upon ourselves, or do we turn to the LORD, asking for his help?

As we earnestly seek God, it requires that we put our faith in him alone. McConville rightly notes that the trustworthiness of God cannot be known "until one begins to make decisions on the basis of his promises, staking wealth and welfare on the outcome—just as it is impossible to know with certainty that a chair will bear one's weight without actually sitting on it."[12] Faith is, indeed, the hallmark of God's people throughout the ages (Gen 15:6; Hab 2:4; Rom 1:17; cf. Heb 11:1–40), but this requires that we step out in faith *before* the outcome is certain. Regardless of our circumstances, God is trustworthy, and he wants us to rely upon him *completely*, remembering that "without faith it is impossible to please God" (Heb 11:6).

Prayer and Fasting

Jehoshaphat not only prays, but he calls the entire community to fast (2 Chr 20:3), which demonstrates their utter dependence upon the LORD. Fasting is often associated with mourning, as an expression of heartfelt grief (Judg 20:26; 1 Sam 31:13; 2 Sam 1:12; 1 Chr 10:12), but fasting occurs with prayer under dire circumstances. The Israelites fasted when Samuel prayed on their behalf, as he confessed Israel's sins and pleaded to God for deliverance from the Philistines (1 Sam 7:6). David prayed and fasted when he had pleaded with God that his son might not die (2 Sam 12:16, 22). The prophet Daniel had prayed and fasted when he had confessed the sin of Israel and asked God to restore his people (Dan 9:3). Japhet rightly notes that fasting is "the strongest expression of soul-searching and complete surrender to God."[13] Fasting is prominent in the post-exilic period, when people such as Ezra (Ezra 8:21, 23) and Nehemiah (Neh 1:4) pray and fast. On this occasion, Jehoshaphat leads God's people into a corporate fast, so that they seek God together (2 Chr 20:3; cf. Ezra 8:21, 23; Neh 9:1). He had learnt the hard way that the battle was not won by might, nor by power, but by God's Spirit (Zech 4:6).

In particular situations, earnest prayer is accompanied by fasting in the New Testament. Most notably, Jesus fasted for forty days and nights before being tempted by the devil (Matt 4:2). The early church practiced prayer

---

12. McConville, *I & II Chronicles*, 195.
13. Japhet, *I & II Chronicles*, 787.

and fasting, at which time the Holy Spirit revealed that Barnabas and Saul were to be set apart for God's work (Acts 13:1–4). Similarly, the appointment of elders takes place after prayer and fasting (14:23). Jesus emphasized that fasting should not be done to appear religious or seek approval from others, but rather, people were to fast in secret, so that only God would see (Matt 6:16–18). Whether prayers are done with or without fasting, what is central is that *we pray*. Jesus taught us how to pray, and he taught us that we need to persevere in prayer. The story of Jehoshaphat, along with other stories in the Old Testament when people prayed and fasted, serve as an exhortation to us to seek God amid all circumstances, remembering that God hears and answers prayer.

LISTEN to the Story

¹Then Jehoshaphat rested with his ancestors and was buried with them in the City of David. And Jehoram his son succeeded him as king. ²Jehoram's brothers, the sons of Jehoshaphat, were Azariah, Jehiel, Zechariah, Azariahu, Michael and Shephatiah. All these were sons of Jehoshaphat king of Israel. ³Their father had given them many gifts of silver and gold and articles of value, as well as fortified cities in Judah, but he had given the kingdom to Jehoram because he was his firstborn son.

⁴When Jehoram established himself firmly over his father's kingdom, he put all his brothers to the sword along with some of the officials of Israel. ⁵Jehoram was thirty-two years old when he became king, and he reigned in Jerusalem eight years. ⁶He followed the ways of the kings of Israel, as the house of Ahab had done, for he married a daughter of Ahab. He did evil in the eyes of the LORD. ⁷Nevertheless, because of the covenant the LORD had made with David, the LORD was not willing to destroy the house of David. He had promised to maintain a lamp for him and his descendants forever.

⁸In the time of Jehoram, Edom rebelled against Judah and set up its own king. ⁹So Jehoram went there with his officers and all his chariots. The Edomites surrounded him and his chariot commanders, but he rose up and broke through by night. ¹⁰To this day Edom has been in rebellion against Judah.

Libnah revolted at the same time, because Jehoram had forsaken the LORD, the God of his ancestors. ¹¹He had also built high places on the hills of Judah and had caused the people of Jerusalem to prostitute themselves and had led Judah astray.

¹²Jehoram received a letter from Elijah the prophet, which said:

"This is what the LORD, the God of your father David, says: 'You have not followed the ways of your father Jehoshaphat or of Asa king of Judah. ¹³But you have followed the ways of the kings of Israel, and you have led Judah and the people of Jerusalem to prostitute themselves, just as the house of Ahab did. You have also murdered your own brothers, members of your own family, men who were better than you. ¹⁴So now the LORD is about to strike your people, your sons, your wives and everything that is yours, with a heavy blow. ¹⁵You yourself will be very ill with a lingering disease of the bowels, until the disease causes your bowels to come out.'"

¹⁶The LORD aroused against Jehoram the hostility of the Philistines and of the Arabs who lived near the Cushites. ¹⁷They attacked Judah, invaded it and carried off all the goods found in the king's palace, together with his sons and wives. Not a son was left to him except Ahaziah, the youngest.

¹⁸After all this, the LORD afflicted Jehoram with an incurable disease of the bowels. ¹⁹In the course of time, at the end of the second year, his bowels came out because of the disease, and he died in great pain. His people made no funeral fire in his honor, as they had for his predecessors.

²⁰Jehoram was thirty-two years old when he became king, and he reigned in Jerusalem eight years. He passed away, to no one's regret, and was buried in the City of David, but not in the tombs of the kings.

Listening to the Text in the Story: 1 Chronicles 17:11–15; Psalm 89:34–37

After the death of Jehoshaphat, the Southern Kingdom takes a devastating turn for the worse when Jehoram, son of Jehoshaphat, becomes king. Jehoram not only mercilessly murders his brothers, but he leads Judah into idolatry and is likened to the northern king Ahab. His close relationship with the house of Ahab had been forged through his marriage to Ahab's daughter, Athaliah. We are now entering one of the darkest periods of the Southern Kingdom, which extends further with the rule of his son Ahaziah, followed by the rule of the murderous Athaliah (2 Chr 21–23). These rulers wreak havoc in the kingdom, and their ungodly actions constitute the gravest threat to the line of Judah. Baal worship is introduced into Judah as the house of Ahab exerts its influence on the south. Selman notes that the close relationship with Judah and Israel is symbolized by the names of Judah's kings during this period, noting that no other southern kings are called Jehoram and Ahaziah, yet these names are found among the house of Ahab (Ahab's son is named Ahaziah and his grandson is Jehoram).[1] He concludes that during the rule of Ahaziah and Athaliah, Ahab's dynasty was effectively in control of Judah.[2]

In spite of the rampant idolatry and bloodshed, it is important to bear in the mind that God had promised David: "I will raise up your offspring to succeed you, one of your own sons, and I will establish his kingdom. He is the one who will build a house for me, and I will establish his throne forever" (1 Ch 17:11–12). The psalmist thus affirms the perpetuity of God's covenant with David, as seen in the divine promise: "I will not violate my covenant or alter what my lips have uttered. Once for all, I have sworn by my holiness—and I will not lie to David—that his line will continue forever and his throne endure before me like the sun; it will be established forever like the moon, the faithful witness in the sky" (Ps 89:34–37; cf. Jer. 33:20–26). The Chronicler has these texts in view when explaining why Jehoram was not wiped out—because of "the covenant the LORD had made with David, the LORD was not willing to destroy the house of David. He had promised to maintain a lamp for him and his descendants forever" (2 Chr 21:7). God's covenant with David thus stands behind the story of Jehoram and the ungodly kings that follow.

EXPLAIN the Story

Jehoram Follows in the Sins of Ahab (21:1–7)

Jehoshaphat's succession plan entailed giving the kingdom to his firstborn son, Jehoram. In the ancient world, the firstborn received a double portion of the inheritance (Deut 21:17), yet God's choice was not always based on primogeniture (1 Chr 2:13–15; 3:1–5). The names of Jehoram's six brothers are listed (2 Chr 21:2). They had received gifts of silver and gold from their father, along with fortified cities in Judah, but the *kingdom* had been given to Jehoram. Disaster strikes, however, after Jehoram makes himself secure (v. 4; cf. v. 13). The king massacres all his brothers and some of the rulers of Israel as well. His intention is to eliminate any potential threat to the throne, yet his rule is far more tenuous than he realizes, since he is likened

---

1. Martin J. Selman, *2 Chronicles: A Commentary*, TOTC (Downers Grove, IL, InterVarsity Press, 1994), 437–38.
2. Ibid., 437.

to the infamous northern king Ahab (v. 6). His relationship with Ahab was forged earlier, when he had married Ahab's daughter Athaliah (2 Kgs 8:18; 2 Chr 21:6; cf. 18:1), making Ahab his father-in-law. Now, the dire consequences of this alliance are impacting the spiritual state of the Southern Kingdom, which has spiraled into idolatry. Jehoram is thus described as a king who "did evil in the eyes of the LORD" (21:6). According to the Mosaic covenant, murder required the death penalty (Exod 21:12–14; Lev 24:17), but in spite of his shocking and reprehensible murder of his own brothers, the full weight of God's wrath is withheld because of God's covenant with David. God had promised David that he would always have a "lamp" (Heb. *nir*, 2 Chr 21:7; cf. 1 Chr 17:1–15), a term that is used as a metaphor for David's descendant (1 Kgs 11:36; 15:4; 2 Kgs 8:19; Ps 132:17). This promise signaled the perpetuity of his line, in contrast to the lamp of the wicked that goes out (Job 18:5–6; Prov 13:9; 24:20).[3] Not unlike the lampstands in the temple that give light morning and evening (2 Chr 13:11), David will always have a perpetual lamp. Even though many southern kings do "evil in the eyes of the LORD," such as Rehoboam (12:14), Ahaziah (22:4), Manasseh (33:2), Amon (v. 22), Jehoiakim (36:5), Jehoiachin (v. 9), and Zedekiah (v. 12), God remains faithful to his promise to David—his "light" will not be extinguished.

Edom Revolts against Jehoram as He Forsakes the LORD (21:8–11)

Given what has taken place, it is not surprising to learn that the Edomites rebel against Judah and set up their own king (2 Chr 21:8).[4] Jehoram responds with a military campaign, but he is unable to suppress the rebellion (v. 10; cf. 25:5–22). As a sign of further unrest, Libnah revolts at this time as well (21:10). The Canaanite city of Libnah had been defeated by Joshua and belonged to Judah (Josh 10:29–30; 12:15; 15:42), but the revolt of its inhabitants indicates further instability due to Jehoram's evil reign. It is heartbreaking to read that the king sets up idolatrous places of worship and causes God's people to "prostitute themselves," thereby leading Judah astray (2 Chr 21:11). The language of "prostituting oneself" (Heb. *z-n-h*) is used figuratively by the prophets to describe idolatry (Ezek 16:35; 23:3; Hos 1:2; 2:7; 4:10, etc.). Japhet thus concludes that Jehoram's guilt was his "willful and malicious incitement of

---

3. Ibid., 434.

4. For more information on the Edomites, see the discussions in Chapter 1 on 1 Chr 1:35–42, pp. 28–30; Chapter 18 on 18:12–13, p. 191, and Chapter 54 on 2 Chr 25, pp. 466–69.

the people to the wrong way."[5] Jehoshaphat had brought God's people back to the LORD (2 Chr 19:4), but Jehoram is now accountable for leading them astray (21:11). This was a serious offense that would be met with the severest of punishment (Deut 13:1–8; cf. Deut 30:17–18).

God Brings Judgment against Jehoram (21:12–20)

Given Jehoram's litany of sins, it is not surprising to learn what happens next. The king receives a letter from the prophet Elijah. The letter was probably written earlier, since the prophet had been taken in a whirlwind prior to this time (see 2 Kgs 2). This might explain why his oracle comes in the form of a letter rather than a direct address.[6] The letter is a stinging indictment against Jehoram:

> "This is what the LORD, the God of your father David, says: 'You have not followed the ways of your father Jehoshaphat or of Asa king of Judah. But you have followed the ways of the kings of Israel, and you have led Judah and the people of Jerusalem to prostitute themselves, just as the house of Ahab did. You have also murdered your own brothers, members of your own family, men who were better than you.'" (2 Chr 21:12–13)

God announces that he will strike the king's family, including his sons and wives and everything that belongs to him (v. 14). While the judgment is severe, God takes sin seriously, and he will not allow the guilty to go unpunished.

In fulfillment of Elijah's prophecy, God stirs up the Philistines and Arabs, notably, the two groups who had brought tribute to Jehoshaphat (vv. 16–17; see 17:11). Now the situation has been reversed in a few short years because of this ungodly king. These foreign nations come against Judah and take Jehoram's possessions as plunder (21:16–17). His wives are taken and his sons are killed, except for his youngest son, Ahaziah,[7] whose preservation ensures that David's "light" is not extinguished (v. 17). God strikes Jehoram with an incurable illness that affects his bowels (vv. 18–19; cf. Deut 28:59, 61), and after two years, his bowels finally come out and he dies in great pain. He dies without honor, having reigned eight short years (2 Chr 21:20).

---

5. Japhet, *I & II Chronicles*, 811.

6. See the discussion by Japhet, *I & II Chronicles*, 812.

7. The Hebrew text has Jehoahaz, which is a variant of the name Ahaziah (who is identified in 22:1 as Jehoram's youngest son). Most English translations retain the name Jehoahaz in 21:17 (ESV, KJV, NASB), although the NIV has Ahaziah (probably in an effort to avoid confusion). While the two names in English may seem different, it is helpful to recognize that they both retain the *ahaz* element (as reflected in the Hebrew): Jeho-*ahaz* and *Ahaz*-iah.

LIVE the Story

The Importance of Godly Leadership

As we consider the reign of Jehoram, it is important to recall that Jehoshaphat had entered into an alliance with Ahab many years earlier, through his son's marriage to Athaliah (2 Kgs 8:26; 2 Chr 18:1). The impact of this ungodly alliance was not only seen in Jehoshaphat's own reign (ch. 18), but it continues to spread like the web of a venomous spider. Jezebel had already promoted the worship of Asherah and Baal in the Northern Kingdom (1 Kgs 16:31–33; 18:19), but now Jehoram and his wife wield their ungodly influence over the Southern Kingdom, the significance of which will be seen shortly (2 Chr 22–23). The house of Ahab has, therefore, wreaked havoc in both the Northern and Southern Kingdoms.

Earlier we saw that Asa had taken the bold step to remove his grandmother, Maakah, from her position as queen mother, for she had set up an image for Asherah (15:16; cf. 1 Kgs 15:1, 10). What would have happened if Jehoshaphat had taken a similar step, learning from his ungodly alliance with Ahab that had led to disaster (see 2 Chr 18:1–34; 19:2; 20:35–36)? Instead, he gives the kingdom to his son Jehoram, who is married to *Ahab's daughter* (21:6). This decision served to legitimize this ungodly alliance between Judah and Israel, and it enabled Athaliah to exert even more influence over the Southern Kingdom. Instead of removing Athaliah from having any influence, Jehoshaphat's succession plan would lead the kingdom to the brink of ruin.

By way of contrast, David understood the importance of appointing godly leaders, and he spent much time and energy ensuring that trusted leaders were in place as the kingdom transitioned to his son Solomon (see 1 Chr 23–27).[8] David had also given Solomon fatherly advice, urging him to follow the Lord (22:6–19; 28:9–10, 20). While such warnings were no guarantee, as any parent understands, David had given significant attention to the transition of leadership, urging his leaders to seek the Lord (22:17–19). The character of Israel's leaders mattered, as they have the potential to shape the spiritual climate of the entire community.

The New Testament emphasizes the importance of godly character as a requirement for church leadership (1 Tim 3:1–16; 5:17–25). Paul had left Titus in Crete so that he might appoint elders in every city, reminding him of the godly virtues required of elders (Titus 1:5–9). In the early church, this

---

8. See Live the Story in Chapter 27, pp. 263–65.

not only meant ensuring that godly leaders were in place, but false teachers were to be rebuked to ensure that they would not negatively influence the body.[9] This point is thus made to the church at Thyatira when the angel rebukes them for their failure to remove Jezebel: "Nevertheless, I have this against you: You tolerate that woman Jezebel, who calls herself a prophet. By her teaching she misleads my servants into sexual immorality and the eating of food sacrificed to idols" (Rev 2:20). Ungodly leaders can quickly lead the church astray and exert undue influence on the body. This is precisely what we have seen with Jehoshaphat's decision to appoint Jehoram as king, even though he was married to Ahab's daughter. Jehoshaphat should have taken action prior to his death to ensure that the kingdom was in godly hands, and likewise, church leaders need to ensure that the church is led by godly people. Sometimes this requires courageous steps to confront sin and take disciplinary action, even when leaders are well-known public figures. The story that follows underscores the mayhem that transpires as Athaliah continues to wield her ungodly influence over the kingdom, yet remarkably, amidst this dark period overshadowed by sin, a godly woman will act with great courage and leadership. At great risk to their own lives, she and her husband give their undivided attention to ensure that the kingdom is in the hands of the legitimate heir to the throne and that evil is removed.

---

9. See Live the Story in Chapter 47, pp. 417–19.

CHAPTER 51

2 Chronicles 22:1–12

 ## LISTEN to the Story

¹The people of Jerusalem made Ahaziah, Jehoram's youngest son, king in his place, since the raiders, who came with the Arabs into the camp, had killed all the older sons. So Ahaziah son of Jehoram king of Judah began to reign.

²Ahaziah was twenty-two years old when he became king, and he reigned in Jerusalem one year. His mother's name was Athaliah, a grand-daughter of Omri.

³He too followed the ways of the house of Ahab, for his mother encouraged him to act wickedly. ⁴He did evil in the eyes of the LORD, as the house of Ahab had done, for after his father's death they became his advisers, to his undoing. ⁵He also followed their counsel when he went with Joram son of Ahab king of Israel to wage war against Hazael king of Aram at Ramoth Gilead. The Arameans wounded Joram; ⁶so he returned to Jezreel to recover from the wounds they had inflicted on him at Ramoth in his battle with Hazael king of Aram.

Then Ahaziah son of Jehoram king of Judah went down to Jezreel to see Joram son of Ahab because he had been wounded.

⁷Through Ahaziah's visit to Joram, God brought about Ahaziah's downfall. When Ahaziah arrived, he went out with Joram to meet Jehu son of Nimshi, whom the LORD had anointed to destroy the house of Ahab. ⁸While Jehu was executing judgment on the house of Ahab, he found the officials of Judah and the sons of Ahaziah's relatives, who had been attending Ahaziah, and he killed them. ⁹He then went in search of Ahaziah, and his men captured him while he was hiding in Samaria. He was brought to Jehu and put to death. They buried him, for they said, "He was a son of Jehoshaphat, who sought the LORD with all his heart." So there was no one in the house of Ahaziah powerful enough to retain the kingdom.

> ¹⁰When Athaliah the mother of Ahaziah saw that her son was dead, she proceeded to destroy the whole royal family of the house of Judah. ¹¹But Jehosheba, the daughter of King Jehoram, took Joash son of Ahaziah and stole him away from among the royal princes who were about to be murdered and put him and his nurse in a bedroom. Because Jehosheba, the daughter of King Jehoram and wife of the priest Jehoiada, was Ahaziah's sister, she hid the child from Athaliah so she could not kill him. ¹²He remained hidden with them at the temple of God for six years while Athaliah ruled the land.

Listening to the Text in the Story: Exodus 1–2; Joshua 2:1–24; Judges 4–5

The house of Ahab continues to extend its evil tentacles over the Southern Kingdom during the reign of Ahaziah, the youngest and only surviving son of Jehoram, who becomes king after the death of his father. Under the sway of his malevolent mother, Ahaziah walks in the ways of Israel's northern kings, doing that which is evil in God's sight. Yet Ahaziah's short reign of one year testifies to *another* reality—that God is bringing judgment against him. It is helpful to rehearse briefly the word given by the prophet Elisha, who announces that the northern king Jehu is to execute God's judgment against the house of Ahab. He tells the king: "You are to destroy the house of Ahab your master, and I will avenge the blood of my servants the prophets and the blood of all the LORD's servants shed by Jezebel. The whole house of Ahab will perish. I will cut off from Ahab every last male in Israel—slave or free" (2 Kgs 9:7–8; cf. 1 Kgs 21:17–26). With this prophetic word reverberating in the background, we now turn to the reign of Ahaziah.

 EXPLAIN the Story

Ahaziah Enters an Alliance with the Northern Kingdom (22:1–6)

The people of Jerusalem make Jehoram's youngest son, Ahaziah, king, for his brothers had been killed by raiders who had come against Judah (2 Chr 22:1; cf. 21:16–17). Already introduced, his mother's name was Athaliah, an Omride and daughter of Ahab (22:2; cf. 21:6). Even though a young king of twenty-two years (22:2),[1] his reign will only last for one year. He walks in the ways of the kings of Ahab, influenced by the ungodly counsel of his mother, who is intent on wickedness (v. 3). Ahaziah allies himself with the northern king Joram, forming a coalition against a powerful Aramean king named Hazael (v. 5), reminiscent of Ahab's coalition a few years earlier (18:1–33). The Tel Dan Stela, written in Aramaic, attests to a victory by an Aramean king in the ninth century BC that may well refer to these events, although it requires some reconstruction.[2] Like Ahab before him, Joram is wounded in battle but he flees for safety to Jezreel. The town of Jezreel may have been chosen as a place of recuperation because it was ten miles closer than Samaria.[3] Yet this location reeks of bloodshed, recalling Naboth's innocent blood that had been shed there (1 Kgs 21:1–26; cf. 2 Kgs 9:1–10, 30–37; 10:1–11). With these events casting their foreboding shadow, Joram's arrival at Jezreel has ominous overtones, not only for his own imminent death, but also for Ahaziah, who plans to meet his wounded ally in Jezreel.

Jehu Murders Ahaziah and His Relatives (22:7–9)

While Ahaziah is unaware of the danger that lies ahead, God is providentially at work, for the Chronicler reminds the reader that Ahaziah's downfall was from God (2 Chr 22:7). Even though Ahaziah had simply gone to Jezreel to seek Joram's welfare, God had already anointed Jehu to destroy the house of Ahab (v. 7; cf. 2 Kgs 9:6–10). Ahaziah is not only identified with the house of Ahab by marriage, but by his own evil practices (2 Chr 22:2–4). As the story unfolds, the Chronicler passes over several events recounted in Kings,[4] but what is important to note is that God's judgment is extending to the Southern Kingdom, which includes members of the royal family (v. 8). Even though Ahaziah had attempted to hide from Jehu, he is found, brought to Jehu, and then killed (v. 9; cf. 2 Kgs 9:27). Ahaziah is given a burial, but only out of

---

1. The Hebrew text has forty-two years, although this reading is unlikely, not only in view of 2 Kgs 8:26 (which has twenty-two years), but also since Jehoram's father died at forty years old (2 Chr 21:5, 20). The NIV and other English versions have "twenty-two years" (ESV, NIV, NASB; cf. LXX, "twenty"), but the KJV has "forty-two years."

2. See Kitchen, *On the Reliability*, 36–37; see also Bryant G. Wood, "The Tel Dan Stela and the Kings of Aram and Israel," *BAR*, 4 May 2011, https://biblearchaeology.org/research/topics/amazing-discoveries-in-biblical-archaeology/2233-the-tel-dan-stela-and-the-kings-of-aram-and-israel.

3. Klein, *2 Chronicles*, 314.

4. Such as Joram's death by Jehu (2 Kgs 9:14–26) and the death of Jezebel (vv. 30–37). Some of the details in this story differ from the account in 2 Kings 9; see ibid., 312–31 and Japhet, *I & II Chronicles*, 820–24. In contrast to Kings, Ahaziah's death is located at the end of a series of bloody events; its literary placement at the conclusion identifies it as the climax of the narrative, and it provides a transition to the events that follow (see 2 Chr 22:10).

respect for his grandfather Jehoshaphat, who had sought the LORD with all his heart (2 Chr 22:9). Since members of the royal household had been killed, the Chronicler concludes with the comment: "So there was no one in the house of Ahaziah powerful enough to retain the kingdom" (v. 9). This sets the context for the power-hungry Athaliah to make her next move.

Athaliah Murders the Royal Household, but Joash Is Saved (22:10–12)

After the death of her son, Athaliah seizes the opportunity to take control of the kingdom. She mercilessly massacres the entire royal family (lit. "all the seed of the kingdom," 2 Chr 22:10). The word "seed" (Heb. *zera'*) is important here because God had made promises to David concerning his "seed" (NIV "offspring"; 1 Chr 17:11), and thus, the perpetuity of his line was critical for the fulfillment of this promise. In stark contrast to the murderous and wicked Athaliah, another woman enters the scene. Jehosheba is introduced as the king's daughter, which identifies her as Ahaziah's sister (2 Chr 22:11). Jehosheba courageously steals her young nephew Joash and hides him with his nurse in a bedroom (v. 11). Jehosheba and her husband, Jehoiada, are able to keep Joash hidden in the temple for the next six years while the evil Athaliah remains on the throne (v. 12). Since she is married to a priest, this gives them access to the temple precincts, which will become a safe haven for the infant. This is where the chapter concludes, although it will be taken up in the following chapter when the young boy is seven years old.

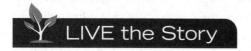

LIVE the Story

Courageous Women of Faith

Athaliah wreaks havoc in the Southern Kingdom, yet, in just a few verses, we are introduced to a devout woman named Jehosheba, whose godly influence in the kingdom is immeasurable. The highly volatile situation under Athaliah required great courage and the willingness to risk her own life. Putting herself at personal risk, she and her husband are able to keep the heir to the throne alive in preparation for the time when he will be anointed as king. Had she been discovered, she would have undoubtedly been killed. Klein thus concludes that Jehosheba is the "daring Davidic descendant whose courageous action saved the Davidic dynasty from extinction."[5]

---

5. Klein, *2 Chronicles*, 322.

Other devout women are recorded in the Old Testament who act with great faith and courage at critical periods in Israel's history. Shiphrah and Puah refused to give heed to the command of the powerful king of Egypt. Out of reverence for God, they courageously risked their own lives, refusing to allow Israelite sons among them to be murdered. When confronted by the king, they held fast to their convictions, fearing God more than the powerful king of Egypt. Through their faith and courage, Israel's infant boys were kept alive (Exod 1:15–21).

The mother of one of these newborn sons defies the king's command and hides her son for three months (2:1–2). She and her husband do this by faith, demonstrating that they were not afraid of the king's edict (Heb 11:23). When they were no longer able to keep him hidden, the infant's mother sacrificially and with great faith puts her son in a basket as she watches him float among the reeds on the Nile. His sister stands at a distance, waiting to see what will happen to her younger brother. When he is draw out of the water by Pharaoh's daughter, she courageously asks whether she might call a nurse from among the Hebrew women (Exod 2:4–7). As a result, the infant boy, named Moses, is providentially not left motherless and his life is preserved (vv. 7–8). Nursing her own son within the royal Egyptian household required yet another act of courage and faith—should her true identify be discovered, one would expect that she and her son would be killed.

The irony in the story is that the Egyptian king had thought that Hebrew *boys* were a threat to his kingdom, but he was oblivious to the significance of these Israelite *women*, who not only take bold and decisive steps to ensure the survival of God's people, but the Israelites continue to increase and become mighty at this time (Exod 1:20). Pharaoh had assumed that women were no threat, since he had only commanded that Israel's *boys* be killed. Yet their courage and faith result in the preservation of *Moses*—the one whom God called to deliver his people and to confront Pharaoh (3:10–22)!

The Scriptures testify to other courageous women, such as Rahab, who risks her own life in an act of faith, resulting in the safety of her entire household (Josh 2:1–24; Heb 11:31). Deborah rises to the challenge with courage and faith when she leads Israel in victory over Sisera's army (Judg 4–5). Even within this story, a woman named Jael shows great courage when Sisera, the commander of the army, enters her tent. Instead of following the king's command, she drives a tent peg into Sisera and kills him (4:17–22; 5:24–27). The irony is that a woman has killed a mighty commander! Esther is another example of a woman who acts courageously and with great faith to preserve her people (Esth 3:13–15; 4:16). The story of Jehosheba thus stands in a line of godly women in the Old Testament who were willing to act courageously and with great faith. They serve as an example for us today, reminding us that God calls each one of us to fear him *more* than those in authority and that sometimes this will require taking bold steps of faith and courage to ensure that God's kingdom work is not thwarted.

LISTEN to the Story

¹In the seventh year Jehoiada showed his strength. He made a covenant with the commanders of units of a hundred: Azariah son of Jeroham, Ishmael son of Jehohanan, Azariah son of Obed, Maaseiah son of Adaiah, and Elishaphat son of Zikri. ²They went throughout Judah and gathered the Levites and the heads of Israelite families from all the towns. When they came to Jerusalem, ³the whole assembly made a covenant with the king at the temple of God.

Jehoiada said to them, "The king's son shall reign, as the LORD promised concerning the descendants of David. ⁴Now this is what you are to do: A third of you priests and Levites who are going on duty on the Sabbath are to keep watch at the doors, ⁵a third of you at the royal palace and a third at the Foundation Gate, and all the others are to be in the courtyards of the temple of the LORD. ⁶No one is to enter the temple of the LORD except the priests and Levites on duty; they may enter because they are consecrated, but all the others are to observe the LORD's command not to enter. ⁷The Levites are to station themselves around the king, each with weapon in hand. Anyone who enters the temple is to be put to death. Stay close to the king wherever he goes."

⁸The Levites and all the men of Judah did just as Jehoiada the priest ordered. Each one took his men—those who were going on duty on the Sabbath and those who were going off duty—for Jehoiada the priest had not released any of the divisions. ⁹Then he gave the commanders of units of a hundred the spears and the large and small shields that had belonged to King David and that were in the temple of God. ¹⁰He stationed all the men, each with his weapon in his hand, around the king—near the altar and the temple, from the south side to the north side of the temple.

¹¹Jehoiada and his sons brought out the king's son and put the crown

on him; they presented him with a copy of the covenant and proclaimed him king. They anointed him and shouted, "Long live the king!"

¹²When Athaliah heard the noise of the people running and cheering the king, she went to them at the temple of the LORD. ¹³She looked, and there was the king, standing by his pillar at the entrance. The officers and the trumpeters were beside the king, and all the people of the land were rejoicing and blowing trumpets, and musicians with their instruments were leading the praises. Then Athaliah tore her robes and shouted, "Treason! Treason!"

¹⁴Jehoiada the priest sent out the commanders of units of a hundred, who were in charge of the troops, and said to them: "Bring her out between the ranks and put to the sword anyone who follows her." For the priest had said, "Do not put her to death at the temple of the LORD." ¹⁵So they seized her as she reached the entrance of the Horse Gate on the palace grounds, and there they put her to death.

¹⁶Jehoiada then made a covenant that he, the people and the king would be the LORD's people. ¹⁷All the people went to the temple of Baal and tore it down. They smashed the altars and idols and killed Mattan the priest of Baal in front of the altars.

¹⁸Then Jehoiada placed the oversight of the temple of the LORD in the hands of the Levitical priests, to whom David had made assignments in the temple, to present the burnt offerings of the LORD as written in the Law of Moses, with rejoicing and singing, as David had ordered. ¹⁹He also stationed gatekeepers at the gates of the LORD's temple so that no one who was in any way unclean might enter.

²⁰He took with him the commanders of hundreds, the nobles, the rulers of the people and all the people of the land and brought the king down from the temple of the LORD. They went into the palace through the Upper Gate and seated the king on the royal throne. ²¹All the people of the land rejoiced, and the city was calm, because Athaliah had been slain with the sword.

Listening to the Text in the Story: Deuteronomy 17:18–20; 1 Chronicles 17:10–14

After hiding the young boy, Joash, Jehoiada the priest reveals his plan to anoint Joash as king, while the bloodthirsty Athaliah remains in control of the kingdom. God had promised David that one of his sons would rule over the kingdom, and this promise gives Jehoiada and the priests confidence to take this next step (see 1 Chr 17:10–15). Jehoiada affirms before those gathered that the "king's son shall reign," reminding them it was "as the LORD promised concerning the descendants of David" (2 Chr 23:3). The royal Davidic genealogy in 1 Chronicles 3:10–14 traces kingship through a singular line of descent, with every king identified as the *son* of the previous king.[1] Notably, Athaliah was not included in the genealogy, for she is an illegitimate usurper!

The other text that stands behind the anointing of Joash is Deuteronomy 17:18–20. Many years earlier, Moses had taught that the king was to write out a copy of the law in the presence of Levitical priests. He was to read it all the days of his life, so that he would learn to the fear the LORD and his heart would not become proud. During the anointing ceremony when Joash is surrounded by Levites, after the crown is placed on his head, he is handed a copy of the covenant (2 Chr 23:11). The centrality of the covenant will be seen in the story that follows.

 EXPLAIN the Story

Joash Is Anointed King (23:1–11)

In a remarkable act of courage, Jehoiada implements his plan to anoint the young boy, Joash, as king in the seventh year (2 Chr 23:1). He makes a covenant with his commanders, some of whom were probably Levites (see 1 Chr 27:5). They were to travel throughout the land of Judah, gathering other Levites and heads of households so that they might be present in Jerusalem (2 Chr 23:1–2). Those assembled enter into a covenant with the king in the house of God, affirming their loyalty to the "son of the king," who was the legitimate heir to the throne (v. 3). Athaliah, the usurper and illegitimate queen (21:6; 22:2, 10–12), must be deposed and the rightful heir restored. Jehoiada stations priests and Levites as gatekeepers at key locations, and those guarding the temple are to ensure that only priests and Levites enter the sacred precincts (23:4–6).[2] With swords in hand, they are commanded to protect the king, which required killing anyone unlawfully entering the temple (v. 7). Jehoiada is taking no chances with the volatile and murderous Athaliah still in power. With fully-armed commanders stationed at their designated posts

---

1. See Live the Story in Chapter 3, Live the Story, The Grace of God Is on Center Stage, pp. 44–46.

2. On the important role of Levitical gatekeepers, see Chapter 26 on 1 Chr 26.

(vv. 8–10) and with all the preparations in place, the king's son is brought into the temple, and the time has finally arrived for the royal crown to be placed on his head (v. 11). At this sacred moment, he is given a copy of the covenant, signaling his sacred role as king over the kingdom of the LORD. Jehoaida and his sons anoint Joash as king and proclaim: "Long live the king!" (v. 11).

Athaliah Is Murdered by Jehoiada (23:12–15)

When Athaliah hears the sounds of jubilation as the people applaud their newly anointed king, she sees the young boy, Joash, standing by the pillar at the entrance of the temple. She takes in the scene, with Levites singing praises to God, while trumpets are sounding and people are rejoicing because the king's son has rightfully been restored to the throne (2 Chr 23:12). The very presence of Joash must have been a great shock to Athaliah, evoking an outburst of rage in her. Seeing the royal crown on *his* head must have infuriated her. She immediately tears her garments and cries out, "Treason! Treason!" (v. 13). Yet no one comes to her aid. Jehoaida tells his officers to bring Athaliah out between the ranks and kill anyone who follows her. The captains seize her and she is put to death, notably, away from the sacred temple, at one of the palace gates (vv. 14–15).

Joash Carries Out Religious Reforms (23:16–21)

With the rightful Davidic king restored to the throne, the people renew their covenant relationship with the LORD (2 Chr 23:16). Loyalty to the LORD required that all foreign gods be destroyed. They tear down the house of Baal and smash the altars and idols used in false worship (v. 17). The LORD had prohibited the worship of other gods, for the covenant entailed an exclusive relationship with the LORD God (Exod 20:1–6). Worship of the Canaanite storm god Baal was especially prominent during the reign of Ahab (1 Kgs 16:28–22:40). He had built a temple for Baal in Samaria, and there had been a staggering 450 prophets of Baal during his reign (16:31–32; 18:20–46), but King Jehu had executed God's judgment against Ahab and the Baal worshipers (2 Kgs 10:18–28). That Baal worship is taking place in *Judah* is due to the ungodly influence of Athaliah on the Southern Kingdom, but Jehoiada restores Yahweh-worship by smashing altars and images of Baal and killing the priest of Baal (2 Chr 23:17). Oversight of the temple is placed in the hands of the Levitical priests, in accordance with David's instructions (1 Chr 23–26). They were to offer burnt offerings to the LORD, according to the law of Moses, which they do with rejoicing and singing (2 Chr 23:18). Gatekeepers are on guard at the temple, ensuring that no unclean person enters the sacred precincts. Finally, in the presence of Israel's leaders and all the people, Joash is brought from the temple to the king's house and is seated on his royal throne (v. 20). The people rejoice and the city is at peace, now that Athaliah has been put to death (v. 21).

LIVE the Story

Confronting Sin in the Church

Athaliah's influence over the Southern Kingdom serves as a warning about making sure that sin is addressed within the covenant community, and it reminds us not to underestimate the influence one ungodly person can have on the flock. Ungodly leaders and false teachers can quickly lead the flock astray. The apostle Paul warned the church at Corinth about the danger of condoning unrepentant sin within the community. His letter to the Corinthians includes addressing the issue of incest, stating that the man who committed incest should be put out of their fellowship (1 Cor 5:1–2). Paul uses the analogy of leaven to illustrate the influence one ungodly person can have on the entire church, posing the question: "Don't you know that a little yeast leavens the whole batch of dough?" (v. 6). He instructs them: "Get rid of the old yeast, so that you may be a new unleavened batch—as you really are" (v. 7). He explains further that he is writing about someone *within* the covenant community who is committing this act, and he concludes with the bold instruction: "Expel the wicked person from among you" (v. 13; see Deut 13:5). While this might seem rather severe, the story of Athaliah underscores the influence one ungodly person can have over an entire community. Moses had warned the Israelites about those who led God's people astray, which would require the severest of penalties (Deut 13:1–9). Jehoiada thus has Athaliah killed. This seems like an extreme measure, yet she has led astray the entire community into the worship of Baal. The repentance of Manasseh demonstrates that God forgives the worst of sinners (2 Chr 33), but it is *unrepentant* sin that is the issue, along with its destructive influence on the entire community.

In the New Testament, church discipline is to be practiced to preserve the holiness of the body (1 Cor 5:7), yet it is intended to lead to restoration and reconciliation (Gal 6:1; Jas 5:20). Paul's teaching to the church at Corinth expresses the hope that a person disciplined will find redemption (1 Cor 5:5). While teaching on church discipline might seem harsh, Paul's point is that a person who continues in unrepentant sin can have undue influence on the body. A study by Lifeway Research in 2018 found that more than half of the one thousand pastors surveyed said that no member in their church had been disciplined during their tenure as pastor or before their tenure. The study concluded that church reprimands are few and far between.[3]

Holding leaders accountable is even more critical. Accordingly, the appointment of godly leaders is an important task, and the whole community is involved in this process (Acts 14:23; 1 Tim 3:1–13; Titus 1:5–9; 1 Pet 5:1–4). Every care needs to be given to ensure that the church is led by godly leaders under the headship of Christ, and those leaders are required to ensure that unrepentant sin is addressed in the flock, remembering that "a little yeast leavens the whole batch of dough." Sin among leaders that is not dealt with within the body can too easily be played out on social media, causing further damage to the reputation of the church. Jehoiada and his wife, Jehosheba, took the courageous step to confront Athaliah's evil leadership, and the godly influence of Jehoiada will continue in the story that follows.

---

3. "Church Rarely Reprimands Members, New Survey Shows," Lifeway Research, April 5, 2018, https://lifewayresearch.com/2018/04/05/churches-rarely-reprimand-members-new-survey-shows/.

CHAPTER 53

2 Chronicles 24:1–27

 LISTEN to the Story

¹Joash was seven years old when he became king, and he reigned in Jerusalem forty years. His mother's name was Zibiah; she was from Beersheba. ²Joash did what was right in the eyes of the LORD all the years of Jehoiada the priest. ³Jehoiada chose two wives for him, and he had sons and daughters.

⁴Some time later Joash decided to restore the temple of the LORD. ⁵He called together the priests and Levites and said to them, "Go to the towns of Judah and collect the money due annually from all Israel, to repair the temple of your God. Do it now." But the Levites did not act at once.

⁶Therefore the king summoned Jehoiada the chief priest and said to him, "Why haven't you required the Levites to bring in from Judah and Jerusalem the tax imposed by Moses the servant of the LORD and by the assembly of Israel for the tent of the covenant law?"

⁷Now the sons of that wicked woman Athaliah had broken into the temple of God and had used even its sacred objects for the Baals.

⁸At the king's command, a chest was made and placed outside, at the gate of the temple of the LORD. ⁹A proclamation was then issued in Judah and Jerusalem that they should bring to the LORD the tax that Moses the servant of God had required of Israel in the wilderness. ¹⁰All the officials and all the people brought their contributions gladly, dropping them into the chest until it was full. ¹¹Whenever the chest was brought in by the Levites to the king's officials and they saw that there was a large amount of money, the royal secretary and the officer of the chief priest would come and empty the chest and carry it back to its place. They did this regularly and collected a great amount of money. ¹²The king and Jehoiada gave it to those who carried out the work required for the temple of the LORD. They hired masons and carpenters to restore the LORD's temple, and also workers in iron and bronze to repair the temple.

¹³The men in charge of the work were diligent, and the repairs progressed under them. They rebuilt the temple of God according to its original design and reinforced it. ¹⁴When they had finished, they brought the rest of the money to the king and Jehoiada, and with it were made articles for the LORD's temple: articles for the service and for the burnt offerings, and also dishes and other objects of gold and silver. As long as Jehoiada lived, burnt offerings were presented continually in the temple of the LORD.

¹⁵Now Jehoiada was old and full of years, and he died at the age of a hundred and thirty. ¹⁶He was buried with the kings in the City of David, because of the good he had done in Israel for God and his temple.

¹⁷After the death of Jehoiada, the officials of Judah came and paid homage to the king, and he listened to them. ¹⁸They abandoned the temple of the LORD, the God of their ancestors, and worshiped Asherah poles and idols. Because of their guilt, God's anger came on Judah and Jerusalem. ¹⁹Although the LORD sent prophets to the people to bring them back to him, and though they testified against them, they would not listen.

²⁰Then the Spirit of God came on Zechariah son of Jehoiada the priest. He stood before the people and said, "This is what God says: 'Why do you disobey the LORD's commands? You will not prosper. Because you have forsaken the LORD, he has forsaken you.'"

²¹But they plotted against him, and by order of the king they stoned him to death in the courtyard of the LORD's temple. ²²King Joash did not remember the kindness Zechariah's father Jehoiada had shown him but killed his son, who said as he lay dying, "May the LORD see this and call you to account."

²³At the turn of the year, the army of Aram marched against Joash; it invaded Judah and Jerusalem and killed all the leaders of the people. They sent all the plunder to their king in Damascus. ²⁴Although the Aramean army had come with only a few men, the LORD delivered into their hands a much larger army. Because Judah had forsaken the LORD, the God of their ancestors, judgment was executed on Joash. ²⁵When the Arameans withdrew, they left Joash severely wounded. His officials conspired against him for murdering the son of Jehoiada the priest, and they killed him in his bed. So he died and was buried in the City of David, but not in the tombs of the kings.

²⁶Those who conspired against him were Zabad, son of Shimeath an Ammonite woman, and Jehozabad, son of Shimrith a Moabite woman. ²⁷The account of his sons, the many prophecies about him, and the record of the restoration of the temple of God are written in the annotations on the book of the kings. And Amaziah his son succeeded him as king.

Listening to the Text in the Story: 2 Chronicles 15:2

Joash is characterized as a godly king who follows the LORD, but events will take a turn for the worse after the death of Jehoiada the priest. A key text that helps explain the reign of Joash is found earlier in Chronicles. During the reign of Asa, the Spirit of God had come upon the prophet Azariah. He had warned God's people that if they forsook the LORD, God would forsake them (2 Chr 15:1–2). This warning reverberates throughout Chronicles as a constant refrain (7:22; 28:6; 29:6–10; 34:25). In the story that follows, the prophet Zechariah gives this same warning to Joash because of his idolatrous practices (24:20), yet it will be met with a hard and unrepentant heart. The outworking of the prophet's message will be seen in the tragic events that follow.

 EXPLAIN the Story

Joash's Godly Reign under the Influence of Jehoiada the Priest (24:1–16)

Joash was seven years old when he was anointed as king, and he reigned for forty years in Jerusalem (2 Chr 24:1). His mother, Zibiah, was from Beersheba, although she did not feature in the earlier story of Joash (22:11–12). At the outset we learn that Joash did what was right in the sight of the LORD, but this is followed by the terse and pregnant statement "all the years of Jehoiada the priest" (24:2; see v. 17), which foreshadows the sorry state of things to come. In the Kings account, the teaching role of Jehoiada is emphasized ("all the years Jehoiada the priest instructed him," 2 Kgs 12:2). Jehoiada selects wives for Joash, who fathers sons and daughters through them (2 Chr 24:3).

The first event that the Chronicler records about Joash is his decision to restore the temple (v. 4; cf. 2 Kgs 12:6), which was necessary because of the neglect and pillage under Athaliah (2 Chr 24:7). Joash gathers priests and

Levites, instructing them to collect money from all Israel so that the temple might be repaired (vv. 4–5). The temple had remained in disrepair for a good many years (see 2 Kgs 12:6), which leads Joash to rebuke the Levites and to ask Jehoiada why he had not required them to collect the tax imposed by Moses (2 Chr 24:6). The law taught that every Israelite twenty years and older was to give an annual contribution toward the tent of meeting (Exod 30:13, 16; cf. Neh 10:32). The negligence of the Levites leads to a new policy: gifts are to be placed in a chest at the gate of the temple. This way contributions can be given directly, rather than requiring the Levites to collect them (2 Chr 24:8). An abundance of provisions are given daily, accompanied by rejoicing (vv. 10–11; cf. 1 Chr 29:9). Having received these contributions, Joash and Jehoiada distribute them to those who had been hired to repair the temple, including masons, carpenters, and workers in iron and bronze (2 Chr 24:13).

The remaining gifts of gold and silver are brought before the king and priest, and they make them into utensils and vessels to be used in the temple (2 Chr 24:14). Burnt offerings are offered to the LORD, signaling the establishment of daily worship (v. 14; cf. Exod 29:42; 1 Chr 16:40; 23:30–31; 2 Chr 2:4; 13:11; 23:18). Yet the statement about worship at the newly restored temple has ominous overtones, for the Chronicler notes that they offered burnt offerings continually "as long as Jehoiada lived" (24:14), a topic already introduced (v. 2). Jehoaida lives a long life, and he is given an honorable burial in the city of David among the kings, "because of the good he had done in Israel and for God and his temple" (v. 16). Yet everything changes with his death.

The People and the King Abandon the LORD (24:17–22)

After the death of Jehoiada, the officials of Judah "paid homage to the king, and he listened to them" (2 Chr 24:17). While people can bow down before a king as an act of deference (e.g., 1 Kgs 1:16, 23, 31), in Chronicles this kind of homage usually takes place in the *religious* sphere, such as when people worship the LORD (1 Chr 16:29; 29:20; 2 Chr 7:3; 20:18; 29:28–30; 32:12) or other gods (7:19, 22; 25:14; 33:3). This may well suggest that something is already awry when the officials bow down before *the king*. While we are not privy to what they say to the king, the story that follows suggests it was not wise counsel, surely not like Jehoiada's godly teaching. What follows is that the temple is abandoned, and the people serve Asherah poles and idols.[1] As a

---

1. For a description of Asherah poles and idols, see 2 Chr 33, pp. 536–37.

consequence, God's wrath is poured out on Judah and Jerusalem (24:18). But God in his compassion sends prophets to call his people to return to him, but they refuse to listen (v. 19; cf. 36:15–16). In spite of their repeated failure to give heed to the prophets, God sends yet *another* prophet, Zechariah, who is clothed with God's Spirit (24:20).

The Spirit of God comes upon specific people at critical moments in the life of the kingdom, bringing words of encouragement and rebuke (15:1; 20:14; 24:20). In this case, God's Spirit "clothed" (NIV "came on"; see comment on pp. 137–38 above) Zechariah, as he had done with Amasai (1 Chr 12:18; cf. Judg 6:34). He is identified as the son of Jehoiada the priest, noting that a number of Jehoiada's sons were first introduced when Joash was anointed king (2 Chr 23:11). Zechariah stands before the people and pronounces God's word with divine authority: "this is what God says." He asks the people why they have disobeyed the LORD's commands and tells them that they will not prosper. Because they have forsaken the LORD, he has forsaken them (24:20). The verb "to forsake, abandon" (Heb. '-z-b) is a covenantal term commonly used by the Chronicler to describe a breach of the covenant (12:1; 15:2; 21:10; 24:20; 28:6; 29:6). The people's idolatry constituted a serious breach of their relationship with the LORD (24:18; see also Deut 28:20; 29:25; cf. 31:6). The prophet Azariah had announced a few years earlier that if his people forsook God, he would forsake them (2 Chr 15:2). This will shortly take place when God raises up the Arameans to defeat Judah.

Instead of Joash and the people repenting, Zechariah is mercilessly stoned to death at the command of the king (24:21). Stoning was reserved for particularly egregious sins, such as child sacrifice (Lev 20:2, 7), blasphemy (24:14, 16, 23), being a medium or spiritist (20:27), breaking the Sabbath (Num 15:35–36), or taking something under the ban (Josh 7:25), but God's people resort to stoning when the word of God or a course of action is defiantly opposed (Num 14:10; 2 Chr 10:18; see Acts 5:26; 7:58; 14:5). God had sent his prophet to Joash, but in Jerusalem the prophet is now stoned to death as a testimony to the king's rebellious heart (cf. Matt 23:34–37). Joash's command to have Zechariah killed is even more heinous, given that his father was Jehoiada, the priest who had risked his life to keep him alive (2 Chr 22:11–12; 23:1–11). In his dying moments, Zechariah prays: "May the LORD see this and call you to account" (24:22). Joash had not remembered the loyalty Zechariah's father had shown him, but Yahweh remembers, as Zechariah's name testifies ("Yahweh has remembered").

The Arameans Defeat Judah, and Joash Is Murdered (24:23–27)

With Zechariah's final words lingering in the background, at the turn of the year the army of Aram marches against Joash, invading Judah and Jerusalem (2 Chr 24:23). His officials are killed (notably, the officials who had led Judah into idolatry, see vv. 17–18), and plunder is brought to the king of Damascus (v. 23; cf. 2 Kgs 12:18). Even though the army of Aram was comprised of "only a few men" in contrast to Joash's "much larger army," they were able to defeat God's people (2 Chr 24:24). God's people are often outnumbered in battle (14:8–11; 16:7–9; 20:12), but when they rely on the LORD, God gives them victory in spite of their small numbers (16:8). This story underscores that "no king is saved by the size of his army" (Ps 33:16), even if he has a much larger army!

Joash's death is filled with ironic reversal: he had "forsaken" God (2 Chr 24:20), but now the army "forsakes" him (v. 25). His own officials "conspire" against him because he had shed the blood of the son of Jehoiada (vv. 25–26), recalling that the people had "plotted" against Zechariah (v. 21). Further, his son Amaziah will also die at the hands of those who "conspire" against him (25:27). Lastly, Joash is killed on his bed (24:25), a tragic reversal of his earlier years, when he had been hidden in a bed chamber in the temple (22:11). As an infant, the bed chamber had been his safe haven, but now it has become his deathbed. The story of Joash thus "begins and ends in a bedroom."[2] Joash is buried in the city of David, although he is not given an honorable burial among the tombs of the kings (24:25; cf. 21:20). Notably, the officials who conspire against him have non-Israelite lineage (24:26; cf. Neh 13:23–27),[3] identifying them with Judah's enemies (cf. 2 Chr 20:1–2, 10, 22). Joash had begun well but finished poorly, and so he becomes a tragic figure in the history of the Southern Kingdom.

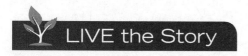

LIVE the Story

The Impact of One Godly Life

The reign of Joash highlights the impact one person can have on an individual king and on an entire community. After Jehoiada dies, the house of God is abandoned, and idolatrous worship is established in the Southern Kingdom. Joash had walked in God's ways, but only while Jehoiada the priest was alive

---

2. Klein, *2 Chronicles*, 348.

3. On the different names and their relationship to 2 Kgs 12:21, see ibid., 349.

to instruct him. We saw earlier (during the reign of Asa) the dire consequences when Israel was without a teaching priest and God's law (2 Chr 15:3–6).[4] And this story provides yet another example. The central role of Jehoiada is seen in the Chronicler's repeated references to him (he is mentioned ten times in the chapter), in contrast to four references in Kings; this indicates that he "plays a much more prominent role in Chronicles than in Kings."[5] After Jehoiada dies, he is given an honorable burial in recognition of "the good he had done in Israel for God and his temple" (24:16). God accomplishes "good things" on behalf of his people (cf. 1 Chr 17:26; 2 Chr 7:10), but now Jehoiada is recognized for the "good things" he has done in Israel. The extent of his godly influence is especially seen in the events that ensue after his death. We watch incredulously as the house of the LORD is abandoned, idolatry is reintroduced in Judah, Zechariah is murdered, Judah is defeated, and Joash is assassinated. All this takes place *after* the death of Jehoiada—one godly life matters.

Jehoiada was a man of faith, a wise counselor, and a faithful servant of the LORD whose godly life influenced an entire community. An example of a godly man of faith who influenced others is missionary and former Gordon-Conwell Theological Seminary faculty member J. Christy Wilson. Having served as a missionary in Afghanistan for over twenty years, his widespread influence in mission organizations is rehearsed by Ken Wilson.[6] But the article draws attention to another aspect of Christy's life that had an impact on hundreds of lives. After being a missionary in Afghanistan, Christy served as a faculty member at Gordon-Conwell Theological Seminary, the school where I teach. Christy was especially known for his commitment to pray for every student, which he did by first memorizing the names of *every* seminary student, including students who had never taken his classes. He even memorized the names of family members of each student, and he prayed for these students daily, using the seminary's "facebook" (this was a spiral-bound booklet produced each year that included the names of every student and their family members); Ken Wilson recalls:

> Christy prayed through the entire Facebook each week, praying for each person individually. When students encountered him on campus for the first time, they would be surprised to hear a professor they had never met

---

4. See Live the Story in Chapter 44, pp. 395–97.
5. Klein, *2 Chronicles,* 334.
6. Ken Wilson, "Life of J. Christy Wilson Jr. (1921–1999) and His Worldwide Discipling Ministry," *Knowing & Doing* (C. S. Lewis Institute), Summer 2017, 1–7, https://www.cslewisinstitute.org/resources/life-of-j-christy-wilson-jr-1921-1999-and-his-worldwide-discipling-ministry/.

address them by name. When Christy and Betty traveled, his Facebook went with them. Christy would drive, Betty would read the names to him, and Christy would pray. He also established a prayer room on campus; every noon, he and a band of students united in prayer for the peoples and nations of the world.[7]

As a faculty member at Gordon-Conwell, I have seen the ongoing influence of Christy's godly life some twenty years after his death. Former students still remember his prayers. They remember times when he stopped them in the hallway to pray for them by name. His legacy continues through the J. Christy Wilson Center for World Missions at Gordon-Conwell. Ken Wilson thus notes that Christy left a "lasting legacy, and the ripple effect of his life continues to spread to people, ethnic groups, and nations throughout the world."[8] To this day, hundreds of prayers are offered every week as students gather daily in this chapel to pray for the nations of the world. Like the priest Jehoiada, Christy lived to a ripe old age, "full of days," and he has been honored because of the "good he had done."

God has given each one of us spheres of influence: in the home, the workplace, in our church, and in our local communities. We could reflect upon people we know who have done good things in their own communities, leaving a godly legacy as their final years are drawing to a close. I know a lady in our church who is in her nineties. She has been a faithful servant of God. She is known as a woman of prayer, and she continues to have a godly influence in our church community. During the COVID-19 pandemic, while isolated at home, sometimes even confined to her bed due to back problems, she has written hundreds of letters and emails, encouraging people to stay firm in the faith. She is someone who will be remembered for the good things she has done. When your eulogy is written, what will people say about *you*? What are the good things you are doing in your local community? How are you investing in the lives of others? One godly life matters. Let us make our lives count for the sake of the kingdom.

---

7. Ibid., 4.
8. Ibid., 5.

LISTEN to the Story

¹Amaziah was twenty-five years old when he became king, and he reigned in Jerusalem twenty-nine years. His mother's name was Jehoaddan; she was from Jerusalem. ²He did what was right in the eyes of the LORD, but not wholeheartedly. ³After the kingdom was firmly in his control, he executed the officials who had murdered his father the king. ⁴Yet he did not put their children to death, but acted in accordance with what is written in the Law, in the Book of Moses, where the LORD commanded: "Parents shall not be put to death for their children, nor children be put to death for their parents; each will die for their own sin."

⁵Amaziah called the people of Judah together and assigned them according to their families to commanders of thousands and commanders of hundreds for all Judah and Benjamin. He then mustered those twenty years old or more and found that there were three hundred thousand men fit for military service, able to handle the spear and shield. ⁶He also hired a hundred thousand fighting men from Israel for a hundred talents of silver.

⁷But a man of God came to him and said, "Your Majesty, these troops from Israel must not march with you, for the LORD is not with Israel—not with any of the people of Ephraim. ⁸Even if you go and fight courageously in battle, God will overthrow you before the enemy, for God has the power to help or to overthrow."

⁹Amaziah asked the man of God, "But what about the hundred talents I paid for these Israelite troops?"

The man of God replied, "The LORD can give you much more than that."

¹⁰So Amaziah dismissed the troops who had come to him from Ephraim and sent them home. They were furious with Judah and left for home in a great rage.

¹¹Amaziah then marshaled his strength and led his army to the Valley

of Salt, where he killed ten thousand men of Seir. ¹²The army of Judah also captured ten thousand men alive, took them to the top of a cliff and threw them down so that all were dashed to pieces.

¹³Meanwhile the troops that Amaziah had sent back and had not allowed to take part in the war raided towns belonging to Judah from Samaria to Beth Horon. They killed three thousand people and carried off great quantities of plunder.

¹⁴When Amaziah returned from slaughtering the Edomites, he brought back the gods of the people of Seir. He set them up as his own gods, bowed down to them and burned sacrifices to them. ¹⁵The anger of the LORD burned against Amaziah, and he sent a prophet to him, who said, "Why do you consult this people's gods, which could not save their own people from your hand?"

¹⁶While he was still speaking, the king said to him, "Have we appointed you an adviser to the king? Stop! Why be struck down?"

So the prophet stopped but said, "I know that God has determined to destroy you, because you have done this and have not listened to my counsel."

¹⁷After Amaziah king of Judah consulted his advisers, he sent this challenge to Jehoash son of Jehoahaz, the son of Jehu, king of Israel: "Come, let us face each other in battle."

¹⁸But Jehoash king of Israel replied to Amaziah king of Judah: "A thistle in Lebanon sent a message to a cedar in Lebanon, 'Give your daughter to my son in marriage.' Then a wild beast in Lebanon came along and trampled the thistle underfoot. ¹⁹You say to yourself that you have defeated Edom, and now you are arrogant and proud. But stay at home! Why ask for trouble and cause your own downfall and that of Judah also?"

²⁰Amaziah, however, would not listen, for God so worked that he might deliver them into the hands of Jehoash, because they sought the gods of Edom. ²¹So Jehoash king of Israel attacked. He and Amaziah king of Judah faced each other at Beth Shemesh in Judah. ²²Judah was routed by Israel, and every man fled to his home. ²³Jehoash king of Israel captured Amaziah king of Judah, the son of Joash, the son of Ahaziah, at Beth Shemesh. Then Jehoash brought him to Jerusalem and broke down the wall of Jerusalem from the Ephraim Gate to the Corner Gate—a section about four hundred cubits long. ²⁴He took all the gold and silver and all the articles found in

the temple of God that had been in the care of Obed-Edom, together with the palace treasures and the hostages, and returned to Samaria.

²⁵Amaziah son of Joash king of Judah lived for fifteen years after the death of Jehoash son of Jehoahaz king of Israel. ²⁶As for the other events of Amaziah's reign, from beginning to end, are they not written in the book of the kings of Judah and Israel? ²⁷From the time that Amaziah turned away from following the LORD, they conspired against him in Jerusalem and he fled to Lachish, but they sent men after him to Lachish and killed him there. ²⁸He was brought back by horse and was buried with his ancestors in the City of Judah.

Listening to the Text in the Story: Genesis 27:1–46; Numbers 20:14–21

Amaziah assumes the throne during a turbulent period after his father Joash was murdered on his bed. The upcoming battle he will fight against the Edomites, one of Israel's neighbors living south-east of the Dead Sea, is central to his reign. Hostility between Judah and the Edomites will erupt later during the reign of Ahaz (2 Chr 28:17), and it will resurface again during the final days of the kingdom (Lam 4:21–22; Ezek 25:12–14; Obad 1:1–21). The longstanding conflict between Israel and Edom, which has its roots in sibling rivalry (Gen 27; Num 20:14–21; cf. Mal 1:4), comes to a crescendo in the Babylonian assault of Jerusalem. Psalm 137 calls God to remember:

> Remember, LORD, what the Edomites did
>   on the day Jerusalem fell.
> "Tear it down," they cried,
>   "tear it down to its foundations!"
> Daughter Babylon, doomed to destruction,
>   happy is the one who repays you
>   according to what you have done to us.
> Happy is the one who seizes your infants
>   and dashes them against the rocks. (vv. 7–9)

Some of these sentiments are reflected in the story that follows. It is important to notice the imagery of rocks used in this psalm and in 2 Chronicles 25:12. The Edomites lived in a mountainous and rugged region south of the Dead

Sea. Their fortress city, Sela, which means "rock" (Heb. *sela*'), testifies to their rugged terrain. The height of the mountains could exceed 5,000 feet, yet this became a metaphor for their pride. God's judgment against them pronounced by the prophet Obadiah employs the mountainous topography as a metaphor for their pride and arrogance (Obad 1:1–21). The prophet announces that the "pride of your heart has deceived you, you who live in the clefts of the rocks and make your home on the heights" (Obad 1:3; cf. Jer 49:16). The Edomites had assumed that no one could bring them down from their elevated place, yet they will be brought down because of the violence done to their brothers (Obad 1:8–10; see Joel 3:19).[1] This mountainous and rugged terrain of the Edomites will be help us listen to the story that follows (2 Chr 25:12).

EXPLAIN the Story

Amaziah Consolidates His Rule (25:1–4)

Amaziah is twenty-five years old when he becomes king (2 Chr 25:1). His lengthy reign of twenty-nine years probably included a period of co-regency with his son, Uzziah.[2] He is introduced as a king who "did what was right in the eyes of the LORD, but not wholeheartedly" (v. 2). The first part of his reign is described favorably. When the kingdom is firmly established, the king executes justice by killing those servants who had assassinated his father (v. 3; cf. 24:25). His actions are seen positively, as Amaziah acts with restraint by not killing their sons, which was in accordance with God's law (Deut 24:16; cf. Jer 31:29–30; Ezek 18:19–24). If Boda is correct that the servants were among the royal family, his restraint is all the more important.[3] Yet the terse but pregnant qualifying comment about the king doing right "but not wholeheartedly" anticipates the sorry state of affairs that follows.

Amaziah Defeats the Edomites (25:5–13)

Amaziah's next action is to prepare for battle against the Edomites (2 Chr 25:5). He musters troops from the tribes of Judah and Benjamin, who are to serve under military commanders according to their clans. Men aged twenty

---

1. For more information on the Edomites, see the discussions in Chapter 1 on 1 Chr 1:35–42, pp. 28–30, Chapter 18 on 18:12–13, p. 191, and Chapter 50 on 2 Chr 21:8–11, pp. 439–40.

2. For a discussion of the dates, a possible co-regency, and the various views by scholars, see Klein, *2 Chronicles*, 354–55.

3. Boda, *1–2 Chronicles*, 361.

years and older are numbered (v. 5; cf. Num 1:2–3, 20–45; 26:2), resulting in thousands of fighting men being mustered for warfare (2 Chr 25:5).[4]

Since the number of men is smaller than armies of earlier kings (cf. 14:8; 17:14–18), it is not surprising that Amaziah seeks to secure mercenaries from Israel, paying one hundred talents of silver (25:6). However, given that military victory was not achieved by the size of an army but by trusting in the LORD (14:11; 16:8; 20:12), this is the first indication that the king's heart is not fully devoted to the LORD. Instead of seeking the LORD, as other kings have done when facing battles (15:4; 20:2–4), his priority is to build his army. He has not taken to heart that a king is not saved by the size of his army (Ps 33:16). Amaziah will go to any length to build a powerful army, even if it means using men from the apostate Northern Kingdom. He surely would have been aware that such alliances were viewed negatively (cf. 2 Chr 18:1; 19:2; 20:35; 22:1–7). Religious compromise, even if for military purposes, would not lead to success (25:7; cf. 14:8–12). When confronted by an unnamed prophet, Amaziah is presented with a choice: "If you fight alone, God will be on your side; if you seek the assistance of those Israelites, you will fail."[5] The choice seems straightforward, but Amaziah's response is revealing. The king wants to know how he will recover the money he has already spent! With divine assurance that he will receive back more than what he has paid, Amaziah dismisses the troops, and they return home furious (25:9–10).

Amaziah leads his army in a decisive victory over the Edomites, killing thousands in the Valley of Salt (v. 11).[6] The account in Kings describes Amaziah's defeat of the Edomite fortress, Sela, which simply means "rock" (Heb. sela'; NIV "cliff" in v. 12; NIV "Sela" in 2 Kgs 14:7), whereas the battle is described in Chronicles in language that evokes divine judgment. We read that the men of Judah "took them to the top of a cliff and threw them down so that all were dashed to pieces" (2 Chr 25:12; cf. Ps 137:7–9). The term "cliff, rock" (Heb. sela') is used in Obadiah's oracle against the Edomites (Obad 1:3; cf. Ps 137:9; Jer 49:16). While this description is not unlike the language used in Psalm 137:7–9 and by the prophet Obadiah when he describes God's judgment against Edom (Obad 1:10–14), it is important to recognize that these texts are in response to the Edomite treatment of Judah during the

---

4. On the meaning of the Hebrew term 'eleph and its meaning as a military unit (rather than a literal headcount), see the discussion in Chapter 12 on 1 Chr 12:23–40, pp. 138–40.

5. Japhet, I & II Chronicles, 863.

6. The Valley of Salt was probably located south of the Dead Sea, in the Great Rift Valley, which corresponds to the Arabah. On the possible locations of Sela, see Dillard, 2 Chronicles, 200.

Babylonian assault against Jerusalem. The story of Amaziah takes place much earlier, however.

Furthermore, the next verse depicts northerners killing thousands in Judah and taking plunder while Amaziah is killing Edomites. The Hebrew text is written to convey simultaneous events (NIV, "Meanwhile"), which may well suggest that something is awry. In other words, while Amaziah is throwing Edomites over cliffs, men from the north raid some of the cities of Judah and kill thousands (2 Chr 25:13).[7] Given that military success is directly related to the spiritual condition of Judah, the slaughter of thousands by northerners seems to cast a dark shadow over Amaziah's actions. Moreover, instead of receiving back what he had paid (v. 19), he faces even more loss as precious goods are plundered from Judah's towns (v. 13; cf. 28:8). The synchronous plot lines seem to imply divine disapproval of Amaziah's excessive violence. If there is any question about the character of the king, it is fully exposed in what takes place next.

Amaziah Worships the Gods of Edom (25:14–16)

After Amaziah returns from slaughtering the Edomites, he takes their gods, but instead of destroying them as David had done (1 Chr 14:12; cf. Deut 7:5), he sets them up as *his gods* (2 Chr 25:14)! He even bows down to them and burns incense to them![8] God sends a prophet to confront the king. He rebukes him for seeking the gods of the Edomites—gods who had not been able to deliver their own people (v. 15). Seeking God is a hallmark of godly leadership (Heb. *d-r-sh*, 1 Chr 22:19; 2 Chr 17:3–4; 18:4, 7; 20:3; 31:21; 34:3), yet Amaziah now seeks help from *foreign gods*. There have already been hints of his divided heart, such as when he mustered his army instead of seeking the LORD. Now his true loyalties are exposed.

Even before the prophet finishes speaking, Amaziah defiantly questions whether *he* has the right to be the king's counselor (2 Chr 25:16)! He demands that the prophet stop speaking, bullying him with a threat of physical retaliation. Throughout Chronicles, listening to wise counsel is a hallmark of godly leadership. The king had his own royal advisers (2 Sam 25:12; 1 Chr 26:14; 27:32-33), and his success was often determined by his ability to give heed to such counsel (2 Chr 10:6-8; 22:3-4; 30:2). With

---

7. Japhet suggests that the cities of Judah may have been located within the northern territory (see 2 Chr 17:2; 19:4), although not all agree (Japhet, *I & II Chronicles*, 865).

8. This may well serve as a warning to the post-exilic community, who were in danger of religious compromise (see the introduction, Life in the Province of Judah and the Diaspora under the Persians, esp. pp. 12–13).

stinging irony, the prophet boldly states that God has "counseled" (NIV "determined"; Heb. *y-'-ts*) to destroy him because the king has not listened to *his* counsel (Heb. *'etsah*). The events that follow are to be interpreted in light of this prophetic word to the king—and we learn that what God "counsels" surely comes to pass.

Amaziah Is Defeated by Israel (25:17–28)

With further play on the verb "to counsel," we read that the king "took counsel" (2 Chr 25:17, ESV). What comes next is that Amaziah foolishly challenges the northern king, Jehoash, to a face-to-face confrontation (v. 17). A parable with sarcastic overtones is uttered by Jehoash, which underscores Amaziah's folly—it is sheer madness to think that a mere thistle could enter into a marriage alliance with a towering cedar of Lebanon (v. 18)! Now the disreputable northern king is mocking the southern king for his pride and arrogance, warning him to stay home (v. 19). But in his pride Amaziah refuses to listen, and God is providentially at work, bringing judgment against his people because they have sought the gods of Edom (v. 20; see v. 16). Under the Mosaic covenant, failure to obey God's commands would lead to military defeat (Lev 26:17; Deut 28:25–26; cf. 2 Chr 36:14-17), and this is precisely what happens next.

The battle takes place at Beth-Shemesh, a town on the border of Judah's territory (2 Chr 25:21). Details about the battle are not provided, but Judah is defeated and the people flee to their tents. Jehoash captures Amaziah, brings him back to Jerusalem, and breaks down a section of the city wall between two gates, thereby making Jerusalem vulnerable (v. 23).[9] Jehoash then takes gold, silver, and utensils from the temple that had been in the care of Obed-Edom (the Levitical family that served as gatekeepers and had oversight of the storehouses; cf. 1 Chr 15:18; 26:8, 15) and brings them to Samaria, along with captives (2 Chr 25:24). Amaziah may have been among the captives, at which time some suggest Uzziah would have ruled as co-regent. What is important is that his demise is due to his turning away from the Lord. He flees to Lachish because people had "conspired" against him (Heb. *q-sh-r*, v. 27), recalling the events that had led to his own father's death when his officials conspired against him (Heb. *q-sh-r*, 24:25–26). While fleeing to Lachish, Amaziah is killed and his body is brought back to Jerusalem where he is buried with his fathers (25:27–28).

---

9. For a discussion of the possible locations of the two gates, see Klein, *2 Chronicles*, 362.

LIVE the Story

The Importance of Wholehearted Devotion to the LORD

Amaziah is a tragic figure who makes a series of mistakes and errors in judgment due to his pride and over-confidence in his abilities. To be sure, he is introduced as a king who did what was right in the eyes of the LORD, but the attentive reader is waiting to see what the terse but pregnant comment means: "but not wholeheartedly" (2 Chr 25:2). Initially, the king acts with restraint, thereby following God's law (vv. 3–4). His military census seems *somewhat* harmless, not done in complete defiance of God, yet the careful reader knows that seeking the LORD is the cardinal virtue in Chronicles, and this should have been his *first* response. His next action of acquiring mercenaries from the north is logical from a human perspective, but again, the attentive reader recognizes that any alliance with the apostate Northern Kingdom is doomed to fail—something that Amaziah has failed to grasp. When confronted by a prophet, the king agrees to allow the soldiers to return home, but his motivation is somewhat troubling, since he is induced by the prospect of recovering the money he has outlaid—and with assurance that he will receive even more back. Things seem to unravel further when the cities of Judah are raided and people are killed, as this is taking place while the king is away fighting his own battle, using excessive force on his enemy. In spite of these misgivings, the tragedy of this figure is seen in what happens next.

After defeating the Edomites, instead of destroying their idols as David had done (1 Chr 14:12; cf. Deut 7:5; 12:3), we watch incredulously as he sets them up as *his* gods, and even bows down before them—the so-called idols that were unable to save their own people! The absence of seeking God earlier, which reflects the posture of his heart, is now exposed as he seeks the gods of the Edomites. This indicates that the king's heart was not fully devoted to the LORD from the beginning. When rebuked by a prophet, even though the king listened to a prophet earlier (although repentance was wanting), now the king is outraged that a prophet would give *him* counsel! Since the prophet's rebuke has come directly from God—this means that Amaziah is commanding *God* to stop speaking.

Another key indicator of the tragic life of this king is the hubris that comes as a result of his victory, leading him to make a serious error in judgment. While Amaziah is oblivious to his error, it is made known to him by the northern king, who recognizes the pride of his heart: "You say to yourself that you have defeated Edom, and now you are arrogant and proud" (2 Chr

25:19). His heart has become lifted up in pride, precisely what Moses had warned about many years earlier (Deut 17:20). Instead of giving glory to God for his success, he attributes the success *to himself.* This is not unlike the boastful Nebuchadnezzar, who congratulated himself on his own achievements (Dan 4:30). Such self-exaltation is not only unbecoming, especially by people called to walk *humbly* before their God, but it entails a serious misplacing of honor, robbing God of what is due to him. Amaziah seeks to glorify himself (2 Chr 25:19), but God's people were to give glory and honor to God (Pss 22:23; 50:23; 86:12). These are the very words they had sung when the ark was brought into Jerusalem: "Ascribe to the LORD, all you families of nations, ascribe to the LORD glory and strength. Ascribe to the LORD the glory due his name; bring an offering and come before him. Worship the LORD in the splendor of his holiness (1 Chr 16:28–29).

The story of Amaziah is a warning against pride and self-glorification, but underlying his pride we find a heart not fully devoted to the LORD. Klein thus makes the insightful comment that the "Chronicler's observation about Amaziah's heart prepares the reader for Amaziah's apostasy in the second half of his life and for his misguided hiring of mercenaries in the first half of his life. Hence, even the first part of his life was not with a whole heart."[10] When considering how to apply this story, Jesus's teaching may come to mind, when he emphasizes that he did not glorify himself, but the Father glorifies him (John 8:54; see also 13:32; 14:13; 16:14; 17:1, 5), and we could think of his stirring words that anticipate his death on the cross: "Father, glorify your name!" (12:28; cf. vv. 23, 27). Jesus's desire to glorify the Father stands in stark contrast to Amaziah's self-glorification. We might even recall the well-known Westminster Shorter Catechism: "Man's chief end is to glorify God, and to enjoy him forever." To be sure, we are to glorify God, not ourselves.

But the story of Amaziah is really about the state of his *heart.* Moses had taught that God's people were to love the LORD their God with all their heart (Deut 6:5), and Jesus reinforced that this was the greatest and foremost of all the commandments (Matt 22:37–38). Yet our hearts can easily be swayed, and our loyalties are more fickle than we care to admit. Other priorities and desires can assume first place in our lives, slowly eroding away our devotion to the LORD. Tim Keller notes in his book *Counterfeit Gods* that, while external objects of worship are revered in many parts of the world, idolatry in the human heart is universal (cf. Ezek 14:3). He explains how these idols deeply lodged in the heart start to have priority in our lives:

---

10. Klein, *2 Chronicles,* 355.

God was saying that the human heart takes good things like a successful career, love, material possessions, even family, and turns them into ultimate things. Our hearts deify them as the center of our lives, because, we think, they can give us significance and security, safety and fulfillment, if we attain them.[11]

He uses the example of the One Ring in *The Lord of the Rings*. The One Ring makes characters willing to do anything, noting that it "turns the good thing into an absolute that overturns every allegiance or value."[12] This is what happened in Amaziah's life. His allegiance to the LORD took second place, for worldly success, financial gain, honor, and even his position as king were more important to him than submission to the LORD, and his heart became hardened as a result. Like the dehumanizing effect of Sauron's Ring, the king's character slowly contorts, and his reality is distorted by his pride. By way of contrast, David, a man after God's heart, exhorts his son Solomon to serve the LORD with a "wholehearted devotion," recognizing the "LORD searches every heart and understands every desire and every thought" (1 Chr 28:9). God searches *our* hearts and he understands *our* desires and thoughts. This story is a reminder that God wants us to serve him with an undivided heart, echoing David's prayer: "Create in me a pure heart, O God, and renew a steadfast spirit within me" (Ps 51:10).

---

11. Timothy Keller, *Counterfeit Gods: The Empty Promises of Money, Sex, and Power, and the Only Hope that Matters* (New York: Penguin Books, 2011), xvi.

12. Ibid., ivii.

CHAPTER 55

2 Chronicles 26:1–23

 LISTEN to the Story

¹Then all the people of Judah took Uzziah, who was sixteen years old, and made him king in place of his father Amaziah. ²He was the one who rebuilt Elath and restored it to Judah after Amaziah rested with his ancestors.

³Uzziah was sixteen years old when he became king, and he reigned in Jerusalem fifty-two years. His mother's name was Jekoliah; she was from Jerusalem. ⁴He did what was right in the eyes of the LORD, just as his father Amaziah had done. ⁵He sought God during the days of Zechariah, who instructed him in the fear of God. As long as he sought the LORD, God gave him success.

⁶He went to war against the Philistines and broke down the walls of Gath, Jabneh and Ashdod. He then rebuilt towns near Ashdod and elsewhere among the Philistines. ⁷God helped him against the Philistines and against the Arabs who lived in Gur Baal and against the Meunites. ⁸The Ammonites brought tribute to Uzziah, and his fame spread as far as the border of Egypt, because he had become very powerful.

⁹Uzziah built towers in Jerusalem at the Corner Gate, at the Valley Gate and at the angle of the wall, and he fortified them. ¹⁰He also built towers in the wilderness and dug many cisterns, because he had much livestock in the foothills and in the plain. He had people working his fields and vineyards in the hills and in the fertile lands, for he loved the soil.

¹¹Uzziah had a well-trained army, ready to go out by divisions according to their numbers as mustered by Jeiel the secretary and Maaseiah the officer under the direction of Hananiah, one of the royal officials. ¹²The total number of family leaders over the fighting men was 2,600. ¹³Under their command was an army of 307,500 men trained for war, a powerful force to support the king against his enemies. ¹⁴Uzziah provided shields,

spears, helmets, coats of armor, bows and slingstones for the entire army. [15]In Jerusalem he made devices invented for use on the towers and on the corner defenses so that soldiers could shoot arrows and hurl large stones from the walls. His fame spread far and wide, for he was greatly helped until he became powerful.

[16]But after Uzziah became powerful, his pride led to his downfall. He was unfaithful to the LORD his God, and entered the temple of the LORD to burn incense on the altar of incense. [17]Azariah the priest with eighty other courageous priests of the LORD followed him in. [18]They confronted King Uzziah and said, "It is not right for you, Uzziah, to burn incense to the LORD. That is for the priests, the descendants of Aaron, who have been consecrated to burn incense. Leave the sanctuary, for you have been unfaithful; and you will not be honored by the LORD God."

[19]Uzziah, who had a censer in his hand ready to burn incense, became angry. While he was raging at the priests in their presence before the incense altar in the LORD's temple, leprosy broke out on his forehead. [20]When Azariah the chief priest and all the other priests looked at him, they saw that he had leprosy on his forehead, so they hurried him out. Indeed, he himself was eager to leave, because the LORD had afflicted him.

[21]King Uzziah had leprosy until the day he died. He lived in a separate house—leprous, and banned from the temple of the LORD. Jotham his son had charge of the palace and governed the people of the land.

[22]The other events of Uzziah's reign, from beginning to end, are recorded by the prophet Isaiah son of Amoz. [23]Uzziah rested with his ancestors and was buried near them in a cemetery that belonged to the kings, for people said, "He had leprosy." And Jotham his son succeeded him as king.

Listening to the Text in the Story: Leviticus 13–14; Numbers 12:1–15; Deuteronomy 17:14–20; 2 Kings 15:1–7; Sumerian King List, Turin Royal Canon

With the unexpected death of Amaziah, the enthronement of his son Uzziah provides hope to the Southern Kingdom. Yet, just as in the reigns of his father and grandfather before him, Uzziah's reign begins with blessing and victory but ultimately ends in judgment and disgrace (2 Chr 24:19–21;

25:15–16; 26:18–19). The turning point from blessing to divine discipline in this account comes in the dramatic confrontation between the king and the high priest over the offering of incense in the temple. In order to listen to the story and its historical tensions, it is important to consider the role of kingship in the ancient Near East.

Royal ideology in the ancient Near East envisions the king as a surrogate for the gods.[1] In this worldview, kingship is a reflection of the rule of the gods on earth through a representative who exercises "sacral kingship." In the ancient world, kings serve the gods by building and maintaining temples, offering sacrifices, and presiding over religious ceremonies. Worship was mediated by the king, who becomes the link between heaven and earth. Ancient Near Eastern kings are invested with full political and religious authority to represent the rule of the gods on earth. By contrast, Israelite kings had limitations placed on them, especially in relation to their power and prestige (Deut. 17:14–20). The law expressly aims at keeping a king's heart from being lifted up in pride above his fellow Israelites, for the king was to meditate on God's law (v. 20). Since the king was vulnerable to the enticement of power and prestige accorded to his office, he is commanded to cultivate humble dependence on the LORD. Rather than wielding unrestrained power like the rulers of the nations, an Israelite king was always to remember that he was under the authority of God and his word.

Limitations were also placed upon the king in relation to his officiating at the temple. Israelite kings were permitted to worship in the temple, and they were invested with authority to lead the nation into worship, but unlike sacral kingship of the ancient Near East, serving at the altar and offering incense were the exclusive prerogative of the Aaronic priesthood (Exod 28–29; Num 3:1-3; 17:40). The priests alone were qualified to approach the Holy One of Israel. Accordingly, while David had brought up the ark to Jerusalem, only the Levites were permitted to physically handle it (1 Chr 15:1–15). Similarly, King Hezekiah will decree the celebration of the Passover, yet only the priests will be permitted to oversee the offering of sacrifices (2 Chr 30:13–21). The restrictions placed upon Israelite kings, along with the specific role given to the priesthood, provide the background for understanding the nature of Uzziah's sin and why his offering of incense provokes such severe censure from the LORD.

---

1. See the *Sumerian King List* (Electronic Text Corpus of Sumerian Literature, *Sumerian King List*, http://etcsl.orinst.ox.ac.uk/section2/tr211.htm) or the *Turin Royal Canon* (http://www.ancient-egypt.co.uk/turin/pages/turin_royal_canon.htm).

EXPLAIN the Story

The Early Days of Uzziah's Successful Reign (26:1–5)

Uzziah becomes king at the age of sixteen following the assassination of his father, Amaziah (2 Chr 26:1). His reign of fifty-two years is one of the longest in the history of Judah, second only to the reign of Manasseh (33:1). Uzziah is evaluated by the Chronicler as a king who did what was "right in the eyes of the LORD" (26:4). Yet his approval is contingent upon his seeking (Heb. *d-r-sh*) the LORD, an exemplary attitude among kings which was notably absent in Israel's first king (1 Chr 10:13–14). As long as Uzziah follows Zechariah's instruction in the fear of the LORD (2 Chr 26:5; cf. Deut 17:19), he experiences the blessings of the covenant in military success and agricultural abundance (cf. Lev 26:4–6).

Uzziah Extends Judah's Boundaries (26:6–15)

Success characterizes Uzziah's foreign and domestic ventures. In a bid to regain the prestige of Solomon's days, Uzziah aggressively extends the boundaries of Judah by leading campaigns in the coastal plain against the Philistines, including going up against key cities such as Gath and Ashdod (2 Chr 26:6). He defeats Arab tribes to the south, securing important caravan routes across the Sinai region. Earlier, Solomon's fleet had sailed from the southern port of Elath as he extended his trade to distant lands (8:17–18). The kingdom is clearly expanding and flourishing, as the archaeological record testifies,[2] yet it is important to recognize that Uzziah's success is due to God's help.[3] The verb "to help" (Heb. *'-z-r*, 26:7) is central to this story (vv. 13 [NIV "support"], 15), and it is reflected in the priest named Azariah ("Yahweh has helped" or "Yahweh is my help," cf. v. 15), which is an alternative name for Uzziah (2 Kgs 15:1). Reminiscent of the glory days of Solomon, Uzziah receives tribute from the nations, with his fame extending to the borders of Egypt (2 Chr 26:8; cf. 9:1, 14).

Uzziah's domestic achievements are no less impressive: he hews out cisterns in the Judean wilderness for his flocks and herds and plants royal vineyards in the hill country (26:10). Like others before him, Uzziah conscripts a standing army, fully equipped and fitted for battle (v. 11; cf. 17:12–19). He fortifies the

---

2. Hoerth, *Archaeology & the Old Testament*, 330.

3. On the topic of divine help, see the discussions on David (Chapter 12 on 1 Chr 12, pp. 130–32), Asa (Chapter 43 on 2 Chr 14:11, p. 388), Jehoshaphat (Chapter 47 on 2 Chr 18:31, p. 416), and Hezekiah (Chapter 61 on 2 Chr 32:8, pp. 526–27).

walls of Jerusalem and commissions the construction of innovative defensive weaponry for shooting arrows and slinging stones from the towers of the city wall (26:14–15). God's blessing is upon Uzziah, and God grants him victory and success (vv. 7, 13, 15). In all this, he is strengthened, for he has been wondrously helped (v. 15).

Uzziah Is Unfaithful and Oversteps His Boundaries (26:16–23)

Uzziah lives up to his name meaning "Yahweh is my strength," but tragically, as he grows strong, he proves unfaithful to the LORD who has strengthened him (2 Chr 26:16; cf. 12:1). Enticed by success, Uzziah grasps at extending his own authority when he enters the temple to offer incense on the golden altar (26:16). The offering of incense was a sacral rite entrusted to the priesthood; theirs was the exclusive prerogative to burn incense on the golden altar every morning and evening (Exod 30:7–8; 1 Chr 6:49). It is no small matter that Uzziah's seizing of unsanctioned authority is judged as an act of "unfaithfulness," that is, presumption with regard to holy things (2 Chr 26:16, 18; cf. Josh 7:1).

The high priest, along with eighty other priests, opposes the king as he stands poised to violate the holiness of the sanctuary, but Uzziah, in obstinate rage, insists on his royal privilege (2 Chr 26:18). Standing by the altar with censer in hand, leprosy suddenly "breaks out" (Heb. *z-r-ḥ*, lit. "shines") on his forehead (v. 19). This was a sign that no one could mistake. Uzziah is reprimanded in a measured way, marked as unclean on the very spot where the high priest is marked as consecrated to the LORD. Israel's high priest was endowed with a golden frontlet on his forehead that was inscribed with the epithet "Holy to the LORD." The frontlet was a mark of the high priest's consecration and the consecration of Israel's offerings before the LORD (Exod 28:36–38). The *shining* golden frontlet on the priest's forehead signified acceptance; the *shining* leprous breakout on the king's forehead signified rejection.[4] Uzziah is conspicuously branded as disqualified from the temple and the worshiping community.

It is important to understand that Uzziah's attempt to offer incense in the temple is not a genuine expression of worship, but rather an overstepping of his bounds to usurp the priesthood's sacral privileges.[5] In a similar overstepping

---

4. I am grateful for Christine Palmer's insight on this section and what follows.

5. Merrill surveys the priestly role of David in particular, but he notes that in this instance, Uzziah has overstepped the boundaries of priestly ministry: "The infraction was not that of a king functioning cultically, but of a king undertaking a cultic ministry limited to another order of priests" (Merrill, "Royal Priesthood," 61).

of bounds, Saul's presumption to offer sacrifice leads to his rejection by God (1 Sam 13:7–14). Uzziah's punishment of leprosy further sheds light on his particular sin. When Miriam had challenged Moses's leadership in the wilderness and grasped at unsanctioned authority, God had punished her with an outbreak of *leprosy* (Num 12:1–15).[6] Her skin disease is interpreted as chastisement and likened to a father's shaming (v. 14). Sufferers of leprosy are regarded as ritually unclean and must be quarantined outside the camp. Separation from the covenant people is symbolic of a living death, and so the leper acts as one who has been defiled by death—he must rend his clothes, dishevel his hair, and cry out in the presence of others, "Unclean, unclean" (Lev 13:45–46). Yet this temporary alienation from the covenant community allows for the possibility of repentance, healing, and restoration (14:1–32). Accordingly, after a period of seven days, Miriam is healed and restored to the worshiping community.

Yet Uzziah's defiling skin disease has a different outcome. He is quarantined in a separate house and is forced to turn over the administration of the government to his son, Jotham, in a period of co-regency (2 Chr 26:21). Perhaps had he humbled himself and sought the LORD, as did Hezekiah (32:24–26), he might have been healed. But instead, Judah's king dies unclean, unrepentant, and alienated from the community, thus he is buried in a cemetery belonging to the kings—but not with the kings (26:23). A limestone epitaph survives as testimony that even after his death, Uzziah's disease still marks him. When Jerusalem expanded during the Second Temple period, his bones had to be unearthed and reburied outside the new city limits. A plaque was inscribed at that time with the warning: "Here were brought the bones of Uzziah, king of Judah—do not open!"[7] It is in such a dramatic moment of national crisis that Isaiah is called as prophet to an unclean people, to proclaim the holiness of Israel's heavenly King (Isa 6:1–3; cf. 2 Chr 26:22).

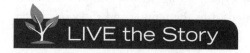

LIVE the Story

Warning against Pride

This memorable narrative of Judah's leprous king exposes the dark sin of pride. At some point in the waves of success enjoyed by Uzziah, his reliance

---

6. Biblical leprosy is not to be identified as Hanson's disease, but it is a more general scaly skin disease (perhaps like psoriasis, fungal infections, or eczema).

7. *Epitaph of King Uzziah of Judah*, Displayed in the Israel Museum in Jerusalem. https://www .imj.org.il/en/collections/353190.

on God waned, and his reliance upon himself and his own strength swelled. Perhaps this is because he failed to abide in the fear of the Lord which instructed him to "not consider himself better than his fellow Israelites" (Deut 17:20).

Pride is the exaltation of oneself against God and against others. It is a malady of the human heart that becomes the breeding ground for all other sin. Pride is a dangerous temptation in leadership, especially when a ministry has been blessed with success. We tend to lose sight that it is the *Lord* we serve and not ourselves, and that *his* fame is our deepest joy, not our own reputation. We are apt to interpret our God-given success as arising from our own resources and capabilities and to absorb all recognition without reference to the Lord, who has gifted us and honored us by calling us into his service.

Inevitably, pride drives us to exceed our boundaries and grasp at that which has not been given to us. We overlook the giftedness of others and fail to give heed to wise counsel, as has been a constant refrain in Chronicles. All who are privileged to serve in leadership must be reminded that the way to greatness in God's kingdom is through humility (Matt 20:26), and the most important quality of a leader is godliness. We must guard our hearts and abide in the fellowship of the Lord, who is the source and definer of success. One of the most treasured ways we can practice daily dependence on the Lord is, like the kings of old, to study his word. There we encounter a Savior whose leadership is of an entirely different order than that of the world.

Although equal to God and sharing in his glory, Christ did not regard his privileged position within the Godhead as a divine right to remain distant from the plight of humanity, but he willingly divested himself of rank and glory to become incarnate in the world he himself created. He did not grasp at advantage, but he humbled himself to take on the role of a suffering servant, even to the point of a shameful death on a cross (Phil 2:6–8). In a radical departure from all expectations, Jesus acquires the kingdom through humble obedience to the Father's will and submission in pouring out his very life unto death. Humiliation is the path to his exaltation (vv. 9–11).

This message is one which permeates Jesus's teaching: "Whoever wants to become great among you must be your servant, and whoever wants to be first must be slave of all. For even the Son of Man did not come to be served, but to serve, and to give his life as a ransom for many" (Mark 10:43–45). Christ's servant posture, generous self-giving, and sacrificial obedience is the mindset all believers must embrace (Phil 2:5). Those who follow him have a high calling, not to greatness but to service, not to privilege but to self-giving. Cruciform living is the definitive antidote to pride.

CHAPTER 56

2 Chronicles 27:1–9

 ## LISTEN to the Story

¹Jotham was twenty-five years old when he became king, and he reigned in Jerusalem sixteen years. His mother's name was Jerusha daughter of Zadok. ²He did what was right in the eyes of the LORD, just as his father Uzziah had done, but unlike him he did not enter the temple of the LORD. The people, however, continued their corrupt practices. ³Jotham rebuilt the Upper Gate of the temple of the LORD and did extensive work on the wall at the hill of Ophel. ⁴He built towns in the hill country of Judah and forts and towers in the wooded areas.

⁵Jotham waged war against the king of the Ammonites and conquered them. That year the Ammonites paid him a hundred talents of silver, ten thousand cors of wheat and ten thousand cors of barley. The Ammonites brought him the same amount also in the second and third years.

⁶Jotham grew powerful because he walked steadfastly before the LORD his God.

⁷The other events in Jotham's reign, including all his wars and the other things he did, are written in the book of the kings of Israel and Judah. ⁸He was twenty-five years old when he became king, and he reigned in Jerusalem sixteen years. ⁹Jotham rested with his ancestors and was buried in the City of David. And Ahaz his son succeeded him as king.

Listening to the Text in the Story: Proverbs 4:26; 21:29

Jotham rules as co-regent during the last few years of his father's sullied life, but with the death of Uzziah, Jotham becomes sole monarch. His short reign is characterized positively by the Chronicler, and later we read that he grew powerful because "he walked steadfastly before the LORD his God" (2 Chr 27:6). The book of Proverbs gives numerous warnings about walking in the ways of the wicked (Prov 1:15; 2:12; 4:14, 19; 5:8; 7:25, etc.), which is in contrast to the ways of the righteous who walk in integrity (2:20; 9:6; 11:5; etc.). Walking in the way of righteousness requires wisdom, and thus Proverbs teaches: "Give careful thought to the paths for your feet and be steadfast in all your way" (4:26). Similarly, another proverb teaches that the "upright give thought to their ways" (21:29). This kind of thoughtful ordering of life before the LORD characterizes our next king.

 EXPLAIN the Story

Jotham Fortifies the Kingdom (27:1–9)

Jotham rules in Jerusalem, and his mother, Jerusha, is introduced as the daughter of Zadok (2 Chr 27:1). This may suggest a marriage between the royal and priestly families (cf. 22:11). The king is likened to his father, Uzziah, although the comment is made that he did not enter the temple of the LORD—a sacred offense committed by his father that resulted in swift judgment (27:2; cf. 26:16–21). Even though Jotham's character is commended, the people "continued their corrupt practices" (27:2), not unlike Isaiah's unflattering description (Isa 1:4). As with other kings before him, Jotham gives his attention to fortifying Jerusalem, which included building defensive walls (2 Chr 27:3). Cities in Judah are built during his reign, along with forts and towns in the wooded areas (v. 4).

Jotham wages war against the Ammonites, one of Judah's neighbors who have already been introduced (2 Chr 27:5; cf. 1 Chr 18:11; 19:1–15; 20:1–3; 2 Chr 20:1, 22). Reminiscent of his father Uzziah's reign (26:8), the Ammonites give tribute to Jotham, including one hundred talents of silver and large amounts of wheat and barley (27:5). Yet when Uzziah had become strong, he became proud (26:8, 16). By contrast, Jotham strengthens himself by walking steadfastly before the LORD his God (27:6). As we observed above, his life reflects an exemplary path of wisdom (Prov 4:26; 21:29). The final comment that he walked before the LORD *his* God underscores his covenantal relationship with the LORD. This is the source of his strength as he orders his ways before his God. The Chronicler concludes by noting that other things done by Jotham are recorded in the book of Kings (see 2 Kgs 15:32–38). The wars that were part of his reign perhaps hint at the conflict brewing in the north (see 15:37; 2 Chr 28). Jotham dies and is buried in the city of David.

LIVE the Story

Strength by Walking Steadfastly with the LORD

The kings of Judah face enormous pressures and challenges that require strength and courage, but they are never to forget that strength comes from the LORD. Jotham had watched as his father died in isolation, excluded from ceremonial aspects of leadership. His father's strength had led to his pride (2 Chr 26:15–16), causing him to overstep his royal boundaries. Even though Jotham had military success and received tribute (27:5), his fame does not lead to pride. Here we find two different responses to fame. Instead of becoming proud, Jotham "grew powerful because he walked steadfastly before the LORD his God" (v. 6). The verb "to grow strong, powerful" (Heb. *kh-z-q*) appears throughout Chronicles, but focus is not simply on the strength of a particular king, but the *source* of his strength. Chronicles teaches that strength and courage are needed to do God's work (1 Chr 22:13; 28:10, 20; 2 Chr 15:7), and many of us can surely relate to this. Yet we are not to forget that strength ultimately comes from God, as he helps us and strengthens us.

We noted earlier the words of Hanani the prophet, who had encouraged God's people with these words: "For the eyes of the LORD range throughout the earth to strengthen those whose hearts are fully committed to him" (2 Chr 16:9).[1] These timely words serve as an exhortation for us as we remember that strength comes from the LORD. The Scriptures resound with the promise that God strengthens his people as they wait for him (Ps 46:1–3; Isa 40:31; 41:10; 2 Cor 12:10; Eph 6:10). This gives us courage and strength to face life's challenges, which we do in the strength that God gives. The apostle Paul understood that when he was weak, he was indeed strong (2 Cor 12:10), for he was able to do all things through Christ "who strengthens me" (Phil 4:13; cf. Eph 6:10; 1 Pet 5:10). This was the testimony of Jotham, who grew strong because he established his ways before the LORD his God (2 Chr 27:6).

---

1. On the topic of strength in leadership, see the discussions in Chapter 41 on 2 Chr 12 and Chapter 43 on 2 Chr 14.

CHAPTER 57

2 Chronicles 28:1–27

 ## LISTEN to the Story

¹Ahaz was twenty years old when he became king, and he reigned in Jerusalem sixteen years. Unlike David his father, he did not do what was right in the eyes of the LORD. ²He followed the ways of the kings of Israel and also made idols for worshiping the Baals. ³He burned sacrifices in the Valley of Ben Hinnom and sacrificed his children in the fire, engaging in the detestable practices of the nations the LORD had driven out before the Israelites. ⁴He offered sacrifices and burned incense at the high places, on the hilltops and under every spreading tree.

⁵Therefore the LORD his God delivered him into the hands of the king of Aram. The Arameans defeated him and took many of his people as prisoners and brought them to Damascus.

He was also given into the hands of the king of Israel, who inflicted heavy casualties on him. ⁶In one day Pekah son of Remaliah killed a hundred and twenty thousand soldiers in Judah—because Judah had forsaken the LORD, the God of their ancestors. ⁷Zikri, an Ephraimite warrior, killed Maaseiah the king's son, Azrikam the officer in charge of the palace, and Elkanah, second to the king. ⁸The men of Israel took captive from their fellow Israelites who were from Judah two hundred thousand wives, sons and daughters. They also took a great deal of plunder, which they carried back to Samaria.

⁹But a prophet of the LORD named Oded was there, and he went out to meet the army when it returned to Samaria. He said to them, "Because the LORD, the God of your ancestors, was angry with Judah, he gave them into your hand. But you have slaughtered them in a rage that reaches to heaven. ¹⁰And now you intend to make the men and women of Judah and Jerusalem your slaves. But aren't you also guilty of sins against the LORD your God? ¹¹Now listen to me! Send back your fellow Israelites you have taken as prisoners, for the LORD's fierce anger rests on you."

¹²Then some of the leaders in Ephraim—Azariah son of Jehohanan, Berekiah son of Meshillemoth, Jehizkiah son of Shallum, and Amasa son of Hadlai—confronted those who were arriving from the war. ¹³"You must not bring those prisoners here," they said, "or we will be guilty before the LORD. Do you intend to add to our sin and guilt? For our guilt is already great, and his fierce anger rests on Israel."

¹⁴So the soldiers gave up the prisoners and plunder in the presence of the officials and all the assembly. ¹⁵The men designated by name took the prisoners, and from the plunder they clothed all who were naked. They provided them with clothes and sandals, food and drink, and healing balm. All those who were weak they put on donkeys. So they took them back to their fellow Israelites at Jericho, the City of Palms, and returned to Samaria.

¹⁶At that time King Ahaz sent to the kings of Assyria for help. ¹⁷The Edomites had again come and attacked Judah and carried away prisoners, ¹⁸while the Philistines had raided towns in the foothills and in the Negev of Judah. They captured and occupied Beth Shemesh, Aijalon and Gederoth, as well as Soko, Timnah and Gimzo, with their surrounding villages. ¹⁹The LORD had humbled Judah because of Ahaz king of Israel, for he had promoted wickedness in Judah and had been most unfaithful to the LORD. ²⁰Tiglath-Pileser king of Assyria came to him, but he gave him trouble instead of help. ²¹Ahaz took some of the things from the temple of the LORD and from the royal palace and from the officials and presented them to the king of Assyria, but that did not help him.

²²In his time of trouble King Ahaz became even more unfaithful to the LORD. ²³He offered sacrifices to the gods of Damascus, who had defeated him; for he thought, "Since the gods of the kings of Aram have helped them, I will sacrifice to them so they will help me." But they were his downfall and the downfall of all Israel.

²⁴Ahaz gathered together the furnishings from the temple of God and cut them in pieces. He shut the doors of the LORD's temple and set up altars at every street corner in Jerusalem. ²⁵In every town in Judah he built high places to burn sacrifices to other gods and aroused the anger of the LORD, the God of his ancestors.

²⁶The other events of his reign and all his ways, from beginning to end, are written in the book of the kings of Judah and Israel. ²⁷Ahaz rested with his ancestors and was buried in the city of Jerusalem, but he was not

placed in the tombs of the kings of Israel. And Hezekiah his son succeeded him as king.

Listening to the Text in the Story: 2 Kings 16:1–18; Isa. 7:1–9

The kingdom spirals into idolatry during the reign of Ahaz. Instead of establishing his ways before God as his father had done (2 Chr 27:6), Ahaz walks in the ways of the northern kings of Israel (28:2). His reign stands in stark contrast to the flourishing period under David, ushering in some of the darkest days in the kingdom. During this period of apostasy, Judah is attacked by the Aramean king Rezin and by the northern king Pekah.[1] Thousands are killed and others are taken captive to Damascus and to Samaria—because Judah has forsaken the LORD (vv. 5–6). It is important to bear in mind that at this time God raises up the prophet Isaiah to speak directly to Ahaz (Isa 7:1–9). When facing a military attack, Isaiah exhorts the king with these words: "Be careful, keep calm and don't be afraid. Do not lose heart because of these two smoldering stubs of firewood—because of the fierce anger of Rezin and Aram and of the son of Remaliah" (v. 4). Even though Isaiah is not mentioned in Chronicles, his prophetic role underscores that God does not leave Ahaz without godly counsel. The prophet even warns the king that if he does not stand firm in his faith, he will not stand (v. 9). As the story unfolds, it is clear that Ahaz has a hard heart, refusing to trust in the LORD. Instead of turning from his evil ways, he plunges even deeper into idolatry, provoking the LORD to anger.

 EXPLAIN the Story

The Moral Decline of the Kingdom under Ahaz (28:1–4)

Ahaz now rules on the throne in Jerusalem, but the Chronicler notes that, unlike David, Ahaz "did not do what was right in the eyes of the LORD" (2 Chr

---

1. In the Kings account, Rezin and Pekah form an alliance against Judah (known as the Syro-Ephramite war; see 2 Kgs 16:5–6). In Chronicles, Aram attacks first, then Israel, resulting in thousands of casualties and captives. For a helpful outline of events, along with an in-depth historical analysis, see Merrill, *1 & 2 Chronicles*, 487–91. Oded argues that the northern alliance was motivated by a desire to regain control of the Transjordan region, noting that the hostilities between the north and Judah had already begun during the reign of Jotham (2 Kgs 15:37); see Bustenay Oded, "The Historical Background of the Syro-Ephramite War Reconsidered," *CBQ* 34 (1972): 153–64.

28:1).[2] Rather than seeking the LORD, he is likened to the kings of Israel and is credited with making molten images for Baal (v. 2). This introduction is reminiscent of kings such as Jehoram (21:5–6, 13) and Ahaziah (22:2–4) and the rampant idolatry that has taken place at various times (21:11; 23:17). Notably, Ahaz makes "metal images" (NIV "idols," NASB "molten images"; Heb. *masseka*), a term rarely used in Chronicles (28:2; 34:3, 4). The Hebrew word *masseka* not only recalls Israel's golden calf worshiped at Sinai (Exod 32:4, 8; Deut 9:12, 16; Neh 9:18; Ps 106:19), but also the two golden calves made by Jeroboam (1 Kgs 14:9; 2 Kgs 17:16). Ahaz plunges the Southern Kingdom into their darkest years, for they have now become like the apostate Northern Kingdom. It is heart-wrenching to see the depth of idolatry embraced by the Southern Kingdom of Judah, something that will not be fully eradicated until Josiah (2 Chr 34:3–4). Abijah's earlier condemnation that the Northern Kingdom had worshiped "no-gods" now serves as a stinging indictment against Judah (13:8–12; cf. Isa 2:8, 20).

Worship of the Canaanite god Baal was rampant in Israel from their earliest period (Judg 2:11, 13; 3:7; 8:33; 10:6; 1 Sam 7:4; 12:10), but it was especially widespread during the reign of the northern king Ahab, demonstrated by the high number of false prophets—Elijah alone is God's prophet among the staggering 450 prophets of Baal (1 Kgs 18:22)! Now, Baal is worshiped in the Southern Kingdom, and Ahaz even burns incense in the Hinnom valley and sacrifices his own children there (2 Chr 28:3; cf. 33:6). The Hinnom valley, located on the outskirts of Jerusalem, was not only a place for burning waste, but it was known as the place of child sacrifice (Jer 7:31–32; Ezek 16:20–21). Offering up of children as sacrifices was strictly prohibited and utterly offensive to God (Lev 20:2–3; Deut 18:10; 2 Kgs 17:17; Ps 106:37–38). The stench of these abominable practices will arise from high places throughout the land (2 Chr 28:4). Not surprisingly, Ahaz's actions are likened to the abominations of the nations that had evoked God's wrath, resulting in their expulsion from the land (v. 3; cf. Lev 18:24–30). This portentous comment hints at the exile that is to come (2 Chr 28:5, 8).

Judah Is Defeated by Aram and Israel (28:5–8)

God gives Ahaz into the hands of the Aramean king Rezin, and Judah is defeated, resulting in thousands of prisoners being brought to Damascus (2 Chr 28:5). Solomon had rehearsed in his well-known prayer various

---

2. On the dating of the reign of Ahaz and his co-regency with Amon in 735–732 BC, see Edwin R. Thiele, *The Mysterious Numbers of the Hebrew Kings* (Grand Rapids: Zondervan, 1983), 133–34.

scenarios that would come upon God's people if they sinned against the LORD (ch. 6). One of these circumstances entailed being defeated by an enemy and being brought into captivity (vv. 36–38). This is precisely what is taking place now, and Judah experiences her own exile to Damascus, the capital city of the Arameans. God also delivers Judah into the hands of the northern king Pekah, now using the idolatrous northern king as an instrument of his judgment (28:6). A great massacre takes place, and key leaders are killed (vv. 6–7). Thousands of Judeans are taken captive and brought to Samaria, including women and children, but a prophet intervenes (v. 8).[3]

The Prophet Oded Speaks to Pekah, Resulting in the Release of the Captives (28:9–15)

A prophet named Oded meets the northern army upon their return to Samaria (2 Chr 28:9). He states plainly that the northerners have been victorious because of God's judgment against Judah, but he rebukes them for their violence done in rage (v. 9). Further, he announces that their intention to subjugate the Judean captives will be met with divine judgment—they are adding to their own guilt. Oded tells them to return their fellow Israelites and warns them that God's anger is burning against them. Some of the leaders of Ephraim respond by instructing the army to return the Judean captives, in recognition of their own guilt and transgressions (vv. 12–13). Under the leadership of four Ephraimite men, the captives are clothed, given food and drink, anointed, and returned to Jericho (v. 15).

Ahaz Turns to a Foreign Power and to Idols for Help (28:16–27)

Ahaz had sought help from Tiglath-Pileser while facing the northern aggression from Pekah and Rezin instead of giving heed to the prophet Isaiah (2 Kgs 16:7–9; cf. Isa 7–8). Tiglath-Pileser's western advance into Palestine in 734–732 BC results in the annexing of Damascus, the death of Rezin, and the exile of northerners (2 Kgs 15:29; 16:7–9; see also 1 Chr 5:6, 25–26).[4] Ahaz not only faces a deadly assault from the north, but also from the east,

---

3. The text records that 120,000 military men were killed in one day (28:6). For the meaning of the Hebrew word "thousand" (Heb. *'eleph*) as a military unit (rather than a literal headcount), see the discussion in Chapter 12 on 1 Chr 12:23–40, pp. 138–40. The same principle applies to 28:8, which states that 200,000 thousand captives were taken, suggesting a smaller social unit of women and children (rather than a literal headcount).

4. For the impact of Tiglath-Pileser's successful campaign into Palestine, including deportations, population shifting, and the appointment of governors, see Bustenay Oded, "Observations of the Methods of Assyrian Rule in Transjordanian after the Palestine Campaign of Tiglath-Pileser III," *JNES* 29 (1970): 177–86.

suffering defeat by the Edomites, who take Judean captives (2 Chr 28:17). The military crisis is exacerbated by an invasion from the west, coming from the troublesome Philistines, who overthrow a number of cities on Judah's western front, making the Southern Kingdom vulnerable (v. 18). Judah's military defeat on several fronts is due to Ahaz's "unfaithfulness" (Heb. *ma'al*, v. 19), a key term used by the Chronicler that characterizes kings such as Saul (1 Chr 10:13), Rehoboam (2 Chr 12:2), Uzziah (26:16), and Manasseh (33:19). Ahaz has been more unfaithful than his predecessors, and he is charged with causing unrestraint in Judah, reminiscent of the golden calf story when the Israelites were "running wild" (Exod 32:25). God humbles Judah at this time through military defeat, but instead of repenting and seeking help from the LORD, Ahaz seeks help from Assyria. Despite some initial relief (cf. 2 Kgs 16:9), the Chronicler notes that the ultimate outcome was further distress instead of being strengthened (2 Chr 28:20). Even though Ahaz seeks to buy Tiglath-Pileser's favor by giving him precious items from the temple and from his palace (v. 21; cf. 2 Kgs 16:7–8), this does not help him (2 Chr 28:21). Help comes from the LORD, as Asa had prayed many years earlier: "LORD, there is no one like you to help the powerless against the mighty. Help us, LORD our God, for we rely on you, and in your name we have come against this vast army. LORD, you are our God; do not let mere mortals prevail against you" (14:11).[5] But Ahaz refuses to call out to God. He prefers to rely on his own devices, and there is no limit to what he will do.

In his distress, it is heartbreaking to watch Ahaz become even more unfaithful. He sacrifices to the gods of Damascus, hoping that *their gods* will help him (28:23). Yet this will be his downfall, and things get even worse. Ahaz not only gives away sacred items from the temple, but we watch in disbelief as he closes the doors of the temple. This is the very place where Solomon had exhorted his people to pray (ch. 6), but Ahaz defiantly shuts its doors. Instead, he sets up idolatrous worship in every city of Judah, and incense is now burned to other gods throughout the land (28:24–25). This is where the story of Ahaz leaves us—with the temple closed for business and the stench of idolatrous incense filling the Southern Kingdom. This is the spiritual decline of the kingdom that Ahaz leaves behind after his death (vv. 26–27). This is also the kingdom Hezekiah inherits, but, as we will see shortly, his reign ushers in one of the greatest periods in the Southern Kingdom.

---

5. On the important topic of "help" coming from God, see the discussion in Chapter 12 on 1 Chr 12.

LIVE the Story

A Heart Riddled with Idolatry

Ahaz was driven by success. He is especially known for adopting the cultural and religious practices of the nations around him, even willing to abandon the LORD to achieve his so-called success. No expense is spared to achieve success, for this king is even willing to sacrifice his own children on the altar. Yet, in the final analysis, his kingship is one of utter failure. He will leave no lasting legacy in Israel, only rubble. Remarkably, all of his so-called achievements will be undone in a just a few short days by his son Hezekiah. As Klein notes: "The 'filth' of sixteen years of the reign of Ahaz is wiped out in sixteen days!"[6] His house had been built on sand, and it came quickly tumbling down. What is left of his legacy are stories of a desperate king who was willing to sell his soul to achieve success. Yet the very success he so desperately desired was unattainable, and his reign is remembered for its utter failure.

As we observed earlier, Tim Keller has written on contemporary forms of idolatry in his book *Counterfeit Gods*.[7] In our contemporary context, the picture we often have of idolatry is a primitive view of people bowing down before cult statues. While worship of cult statues continues throughout the world, Keller explores other forms of idolatry in the West, noting that idolatry is nevertheless present, even in the absence of cult statues. He argues that every culture "has its shrines—whether office towers, spas and gyms, studios or stadiums—where sacrifices must be made in order to procure the blessings of the good life and ward off disaster."[8] While we may live in a society that does not bow before cult statues or burn incense to gods, he argues that we "perform a kind of child sacrifice, neglecting family and community to achieve a higher place in business and gain more wealth and prestige."[9] Being driven by wealth, security, and success, we can easily—and sometimes inadvertently—adopt the practices of contemporary culture that undermine and erode our relationship with God. Instead of our relationship with God having first place in our lives, we can live a syncretistic "religious" life, unwittingly serving both God and other things that become our source of happiness and security. Keller thus

---

6. Klein, *2 Chronicles*, 419; see also the discussion in Chapter 59 on 2 Chr 30.

7. Keller, *Counterfeit Gods*. See Live the Story in Chapter 54, pp. 470–72. Another helpful book on this topic is Christopher J. H. Wright, *"Here Are Your Gods": Faithful Discipleship in Idolatrous Times* (Downers Grove, IL: IVP Academic, 2020).

8. Keller, *Counterfeit Gods*, xiv.

9. Ibid.

writes, "Every human being must live for something. Something must capture our imaginations, our heart's most fundamental allegiance and hope. . . . If we look to some created thing to give us the meaning, hope, and happiness that only God himself can give, it will eventually fail to deliver and break our hearts."[10] Ahaz had sought help from foreign gods and a foreign king, but they had failed to deliver. His "religious" activity was not directed toward God but to his so-called "gods" that he perceived were the answer to his problems. Yet his attempts at success without God led to failure and ruin.

Keller offers practical advice about how to identify our idols. He suggests asking ourselves the question: What do you enjoy daydreaming about? What occupies your mind? He makes the insightful observation that "the true god of your heart is what your thoughts effortlessly go to when there is nothing else demanding your attention."[11] The second way he recommends identifying our idols is by asking the question: What are you spending your money on? He notes: "Your money flows most effortlessly to what you love."[12] The third test requires us to question what we are living for, and in this case, he suggests that when we are deeply disappointed or in despair about not achieving a goal or a dream, then we have found our real god. He thus concludes: "Idolatry is not just a failure to obey God, it is a setting of the heart on something besides God."[13]

In the story of Ahaz, the human heart is on display—a heart riddled with idolatry that seeks success and security without God. Keller writes that idols must not simply be smashed down, but replaced with something else.[14] Ahaz's son Hezekiah will, indeed, smash down the idols that his father had built. But the story that follows is so much more—it shows us the steps to be taken to remedy the insidious problem of idolatry. It comes through purging, consecration, and repentance. Yet ultimately, there is restoration only because the LORD God is gracious. He hears and answers prayers. And he forgives, restores, and heals.

---

10. Ibid., 3.

11. Ibid., 168.

12. Ibid.

13. Ibid., 171.

14. Ibid., 93. See also Manasseh, who removes the idols but replaces them with altars to the LORD (2 Chr 33:15–16).

CHAPTER 58

2 Chronicles 29:1–36

 ## LISTEN to the Story

¹Hezekiah was twenty-five years old when he became king, and he reigned in Jerusalem twenty-nine years. His mother's name was Abijah daughter of Zechariah. ²He did what was right in the eyes of the LORD, just as his father David had done.

³In the first month of the first year of his reign, he opened the doors of the temple of the LORD and repaired them. ⁴He brought in the priests and the Levites, assembled them in the square on the east side ⁵and said: "Listen to me, Levites! Consecrate yourselves now and consecrate the temple of the LORD, the God of your ancestors. Remove all defilement from the sanctuary. ⁶Our parents were unfaithful; they did evil in the eyes of the LORD our God and forsook him. They turned their faces away from the LORD's dwelling place and turned their backs on him. ⁷They also shut the doors of the portico and put out the lamps. They did not burn incense or present any burnt offerings at the sanctuary to the God of Israel. ⁸Therefore, the anger of the LORD has fallen on Judah and Jerusalem; he has made them an object of dread and horror and scorn, as you can see with your own eyes. ⁹This is why our fathers have fallen by the sword and why our sons and daughters and our wives are in captivity. ¹⁰Now I intend to make a covenant with the LORD, the God of Israel, so that his fierce anger will turn away from us. ¹¹My sons, do not be negligent now, for the LORD has chosen you to stand before him and serve him, to minister before him and to burn incense."

¹²Then these Levites set to work:

from the Kohathites,

Mahath son of Amasai and Joel son of Azariah;

from the Merarites,

Kish son of Abdi and Azariah son of Jehallelel;

from the Gershonites,

Joah son of Zimmah and Eden son of Joah;
¹³from the descendants of Elizaphan,
  Shimri and Jeiel;
from the descendants of Asaph,
  Zechariah and Mattaniah;
¹⁴from the descendants of Heman,
  Jehiel and Shimei;
from the descendants of Jeduthun,
  Shemaiah and Uzziel.

¹⁵When they had assembled their fellow Levites and consecrated themselves, they went in to purify the temple of the LORD, as the king had ordered, following the word of the LORD. ¹⁶The priests went into the sanctuary of the LORD to purify it. They brought out to the courtyard of the LORD's temple everything unclean that they found in the temple of the LORD. The Levites took it and carried it out to the Kidron Valley. ¹⁷They began the consecration on the first day of the first month, and by the eighth day of the month they reached the portico of the LORD. For eight more days they consecrated the temple of the LORD itself, finishing on the sixteenth day of the first month.

¹⁸Then they went in to King Hezekiah and reported: "We have purified the entire temple of the LORD, the altar of burnt offering with all its utensils, and the table for setting out the consecrated bread, with all its articles. ¹⁹We have prepared and consecrated all the articles that King Ahaz removed in his unfaithfulness while he was king. They are now in front of the LORD's altar."

²⁰Early the next morning King Hezekiah gathered the city officials together and went up to the temple of the LORD. ²¹They brought seven bulls, seven rams, seven male lambs and seven male goats as a sin offering for the kingdom, for the sanctuary and for Judah. The king commanded the priests, the descendants of Aaron, to offer these on the altar of the LORD. ²²So they slaughtered the bulls, and the priests took the blood and splashed it against the altar; next they slaughtered the rams and splashed their blood against the altar; then they slaughtered the lambs and splashed their blood against the altar. ²³The goats for the sin offering were brought before the king and the assembly, and they laid their hands on them. ²⁴The priests then slaughtered the goats and presented their blood on the altar

for a sin offering to atone for all Israel, because the king had ordered the burnt offering and the sin offering for all Israel.

²⁵He stationed the Levites in the temple of the LORD with cymbals, harps and lyres in the way prescribed by David and Gad the king's seer and Nathan the prophet; this was commanded by the LORD through his prophets. ²⁶So the Levites stood ready with David's instruments, and the priests with their trumpets.

²⁷Hezekiah gave the order to sacrifice the burnt offering on the altar. As the offering began, singing to the LORD began also, accompanied by trumpets and the instruments of David king of Israel. ²⁸The whole assembly bowed in worship, while the musicians played and the trumpets sounded. All this continued until the sacrifice of the burnt offering was completed.

²⁹When the offerings were finished, the king and everyone present with him knelt down and worshiped. ³⁰King Hezekiah and his officials ordered the Levites to praise the LORD with the words of David and of Asaph the seer. So they sang praises with gladness and bowed down and worshiped.

³¹Then Hezekiah said, "You have now dedicated yourselves to the LORD. Come and bring sacrifices and thank offerings to the temple of the LORD." So the assembly brought sacrifices and thank offerings, and all whose hearts were willing brought burnt offerings.

³²The number of burnt offerings the assembly brought was seventy bulls, a hundred rams and two hundred male lambs—all of them for burnt offerings to the LORD. ³³The animals consecrated as sacrifices amounted to six hundred bulls and three thousand sheep and goats. ³⁴The priests, however, were too few to skin all the burnt offerings; so their relatives the Levites helped them until the task was finished and until other priests had been consecrated, for the Levites had been more conscientious in consecrating themselves than the priests had been. ³⁵There were burnt offerings in abundance, together with the fat of the fellowship offerings and the drink offerings that accompanied the burnt offerings.

So the service of the temple of the LORD was reestablished. ³⁶Hezekiah and all the people rejoiced at what God had brought about for his people, because it was done so quickly.

Listening to the Text in the Story: Leviticus 11:44–45

The low point of the kingdom under Ahaz is followed by a period of religious reform under his son, Hezekiah. At the outset, Hezekiah summons Judah's priests and Levites to consecrate themselves and the house of God and to remove the filth from the holy place (2 Chr 29:5). During the period of Moses, God had revealed to his people that they had been set apart as holy, for God was holy (Lev 11:44–45; 19:2; 20:26). Since the temple was the place where God dwelt, this meant that Israel's priests and Levites had to be consecrated so that they could serve before a holy God (cf. Exod 29:1–30; Lev 8:1–10:20). The high frequency of the verb "to be holy, consecrate" (Heb. *q-d-sh*) in these chapters underscore this central concern of Hezekiah as he seeks to reestablish worship in the temple (2 Chr 29:5, 15, 17, 19, 33, 34; 30:3, 8, 15, 17, 24, etc.). Moreover, Ahaz's abominable actions had polluted the holy place, putting the entire community at risk, like a deadly contagion requiring urgent attention.[1] The significance of Hezekiah's reforms at this critical moment in Judah's history cannot be underestimated, and it was surely not lost on the Chronicler, who saw Hezekiah as one of Israel's greatest kings, comparable only to David and Solomon.

In contrast to the single verse devoted to Hezekiah's reforms in Kings (2 Kgs 18:4), the Chronicler spends *three* chapters rehearsing the widespread religious reforms accomplished at this time (2 Chr 29–31). Hezekiah's reign is depicted in language reminiscent of the unified kingdom under Solomon and David.[2] As will be seen shortly, his invitation to the northern tribes to join the Passover celebration signals a reversal of the division that had begun under Rehoboam, as northerners humble themselves, return to the LORD, and joyfully celebrate with their brethren.

EXPLAIN the Story

Hezekiah Purges Judah and the Temple Is Cleansed (29:1–19)

With the death of his father, Ahaz, after a period of co-regency, Hezekiah now becomes sole ruler over a kingdom that has been in serious spiritual decline.[3] The events that follow probably take place in his first year as sole monarch, while noting that the dates for Hezekiah's reign are not easily

---

1. For a helpful discussion on the meaning of holiness, along with other cultic terms used in Leviticus, see Gordon J. Wenham, *Leviticus*. NICOT (Grand Rapids: Eerdmans, 1979), 19–25.

2. For a list of similar features, see Klein, *2 Chronicles*, 413; see also the discussion in Chapter 59 on 2 Chr 30.

3. On the date and chronology, see the note in Chapter 57 on 2 Chr 28:1, p. 486n2.

resolved.[4] Japhet notes that the chronology of Hezekiah is "one of the most debated issues in the reconstruction of biblical chronology."[5] From the outset Hezekiah is characterized favorably as a king who "did what was right in the eyes of the LORD, just as his father David had done" (2 Chr 29:2). Hezekiah's first priority is to open the doors of the temple and repair them. Given that his father Ahaz had closed them (vv. 3, 7; cf. 28:24), the young king's first action represents a bold and courageous repudiation of his father's ungodly legacy. Next, he gathers priests and Levites and instructs them to consecrate themselves and remove the impurity from the holy sanctuary (29:5). The verb "to be holy, consecrate" (Heb. *q-d-sh*) is used throughout these chapters,[6] along with the Hebrew noun *qodesh* "sacred, holy" used to describe the *sanctuary* (vv. 5, 7; 30:19), the *consecrated* animals (29:33), and the *holy* dwelling place (30:27). Under Hezekiah's leadership, a major purging takes place, therefore. He recognizes that his central task is to set right the kingdom after years of neglect. That the language of holiness permeates the narrative underscores that the temple, along with Judah's priests and Levites, needed to be consecrated so that worship before a holy God can be reestablished.

Given the extent of idolatry that had taken place under Ahaz, the Levites are given the sacred task of removing "all defilement from the sanctuary" (29:5). The term "filth, defilement" (Heb. *nidda*) occurs over thirty times in the Old Testament. It is used in Leviticus for ritual uncleanness (Lev 5:3; 7:20–21; 14:19; 15:3; 16:16–19; 18:19; 22:3, etc.), but it is also used to describe the ungodly state of Judah during the final days of the kingdom (Ezek 36:18), which may be compared to the uncleanness of the nations (Ezra 9:11). Since this marks the only occurrence of the term in Chronicles, it underlines the gravity of Judah's sin brought about by the abominable practices of Ahaz, and as such, it indicates that Judah is on the brink of ruin if this defilement is not quickly removed.

Hezekiah confesses the sins of their forefathers, acknowledging that they had been "unfaithful; they did evil in the eyes of the LORD our God and

---

4. The account in Kings states that Samaria fell to the Assyrians in the sixth year of Hezekiah's reign (2 Kgs 18:9–10), suggesting that Hezekiah's rule began six years *prior* to the fall of the north. This would locate his initial reforms and the Passover in the period prior to the fall of Samaria, but the text implies that the fall of the north has already taken place (2 Chr 30:6, 9). Merrill thus suggests (as others have done) that there may have been a period of co-regency (*1 & 2 Chronicles*, 501). Accordingly, Hezekiah's sole reign would begin in 715 BC, what the Chronicler identifies as the first year of his (sole) reign. For a more extensive discussion of the issues, see Japhet, *1 & II Chronicles*, 935–36.

5. Ibid., 935.

6. For a list of biblical references, see Listen the Story above.

forsook him. They turned their faces away from the LORD's dwelling place
and turned their backs on him" (2 Chr 29:6). The term "unfaithful" (Heb.
ma'al), which is a key term in Chronicles,[7] was used to describe King Ahaz,
who was very unfaithful to the LORD (28:19, 22). Yet Hezekiah now confesses
their unfaithfulness (cf. Lev 26:40) and their blatant rebellion against God and
his temple. The deplorable state of affairs is seen in the closing of the temple
doors and in the lights being snuffed out, like a vacant and rundown building
that was no longer in use. Judah had forgotten that worship of the LORD
God was at the center of their life. They had been set apart as a worshiping
and witnessing community, but instead of giving glory to God among the
nations, they had become an object of "dread and horror and scorn" under
his wrath (2 Chr 29:8; cf. Jer 29:18). Death and exile have come because of
their unfaithfulness (2 Chr 29:9), as witnessed by the calamitous and chaotic
events that had transpired during Ahaz's reign (28:5–8, 17–18, 20–21). Much
is at stake at this critical juncture in the kingdom, and this is surely not lost
on the young king Hezekiah.

As other kings have done before him (15:12; 23:16), Hezekiah enters into
a covenant with the LORD as he pledges his unswerving loyalty (29:10). He
exhorts the Levites not to be at ease amid such dire circumstances, but rather,
like a father, he tenderly reminds them of their sacred calling—they have been
chosen to serve and to minister before the LORD (v. 11). The king summons
them at this perilous time to fulfill their divinely appointed duties. Names of
seven Levitical families are rehearsed (vv. 12–14), with two names representing
each family, beginning with the three prominent families of Kohath, Merari,
and Gershon (v. 12; cf. 1 Chr 6:16–48), followed by Elizphan (2 Chr 29:13; cf.
1 Chr 15:8) and concluding with the three musical families of Asaph, Herman,
and Jeduthun (2 Chr 29:13–14; cf. 1 Chr 25:1–7). After being consecrated,
they proceed to purify the house of the LORD, according to the commandment
of the king (2 Chr 29:15). The verb "to purge, purify" (Heb. *t-h-r*) occurs in
the book of Leviticus, but in Chronicles it appears in connection with the
two great reformers: Hezekiah (vv. 15, 16, 18; 30:18) and Josiah (34:3, 5, 8),
signaling their important task in Judah. The priests enter the temple to purify
it and remove anything unclean (29:16). The Levites bring the unclean objects
to the Kidron Valley, a burial site that had been used for the disposal of foreign
cult objects (v. 16; see 15:16; 30:14; Jer 31:40). Consecration of the temple
begins on the first day of the first month, the day Hezekiah had opened the

---

7. See the discussion in Chapter 10 on 1 Chr 10:13 for a brief study on "unfaithfulness,"
pp. 118–20.

temple (2 Chr 29:3), and it continues over the course of sixteen days. As noted earlier, Klein comments that the "'filth' of sixteen years of the reign of Ahaz is wiped out in sixteen days!"[8] The priests report to Hezekiah that the temple and its sacred furniture have been fully cleansed, and the utensils discarded by Ahaz have been retrieved, consecrated, and returned to the temple. Now that Hezekiah has received the official "clean" verdict, the temple is ready for sacrifices to be offered and atonement to be made.

Hezekiah Restores Temple Worship (29:20–36)

Hezekiah rises early the next morning, a description not simply indicating he was an early riser, but rather, it suggests here a person eager to follow God's instructions (Gen 20:8; 21:14; 22:3; etc.). The king assembles city officials at the temple, and they bring with them seven bulls, rams, and lambs, along with seven male goats "as a sin offering for the kingdom, for the sanctuary and for Judah" (2 Chr 29:21). The number seven is commonly featured in priestly rituals, and here it underscores the gravity of Judah's sin and the need for complete atonement for the kingdom. After the priests sacrifice the bulls, rams, and lambs, they take their blood and splash it on the altar (v. 22; cf. 35:11), as priests had done in earlier times (Lev 1:5, 11; 3:2, 8, etc.). The male goats, which were for the sin offerings (cf. 4:23–24), are brought before the king and the assembly; they lay hands on the goats, as has been the practice from ancient times (2 Chr 29:23–24; cf. Lev 4:4, 15, 16:21, etc.). The goats are slaughtered, and their blood is used to purge the altar and atone for all Israel, in accordance with the command of the king (2 Chr 29:24).

Hezekiah assembles the Levitical singers with their musical instruments, recalling other times when God's people gather to praise the LORD (v. 25; cf. 1 Chr 13:8; 15:16–28; 16:4–43; 2 Chr 5:11–14; 7:6). King David had appointed the Levites to lead the gathered assembly in worship (29:25–26).[9] With everything now in place, as the burnt offering is being offered on the altar, singing to the LORD begins as the sacred assembly worships God, accompanied by cymbals, harps, lyres, and trumpets.

The scene shifts as "the king and everyone present with him knelt down and worshiped" (v. 29). Solomon had knelt down before God when he had prayed at the dedication of the temple, and all Israel had knelt before God "on the pavement with their faces to the ground" when the temple had been filled with God's glory (7:3). Now, we again encounter God's people kneeling

---

8. Klein, *2 Chronicles*, 419.

9. For a description of musicians, along with ancient musical instruments, see the discussion in Chapter 25 on 1 Chr 25.

before the LORD in worship. The king instructs the Levites to sing praises to the LORD using the songs written by Israel's two well-known and beloved musicians, David and Asaph. Compare this scene of worship with Judah's stiff-necked posture under Ahaz, when God's people had turned their back on the LORD (29:6). What a different state of affairs under the godly leadership of Hezekiah—the people are now kneeling before the LORD their God. The Chronicler summarizes this joyous occasion: "So they sang praises with gladness and bowed down and worshiped" (v. 30), underscoring again the importance of joyful worship, a theme that reverberates throughout Chronicles like a delightful melody rising up to God.[10]

Now that the people have dedicated themselves to the LORD, Hezekiah instructs the assembly to "draw near" (Heb. *n-g-sh*) and bring their sacrifices and thank offerings to the LORD (v. 31). The Hebrew idiom describing their dedication to God (Heb. *m-l-'hayyad*; lit. "to fill the hand") is commonly rendered "to ordain" in priestly contexts (Exod 28:41; 29:9, 29, 33, etc.), but now it has been applied to the entire assembly. Similarly, the language of "drawing near" (Heb. *n-g-sh*) not only recalls the times when Moses had "drawn near" to the LORD (20:21; 24:2), but this verb is also used to describe Israel's priests who approach God at Mount Sinai (19:22) and in the tabernacle after they are consecrated (28:43; 30:20; Lev 21:21, 23, etc). Hahn thus suggests that the gathered assembly (Heb. *qahal*) is being depicted by the Chronicler as the "reconstitution of the children of Israel in their original vocation at Sinai to be a 'kingdom of priests and a holy nation' (Exod. 19.6)."[11] This anticipates the time when all of God's people will be called his priests (cf. Isa 61:6). Having dedicated themselves to the LORD, the people bring sacrifices and thank offerings, and those willing offer burnt offerings to God, not under compulsion but freely to the LORD (2 Chr 29:31; cf. Exod 35:22; 1 Chr 28:21). The people bring bulls, rams, and male lambs to be offered as burnt offerings to the LORD, along with six hundred bulls and three thousand sheep to be offered as sacrifices (2 Chr 29:33). While these numbers pale in light of the sacrifices Solomon offered at the dedication of the temple when all the tribes were present (cf. 7:5), these quantities are not insignificant, given that they are brought from the much smaller Southern Kingdom. Animals were costly, especially those fully burnt on the altar, yet an abundance of sacrifices are generously offered at this time. With insufficient priests to skin all the animals, the Levites are required to assist in the task until other priests had

---

10. On the topic of joy, see Live the Story in Chapter 34, pp. 319–21.
11. Hahn, *The Kingdom of God*, 174.

consecrated themselves. Finally, we read that "Hezekiah and all the people rejoiced at what God had brought about for his people, because it was done so quickly" (29:36). That it had been done "quickly" suggests that the sovereign hand of God was at work (cf. Isa 29:5–6; 48:3; Jer 6:26; 15:8; 51:8; Mal 3:1).

 LIVE the Story

Putting God First

Hezekiah's reforms signify a repudiation of all that his father Ahaz had done. His father had closed the temple doors, but Hezekiah now opens them and purges the temple of his father's abominable objects. Ahaz had discarded temple vessels, but Hezekiah now restores them. It is easy to miss the personal element of Hezekiah's actions, watching as aloof bystanders who fail to recognize what was required of the king when he repudiated the legacy of his father. We may also recall that when Asa had become king, he had taken the bold decision to remove his grandmother from her position as queen mother, and he destroyed the Asherah that she had built (2 Chr 15:16). As with Hezekiah, one would expect this to cause a rift in the family, but it was required of Asa in order to put God first in his life and to ensure that idolatry did not take root in the kingdom. The Ten Commandments taught that the Israelites were to honor their father and mother (Exod 20:12), yet the same law taught that if anyone from among one's own family enticed a person to go after other gods, the family was not to yield to them, but instead, they were to face the severest of punishment (Deut 13:6–10). God requires absolute loyalty, even above family members.

When God called Gideon he had told him to take down the altar of Baal that his father had built. As with Hezekiah, Gideon was required to take action against his own father, facing the anger of his father's household and men from the city (Judg 6:25–27). But unlike Hezekiah, God had asked Gideon to take this action while his father was still alive. Giving priority to God, even above one's own parents, is already foreshadowed in the Levites, who had shown devotion to God, putting concerns for God's holiness above their family (Deut 33:8–9; see Exod 32:25–29). The Levites had put God first and they were set apart for his service. As followers of Jesus, nothing less is required of us today, and sometimes this requires us to go against our parents.

Jesus taught his disciples that he had come to set a man against his father and a daughter against her mother, teaching that anyone "who loves their father or mother more than me is not worthy of me" (Matt 10:37; see also

Luke 14:26). McConville suggests that Jesus's teaching on discipleship means that the Levitical principle "is extended to all who would be disciples."[12] Jesus thus requires absolute loyalty, and even though familial relationships were highly regarded in the ancient world (as they are today), they must not come before Jesus. Nothing less is required of us today. Hezekiah stands as an example of a king whose loyalty to God was over and above his loyalty to his father. Because of his willingness to do what was good and right before the LORD, Judah turns back to the LORD. As we reflect upon this story, it is important to remember the human element in the story and the kind of devotion to God that Hezekiah embodies. Jesus calls us to put him *first* in our lives, and for some, this will mean living with the scorn or ridicule of parents. For those in the Muslim world, the stakes are even higher, but Jesus demands our undivided loyalty.

The book *Seeking Allah, Finding Jesus* by Nabeel Qureshi is a reminder of the cost involved by Muslims who convert to Christianity. Nabeel's family had moved to California after immigrating to the United States from Pakistan. While at university, he debated the tenets of the Christian faith with a fellow student and Christian, David Wood. After many conversations and a series of dreams, Nabeel recalls his conversion in an interview with Christianity Today. He recalls reading his New Testament fervently and was unable to put it down. He came across Matthew 10:37, which taught him that he must love God more than his mother and father. He records his initial response: "'But Jesus,' I said, 'accepting you would be like dying. I will have to give up everything.'" After reading the next verse about taking up his cross and following after Jesus, he recalls the significance of this verse for his own life: "Jesus was being very blunt: For Muslims, following the gospel is more than a call to prayer. It is a call to die." It was at this time that Nabeel knelt at the foot of his bed and gave his life to Christ. He recalls that a few days later "the two people I loved most in this world were shattered by my betrayal. To this day my family is broken by the decision I made, and it is excruciating every time I see the cost I had to pay."[13] Nabeel weighed up the cost of following Jesus, and for him, the greatest cost was the breach in his relationship with his parents. He recognized, however, that he was required to put Jesus first, even above his parents, whom he loved dearly. His journey of faith would mean taking further steps that would alienate him from his parents, which included leaving

---

12. McConville, *Deuteronomy*, 297.
13. See the blog by Justin Taylor, "Nabeel Qureshi (1983–2017), The Gospel Coalition, September 16, 2017 (https://www.thegospelcoalition.org/blogs/justin-taylor/nabeel-qureshi-1983-2017/).

medicine to enter full time ministry.[14] Nabeel ended up fighting a yearlong battle with cancer, and in 2017 he went to be with his Lord. His story is just one of many brothers and sisters around the world who have taken seriously the call to follow Jesus, putting him first above family and friends. Putting Jesus first and living our lives to please him does not always mean estrangement from family members, but it can result in the more subtle disapproval from parents or siblings. Whatever the situation, the reality is that following Jesus requires us to take up our cross daily and follow him, putting him first in our lives. Living according to the ethics of the kingdom puts us in conflict with the values of the world, and sometimes these conflicts can occur in one's own family. The actions Hezekiah takes to destroy the altars his father had built and to eradicate anything associated with his idolatrous reign were necessary for him so that he might worship the LORD and serve him faithfully. As Christians, we are required to put Jesus first and seek first *his* kingdom, no matter the cost.

---

14. For the full story, see Nabeel Qureshi, *Seeking Allah, Finding Jesus: A Devout Muslim Encounters Christianity* (Grand Rapids: Zondervan, 2014).

LISTEN to the Story

¹Hezekiah sent word to all Israel and Judah and also wrote letters to Ephraim and Manasseh, inviting them to come to the temple of the LORD in Jerusalem and celebrate the Passover to the LORD, the God of Israel. ²The king and his officials and the whole assembly in Jerusalem decided to celebrate the Passover in the second month. ³They had not been able to celebrate it at the regular time because not enough priests had consecrated themselves and the people had not assembled in Jerusalem. ⁴The plan seemed right both to the king and to the whole assembly. ⁵They decided to send a proclamation throughout Israel, from Beersheba to Dan, calling the people to come to Jerusalem and celebrate the Passover to the LORD, the God of Israel. It had not been celebrated in large numbers according to what was written.

⁶At the king's command, couriers went throughout Israel and Judah with letters from the king and from his officials, which read:

"People of Israel, return to the LORD, the God of Abraham, Isaac and Israel, that he may return to you who are left, who have escaped from the hand of the kings of Assyria. ⁷Do not be like your parents and your fellow Israelites, who were unfaithful to the LORD, the God of their ancestors, so that he made them an object of horror, as you see. ⁸Do not be stiff-necked, as your ancestors were; submit to the LORD. Come to his sanctuary, which he has consecrated forever. Serve the LORD your God, so that his fierce anger will turn away from you. ⁹If you return to the LORD, then your fellow Israelites and your children will be shown compassion by their captors and will return to this land, for the LORD your God is gracious and compassionate. He will not turn his face from you if you return to him."

¹⁰The couriers went from town to town in Ephraim and Manasseh, as far as Zebulun, but people scorned and ridiculed them. ¹¹Nevertheless, some from Asher, Manasseh and Zebulun humbled themselves and went to Jerusalem. ¹²Also in Judah the hand of God was on the people to give them unity of mind to carry out what the king and his officials had ordered, following the word of the LORD.

¹³A very large crowd of people assembled in Jerusalem to celebrate the Festival of Unleavened Bread in the second month. ¹⁴They removed the altars in Jerusalem and cleared away the incense altars and threw them into the Kidron Valley.

¹⁵They slaughtered the Passover lamb on the fourteenth day of the second month. The priests and the Levites were ashamed and consecrated themselves and brought burnt offerings to the temple of the LORD. ¹⁶Then they took up their regular positions as prescribed in the Law of Moses the man of God. The priests splashed against the altar the blood handed to them by the Levites. ¹⁷Since many in the crowd had not consecrated themselves, the Levites had to kill the Passover lambs for all those who were not ceremonially clean and could not consecrate their lambs to the LORD. ¹⁸Although most of the many people who came from Ephraim, Manasseh, Issachar and Zebulun had not purified themselves, yet they ate the Passover, contrary to what was written. But Hezekiah prayed for them, saying, "May the LORD, who is good, pardon everyone ¹⁹who sets their heart on seeking God—the LORD, the God of their ancestors—even if they are not clean according to the rules of the sanctuary." ²⁰And the LORD heard Hezekiah and healed the people.

²¹The Israelites who were present in Jerusalem celebrated the Festival of Unleavened Bread for seven days with great rejoicing, while the Levites and priests praised the LORD every day with resounding instruments dedicated to the LORD.

²²Hezekiah spoke encouragingly to all the Levites, who showed good understanding of the service of the LORD. For the seven days they ate their assigned portion and offered fellowship offerings and praised the LORD, the God of their ancestors.

²³The whole assembly then agreed to celebrate the festival seven more days; so for another seven days they celebrated joyfully. ²⁴Hezekiah king of Judah provided a thousand bulls and seven thousand sheep and goats

for the assembly, and the officials provided them with a thousand bulls and ten thousand sheep and goats. A great number of priests consecrated themselves. [25]The entire assembly of Judah rejoiced, along with the priests and Levites and all who had assembled from Israel, including the foreigners who had come from Israel and also those who resided in Judah. [26]There was great joy in Jerusalem, for since the days of Solomon son of David king of Israel there had been nothing like this in Jerusalem. [27]The priests and the Levites stood to bless the people, and God heard them, for their prayer reached heaven, his holy dwelling place.

Listening to the Text in the Story: Exodus 12:1–28; Deuteronomy 16:1–8; 1 Chronicles 13:1–14; 2 Chronicles 7:14.

The jubilant tone of worship continues as Hezekiah makes preparations to celebrate the Passover. Israel's deliverance from slavery in Egypt was commemorated each year during the Passover meal, celebrated on the first month of the calendar (Exod 12:2). On the fourteenth day of the month, at twilight, each household was to kill an unblemished lamb, roast it, and eat it together as a family meal, along with unleavened bread and bitter herbs (vv. 3–6). Foreigners living among the Israelites could participate, but only after they had been circumcised (vv. 43–49). The significance of the Passover during the reign of Hezekiah is that it was celebrated in Jerusalem, and it includes the northern tribes of Ephraim, Manasseh, Issachar, and Zebulun. This joyous celebration represents a reunification of the tribes, hearkening back to the united and flourishing kingdom under David and Solomon.

Given that the tribes had been divided from the time of Rehoboam onward, the initiative by Hezekiah marks a reversal of the dissolution of the tribes, presenting a powerful vision for a unified people of God.[1] Rehoboam had attempted to restore the kingdom through military intervention (2 Chr 11:1), but the unity of estranged tribes will be accomplished through self-humbling, prayer, and seeking God's face (7:14). Standing behind the restorative process is a gracious God who forgives, hears, and heals. It is fitting that this reconciliation takes place at Passover—a celebration that commemorates Israel's mighty

---

1. For an insightful analysis of this story, see M. Patrick Graham, "Setting the Heart to Seek God: Worship in 2 Chronicles 30.1–31.1," in *Worship and the Hebrew Bible: Essays in Honor of John T. Willis*, eds. M. Patrick Graham, et al., JSOTSup 284 (Sheffield: Sheffield Academic Press, 1999): 124–41, esp. 130–35.

deliverance. The same mighty God who redeemed Israel by an outstretched arm is now at work restoring his people. This surely is an occasion for great rejoicing.

EXPLAIN the Story

Hezekiah Invites All Israel and Judah to Celebrate the Passover (30:1–9)

The vision for a restored and unified people of God reverberates throughout this chapter, beginning with Hezekiah's invitation to "all Israel and Judah" (2 Chr 30:1). The term "all Israel" is used throughout Chronicles to underscore a vision for a united people of God, as in the days of Solomon and David.[2] The celebration in the story that follows presents a vision for the returnees living in Jerusalem, who are comprised of people from northern and southern tribes (cf. 1 Chr 9:1).

Moses had taught that the Passover meal would one day be celebrated at a central location ("the place") chosen by God (Deut 16:1–8). The Passover was celebrated earlier in Israel's history during the days of the judges (2 Kgs 23:22; 2 Chr 35:18), but since Jerusalem has now been identified as "the place" anticipated by Moses (1 Chr 22:1–2; 2 Chr 3:1), the gathering of the tribes in Jerusalem marks a historic moment in the story of God's people. Hezekiah thus summons all Israel to "come to the temple in Jerusalem" to celebrate the Passover (30:1).

The Passover was to be celebrated in the first month, but the second month has now arrived since there had been insufficient consecrated priests and the people had not yet assembled in Jerusalem (2 Chr 30:2–3). A decision is made by the king and the people to celebrate the festival in the second month, for the plan "seemed right both to the king and to the whole assembly" (v. 4). Hezekiah not only invites Judah to the celebration, but he also extends an invitation to the northern tribes of Ephraim and Manasseh, sending "a proclamation throughout Israel, from Beersheba to Dan" (v. 5). Often given in reverse order, the expression "from Dan to Beersheba" represents the northern and southern borders of the land, underscoring the extent of Hezekiah's far-reaching invitation.

Hezekiah appoints couriers to travel throughout Israel and Judah. They carry with them letters from the king, calling their fellow Israelites to return

---

2. See Live the Story in Chapter 7, pp. 95–98.

to the LORD, the God of their forefathers (2 Chr 30:6). The summons to "return" (Heb. *sh-w-b*) to the LORD is deeply embedded in Israel's traditions (Deut 30:1–10; cf. Neh 1:8–9; 9:29; Zech 1:4, 6; Mal 3:7), and it was central to Solomon's prayer (2 Chr 6:24–31). The letters pass among those who had escaped the deportation by the Assyrian kings (30:6; cf. 2 Kgs 17; 1 Chr 5:26), warning them not to be like their forefathers and fellow Israelites, who had been unfaithful to the LORD (2 Chr 30:7; see 28:19, 22). They are not to be "stiff-necked" like their ancestors (30:8), an idiom that depicts someone unwilling to repent (Deut 10:16; Neh 9:16, 17, 29), but instead, they are to "submit" to the LORD, expressed by the idiom "to give a hand" (Heb. *n-t-n yad*; 2 Chr 30:8; cf. Ezra 10:19; Lam 5:6).[3]

Hezekiah exhorts them to yield to the LORD and come to the sanctuary and serve the LORD (2 Chr 30:8). Yet they must first repent, and when they do, there is the hope that their kinsmen will find mercy from their captors and be free to return to the land. Underlying his offer of restoration is the unchanging character of God, as the letters stated plainly: "for the LORD your God is gracious and compassionate. He will not turn his face from you if you return to him" (v. 9). This is the hallmark of the character of God that is appealed to throughout the Old Testament (Exod 34:6; Neh 9:17, 31). Moses surely understood this as he prayed on behalf of Israel, and Hezekiah now recalls the character of the LORD, underscoring that God's kindness leads to repentance. Unlike their forefathers, who had turned their backs on God (2 Chr 29:6), God would not turn his face away from them.

Some from the Northern Tribes Respond Positively to the Invitation (30:10–12)

The couriers pass through the region of Ephraim and Manasseh as far as Zebulun, but their invitation is met with scorn and mocking (2 Chr 30:10). Nevertheless, all is not lost, as some from Asher, Manasseh, and Zebulun humble themselves and come to Jerusalem (v. 11). Their physical journey to Jerusalem thus signifies a spiritual return to the LORD.[4] Humbling oneself is the first and necessary step in repentance (7:14), and examples are found elsewhere in Chronicles (12:6–7, 12; 32:26; 33:12; 34:27). The humbling of the northerners is seen in their decision to respond to the invitation, even at the risk of being mocked by their fellow Israelites. The northerners had belonged to the apostate kingdom, but their recent history would have led to

---

3. On the idiom "to fill the hand," see the commentary in Chapter 29 on 1 Chr 29:5, pp. 277–78, and Chapter 58 on 2 Chr 29:31, p. 498.

4. Graham, "Setting the Heart to Seek God," 135.

an increased animosity because of their maltreatment of Judeans (see ch. 28). In light of this, one wonders how the southerners were able to accept these returnees, with the bloodshed and captivity of their loved ones still fresh in their national conscience. Perhaps the Judeans had felt some level of compassion for their fellow Israelites who had suffered great loss and humiliation under the Assyrians.

Whatever misgivings they may have had, the Chronicler gives us a window into how this kind of heartfelt and deeply moving reconciliation was possible—by the sovereign God at work on the human heart. Thus, at this critical moment in the story, we are told that God's hand was on Judah to give them "unity of mind to carry out what the king and his officials had ordered, following the word of the LORD" (2 Chr 30:12). This kind of "one heart" could only come about through God's intervention (Jer 32:39; Ezek 11:19). Former hostilities would need to be set aside, but it was ultimately the hand of God that enabled Judah to receive their estranged brethren. Perhaps the prodigal Israelites would see in Judah's welcome the very face of God, as Jacob had seen in his brother's acceptance many years earlier (Gen 33:10).

All Israel Gathers to Celebrate the Passover (30:13–20)

A large crowd of people assembles in Jerusalem to celebrate the Passover and the Festival of Unleavened Bread, recalling that both festivals commemorate the Exodus from Egypt (Exod 12:8, 39; Deut 16:1–4).[5] Over the course of seven days, the Israelites had been instructed to eat bread without yeast, but the seventh day was a holy celebration to the LORD (Lev 23:5–8). As God's people prepare for the festival, they remove the altars in Jerusalem made by Ahaz (2 Chr 28:24) and throw them into the Kidron valley (30:14), a dumping area for unclean items (29:16). They slaughter the Passover lamb on the fourteenth day of the second month, notably, one month later than the law prescribed (30:15). The priests and Levites had been ashamed of themselves, but they are consecrated and proceed to offer burnt offerings to God (v. 15). They take up their regular positions according to the law of Moses, and the priests sprinkle blood received from the Levites (v. 16; cf. 35:11). Laity usually sacrificed their own animals at the Passover since it was a family meal (Exod 12:6; Deut 16:6), but many in the assembly had not consecrated themselves, so the Levites assume this responsibility for those who were ceremonially unclean.

The question now arises how the northerners from the tribes of Ephraim,

---

5. For a helpful discussion of the Feasts of Passover and Unleavened Bread (and a history of scholarship), see McConville, *Law and Theology in Deuteronomy*, 99–123.

Manasseh, Issachar, and Zebulun—those who had responded to Hezekiah's invitation—can participate in the Passover, for they had not yet "purified themselves" (2 Chr 30:18). The law taught that those who were ceremonially unclean were not allowed to participate in the Passover meal (Num 9:6–7), but a provision was made that they could celebrate it a month later (vv. 9–12). This provision does not resolve the problem in this situation, since they were already a month late (2 Chr 30:2). Instead of being precluded from participating, the people eat of the Passover even though it was "contrary to what was written" (v. 18). This presents a serious problem, but Hezekiah intercedes on their behalf by appealing to God directly with prayer: "May the LORD, who is good, pardon" (v. 18). Hezekiah appeals to the goodness of the LORD as he asks for forgiveness. The verb translated as "pardon" is elsewhere often translated as "atone" (Heb. *k-p-r*). Israel's priests were given the sacred task of making atonement on behalf of the people, which required the blood of an animal (Lev 4:20, 26, 31, 35; cf. 17:11). But in his prayer, Hezekiah asks God directly to "atone," something that Moses had done when he had interceded on Israel's behalf during the golden calf story (Exod 32–34). He had mediated between God and the people through intercessory prayer as he had sought to "make atonement" for Israel's sin (Heb. *k-p-r*, 32:30). God's gracious character preserved Israel back then, as it does during the time of Hezekiah. The king prays for those who had set their heart to seek the LORD even though they were not ritually clean (2 Chr 30:17). Hezekiah's prayer reminds us that worship "is not the glorious work of a perfect people, but the humble offering of flawed humans to God."[6]

It is important to recognize that echoes of 2 Chronicles 7:14 permeate this story. This means that the events described in this chapter explain *how* 2 Chronicles 7:14 is to be applied in the community. Rather than praying this for others, each action is being done by the participants: the northerners *humbled themselves* (Heb. *k-n-ʿ*, 30:11), *turned* from their evil ways (Heb. *sh-w-b*, vv. 6–9), and *sought* God (Heb. *d-r-sh*, v. 19). Hezekiah *prayed* for them (Heb. *p-l-l*, v. 18), asking that God might *pardon* them (expressed by the verb "atone," Heb. *k-p-r*, v. 18), and God *heard* (Heb. *sh-m-ʿ*, v. 20). The final outcome is that the people were *healed* (Heb. *r-p-ʾ*, v. 20). The verb "to heal" (Heb. *r-p-ʾ*) can refer to physical healing from a sickness and disease (e.g., Lev 13:18, 37; 14:3; Deut 28:27, etc.), but physical healing can include the idea of restoration (since some maladies come as a result of sin).[7] As the

---

6. Graham, "Setting the Heart to Seek God," 136.

7. For example, the wrath of God was upon Miriam, and a skin disease broke out on her body. Moses asks God to heal her, but in this case, her disease was a result of God's wrath; thus "healing"

psalmist prays: "Have mercy on me, LORD; heal me, for I have sinned against you" (Ps 41:4; cf. 103:3). Since the northerners had not adequately prepared to eat the Passover meal, their healing means that any potential wrath has been averted, but it also suggests that they have been restored into fellowship with the LORD and each other, demonstrated in their shared meal and in the peace offerings that follow.

The Joyful Celebration Continues and Thousands of Sacrifices Are Offered (30:21–27)

The united people of God, identified by their common ancestral father Israel (2 Chr 30:21), joyfully celebrate the Festival of Unleavened Bread over seven days (v. 30:21; cf. Exod 23:15; Lev 23:6–8). Israel's festivals were occasions for great joy (Deut 16:10–11, 13–14). Thus, their singing, which was accompanied by musical instruments, resounds with joyful praise (2 Chr 30:21; see also 1 Chr 15:16; 2 Chr 20:27; 23:18; 29:30).[8] This is a meal shared as the united people of God. Hezekiah speaks tenderly to the Levites, who had shown insight as they carried out their cultic duties. Over the course of seven days, peace offerings are sacrificed and praises are offered to the LORD. The whole assembly decides to continue the celebration for another seven days, reminiscent of the two-week celebration during the time of Solomon (7:8–9). The festival is underwritten by the generosity of King Hezekiah, who provides sacrifices in abundance (30:24).

The picture of a unified people of God is highlighted in the description of those present in Jerusalem. In addition to those from the tribe of Judah, there were priests and Levites, people from northern tribes, and foreigners who had come from the land of Israel, along with foreigners who were living in Judah (v. 25). This is a wonderful description of a united and multi-ethnic people of God. From Israel's earliest period, foreigners could participate in the Passover, provided that they were circumcised (Exod 12:48–49; Num 9:14; cf. Gen 17:12–13). A large number of foreigners living in the land of Israel had been conscripted to work on the temple (1 Chr 22:2; 2 Chr 2:17–18), but here the reference probably includes those who had been brought into northern cities by the Assyrians through their policy of population shifting (2 Kgs 17:24–41). Here we see a vision not only for a united people of God, but also an international people gathered together for worship in Jerusalem. This is table fellowship at its best—as those from all the tribes and from

---

entails physical restoration, but it also means the cessation of God's wrath (Num 12:11, 13; cf. Gen 20:17; Exod 15:26; 1 Sam 6:3).

8. See Live the Story in Chapter 34, pp. 319–21.

the nations eat together in the presence of the LORD. The description of the celebration concludes with an emphasis on great joy, noting that nothing like this had taken place since the days of Solomon (2 Chr 30:26). The festival concludes with a blessing given by the Levitical priests (cf. Num 6:22–27), along with an affirmation that their prayer has been heard by God in his holy dwelling—in heaven itself.

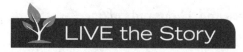

LIVE the Story

A Vision for Reconciliation

A vision for a united people of God has been a prominent theme throughout Chronicles, beginning with the opening genealogies intended to demonstrate that all the tribes trace their lineage back to one ancestral father, Israel (1 Chr 2–8).[9] In the Passover celebration, we see firsthand what is required to accomplish the hard work of reconciliation among estranged tribes. Hezekiah's invitation to the northern tribes is remarkable, given what had taken place in their recent history (2 Chr 28:5–15). Underlying this story is God's plan for a united people of God. The kingdom had been divided for two hundred years, but this is a climactic moment of reconciliation and unity, a foretaste of what is to come. This is what the prophet Ezekiel prophesied: "I will make them one nation in the land, on the mountains of Israel. There will be one king over all of them and they will never again be two nations or be divided into two kingdoms" (Ezek 37:22). This united and restored kingdom would have one Davidic king ruling over them. This is the vision that saturates Chronicles. It is seen in the flourishing kingdoms of David and Solomon, but after the tragic division under Rehoboam, glimpses of it are seen during the reign of Hezekiah. It is not accomplished by coercion or military force, but rather by self-humbling, repentance, prayer, and forgiveness. In this story we see *how* reconciliation takes place in accordance with God's promise given to Solomon in 2 Chronicles 7:14.

In this story we encounter the sovereign and gracious hand of God at work. As the repentant northerners arrive in Jerusalem, it is *God's hand* upon Judah, giving them "unity of mind to carry out what the king and his officials had ordered, following the word of the LORD" (30:12). This one-mindedness is a divine gift, anticipating what God will do when he restores his people and gives them "one heart" (Jer 32:39; Ezek 11:19; see Acts 4:32). The unification

---

9. See the introduction, Genre, pp. 7–8, and Live the Story in Chapter 7, pp. 95–98.

of Judah with their estranged brethren takes us to the heart of the reconciling work of God. It provides an example to the returnees living in Jerusalem, who were from Judah, Benjamin, and Levi, but also from Ephraim and Manasseh (1 Chr 9:1). As Hahn notes, Hezekiah is a "model leader for the post-exilic community. The Chronicler urges his contemporaries to follow the priorities that Hezekiah establishes and the steps he takes to renew the kingdom."[10] But this story also speaks to our context as it anticipates the unity accomplished through Jesus, as old hostilities are broken down and people become *one* in Christ (Eph 2:11–22).

The reality of the reconciling work of Christ is powerfully illustrated in the story of a Sudanese man name Brother Yassir. As a child, Yassir grew up in a devout Sunni Muslim family and was instructed and radicalized in the Qur'an, memorizing it and learning its doctrines. When he was at school, one day he and another boy took their classmate Zachariah into the forest to kill him. They beat him as he screamed out, and after breaking his bones, they left him there to die. Zachariah was a Christian, and Yassir viewed him as an infidel.

Yet God was at work in Yassir's family. His uncle, who was a fanatical Muslim, was known for his persecution of Christians. Yet, one day he would encounter Jesus, which would finally lead to his imprisonment. Through a series of events, Yassir also became a Christian, and as a result, his family disowned him. Yassir left Sudan and continued his education, finally serving as a lecturer and pastor of migrant churches in Germany. Twenty-five years later when Yassir was in Egypt teaching at a pastor's conference, he noticed a pastor in the audience while he was speaking, who was blind in one eye and physically weak. This man was weeping. Yassir was curious, so he went to speak with him afterward. The man proceeded to tell him that he was Zachariah, the young boy Yassir had left for dead twenty-five years earlier. Zachariah opened his Bible, and there Yassir saw his own name written on the first page. Zachariah told him that he had not stopped praying for him for twenty-five years, praying that he might become a Christian. As Yassir stood in front of Zechariah and saw what the beating had done to him, he was moved by his loving heart. He thought to himself, "What kind of religion can make one love an enemy so much!"[11] This deeply moving story of reconciliation is at the heart of the gospel, and it underscores the kind of reconciliation that is possible in Christ, something anticipated in the story of Hezekiah as God's hand is upon his people, giving them "one heart."

---

10. Hahn, *The Kingdom of God*, 173.

11. This story is recounted by Hikmat Kashouh, *Following Jesus in Turbulent Times: Disciple-Making in the Arab World* (Cumbria, CA: Langham Global Library, 2018), 23–25.

Vision for an "Assembly of Nations"

In this chapter, all Israel celebrates the Passover, and we see that foreigners join in the Passover celebration and partake of the shared meal. Sometimes we can (wrongly) assume that the old covenant was exclusively Jewish, whereas the new covenant is now open to people from all nations. But this overlooks the fact that foreigners were always among the people of God (cf. Gen 17:13–14; Exod 12:38; Josh 8:33), and they were subject to the law like the native-born (Lev 16:29; 17:15; 24:22; Num 15:29). God loved the foreigners, and Israel was to do the same, remembering they were once foreigners (Lev 19:34; Deut 10:18–19). Foreigners had also worked on the temple in great numbers (1 Chr 22:2; 2 Chr 2:17), contributing to the theme that foreigners were building up God's house, and they were invited to pray to the LORD (6:32–33). Foreigners are therefore included in this Passover celebration, as they were from Israel's earliest times (Exod 12:43–49; Num 9:14).

The sacred assembly that gathers for this festival includes both northern and southern tribes and foreigners in their midst (2 Chr 30:25). The term "assembly, sacred assembly" is used to describe the people gathered for worship (Heb. *qahal*, vv. 2, 24, 25; rendered "crowd" in NIV in vv. 13, 17), and it has its roots in God's promise to Israel that he would become a "*community of nations*" (Heb. *qahal*, Gen 35:11). It is important to bear in mind that the Greek word used in the Septuagint to translate *qahal* in this story is *ekklesia* (2 Chr 30:2, 4, 13, 17, 23, 24, 25 [2x]), the same Greek word translated as "church" in the New Testament (Matt 16:18; 18:17; Acts 5:11; 8:1, etc.).[12] The church is not the building but the "gathered" people of God. During the time of Hezekiah, the sacred assembly gathers in worship, sharing table fellowship as they remember their mighty deliverance. This celebration anticipates the reconciling work in Christ and the table fellowship among believers who celebrate the Lord's Supper as a unified *ekklesia*.

Yet Graham laments that our churches today often have what he calls a "pseudo-fellowship," which is sadly "more illusion than reality—a gathering for a brief time of people from similar socio-economic grounds who agree on little of religious significance—and worship is fashioned on the basis of market research to appeal to current human aesthetics, ideology and convenience—by, to and for oneself."[13] He argues that Chronicles has something to offer the contemporary American church. The vision of worship it presents has to do

---

12. On this topic, see Live the Story, Worship of God Continues in the Church in Chapter 15, pp. 161–63.

13. Graham, "Setting the Heart to Seek God," 141.

with the heart; it is "an occasion for joy, thankfulness, generosity, healing, reconciliation and a time for God to empower and enthuse his people."[14] The sharing of a meal by the "sacred assembly" gathered in Jerusalem anticipates what will become a reality in the *ekklesia*, where there is no longer Jew or Greek, slave or free, but all are one in Christ. Hays thus writes that "the church's unity at table across ethnic boundaries is an outward and visible sign of the breaking down of these barriers, a prefiguration of the eschatological banquet of the people of God."[15] This Passover meal shared by God's people during the time of Hezekiah is a foretaste of the heavenly banquet when the tribes of Israel and the nations join together in worship around God's throne (Rev 7:4–9). This gives significance to our weekly gatherings. Worship is the time for the "reorientation of the human heart—to remember what God has done in the past and to infuse the present with home for a future life of well-being and communion with God."[16] Israel's worship and joyful singing lasted for two weeks, but ours will last for all eternity. This is the vision set before us in Chronicles. May our communities and churches be places that testify to the redemptive and reconciling work of Christ, as people from all nations, tribes, people, and tongues gather together for worship, united in joyful praise unto our Lord.

---

14. Ibid.

15. Richard B. Hays, *The Moral Vision of the New Testament: A Contemporary Introduction to New Testament Ethics* (New York: Harper Collins), 440.

16. Graham, "Setting the Heart to Seek God," 141.

LISTEN to the Story

¹When all this had ended, the Israelites who were there went out to the towns of Judah, smashed the sacred stones and cut down the Asherah poles. They destroyed the high places and the altars throughout Judah and Benjamin and in Ephraim and Manasseh. After they had destroyed all of them, the Israelites returned to their own towns and to their own property.

²Hezekiah assigned the priests and Levites to divisions—each of them according to their duties as priests or Levites—to offer burnt offerings and fellowship offerings, to minister, to give thanks and to sing praises at the gates of the LORD's dwelling. ³The king contributed from his own possessions for the morning and evening burnt offerings and for the burnt offerings on the Sabbaths, at the New Moons and at the appointed festivals as written in the Law of the LORD. ⁴He ordered the people living in Jerusalem to give the portion due the priests and Levites so they could devote themselves to the Law of the LORD. ⁵As soon as the order went out, the Israelites generously gave the firstfruits of their grain, new wine, olive oil and honey and all that the fields produced. They brought a great amount, a tithe of everything. ⁶The people of Israel and Judah who lived in the towns of Judah also brought a tithe of their herds and flocks and a tithe of the holy things dedicated to the LORD their God, and they piled them in heaps. ⁷They began doing this in the third month and finished in the seventh month. ⁸When Hezekiah and his officials came and saw the heaps, they praised the LORD and blessed his people Israel.

⁹Hezekiah asked the priests and Levites about the heaps; ¹⁰and Azariah the chief priest, from the family of Zadok, answered, "Since the people began to bring their contributions to the temple of the LORD, we have had enough to eat and plenty to spare, because the LORD has blessed his people, and this great amount is left over."

¹¹Hezekiah gave orders to prepare storerooms in the temple of the LORD,

and this was done. [12]Then they faithfully brought in the contributions, tithes and dedicated gifts. Konaniah, a Levite, was the overseer in charge of these things, and his brother Shimei was next in rank. [13]Jehiel, Azaziah, Nahath, Asahel, Jerimoth, Jozabad, Eliel, Ismakiah, Mahath and Benaiah were assistants of Konaniah and Shimei his brother. All these served by appointment of King Hezekiah and Azariah the official in charge of the temple of God.

[14]Kore son of Imnah the Levite, keeper of the East Gate, was in charge of the freewill offerings given to God, distributing the contributions made to the LORD and also the consecrated gifts. [15]Eden, Miniamin, Jeshua, Shemaiah, Amariah and Shekaniah assisted him faithfully in the towns of the priests, distributing to their fellow priests according to their divisions, old and young alike.

[16]In addition, they distributed to the males three years old or more whose names were in the genealogical records—all who would enter the temple of the LORD to perform the daily duties of their various tasks, according to their responsibilities and their divisions. [17]And they distributed to the priests enrolled by their families in the genealogical records and likewise to the Levites twenty years old or more, according to their responsibilities and their divisions. [18]They included all the little ones, the wives, and the sons and daughters of the whole community listed in these genealogical records. For they were faithful in consecrating themselves.

[19]As for the priests, the descendants of Aaron, who lived on the farmlands around their towns or in any other towns, men were designated by name to distribute portions to every male among them and to all who were recorded in the genealogies of the Levites.

[20]This is what Hezekiah did throughout Judah, doing what was good and right and faithful before the LORD his God. [21]In everything that he undertook in the service of God's temple and in obedience to the law and the commands, he sought his God and worked wholeheartedly. And so he prospered.

Listening to the Text in the Story: Numbers 18:21–32; Deuteronomy 14:22–29

With the joyful celebration of Passover resounding in the hearts and minds of God's people, the land is purged of idolatrous altars and high places. Hezekiah reappoints priests and Levites so that they might serve in the reopened temple, thereby ensuring that daily sacrifices and praises are offered to the LORD. From Israel's early days, the Levites had been set apart to serve in the tabernacle, but this required that the Israelites give a tithe so that the Levites could be compensated for their service (Num 18:21–32).[1] Even the Levites were to tithe, as this was as a provision for the priests (v. 28; Neh 10:35–39; 12:47). Underlying the tithe-law was the fact that God had generously given land and its abundance to his people. In response, they were required to reciprocate by giving back to the LORD through their tithes and offerings. The tithe was a provision for the Levites who were dispersed among the tribes, and as cult personnel without inherited land, they had the right to receive an income. The tithe had the character of a tax or sacral levy that was not to be neglected (Deut 14:27). A portion of the tithe was consumed by the offeror and his family in the presence of the LORD, which was an occasion for rejoicing as they partook of God's blessing (vv. 22–27). The third-year tithe, in addition to providing for the Levites also provided for the alien, the orphan, and the widow, and as such, it was given over in its entirety (vv. 28–29).

The tithe was also important in the post-exilic community after the temple had been rebuilt (Neh 10:37–38; 12:44–47; 13:12). Yet it had apparently been neglected, resulting in Levites and singers not receiving what was due to them—something Nehemiah seeks to set right (13:10–11). In the post-exilic period, the prophet Malachi rebukes God's people for withholding the tithe, charging them of robbing God (Mal 3:8–10). With this context in view, the reinstitution of the tithe and the generosity of the people under the godly leadership of Hezekiah provide an important example for the post-exilic community. This story is instructive for our contemporary context as well.

EXPLAIN the Story

The Celebration Concludes with the Purging of Idolatrous Objects (31:1)

Following the Passover celebration, the people purge the land of sacred pillars, Asherim, high places, and idolatrous altars (2 Chr 31:1).[2] King Ahaz

---

1. McConville traces the history of interpretation of the tithe (and some of the problematic issues for interpretation) and concludes that each reiteration of the tithe-law in the Pentateuch gives only a partial picture, with certain aspects being omitted in each text (since the tithe-law would have been assumed by the readers). For an insightful discussion, see McConville, *Law and Theology in Deuteronomy*, 68–87.

2. For a description of these religious items, see the discussion in Chapter 63 on 2 Chr 34:3–7, pp. 546–47.

had set up idolatrous worship throughout the land (28:1–4, 23–25), but these abominable objects and altars are now destroyed in accordance with what Moses had prescribed in the law (Deut 7:5; 12:3). The destruction of foreign cult objects not only takes place in Judah and Benjamin, but it also extends to the northern region of Ephraim and Manasseh (2 Chr 31:1). People from these tribes had returned to the LORD and had participated in the Passover celebration (30:11, 18), but now the residue of their idolatry is purged. True worship of the LORD God requires the destruction of false gods and their altars (see 33:15; 34:3–7). The purging that had begun in Jerusalem is now reaching beyond the city so that the holiness of Jerusalem is extending outward to encompass the rest of the land.[3] After purging the land, the people return to their homes; this brings to completion the events described in 2 Chronicles 29–30.

Hezekiah Appoints Priests and Levites for Their Service (31:2–10)

Hezekiah reappoints priests and Levites by their divisions, which was according to what David had prescribed (2 Chr 31:2; cf. 8:14; 29:25–30). Judah's priests were to offer burnt offerings and fellowship offerings. The Levitical singers were to serve, thank, and praise the LORD (31:2). Burnt offerings were offered daily to the LORD (v. 3; cf. 2:4; 8:13), and Hezekiah generously makes provisions for them, as Solomon had done earlier (cf. 2 Chr 8:12–13). The king instructs the people to give their portion for the priests and Levites so that they might devote themselves to the law of the LORD (31:4). Since Israel's priests and Levites had been given the sacred task of teaching the law (Deut 17:9–13; 33:9–10; 2 Chr 17:9; Ezra 7:10),[4] the tithes received were necessary for their livelihood.

As soon as the order is given, the Israelites give their firstfruits of grain, new wine, oil, honey, and from their produce of the field, which is set aside for the priests (2 Chr 31:5; cf. Num 18:12–13). The abundance of produce collected serves as testimony to God's blessing on them (see Deut 12:5–7). Over the course of a few months, their consecrated gifts are placed in heaps. Upon seeing the abundance given, Hezekiah and the leaders bless the LORD (2 Chr 31:8), reminiscent of the blessing of David and Solomon (1 Chr 16:2; 29:10; 2 Chr 6:3). When Hezekiah asks about all the abundance he sees, the chief priest, Azariah, tells him that such generosity has meant that the priests

---

3. Graham, "Setting the Heart to Seek God," 135–36.
4. On the priority of teaching God's word, see Live the Story in Chapter 46, pp. 408–10.

and Levites have plenty to eat, and there is even a great quantity left over—a sign of God's blessing (31:9–10; cf. Deut 28:11)!

The Tithes Are Faithfully Distributed to the Priests and Levites (31:11–19)

Hezekiah instructs the priests and Levites to prepare rooms in the house of the LORD where the contributions, tithes, and dedicated gifts are to be stored (2 Chr 31:11). Oversight of the contributions is given to Konaniah and his brother Shemei, but ten other Levites are appointed, bringing the number to twelve (vv. 12–13). Hezekiah and Azariah work harmoniously together, underscoring an "ideal sharing of power."[5] A Levite named Kore, who was a gatekeeper of the important East Gate, is put in charge of the freewill offerings and their distribution (v. 14; cf. 1 Chr 9:17–18; 26:16). With the faithful assistance of other Levites, the contributions are distributed equitably ("old and young alike," 2 Chr 31:15) to the priests who serve in the temple, along with priests who live outside Jerusalem, according to their genealogical record (vv. 15–16). Provisions were given to Levites aged twenty years and upward[6] who were registered by their offices, according to their divisions (v. 18).[7] Priests who were dispersed among the cities receive their portion, along with the Levites who had been registered (v. 19).

Hezekiah's Faithfulness to the LORD (31:20–21)

The chapter concludes with an affirmation of all that Hezekiah had done throughout Judah. Hezekiah did "what was good and right and faithful before the LORD his God" (2 Chr 31:20). His faithfulness is further described in what follows: "In everything that he undertook in the service of God's temple and in obedience to the law and the commands, he sought his God and worked wholeheartedly" (v. 21). In contrast to his father's ungodly legacy, Hezekiah is building a godly reputation, and unlike his father's unsuccessful reign, Hezekiah is prospering under God's blessing (v. 21).

---

5. Klein, 2 Chronicles, 451. On the dual leadership of king and priest, see Hagg 1:1, 12; 2:4; Zech 4:14; 6:11–15, etc.

6. The age when a Levite began his service seems to vary (see Num 4:3; 8:24; 1 Chr 23:3, 24; Ezra 3:8). Even in this chapter, the eligible age for priestly provision is three years old (31:16), the age associated with weaning. While three years old may seem unusual, it may well be that after weaning, infants were included in the provision for priestly families.

7. The various offices of Levites according to their divisions are given in 1 Chr 25-26, which include musicians (ch. 25), gatekeepers (26:1-19), treasurers (vv. 20-28), and officers and judges (vv. 29-32).

LIVE the Story

Generosity

The Israelites were required to give a tithe of their produce as compensation to the Levites for their service (Num 18:21–32; Deut 14:22–29). Since priests and Levites were needed to serve in the reopened temple, Hezekiah had instructed the people to give their tithe. The people responded with great generosity—something that causes the king to praise the LORD. The important topic of generosity has already been explored, and it is again seen in this story.[8] While the tithe was required of every Israelite, the concept of generosity and self-sacrifice is embedded in the command, since it was given in response to God's generosity of land.[9]

When considering the New Testament teaching about the tithe, minimal attention is given to it, although when Jesus does teach on it, he rebukes the Pharisees for their legalism, which had resulted in their neglecting the weightier matters of justice and mercy (Matt 23:23; Luke 11:42; 18:9–14).[10] Although the tithe is hardly mentioned, Jesus does have much to say about giving and generosity. He emphasizes the importance of both generosity and sacrificial giving (Mark 12:41–44; Luke 21:1–4; cf. 6:38); he warns against covetousness and greed (12:13–21); he exhorts his disciples to store up treasure in heaven (Matt 19:16–26; Luke 12:33–34; 18:22); and he teaches that it is more blessed to give than to receive (Acts 20:35). Generosity was evident in the early church, which included sharing resources and caring for those in need (2:43–47; 4:32–37; 11:29–30; 1 Cor 16:1–4; 1 Tim 6:17–19). Paul commends the Macedonian churches for their generosity and giving amid their poverty, which served as an example to the Corinthians (2 Cor 8:1–9:15).

Generosity is a virtue that ought to be cultivated in our lives today. A recent study by Barna affirms that nine in ten practicing Christians agree that generosity is either "extremely" or "very" important to them. Yet the same study shows that only thirteen percent of Millennials and only six percent of Gen Z give money on a frequent basis. The study tracks generational attitudes toward giving, noting that student debt and lack of good teaching

---

8. See the discussion in Chapter 29 on 1 Chr 29 and, especially, Live the Story, pp. 282–84.

9. McConville, *Law and Theology in Deuteronomy*, 82–86.

10. For a helpful summary of two main views of the tithe, see William Barcley, "The Bible Commands Christians to Tithe," The Gospel Coalition, March 28, 2017, https://www.thegospelcoalition.org/article/bible-commands-christians-to-tithe/, and Thomas Schreiner, "7 Reasons Why Christians Are Not Required to Tithe," The Gospel Coalition, 28 March 2018, https://www.thegospelcoalition.org/article/7-reasons-christians-not-required-to-tithe/.

on personal finances seem to adversely impact giving in younger Christians. The study concludes that it is "important for church leaders to communicate to their congregation that generosity is not solely about financial gifts, but about discipling Christians for long-term and whole-hearted expressions of generosity—wherever they are in life."[11] In a time where consumerism has become pervasive in the church and individualism seems to have influenced how we view our personal finances, the kind of generosity seen during the time of Hezekiah and the generosity and self-sacrifice inherent in the tithe-law stands as a call for us to consider carefully whether our giving to the LORD is characterized by generosity and self-sacrifice. This may also require teaching younger generations on the importance of generosity, along with practical teaching on personal finances. The generosity of God's people at the time of Hezekiah results in the priests and Levites being fully satisfied, and there is even much left over—causing the king to praise the LORD. This serves as a challenge to give in our own local church to ensure that the needs of the pastors and staff are met; as McConville notes, even the Levites were "not to be offered mere crumbs," but they had the potential to build up personal or family wealth.[12]

Supporting our Modern-Day Levites

The tithe provided for priests and Levites, but in this passage emphasis is given to their role as teachers. The tithe was necessary, therefore, so that they "could devote themselves to the Law of the LORD" (2 Chr 31:4).[13] Ezra is a powerful example of a Levite who "devoted himself to the study and observance of the Law of the LORD, and to teaching its decrees and laws in Israel" (Ezra 7:10).

The New Testament teaches that ministers of the gospel were to receive their living from the gospel (1 Cor 9:14; cf. Matt 10:10; Luke 10:7). Accordingly, Paul and Barnabas had the right to "not work for a living" (1 Cor 9:6), although Paul did not avail himself of this right. Paul taught that the laborer was worthy of his wages (1 Tim 5:18), recognizing that elders work hard at preaching and teaching (v. 17). In our contemporary context, one may well wonder whether the amount of debt incurred by seminary students represents a failure of the church to meet the needs of those who have dedicated themselves to teaching

---

11. For a helpful analysis of giving according to age-groups, see the 2019 Barna study, "Why the Generations Approach Generosity Differently," June 19, 2019 (https://www.barna.com/research/generations-generosity/).

12. McConville, *Deuteronomy*, 297.

13. On the role of the teaching role of the priests and Levites, see Live the Story in Chapter 46, pp. 408–10.

God's word.[14] In 2019, forty percent of graduating seminary students had incurred an average debt of $33,000 from their undergraduate degree, but forty-five percent reported taking on an additional average debt of $34,000 while at seminary.[15] In Israelite society, the tithe provided the necessary support for Israel's teachers so they could devote themselves to the study and teaching of the law, but in our contemporary context, the burden of studying God's word falls on seminary students, who are often required to take on debt to pay for their theological education.

Given that the word of God is central to the life and well-being of the church,[16] this story raises the question of whether we have neglected this important task of ensuring that the needs of the "Levites" in our midst are being met. While local churches provide for the needs of their pastor through their tithes and offerings, the increasing level of debt incurred by seminary students who are preparing for ministry ought to cause us to rethink whether the church ought to be more actively providing for these students. Coupled with an aging clergy, this need is even more urgent.[17]

We noted earlier that George Whitefield's ministry was supported by the gospel patron, Lady Huntington.[18] She was known to have used her financial resources to cover the living expenses of seminary students. Rinehart notes that a staggering half her annual income was used for their food, clothing, and ministry trips.[19] She had intentionally lived sacrificially herself, taking a "sparing hand" for her own needs, so that she might use her resources to prepare ministers of the gospel. Underlying her generosity and sacrificial giving was an unswerving commitment to the gospel. What a blessing it would be for students to leave seminary without debt so that they can devote themselves to the ministry of the word. This cannot be done without the generosity and self-sacrifice of God's people, a topic worth further reflection as we seek to *live* the story.

---

14. For some helpful statistics, along with suggestions how students and institutions can alleviate student debt, see the report by Sharon L. Miller, Kim Maphis Early, and Anthony T. Ruger, "A Call to Action: Lifting the Burden," April 2014, Auburn Center for the Study of Theological Education, chrome-extension://efaidnbmnnnibpcajpcglclefindmkaj/https://auburnseminary.org/wp-content/uploads/2016/05/LiftingTheBurden-Final.pdf.

15. Cited by JoAnn Deasy, "How Seminaries are Addressing Students' Ballooning Debt," Good Faith Media, August 29, 2019 (https://goodfaithmedia.org/author/jo-ann-deasy/).

16. For a description of the dire consequences when God's law is not taught (cf. 2 Chr 15:3–6), see Live the Story in Chapter 44, pp. 395–97.

17. For statistics from a Barna study on aging Protestant clergy, see Live the Story in Chapter 27, p. 264.

18. See Live the Story in Chapter 29, pp. 282–84.

19. Rinehart, *Gospel Patrons*, 87.

LISTEN to the Story

¹After all that Hezekiah had so faithfully done, Sennacherib king of Assyria came and invaded Judah. He laid siege to the fortified cities, thinking to conquer them for himself. ²When Hezekiah saw that Sennacherib had come and that he intended to wage war against Jerusalem, ³he consulted with his officials and military staff about blocking off the water from the springs outside the city, and they helped him. ⁴They gathered a large group of people who blocked all the springs and the stream that flowed through the land. "Why should the kings of Assyria come and find plenty of water?" they said. ⁵Then he worked hard repairing all the broken sections of the wall and building towers on it. He built another wall outside that one and reinforced the terraces of the City of David. He also made large numbers of weapons and shields.

⁶He appointed military officers over the people and assembled them before him in the square at the city gate and encouraged them with these words: ⁷"Be strong and courageous. Do not be afraid or discouraged because of the king of Assyria and the vast army with him, for there is a greater power with us than with him. ⁸With him is only the arm of flesh, but with us is the LORD our God to help us and to fight our battles." And the people gained confidence from what Hezekiah the king of Judah said.

⁹Later, when Sennacherib king of Assyria and all his forces were laying siege to Lachish, he sent his officers to Jerusalem with this message for Hezekiah king of Judah and for all the people of Judah who were there:

¹⁰"This is what Sennacherib king of Assyria says: On what are you basing your confidence, that you remain in Jerusalem under siege? ¹¹When Hezekiah says, 'The LORD our God will save us from the hand of the king of Assyria,' he is misleading you, to let you die of hunger and thirst. ¹²Did not Hezekiah himself remove this god's

high places and altars, saying to Judah and Jerusalem, 'You must worship before one altar and burn sacrifices on it'?

¹³"Do you not know what I and my predecessors have done to all the peoples of the other lands? Were the gods of those nations ever able to deliver their land from my hand? ¹⁴Who of all the gods of these nations that my predecessors destroyed has been able to save his people from me? How then can your god deliver you from my hand? ¹⁵Now do not let Hezekiah deceive you and mislead you like this. Do not believe him, for no god of any nation or kingdom has been able to deliver his people from my hand or the hand of my predecessors. How much less will your god deliver you from my hand!"

¹⁶Sennacherib's officers spoke further against the LORD God and against his servant Hezekiah. ¹⁷The king also wrote letters ridiculing the LORD, the God of Israel, and saying this against him: "Just as the gods of the peoples of the other lands did not rescue their people from my hand, so the god of Hezekiah will not rescue his people from my hand." ¹⁸Then they called out in Hebrew to the people of Jerusalem who were on the wall, to terrify them and make them afraid in order to capture the city. ¹⁹They spoke about the God of Jerusalem as they did about the gods of the other peoples of the world—the work of human hands.

²⁰King Hezekiah and the prophet Isaiah son of Amoz cried out in prayer to heaven about this. ²¹And the LORD sent an angel, who annihilated all the fighting men and the commanders and officers in the camp of the Assyrian king. So he withdrew to his own land in disgrace. And when he went into the temple of his god, some of his sons, his own flesh and blood, cut him down with the sword.

²²So the LORD saved Hezekiah and the people of Jerusalem from the hand of Sennacherib king of Assyria and from the hand of all others. He took care of them on every side. ²³Many brought offerings to Jerusalem for the LORD and valuable gifts for Hezekiah king of Judah. From then on he was highly regarded by all the nations.

²⁴In those days Hezekiah became ill and was at the point of death. He prayed to the LORD, who answered him and gave him a miraculous sign. ²⁵But Hezekiah's heart was proud and he did not respond to the kindness shown him; therefore the LORD's wrath was on him and on Judah and

Jerusalem. ²⁶Then Hezekiah repented of the pride of his heart, as did the people of Jerusalem; therefore the LORD's wrath did not come on them during the days of Hezekiah.

²⁷Hezekiah had very great wealth and honor, and he made treasuries for his silver and gold and for his precious stones, spices, shields and all kinds of valuables. ²⁸He also made buildings to store the harvest of grain, new wine and olive oil; and he made stalls for various kinds of cattle, and pens for the flocks. ²⁹He built villages and acquired great numbers of flocks and herds, for God had given him very great riches.

³⁰It was Hezekiah who blocked the upper outlet of the Gihon spring and channeled the water down to the west side of the City of David. He succeeded in everything he undertook. ³¹But when envoys were sent by the rulers of Babylon to ask him about the miraculous sign that had occurred in the land, God left him to test him and to know everything that was in his heart.

³²The other events of Hezekiah's reign and his acts of devotion are written in the vision of the prophet Isaiah son of Amoz in the book of the kings of Judah and Israel. ³³Hezekiah rested with his ancestors and was buried on the hill where the tombs of David's descendants are. All Judah and the people of Jerusalem honored him when he died. And Manasseh his son succeeded him as king.

Listening to the Text in the Story: 2 Kings 18–19; Isaiah 36–37; Siloam Inscription, Sennacherib Prism.

Hezekiah has acted with great faithfulness, purging Judah of idolatry and reestablishing worship at the temple in Jerusalem (2 Chr 29–30). Yet it is disconcerting to learn—and perhaps not coincidental—that amid a time of renewal, an aggressive assault comes from a powerful Assyrian king whose emissaries arrive in Jerusalem, demanding that God's people submit to him. These words of intimidation and blasphemy are spoken at the very place where all Israel has gathered to worship the LORD God. As we read this account in Chronicles, it is important to bear in mind that this story is recorded in Kings and in Isaiah (2 Kgs 18–19; Isa 36–37).[1]

---

1. For a detailed analysis of the similarities and differences of the accounts, see Japhet, *I & II Chronicles*, 974–98 and Klein, *2 Chronicles*, 456–70.

In the story that follows, Hezekiah is able to block off the water supply from outside Jerusalem that comes from the Gihon Spring (2 Chr 32:3–4, 30). He was able to redirect the water by building another tunnel that becomes part of Jerusalem's extensive water system. Remarkably, an inscription found chiseled into the wall of the tunnel at its lower entrance south of the temple describes this event. The partial inscription etched in stone records what took place as the men were digging: "And when the tunnel was driven through, the quarrymen hewed (the rock), each man toward his fellow, axe against axe; and the water flowed from the spring toward the reservoir for 1,200 cuts, and the height of the rock above the head(s) of the quarrymen was 100 cubits."[2] This tunnel can be visited in Israel today, and the adventurous can even wade through its dark passageway.

In the story that follows, envoys sent by the Assyrian king Sennacherib arrive in Jerusalem. An ancient text known as the Sennacherib Prism records the disloyalty of those in the western region of the empire that eventually leads to Sennacherib's assault against Palestine and his defeat of cities belonging to Judah.[3] An excerpt from this text highlights what happens to Hezekiah and Jerusalem:

As to Hezekiah, the Jew, he did not submit to my yoke, I laid siege to forty-six of his strong cities, walled forts and to the countless small villages in their vicinity, and conquered them by means of well-stamped earth-ramps, and battering-rams brought near to the walls, combined with the attack by foot soldiers, using mines, breeches, as well as sapper work. I drove out of them 200,150 people, young and old, male and female, horses, mules, donkeys, camels, big and small cattle beyond counting, and considered them booty. Himself I made a prisoner in Jerusalem, his royal residence, like a bird in a cage.[4]

The prism gives insight into this critical moment in Israel's history during the reign of Hezekiah, and it underscores the dire threat of invasion that is at hand. Hezekiah has shown himself faithful to the Lord, but the bully tactics of Sennacherib's messengers would cause even the strongest of kings to be

---

2. "The Siloam Inscription," trans. W. F. Albright (*ANET*, 321). For a description and picture of the inscription, see Hoerth, *Archaeology & the Old Testament*, 342–47.

3. For a helpful overview of the political climate and alliances forged at this time, see ibid., 341–53. Included in Hoerth's discussion are pictures of the Sennacherib Prism and the Lachish Reliefs, as well as a detailed chronology of events. Merrill has also provided an extended description of the Assyrian conquests (see *1 & 2 Chronicles*, 548–53).

4. Sennacherib (704–681): "The Siege of Jerusalem," trans. A. Leo Oppenheim (*ANET*, 288).

gripped with fear, even a faithful king like Hezekiah. How will he respond at this moment of national crisis?

Hezekiah Exhorts the People to Trust in the LORD (32:1–8)

The story of Sennacherib's invasion of Judah is introduced as follows: "After all that Hezekiah had so faithfully done" (2 Chr 32:1; cf. 31:20). This not only gives a positive assessment of Hezekiah's religious reforms (chs. 29–30), but it indicates that the Assyrian attack is not to be interpreted as God's judgment. On the contrary, the assault comes after Hezekiah's *faithful* actions. This may even suggest that there is a spiritual component to this assault lurking below the surface, seen in the blasphemous words of Sennacherib's messengers as they mock the LORD God and raise doubt about God's ability to deliver his people.[5] The attack of Sennacherib is dated to 701 BC, the fourteenth year of Hezekiah, which locates it after the fall of the Northern Kingdom to the Assyrians (2 Kgs 18:9–13). The Assyrian king Sennacherib had laid siege to the fortified cities of Judah (2 Chr 32:1), imposing on Hezekiah tribute of gold and silver, which he had paid from the treasuries of the temple and the palace (2 Kgs 18:14–16).

The story is picked up with Hezekiah's plan to protect the supply of fresh water, for he knows that Sennacherib intends to wage war against Jerusalem (2 Chr 32:3). With the counsel and support from his officers and military, along with the support of the people, they are remarkably able to block off the water supply from outside the city, thereby preventing the Assyrians from having access to it (vv. 3–5, 30). Hezekiah repairs the broken sections of the wall and fortifies it with defensive towers.[6] He makes weapons and shields, and he appoints military officers over the people (vv. 5–6). The king gathers the people to the city gate and encourages them with the assuring words: "Be strong and courageous" (v. 7; cf. Josh 1:5–7; 1 Chr 28:20). The people were not to be fearful, for Hezekiah reminds them: "With him is only the arm of flesh, but with us is the LORD our God to help us and to fight our battles" (2 Chr 32:8). The Assyrians were mere mortals, but the LORD God was with his people to help them, as Asa understood when he had faced a

---

5. For further discussion on the spiritual nature of Israel's battles, see Live the Story in Chapter 14, pp. 153–54, and Chapter 19, pp. 199–201.

6. Scholars have estimated that Hezekiah's fortifications may have more than tripled the size of Jerusalem from forty acres to 140 acres (Merrill, *1 & 2 Chronicles*, 531n59).

great multitude: "LORD, there is no one like you to help the powerless against the mighty. Help us, LORD our God, for we rely on you, and in your name we have come against this vast army. LORD, you are our God; do not let mere mortals prevail against you" (14:11). God has helped his people in the past, and he can be relied upon to do so again. In view of the military strength of the Assyrians and the gruesome treatment of their foes (see below), the stance taken by Hezekiah is a remarkable act of courage and faith.

Sennacherib's Messengers Mock the Living God (32:9–19)

Assyrian emissaries arrive in Jerusalem while Sennacherib is besieging Lachish, a city belonging to Judah located thirty miles southwest of Jerusalem (2 Chr 32:9). Lachish was a well-fortified city that was protected by massive fortifications, stone walls, and an extensive gate complex. Yet these extensive fortifications could not protect the city from the might of the Assyrian army (cf. Mic 1:13). Stone wall reliefs originally in Nineveh depict the conquest of Lachish in extraordinary detail. Towering wall reliefs comprised of twelve stone slabs, extend eighty feet in length and eight feet in height. Etched into stone were artistic depictions of siege engines battering walls, infantry soldiers storming the city, prisoners being stripped naked, and captives impaled on stakes and flayed alive, while women, children, and precious objects are taken as plunder, only to be paraded as trophies of war before the victorious Sennacherib seated on his throne.[7] The emissaries come with a word from the mighty king Sennacherib: "On what are you basing your confidence, that you remain in Jerusalem under siege?" (2 Chr 32:10). Sennacherib taunts the people by suggesting that Hezekiah was deceiving them. Implicit in their taunt is that God is unable to deliver his people (v. 11). Hunger and thirst were the grim realities of warfare, and now the messengers suggest this will be their fate if they do not submit to Sennacherib.

Next, the emissaries mock Hezekiah's religious reforms by attacking his role in centralizing worship (2 Chr 32:12). They wrongly assume that the destruction of high places and altars throughout the land reflects poorly upon the king. But the attentive reader knows that purging the land of idols was a testimony to Hezekiah's *faithfulness* (30:14; 31:1). Their false claims have the unintended effect of stressing that Hezekiah's actions were "wholly acceptable, and to show the blasphemy of the Assyrians."[8] Their blasphemy

---

7. See Osama S. M. Amin, "Siege of Lachish Reliefs at the British Museum," 7 February 2017, https://etc.worldhistory.org/photos/siege-lachish-reliefs-british-museum/.

8. Richard J. Coggin, *The First and Second Books of the Chronicles*, The Cambridge Bible Commentary (Cambridge: Cambridge University Press, 1976), 282.

leads to another serious and fatal miscalculation. With much hubris, they boast in Sennacherib's military victories accomplished by *their* gods, and in doing so, they assume that Yahweh is unable to deliver his own people—a serious miscalculation (32:13–14)! The verb "to deliver, save" (Heb. *n-ts-l*) is a central theme in this story (vv. 11, 13, 14 [2x], 15 [2x], 17 [2x]). The messengers fail to recognize that Yahweh has distinguished himself from other gods, for he alone can deliver his people (1 Chr 16:35; Isa 44:17, 20). The prophet Isaiah understood that God's arm was not so short that it could not save (50:2). The LORD was, indeed, *unlike* the gods of the nations—there was none like him (44:6–8; 45:5–7, 20–25; 46:5–9, etc.). He was surely able to save his people.

The Assyrians had achieved remarkable military success, and this reflected poorly on the so-called gods of the defeated nations, but the messengers make the bold and audacious claim that *no god* of any nation or kingdom has been able to deliver their people from the Assyrian might. They insist that the people not *believe* Hezekiah (Heb. *'aman*, cf. 2 Chr 20:20), and they boldly claim that such faith rests in a false hope: "How much less will your god deliver you from my hand!" (32:15). Sennacherib's attack against Jerusalem is ultimately an attack against the LORD himself, and thus the insults that continue in the form of letters mock the God of Israel (v. 17). They overconfidently claim that, like the gods of the nations that are unable to defeat the Assyrians, so too, the "god of Hezekiah will not rescue his people from my hand" (v. 17). Perhaps the Northern Kingdom is in view, which had been defeated by the Assyrians, yet this was not due to God's inability to save his people. On the contrary, the Northern Kingdom had worshiped golden calves (the "no-gods"), and they surely were unable to deliver (cf. 13:8–9).

The messengers taunt those on the wall, shouting their blasphemous words aloud, hoping to incite fear by those responsible to protect the wall. The final assessment by the Chronicler is that the messengers "spoke about the God of Jerusalem as they did about the gods of the other peoples of the world—the work of human hands" (32:19). The Scriptures resound with the message that the gods of the nations were mere idols, made by human hands (1 Chr 16:26; Isa 2:8, 20; Hab 2:18); they were not gods after all, for there was only one God, the LORD God, and he alone is able to save (Isa 43:10–13; 44:6–8; 45:5–7, 21–22).

Hezekiah's Prayer and God's Deliverance (32:20–23)

What happens next brings us to the heart of the story—*prayer*. Upon hearing these bully tactics intended to publicly denounce the character of the LORD, Hezekiah and Isaiah the prophet "cried out in prayer to heaven about this"

(2 Chr 32:20; cf. 2 Kgs 19:1–36; Isa 37:1–35). In the parallel accounts, Hezekiah asks Isaiah to lift up a prayer (2 Kgs 19:4; Isa 37:4) and the king prays by himself in the temple (2 Kgs 19:14–19; Isa 37:14–20), but in Chronicles they are united in prayer, with one voice crying out to God. The verb "to pray" (Heb. *p-l-l*) occurs at key places in Chronicles, especially in Solomon's prayer (2 Chr 6:19, 20, 21, 24, etc.), but also elsewhere (7:1, 14; 30:18; 32:24; 33:13). The second verb, "to cry out" (Heb. *z-'-q*) recalls the time when the Hagrites had cried out to God amid the battle (1 Chr 5:20), and it recalls Jehoshaphat's desperate cry for help (2 Chr 18:31). In both circumstances, God had answered their pleas, as Jehoshaphat had affirmed publicly—when his people cry out to God amid their distress, he will hear and answer (20:9). Even though the content of Hezekiah's prayer is not recorded in Chronicles, what matters is that he and Isaiah *prayed* to the LORD (cf. 2 Kgs 19:20; Isa 37:21).

God answers Hezekiah's prayer by sending an angel to destroy the Assyrian army (2 Chr 32:21; see 2 Kgs 19:35–36; Isa 37:36–37). Notice that just *one angel* defeats the mighty Assyrian army! Sennacherib returns in shame to his own land (2 Chr 32:21; cf. 2 Kgs 19:37). Thus, although Sennacherib boasted of his victory over Hezekiah, he was unable to conquer Jerusalem, and the king remained unharmed. In fact, we read that Sennacherib was finally slaughtered by his sons in the "temple of his god" (2 Chr 32:21), and another son, Esarhaddon, became king in his place (2 Kgs 19:37).[9] The irony is that these so-called powerful Assyrian gods were unable to save Sennacherib from his own sons, who assassinate him while he is worshiping in the temple. Sennacherib's death takes place twenty years after his attack against Jerusalem (dated to 681 BC), but its placement at the end of this story is for theological reasons, explaining the fate of the king who had mocked the LORD God. The story concludes with an affirmation that the LORD saved Hezekiah and the people from the hand of Sennacherib (2 Chr 32:22). God *is* able to deliver his people after all (cf. Dan 3:16–18, 25–27; 6:20–22). Finally, people from the surrounding nations bring offerings to the LORD and costly gifts to Hezekiah, exalting him in the sight of the nations (2 Chr 32:23; cf. 1 Chr 14:17; 2 Chr 17:11; 26:8). This recalls the flourishing kingdom under Solomon, and it indicates that the LORD is being exalted among the nations (cf. 1 Chr 16:28–31).[10]

---

9. An inscription of Esarhaddon describes the animosity between the king and his older brothers (because Sennacherib had chosen Esarhaddon to succeed him). This inscription hints at some of the family strife that seems to be reflected in Sennacherib's murder by his sons (see "The Fight for the Throne," trans. A. Leo Oppenheim [*ANET*, 289–90]).

10. See the discussion in Chapter 38 on 2 Chr 9 and, especially, Live the Story, pp. 359–60.

Hezekiah's Illness and Pride, and the Final Years of His Life (32:24–33)

The story of Hezekiah's illness is rehearsed briefly next (2 Chr 32:24–26). The Chronicler's omission of a number of details found elsewhere (cf. 2 Kgs 20:1–11; Isa 38:1–22) allows him to focus on two key themes that are prominent in Chronicles: pride and humbling oneself. The Chronicler notes that "Hezekiah's heart was proud and he did not respond to the kindness shown him" (2 Chr 32:25). Instead of responding with thankfulness to the LORD, Hezekiah became proud, reminding us that, in Chronicles, success and faithfulness can easily lead "to pride and self-reliance. More often than not, this temptation comes in the form of riches and power or a military alliance with a foreign power."[11] Hezekiah should have responded to God in thankfulness for the benefit that had been shown to him (v. 25; cf. Ps 103:3–5). God's wrath comes as a result, leading Hezekiah and the people to humble the pride of their heart (2 Chr 35:25–26). The verb translated as "repent" in the NIV is the verb "to humble oneself" (Heb. k-n-$'$), recalling the important passage in 2 Chronicles 7:14.[12] As a result, God's wrath is averted.

The reign of Hezekiah is now drawing to a conclusion (32:27–33). Hezekiah has great riches and honor, reminiscent of the flourishing kingdom under David and Solomon (1 Chr 29:12, 28; 2 Chr 9:22-28). With such wealth, the king makes treasuries to store his silver and gold, his precious stones, spices, shields, and all kinds of valuables, and he builds storehouses for his abundance of produce and animals (32:27–28). Hezekiah is remembered for protecting the water supply, and he prospered in all that he did (v. 30; cf. 1 Chr 22:11; 29:23; 2 Chr 7:11). Envoys had come from Babylon to inquire about the miraculous sign (32:31; cf. 2 Kgs 20:12–13); but Hezekiah had unwisely shown them his royal treasures (2 Chr 32:31), which would later be carried to Babylon (cf. 2 Kgs 20:14–19; Isa 39:1–8). God was testing Hezekiah so that he might see what was in his heart (2 Chr 32:31; cf. Deut 8:2). While further details are not given, the Chronicler makes reference to other events in Hezekiah's reign and his "acts of devotion" that have been recorded in other sources (2 Chr 32:32). When considering Hezekiah's life as a whole, he has served God faithfully, and he is surely remembered as one of Judah's greatest kings. Thus it is fitting that after he dies, he is given an honorable burial among the tombs of the Davidic kings (v. 33).

---

11. Hahn, *The Kingdom of God*, 168. On the danger of pride, see Live the Story, The Dangers of Success without Humility, in Chapter 45, p. 403.

12. See the discussion in Chapter 36 on 2 Chr 7:14, pp. 338–41.

LIVE the Story

Facing Opposition with Spiritual Weapons

At the outset of this chapter we are told that Sennacherib invaded Judah "after all that Hezekiah had so faithfully done" (2 Chr 32:1), which recalls the religious reforms recorded in chs. 29–31. The events described in the previous chapters mark a reversal of the division that had begun under Rehoboam, as tribes from the north and south are united in their worship of the LORD. This has come about because God's sovereign hand was giving his people "unity of mind" (30:12), and it stands at the center of God's plan of restoration (Ezek 37:15–24). That Sennacherib's invasion takes place amidst a context of repentance and reconciliation hints at a deeper level of opposition that is beyond a mere military battle. Similarly, when David was anointed king over all Israel—something that had signaled a key moment in God's plan of redemption—the next thing that happens is that the Philistines wage war against him (1 Chr 14:8). It would appear that such attacks are motivated by something more than simply a military encounter. It is important to recognize that when nations attack the Davidic king and God's people, this is tantamount to an attack against God himself, recalling that the king rules over the kingdom of God (cf. Pss 2:1–12; 83:1–18).

The spiritual aspect of the attack is seen in the messengers' attempt to undermine and ridicule Israel's God. With bullying tactics that are intended to evoke fear and to intimidate, they make derogatory remarks about Hezekiah's centralization of worship—something that is, indeed, a testimony to his faithfulness. With much hubris, they overestimate the ability of their gods and boldly assert that the LORD is unable to deliver his people. Yet their claims will turn out to be *false*, for the LORD does deliver his people, and ironically, their own gods are unable to save their king. There are other times when God's people face bullying tactics, requiring them to pray and trust in God. Daniel faced opposition when three of Darius's men maliciously accuse him, yet Daniel prays and trusts in God (Dan 6:1–24). Nehemiah faced opposition when rebuilding the walls of Jerusalem, yet he and those with him pray and trust that God will fight their battles (Neh 4:1–23). These kind of scare tactics and false accusations are seen in the story of Hezekiah, and like other godly leaders, his response is to pray and cry out to his God.

These stories remind us that when we face opposition, there is sometimes a spiritual reality to conflicts because we are citizens of the kingdom of God. The New Testament teaches that a spiritual battle is taking place between the kingdom of God and the kingdom of darkness, with the ultimate adversary being Satan himself and his demons (Matt 4:1–11; 12:25–26; Luke 10:18–19; Acts 26:18; cf. 1 Thess 2:18). In view of this spiritual reality, God's people are to be aware of the wiles of the enemy and not give Satan any foothold (1 Cor 7:5; 2 Cor 2:10–11; 11:14). Hostile forces at work ought to cause us to be spiritually alert and praying at all times. The apostle Paul exhorts the church at Ephesus to be strong in the Lord and stand firm against the schemes of the devil, reminding them that "our struggle is not against flesh and blood, but against the rulers, against the authorities, against the powers of this dark world and against the spiritual forces of evil in the heavenly realms" (Eph 6:12). This kind of spiritual battle is to be fought with spiritual weapons (vv. 13–17), and prayer is central (v. 18). When Hezekiah faced the taunting words of the messengers, he did not call up his military; he prayed (2 Chr 32:20; Isa 37:21). Similarly, when Jehoshaphat faced a multitude coming against Jerusalem, he did not call up his military, but instead, he set his face to seek the LORD (2 Chr 20:3–4). When Esther faced the threat of Haman, who was attempting to destroy Jews in Susa, God's people had prayed and fasted (Esth 4:1–3, 16–17). Battles are fought by prayer as we rely upon God for deliverance.

Paul reminds believers at Corinth that "though we live in the world, we do not wage war as the world does" (2 Cor 10:3). Nor do we fight with "weapons of the world" (v. 4). Hezekiah recognized that the mighty Assyrian king's strength was *only flesh*, but "with us is the LORD our God to help us and to fight our battles" (2 Chr 32:8). The simple song *Surrounded* by Michael W. Smith reminds us of the reality of God's presence when facing opposition. After repeating the words, "This is how I fight my battles," the refrain continues: "It may look like I'm surrounded but I'm surrounded by You."[13] As we face opposition, may we be strengthened by God's power at work in us. May we be on the alert, aware of the wiles of the enemy, and praying at all times. We, too, can be strong and courageous, for our God is with us, strengthening us by the power of his might and assuring us that the battle has already been won (Col 2:15).

---

13. Michael W. Smith, "Surrounded (Fight My Battles)"; see https://www.youtube.com/watch?v=WamhEa4M7us.

CHAPTER 62

2 Chronicles 33:1–25

 LISTEN to the Story

¹Manasseh was twelve years old when he became king, and he reigned in Jerusalem fifty-five years. ²He did evil in the eyes of the LORD, following the detestable practices of the nations the LORD had driven out before the Israelites. ³He rebuilt the high places his father Hezekiah had demolished; he also erected altars to the Baals and made Asherah poles. He bowed down to all the starry hosts and worshiped them. ⁴He built altars in the temple of the LORD, of which the LORD had said, "My Name will remain in Jerusalem forever." ⁵In both courts of the temple of the LORD, he built altars to all the starry hosts. ⁶He sacrificed his children in the fire in the Valley of Ben Hinnom, practiced divination and witchcraft, sought omens, and consulted mediums and spiritists. He did much evil in the eyes of the LORD, arousing his anger.

⁷He took the image he had made and put it in God's temple, of which God had said to David and to his son Solomon, "In this temple and in Jerusalem, which I have chosen out of all the tribes of Israel, I will put my Name forever. ⁸I will not again make the feet of the Israelites leave the land I assigned to your ancestors, if only they will be careful to do everything I commanded them concerning all the laws, decrees and regulations given through Moses." ⁹But Manasseh led Judah and the people of Jerusalem astray, so that they did more evil than the nations the LORD had destroyed before the Israelites.

¹⁰The LORD spoke to Manasseh and his people, but they paid no attention. ¹¹So the LORD brought against them the army commanders of the king of Assyria, who took Manasseh prisoner, put a hook in his nose, bound him with bronze shackles and took him to Babylon. ¹²In his distress he sought the favor of the LORD his God and humbled himself greatly before the God of his ancestors. ¹³And when he prayed to him, the LORD was moved by his entreaty and listened to his plea; so he brought

him back to Jerusalem and to his kingdom. Then Manasseh knew that the LORD is God.

[14]Afterward he rebuilt the outer wall of the City of David, west of the Gihon spring in the valley, as far as the entrance of the Fish Gate and encircling the hill of Ophel; he also made it much higher. He stationed military commanders in all the fortified cities in Judah.

[15]He got rid of the foreign gods and removed the image from the temple of the LORD, as well as all the altars he had built on the temple hill and in Jerusalem; and he threw them out of the city. [16]Then he restored the altar of the LORD and sacrificed fellowship offerings and thank offerings on it, and told Judah to serve the LORD, the God of Israel. [17]The people, however, continued to sacrifice at the high places, but only to the LORD their God.

[18]The other events of Manasseh's reign, including his prayer to his God and the words the seers spoke to him in the name of the LORD, the God of Israel, are written in the annals of the kings of Israel. [19]His prayer and how God was moved by his entreaty, as well as all his sins and unfaithfulness, and the sites where he built high places and set up Asherah poles and idols before he humbled himself—all these are written in the records of the seers. [20]Manasseh rested with his ancestors and was buried in his palace. And Amon his son succeeded him as king.

[21]Amon was twenty-two years old when he became king, and he reigned in Jerusalem two years. [22]He did evil in the eyes of the LORD, as his father Manasseh had done. Amon worshiped and offered sacrifices to all the idols Manasseh had made. [23]But unlike his father Manasseh, he did not humble himself before the LORD; Amon increased his guilt.

[24]Amon's officials conspired against him and assassinated him in his palace. [25]Then the people of the land killed all who had plotted against King Amon, and they made Josiah his son king in his place.

Listening to the Text in the Story: Deuteronomy 30:11–15; 2 Kings 21:10–18; 2 Chronicles 7:14

The Southern Kingdom spirals into one of its darkest periods during the reign of Manasseh, marked by the proliferation of idolatry and abominable pagan practices that signal a drastic reversal of the flourishing kingdom under

Hezekiah. The young king Manasseh not only establishes worship of Baal, Asherah, and the host of heaven, but idolatrous worship even takes place in the temple. It is heart-wrenching to learn that the king adopts the deplorable practice of child sacrifice. The dire state of the kingdom is highlighted in the Kings account, where the sins of Manasseh are given as the reason for God's impending judgment against Jerusalem and Judah (2 Kgs 21:10–16; cf. Jer 15:4). God has been merciful to his people, but he will by no means leave the guilty unpunished, and his judgment will surely be forthcoming.

Yet alongside this dismal period in the kingdom stands God's offer of restoration, reminding us that God's mercy triumphs over judgment. Moses had seen from afar that if God's people returned to the LORD, he would graciously restore his people: "the LORD your God will restore your fortunes and have compassion on you and gather you again from all the nations where he scattered you. Even if you have been banished to the most distant land under the heavens, from there the LORD your God will gather you and bring you back" (Deut 30:3–4). This is exactly what Solomon had rehearsed in his prayer of dedication (2 Chr 6:24–25, 36–39), and, as we will see shortly, God's promise of 2 Chronicles 7:14 lies behind the story of Manasseh. In the final analysis, even though the period begins so wretchedly, it resounds with hope and restoration. The depravity of Manasseh's heart sets the context for his reign, but it ultimately casts a spotlight on the divine grace that shines forth as a ray of hope upon a dark land. Manasseh's restoration will lead to a profound change of heart, and it is intended to instill hope in the returnees and in our lives today as we witness the remarkable restoration that occurs when a repentant sinner encounters the living God.

EXPLAIN the Story

Manasseh's Litany of Sins (33:1–9)

Manasseh becomes king at the young age of twelve years old, and he reigns for fifty-five years, identifying him as the longest ruling monarch in the Southern Kingdom (2 Chr 33:1). A co-regency with Hezekiah of approximately ten years would mean his sole reign would still extend to forty-five years,[1] identifying Esarhaddon (681–669 BC; cf. 2 Kgs 19:37) and Ashurbanipal (668–633 BC) as the Assyrian rulers during this period.

---

1. See Klein for a discussion on the dates for Manasseh, including a potential co-regency with Hezekiah (Klein, *2 Chronicles*, 478).

It is notable that Manasseh's name is recorded in Assyrian royal annals. One prism records that Esarhaddon had received building materials for his palace from twenty-two vassal kings, one of whom is identified as Manasseh. Another text lists Manasseh among those who had paid tribute to Ashurbanipal and had provided military assistance when the king campaigned in Egypt.[2] While not mentioned in the biblical account, these foreign alliances paint an even more negative picture of Manasseh, for reliance upon foreign kings meant that the king was not trusting the LORD (cf. 2 Chr 19:2; 20:35). The Chronicler notes at the outset that Manasseh did evil in God's sight, following the "detestable practices of the nations," the practices that had resulted in God driving out the nations from their land (33:2). His abominable practices include building altars for Baal, making images of Asherah, and worshiping the host of heaven (v. 3). Worship of Baal was not only prominent in the Northern Kingdom (2 Kgs 17:16), especially during the reign of Ahab (1 Kgs 16:31–32; 18:22), but also in periods of the Southern Kingdom (2 Chr 23:17; 24:7). Similarly, worship of the female Canaanite goddess Asherah, often represented with a pillared base ("Asherah poles"), was widespread during Ahab's reign (1 Kgs 16:33; 18:19), but Judah was not exempt from this idolatry (2 Kgs 21:2, 7; 2 Chr 24:18; 31:1). Even though such pagan practices were prohibited (Deut 7:5; 12:3; 16:21, etc.), the archaeological record testifies that thousands of terracotta figurines have been found in Israel and Judah.[3] While not all scholars identify them with the cult of Asherah, their presence indicates that Judah is not exempt from pagan religious practices.

Manasseh builds two altars in the temple for all the host of heaven (2 Chr 33:4). What an affront against the living God that worship of celestial bodies, something strictly prohibited under the law (Deut 4:19; 17:3; cf. 2 Kgs 17:16), is now taking place *in the temple* (cf. Ezek 8:16)! The temple had been built and consecrated as a holy place where God's name would dwell. This is the holy sanctuary where God's presence dwelt above the richly carved cherubim that flanked the ark of the covenant. The Chronicler has given careful attention to describe every detail of the temple's construction and its sacred furniture, followed by Solomon's extended prayer of dedication (2 Chr 1–7), but now this glorious temple has been hideously defiled by pagan worship. Guilt lies with Manasseh alone—he alone is the subject of a series of verbs that underscore his detestable practices, which include building altars for Baal,

---

2. See Essarhaddon (680–669): "The Syro-Palestinian Campaign," Prism B, trans. A. Leo Oppenheim (*ANET*, 291, 294).

3. King and Stager, *Life in Biblical Israel*, 348–51.

making Asherah poles, worshiping the starry hosts, and even building altars in the temple for idolatrous worship (33:2-5).

The litany of sins climaxes with the statement that Manasseh sacrificed his own children in the Valley of Ben Hinnom, a deplorable waste place used for child sacrifice (2 Chr 33:6; cf. Jer 7:31–32; Ezek 16:20–21). Child sacrifice was something that characterized the nations, and it was utterly abhorrent in God's eyes (Lev 20:2–3; Deut 12:31).[4] Yet the list of sins continues with the statement that Manasseh "practiced divination and witchcraft, sought omens, and consulted mediums and spiritists" (2 Chr 33:6; cf. Deut 18:9–13). It is not surprising to read, therefore, that Manasseh did "much evil in the eyes of the LORD, arousing his anger" (2 Chr 33:6). Manasseh even puts the image he had made *in the temple*—the very place which had been chosen as the place where God's name would dwell (v. 7). The section concludes with an indictment against Manasseh for leading Judah and the inhabitants of Jerusalem astray, so that they did "more evil than the nations the LORD had destroyed before the Israelites" (v. 9; see Lev 18:24–30). This is surely a tragic state of affairs, and it marks one of the darkest periods in the Southern Kingdom.

Judgment, Repentance, and Restoration (33:10–20)

God speaks to Manasseh and the people through his prophets, but since they pay no attention, he brings the commanders of the Assyrian army against them (2 Chr 33:10–11; cf. 2 Kgs 21:10–16).[5] The humiliating events that take place focus on Manasseh. The army captures him with a hook in his nose. He is bound with bronze shackles and brought to Babylon (2 Chr 33:11), foreshadowing what lies ahead for Zedekiah (36:6). A stele of Esarhaddon celebrating his victory over Egypt depicts two defeated foes before the king, showing the practice of piercing an enemy's nose or lip, with some kind of hook or ring placed in the hole, enabling the enemy to be brought to submission. The description of Manasseh's capture and exile to Babylon is not far removed from this scene that depicts both kings kneeling in submission before the powerful Assyrian king.[6]

But the humiliating circumstances will bring about a humbling in Manasseh's heart that changes the trajectory of his life. We learn that in his

---

4. See comment in Chapter 57 on 2 Chr 28:3, p. 486.

5. Scholars are uncertain when this took place and how it relates to the political circumstances of the period. For a summary of scholarship (which includes eight possible reconstructions!), see Klein, *2 Chronicles*, 473–77. While the exact circumstances remain uncertain, this need not preclude the account from being historical. Isaiah had already prophesied that some of Hezekiah's sons would be taken to Babylon (2 Kgs 20:16–19).

6. See Hoerth, *Archaeology & the Old Testament*, 355; cf. *ANEP*, 447.

distress "he sought the favor of the LORD his God and humbled himself greatly before the God of his ancestors" (33:12). While times of distress can lead to a hardening of the heart (28:22), the desired outcome is a turning to God (1 Chr 21:13; 2 Chr 15:4). Now, Manasseh appeals to God's favor (lit. his "face"), as Moses had done many years earlier (Exod 32:12; cf. Dan 9:13). In his distress, he "humbled himself greatly" (2 Chr 33:12) before God, recalling the important promise of 2 Chronicles 7:14 ("if my people . . . will humble themselves").[7]

What is truly remarkable is that even though Manasseh is the *worst* southern king, and even though he is known for his litany of sins, the LORD hears his prayer, for when Manasseh prayed "the LORD was moved by his entreaty and listened to his plea; so he brought him back to Jerusalem and to his kingdom" (33:13). This verse encapsulates the theology that permeates Solomon's prayer of dedication (6:12–42) and God's response to him (7:14). Solomon had envisaged a variety of adverse circumstances that would come upon God's people because of their sin, but they were exhorted to pray, to plead for mercy, and to repent. If they did this while captive in a far-off land, God would hear, forgive, and restore (6:36–39). Accordingly, when Manasseh "prayed" (33:13; Heb. *p-l-l*; cf. 6:19, 20, 21, 24, etc.), God "listened to" (Heb. *sh-m-'*, 33:13; cf. 6:19, 20, 21, 23, etc.) "his plea" (33:13; cf. 6:19, 29, 35), and "restored" him (Heb. *sh-w-b*; 33:13; cf. 6:25). Manasseh's sin is met with God's lavish grace, and thus he "furnishes the most explicit and dramatic example of the efficacy of repentance in the whole of the Chronicler's work."[8] Manasseh's restoration embodies the outworking of Solomon's prayer, and as noted by Dillard, the Chronicler will "seek again and again to demonstrate the realization in Israel's history of the principles announced in Solomon's prayer and in God's response."[9] Manasseh's restoration is a profound testimony to the mercy of God shown to a repentant sinner.

The spiritual transformation in Manasseh's life is seen in what happens next, for we read that "Manasseh knew that the LORD is God" (2 Chr 33:13). It is through answered prayer and God's mercy shown to him that the king discovers for himself that the LORD is God. Unlike the deaf and dumb idols he had worshiped, he now experiences the reality of the living God, who hears and answers prayer. The idols were not gods after all. Answered prayer is a powerful testimony that the LORD is God (cf. 1 Kgs 18:37), reminiscent of

---

7. For occurrences of this verb (Heb. *k-n-'*) in Chronicles, see the discussion in Chapter 36 on 2 Chr 7:14, pp. 388–41.

8. Williamson, *1 and 2 Chronicles*, 389.

9. Dillard, *2 Chronicles*, 7.

Israel's declaration many years earlier when Elijah's prayer was answered: "The LORD—he is God! The LORD—he is God!" (v. 39).

Upon returning to Jerusalem, Manasseh rebuilds the city wall and stations military commanders in the fortified cities of Judah (2 Chr 33:14). But what takes place next is a further testimony to the spiritual transformation that has occurred in his life. He removes the foreign gods and the idol from the temple, along with the altars he had made, and he throws them out of the city (v. 15). This is a king whose life had been riddled with idolatry, witchcraft, divination, and sorcery, and he had shed much innocent blood, including sacrificing his own sons. But now, Manasseh gets rid of the foreign gods associated with pagan worship (v. 15; cf. Gen 35:1–4; Josh 24:14, 23; Judg 10:16; 1 Sam 7:3–4), because the LORD has become his God.

Manasseh does not simply remove the foreign gods, but he *replaces* them with worship of the LORD—he restores the altar of the LORD and sacrifices fellowship offerings and thank offerings on it.[10] These are tangible and heartfelt expressions of a restored sinner who responds in gratitude to the LORD (2 Chr 33:16). Moreover, this changed king, who had previously led Judah astray, now instructs Judah to serve the LORD. While the high places remain, instead of being places of idolatry (21:11; 28:4; 33:3), sacrifices are offered to the LORD (v. 17). Manasseh's reforms mark a significant reversal of the rampant idolatry that had characterized his reign before he had encountered God's grace in Babylon. The high places will nevertheless remain until Josiah destroys them a few years later (34:3). The reign of Amon indicates that some images remained (33:22), suggesting that the religious reforms were limited in scope.

As the reign of Manasseh draws to a close, the Chronicler notes that his reign has been recorded elsewhere, and prophets had courageously spoken in the name of the LORD to him (2 Chr 33:18–19). These prophets underscore God's relentless pursuit of Manasseh, yet it is notably only after Manasseh had been brought to Babylon that he finally repents. God sometimes uses difficult circumstances to bring his people to their senses. Manasseh will not only be remembered for his idolatrous practices before he humbled himself, but also for his prayer and how God was moved by his entreaty, thereby underscoring the centrality of Manasseh's conversion.[11] His sin does not have the final word, for prayer, repentance, and restoration have been beautifully woven into his story. He is a sinner who found God's mercy. Manasseh is not buried in the royal tombs but in his palace (v. 20), indicating that he died with less honor

---

10. On this topic, see Live the Story in Chapter 57, pp. 489–90.
11. Selman, *2 Chronicles*, 524.

than his father, Hezekiah (32:33). In Chronicles, a number of kings begin well but finish poorly. Manasseh starts poorly but finishes well because of God's mercy. This story provides hope for the exilic community, and it surely provides hope for us today.

The Short Reign of Amon (33:21–25)

After Manasseh dies and is buried in his palace, his son Amon becomes king (2 Chr 33:21). The story of the kingdom takes a tragic turn for the worse, however. Amon does evil in the sight of God, something that had characterized the early period in Manasseh's reign. He sacrifices to the carved images that his father had made, yet, unlike Manasseh, he does not humble himself before the LORD but *increases* his guilt (v. 23). His failure to humble himself will not only lead to his downfall, but it anticipates the last king, Zedekiah, who refuses to humble himself (36:12). Amon reigns for two short years before his officials conspire against him and assassinate him. The people in turn kill all those who had plotted against Amon, and they make his son Josiah king (33:25).

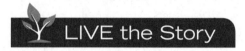

LIVE the Story

God's Lavish Grace

Manasseh had spent his early years in rebellion against the LORD, following after the practices of the nations, which would even lead him to shed innocent blood and to sacrifice his own children on the altar. In fact, his actions were decidedly *worse* than the nations whom the LORD dispossessed. Yet it was not until he was in Babylon—removed from his throne, exiled from his land, and in fetters in Babylon with a hook in his nose—that he came to his senses. His dire circumstances caused him to turn to God in prayer and to seek God's mercy, precisely what Solomon had rehearsed in his prayer when he spoke about God's people having a "change of heart" while in captivity, where they would "repent and plead" with God (2 Chr 6:37) and turn back to him "with all their heart and soul in the land of their captivity" (vv. 37–39). This is what happened to Manasseh. His distressing circumstances caused him to turn to the LORD.

While we would not wish adverse circumstances on anyone, God sometimes uses them to bring people to himself. This is what happened to the prodigal son described by Jesus in a parable, who not only squandered his father's estate with loose living, but he ended up taking the lowly and degrading job of feeding swine (Luke 15:11–32). While in his desperate state, he would have gladly eaten the carob pods the pigs were eating, yet it was at this time that he "came to his senses" (v. 17). While facing adversity, this lost son realized he had sinned against his father, and like Manasseh, he repented and encountered the Father's lavish grace.

The story of Christopher Yuan's journey of faith is the story of a prodigal whose adverse circumstances were used by God to restore him back to himself. Christopher grew up in a wealthy neighborhood in Chicago. After high school, he entered dental school in Louisville, Kentucky, following in the footsteps of his father, who had his own dental practice. But while at college, he began to squander away his life, visiting gay clubs, going to parties, having casual sexual relationships, taking drugs, and finally, becoming a highly prosperous and successful drug dealer.

In the meantime, his atheist mother, Angela, who was living in an emotionally bankrupt marriage, came to the Lord. As she grew in her faith (and her husband later came to faith as well), she became burdened by her prodigal son, causing her to spend hours in her prayer closet, which was her bathroom. She spent countless hours praying for her son and asking God to restore him. But Christopher's fast-paced lifestyle caught up with him when he was busted by the police and found in possession of a large amount of illegal drugs, resulting in a six year prison sentence. While being locked in a tiny cell in a high security prison in Atlanta, he recalls noticing graffiti on his cell wall. As he looked up, he saw something scribbled on the wall, hardly legible: *If you're bored, read Jeremiah 29:11.*

In his tiny cell was a small desk and chair bolted to the floor, a metal toilet and a sink, and a rusty old locker. He began to rummage through the locker, finding empty cereal boxes, paper, foam bowls, and napkins. But he recalls his hand hitting something at the back of the locker that felt like the corner of a book—it was *a Bible*. He flicked through its pages, searching for Jeremiah 29:11. As he read that God had plans to give him hope and a future, a glimmer of hope was ignited in his heart. He kept reading: "Then you will call on me and come and pray to me, and I will listen to you" (v. 12). He read that if he sought God with all his heart, God would bring him back from "nations and places from which I have banished you" (v. 14). He recalls: "The thought that God could restore me and bring me back from captivity resonated with my spirit."[12] God did have a plan to restore Christopher, and the events that follow are told in his memoir, *Out of a Far Country*, a story about two prodigals

---

12. Christopher and Angela Yuan, *Out of a Far Country: A Gay Son's Journey to God. A Broken Mother's Search for Hope* (Colorado Springs: Waterbrook Press, 2011), 149.

who find God. His mother, Angela, had prayed that God would use her son's imprisonment to bring him to the Lord, and this is exactly what happened. While incarcerated, Christopher began to read his Bible, and he even started Bible studies with fellow inmates.

With many inspiring stories that follow, the book concludes with Christopher's six-hour journey back to Chicago with his parents after he had been released from prison. When he finally arrived at his home, he noticed a yellow ribbon tied around the tree in the front yard. He paused to recall the familiar story encapsulated in the song, "Tie a Yellow Ribbon Round the Ole Oak Tree," which was about an inmate returning from prison who had asked his sweetheart to tie a ribbon around the tree in their front yard if she would still have him.[13] The released prisoner tells the bus driver that, if there is no ribbon in the front yard, he should just drive by. To his surprise, when the bus approached the house (and with his fellow travelers shouting for joy!), he saw one hundred ribbons tied around the tree!

As Christopher saw the yellow ribbon tied to the tree in front of *his* house, he felt unworthy of the love his parents had showed him. They had waited for him all these years. As his eyes filled with tears, his heart "flooded with the understanding of grace and forgiveness that had been given to me."[14] As he approached the front door, he could hear a faint sound of music, only to find a CD player inside the hallway playing the song, *Tie a Yellow Ribbon*. As he entered the house, he was overwhelmed when he saw more than a hundred yellow ribbons attached to different places in the room. Each yellow ribbon had a signature on it, with words of encouragement written by those who had prayed for him. This is a story of God's lavish grace and restoration.

Christopher's journey with God did not stop the day he returned home—it was just the beginning, for he went on to receive a bachelor's degree from Moody Bible Institute and a master's degree from Wheaton College. He now teaches at Moody Bible Institute, and he has an international ministry, as he speaks in various contexts about God's desire for prodigals to return to him. These stories of restoration—whether Manasseh's, Christopher's, or our own—can be recounted across the globe as a testimony to a gracious and loving Father who lavishly welcomes the repentant sinner, leading to transformation and hearts filled with worship.

---

13. Ibid., 199. The song is based on a true story of a Civil War soldier who was returning from prison, but in the original story yellow handkerchiefs were tied to the oak tree instead of yellow ribbons.

14. Ibid., 200.

CHAPTER 63

2 Chronicles 34:1–33

 LISTEN to the Story

¹Josiah was eight years old when he became king, and he reigned in Jerusalem thirty-one years. ²He did what was right in the eyes of the LORD and followed the ways of his father David, not turning aside to the right or to the left.

³In the eighth year of his reign, while he was still young, he began to seek the God of his father David. In his twelfth year he began to purge Judah and Jerusalem of high places, Asherah poles and idols. ⁴Under his direction the altars of the Baals were torn down; he cut to pieces the incense altars that were above them, and smashed the Asherah poles and the idols. These he broke to pieces and scattered over the graves of those who had sacrificed to them. ⁵He burned the bones of the priests on their altars, and so he purged Judah and Jerusalem. ⁶In the towns of Manasseh, Ephraim and Simeon, as far as Naphtali, and in the ruins around them, ⁷he tore down the altars and the Asherah poles and crushed the idols to powder and cut to pieces all the incense altars throughout Israel. Then he went back to Jerusalem.

⁸In the eighteenth year of Josiah's reign, to purify the land and the temple, he sent Shaphan son of Azaliah and Maaseiah the ruler of the city, with Joah son of Joahaz, the recorder, to repair the temple of the LORD his God.

⁹They went to Hilkiah the high priest and gave him the money that had been brought into the temple of God, which the Levites who were the gatekeepers had collected from the people of Manasseh, Ephraim and the entire remnant of Israel and from all the people of Judah and Benjamin and the inhabitants of Jerusalem. ¹⁰Then they entrusted it to the men appointed to supervise the work on the LORD's temple. These men paid the workers who repaired and restored the temple. ¹¹They also gave money to the carpenters and builders to purchase dressed stone, and timber for

joists and beams for the buildings that the kings of Judah had allowed to fall into ruin.

¹²The workers labored faithfully. Over them to direct them were Jahath and Obadiah, Levites descended from Merari, and Zechariah and Meshullam, descended from Kohath. The Levites—all who were skilled in playing musical instruments—¹³had charge of the laborers and supervised all the workers from job to job. Some of the Levites were secretaries, scribes and gatekeepers.

¹⁴While they were bringing out the money that had been taken into the temple of the LORD, Hilkiah the priest found the Book of the Law of the Lord that had been given through Moses. ¹⁵Hilkiah said to Shaphan the secretary, "I have found the Book of the Law in the temple of the LORD." He gave it to Shaphan.

¹⁶Then Shaphan took the book to the king and reported to him: "Your officials are doing everything that has been committed to them. ¹⁷They have paid out the money that was in the temple of the LORD and have entrusted it to the supervisors and workers." ¹⁸Then Shaphan the secretary informed the king, "Hilkiah the priest has given me a book." And Shaphan read from it in the presence of the king.

¹⁹When the king heard the words of the Law, he tore his robes. ²⁰He gave these orders to Hilkiah, Ahikam son of Shaphan, Abdon son of Micah, Shaphan the secretary and Asaiah the king's attendant: ²¹"Go and inquire of the LORD for me and for the remnant in Israel and Judah about what is written in this book that has been found. Great is the LORD's anger that is poured out on us because those who have gone before us have not kept the word of the LORD; they have not acted in accordance with all that is written in this book."

²²Hilkiah and those the king had sent with him went to speak to the prophet Huldah, who was the wife of Shallum son of Tokhath, the son of Hasrah, keeper of the wardrobe. She lived in Jerusalem, in the New Quarter.

²³She said to them, "This is what the LORD, the God of Israel, says: Tell the man who sent you to me, ²⁴'This is what the LORD says: I am going to bring disaster on this place and its people—all the curses written in the book that has been read in the presence of the king of Judah. ²⁵Because they have forsaken me and burned incense to other gods and aroused my

anger by all that their hands have made, my anger will be poured out on this place and will not be quenched.' ²⁶Tell the king of Judah, who sent you to inquire of the LORD, 'This is what the LORD, the God of Israel, says concerning the words you heard: ²⁷Because your heart was responsive and you humbled yourself before God when you heard what he spoke against this place and its people, and because you humbled yourself before me and tore your robes and wept in my presence, I have heard you, declares the LORD. ²⁸Now I will gather you to your ancestors, and you will be buried in peace. Your eyes will not see all the disaster I am going to bring on this place and on those who live here.'"

So they took her answer back to the king.

²⁹Then the king called together all the elders of Judah and Jerusalem. ³⁰He went up to the temple of the LORD with the people of Judah, the inhabitants of Jerusalem, the priests and the Levites—all the people from the least to the greatest. He read in their hearing all the words of the Book of the Covenant, which had been found in the temple of the LORD. ³¹The king stood by his pillar and renewed the covenant in the presence of the LORD—to follow the LORD and keep his commands, statutes and decrees with all his heart and all his soul, and to obey the words of the covenant written in this book.

³²Then he had everyone in Jerusalem and Benjamin pledge themselves to it; the people of Jerusalem did this in accordance with the covenant of God, the God of their ancestors.

³³Josiah removed all the detestable idols from all the territory belonging to the Israelites, and he had all who were present in Israel serve the LORD their God. As long as he lived, they did not fail to follow the LORD, the God of their ancestors.

Listening to the Text in the Story: Deuteronomy 28:15–68; Jeremiah 11:3

The crisis in the kingdom brought about by Amon's murder is resolved when the people of the land step in to make his son Josiah king and kill those who had been disloyal (2 Chr 33:24–25). Amid this turbulent period, the young boy Josiah unexpectedly finds himself sole monarch over the kingdom, thrust onto the throne when he is a mere eight years old (640 BC). The story of his reign can be divided into several key periods, beginning with the young king seeking the LORD and purging Judah and Israel (34:1–7), followed by the discovery of the law in the temple, which leads to further reforms and covenant renewal (vv. 8–33), and the celebration of the Passover (35:1–19). Josiah's reign concludes with his untimely death at the hands of an Egyptian Pharaoh because of his failure to listen to God's word (vv. 20–27).

Listening to the text in this story requires rehearsing briefly the Mosaic covenant, which is central to the account that follows. When God entered into a covenant with his people at Sinai, they had agreed to obey his laws (Exod 20, 24). As with other ancient covenants, blessings and curses were part of this legally-binding arrangement, and God had promised to bless his people if they obeyed him but curse them if they disobeyed (Lev 26:1–39; Deut 27–28). After a series of curses proclaimed on Mount Ebal, the final words were spoken by the Levites: "'Cursed is anyone who does not uphold the words of this law by carrying them out.' Then all the people shall say, 'Amen!'" (Deut 27:26; see Jer 11:3). Amidst a long list of curses (Deut 28:15–68), Moses explains to Israel that all these curses will come upon them if they fail to obey his laws (v. 45). These curses lie behind the words of Huldah the prophetess and her pronouncement that divine judgment against Judah will be forthcoming. Yet Josiah humbles himself, and his repentance forestalls God's wrath. It is surely coming, but it will take a few more years as we now enter the final days of the Southern Kingdom.

EXPLAIN the Story

Josiah Seeks the Lord and Purges Judah of Idolatry (34:1–7)

Josiah is introduced as a king who did what was right in the sight of the Lord, walking in the way of his father David (2 Chr 34:1–2; cf. 29:2).[1] That he did not turn to the right or left underscores his obedience to the Lord (Deut 5:32; 17:11), in accordance with the requirement for a godly king (v. 20). In the eighth year of his reign, while still a youth, he began to seek the Lord (Heb. *d-r-sh*, 2 Chr 34:3).[2] As has been noted elsewhere, seeking the Lord

---

1. While there are similarities between Josiah and Hezekiah, the number of chapters devoted to Hezekiah gives him a heightened status in Chronicles. Moreover, Josiah's death is reminiscent of kings like Ahab, putting him in a less favorable light (Boda, *1–2 Chronicles*, 412–13).

2. The account in Kings does not mention this earlier period, but Chronicles seems to suggest that there was an early period of purging, initiated by the king after he had sought the Lord (34:1–7). Thus a second phase of reforms is associated with the finding of the law, at which time the entire community is involved (vv. 29–33). Klein notes that there are other examples of kings whose early reforms are followed by a second phase of reforms, which come as a result of a prophetic word (Klein, *2 Chronicles*, 393–94).

is the hallmark of a godly king, and it is expected of the entire community (1 Chr 22:19; 2 Chr 1:5; 14:4, 6; 15:2, 12; 17:4; 20:3, etc.). Josiah's piety leads to a purging of Judah and Jerusalem in the twelfth year of his reign (34:3), dated to 628 BC when the king was twenty years old, an important age of responsibility in Israelite society (Num 1:3; 26:2; 1 Chr 23:24; 2 Chr 31:17). Notably, this is only one year prior to the word of God coming to Jeremiah (Jer 1:1–2). At this time, the king purges Judah and Jerusalem of "high places, Asherah poles and idols" (2 Chr 34:3). High places had remained during the reign of Manasseh, although only the LORD had been worshiped there (33:17). The kingdom had spiraled back into idolatry under Josiah's father, Amon (vv. 22–23). Josiah now ensures that the high places are eradicated, signifying a more extensive purging than what had been done previously (15:17; 20:33; 33:17). Asherah poles and molten images are destroyed, which seem to have been left over from Manasseh's reign (vv. 19, 22).

Altars for Baal and incense altars are destroyed, recalling the instructions given by Moses when the Israelites were to enter the land (2 Chr 34:4; see Deut 7:5; 12:3). Idolatrous objects are broken into pieces and ground into powder, as Moses had done with Israel's golden calf (Exod 32:20). Josiah sprinkles their ashes on the graves of those who had sacrificed to these idols and burns the bones of the false priests (2 Chr 34:4–5; cf. 1 Kgs 13:2). His purging extends to the northern region among the cities in the territory of Manasseh, Ephraim, and Simeon, even as far as Naphtali. The Northern Kingdom had been defeated by the Assyrians in 722 BC, almost one hundred years earlier, but foreigners had been brought into the region, and various idolatrous practices remained (2 Kgs 17). In addition to these factors, the Assyrian Empire had been waning in the region, which may have given Josiah the opportunity to extend his influence in the north. Josiah destroys foreign altars, Asherah poles, carved images, and incense altars throughout Israel as he had done in Judah, and he then returns to Jerusalem (2 Chr 34:6–7).

Josiah Repairs the Temple (34:8–13)

In the eighteenth year of his reign (622 BC), Josiah sends Shaphan the scribe, Maaseiah the ruler of the city, and Joahaz the recorder to repair the house of God (2 Chr 34:8). They bring the money that had been collected by the Levites to Hilkiah the high priest. Contributions had come from Judah and Benjamin, but also from Manasseh, Ephraim, and the remnant of Israel, which refers to those who had survived the deportation (v. 9). The money collected is used for supplies and repairs to the temple, indicating there had been deferred maintenance due to the neglect of previous kings. The workers labor faithfully under the leadership of the Levites, who assume various responsibilities, including playing music to accompany the hard labor!

The Law Is Found and the Covenant Is Renewed (34:14–33)

Something remarkable happens when the contributions are deposited in the temple: Hilkiah the high priest finds the book of the law of the LORD given by Moses (2 Chr 34:14). The scroll that was found was probably Deuteronomy.[3] The leaders bring the book to Josiah, and they give the king a progress report about the work that had been done and the money that had been paid to workers (vv. 15–17). But then Shaphan reads from the scroll that had been found (v. 18), where it hearkens back to the curses of the Mosaic covenant found in Deuteronomy (Deut 27–28; Deut 29:21; cf. Lev 26:14–39).[4] That the law was "given through Moses" (2 Chr 34:14) underscores its antiquity and authority, and it is consistent with references elsewhere that attribute authorship to Moses (e.g., Lev 10:11; 26:46; Num 36:13; 2 Chr 33:8; Neh 8:14; 9:14; 10:29).[5]

When Josiah hears the words of the law, with a stirring and heartfelt conviction of sin he tears his garments and commands Hilkiah, Shaphan, and his son Ahikam, along with two other leaders, to inquire of the LORD, because he is concerned about God's great wrath (2 Chr 34:21).[6] He recognizes that "those who have gone before us have not kept the word of the LORD; they have not acted in accordance with all that is written in this book" (v. 21). The Mosaic covenant required obedience to the law (Exod 24:3, 7; Lev 18:5), and failure to do so would lead to God's wrath, coming in the form of curses (Deut 27–28). No wonder Josiah tears his clothes and weeps when he hears these words.

The royal delegation seeks out Huldah the prophetess, who lived in Jerusalem (2 Chr 34:22). Her husband's grandfather looked after garments (probably priestly vestments), which would require the family to live in proximity to the temple (v. 22). She immediately gives her response, which entails a prophetic word for the king, directly from the LORD, the God of Israel. She warns him that God is about to bring great calamity upon Jerusalem and its

---

3. See Dillard, *2 Chronicles*, 280–81.

4. The "book of the law" can also refer to a larger corpus (cf. Deut 31:26; 2 Chr 17:9; Neh 8:3).

5. Some scholars argue that Deuteronomy was written by Josiah to support his reforms (thus dating Deuteronomy to the seventh century BC), but it is preferable to attribute Deuteronomy to Moses (albeit with some later editorial work), which is congruent with the Chronicler's emphasis on Moses as author ("by the hand of Moses," 34:14). This does not preclude later editorial work and updates (e.g., Deut 34:1–12). See the discussion by Merrill, *1 & 2 Chronicles*, 614–17.

6. The leadership role of this family is seen in the prominence of Gedaliah, son of Ahikam, who later serves as governor (2 Kgs 25:22; Jer 39:14; 40:5, 9, 11), as pointed out by Klein (*2 Chronicles*, 503n79).

inhabitants that would be in the form of "all the curses written in the book" (v. 24). The people have forsaken God and burnt incense to other gods, thereby arousing his unquenchable anger (v. 25). Yet the prophetess announces that, because Josiah was tender-hearted and has humbled himself before God, his cries have been heard (v. 27). Josiah's penitent response to the word of God recalls 2 Chronicles 7:14, for the king humbles himself before God. Huldah thus announces that the king will be buried in peace, for he will not witness the disaster that God is about to bring on Jerusalem, which will take place a few short years after his death (see ch. 36).

After hearing these words, Josiah gathers his elders and goes up to the temple (2 Chr 34:30). The entire community joins him as they gather to hear the scroll of the covenant read by the king (v. 30; cf. Exod 24:7). Standing in his place, the king makes a covenant in the presence of the LORD to follow him and "keep his commands, statutes and decrees with all his heart and all his soul, and to obey the words of the covenant written in this book" (2 Chr 34:31). The renewal of the covenant is reminiscent of previous kings, when God's people had returned to the LORD (15:12–14; 29:10; cf. Deut 29:10–15). The terms "commands," "statutes," and "decrees" are technical terms that are prominently used in Deuteronomy to refer to the stipulations of the covenant.[7] Josiah pledges his full allegiance ("heart and soul") to the LORD (cf. Deut 6:5; 11:13). The people join him in the renewal of the covenant (2 Chr 34:32), which is followed by the removal of detestable idols and a purging that extends beyond the borders of Judah. The renewal under Josiah marks a key moment in the history of the Southern Kingdom, but there are hints that this obedience will be short-lived, as suggested by the statement that the people followed the LORD "as long as he lived" (v. 33), something we have already seen in the life of Jehoiada (24:2, 17).[8] Not surprisingly, even though "detestable things" are removed, they will later reappear (36:8, 14), and God's wrath that had been forestalled is surely coming in the days ahead (34:21; 36:16).

LIVE the Story

Seeking the LORD While a Youth

Josiah became king when he was eight years old, but at the age of sixteen he devoted himself to seeking the LORD (2 Chr 34:3). When he was twenty years

---

7. Merrill, *1 & 2 Chronicles*, 583.
8. See Live the Story in Chapter 53, pp. 460–62.

old, he purged Judah and Jerusalem of idolatry—what had remained from his father's and grandfather's reigns. In Israelite society, the age of twenty was a threshold that moved someone into adult responsibilities such as being eligible to go to war (Num 1:3; 1 Chr 27:23; 2 Chr 25:5) and, if a Levite, serving as temple personnel (1 Chr 23:24; 2 Chr 31:17). Sometimes God calls someone from an early age for a particular task: Samuel was a boy when God called him (1 Sam 2:18, 26; 3:8), and while a youth he was given the difficult task of pronouncing judgment against Eli and his household (vv. 10–21). Jeremiah was a youth when God called him to be a prophet (Jer 1:4–7), and he, too, was called to a difficult task to make known God's judgment against Judah. Josiah not only sought the LORD at a young age, but he was humble, tender-hearted toward God, and submitted to the abiding authority of God's word (2 Chr 34:19–21, 26–27, 31–33), resulting in covenant renewal and the revitalization of the kingdom at a critical period in Israel's history.

There are many examples from church history of people who began serving the LORD at a young age. In the book *To the Golden Shore*, the moving story of the first Baptist missionaries sent out from Salem, Massachusetts, is told by Courtney Anderson. One of the missionaries, Adoniram Judson (1788–1850), received his calling at the tender age of twenty while studying at Andover Theological Seminary. After being stirred by a sermon he had read by a British missionary who had served in India, he would receive the call the following year:

> It was during a solitary walk behind the woods in the college, while meditating and praying on the subject, and feeling half inclined to give it up, that the command of Christ, "Go into all the world and preach the Gospel to every creature," was presented to my mind with such clearness and power, that I came to a full decision, and though great difficulties appeared in my way, resolved to obey the command at all events.[9]

In the prime of life, Adoniram and his new wife, Ann, decided to serve God as missionaries. The ordination of Adoniram and four other men was held at the historic Tabernacle Church in Salem, Massachusetts, on a blistering and frigid day on February 6, 1812. People traveled on horseback, on foot, and on sleighs through the blistering snow, coming from local towns but even from Boston and as far north as Gloucester. The historic Tabernacle Church was

---

9. As cited by C. Anderson, *To the Golden Shore: The Life of Adoniram Judson* (Boston: Little, Brown and Company, 1956; repr., Valley Forge, PA: Judson Press, 1987), 57.

bursting with people as the aisles were filled with congregants, and dignitaries and clerics crowded the platform upon which the lofty pulpit stood. During a moving commissioning service, five men and the whole congregation knelt before the Lord, with sighing and weeping heard throughout the assembly as solemn promises were made. In 1812 these young missionaries with their wives sailed out of Derby Wharf in Salem, Massachusetts, responding to the call of the gospel.[10] The story of Adoniram's life included many difficult years ahead. After being ousted from India, he and his wife left for Burma and, providentially, this is where they would focus on evangelism and translation of the Bible into Burmese. At great cost, and with many trials and sufferings along the journey, Adoniram served the Lord for decades, having first received his call when he was twenty years old.

These stories (and many more could be told) serve as a reminder that God uses people of all ages—including youth—for his kingdom purposes. Sometimes parents witness this sense of calling in their own children who are responsive to the Lord from an early age (often to the surprise of parents). It is easy to dismiss this, yet God can be at work in their lives in ways that we can only understand many years later after events have unfolded. We should not look down upon someone because of their youth (1 Tim 4:12; 2 Tim 3:14–15). God can reveal himself to young people who are tender-hearted toward him, and he can call them to a lifetime of service, even in their youth. Such child-like faith is required of all of us, and Josiah is an example of a young person who sought the LORD and was used by God for his kingdom purposes.

---

10. This moving story is recounted in ibid., in the chapters on "Ordination" (103–114) and "Embarkation" (115–121).

LISTEN to the Story

¹Josiah celebrated the Passover to the LORD in Jerusalem, and the Passover lamb was slaughtered on the fourteenth day of the first month. ²He appointed the priests to their duties and encouraged them in the service of the LORD's temple. ³He said to the Levites, who instructed all Israel and who had been consecrated to the LORD: "Put the sacred ark in the temple that Solomon son of David king of Israel built. It is not to be carried about on your shoulders. Now serve the LORD your God and his people Israel. ⁴Prepare yourselves by families in your divisions, according to the instructions written by David king of Israel and by his son Solomon.

⁵"Stand in the holy place with a group of Levites for each subdivision of the families of your fellow Israelites, the lay people. ⁶Slaughter the Passover lambs, consecrate yourselves and prepare the lambs for your fellow Israelites, doing what the LORD commanded through Moses."

⁷Josiah provided for all the lay people who were there a total of thirty thousand lambs and goats for the Passover offerings, and also three thousand cattle—all from the king's own possessions.

⁸His officials also contributed voluntarily to the people and the priests and Levites. Hilkiah, Zechariah and Jehiel, the officials in charge of God's temple, gave the priests twenty-six hundred Passover offerings and three hundred cattle. ⁹Also Konaniah along with Shemaiah and Nethanel, his brothers, and Hashabiah, Jeiel and Jozabad, the leaders of the Levites, provided five thousand Passover offerings and five hundred head of cattle for the Levites.

¹⁰The service was arranged and the priests stood in their places with the Levites in their divisions as the king had ordered. ¹¹The Passover lambs were slaughtered, and the priests splashed against the altar the blood handed to them, while the Levites skinned the animals. ¹²They set aside the burnt offerings to give them to the subdivisions of the families of the

people to offer to the LORD, as it is written in the Book of Moses. They did the same with the cattle. ¹³They roasted the Passover animals over the fire as prescribed, and boiled the holy offerings in pots, caldrons and pans and served them quickly to all the people. ¹⁴After this, they made preparations for themselves and for the priests, because the priests, the descendants of Aaron, were sacrificing the burnt offerings and the fat portions until nightfall. So the Levites made preparations for themselves and for the Aaronic priests.

¹⁵The musicians, the descendants of Asaph, were in the places prescribed by David, Asaph, Heman and Jeduthun the king's seer. The gatekeepers at each gate did not need to leave their posts, because their fellow Levites made the preparations for them.

¹⁶So at that time the entire service of the LORD was carried out for the celebration of the Passover and the offering of burnt offerings on the altar of the LORD, as King Josiah had ordered. ¹⁷The Israelites who were present celebrated the Passover at that time and observed the Festival of Unleavened Bread for seven days. ¹⁸The Passover had not been observed like this in Israel since the days of the prophet Samuel; and none of the kings of Israel had ever celebrated such a Passover as did Josiah, with the priests, the Levites and all Judah and Israel who were there with the people of Jerusalem. ¹⁹This Passover was celebrated in the eighteenth year of Josiah's reign.

²⁰After all this, when Josiah had set the temple in order, Necho king of Egypt went up to fight at Carchemish on the Euphrates, and Josiah marched out to meet him in battle. ²¹But Necho sent messengers to him, saying, "What quarrel is there, king of Judah, between you and me? It is not you I am attacking at this time, but the house with which I am at war. God has told me to hurry; so stop opposing God, who is with me, or he will destroy you."

²²Josiah, however, would not turn away from him, but disguised himself to engage him in battle. He would not listen to what Necho had said at God's command but went to fight him on the plain of Megiddo.

²³Archers shot King Josiah, and he told his officers, "Take me away; I am badly wounded." ²⁴So they took him out of his chariot, put him in his other chariot and brought him to Jerusalem, where he died. He was buried in the tombs of his ancestors, and all Judah and Jerusalem mourned for him.

²⁵Jeremiah composed laments for Josiah, and to this day all the male and female singers commemorate Josiah in the laments. These became a tradition in Israel and are written in the Laments.

²⁶The other events of Josiah's reign and his acts of devotion in accordance with what is written in the Law of the LORD—²⁷all the events, from beginning to end, are written in the book of the kings of Israel and Judah.

Listening to the Text in the Story: Exodus 12:1–28; 2 Chronicles 30:1–27

Having renewed the Mosaic covenant and pledged allegiance to the LORD, Josiah makes preparations for the Passover in the eighteenth year of his reign (2 Chr 35:19). The Passover commemorated Israel's deliverance from slavery and marked the beginning of their religious calendar (Exod 12:1–28).[1] The festival in this story is reminiscent of the Passover celebrated by the united people of God during the reign of Hezekiah (2 Chr 30:1–27). Its importance is underscored by the fact that the Chronicler has significantly expanded what was merely a brief comment in Kings (2 Kgs 23:21–23). As we will see shortly, when the Passover under Josiah is compared to the earlier celebration under Hezekiah (2 Chr 30), the tone of the festival is surprisingly less jubilant than what we might expect, and there is a disconcerting absence of singing and praises to the LORD. To be sure, Josiah ensures that everything is done properly according to the law, but the cumulative effect is that a more somber picture is being painted, perhaps even suggesting that Josiah's impending death is casting a foreboding shadow over the festival.

Even more to the point, all the features that made Hezekiah's Passover celebration so moving—including those aspects that were not done according to the law—point to the heartfelt devotion of the people. This is curiously missing at this time, perhaps hinting at the lack of spiritual fervor that will characterize the final days of the kingdom. The chapter concludes with the death of Josiah by an Egyptian pharaoh (35:20–24), followed by the prophet Jeremiah chanting a lament for him (v. 25). The dark shadow of Josiah's death thus leads to mourning, not joy, and it signals that the final days of the kingdom are at hand.

It is important to bear in mind that Jeremiah begins his prophetic ministry in 627 BC, in the thirteenth year of Josiah (Jer 1:2). God also raises up the

---

1. For the background of the Passover, see the discussion in Chapter 59 on 2 Chr 30, p. 504.

prophet Zephaniah during the days of Josiah (Zeph 1:1), who pronounces judgment against Judah and the inhabitants of Jerusalem. Notably, the prophet makes reference to the worship of Baal and the host of heaven and to those who bow down and swear by Milcom (Zech 1:4–5). Josiah had destroyed foreign idols and their altars at the beginning of his reign (2 Chr 34:4–7), but Zephaniah announces judgment against "those who turn back from following the LORD and neither seek the LORD nor inquire of him" (Zeph 1:6; see also Zeph 2:3). The verbs "to seek" (Heb. *b-q-sh*) and "to inquire" (Heb. *d-r-sh*) are key terms used in Chronicles, noting that seeking the LORD is the cardinal virtue. That the people have not sought the LORD may well be indicative of the spiritual state of the kingdom that is suggested in the less-than-jubilant tone of the Passover.

EXPLAIN the Story

Josiah Prepares for the Passover Festival (35:1–19)

The Passover takes place on the fourteenth day of the first month (2 Chr 35:1), which is in accordance with the law (Exod 12:6; Lev 23:5). Priests are appointed to their duties, and the king encourages them in their service. The Levites, here identified as teachers (see 2 Chr 17:7–9; Ezra 8:16; Neh 8:7), are instructed to bring the ark of the covenant into the temple (2 Chr 35:3; cf. 1 Chr 15:2).[2] It is uncertain why the ark was not in the temple at this time, but it may have been neglected or even removed during the idolatrous reigns of Manasseh or Amon. Attention to the ark speaks of Josiah's piety (cf. 13:3), but this is the last time it is mentioned in Chronicles. It may have been taken as plunder by the Babylonians or even destroyed (see possibly Lam 2:1), although we cannot be certain.

Josiah instructs the Levites to prepare the Passover according to their divisions (2 Chr 35:5–6), which was based on the three Levitical families of Gershon, Kohath, and Merari (1 Chr 23–24). The Passover was originally celebrated in individual households (Exod 12:3–6; Deut 16:5–6), but the move toward centralization under Hezekiah (2 Chr 30:13–20; cf. Deut 12) has now become formalized, although the family character of the festival remains. The Levites are to represent the laity as they sacrifice the Passover animals on behalf of their fellow Israelites. Josiah contributes large quantities of lambs and

---

2. For a description of the ark of the covenant and how it was to be transported, see the discussions in Chapter 13 on 1 Chr 13, pp. 143–46, and Chapter 15 on 1 Chr 15, pp. 157–60.

goats for the Passover (cf. Exod 12:5; Deut 16:2), along with bulls that are offered up to God—all are from his own royal estate (2 Chr 35:7). The large quantities given signal the king's generosity, a godly leadership quality (1 Chr 29:12–14; 2 Chr 30:24).[3] Josiah's political and religious leaders follow him, as they generously give freewill offerings (35:8–9; cf. 1 Chr 29:5, 6, 9, 14, 17). The total number of animals indicate that the festival was substantially larger than the Passover under Hezekiah (2 Chr 30:24).[4]

With the priests standing at their appointed stations and the Levites in their divisions, animals are slaughtered and skinned while the priests splash their blood on the altar (35:10–11), recalling the blood placed on Israelite doorposts in the first Passover (Exod 12:7, 13). Portions used as burnt offerings are given to the people, who are to offer them to the LORD through the priests. Following correct protocol, the Passover animals are roasted over fire (2 Chr 35:13; cf. Exod 12:8–9; Deut 16:7), whereas other sacrifices are cooked in pots (cf. Exod 29:31; Lev 8:31). The Levites quickly bring the meat to the people (2 Chr 35:13), enacting the haste associated with the Passover meal (Exod 12:11).

Having served the people, the Levites prepare the Passover for themselves and for the priests, although they have to wait until evening due to the amount of work required for such a large festival (2 Chr 35:14). Finally, the singers, the sons of Asaph, and the gatekeepers who were stationed at the gates remain at their posts while the Levites prepare the Passover for them. Those assembled included some from the northern tribes, as had been the case under Hezekiah (v. 17; cf. 30:6, 18, 21). The Feast of Unleavened Bread is celebrated for seven days, as the law prescribed (Exod 23:15). This festival, dated to the eighteenth year of Josiah's reign (622 BC), marks a high point in the history of the Southern Kingdom (2 Chr 35:18–19). King Hezekiah had celebrated the Passover earlier (ch. 30) but, unlike Hezekiah, Josiah celebrates it according to God's law on the fourteenth day of the *first* month (35:1; cf. Num 9:2-5). Yet, tragically, this will be the last celebration for a long time, since Judah is about to go into exile in a few short years.

Josiah Is Killed by Pharaoh Necho (35:20–27)

The events leading to Josiah's death are now rehearsed, which takes place more than a decade after the Passover, dated to 609 BC. The story is introduced

---

3. On this topic, see Live the Story in Chapter 29, pp. 282–84.

4. While some scholars think the numbers may be exaggerated, Dillard argues they are reasonable in view of the size of the population, which has been estimated to be around 300,000 (Dillard, *2 Chronicles*, 290).

with Pharaoh Necho (609–594 BC) marching to Carchemish to wage war against the Babylonians, with Josiah planning to meet him (2 Chr 35:20). Hamath marked the northern border of Israel (1 Chr 13:5; 2 Chr 7:8; 8:3), but Carchemish was located even further north on the Euphrates River, west of Haran. The Assyrian Empire had been on the decline, with several of their cities already defeated. In an effort to suppress the Medo-Babylonian coalition under Nabopolassar (Nebuchadnezzar's father), Necho sought to provide reinforcements for the waning Assyrians.[5] This required his army to march through the land of Israel, a region that was a buffer zone between the two great empires east and southwest. Josiah travels northward to Megiddo in an attempt to intercept the Egyptians so that he might protect the important route through Israel. Boda thus notes that it was "most likely that control over the pass at Megiddo was in dispute. The pass would be important for Neco to control because it was essential to secure his communication lines and escape route back to Egypt, especially in case a retreat was necessary."[6] But Necho sends messengers to Josiah, telling him that he has no dispute with him, for his war was with another house (35:21). Necho even tells Josiah that God has told him to act quickly and that Josiah was to stop opposing God, who was with him, lest God destroy him (v. 21). Josiah refuses to give heed, but instead, he disguises himself, recalling the folly of the notorious king Ahab (18:29). The final indicting comment is made that Necho's words were "at God's command" (35:22). While some may question whether a non-Israelite king could speak on behalf of God, there are other occasions when God uses non-Israelites to perform his purposes (36:22–23; Isa 44:24–28; 45:1–4). Josiah's failure to give heed to God's command—even though from an unlikely messenger—identifies Josiah with other kings who started well but finished poorly (such as Solomon, Asa, Jehoshaphat, Joash, and Uzziah). This reminds us that even the best of kings fail in some way, and as Dillard notes, "Josiah's failure drives us to look for yet another son of David who will rule the people of God in righteousness without lapse."[7]

Josiah is shot by archers and badly wounded in battle (2 Chr 35:23), providing another literary connection with the infamous Ahab, thereby casting a negative shadow over Josiah at the end of his life (18:33). Having been wounded, Josiah instructs his servants to take him away. They put him in a chariot and bring him back to Jerusalem, where he is buried in the tombs of

---

5. For a concise history of the rise of Babylonia, see Merrill, *1 & 2 Chronicles*, 617–619.
6. See also the helpful map outlining the routes, Boda, *1–2 Chronicles*, 420.
7. Dillard, *2 Chronicles*, 293.

his ancestors (35:24).[8] Josiah's death leads to further Egyptian dominance, but they will be defeated in 605 BC by Nebuchadnezzar (Jer 46). This watershed battle marks a turning point in the political landscape of the ancient Near East, and it will directly impact Judah in the coming days. In the meantime, all Judah and Jerusalem mourn for Josiah, and Jeremiah composes laments for him that become part of Israel's traditions. The Chronicler concludes by noting that other events, including Josiah's acts of devotion, are recorded in the book of the kings of Israel and Judah (2 Chr 35:26–27).

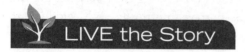

LIVE the Story

God Will Turn Israel's Mourning into Joy

King Josiah carefully follows what Moses had prescribed in the law (2 Chr 35:6, 12) and what David had instituted concerning the cult (vv. 4, 15).[9] By way of contrast, when Hezekiah had celebrated the Passover, he had made several concessions, requiring him to ask God to pardon those who had not consecrated themselves (30:17–18).[10] King Josiah can surely be commended for his adherence to the law. His introduction underscores that he was a king who did not turn aside to the right or the left (34:2; cf. Deut 5:32; 17:11, 20; 28:14; Josh 1:7). His obedience to the word of God was critical, since failure to obey it would lead to God's wrath (2 Chr 34:21). Accordingly, the Chronicler had introduced Josiah by saying that he did what was "right in the eyes of the LORD and followed the ways of his father David" (v. 2). Apart from the final episode, Josiah is exemplary in his devotion to the LORD, his submission to the abiding authority of Scripture, and his commitment to carefully follow God's law.

Yet there is something wanting in the Passover festival when it is compared to the earlier celebration under Hezekiah. To be sure, all the procedures are carefully followed and the devotion of the king is not to be questioned, but there is no joy, no singing of praises to the LORD, no prayers, and no blessing. King David had appointed the Levitical musicians to make a "joyful sound" with their musical instruments (1 Chr 15:16; cf. v. 25), and when God's

---

8. The account in Kings has Josiah being killed in Megiddo, and then his body is brought back to Jerusalem (2 Kgs 23:30). Merrill resolves this by interpreting the Kings narrative to indicate that the blow causing his death was inflicted at Megiddo, although the king's actual death was in Jerusalem (Merrill *1 and 2 Chronicles*, 596n87).

9. See De Vries, "Moses and David as Cult Founders," 619–30.

10. See the discussion in Chapter 59 on 2 Chr 30, pp. 505–10, for the concessions made by Hezekiah.

people gathered there was usually great joy (29:9, 17, 22). When Jehoiada had appointed Levitical priests to offer burnt offerings, it was done according to the law of Moses, but notably, "with rejoicing and singing, as David had ordered" (2 Chr 23:18). During the time of Hezekiah, the festivities took place over seven days "with great rejoicing, while the Levites and priests praised the LORD every day with resounding instruments dedicated to the LORD" (30:21). The festival was extended for another seven days, but this simply meant that "for another seven days they celebrated joyfully" (v. 23). Thus it was characterized as a time of "great joy in Jerusalem" (v. 26). The more somber tone of the festival during the time of Josiah is even more noticeable when one considers that joy is an important theme in Chronicles, as Hahn notes: "Chronicles, in a way unmatched elsewhere in the Bible, depicts the worship of God as a joyous, heartfelt affair."[11] As noted earlier, joy experienced in Jerusalem during Hezekiah's time was in fulfillment of God's promise to Moses (Deut 12:7, 12, 18). Accordingly, the psalms resound with songs of joy (Pss 9:2; 21:1; 32:11; 33:21; 40:16, etc.).

Josiah's heart was clearly devoted to the LORD, and he had humbled himself when the law had been read to him, yet there is no indication that the people responded in the same way. Josiah had torn his garments (2 Chr 34:19), but there is no such response by the people when the law was read to them (v. 30). Their almost stoic response is in stark contrast to the returnees, who had wept when they heard the word of God (Neh 8:9) and had rejoiced in their God (vv. 10, 12, 17; cf. 12:27, 44). Instead of a joyful celebration in this story, its less than jubilant tone turns to mourning and lament as the people grieve over the death of their king. This ushers in a bleak period, for the kingdom is about to come to an end.

It is important to recognize that the restoration envisaged by the prophets would mean that Israel's mourning would be turned to joy, as the prophet announces: "I will turn their mourning into gladness; I will give them comfort and joy instead of sorrow" (Jer 31:13; cf. Ps 14:7). The prophet Isaiah had also taught that the restoration would be characterized by joy: "Those the LORD has rescued will return. They will enter Zion with singing; everlasting joy will crown their heads. Gladness and joy will overtake them, and sorrow and sighing will flee away" (Isa 51:11; cf. 35:1–10). Even though weeping may stay for the night, joy comes in the morning (Ps 30:5, 11).

While there is an initial period of restoration after the exile, when God's

---

11. Hahn, *The Kingdom of God*, 127. See Hahn for an extensive list of passages in Chronicles where joyful worship is mentioned (127). For the topic of joy, see Live the Story in Chapter 34, pp. 319–21.

people return to Zion and rejoice (Neh 8:10, 12, 17; 12:27; 12:44), the full restoration is not realized until the Messiah arrives, and his birth is marked by—yes, joy! Through his mighty redemption that takes place on Passover, Jesus is the sacrificial Lamb of God who takes away the sin of the world. He is the one who redeems his people and establishes the new covenant, and this surely brings great joy (Acts 13:52; 16:34; I Pet 1:8), a joy that is given by the Spirit (Luke 10:21; Rom 14:17; Gal 5:22; 1 Thess 1:6). The restoration would bring joy to God's people, but the full restoration accomplished by Jesus brings everlasting joy. I'm reminded of the old chorus that repeats the simple yet profound message of hope taken directly from Isaiah:

> Therefore the redeemed of the Lord shall return,
> And come with singing unto Zion;
> And everlasting joy shall be upon their head.
> They shall obtain gladness and joy;
> And sorrow and mourning shall flee away.

May this song taken directly from Scripture overflow in our own hearts and minds as we rejoice in God's promise of restoration that is fulfilled in our Lord and Redeemer. May *his* joy be upon our head, and may sorrow and mourning flee away as we await the coming of his everlasting kingdom—where there will no longer be mourning, sorrow, or pain (Rev 21:4)

CHAPTER 65

2 Chronicles 36:1-23

 LISTEN to the Story

¹And the people of the land took Jehoahaz son of Josiah and made him king in Jerusalem in place of his father.

²Jehoahaz was twenty-three years old when he became king, and he reigned in Jerusalem three months. ³The king of Egypt dethroned him in Jerusalem and imposed on Judah a levy of a hundred talents of silver and a talent of gold. ⁴The king of Egypt made Eliakim, a brother of Jehoahaz, king over Judah and Jerusalem and changed Eliakim's name to Jehoiakim. But Necho took Eliakim's brother Jehoahaz and carried him off to Egypt.

⁵Jehoiakim was twenty-five years old when he became king, and he reigned in Jerusalem eleven years. He did evil in the eyes of the LORD his God. ⁶Nebuchadnezzar king of Babylon attacked him and bound him with bronze shackles to take him to Babylon. ⁷Nebuchadnezzar also took to Babylon articles from the temple of the LORD and put them in his temple there.

⁸The other events of Jehoiakim's reign, the detestable things he did and all that was found against him, are written in the book of the kings of Israel and Judah. And Jehoiachin his son succeeded him as king.

⁹Jehoiachin was eighteen years old when he became king, and he reigned in Jerusalem three months and ten days. He did evil in the eyes of the LORD. ¹⁰In the spring, King Nebuchadnezzar sent for him and brought him to Babylon, together with articles of value from the temple of the LORD, and he made Jehoiachin's uncle, Zedekiah, king over Judah and Jerusalem.

¹¹Zedekiah was twenty-one years old when he became king, and he reigned in Jerusalem eleven years. ¹²He did evil in the eyes of the LORD his God and did not humble himself before Jeremiah the prophet, who spoke the word of the LORD. ¹³He also rebelled against King Nebuchadnezzar, who had made him take an oath in God's name. He became stiff-necked and hardened his heart and would not turn to the LORD, the God of Israel. ¹⁴Furthermore, all the leaders of the priests and the people became more and more unfaithful, following all the detestable practices of the nations and defiling the temple of the LORD, which he had consecrated in Jerusalem.

¹⁵The LORD, the God of their ancestors, sent word to them through his messengers again and again, because he had pity on his people and on his dwelling place. ¹⁶But they mocked God's messengers, despised his words and scoffed at his prophets until the wrath of the LORD was aroused against his people and there was no remedy. ¹⁷He brought up against them the king of the Babylonians, who killed their young men with the sword in the sanctuary, and did not spare young men or young women, the elderly or the infirm. God gave them all into the hands of Nebuchadnezzar. ¹⁸He carried to Babylon all the articles from the temple of God, both large and small, and the treasures of the LORD's temple and the treasures of the king and his officials. ¹⁹They set fire to God's temple and broke down the wall of Jerusalem; they burned all the palaces and destroyed everything of value there.

²⁰He carried into exile to Babylon the remnant, who escaped from the sword, and they became servants to him and his successors until the kingdom of Persia came to power. ²¹The land enjoyed its sabbath rests; all the time of its desolation it rested, until the seventy years were completed in fulfillment of the word of the LORD spoken by Jeremiah.

²²In the first year of Cyrus king of Persia, in order to fulfill the word of the LORD spoken by Jeremiah, the LORD moved the heart of Cyrus king of Persia to make a proclamation throughout his realm and also to put it in writing:

²³"This is what Cyrus king of Persia says:

"'The LORD, the God of heaven, has given me all the kingdoms of the earth and he has appointed me to build a temple for him at

Jerusalem in Judah. Any of his people among you may go up, and may the LORD their God be with them.'"

Listening to the Text in the Story: 2 Chronicles 34:24–25; Jeremiah 29:10

After the death of Josiah, Necho's focus is to suppress the Babylonian threat. This gives Judah a short reprieve, enabling the people to appoint Josiah's son Jehoahaz king in place of his father. As we enter this stormy period that is fraught with political unrest, it is important to recognize that God's judgment is now at hand, which will climax in the final Babylonian assault. God had promised David that his son would rule over his everlasting throne and kingdom (1 Chr 17:1–15), but the recipient of this promise was required to obey God's law (22:11–13; 28:5–7; 2 Chr 7:17–22). Only a righteous king would rule over God's everlasting kingdom. It is not insignificant that the last four kings do evil in God's sight (36:5, 9, 12), culminating in the last king, Zedekiah, who refuses to humble himself but stiffens his neck and hardens his heart against the LORD (vv. 12–13).

The discovery of the law during the reign of Josiah provides an important lens through which to read the events that follow in this final period. When Josiah had heard the words of the law, he recognized that "Great is the LORD's anger that is poured out on us because those who have gone before us have not kept the word of the LORD; they have not acted in accordance with all that is written in this book" (34:21). The king had sought confirmation through Huldah the prophetess, who had given this response:

"'This is what the LORD says: I am going to bring disaster on this place and its people—all the curses written in the book that has been read in the presence of the king of Judah. Because they have forsaken me and burned incense to other gods and aroused my anger by all that their hands have made, my anger will be poured out on this place and will not be quenched.'" (vv. 24–25)

Josiah's penitent heart had forestalled God's wrath against Judah during his lifetime (vv. 27–29), but his death means that God's wrath is inevitable (36:16) and the covenant curses will shortly come upon Judah (34:24; cf. Deut 28:15–68). This is the tragic story that lies before us.

Yet it is not the full picture, for something else reverberates throughout

Chronicles—it is the abiding assurance that if God's people return to the LORD, he will restore them and bring them back to Jerusalem (2 Chr 6:24–31, 36–39; 7:14; cf. Lev 26:40–46; Deut 30). This leads to the second key text that informs this final chapter. God had told the prophet Jeremiah: "When seventy years are completed for Babylon, I will come to you and fulfill my good promise to bring you back to this place" (Jer 29:10). The rise of King Cyrus in 539 BC and the return of God's people from exile will come about in fulfilment of God's word through the prophet. The Chronicler concludes his magisterial work with this prophecy in view (2 Chr 36:20–21; cf 1 Chr 9:1). In the final analysis, this hope of restoration shapes his entire work and it stands as an invitation, reminding us that the sovereign God is still at work restoring his people.

EXPLAIN the Story

The Ungodly Reigns of Jehoahaz, Jehoiakim, and Jehoiachin (36:1–9)

With the sudden death of Josiah, his fourth-born son, Jehoahaz (who is also known as Shallum, 1 Chr 3:15), is placed on the throne (2 Chr 36:1). Described in Kings as doing evil in God's sight (2 Kgs 23:32; cf. Jer 22:11–17), he will only reign for three short months. Pharaoh Necho had initially focused on the Babylonian threat, but his attention turns to Israel with his military outpost in northern Riblah in the region of Hamath (2 Kgs 23:33). King Jehoahaz is deposed and imprisoned there before being brought to Egypt where he dies (2 Chr 36:3–4; cf. 2 Kgs 23:33–34; Jer 22:11–12). Tribute is imposed upon Judah, and Necho places Jehoahaz's brother Eliakim on the throne. Demonstrating his powerful suzerainty over his "puppet king," Necho changes Eliakim's name to Jehoiakim. He, too, is required to pay tribute, which he pays by imposing tax on the inhabitants of Jerusalem (2 Kgs 23:35). Jeremiah gives a number of prophetic oracles at this time (Jer 25:1; 26:1; 35:1; 36:1, etc.), including words against Jehoiakim (22:18–23). The king's response to the word of God stands in stark contrast to Josiah's tender heart (2 Chr 34:19, 27). Unlike Josiah, when Jehoiakim hears God's word read to him, he throws the scroll into a fire—burning up the Scriptures (Jer 36:1–26)! Yet God will announce his judgment against him and Jerusalem because they have not given heed to his word (36:31).

In the meantime, Nebuchadnezzar's defeat of Necho at Carchemish in 605 BC marks a decisive turn of events that directly impact Judah, enabling him to exert his control over the region. Jehoiakim is required to pay tribute, but the account in Kings notes that he rebels, leading to an assault against the kingdom (2 Kgs 24:1–7). The Chronicler picks up the story with Nebuchadnezzar coming against Jehoiakim, binding him in chains so that he might be brought to Babylon, reminiscent of Manasseh earlier (2 Chr 36:6; cf. 33:11).[1] Vessels from the temple are plundered and brought to Babylon, and Nebuchadnezzar places them in *his* temple (36:7). Jehoiakim's reign concludes with a reference to the "detestable things he did" (v. 8), perhaps summarizing what is said about him elsewhere (Jer 22:17), but also identifying him with Ahaz (2 Chr 28:3) and Manasseh (33:2; cf. 34:33). After Jehoiakim's death, his son Jehoiachin (also known as Jeconiah) becomes king, but his reign is short-lived. He is identified as a king who did "evil in the eyes of the LORD" (36:9; cf. Jer 22:24–25; 52:31–34).

God's Wrath Comes against His People for Their Unfaithfulness (36:10–21)

Nebuchadnezzar comes against Jerusalem in 597 BC and takes Jehoiachin to Babylon (2 Chr 36:10). The royal family and leading citizens are among the deportees, along with valuable vessels from the temple (2 Kgs 24:10–16). The Babylonian Chronicle records this event, describing Nebuchadnezzar and his army encamped against the city of Judah. He captures Jehoaichin and appoints his choice of king.[2] Nebuchadnezzar places Jehoiachin's uncle, Mattaniah, on the throne and changes his name to Zedekiah (v. 17; cf. 2 Chr 36:10). He is Josiah's third-born son (1 Chr 3:15).

We are now in the final decade of the kingdom. At the outset we are told that Zedekiah "did evil in the eyes of the LORD his God and did not humble himself before Jeremiah the prophet, who spoke the word of the LORD" (2 Chr 36:12; cf. Jer 37:1–2). Throughout Chronicles we have seen how important it is to humble oneself before God (2 Chr 12:6–7, 12; 32:26; 33:12, 19; 34:27), and failure to do so leads to judgment (28:19; 33:23; 36:12). The charge that Zedekiah did not humble himself will have disastrous ramifications. God had sent the prophet Jeremiah to warn the king that judgment was surely coming

---

1. The Hebrew text notes that Nebuchnezzar's intent was to bring Jehoiakim to Babylon (2 Chr 36:6). Although it does not state directly that Jehoiakim *was* brought to Babylon, this seems to be implied (cf. Dan 1:2). It is possible that the king was brought there temporarily but later returned for reasons unknown to us. The Kings account indicates he slept with his fathers (2 Kgs 24:6), but the usual death notice is absent in Chronicles (2 Chr 36:8), contributing to the theme of exile and leaving some level of ambiguity.

2. The Babylonian Chronicle is on display in the British Museum (see https://www.british museum.org/collection/object/W_1896-0409-51).

(Jer 21:1–14; 27:1–22; 37:1–21; 38:1–28), but the king is ardent in his refusal to give heed to the word of the LORD.

Zedekiah not only rebels against Nebuchadnezzar (2 Chr 36:13; cf. Ezek 17:11–17), but his obstinacy is emphasized by the description of being "stiff-necked" (2 Chr 36:13), which recalls the description of the Israelites in the golden calf story (Exod 32:9; 33:3; 34:9). Zedekiah refuses to "return" to the LORD, the posture of repentance so necessary in order for God to forgive and restore (2 Chr 6:23, 24, 26, 37, 38, 42; 7:14, etc.). The Chronicler further notes that all the leaders of the priests and the people "became more and more unfaithful, following all the detestable practices of the nations" (36:14). This statement testifies to the utter depravity of the leaders and suggests that their unfaithfulness has come to a crescendo, especially in light of the repeated emphasis on "unfaithfulness" leading up to this very moment (cf. 1 Chr 9:1).[3] That their behavior is likened to the detestable practices of the nations indicates that they have now become like their *worst* kings, such as Ahaz (2 Chr 28:3), Manasseh (33:2), and Jehoiakim (36:8).

Finally, the Chronicler states the unthinkable—they have *defiled the temple* (2 Chr 36:14). This is the temple that Solomon had spent seven years building, acquiring some of the finest of materials in the ancient Near East and securing expert craftsmen to ensure it was glorious and fitting for the LORD God (chs. 2–7). This is the temple that was a microcosm of God's glorious and exalted heavenly throne, which had been consecrated as sacred space with a holy God dwelling in Israel's midst. Now God's own people, who had been set apart as a holy people, have defiled it. Given the centrality of the temple in Chronicles, this is unimaginable. The prophets Jeremiah and Ezekiel make known that the temple had become unclean because of the detestable idols that had been placed in it (Jer 7:30; 32:34; Ezek 5:11). Israel's idolatry had been an incessant problem since their time in Egypt (20:7, 18, 30, 31; 23:3, 5, 7, etc.). The cumulative effect was that the people had become unclean, and as a result, God's presence had tragically left the temple, which is followed by his judgment on Jerusalem (chs. 8–11). The picture of devastation is now complete—God's holy temple that he had consecrated in Jerusalem has become *defiled*.

The Chronicler shifts to focus on God's response to Israel's repeated sin: "The LORD, the God of their ancestors, sent word to them through his messengers again and again, because he had pity on his people and on his dwelling place" (2 Chr 36:15). As we have traversed the stories of the kings, we have

---

3. On the term "unfaithful," see the discussion in Chapter 10 on 1 Chr 10:13, pp. 118–20.

seen how often God has sent his prophets to bring rebuke and correction to his people, calling them to return to the LORD. God has shown pity on his people and his holy dwelling place, but the time has now arrived when he will no longer show pity. The prophet Ezekiel announces that because his people have defiled the temple with their vile images and detestable practices, God will not look on them with pity or spare them (Ezek 5:11; 7:4). The book of Lamentations shows the devastating circumstances when his people fall under divine wrath without pity (Lam 2:2, 17, 21; 3:43), as they are left to the ruthless Babylonians (2 Chr 36:17; Jer 21:7).

Instead of giving heed to the prophets, the people had "mocked God's messengers, despised his words and scoffed at his prophets" (2 Chr 36:16). Such disdain for God's prophets and his word means that his wrath is aroused until there was "no remedy" (v. 16). God had promised earlier during the reign of Solomon that if his people humbled themselves, prayed, and turned from their evil ways, he would heal the land (7:14; cf. 30:20).[4] Yet without repentance, there can be no healing, only God's wrath (Jer 8:14–15; 14:19–20), as Proverbs wisely states, "Whoever remains stiff-necked after many rebukes will suddenly be destroyed—without remedy" (Prov 29:1).

The Babylonian siege of Jerusalem is described next, although the ruthless military tactics of Nebuchadnezzar (especially what happens to Zedekiah and his sons) are not rehearsed here (cf. 2 Kgs 25:1–21). Instead, the slaughter of those who had sought refuge in the temple is recounted, which was due to God's judgment—*he* gave them into the hand of the Chaldean king (2 Chr 36:17). Nebuchadnezzar plunders the temple and the royal treasuries, bringing the precious vessels to Babylon (v. 18; cf. Dan 1:2; 5:1–5). Those who escape the sword are brought into exile to Babylon. Other events that take place in Jerusalem and in Egypt are told elsewhere (2 Kgs 25:22–26; Jer 40–44), but the Chronicler concludes his account by noting that those in Babylon became servants of Nebuchadnezzar and his sons "until the kingdom of Persia came to power" (2 Chr 36:20). This signals that the restoration is at hand.

In 539 BC, the Persian king Cyrus defeats Babylon.[5] This watershed moment in the history of the ancient Near East is recorded in the ancient Cyrus Cylinder.[6] It is even more significant in God's redemptive plan, for it signals that his promised restoration has arrived, and thus it marks a new

---

4. On the verb "to heal," see the commentary on 2 Chr 7:14, pp. 338–41.

5. For a brief history of this period, see the introduction, Life in the Province of Judah and in the Diaspora under the Persians, pp. 10–13.

6. The Cyrus Cylinder is located in the British Museum; see www.britishmuseum.org/collection /object/W_1880-0617-1941.

beginning. Moses had taught many years earlier that the land was to enjoy a Sabbath rest every seven years (Lev 25:1–7; 26:43). The seventy years are calculated with this teaching in view (2 Chr 36:21), as God is reclaiming his sabbatical years (Jer 25:11–12; 29:10).[7] But this has further significance for the Chronicler's view of the exile. Instead of simply being interpreted as God's judgment, the exile is perhaps intended to be seen as a "time of Sabbath rest, a time of restoration and purification in the Chronicler's version," which means that the rise of the Persian king represents a "new beginning."[8] Jonker notes further that the Chronicler "did not want his contemporaries to see this new phase as a new exile—this time within their own land. He rather wanted them to realize that the Persian era was a new beginning."[9] The Chronicler's earlier account of the returnees had resounded with hope and optimism for what God will do in the days ahead (1 Chr 9:2).[10] Now the Chronicler concludes his sacred history with hope for what lies ahead, a new beginning of sorts after a Sabbath rest, as God's people are invited to go up to Jerusalem.

The Restoration from Exile Begins with the Decree of Cyrus (36:22–23)

The return of God's people to Jerusalem takes place because God "moves" or "stirs" the heart of Cyrus (Heb. ʿ-w-r, 2 Chr 36:22; cf. 1 Chr 5:26; 2 Chr 21:16; Ezra 1:1). This reminds us that God has a sovereign plan that will surely be accomplished, and he can use whomever he chooses (Dan 2:21; 4:17, 25–26). Stirred by God himself, Cyrus sends out a proclamation allowing the exiles to return to Jerusalem. The Persian king acknowledges that the LORD, the God of heaven, has given him all the kingdoms of the earth, and he has appointed him to build God's house in Jerusalem (2 Chr 36:23). This is in accordance with Isaiah's prophecy that Cyrus would rebuild Jerusalem (Isa 44:26–28; 45:13). The Chronicler leaves his readers with these words of encouragement: "Any of his people among you may go up, and may the LORD

---

7. Various views are proposed by scholars regarding how the seventy years are to be calculated (cf. Zech 1:12; 7:5), which include the following: a) the death of Josiah in 609 BC until the rule of Cyrus in 539 BC; b) the destruction of Jerusalem in 586 BC until its rebuilding in 516 BC; c) a non-literal seventy years that conveys the idea of completeness; and d); the seventy years is extended to "seventy sevens," which is fulfilled with the coming of the Messiah (Dan 9:24). Japhet argues, however, that for the Chronicler, the seventy years is "not a chronological datum which may be explained by various calculations, but a historical and theological concept: a time limit for the duration of the land's desolation, established by a divine word through a prophet (Japhet, *I & II Chronicles*, 1076).

8. Louis Jonker, "The Exile as Sabbath Rest: The Chronicler's Interpretation of the Exile," *OTE* 20:3 (2007): 703–719, esp. p. 715.

9. Ibid., 714.

10. See Live the Story in Chapter 9, pp. 113–14.

their God be with them" (2 Chr 36:23). Those who were among the returnees have already been described (cf. 1 Chr 9), but the Chronicler now concludes his magisterial work with an invitation to go up to Jerusalem, which comes with the assurance that God is with his people!

LIVE the Story

The Davidic King Has Arrived

We have traversed the stories of Israel's kings, praising God for his work among his people while lamenting during Israel's darkest years. We have seen throughout our study that God has been faithful to his promises made to David, for he will surely have a son ruling over his kingdom. The stories of Davidic kings show us that, in spite of some outstanding leaders who serve God faithfully, every king fails in some way, even the best and most beloved kings. We watched as the young shepherd boy was anointed as king and rose to the challenge, defeating Israel's enemies with God's help. He worked tirelessly to organize the kingdom and appoint trusted leaders, instructing them to give their undivided support to Solomon. His generosity and devotion to the LORD has stirred our heart and caused us to reflect upon the greatness of our God. Yet David's military census tragically resulted in thousands being killed as he faced the dire consequences of his sin. Solomon is the cosmopolitan, temple-building king who gave his undivided attention to ensure that God's temple was glorious and worthy of his God. His deeply moving prayer brought us before God's heavenly throne, and his flourishing kingdom led to God's name being exalted among the nations. Yet there are hints at the end of his reign that he cared more about his wealth and fame than seeking God. Asa established major religious reforms and trusted God amidst the battle, but later in his life he allied himself with Baasha and failed to give heed to the prophet Hanani. He was plagued with a severe foot disease in his final years, yet even in his illness he did not seek God. Jehoshaphat is another beloved king, known for building up the kingdom and ensuring that God's law is taught. After a serious mistake that almost cost him his life, he led God's people in prayer and fasting and emerges as an outstanding and unforgettable leader who trusted God amidst insurmountable circumstances. This is surely a high point in his reign, yet later in life he allied himself with the northern Ahaziah, which led to God's judgment. Stories of other kings who are known for their great accomplishments could be remembered, kings such as Uzziah, Hezekiah, and Josiah, but at the same time, every king fails in some way. Any lingering hope for a righteous Davidic king is utterly shattered with the last four kings, who do evil in God's sight, culminating in King Zedekiah, who stiffens his neck and fails to give heed to God's word through his prophets.

The story of Israel's kings underscores that in the final analysis, every king is found wanting. Yet, their failures stir in the prophets an undying hope that God will raise up a righteous king in fulfillment of his promise to David. Isaiah prophesied that one day a child would be born. He would reign on the throne of David and over God's everlasting kingdom (Isa 9:6–7). He would be called "Wonderful Counselor, Mighty God, Everlasting Father, Prince of Peace" (v. 6; cf. Isa 11:1–5). The prophet Micah prophesied that a ruler would come forth from Bethlehem, and his rule would extend to the ends of the earth (Mic 5:2, 4). Jeremiah, too, prophesied that God would raise up a righteous Davidic king:

> "The days are coming," declares the LORD,
>   "when I will raise up for David a righteous Branch,
> a King who will reign wisely
>   and do what is just and right in the land.
> In his days Judah will be saved
>   and Israel will live in safety.
> This is the name by which he will be called:
>   The LORD Our Righteous Savior." (Jer 23:5–6)

God had promised David that one of his sons would rule over God's everlasting kingdom and that his throne would be established *forever* (1 Chr 17:11, 14). The Chronicler has highlighted that, in spite of serious threats along the way, the line of David has been preserved and thus David's "lamp" has not gone out (1 Kgs 11:36; 2 Kgs 8:19; 2 Chr 21:7; cf. 1 Chr 3:1–24). Even though the returnees are living in Jerusalem without a king on the throne, God has not forgotten his promise. The prophet Zechariah saw from afar that a king would one day return to Jerusalem. Humble and mounted on a donkey, he would be endowed with salvation, the very salvation David knew could only come from God. This king would speak peace to the nations and his dominion would extend to the ends of the earth (Zech 9:9–10). This is the king that Israel is waiting for. This is the expectation that reverberates throughout Chronicles as the stories of Israel's beloved kings are rehearsed. Kings such as David, Solomon, and Hezekiah provide a vision for a united and flourishing kingdom, an eschaton of sorts, anticipating the time when God would fulfill his promise to raise up a son of David to rule over God's kingdom. Thus the Chronicler lived in hope that the sure promises given to David would one day be fulfilled.

God's promise to raise up a righteous Davidic king comes to fulfillment with the birth of the Messiah, as Matthew traces Jesus's ancestry through the royal line of David (Matt 1:1–17). Jesus is the king born in Bethlehem, in fulfillment of God's promise through Micah (2:1–12). He will be called "the Son of the Most High. The Lord God will give him the throne of his father David" (Luke 1:32). He is the long-expected king, and he calls people to enter *his* kingdom.

This is the story that has been traced so beautifully and patiently in Chronicles. Even though the returnees were living at a time when there was no king on the throne and they were struggling as a small province of Yehud amidst a vast Persian Empire, they were not to lose heart. They were to lift their eyes beyond their circumstances to see signs of God's heavenly kingdom. They were to return to their sacred history—the *Scriptures*—and understand that God was sovereignly at work accomplishing his plan through history. We are always, as Bauckham and Hart write, "beginning from the biblical narratives, which open up for us possibilities for our own future with the future of Jesus Christ." This means, therefore, that we are "figuratively starting again from Jerusalem on our way to the ends of the earth."[11] The Chronicler concludes his writing with the invitation to go up to Jerusalem—always starting from Jerusalem before being sent out to the world. His invitation ultimately resounds with *hope*—not in the Persian king but in the King of Kings who stands behind the invitation with his plan to forgive and restore his people.

For the Christian, the story of redemption is brought to a climax with the coming Messiah, and we are invited to become citizens of his heavenly kingdom. This is the kingdom we seek to embody, cultivating the virtues of prayer, worship, seeking God's face, humility, repentance, trusting in God, obedience to his word, and listening to the Spirit. We are set apart to be a worshiping and witnessing community, a sacred assembly among the nations in a world that desperately needs a new story. We do not lose heart when things go awry, for even amid persecution and difficulties, the kingdom of God continues to grow and God's rule is being established. We are called to seek *first* his kingdom and to proclaim the gospel of the kingdom to all nations (Matt 6:33; 24:14). We have a message for the world: "Our God Reigns!" And like the returnees, we live in hope that God will return and restore all things, resounding with the words of hope: "Come, Lord Jesus, Come!"

---

11. Bauckham and Hart, *Hope Against Hope*, 21.

Scripture Index

Numbers

Deuteronomy

Joshua

Judges

2 Kings

1 Chronicles

2 Chronicles

Proverbs

Isaiah

Jeremiah

Lamentations

Ezekiel

John

Acts

Subject Index

Author Index